インドネシアの王都出土の肥前陶磁
—トロウラン遺跡 ほか—

坂井 隆 編

坂井 隆／大橋康二 著

雄山閣

口絵 1：トロウラン遺跡　Trowulan

トロウラン遺跡：ティクス水浴場跡（1984 年三上次男撮影）
Candi Tikus (the holy bath), Trowulan in 1984 by Prof. Mikami Tsugio

トロウラン遺跡：バジャン・ラトゥ門
Bajang Ratu Gate, Trowulan

口絵2：トロウラン遺跡　Trowulan

トロウラン遺跡：スガラン貯水池
Segaran Reservoir ruins, Trowulan

トロウラン遺跡：クダトン地区建物跡
A building ruins in Kedaton, Trowulan

口絵 3：トロウラン遺跡　Trowulan

トロウラン遺跡：発掘された居住遺構
An excavated residence ruins, Trowulan

トロウラン遺跡：発掘された別の居住遺構
Another excavated residence ruins, Trowulan

口絵4：トロウラン遺跡　Trowulan

トロウラン遺跡：旧ポント邸（1984 年三上次男撮影）
Former house of M. Pont, Trowulan in 1984 by Prof. Mikami Tsugio

トロウラン遺跡：ポント寄贈の元青花片（ジャカルタ国立博物館）
Yuan under-glaze cobalt blue shards contributed by M. Pont to Jakarta National Museum

口絵 5：トロウラン遺跡　Trowulan

トロウラン遺跡：トロウラン遺跡博物館の陶磁片屋外収蔵場所
The ceramic shards storage in Trowulan Site Museum

トロウラン遺跡：2013 年陶磁片整理調査
Analysis work of ceramic shards in 2013, Trowulan Siite

口絵6：バンテン・ラーマ遺跡　Banten Lama

バンテン・ラーマ遺跡：スロソワン王宮跡全景
Panorama of the Surosowan Palace ruins, Banten Lama

バンテン・ラーマ遺跡：スロソワン王宮内の水浴場跡
A bath structure ruins in the Surosowan Palace, Banten Lama

バンテン・ラーマ遺跡：スピルウィク要塞内に残る市壁
The City Wall ruin of Banten Lama in the Spilwijk Fort

ティルタヤサ遺跡：「スルタンの土地」
The 'Land of Sultan' in Tirtayasa

ティルタヤサ遺跡：スジュン水門跡
The water gate ruins of Sujung, Tirtayasa

口絵8：ソンバ・オプー城跡　Somba Opu Fort

ソンバ・オプー城跡：南西側城壁
The southwestern wall of Somba Opu Fort

ソンバ・オプー城跡：西城壁北方向
Northern direction of the western wall, Somba Opu Fort

口絵 9：ブトン・ウォリオ城跡　Buton Wolio Fort

ブトン・ウォリオ城跡：北東端堡塁
The northeast end bastion of Buton Wolio Fort

ブトン・ウォリオ城跡：南側堀跡の発掘調査
The excavation research of the southern moat, Buton Wolio Fort

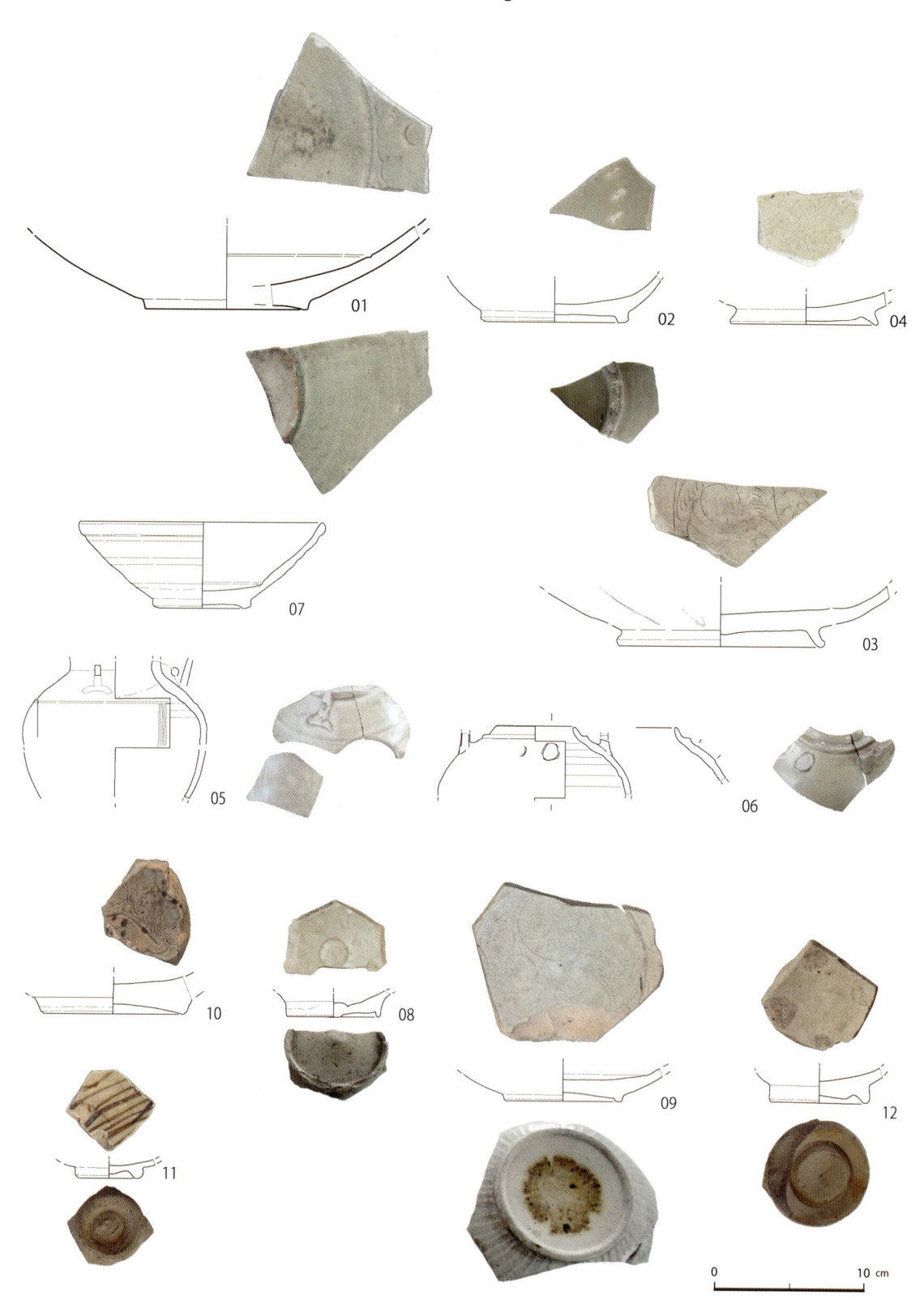

Fig.1　トロウラン遺跡　Ⅰ-1 期　Trowulan Site, Ⅰ-1 period, 中国陶磁 Chinese ceramics

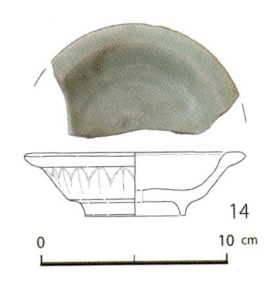

14

0 _____ 10 cm

Fig.2　トロウラン遺跡　Ⅰ-2 期
Trowulan Site, Ⅰ-2 period, 中国陶磁 Chinese ceramics

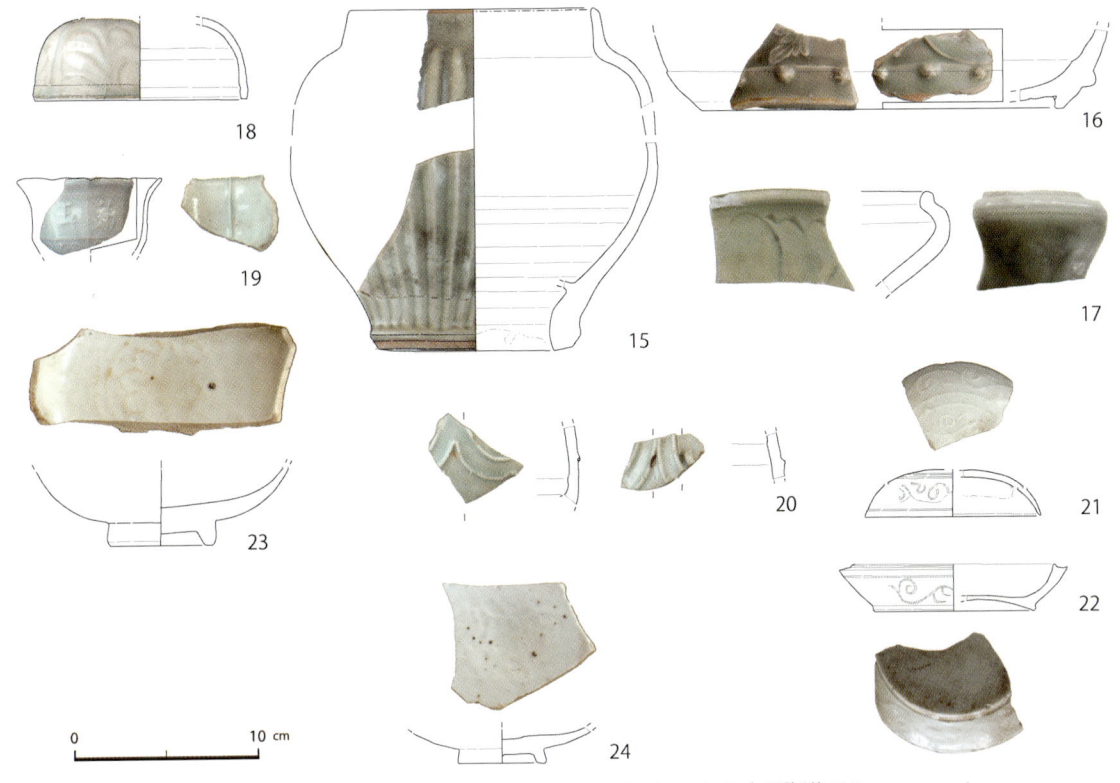

18

19

15

16

17

23

20

21

22

24

0 _____ 10 cm

Fig.3　トロウラン遺跡　Ⅱ-1 期　Trowulan Site, Ⅱ-1 period, 中国陶磁 Chinese ceramics

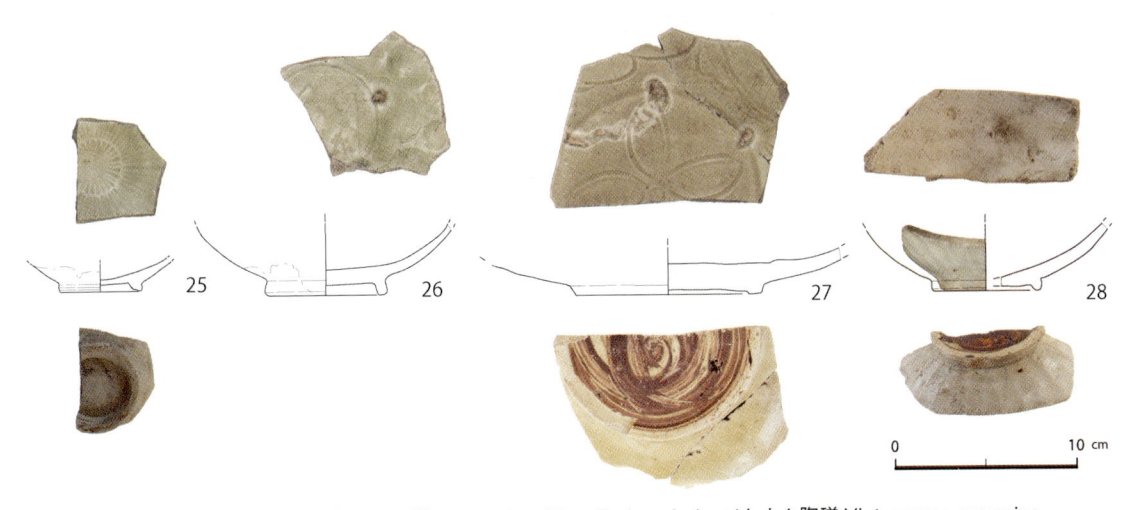

25　　26　　27　　28

0 _____ 10 cm

Fig.4　トロウラン遺跡　Ⅱ-1 期　Trowulan Site, Ⅱ-1 period, ベトナム陶磁 Vietnamese ceramics

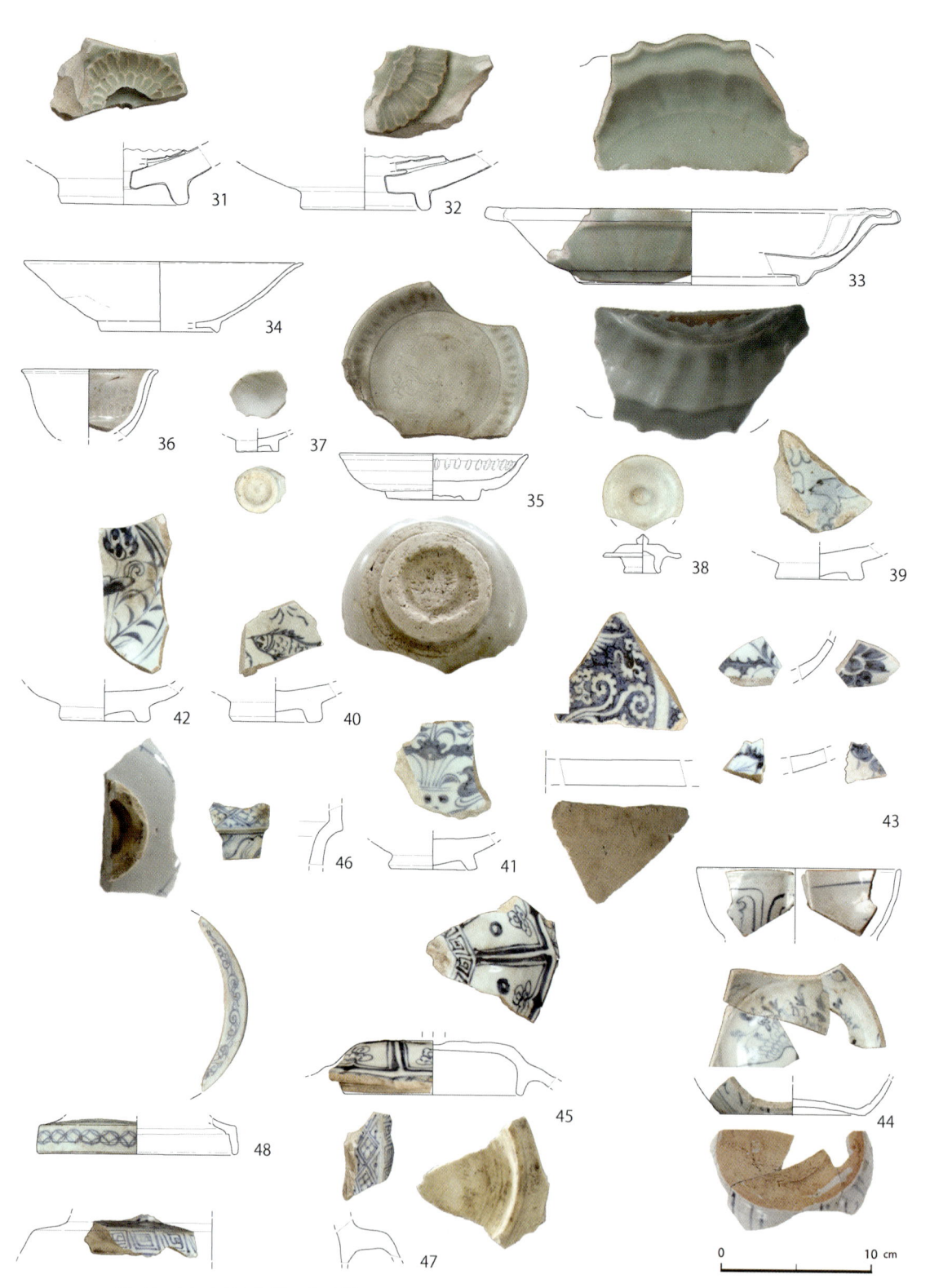

Fig.5　トロウラン遺跡　Ⅱ-2 期　Trowulan Site, Ⅱ-2 period, 中国陶磁 Chinese ceramics

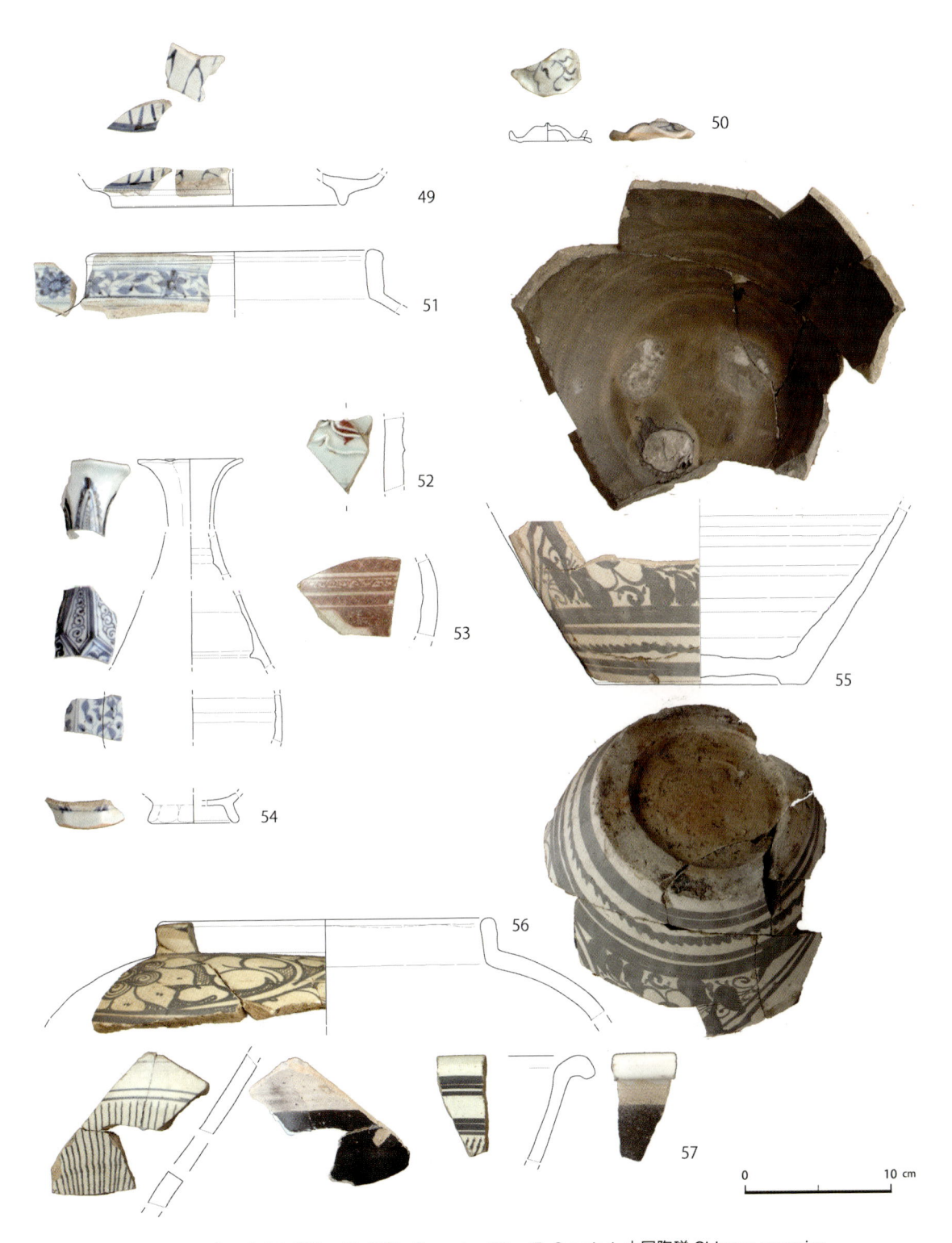

49

50

51

52

53

54

55

56

57

0　　　　　　　　　　10 cm

Fig.6　トロウラン遺跡　Ⅱ-2 期　Trowulan Site, Ⅱ-2 period, 中国陶磁 Chinese ceramics

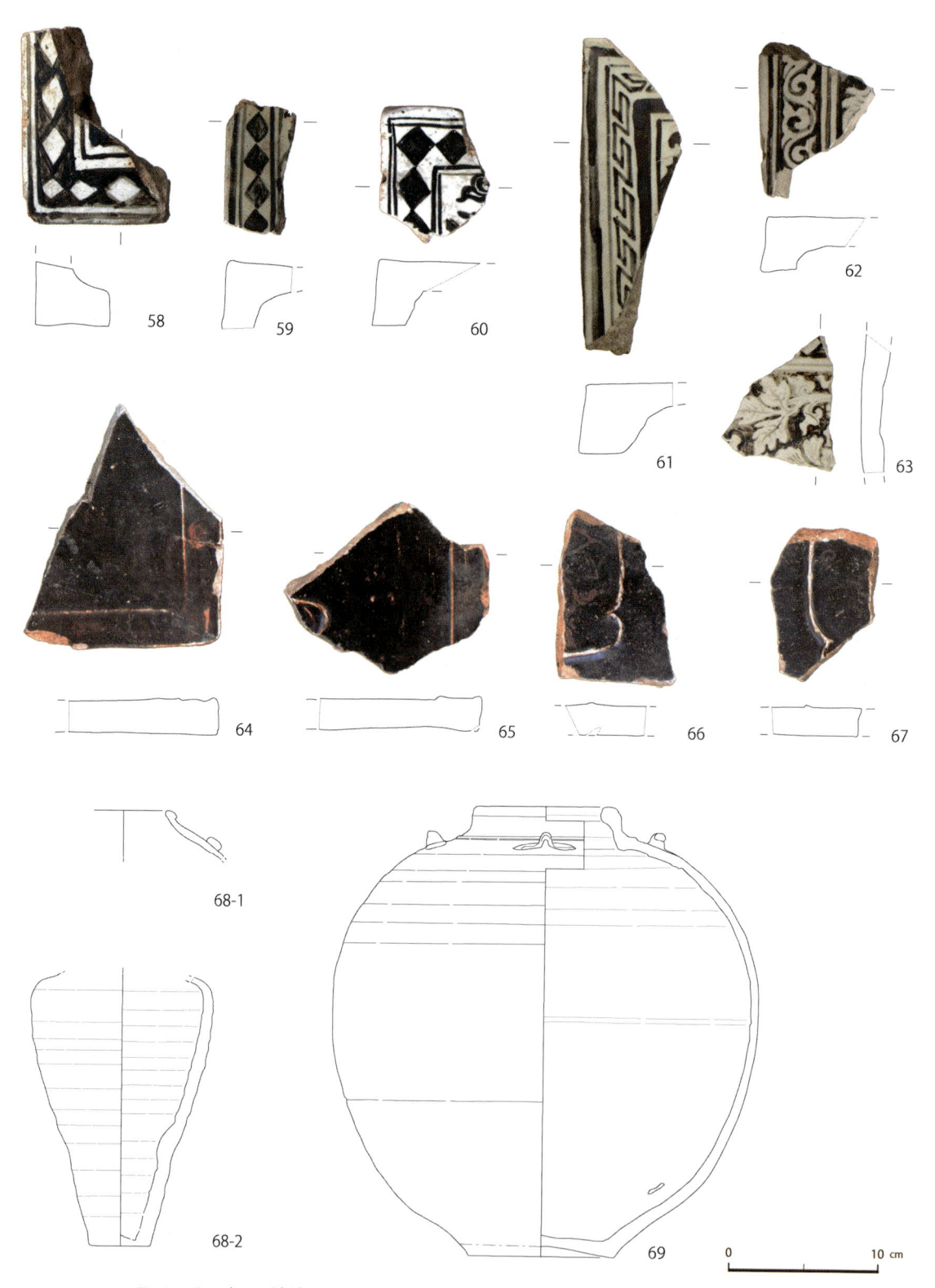

Fig.7　トロウラン遺跡　Ⅱ-2 期　Trowulan Site, Ⅱ-2 period, 中国陶磁 Chinese ceramics

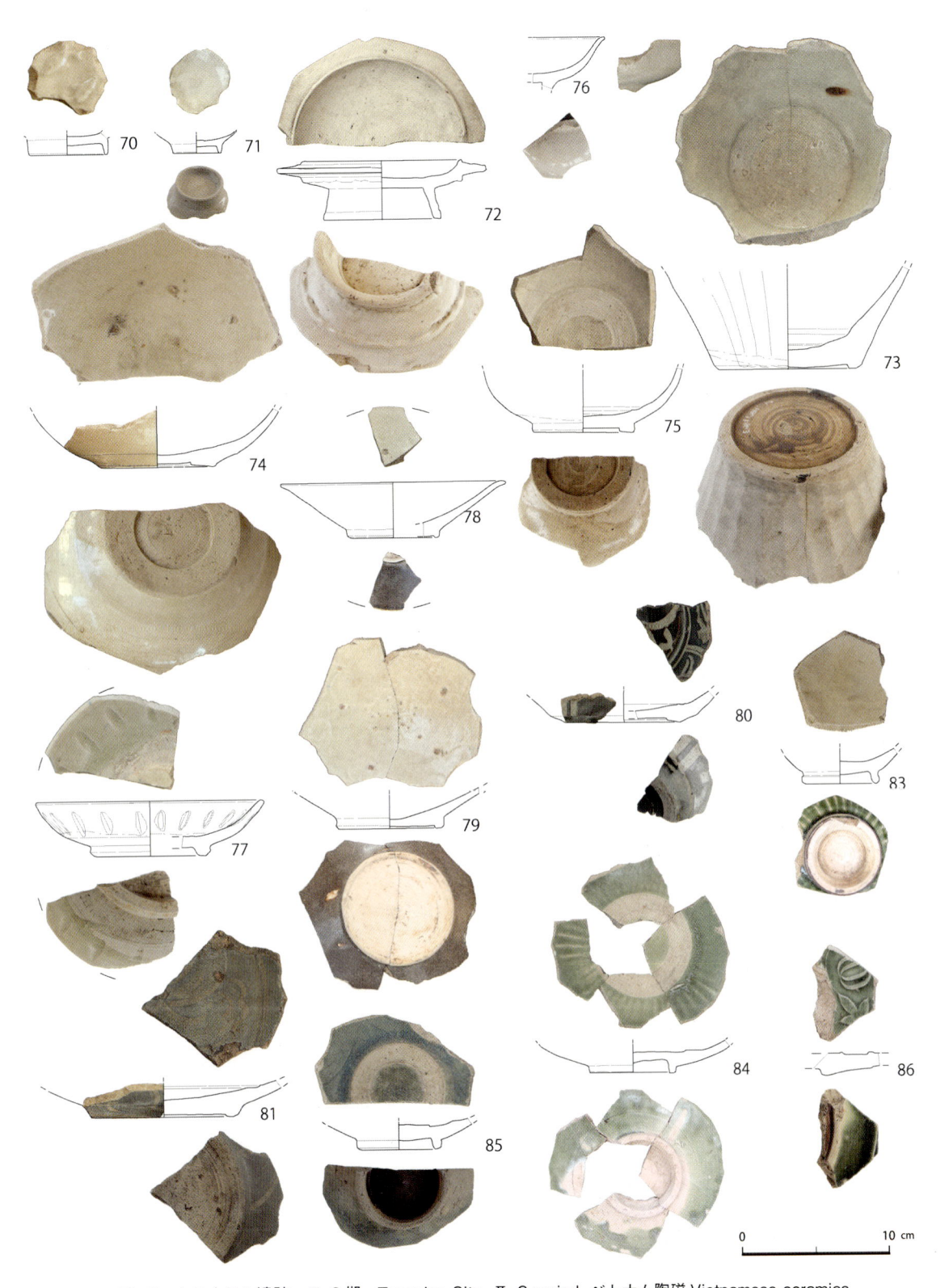

Fig.8　トロウラン遺跡　Ⅱ-2 期　Trowulan Site, Ⅱ-2 period, ベトナム陶磁 Vietnamese ceramics

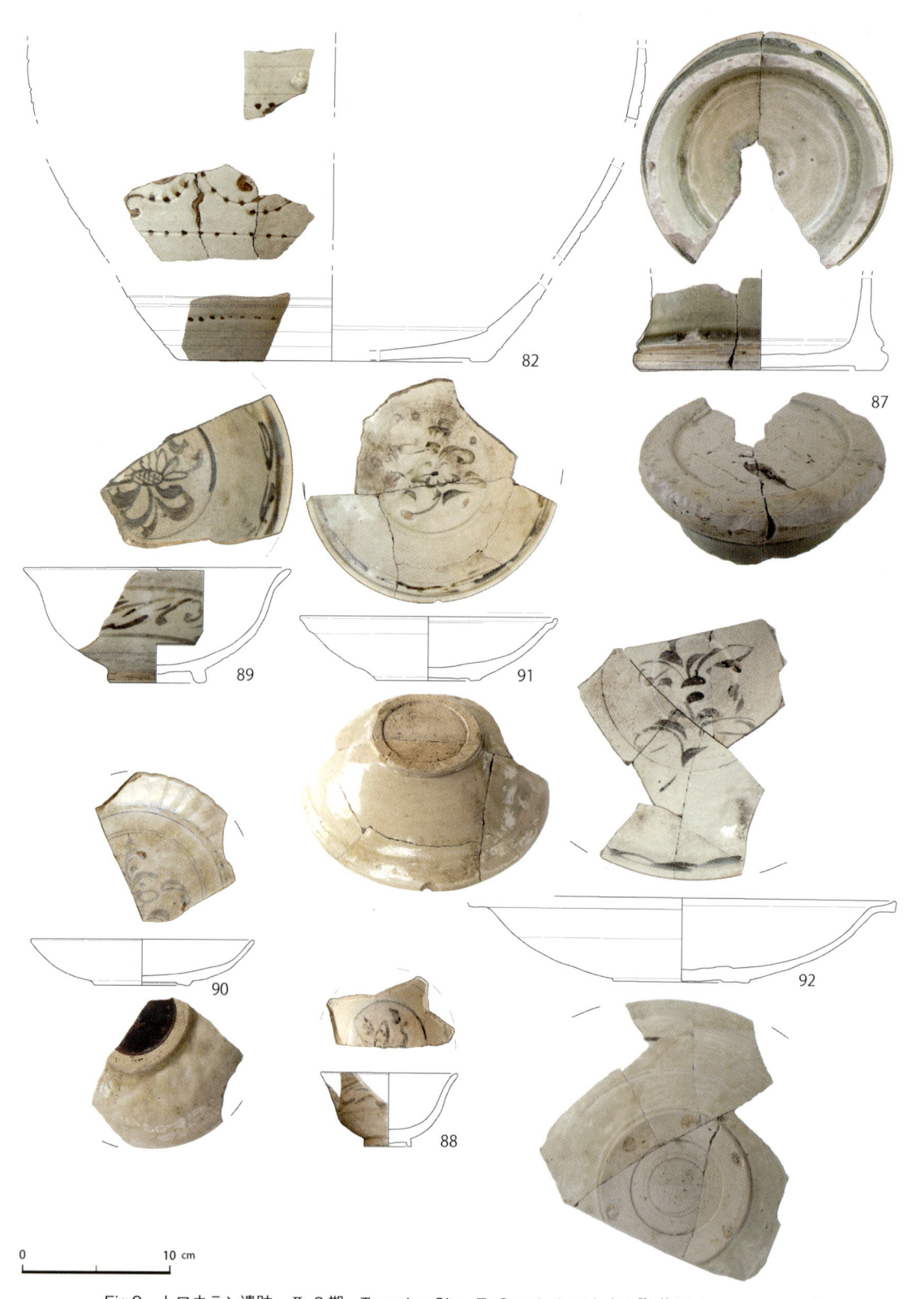

Fig.9　トロウラン遺跡　Ⅱ-2 期　Trowulan Site, Ⅱ-2 period, ベトナム陶磁 Vietnamese ceramics

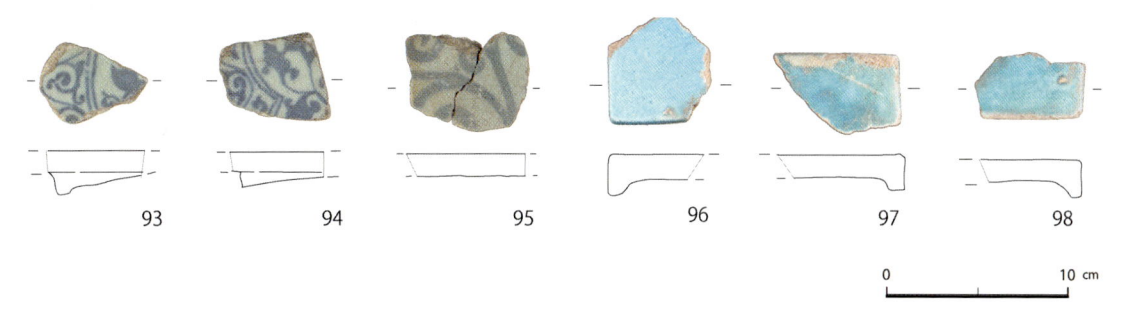

93　94　95　96　97　98

0　10 cm

Fig.10　トロウラン遺跡　Ⅱ-2 期　Trowulan Site, Ⅱ-2 period, イスラーム陶器 Islamic ceramics

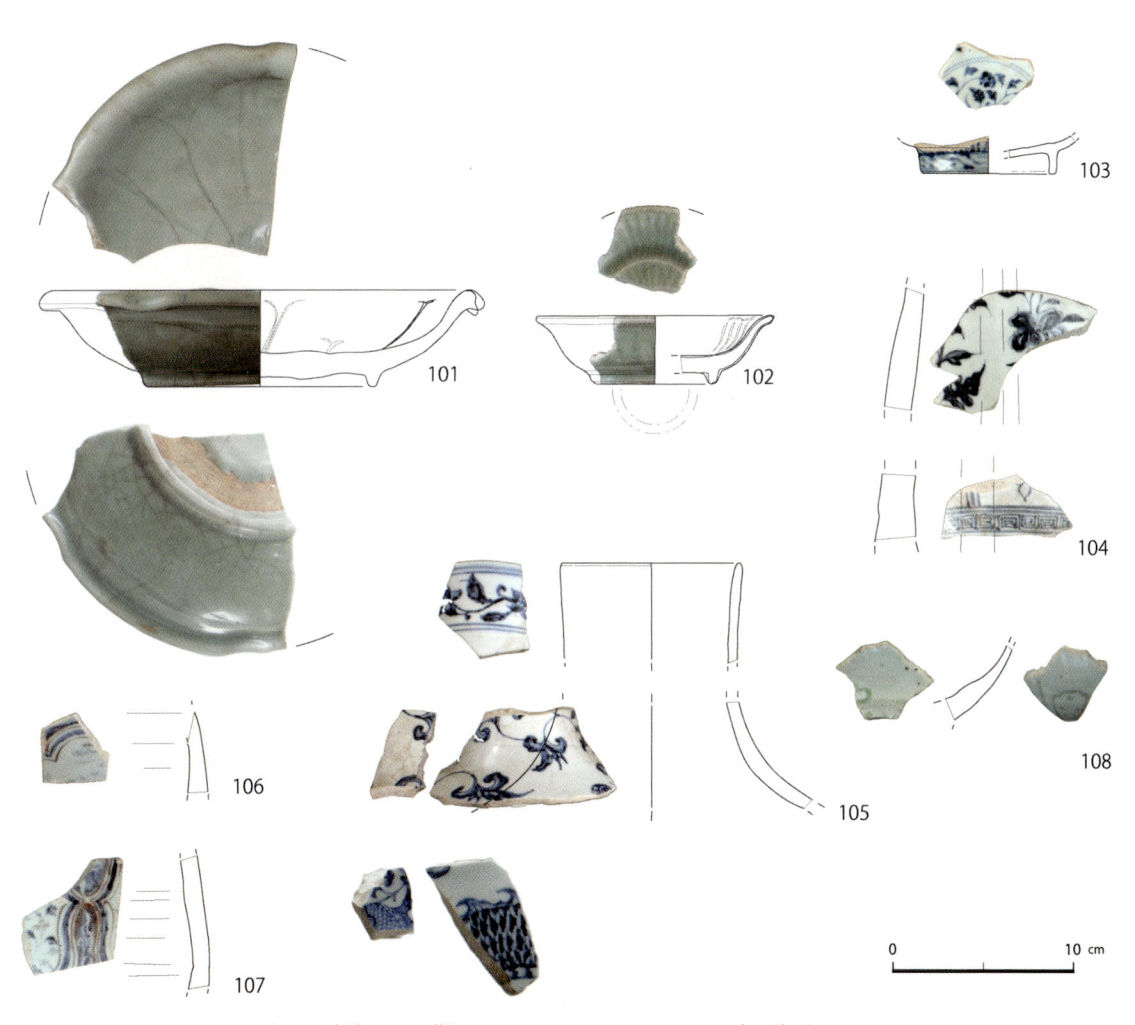

0　10 cm

Fig.11　トロウラン遺跡　Ⅲ-1 期　Trowulan Site, Ⅲ-1 period, 中国陶磁 Chinese ceramics

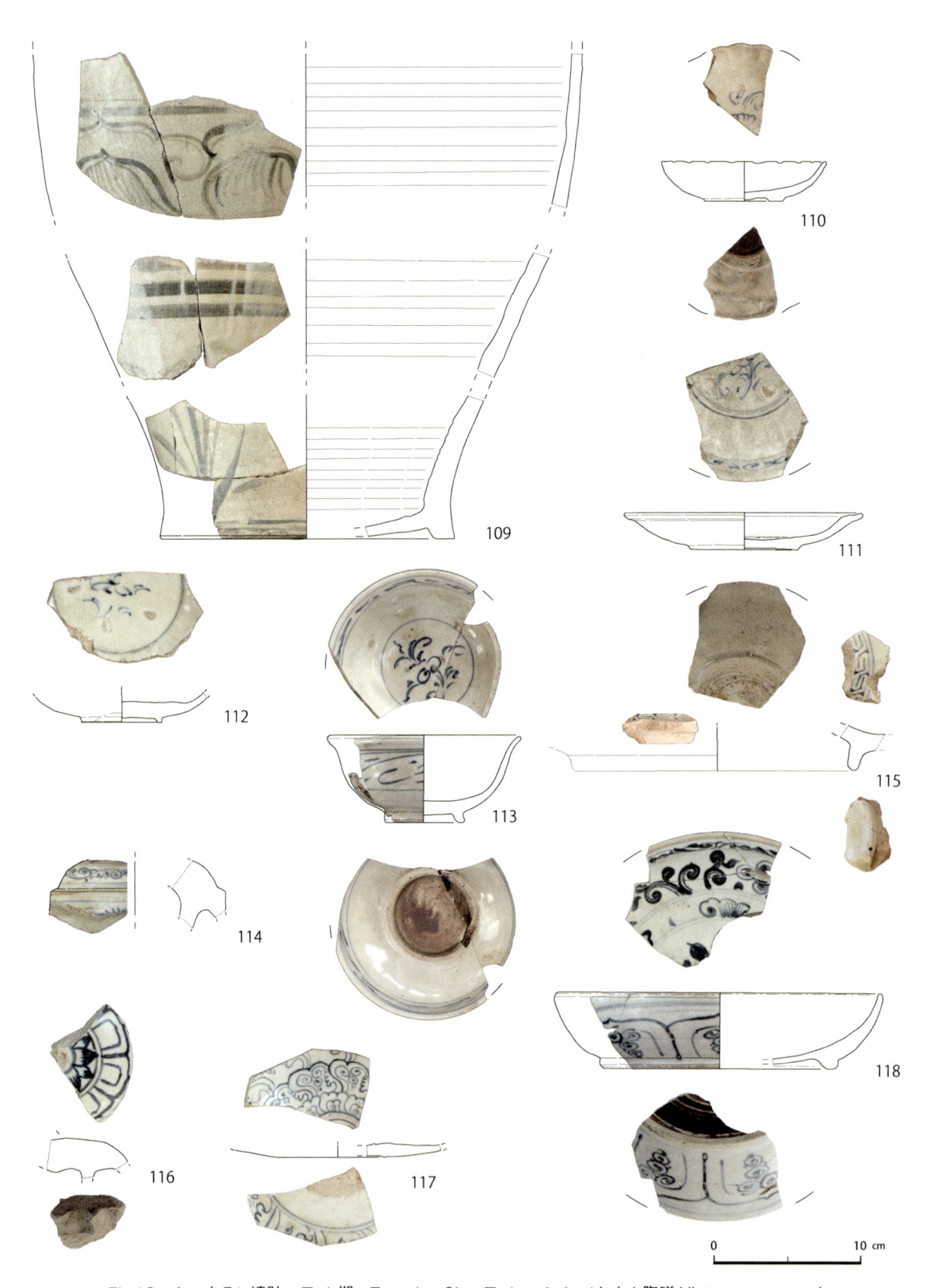

Fig.12　トロウラン遺跡　Ⅲ-1 期　Trowulan Site, Ⅲ-1 period, ベトナム陶磁 Vietnamese ceramics

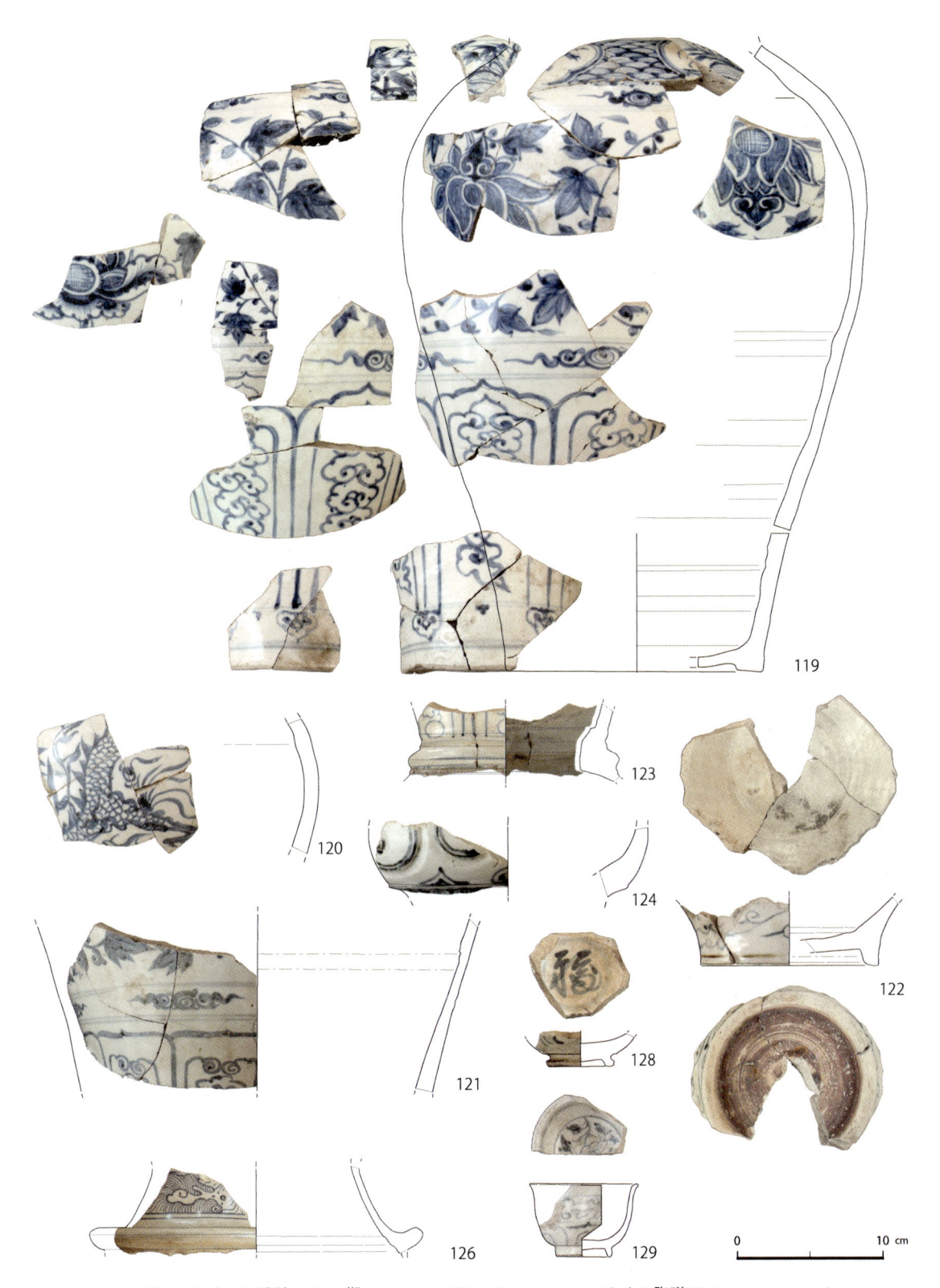

Fig.13　トロウラン遺跡　Ⅲ-1 期　Trowulan Site, Ⅲ-1 period, ベトナム陶磁 Vietnamese ceramics

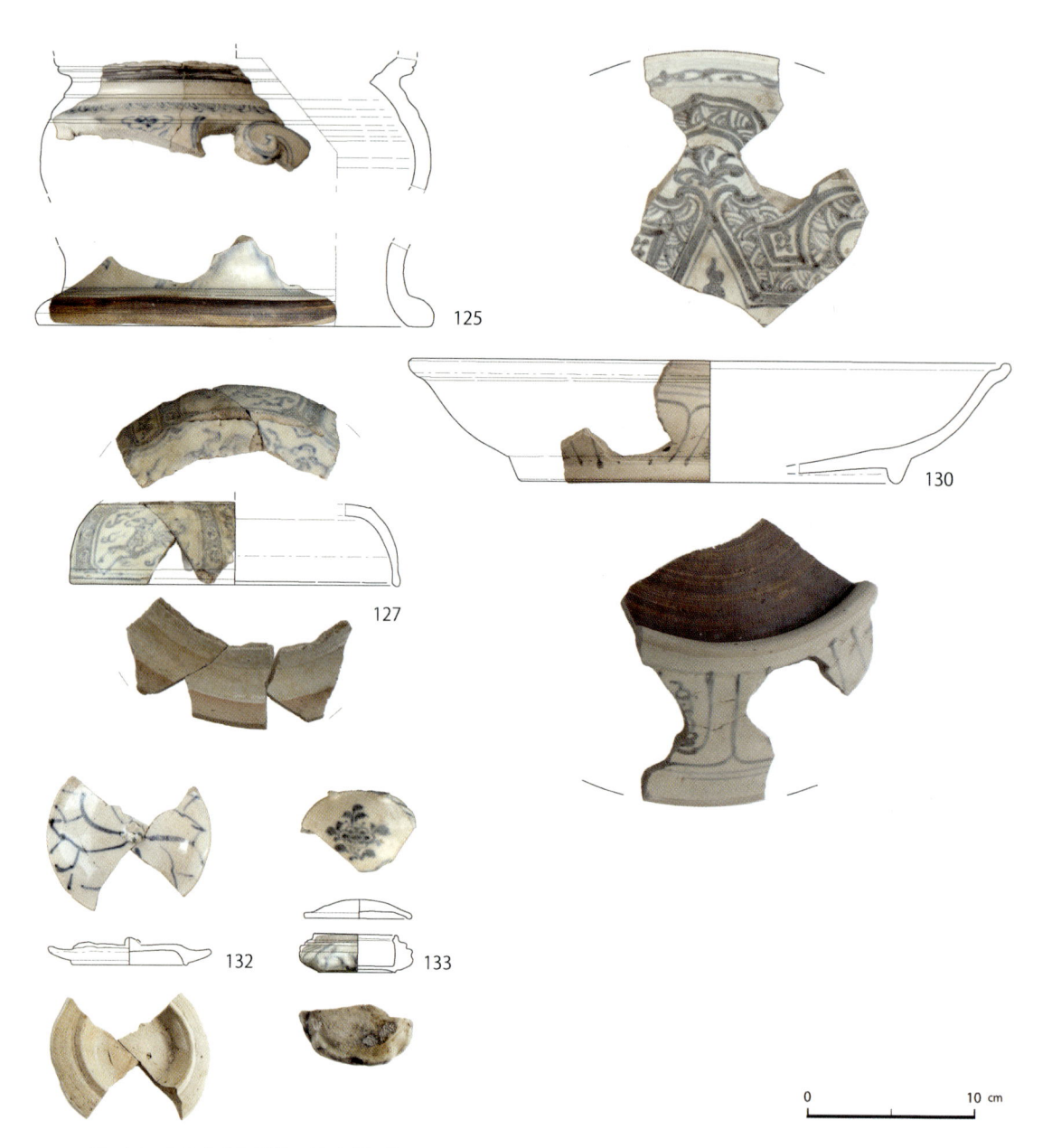

Fig.14　トロウラン遺跡　Ⅲ-1 期　Trowulan Site, Ⅲ-1 period, ベトナム陶磁 Vietnamese ceramics

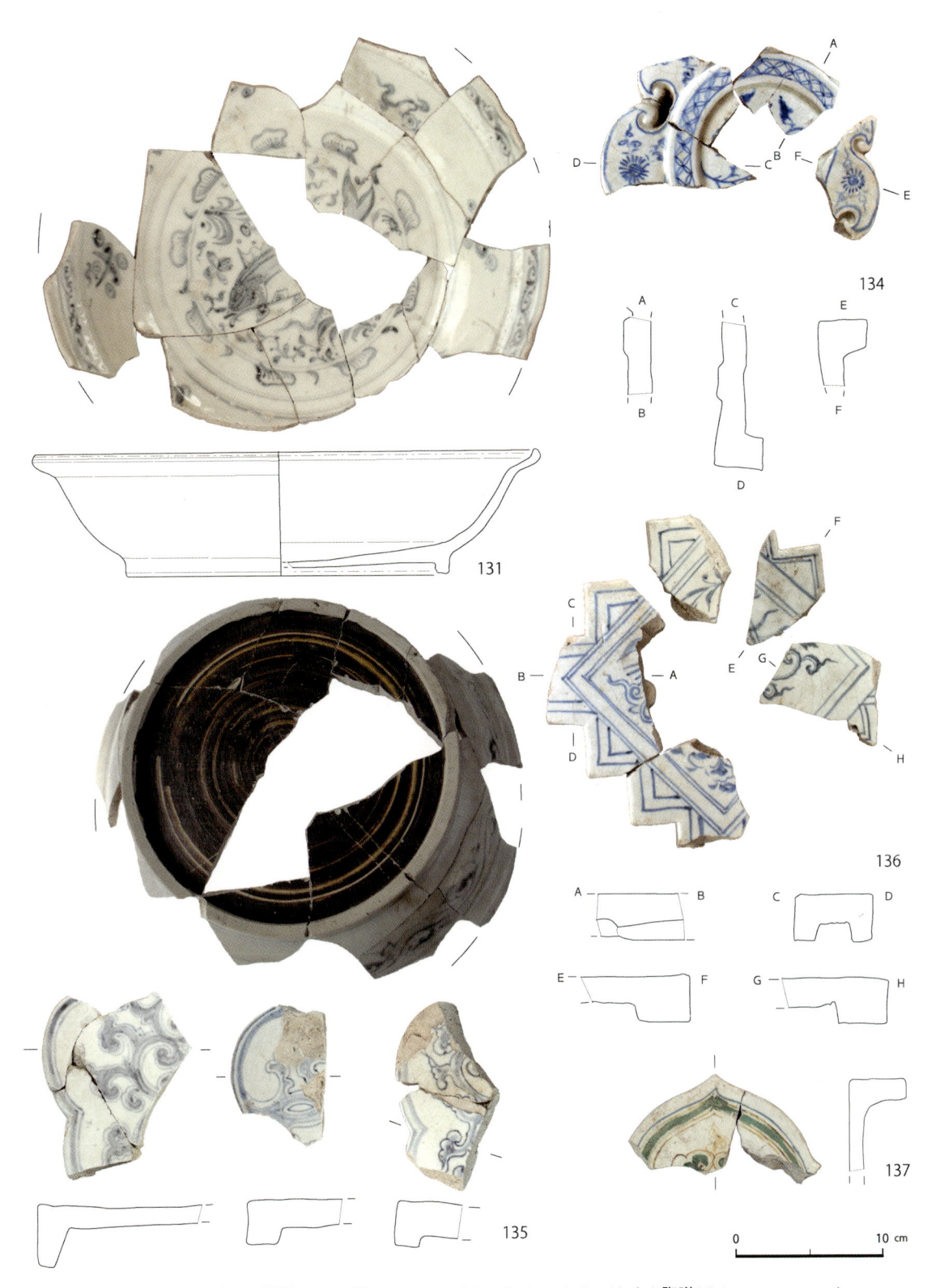

Fig.15　トロウラン遺跡　Ⅲ-1 期　Trowulan Site, Ⅲ-1 period, ベトナム陶磁 Vietnamese ceramics

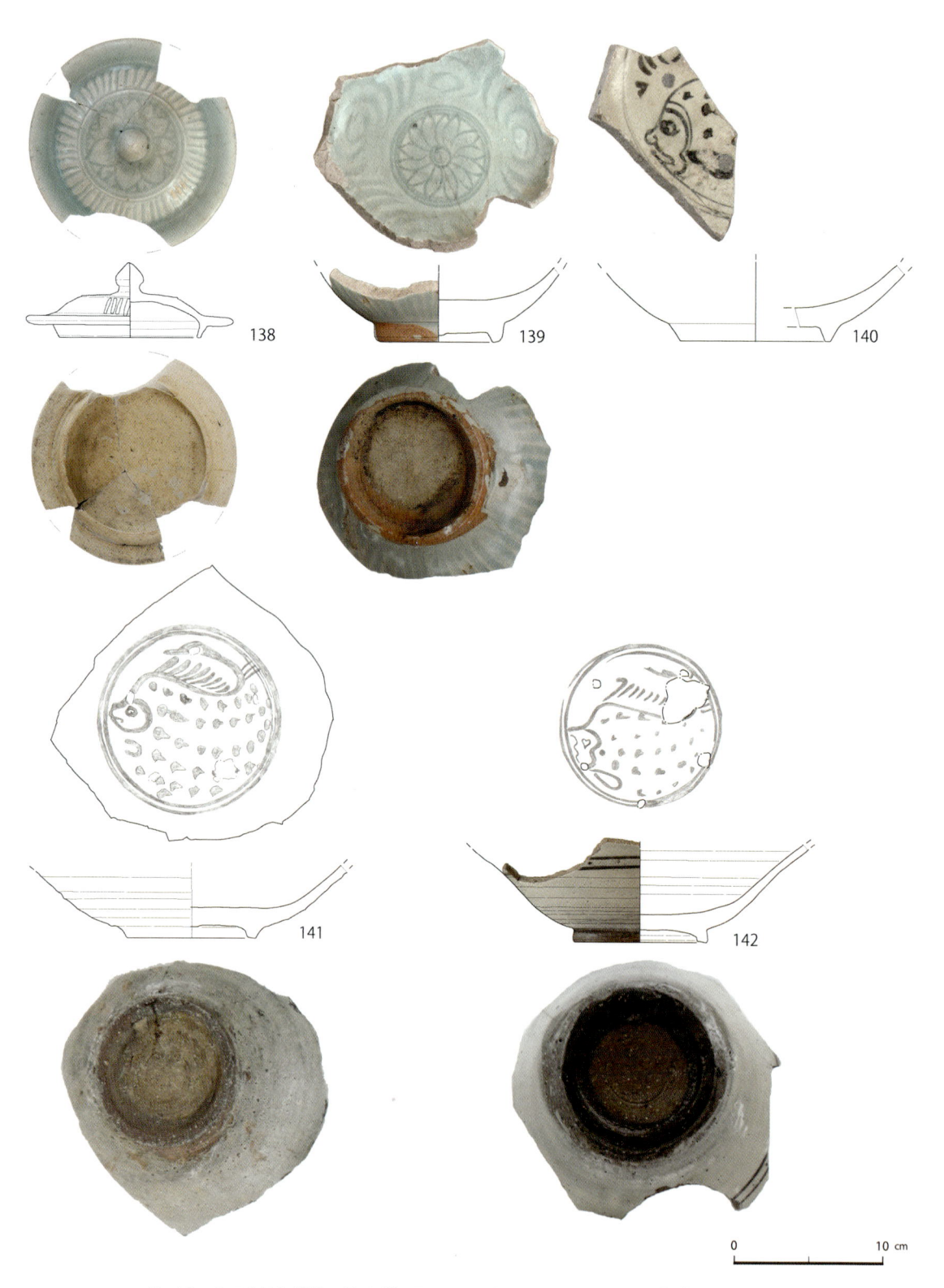

Fig.16 トロウラン遺跡 Ⅲ-1 期 Trowulan Site, Ⅲ-1 period, タイ陶磁 Thailand ceramics

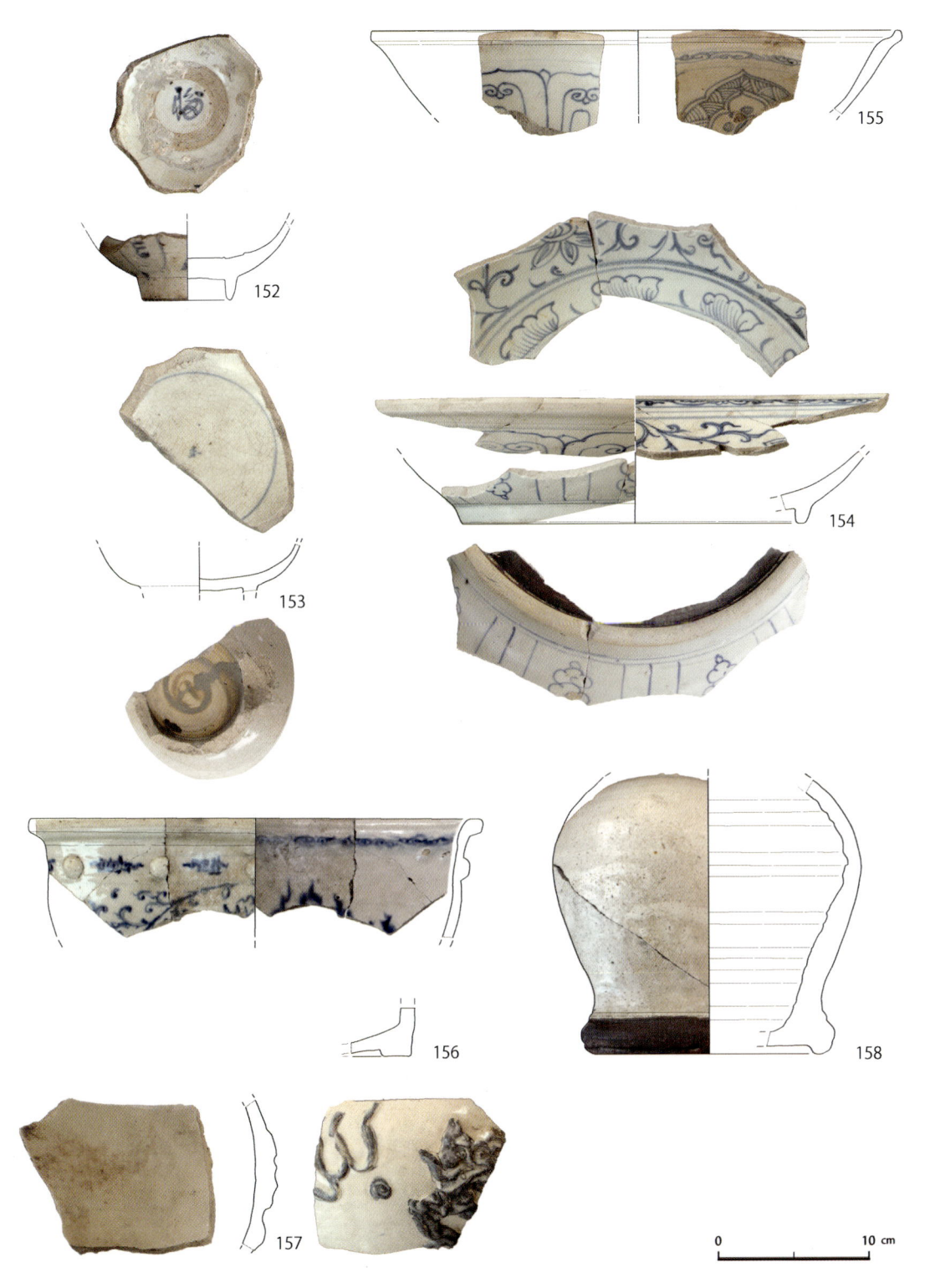

Fig.17　トロウラン遺跡　Ⅲ-2 期　Trowulan Site, Ⅲ-2 period, ベトナム陶磁 Vietnamese ceramics

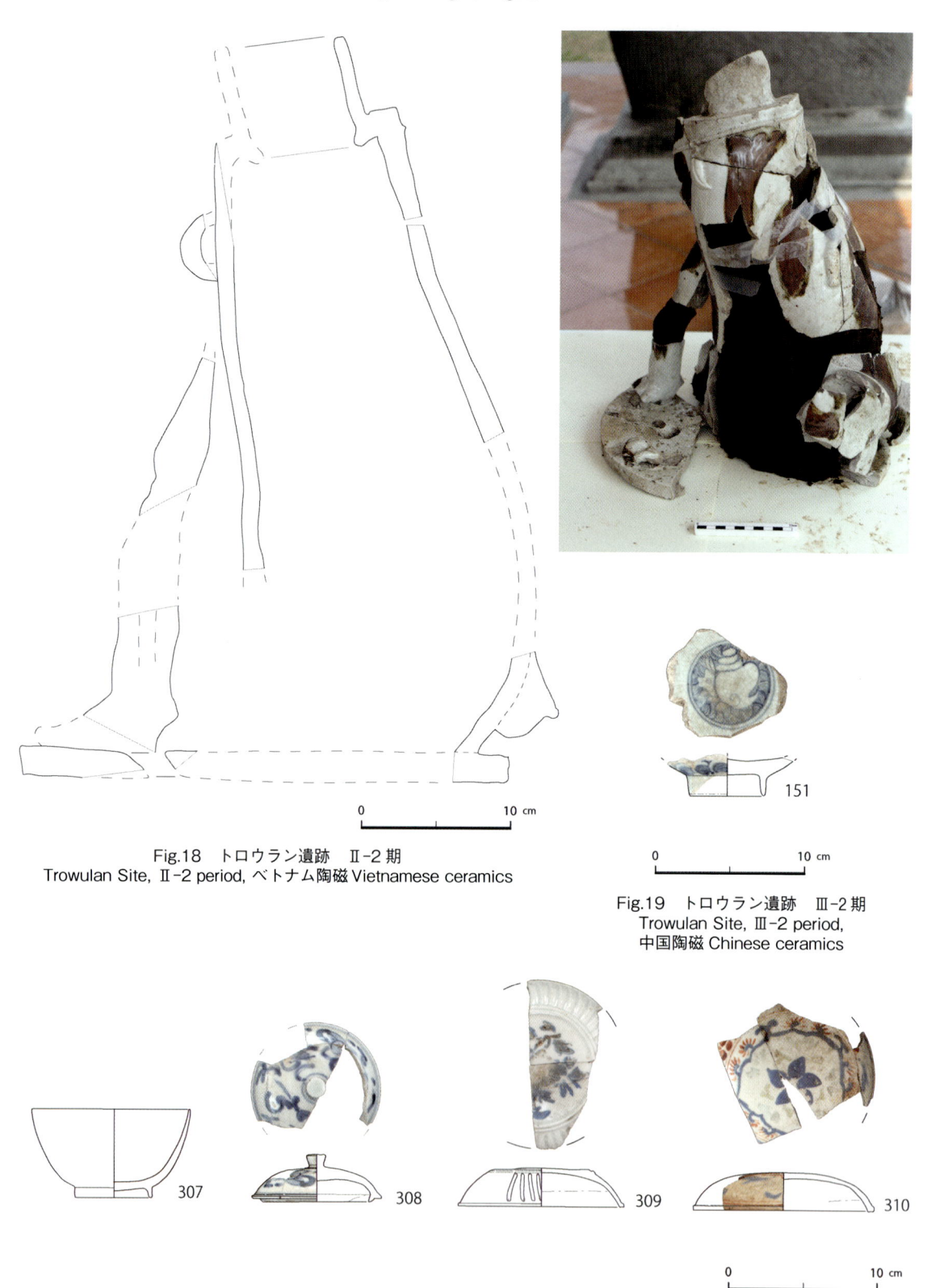

Fig.18　トロウラン遺跡　Ⅱ-2 期
Trowulan Site, Ⅱ-2 period, ベトナム陶磁 Vietnamese ceramics

151

Fig.19　トロウラン遺跡　Ⅲ-2 期
Trowulan Site, Ⅲ-2 period,
中国陶磁 Chinese ceramics

307　308　309　310

Fig.20　トロウラン遺跡　Ⅴ-2 期　Trowulan Site, Ⅴ-2 period, 肥前陶磁 Japanese Hizen ceramics

まえがき

　『陶磁の道』を提唱した三上次男は、1984年にインドネシアのトロウラン遺跡を訪ねている。その時、開始されたばかりのティクス水浴場跡やブラフ寺院跡の修復現場を見学し、また発見された陶磁片について案内をしたアブー・リドと意見を交わしている。

　トロウラン遺跡は三上が十代後半だった1920年頃に、インドネシア生まれのオランダ人建築家マクレーヌ・ポントが地元の貴族クロモジョヨ・アディネゴロと共に最初に調査を行った。その嚆矢をなしたのは、アディネゴロが発掘したティクス水浴場跡であった。修復や発掘によってすでに大量の陶磁片が地上に現れたが、ポントの友人でもあったファン・オルソイ・デ・フリーネスはそれに大きな興味を示した。そして彼はインドネシアにもたらされた陶磁器に恋い焦がれ、一生をかけて膨大な蒐集を行った。

　彼の蒐集品は後にジャカルタ国立博物館に寄贈されて、その陶磁室を形成することになる。三上を案内したアブー・リドは彼を手伝った助手であり、トロウラン遺跡の陶磁片は長く同博物館陶磁室で破片の状態のまま唯一常設されていた展示品だった。

　三上の訪問から約20年後、私たちはポントたち以来長年採集されてきたトロウラン遺跡の陶磁片を調査することになった。それは、それまでに行ってきたインドネシアの4王都遺跡での陶磁片調査を振り返るのにふさわしい内容だった。

　ここに彼ら先学たちの歩みを蘇らせ、また大きく新たな研究の道を切り拓く企図を込めて本書を刊行する。学恩に報いる意味だけでなく、私たち自身の四半世紀の試みをまとめるものでもある。

　最後に、本書の刊行に多大なご支援を賜わった公益財団法人出光文化福祉財団に対し、心よりの謝意を述べたい。

2018年1月

坂井　隆

◎インドネシアの王都出土の肥前陶磁—トロウラン遺跡ほか—◎目次

Hizen wares excavated from Royal Capital Sites in Indonesia
— Trowulan and other sites—

Translated by
Nicole Coolidge Rousmaniere

I トロウラン遺跡と4王都遺跡

1. 調査の経緯

　トロウラン Trowulan 遺跡はインドネシア共和国東部ジャワ州モジョクルト県トロウラン郡に位置し、ジャワ島第二の長さを持つブランタス川の下流右岸にあたる。そこは河口の港スラバヤからは約60km遡った平地で、東約25kmには聖山プナングンガンを望む場所である。

　トロウラン遺跡博物館に収蔵されていた未整理の陶磁片に対するインドネシア国立考古学研究センターの分類調査実施にあたって私たちは協力を行なった。同センターのナニッ・ハルカンティニンシ・ウィビソノ Naniek Harkantiningsih Wibisono 上級研究員が主導した調査は、2012年1月・13年4月そして15年8月の3回にわたって行なわれた。第1・2回の調査成果については2014年にすでに概要報告[1]を著したが、それは15%程度の重要な種類に限ったものだった。そのため2015年の調査では、本書での本報告に資するべく実測図作成など補足的な作業を行なった。

　そのような経緯からすれば、本書は本来トロウラン遺跡陶磁片調査の本報告のみでも十分であった。しかしトロウラン遺跡出土陶磁の内容は、私たちが過去25年間従事してきたインドネシアでの陶磁片調査協力[2]を総括するのに極めてふさわしい内容を含んでいた。過去に行なった陶磁片調査協力は、次の通りである（map 1 参照）。

　　1993・97年　ジャワ島バンテン・ラーマ Banten Lama 遺跡[3]

　　1997・99・2001－06年　ジャワ島ティルタヤサ Tirtayasa 遺跡[4]

　　2001年　スラウェシ島ソンバ・オプー Somba Opu 城跡[5]

　　2004－06　スラウェシ島ブトン・ウォリオ Buton Wolio 城跡[6]

　第II章で詳述するように、これら4遺跡での陶磁貿易の中心的な年代は16世紀から18世紀であった。もともと私たちのインドネシアでの調査協力の契機は肥前陶磁輸出状況の確認だったが、それにふさわしい時期の遺跡群であった。しかし実際には、極めて短期間しか存続しなかったティルタヤサ遺跡を除いて、他の3遺跡では15世紀以前の陶磁片を

1　坂井・大橋 2014

2　1991年より2007年までは任意団体のバンテン遺跡研究会として、また2007年以降はNPO法人アジア文化財協力協会として行なってきた（同協会 Web-Site 参照）。

3　大橋・坂井 1999

4　坂井編 2000・04・07

5　坂井編 2004

6　坂井編 2007

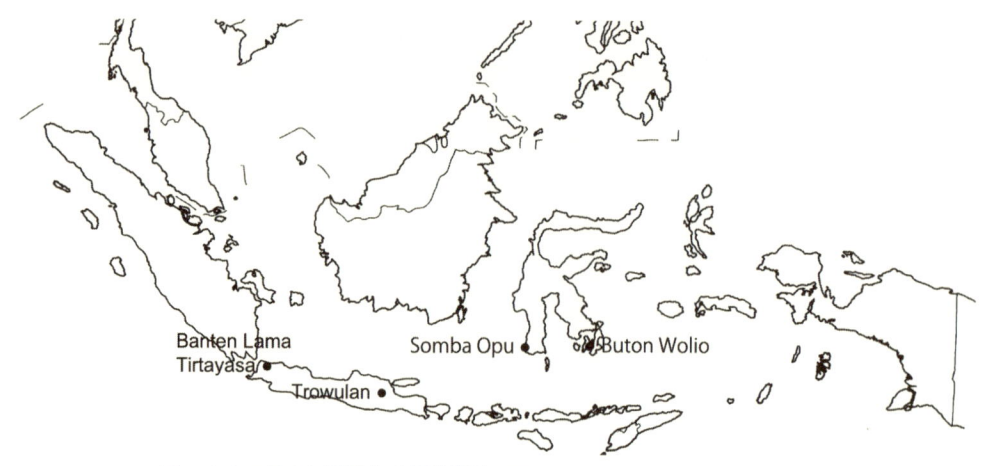

Map 1　トロラウン遺跡と 4 王都遺跡　Trowulan & 4 ancient capital sites

少なからず確認していた。

　トロウラン遺跡の陶磁片の中心的な年代は 13 世紀末から 16 世紀初頭だが、ここでも 17 世紀の肥前陶磁を少量検出したのみならず、13 世紀よりはるかに古い陶磁片も数多く発見したのである。つまりトロウランは他の 4 遺跡より基本的には古いが、完全に切り離された存在ではなく関連性があった。同時にインドネシアでの 9・10 世紀の初期陶磁貿易を考える上でも重要な存在であることも判明した。そのような状況に基づいて、本書は単にトロウラン遺跡陶磁調査の報告としてよりも、インドネシアでの陶磁貿易全体を見渡す視点での内容とすることになった。

　トロウラン遺跡の内容及びそこでの陶磁片調査の経過は重要なので、概要報告と重複するものの本書でも記したい。他の 4 遺跡については基本的に報告済みのため、個々の詳細な内容は省く形での紹介となる。東南アジア島嶼部に大きく広がるインドネシアでの陶磁貿易全体を見渡すことが、本書の最大の目的である。

2. トロウラン遺跡

　トロウラン遺跡は、マジャパイト王国の王都跡の大規模な遺跡である。

　マジャパイト王国は、5 世紀以来インド文化の影響を受けてジャワ島に連綿として樹立されたヒンドゥ・ジャワ王権の最後にして最大のものである。13 世紀末のモンゴル帝国のジャワ遠征を契機としてクルタラジャサ・ジャヤワルッダナ（ラデン・ウィジャヤ）王（在位 1293 – 1309）によって 1293 年に建国され、14 世紀後半のラジャサナガラ（ハヤム・ウルク）王（在位 1350 – 89）の時代には名宰相ガジャ・マダの補佐によって現在のインドネシアの領域に匹敵する範囲に影響力を及ぼしたとされる。その後 15 世紀初頭には明の鄭和の来訪を受ける勢いを保ったものの、15 世紀後半にはジャワ島北岸に発展したイスラーム港市の台頭により急速に力を失った。そして 1527 年頃には、ドゥマッを中心とする新興の

イスラーム港市国家の攻撃で王都トロウランは陥落したとされる。

　マジャパイトの凋落はジャワ島のイスラーム化と同じ現象であり、世界最大のイスラーム人口を有する現代のインドネシアのイスラーム教徒にとって大きな意味のあるできごとだった。しかしジャワの伝統的イスラーム信仰の中で、マジャパイトは決して否定的な存在にはなっていない。ドゥマッに始まるジャワのイスラーム王権は、マジャパイト王と繋がる系譜伝承[7]を有している。

　オランダ植民地時代の 1920 年前後にトロウランの学術的調査はマクレーヌ・ポント（1884-1971）とクロモジョヨ・アディネゴロによって開始されたが、インドネシア独立を目指す民族主義者たちには、マジャパイトは理想的な過去の栄光と考えられた。そのため独立後の 1950 年代末にはトロウランは重点的な調査研究対象となり、2009 年には世界文化遺産の国内候補になっている。

遺跡の概要

　トロウラン遺跡の状態を見てみよう。

　1976 年から開始された考古学研究センターによる調査での特に重要な発見は、航空写真によるトロウラン全体を覆うように格子状に配された運河網の存在である。城壁状の施設が全く発見されない中でトロウラン遺跡の範囲は現在 9×11km と推定されているが、その中心部分にこの運河網が存在した。遺跡の中心部（約 4km 四方）は、大きく次のような 4 地区遺構群に分けられる。

(1) クダトン地区

　運河網の中心に位置し、さまざまなレンガ造遺構が発見されてきている。中でも基壇のみが残るクダトン寺院に隣接して、何回も立て直されたレンガ建築が眼を惹く。その西には八角形に加工された長大な高床建物の礎石群が残り、また南側ではスントノレジョ居住跡が発掘されている。後者では六角形の無釉磚で敷き詰められた床面が、きれいに発見された。クダトンとはジャワ語で宮殿を指すクラトンに似た語調であるため、この地区にトロウランの中枢部があった可能性は大きい。南に接するトロロヨ地区には、1368 年のヒジュラ暦年を記すトロウラン最古のイスラーム墓群がある。

(2) スガラン池地区

　クダトンから 1.5km ほど北に位置する長方形の人造湖スガラン池（約 370×150m）を中心とする部分で、池の南西側ではやはりレンガ造の大規模な居住跡が 2 ヶ所発掘されている。また池の北東側で運河に沿った場所に、チャンパ王女の墓と伝えられる 1448 年の紀

7　現在まで伝わる伝承ではマジャパイトの王名は初代王より全てブラウィジャヤとなっているが、同時代の金石文にはそのような王名はない。王の通称ラデン・ウィジャヤやハヤム・ウルクの名も後の伝承名である。

年銘を持つイスラーム墓が残っている。トロウラン博物館は、ここの居住跡発見地に近接して建設された。

（3）北方寺院群

　スガラン池の北北西約2kmには、現存する最大のレンガ造寺院であるブラフ寺院跡がある。周辺には他にも寺院跡が散在し、宗教的地域と想定することもできる。ブラフの真東約2kmには、レンガ造の割れ門ウリンギン・ラワン門が残っている。

（4）東方寺院群

　クダトンの東約2kmには、寺院の門と考えられるレンガ造のバジャン・ラトゥ門がある。東部ジャワ様式のヒンドゥ寺院本殿建築の礼拝室を刳り貫いて門としたもので、割れ門よりは古い型式である。さらにその1km弱東には、ティクス水浴場跡が位置する。1914年にアディネゴロによって発見され、東に聖山プナングンガン（1653m）やその南側のアルジュノ山群（3389m）への眺望がある。プナングンガン山中から山麓には、ジョロトゥンド水浴場跡（977年）やブラハン水浴場跡（1042年）などの祭祀遺跡やジャウィ（1300年）などの寺院跡などが数多く発見されている。

陶磁片の調査

　だがトロウランでの陶磁片研究の進展には時間がかかり、1920年代にファン・オルソイ・デ・フリーネス（1886-1964）が関心を示して以降、長い空白期間が続いた。出土元青花とベトナムタイルへの接近は、1970年代末から80年代にかけて繭山康彦が最初に行なった[8]。また盗掘資料を中心としたものだが、ベトナムタイルへの関心もジョン・ガイによって継続された[9]。両者の研究は確実な発掘資料には基づいてはいないが、当時の状況の中では大きな刺激を与えたと言える。

　1990年代初めに考古学研究センターが大規模な分布調査を行なったものの、結果的に私たちのカウンターパートであるナニッ・ウィビソノがマリー・デュポワザと連名で初めての図録を刊行したのは、2007年のことである[10]。これは考古学研究センターが行なった調査で検出された陶磁片が対象であり、トロウラン博物館保管のものではないが、トロウラン遺跡出土陶磁片についての初めての学術報告となった。そして2010年には亀井明徳とジョン・ミクシッが、シンガポール大学の所蔵するトロウラン出土とされる青花陶磁片

8　繭山 1977・85

9　Guy 1989a

10　Duppoizat & Naniek, 2007　そこには景徳鎮陶磁として35点の文様のある青花または釉裏紅があった（25点を元代とする）。掲載写真がどのくらい出土量全体を反映しているかは不明だが、元代のものでは、略描様式と至正様式の混在を示している。またベトナム陶器として掲載された破片には、青磁・褐釉・鉄絵・鉄釉白花・青花・五彩そして陶製塑像（青磁・青花・白釉・白釉褐彩）が含まれていた。

の詳細な整理報告書を刊行した[11]。

　ここで私たちの調査対象となった陶磁片の来歴を記したい。

　オランダ人建築家マクレーヌ・ポントは、1921−24年に初めてトロウランの発掘調査を行なった。彼はナーガラクルターガマ[12]に記された王都の姿の再現を試み、建築家としての復元図作成も試みた。アディネゴロの協力で1924年にトロウランに建てられたポントの家は実質的には博物館として機能し、陶磁片を含む多くの出土品がここに集められた。

　ポントは陶磁片自体への理解は少なかったが、家の庭に陶磁片の集積場（野外収蔵施設）を設けた。ファン・オルソイ・デ・フリーネスは、ポントの集めた資料の中から重要なものの抽出を行なった[13]。インドネシア独立後の1960年代初頭になって、トロウラン遺跡の調査は重要な国家プロジェクトの1つとして位置付けられ、旧ポント邸は当時の考古庁の分室となった。やがてポント邸跡は東部ジャワ文化財管理事務所になって、博物館機能は陶磁片を含め97年に建設されたトロウラン博物館へ移された。

　それらの陶磁片は、博物館の構内にある旧ポント邸と同様の野外陶磁片集積場（約3×2×0.5m）に収納された。一部の陶磁片にはポントの調査による注記がされてあり、ポント以降絶えず収納され続けてきた破片と考えられる。博物館建設後に発見された陶磁片は建物内に袋詰めされており、この集積場に袋なしに納められていた破片は全て施釉陶磁のみであることからも、ポント時代以来のトロウランでの出土資料であることは間違いない。しかしほとんどが出土地点情報を欠いていた。

3. 4 王都遺跡

　4王都遺跡とは、ジャワ島西部にあったバンテン王国の王都バンテン・ラーマと離宮跡のティルタヤサ遺跡、そしてスラウェシ島南部ゴワ王国王都のソンバ・オプー城と南東部ブトン王国王都のウォリオ城である。これらはいずれもイスラーム王国の権力中枢であるとともに、ウォリオ城を除いて最終的にオランダによって破壊されて遺跡となった[14]。

　それぞれの概要を記してみよう。

11　亀井・ミクシック2010　残念ながら対象となった陶磁片はトロウラン出土の蓋然性が高いものの、盗掘品のため由来を証明することはできない。

12　1365年に宮廷詩人プラパンチャがマジャパイトの状態を記した讃歌で、1894年にロンボク島で発見された。デーサワルナナが本来の名称。

13　全て大皿と思われる至正様式元青花7片の他に中国陶磁では磁州窯の翡翠釉鉢片もあり、またベトナム青花・五彩タイルとターコイズブルー色のイスラームタイルも含んでいた。それらは最近まで長く、ジャカルタ国立博物館の陶磁器部門で唯一の展示陶磁片となっていた。

14　13世紀末以降、多数のイスラーム王国が現在のインドネシア領域に生まれたが、マジャパイトのような広大な地域へ影響力を持ったものはなかった。そのため大小のイスラーム王国は各地にあるが、オランダと抗争して廃墟になったイスラーム王宮は他にスマトラ北端のアチェ王国を除けば多くない。

3-1. バンテン・ラーマ遺跡

　バンテン・イスラーム王国は、16 世紀初頭にジャワとスマトラの間のスンダ海峡に誕生した王権である。王統の由来は必ずしも明確ではないが、中部ジャワに誕生したイスラーム王国ドゥマッの系譜を引くとともに、創始者のファタヒラはスマトラ北端アチェのサムドゥラ・パサイ出身のイスラーム学者とされている。確実なことは、1527 年には王都バンテンに次ぐ重要港市スンダ・クラパ（後のバタヴィア、現在のジャカルタ）までが、バンテン王国の支配下に入っていたことである。

　もともとスンダ海峡地域はコショウの産地として知られ、早くからインド系文化が根付いていた。この地域の重要性の証しは、バンテン川の河口から 10 km 強に位置する堀で囲まれたバンテン・ギラン遺跡である。ここは前イスラーム時代の拠点で、12・13 世紀を中心に大量の貿易陶磁が出土している。1511 年のポルトガルによるマラッカの占領は、ムスリム商人の東西交易ルートとしてのマラッカ海峡忌避を生み出したが、コショウを産するスンダ海峡のバンテンは重要な代替ルートの要地となった。そして 1596 年、アジアに最初にやってきたオランダ人は南アフリカから一直線にバンテンに向かい、ここでコショウを手に入れた[15]。

　やがてオランダは 1619 年バンテンの内部対立に乗じてスンダ・クラパを占領しバタヴィアと改称するが、以後約 1 世紀半の間、さまざまな紆余曲折はあるもののバタヴィアとバンテンは基本的には相互補完的な機能を持つ東南アジア島嶼部最大の港市として並存した。政治的な力関係は 1682 年以降バタヴィアのオランダ東インド会社が圧倒的な優位に立つが、バンテンが築いていたアジアネットワークは 18 世紀中葉に起きた第 2 次内乱にオランダが関与するまで維持されていた。18 世紀後半にはバンテンのスルタンは完全なオランダの傀儡でしかなくなるが、それでも同様の立場に置かれた他のジャワのいずれの王権とも異なって、1809 年の王宮破壊そして 1832 年の最後のスルタン追放という過程により王国は完全に消滅させられた。1799 年に東インド会社から引き継いだオランダ植民地政府にとって、存続を許されないような存在だったと言える。

　17 世紀後半には 10 万人の人口があったとされるバンテン川河口のバンテンは、王国消滅以後は農村のバンテン・ラーマ（「古バンテン」）になってしまい、わずかに大モスクと華人寺院観音寺だけがかつての姿を思いおこさせる存在だった。そのようなバンテン・ラーマに対して初めてなされた研究が、1900 年にセルリエルが行なった 36 ヶ所に及ぶ残存地名の収録である[16]。しかし最初の考古学的な調査の開始は、1968 年のインドネシア大学と国立文化財研究センターの共同での表面採集まで待たねばならなかった。8 年経った

15　ここで彼らは華人などアジア中の貿易商と出会っている。それはこの時点での陶磁貿易の華やかさを想定させるものだった。

16　Serruriel 1902

1976年、改組された国立考古学研究センターはインドネシア大学との協力の下、ラーマでの最初の発掘調査を実施した。ハッサン・アムバリィが指導したこの調査は、インドネシア考古学の中で新しく確立されたイスラーム文化考古学という研究部門での初めての本格的な発掘調査であった。2年後に公刊された調査報告書[17]は、その後のバンテンのみならずイスラーム文化考古学の方向を示した記念碑的な研究成果であった。

　ラーマでの発掘調査はその後も毎年継続して進められたが、同時に調査の中心となったスロソワン王宮跡などを始めとする遺跡の保存活動が開始された。そのような発掘調査と遺跡保存活動の最初の成果が、1988年にハッサンとハルワニ・ミフロブらによって編集されて『バンテン考古学資料集』[18]として公刊された。ここで初めて調査状況から検出遺構また陶磁片を含む出土遺物の代表的なものが、写真と共に提示されることになった。

遺跡の概要

　バンテン・ラーマ遺跡は市壁で囲まれた部分を城内とし、その外側が華人街のあった西城外、そして大市場が位置した東城外に分かれる。また城内は、南東から北西に貫流するバンテン川を境にして、王宮やイスラーム大寺院のある左岸と海に面した右岸に区分できる。

(1) 城内左岸

　スロソワン王宮跡は城内の中心で、北側の王宮前広場を隔てて現在も多くの参拝者で賑わう大モスクに接する。現在の王宮跡の城壁（高3m、最大幅14m、東西282×南北140m、内部面積約23,600㎡）は四隅に星形稜堡を伴う長方形で、1680年に亡命オランダ人技術者が築造したものである。内部で発掘調査されたのは、北西側の正門近くを中心とする一帯で、レンガで築かれた儀礼的な建物の一部・水浴場・上水道施設などが検出されている。城壁北外側の調査でも多くの建物基礎が確認されており、現城壁建造以前の時期も当然存在する。

(2) 城内右岸

　カイボン宮殿跡はスロソワン王宮跡から南東へ約500m離れる。19世紀初頭に建立された最後のスルタンの王母宮殿と言われ、割れ門が連なるレンガ積壁とモスク跡、そして本殿の一部が現存する。しかしここで発見された陶磁片は17世紀代のものも少なくない。17世紀にはバンテン川が城内に入る右岸地点にあたっており、当時の何らかの施設が存在した可能性がある。

17　Hasan et al. 1978
18　Hasan et al. 1988

(3) 西城外

　スピルウィク要塞跡は、旧バンテン川の河口部右岸に位置する。この要塞はオランダが1685年に築いたもので、珊瑚石灰岩による変形四角形の構造である。この要塞内部には、市壁（下幅約1.5m、高さ約4m）が取り込まれている。旧バンテン川河口対岸のパベアン（税関地区）には、18世紀後半以降に建立された華人寺院観音寺がある。

　華人街跡（パチナン）はスロソワン王宮跡の西約600m方向で、モスク跡と19世紀前半の華人墓が残っている。ここが華人地区になったのは1630年代以降で、1590年代の木柵に囲まれた華人地区は観音寺のあたりにあった。

(4) 東城外

　スロソワン王宮跡の北東約700mには、木柵で囲まれたかつての大市場があった。現在も活気があるカランガントゥ港とその市場にあたる。現在遺跡博物館に展示されている青銅巨砲「キ・アムッ」は、20世紀初頭にはここにあった。

陶磁片の調査

　1976年の最初の発掘調査以来、大量の陶磁片が出土した。85年にはスロソワン王宮の前に建てられた遺跡博物館が開館したが、当時インドネシアでは珍しい存在であったこの遺跡博物館には西部ジャワ等地域文化財管理事務所も併設され、文化財保護行政の中心となった。調査で出土した陶磁片は、この博物館の屋外で収蔵されるようになった。

　そして1993・97年に整理した陶磁片は、その収蔵品である。1989年、大橋は博物館で最初の陶磁片調査を行なった。この陶磁片は整理作業直前に隣接する考古学研究センター事務所に移管されたが、全て出土遺跡と層位の来歴が注記されていた。基本的にはスロソワン王宮跡の出土で、一部はスピルウィク要塞跡など他地区の出土資料も含まれていた。

3-2. ティルタヤサ遺跡

　バンテン・ラーマから東に20kmの位置にあるティルタヤサ大スルタン（在位1651-78）の退位後の離宮跡である[19]。

　大スルタンはバンテンの歴代スルタンの中で最も英明と言われ、オランダ東インド会社と対抗する富国強兵政策を行なった。特に経済の根幹をなす貿易について、従来は特産のコショウを背景に来航する外国商人に徴税する受け身の姿勢だったが、彼は独自の商船隊をアジア各地に派遣するような積極策を実施した。そして他のイスラーム王国と同盟関係を築いて、オランダ東インド会社を包囲するような外交政策を行なう。

　また経済政策の別の1つが、1663年頃から開始したティルタヤサ地域での灌漑開発で

19　Guillot 1990

ある。運河網の建設により水位の高いこの地域の排水施設を完備させ[20]、そのことによって大規模な水田開発を成し遂げた。ティルタヤサとはジャワ語で大いなる水を意味するが、それはまさしく運河網建設による灌漑開発を指している。

そのような地域に、息子のハジ・スルタンに譲位した大スルタンは離宮を築いた。しかし父子の間で対オランダ政策は180度異なっていたため、まもなく両者は深刻な対立状態に至った。そしてそれは1682年2月から始まった内戦となってしまい、劣勢なハジ・スルタンに加勢したオランダとの戦争に転じた。同年末にオランダ軍は離宮を占領し、翌年3月には大スルタンは降伏を余儀なくされた。そして離宮は、足掛け5年という短い歴史を終えることになった。

遺跡の概要

遺跡はティルタヤサ村役場の東側に広がっている。役場の北北東約100mにはティルタヤサ大スルタン廟があり、その南側の南北に長い長方形の空間（90×50m）が「スルタンの土地」と呼ばれている。さらに南北に走る低地（幅約15m）を隔てた東地区にはより広い南北に長い長方形の空間（130×90m）がある。共に村民の共同墓地として使われている。

東地区には、北西隅部に土塁（下幅5m、高さ1m弱）で囲まれた長方形の空間（50×25m）がある。一方、村役場の西隣には周辺で最も高い小丘グヌン・スウが位置する。オランダ人が描いたティルタヤサ離宮攻略図には、城内の中央に旗が立てられた三角錐形の丘が描かれている。現状でこの旗の丘を捜すとするなら、グヌン・スウ以外には考えられない。

東地区から現在の村道を挟んだ南側には、精米工場跡地の多角形状の空間（約120×120m）が見られる。その西側と南側は屈曲する小川が境をなすが、この南端には「スルタン道」と呼ばれる旧道が南東へ向かっている。この「スルタン道」の近くからは、かつて大量の中国銭が発見されたと言う。

これら遺跡地とティルタヤサ村集落の西から南にかけて、東のウジュン川と西のドゥリアン川を結ぶティルタヤサ大王時代築造とされる運河が走り、さらにその途中からウジュン川に向かう別の運河が分岐している。

ティルタヤサ遺跡は文化財事務所による1993年の範囲確認緊急調査により、初めて本格的な調査と保存活用の手が入った。村の共同墓地として使用されている遺跡地では、建物の構造材である珊瑚石灰岩やレンガなどが大量の陶磁片と共に造墓活動により地上に現れている。

20　実際に運河網の中でレンガ造の水門を発見した（坂井編2007、pp.42-45）。

陶磁片の調査

　1992年10月14日から18日までバンテン・ラーマで行われたインドネシア出土日本陶磁国際セミナーの際、参加した6人の日本人研究者は初めてティルタヤサ遺跡を訪ねた。そしてそこで膨大な肥前陶磁片が地上に散布していることを知った。

　その後1997年、私たちバンテン遺跡研究会とインドネシア国立考古学研究センターは第1次共同発掘調査を実施した[21]。第1次調査出土遺物の整理を含む第2次調査は、結局、インドネシアの政情安定後の1999年7月〜8月にようやく行なうことができた。以後同様のティルタヤサ遺跡での調査は、2001年8〜9月・2002年9月・2004年10月・2005年11月そして2006年8月〜9月の7次に及んだ。離宮跡の調査は第1次から5次までで、第5次以降は運河の水門跡が中心となった。

　「スルタンの土地」に離宮跡が位置していることは間違いなく、私たちはその城壁基礎の一部を発見している。しかしここは住民墓地として使われており、上述のように彼らの造墓活動により日々地下の遺構が破壊されると共に陶磁片が大量に地上に現れる関係がある。そのため発掘調査によって地下の原位置で陶磁片を確認することは、絶えず困難になっている[22]。離宮としての利用期間が極めて短いために地上散布陶磁片は意味がないわけではないが、厳密な出土状態を把握するのが難しいという制約がこの遺跡の陶磁片調査には含まれていた。

3-3. ソンバ・オプー城

　ジャワ島の北東側にジャワ海を挟んで位置するスラウェシ島は、不思議なK字形をした東部インドネシアの大島である。その南部に住むブギス人とマカッサル人は、インドネシア有数の海洋民として名高い。両民族はバンテン王国と同時期の17・18世紀にいくつものイスラーム王国を樹立し、バンテンとも深い関係があった。特にバンテン最盛期のティルタヤサ大王の娘婿であったマカッサル人シェフ・ユスフは、大王と共に反オランダ抵抗を続けたイスラーム指導者として知られている。

　ゴワ王国はマカッサルを本拠地として、マルク諸島の香料貿易に大きく関与した海上王国である。16世紀後半に隣接するタロ王国と連合してスラウェシ島南部の覇権を握るや、東のマルク諸島にも勢威を延ばした。そして1605年にタロ王である宰相アラウッディンがイスラーム教に改宗するに伴い、東南アジア群島部東部における香料貿易に大きな影響を及ぼした最強のイスラーム王国となった。

　ゴワ第16代王ハサヌッデイン（在位1653−69）は生涯のほとんどをオランダ東インド

21　この調査は、日本とインドネシアの間で行なわれた初めての共同発掘調査となった（坂井編2000）。
22　同様の状況は、レンガ用粘土の採掘が大規模になされているトロウランでも見られる。インドネシアの遺跡の保存は、住民生活安定との深い関係がある。

会社との戦いに費やし、今日のインドネシアでも良く知られた民族英雄の一人である。マルク諸島での香料貿易の覇権がオランダとの争いの最大要因だが、強力な艦隊を持っていたため抗争の最後の段階（1666－69）は、マカッサル戦争として知られている。

遺跡の概要

ソンバ・オプー城跡は、現在のマカッサルの中心部にあるウジュンパンダン（ロッテルダム）要塞跡から南に約5km強離れた位置に残っている。マカッサルは、マカッサル海峡に面する南スラウェシ西海岸の南端に近い場所である。ジェネベラン川本流の河口からは2kmほどの右岸にあたるが、すぐ北東側には同川の放水路が流れている。もともとゴワ王国の本拠は、4kmほど同川を遡ったゴワ城跡にあったが、17世紀初頭以前には当時の海岸線に位置したソンバ・オプーが拠点港市としての役割を果たし始めたようである。

1630年代にはその中心に、正方形の平面で堡塁を持つ同城が築造されていた。1669年、ハサヌディン王が度重なるオランダとの最後の戦闘に敗北したことで、この城郭の実質的な機能はなくなった。現存している遺構は、南辺全体（長約650m）とそれに続く東西両辺の南端部（各長約100m）のレンガ積城壁のみである。城壁は東南アジア群島部地域のものとしてはかなり厚く、南辺の幅は3.7～4.1mあり、改修痕が明瞭な西辺の幅は10.5mを測る。南辺は中央部3分の1が100mほど突出しており、南西隅には円形堡塁、そして西辺には丸馬出が見られる。

陶磁片の調査

2001年に南・南東スラウェシ文化財管理事務所よりマカッサルのソンバ・オプー城跡出土の陶磁片について共同整理の依頼があり、同年9月事務所内での整理調査を行なった。これはスラウェシにおける日本が関与した初めての学術的な陶磁器調査となった。マカッサル周辺では古墓を盗掘しての陶磁器収集が、戦前から盛んであった。そしてその最も多い流出先は、現在まで日本の骨董市場である。そのような環境の中で、陶磁片についての共同調査を実施した。

陶磁片はソンバ・オプー城跡の整備に伴って出土したもので、文化財管理事務所に保管されていた。出土した陶磁片の一部は城内にある博物館に展示されていたが、大部分はウジュンパンダン要塞跡内の文化財管理事務所内で保管されていた。

スラウェシ南部は陶磁器が大量に残されている地域として、オランダ植民地時代から関心を呼んでいた。ジャカルタ国立博物館のファン・オルソイ・デ・フリーネスコレクションやインドネシアで伝世された肥前陶磁を集めた進藤夫妻コレクションの多くの部分は、スラウェシ南部で蒐集されたものであった。ただ残念ながらスラウェシ出土の陶磁器について学術的な検討は、私たちの調査以後も極めて少ないと言わざるをえない。

3-4. ブトン・ウォリオ城

　南東スラウェシのブトン島ウォリオ城跡について、一般には知られていない。この城を中心に16世紀から20世紀まで存続していたとされるブトン・イスラーム王国も、インドネシアに数あるイスラーム王国の中で決して有名な存在ではない。公刊のインドネシア史でも、僅かに1630年代にマカッサルのゴワ王国の攻撃を受けてその従属下に入り、1650年代からのゴワとオランダの戦争の中で、何回かの戦闘がブトンで起きたことが記されているだけである。

　しかし14世紀頃すでに初期王権が、ブトン島で誕生していた。伝承中での先イスラーム時代の王名の多くは、ヒンドゥ・ジャワ文化の影響が強く感じられる。16世紀にイスラームの影響がブトン地域に達し、1540年第6代王ラ・キラポントはイスラーム教に改宗したとされるが、それはゴワのイスラーム化より半世紀以上早い。

　そして16世紀末頃にはイスラーム王国としての体制が確立し、オランダの記録によれば1613年にはウォリオ城は築造途上だった。香料貿易の覇権をめぐる争いが、マルク諸島への航路上に位置するブトンの戦略的重要性を高めたことが理由と考えられる。そして王国の領域に次々と城郭が建設されるようになった。外的な要因としてはマカッサル戦争の波及があるが、また内的な理由もあった。スルタンは3系統の王族から貴族たちによって選ばれる制度だったが、それは内部抗争の可能性を常に孕んでいた。その結果、比較的短期間にスルタン位継承が相次ぎ、権力を握った貴族の存在を示すため多くの城郭が築かれた。最後に城郭が建設された19世紀代でも、ブトンの全人口は約10万人だった。そのような乏しい人的資源の中で、ブトンの権力者たちは城郭建設による防衛強化に関心を寄せ続けた。

　結果的にブトンはオランダと協力関係を維持して、ゴワのように直接攻撃されることはないまま、王国としての体裁はインドネシア独立以後まで保つことができた。

遺跡の概要

　旧ブトン王国領域全体の100近い城跡伝承地の中で、貴族末裔たちがなお城内に居住するウォリオ城跡は、スルタン以下の王国支配層が居住した最大規模の王城である。

　ブトン水道に面するバウバウ港郊外のバウバウ川左岸の隆起サンゴ礁急崖上に位置するウォリオの城壁は、北と東の両壁が長く、西壁が短い変形四角形（北壁約440m、東壁約390m、西壁約270m、南壁約1450m）を呈する。北東隅が極端な狭角をなすが、丘陵の背が北東方向に向かって狭くなる地形に対応したものである。城壁は人頭大のサンゴ石灰岩を積み上げて築造し、北壁と東壁では急峻な崖の上に8〜10mの高さを測り、崖面ではない西壁と南壁では3〜5mと低いが外側には堀が走っている。全長約2.6kmを測る城壁には14ヶ所の城門と18ヶ所の堡塁が見られる。

　ブトン水道を見下ろすウォリオ城内部には 18 世紀に遡る王宮モスクが現存するほか、歴代スルタンの墓や最後のスルタンの邸宅が残っている。

陶磁片の調査

　1980 年代よりウォリオ城の城壁修復が始まり、その工事で人骨と共に出土した大量の陶磁片が城内の城跡修復事務所内に保管されていた。城内は基本的に居住と埋葬が併用される場所で、現存建物以外の空白地もほとんど過去の埋葬場所と考えられ、多数の副葬された陶磁片が地上に散乱している。

　2002 年 9 月の予備調査で確認した陶磁片は、磁器だけで推定個体数 5,983 個（底部片を計算）に達した。その量から、個々の墓に納められていた陶磁器の数量は、予想以上に大きな数になることが想定できる[23]。インドネシア国立考古学研究センターと共同の発掘調査は 2004 年 11 月・2005 年 11 〜 12 月・2006 年 9 月に行なったが、併行して陶磁片整理も実施した。そのため対象陶磁片の大部分は 1980 年代以降の城壁修復工事で発見されたものだが、僅かな部分は発掘調査での出土遺物である。

23　本来、城内の住民は王国貴族の末裔であり、一程度量の陶磁器伝世品を所有していた可能性が高いが、調査時点では全く確認できなかった。ある時点で骨董商の大規模な買い付けが起きた可能性が推定できる。

Ⅱ トロウラン遺跡と4王都遺跡出土の貿易陶磁器

　インドネシアでの出土貿易陶磁器の整理分析を、インドネシア国立考古学研究センターと協力して始めたのは、1993年のバンテン・ラーマ遺跡出土品からである。その後ティルタヤサ遺跡出土品の整理・分析を行なう。その後、スラウェシ島に移り、ソンバ・オプー城、ブトン・ウォリオ城の整理を行なった。これらの整理分析で、15世紀以降のインドネシアにおける貿易陶磁器の傾向をある程度把握できたが、それ以前の状況は分からなかった。

　そこで、東部ジャワのマジャパイト王国の都であったと考えられるトロウラン遺跡出土品に注目し、2012年1月以降3回、整理分析を行なった。その結果、13世紀以降の豊富な貿易陶磁器の資料を得て、インドネシアにおける貿易陶磁器の傾向を知ることができるようになった。

　その傾向を記述するに当たって、概略、次のように時期区分を行なった。括弧書きの世紀表示はあくまでも参考までに表記したということでご了承いただきたい。この時期区分ごとに、さらに遺跡ごと、産地ごとに説明した。

> Ⅰ-1期（9世紀～13世紀）
>
> Ⅰ-2期（13～14世紀前半）
>
> Ⅱ-1期（マジャパイト王国成立の13世紀末～14世紀）
>
> Ⅱ-2期（14世紀、特に後半中心）
>
> Ⅲ-1期（15世紀、特に前半中心）
>
> Ⅲ-2期（15世紀後半～16世紀初）
>
> Ⅳ-1期（15世紀末～16世紀中葉）
>
> Ⅳ-2期（16世紀後半～17世紀初）
>
> Ⅴ-1期（17世紀前半頃）
>
> Ⅴ-2期（17世紀後半～18世紀初）
>
> Ⅵ-1期（18世紀前半頃）
>
> Ⅵ-2期（18世紀後半頃）
>
> Ⅶ-1期（19世紀前半頃）
>
> Ⅶ-2期（19世紀後半頃）

　遺跡の順は、その遺跡の主要な年代が古いほうから配列した。つまり、トロウラン遺跡、ソンバ・オプー城、ブトン・ウォリオ城、バンテン・ラーマ遺跡、ティルタヤサ遺跡の順である。

1. Ⅰ-1期（9世紀〜13世紀）

トロウラン遺跡

　トロウラン遺跡からは、豊富な内容の輸入陶磁器が見られる。今回整理した膨大な陶磁器片は、発掘調査や採集などによって集められたものである。

　この陶磁器片の整理調査を行なった。産地・種類をもとに分類し、基本的に口縁部もしくは底部が残る破片の個数から推定個体数を算出した。総数は 7,557 個体に上る。

(1) 中国の陶磁器

　マジャパイト王国成立以前と考えられる陶磁器である。

　中国の青磁、白磁、青白磁などのほか、黄釉褐彩陶器 1 点がある。青磁は越州窯（浙江省）、龍泉窯（浙江省）、同安窯（福建省）系などがあり、白磁は福建地方のものが多いと思われる。青白磁は景徳鎮窯（江西省）などのものである。黄釉褐彩陶器は長沙窯（湖南省）産である。

〈青磁〉

●越州窯系

　Fig.1-01　盞形の青磁であり、台状に削り出された底部はいくらかアーチ状に抉り込まれる。この底部を無釉とするが、窯詰め時の目跡のような焼けムラが見られる。同様の底部の青磁碗は浙江省蕭山窯[1]で出土しているが、これは外側面に櫛描き文が底部から上方に引かれている。また内側面の花文は線彫りで表されるが、越州上林湖窯の青磁碗[2]に類例が見られる。

　Fig.1-02　輪高台の青磁碗である。白い独特の目跡が見込周囲をめぐり、高台畳付にもその痕跡がある。同類は西部ジャワ発見とする例[3]があり、また同様の目跡の例は、越州上林湖窯（皮刀山）で出土[4]している。

　Fig.1-03, 04　内面に線彫りの花唐草文、外側面に蓮弁をヘラ彫りした大きい皿。高台が撥形に作られる。Fig.1-03 は無釉か、釉が剥落したもの。年代は 10 世紀頃と考えられる[5]。

　Fig.1-05　珍しい耳付きの瓜形壺である。耳は駒状の板に穴をあけた耳を縦に貼り付け、その前面に型で作った飾り板を直角に貼り付ける。肩に沈線を施し、それから胴部に縦方向の二条線を陽刻している[6]。

1　出光美術館 1982- 図45・46　年代は南朝（420-589）とする。
2　慈渓市博物館 2002 の 42 頁　唐代とする。
3　Adhyatman 1981-No.195　9-10 世紀とする。
4　慈渓市博物館 2002 彩版 10　唐代としている。
5　越州窯寺龍口窯出土品に似通った線彫り文と撥形で輪花の皿がある（浙江省文物考古研究所他 2002 の 82 頁）。
6　この類例は上海博物館に 1 例あり、蓋が付く長頸の四耳壺である（上海人民美術出版社 1981 図203）。北宋とする。

Fig.1-06　かぶせ蓋が付くと考えられる壺の口縁部である[7]。2種類の耳が各2個付くと考えられる。

〈白磁〉

●中国の窯

Fig.1-07, 08 は福建地方産が主と思われる。口縁玉縁形碗（Fig.1-07）や、口縁部を小さく外に折る碗があり、櫛描き文を施した碗（Fig.1-08）もある。

〈青白磁〉

●景徳鎮窯

Fig.1-09, 10 は碗であるが、ほかに瓶や蓋が見られる。

〈黄釉鉄彩〉

●長沙窯

Fig.1-11 は黄釉に鉄顔料で線描きした皿である。

〈その他〉

●中国の窯

Fig.1-12 は白濁釉を施した皿。見込の釉を四角く釉剥ぎし、そこに目を置いて窯詰めしたもの。外底は無釉であり、高台畳付に茶色い目跡が見られる。

バンテン・ラーマ遺跡

（1）中国の陶磁器

Fig.21-13 は黄釉褐彩水注。外面に貼り付け文を施す[8]。1個体。9世紀。長沙窯。

13

Fig.21　バンテン・ラーマ遺跡
Banten Lama Site, I-1 period, 中国陶磁 Chinese ceramics

7　類例としては海塩県博物館所蔵の「双耳有蓋罐」がある（上海人民美術出版 1981図165）。五代とする。

8　類例は小学館 1976a図248 にある。貼り付け文は人物。

2.　Ⅰ-2期（13～14世紀前半）

トロウラン遺跡

(1) 中国の陶磁器
〈青磁〉
● 龍泉窯

Fig.2-14 は外側面にヘラ彫りで鎬蓮弁を施し、高台畳付を無釉とした上質の皿である。見込には魚文を貼り付けで表す。

3.　Ⅱ-1期（13世紀末～14世紀）

トロウラン遺跡

量的に増加する。14世紀でも14世紀前半の可能性が高いものまでをここで扱う。

(1) 中国の陶磁器
〈青磁〉
● 龍泉窯

Fig.3-15 はヘラ彫りによる鎬蓮弁文を深く表した酒海壺。口縁と高台畳付を無釉とし、底部は別に作った底板を焼成時に青磁釉で熔着する構造に作られている。27個体出土。同類の青磁蓋も出土している[9]。

Fig.3-16 は外面に牡丹唐草文と思われる文様を貼り付けし、高台際に擂座を貼り付け、太鼓胴と呼ばれる器形の蓋付鉢である[10]。

Fig.3-17 は外面にヘラ彫りで蓮弁文を表した鉢[11]。中国などでは「浄水鉢」と記される向きもある。

〈青白磁〉
● 景徳鎮窯

Fig.3-18 は蓋物の蓋であり、ヘラ彫り文様を施す。12世紀～14世紀前半。

Fig.3-19 は型押し成形による八角坏。外面に「金玉満堂」の文字、腰部に蓮弁文を型による陽刻で表す。口縁部と内面の区画線をビーズ繋ぎ線で表す[12]。

Fig.3-20 は瓶の外面に窓枠をビーズ繋ぎ線で二重にめぐらす。右の破片の窓内に貼り付け文が見られる。類品はハンガリーのルイ大王（在位1342-82）の紋章のある金属加工が

9　類品は横浜市金沢区称名寺境内出土品（重文、小学館1981図33）や、韓国・新安沖引揚げ品（国立中央博物館1977図59～60）に見られる。

10　類品は静嘉堂文庫美術館所蔵品（重文、平凡社1997図71）があり、鴻池家伝来と言われる。

11　新安沖引揚げ品中に類似の例が見られる（国立中央博物館1977図107～109）。

12　外面の文様は異なるが、類品は香港大学馮平山博物館1992の図121の高足坏がある。

施されていたものであり、1325年頃と推測されている[13]。他に大徳2（1298）年、または3年の墨書銘をもつ白磁仏像からビーズ繋ぎ線文が13世紀末には始まっていると考えられている。本遺跡出土の磁器にもビーズ繋ぎ線文の例は多く、14世紀頃のものと考えられる。

〈白磁〉

●中国の窯

Fig.3-21, 22は型押し成形で外面に唐草文を陽刻した合子。ソンバ・オプー城出土の白磁合子（Fig.22-29）に似通っている。

●景徳鎮窯

Fig.3-23, 24は内面に型による陽刻文を施した碗。外底は無釉。

（2）ベトナムの陶磁器

〈青磁〉

Fig.4-25は型成形により内面に菊花を多重に表した小碗。釉は黄みを帯び、外底は無釉である。削り出しの高台内に粗い鬆が生じる。おそらく14世紀と考えられる[14]。

Fig.4-26左は型成形により、内側面に丸文を表す。見込周囲に沈線を陰刻し、茶色の小さな目跡が見られる。外底は無釉[15]。

Fig.4-27は見込周囲に沈線を引き、見込に草花と思われる文様をヘラ彫りし、内側面にもヘラ描き文が見られる皿。高台内は鉄泥を塗り、いわゆるチョコレートボトムとする[16]。

〈白磁〉

Fig.4-28は外面に鎬蓮弁文を施した碗。高台内は鉄泥を塗り、高台畳付を除き、内外に白釉をかける。見込には小さな目跡が残る[17]。

ソンバ・オプー城

（1）中国の陶磁器

●福建

Fig.22-29は福建南部産の大型の白磁合子。型成形で蓋と身に如意頭状の唐草文を陽刻する。13世紀末～14世紀前半[18]。トロウラン遺跡（Fig.3-22）と似通っている。

●中国の窯

Fig.22-30は褐釉の四耳壺。肩部に縦耳を貼り付ける。

---

13 ゲイニエル・フォントヒル瓶と呼ばれる玉壺春形の瓶（小学館1981図43）。

14 類例にNMVH（National Museum of Vietnamese History）2005-Fig.96があり、年代を11～13世紀とするが、町田市立博物館1993図75は13～14世紀とする。

15 類例は愛知県陶磁資料館1987図41（13～14世紀）、National Museum of Vietnamese History（NMVH）2005-Fig.94（11～13世紀）などがある。

16 類例は町田市立博物館1993図87にあり、見込は牡丹文で14～15世紀とする。

17 類例は町田市立博物館1993図43にあり、13～14世紀とする。

18 類例は徳化窯系の安渓魁斗窯にある。

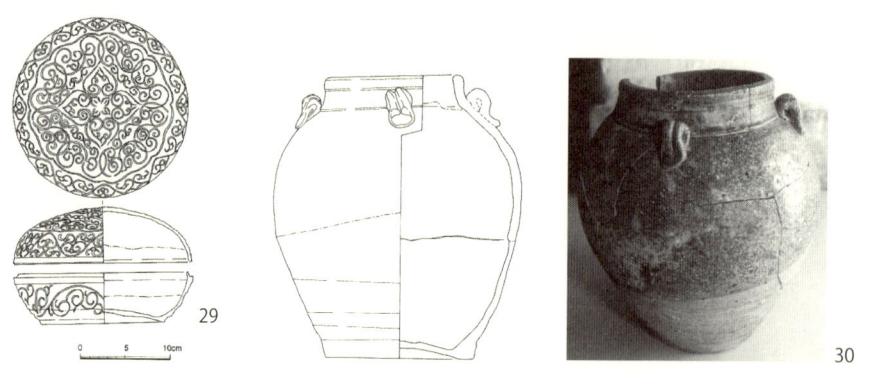

Fig.22　ソンバ・オプー城跡　Somba Opu Fort, Ⅱ-1 period, 中国陶磁 Chinese ceramics

4. Ⅱ-2 期（14 世紀、特に後半中心）

トロウラン遺跡

　量的にさらに増加し、景徳鎮の青花が龍泉窯青磁とともに主となる。元末・明初と推測されるものを中心とする。

(1) 中国の陶磁器
〈青磁〉
●龍泉窯

　Fig.5-31, 32 は大きい鉢の底部片であり、底部中央に円孔を開け、青磁釉を施し、内側に別に型で作った菊花形円板にも青磁釉をかけて見込に置き、焼成時に釉で熔着させたもの。内側面にヘラ彫りで蓮弁文を表し、外面にもヘラ彫り文が見られる。6 個体出土。エジプト・フスタート遺跡などで出土し、イスラーム陶器で模倣品が作られた。

　Fig.5-33 は稜花形の大皿。内外側面に鎬蓮弁文を鋭く表す。高台内を蛇の目釉剝ぎする。

〈白磁〉
●福建か

　Fig.5-34 は口禿の碗。口縁部外面に粘土皺が見られるため、型押し成形でおおよその形を作った後、外側下半から高台部はロクロ削りを施したもの。伏せ焼もしくは合せ口で焼成したものと考えられる。

　Fig.5-35 は内側面にヘラ彫りで蓮弁か菊弁様の文様を施した折縁皿。見込に印花による草花文が施される。日本でビロースクタイプと呼ばれる印花文の碗などに似通っており、14 世紀と推測される。しかも同様の彫文を施し中国磁器の影響を受けた可能性がある皿が、ベトナム白磁に 1 点（Fig.8-77）見られる。

●景徳鎮窯

　Fig.5-36, 37 は Fig.3-23, 24 の碗同様に型によって内面に印花文を施し、高台無釉とし

た小碗。枢府手などとの関わりの中で作られたものと推測され、14世紀と考えられる。Fig.5-36は内側面下半に菊弁文を型で表したもの。

Fig.5-38は水注の蓋と推測される。つまみは宝珠形に作られる[19]。本品は縁の3分の1くらいを欠失しているために、環耳の有無は不明である。

〈青花〉

● 景徳鎮窯

Fig.5-39, 40は高台無釉の碗であるが、見込文様が珍しい。Fig.5-40は魚を描き、Fig.5-39は蛙に吹墨を加える。

Fig.5-41は見込に蓮池水禽文を描いた高台無釉の碗か鉢。高台は厚く削り出され、兜巾を作る。

Fig.5-42はFig.5-41同様に見込に蓮池水禽文を描いた碗。口縁部内外に唐草文を描く陶片もある。

Fig.5-43は内底の地をコバルト（いわゆる「呉須」であるが、本稿ではコバルトと記す）で塗り埋め、白抜き文様で鳳凰と唐草、牡丹かと思われる文様を表した大皿。外底は無釉。内側面も白抜きの牡丹かと思われる文様の葉などが表される[20]。大皿は多種類出土しているが、細片が多い。

Fig.5-44は無釉の平底をもつ片口であり、見込に鳥の文様が描かれ、外側面に蓮弁文がおおらかに表現される。口端は無釉。底部に型押し成形を表す粘土皺が見られ、片口部はほとんど失われ、わずかに根元が残る。一般に片口の例は少なくないが、より精緻な例が多い。

Fig.5-45は八角壺の蓋。蓋の鍔端を下方に折って身の口縁部を包み込むような構造の蓋であり、この時期の大壺の蓋に見られる。八角に作り、各面に蓮弁文を表す。鍔の端は欠失しているが、上面は七宝繋ぎ文、つまみの根元周囲に雷文をめぐらす[21]。

Fig.5-46は口部を鋭く鍵形に折り返した大壺の口縁部[22]。

Fig.5-47, 48は丸形壺の蓋であり、身の口縁部を包み込む二重構造に作られている点で共通である。Fig.5-47は蓋。鍔部に四方襷、下方に折った縁に雷文帯を描く。Fig.5-48は蓋鍔部に唐草、下方に折った縁に七宝繋ぎ文帯を描く[23]。

Fig.6-49は蓮葉形に作り、葉の葉脈をコバルトで描いた壺蓋。同意匠の身は見られない。

Fig.6-50も、Fig.6-49同様に蓮葉形の小壺蓋である。やはり身と思われるものは見ら

---

19 類品は新安沖引揚げ品（国立中央博物館19771図63）にあり、高さ24.1cmとある水注の蓋には、後に金属で取手と連結するための環が付いている。

20 類品はトプカプ宮殿博物館収蔵品 Krahl & Ayers1986-No.556（以下、トプカプ宮殿蔵品）にあり、14世紀中葉とする。口径45.5cm。

21 トロウラン遺跡出土とするミクシッ・亀井の図（Miksic & Kamei 2010-Fig.12）も同類の八角壺蓋。

22 類例は Miksic & Kamei 2010-Fig.4、平凡社 1995図5。

23 こうした丸形壺の蓋の類例は、河北省保定市出土の青花紅釉壺（小学館 1981図52）、沖縄・勝連グスク出土品（亀井他 2008 の149-150頁）などがある。

れなかった。伝世例でも景徳鎮市出土で青花草花文小壺の蓋に釉裏紅で葉脈を表した同様の形の小壺蓋が載った例がある。この種の身の破片は見られるから、もともと蓋と身の文様を統一していなかった可能性がある。

　Fig.6-51 は壺の口縁部であり、ふつうの蓋が載るタイプの直口口縁の端を少し外に肥厚させたものである。

　Fig.6-52 は青花紅釉大壺の胴部片である。胴部の窓枠をビーズ繋ぎ線で二重に表し、その窓内をくぼませ、そこに貼り付け文で透かしを作り、紅釉を施す[24]。

　Fig.6-53 は釉裏紅壺の肩あたりの破片である。銅顔料で釉下に圏線を引き、唐草文帯を表し、その上に七宝繋ぎ文帯、下に鋸歯状蓮弁文帯をめぐらす。その下に如意頭状の文様を描く[25]。

　Fig.6-54 は外側面を八角の面取りを3段に表した瓶。内面は無釉であり、回転成形したものを胴継成形したもの。高台も外面だけ八角に面取りする[26]。

〈鉄絵陶器〉

●磁州窯

　Fig.6-55, 56 は鉄絵壺であるが、Fig.6-55 は壺の下部であり、底部は畳付を幅広く削り出し、無釉とする。外面は白化粧を施し、鉄絵を描き、透明釉をかける。胴部は窓絵を表したもので、Fig.6-56 は口部や上部の破片[27]。

　Fig.6-57 は洗とも呼ばれる鉢。口部を外に折る。内側面に波状線文を引く[28]。

　以上のほか翡翠釉の壺・鉢も出土している。

　Fig.7-58/63 は表面に白化粧を施した素地に鉄で黒い文様を描いた陶板。形は方形と思われる。裏面は縁を作り出す。Fig.7-58/60 は方形の周縁帯に菱の連続文を表すが、Fig.7-58 は地を鉄で塗り埋め、白抜きの菱文とする。Fig.7-61 は斜状の雷文を周縁帯に表し内外に帯状文を鉄で描く。Fig.7-62 は周縁帯に黒地白抜きの唐草文を表す。これらは繭山 1977 の時点や小学館 1984 ではベトナム陶器タイルとして紹介されたが、文様や、形状が方形のみであることなど、中国・磁州窯系の窯でベトナム青花タイルに先行して作られた可能性が高い。14 世紀であろう。

　Fig.7-64/67 は黒褐釉を表面にかけた陶磚。これには白化粧は見られず、裏面周縁の作り出しもない方形の板状陶磚。表面は白土の堆線で方形の外周線を引き、その内に格座間形であろうか、枠取し、鉄釉をかけたうえに枠内に鉄顔料で草花と思われる茶色の文様を

24　類例は河北省保定市出土（小学館 1981 図 52）の 1 対が蓋付で完存するほか、大英博物館デヴィッドコレクション（身のみ、日本経済新聞社 1980 図 43）のほか、モンゴル・オロンスム遺跡出土（亀井他 2009-Fig.9）の胴部細片がある。中国大陸以外での出土例は寡聞にして知らない。

25　類例は揚州文物商店蔵の上部を金属加工した 1 例（亀井他 2005-124 頁）のみである。

26　類例は台湾・国立歴史博物館所蔵品（国立歴史博物館 1992-No.65、高さ 26cm）がある。

27　Fig.6-55 の類例は小学館 1981 図 266（高さ 24.7cm）。Fig.6-56 の肩の花唐草に似通ったものは小学館 1981 図 154 にある。

28　類例は小学館 1981 図 265（口径 45 〜 46cm）。

描く。中国産と推測され、14 世紀であろう。

〈褐釉陶器〉

Fig.7-68 は瓶であり、下部は内外とも無釉である。

Fig.7-69 は壺。

(2) ベトナムの陶磁器

〈白磁〉

Fig.8-70 は見込に双魚文を貼り付けで表したと考えられる碗か皿。高台は薄く丁寧に作られ、畳付にも施釉されている。コバルトの飛斑が見られるので、年代は青花生産が始まっている時期と考えられ、14 世紀後半〜15 世紀初と推測される。

Fig.8-71 は内面に型で陽刻文を表した小坏。見込に七弁の花文、見込周囲に二重の堆線、内側面に草花か唐草を表す。クリーム色の上質な白磁である。本例はホイアン沖[29]引揚げ品の年代より古く、14 世紀後半〜15 世紀前半と考えられる[30]。

Fig.8-72 は外側面に透明釉をかけた台付皿[31]。

Fig.8-73 は外面にヘラ彫りで鎬文を表した壺。外面に白化粧したことが明らかであり、上に透明釉をかけ、高台内は鉄泥を塗る。内面は内底周囲に 1 段付け、内側に小さな目跡がある。本例は 14 世紀頃と推測される[32]。

Fig.8-74 は高台を浅く幅広く削り出し、高台から斜めに広がり、上方に折る器形の鉢。内底に目跡がある[33]。

Fig.8-75 は腰が張る鉢であり、高台畳付の幅は広く削り出す。見込は蛇の目釉剥ぎし、外底無釉。蛇の目釉剥ぎした部分に砂粒の引きずり痕が顕著であり、ベトナム中部産の可能性がある。14 世紀であろう。

Fig.8-76 は腰が張り口縁外反の皿。口禿であり、上質な作りで、高台内は鉄泥を塗る。

Fig.8-77 は粗放な青磁かと思われる小皿。内外側面に粗放なヘラ彫り文が施される。内外面上部に白化粧が施されていると考えられ、上に灰釉のような釉薬がかけられる。見込は蛇の目状に釉剥ぎされ、白い砂状の目が見られる。内面口縁部に沈線が見られ、おそらく 14〜15 世紀前半と考えられる[34]。中国の白磁皿（Fig.5-35）の影響のもとで作られた可能性がある。

29　中部ベトナムのチャム島 Cu Lao Cham 沖で発見された沈没船（Butterfield 2000）。

30　ホイアン沖引揚げ品（Butterfield 2000）は見込の花文が六弁であり中心の表現も異なり、また見込周囲の圏線も一重であり、より粗放に見える。

31　皿内面を無釉とするのは、町田市立博物館 1993 図27〜31 の盤の内底に見られる。器形は大分異なるが、用途は同じである可能性がある。

32　上部の器形は不明であるが、NMVH2005-Fig.82（口径 16cm）の青磁壺の下部に似る。11〜13 世紀とする。

33　類例は町田市立博物館 1993 図50 のような擂座をもつ鉢と推測される。

34　比較的に似通ったものは、町田市立博物館 1993 図113 の褐釉刻花文皿、15〜16 世紀がある。本例はこれより古い可能性が推測される。

〈鉄釉陶器〉

Fig.8-78 は内面に型で草花を陽刻し、外面に鉄釉をかけ分けた碗。内面の透明釉は幾分黄緑色を帯び、見込に目跡が見られる。中国の茶碗の影響と考えられる[35]。

Fig.8-79 は内面に Fig.8-78 に似通った草花を型で陽刻し、内面に透明釉、外側面に鉄釉をかけ分けた鉢。見込には小さい茶色の目跡が 5 ヶ所残る。外底無釉。Fig.8-78 同様に 13～14 世紀と推測される。

〈黒地掻き落とし〉

Fig.8-80, 81 は高台脇を Fig.8-74 などと同様に面を作り、明瞭な稜を作って上方に立ち上がらせ、内底周囲に凹帯をめぐらす。この素地に外底以外に白化粧を施し、鉄顔料を塗り掻き落とし手法で文様を表し、透明釉をかける。Fig.8-80 は高台内に鉄泥を塗る。見込に小さな目跡が見られる。ベトナム陶器でこうした黒地掻き落としの類例は知らない。おそらくは中国磁州窯の元時代の黒地掻き落とし装飾の影響を受けたものと思われる。よって年代は 14 世紀と考えられる。

〈白磁鉄彩〉

Fig.9-82 は透明釉を外面にかけ、文様部分を掻き落とし、そこに鉄釉を塗るが、線状部分には列点状に表現する。また擂座の貼り付けが施された破片もある[36]。一部の破片にコバルトの飛斑があるので、製作年代は青花を作っている時代と考えられる。内底の際に 1 段あり、目跡も認められる。14 世紀後半～15 世紀前半であろう。

〈緑釉〉

Fig.8-83 は外面にヘラ彫りで鎬文を表した上に緑釉をかけ、内面に透明釉をかけた小碗。高台脇には鉄泥を塗るが高台は無釉。高台脇を削り込み低い台付とした碗。

Fig.8-84 は内側面に型で多重の菊花を表し、緑釉をかけた皿。外底は無釉とする。内底は蛇の目釉剥ぎし、製品を直接重ね積みした痕が見られる。

Fig.8-85 は内側面にヘラ彫りで文様を陰刻し、緑釉をかけ、内底は蛇の目釉剥ぎした皿。高台内は鉄泥を塗る。被熱。

Fig.8-86 は内面に型による鋭い陽刻で瓜のような文様を表した大皿。高台も珍しく碁笥底状に丁寧に削り出し、外面下部に深い 1 段を削り出す。高台内に鉄泥を塗る。14～15 世紀前半と推測される。

〈青磁〉

Fig.9-87 は大壺で、外底は無釉であり、高台内は浅く削り込む。内底周囲を成形時にくぼませるのは、青花壺なども同様である。緑釉に近いが、青磁釉と推測される。14～15 世紀。

35　類例は町田市立博物館 1993 図 109 にあり、13～14 世紀とする。大英博物館蔵品は口縁が立ち上がり、天目形に近い。

36　類例は町田市立博物館 1993 図 126 の鉢（口径 35.3cm）であり、14～15 世紀とする。

〈鉄絵陶器〉

Fig.9-88 は腰が張り、口縁外反の小碗。見込に菊のような草花を鉄顔料で描き、外面上部にも圏線を引いた間に唐草状の文様を描く。外底部は無釉。

Fig.9-89 は腰が張り、口縁外反の碗。Fig.9-88 より大振りに作られ、口縁内側に唐草と思われる文様をラフに描く[37]。

Fig.9-90 は型で菊花形に作り、高台畳付を幅広く削り出した小皿。内底は鉄顔料の2条線で白地帯をめぐらし、中央に草花文を描き、黄緑色を帯びた透明釉を外底以外にかける。見込に小さな目跡が見られる。高台内は鉄泥を塗る[38]。

Fig.9-91 は口縁部を折った盤形の中皿。高台は畳付を幅広く削り出す。内面から口縁外側まで白化粧を施し、見込に菊文のような草花、口縁部にラフな唐草を鉄顔料で描く。見込に茶色い小さな目跡が5ヶ所見られる[39]。

Fig.9-92 は Fig.9-91 よりラフな作りの大皿。盤形の皿であり、見込に文様より小さな円凹部を作る。高台畳付は幅広く浅い削りであり、無釉である。内底に1条の圏線を引いた中にラフな草花を鉄顔料で描き、口縁部には唐草の簡略化した文様を描く。見込と高台畳付に茶色の目跡が6ヶ所見られる。Fig.9-91 より後出と考えられる。

〈人形置物類〉

Fig.18：トロウラン遺跡では多くの大型人形置物類の細片が出土している。ベトナム産と考えられるものが多いが、その中で形がある程度復元できた1例をあげる。白磁の素地に鉄釉をかけ分け、大型の犬かと思われる置物。頭部を受ける部分が残り、頸部下に紐が巻かれ、鈴や飾りの垂れた様子が貼り付け文で表される。体部に白地に褐色のまだらを釉で表す。楕円形の板状台部に前脚の下部が残る。14～15世紀前半と推測される。

(3) イスラーム・タイル

Fig.10-93/95 は素地が砂質で粗い。その表面を白釉で覆い、それにコバルトで藍彩を施す。形がわかるものは周縁を作り出す[40]。こうしたイスラーム陶器タイルが王国の14世紀～15世紀前半頃にもたらされ、その影響下でベトナムの青花タイルを特注した可能性が高い。割れた断面をよく見ると、素地は2層になっている。取り付けるときに、内側にモルタル状のものを塗ったものであろうか。

Fig.10-96/98 はターコイズ青の釉をかけた陶磚。粗い素地に白化粧を施し、表面だけ釉をかけたもの。イスラーム陶器と考えられ、14～15世紀前半頃であろう。表面に褐色の目跡が見られる。

37　類例は町田市立博物館 1993 図 136 にあり、14 世紀とする。口径 16.2cm。

38　町田市立博物館 1993 図 147 の青花に似る。

39　類例は町田市立博物館 1993 図 134・135 にある。

40　こうした白釉藍彩のタイルはイスラーム地域では 13～15 世紀に例がある（小学館 1984-218 頁）。六角形や星形タイルが多いが、周縁を作り出す例は知らない。

ブトン・ウォリオ城

(1) 中国の陶磁器

● 龍泉窯と磁州窯

Fig.23-99 左は青磁鎬蓮弁文の壺と見られ、14 世紀。龍泉窯。

Fig.23-99 右は磁州窯系の鉄絵壺の肩部片である。14 世紀。

Fig.23 ブトン・ウォリオ城跡
Buton Wolio Fort, Ⅱ-2 period, 中国陶磁 Chinese ceramics

バンテン・ラーマ遺跡

(1) 中国の陶器

Fig.24-100 は褐釉の大壺。外面に鳳凰のような文様を線彫などで表す[41]。

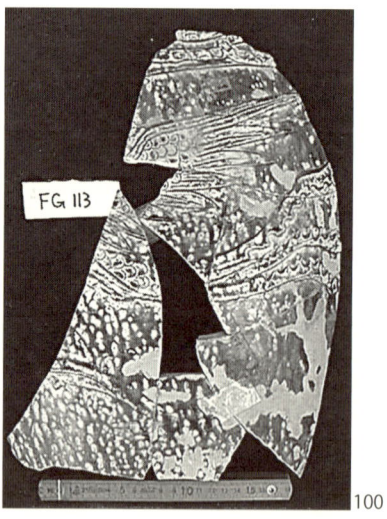

Fig.24 バンテン・ラーマ遺跡
Banten Lama Site, Ⅱ-2 period, 中国陶磁 Chinese ceramics

---

41 類例は Adhyatman & Abu Ridho1984 の p.96 があり、14 世紀とする。

5. Ⅲ-1期 （15世紀、特に前半中心）

明らかに明時代に入るもの。

トロウラン遺跡

(1) 中国の陶磁器

〈青磁〉

●龍泉窯

Fig.11-101 は内面にヘラ描きで蓮弁を表し、見込中央に印花文を押す。花弁に合わせて口縁部を外から押し込み、輪花に作る。高台内は蛇の目釉剥ぎし、窯道具のチャツの熔着痕が見られる。1個体出土。

Fig.11-102 は口縁部外反りの小皿。外側面と内面にヘラ彫りで菊弁を表す。高台内無釉。15世紀前半～中葉と推測される。

〈青花〉

●景徳鎮窯[42]

Fig.11-103 は碗であり、高台畳付のみ丁寧に釉剥ぎされたもの。見込に唐草文、高台に雷文、高台脇に蓮弁文を表す[43]。

Fig.11-104 は大壺であり、外面に縦筋を陰刻し、胴部に花卉文、下方の絞った部分に雷文帯をコバルトで描く。その上に伝世例から蓮弁文をコバルトで描いていることがわかる。本例は明らかに青花である[44]。

Fig.11-105 は胴部に花唐草文と龍文を描き、直口口縁部に区画線間に花唐草文の文様帯をコバルトで描いた天球瓶と呼ばれる器形の大瓶。胴部片2点の龍文部分も同一個体の可能性がある[45]。

Fig.11-106, 107 は青花釉裏紅壺の胴部片。コバルト線と銅線を交互に引いて窓枠と思われる文様を表し、その中に不鮮明な文様が青花と釉裏紅で描かれる。15世紀と推測される。

〈五彩〉

●景徳鎮窯

Fig.11-108 は枢府タイプの白磁素地に緑絵具で文様を描いた皿か鉢と思われる胴部片。内面に型で見込周囲の1段の盛り上げと内側面の陽刻文が見られる。それに緑絵具で文様が描かれ、外側面に蓮弁様の文様を緑絵具で描く。

42　景徳鎮窯は江西省の景徳鎮を中心に焼かれた明時代以降、最大の磁器生産地である。

43　類品は台湾・故宮博物院（国立故宮博物院 1990 図 28）にあり、明初とする。口径 19.6cm。官窯クラスの製品である。

44　伝世例のうち、青花の例は中国・首都博物館蔵の北京市出土の蓋付壺（亀井他 2005-21 頁、総高 65.5cm）で洪武（1368 -98）頃とする。ただし、これは釉裏紅とする見解もある。他に釉裏紅の例が、梅澤記念館蔵品（重文、平凡社 1995 図 22）にあり、高さ 51.2cm。また景徳鎮窯出土品に青花の例がある。

45　類例は松岡美術館蔵品（高さ 42cm）（平凡社 1995 の図 41）で永楽（1403～24）頃とする。

(2) ベトナムの陶磁器

〈鉄絵〉

Fig.12-109 は大壺であり、下部から底部の破片である。底部は高台内を削り込み、外面は白化粧を施す。外底以外に透明釉をかける。Fig.9-88／92 と Fig.12-109 の鉄絵陶器は青花の古式のグループと器形や文様に類似性が認められ、年代的にも近い 14 世紀後半、下っても 15 世紀前半までの中で作られた可能性が高い。

〈青花（五彩含む）〉

Fig.12-110 は型で菊花形に作り、見込に菊と推測される草花をコバルトで描き、二重圏線を引く小皿。高台畳付は幅広く削り出し、その内方は鉄泥を塗る。見込に目跡が見られるなど 14 世紀後半〜15 世紀前半と考えられる。

Fig.12-111, 112 は盤形に作り、内側面を菊弁状にヘラ彫りした小皿。見込に二重もしくは一重の円圏内に草花を描き、口縁部に崩れた唐草をコバルトで描く。Fig.12-111 の皿は高台畳付をとくに幅広く削り出し、無釉であるが、Fig.12-112 の小皿は高台内に鉄を塗る。いずれも見込に小さい目跡が見られ、14 世紀後半〜15 世紀前半と推測される。

Fig.12-113 は腰が張り、口縁外反の碗。外底を除く内外に白化粧を施しコバルトで文様を描くが、圏線は青黒いのに対し、見込の草花・口縁部の崩れた唐草・外側面の崩れた唐草は明るい青で表される。高台内は鉄泥を塗る。本例は 14 世紀後半〜15 世紀前半と思われる[46]。

Fig.12-114 は大壺の蓋と考えられ、景徳鎮青花の 14 世紀に見られた身の口縁部を包み込むような構造の蓋と思われる。外面に唐草文などの文様帯をコバルトで描く。白化粧は認められない。伝世例は知らない。景徳鎮青花の年代からすると、14 世紀後半〜15 世紀前半と推測される。

Fig.12-115 は大壺の蓋であり、特徴的な雷文を描く。この種の雷文は元時代の磁州窯の鉄絵に多く見られたが、その影響を受けたものと考えられ、ベトナム青花の古式のグループにいくらか伝世例がある[47]。蓋の内面には白化粧の塗布が見られ、鍔の内側にはない。

Fig.12-116 は Fig.12-114 同様に二重構造に作った壺蓋。外面に蓮弁を描く。14 世紀後半〜15 世紀前半と推測される。

Fig.12-117 は内底中央に円圏を凸線で表し、焼へたりが見られるが、器台と推測される。無釉の外底は平底であるが、その少し上の釉切れ部に熔着痕が見られるため、台が付

46　類例は町田市立博物館 1993図 145 にあるが、唐草文様の崩れは少なく、器形的にも本例より古式の可能性がある。14 世紀とある。

47　代表的なものとして、日本に伝世したとする龍文瓶「銘白衣」（矢部 1978-11〔高さ 28.7cm〕）の口部に表される。14 世紀と考えられている。蓮弁の表現もより景徳鎮に近く、古様であり、14 世紀、おそらく中葉〜末のベトナム青花の基準資料と言えるだろう。このような瓶の破片が後述の Fig.13-123, 124である。もう 1 点、この雷文や古様の蓮弁文をもつ玉壺春形瓶の例が NMVH2005-No.232 である。同書では 15 〜 16 世紀とするが、文様・器形ともに 14 世紀後半頃の可能性が高い。

けられていた可能性がある。内面に型で陽刻した上にコバルトで3段以上の捻花を描く。外側面にも同様の捻花をコバルトで描く。上手であり、コバルトの特徴から、14世紀後半～15世紀と推測される[48]。

Fig.12-118は大皿。見込周囲に波頭文、内側面に花唐草、口縁部に唐草をコバルトで描く。外側面は蓮弁文を描くが、複弁はないので、ホイアン沖引揚げ品より古いと思われる。口禿。高台内に鉄泥を塗る。年代は14世紀後半～15世紀前半であろう[49]。

Fig.13-119はFig.13-120, 121と同類。胴部に牡丹・蓮花と蓮弁文を描き、肩に格座間形の窓絵を配し、梅鳥、竹などを窓内に描く。窓間の地文は青海波文、下部は蓮弁文とその上に唐草文帯を描く。蓮弁文帯の下には如意頭文帯を描く。14世紀後半～15世紀前半と考えられる[50]。底部は高台を削り出し無釉。内底周囲はくぼむ。外面は底面を除き、白化粧を施す。内面は被熱によると思われる釉のただれが見られる。

Fig.13-120, 121は胴部に雲龍文を描いた大壺と牡丹唐草文大壺の胴部片。蓮弁に複弁がないなどから14世紀後半～15世紀前半と推測される。

Fig.13-122は壺の底部と見られる。下部に唐草文帯を描き、高台を削り出し、高台内は鉄泥を塗る。唐草文の下の圏線は褐色であり、2色の顔料で表現しているタイプ。内底は周囲をくぼませ、その内方に小さな目跡が見られる。外面は白化粧が施されるが内面は透明釉のみである。14世紀後半～15世紀前半と推測される。

Fig.13-123, 124は瓶の一部と考えられる破片。こうした形・文様の類例として、脚注47で述べた龍文瓶（銘白衣）がある。Fig.13-123はこの龍文瓶の頸部下部の凸帯に似ている。Fig.13-124は胴下部と推測されるが、龍文瓶胴部の両側に不遊環が浮彫で表されており、本例も胴部に浮彫の文様が表されている。年代は文様から考えると、銘白衣の瓶より後出の可能性があり、14世紀後半～15世紀前半と推測される。

Fig.14-125は胴部に透かし彫りを施した大型器台。おそらく14世紀後半～15世紀前半と推測される[51]。

Fig.13-126は壺の蓋。鍔が反り返っている。外面に波濤文をコバルトで描く。この波濤文は前述の「銘白衣」瓶（14世紀とする）の台部の波濤文に似通っている。この瓶より後出と思われ、15世紀と推測される。

Fig.14-127は型で甲を平らに作り側面を輪花とした蓋物の蓋。上面の文様は一部が残り、雲や動物の足が見えるが不明。側面は型で窓絵が表され、残存破片の窓内に麒麟と雲、鹿と雲が描かれる。窓間は小さな縦長の窓内に竹らしき植物が描かれ、その両側に小円内の

48　類品が沖縄県首里城（沖縄県埋蔵文化財センター2001の第29図11）で出土している。

49　類例は小学館1984図144の樹鳥文盤があり、15～16世紀とする。

50　類似の大壺は、平凡社1978図78の佐野美術館蔵品（高さ39.5cm）がある。これはトプカブ宮殿博物館蔵の1450年銘瓶同様に蓮弁文に複弁を加え、牡丹唐草の葉に葉脈を描くなど新しい特徴があり、本例のほうが古い。

51　類例は国立ベトナム歴史博物館蔵品（NMVH2005-No.223）があり、台下端と上のくびれ部に鉄泥を塗る。15世紀とする。

文字が3つ並ぶ。文字は異なる3つの文字であることは分かり、各行は同じ文字列の繰り返しと考えられるが、解読できない。文字の円圏の周囲の地文は紗綾形文と推測されるが不鮮明である。内外に白化粧し、透明釉をかけたものであるが、身に当たる部分は釉剥ぎが施されている。景徳鎮青花の影響と考えられ、年代は14世紀後半〜15世紀前半と推測される。

　Fig.13-128は緑釉のFig.8-83などと同様の台を削り出した台付小碗であり、台の側面に鉄泥を塗る。見込には円圏内に「福」字をコバルトで描き、外側面にもコバルトによる文様が見られる。

　Fig.13-129は口縁外反の小碗であり、見込に草花、口縁に唐草、外面下部に蓮弁、上部に唐草をコバルトで描く。15世紀と考えられる。

　Fig.14-130は内面一杯に6弁の唐花文をコバルトで描いた盤形の大皿。口禿。外側面には複弁のない蓮弁を描く。Fig.17-155と比べて線描きが太い点からも、14世紀後半〜15世紀前半と推測される[52]。高台内に鉄泥を塗る。

　Fig.15-131は見込に魚藻文を描いた盤形の大皿。折縁の端を小さく立てるが、さらに指で数ヶ所を押して輪花に作る。稜花形に作る松岡美術館蔵の大皿などは少なくないが、このような輪花は珍しい。見込周囲に波頭文を描くが、ホイアン沖引揚げ品大皿などに描かれる波濤文と大差ない。内側面には宝文を描き、口縁部に唐草文を配す。外側面も唐草文を描き、高台内は鉄泥を塗る。口禿。15世紀であろう[53]。

　Fig.14-132は蓮葉の葉脈をコバルトで描いた壺の蓋。円形にロクロ成形した後、縁を蓮葉形に変形させている。上面は白化粧を塗り、鍔部の身と当たる下面を除き透明釉をかける。つまみは蓮の茎で表す。14世紀後半〜15世紀前半。景徳鎮青花で似通った意匠の蓋（Fig.6-50）も出土しており、景徳鎮の影響と考えられる。

　Fig.14-133は蟹形の合子。外面には白化粧を施す。本例は15世紀と推測される[54]。

〈陶板〉

　Fig.15-134はFig.14-125の器台に通じる透かしを施した縁をもつ青花陶板。左1点は内圏に七宝地文を描く凸帯をめぐらす。縁取りは如意頭形に彫り、菊唐草文を描く。15個体以上出土。これはドゥマッ大モスクには見られないようであり、装飾的にもドゥマッ大モスクの陶板とはかなり異なる。器台は14世紀後半〜15世紀前半と推測されたが、他の多くの陶板がドゥマッ大モスクの例と共通し、15世紀前半の可能性が高いのに対し、本例はより古式の可能性が高い。よって14世紀後半〜15世紀前半とする。

　Fig.15-135は唐草文を描いた青花陶板。左は六弁木瓜型とする（繭山1977 Fig.1-3）陶板の破片。右2点も類似のものだが、唐草の表現など少し異なるため後出の可能性が

52　ジャカルタ国立博物館蔵品（平凡社1978図85）に類似する。

53　見込魚藻文、内側面宝文の類例としては町田市立博物館1993図153（現石洞美術館蔵、15〜16世紀とする）。

54　類例は町田市立博物館1993図209にあり、15〜16世紀とする。

ある[55]。

Fig.15-136 は段十字型の青花陶板。右側の1点は鳳凰文を描くタイプ（繭山1977 Fig.1-5, 6）と推測される。鳳凰の尾を唐草状に表現した部分。他も同類と推測されるが、中央の文様は異なる。

Fig.15-137 はコバルト線の枠内に緑・赤の色絵具で描いた五彩陶板[56]。15世紀。

（3）タイの陶磁器

〈青磁〉

Fig.16-138 は宝珠形のつまみを持つ青磁蓋。内面無釉。甲の部分にヘラ彫りで鎬文を施し、二重圏線内に蓮弁文をヘラ彫りと櫛状工具で表現[57]。

Fig.16-139 は見込中央に蓮華の崩れたと考えられる花をヘラ描きし、区画線を引き、この外周に櫛描きで花形を表す[58]。外側面もヘラ描き鎬文を表し、外底を無釉とする。高台内に比較的径の大きい道具の痕が黒く残る。

〈鉄絵陶器〉

Fig.16-140 は見込に鉄絵で魚文を描いた盤か鉢。内面から外側面にかけて白化粧を施し、鉄絵を描いた上に透明釉を外底以外にかける[59]。見込に窯道具の目跡が見られる。

Fig.16-141, 142 は見込の魚文の下側の輪郭表現を円圏にゆだねたタイプの鉢か皿。この表現の方が Fig.16-140 より後出と言う[60]。

〈灰陶〉

Fig.25-143／146 は炻器質の灰色の陶器壺であり、外面に印花で装飾する。Fig.25-143 は口縁部片。Fig.25-144 は肩部片であり、左下の肩に小さな耳が付く。Fig.25-145 は胴部片であり、右は円盤状に二次加工している。2片とも胴部には象の文様がハンコで押されている。Fig.25-146 は底部片。

胴部に象の文様を押捺装飾した類例は底部の作りの違いから、バンコク国立博物館と唐珍木コレクションのタイプと鹿児島神宮の例がある[61]。Fig.25-146 の底部は鹿児島神宮の方に近いが、別にバンコク国立博物館などのタイプの底部も出土している。また象の文様も、鹿児島神宮や唐珍木コレクションが鼻を上にあげた表現であるのに対し、Fig.25-145

55　この類例は小学館1984図302右上の出土品がある。

56　町田市立博物館1993図259に類似のトロウラン遺跡出土例がある。内面の主文様は異なる。

57　同種の蓮弁文を肩にめぐらし、胴部にヘラ彫りの鎬文を表した壺であり、かつ口部無釉で中蓋をもつ例がある（小学館1984図80、シーサッチャナライ窯、15世紀、口径13.3cm）。

58　類例はナンヤン沈没船引揚げ資料（向井2012図34）にあり、15世紀前半頃と推測される。

59　左の類例は東京国立博物館蔵品（平凡社1978挿図26、径26cm、鉢、スコータイ窯、15世紀とする）やトゥリアン沈没船引揚げ資料（向井2012図24）がある。

60　類例はロンチュエン沈没船引揚げ資料（向井2012図48）にあり、これらはスコータイ窯の15世紀でも中葉の可能性が高い。

61　類例はバンコク国立博物館蔵品、小学館1984図220（高さ50cm、シーサッチャナライ窯、13～14世紀とする）にある。その後の研究では、スパンブリ県バン・バンプーン窯跡のものと考えられており、年代も15世紀前半頃と推定されている（高島2013）。

Fig.25　トロウラン遺跡
Trowulan Site, Ⅲ−1 period, タイ陶磁 Thailand ceramics

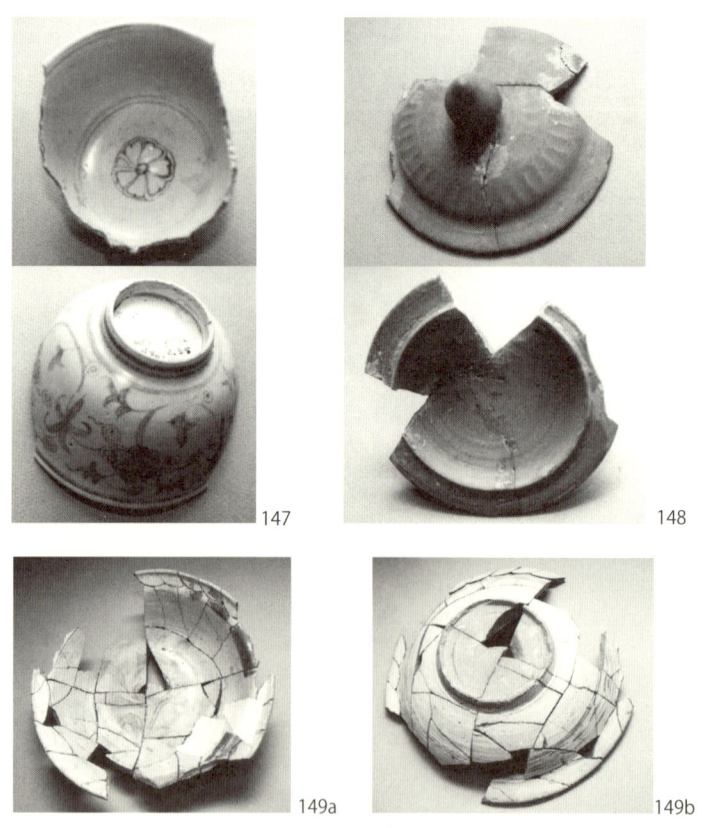

Fig.26　ソンバ・オプー城跡
Somba Opu Fort, Ⅲ−1 period, 中国・タイ陶磁 Chinese/Thailand ceramics

は明らかに鼻を下方、内に巻いている。また、Fig.25-143 のように頸部に凸帯を作るものが多いが、こうした例は今のところ他に見ない。

ソンバ・オプー城

（1）中国の陶磁器
〈青花〉
●景徳鎮窯
Fig.26-147 は口縁外反りに作る青花碗。見込に花文、外面に花唐草文を染付する。

（2）タイの陶磁器
Fig.26-148 は宝珠形のつまみを持つ青磁蓋。甲の部分にヘラ彫りで鎬文を施す。類例はトロウラン遺跡（Fig.16-138）にある。15 世紀前半頃のシーサッチャナライ窯と考えられる。

Fig.26-149 は鉄絵の盤形の大皿。焼成が不十分なため釉が不透明であるが、青磁釉の可能性がある。見込に独特の草花文と外側面にも連続文を施す。文様・器形から、シーサッチャナライ窯の 15 世紀前半頃と推測される[62]。

ブトン・ウォリオ城

（1）ベトナムの陶磁器
〈青花〉
Fig.27-150 は大皿、合子（右上）、碗（右下）などである。左上の大皿は太めの筆致や外側面の蓮弁に複弁がないなどから、15 世紀前半頃と考えられる。右下の碗はトロウラン遺跡例（Fig.12-113）に近いものであろう。右上の合子蓋はトロウラン遺跡でも見られる。

150a

150b

Fig.27　ブトン・ウォリオ城跡
Buton Wolio Fort, Ⅲ-1 period, ベトナム陶磁 Vietnamese ceramics

62　類例は向井 2012 の図 22。

6.　Ⅲ-2期（15世紀後半〜16世紀初）

トロウラン遺跡

マジャパイト王国末期に当たると考えられるもの。

(1)　中国の陶磁器
〈青花〉
●景徳鎮窯

Fig.19-151 は青花碗であり、口縁部が外反と考えられるもの。見込文様は巻貝文である。15世紀末〜16世紀初と推測される。

(2)　ベトナムの陶磁器
〈青花ほか〉

Fig.17-152 は見込に「福」字をコバルトで書き、蛇の目釉剝ぎとした碗。外面腰部に蓮弁文を描くが、「福」字や蓮弁の表現などから、15世紀後半〜16世紀初と推測される[63]。

Fig.17-153 は見込に「正」字をコバルトで小さく書き、円圏をめぐらす碗。高台内の鉄泥はかすれた状態になるのも特徴であり、16世紀にかかる可能性が高い特徴を持つ[64]。

Fig.17-154 は見込周囲に波濤文帯を設け、内側面に花唐草、口縁部に唐草を描く盤形の大皿。外側面に蓮弁文を描き、高台内に鉄泥を塗る。口縁端部は無釉。蓮弁文は複弁を持ち15世紀中葉〜後半と推測される。

Fig.17-155 は内面一杯に6弁の唐花文をコバルトで描いた盤形の大皿。口縁端部は無釉。Fig.14-130 と意匠は類似しているが、コバルト線描がより細く、外側面の蓮弁間に複弁を書き加えている。蓮弁間の複弁はトプカプ宮殿博物館蔵の1450年銘天球瓶に見られ、よりホイアン沖引揚げ品に近いことから、15世紀後半〜16世紀初と推測される[65]。

Fig.17-156 は外面口縁部下に擂座を貼り付けた鉢。胴部に唐草、擂座の間に唐草、口縁部内側にも唐草と思われる文様をコバルトで描く。口縁部無釉。本例は文様に崩れが見られるため、15世紀後半〜16世紀初と推測される[66]。

Fig.17-157, 158 は黄白釉の瓶子形の瓶の胴部に黒土で盛上げ、龍文を表し、透明釉をかけて焼いたもの。底部の縁は鉄泥を塗る。本例も15〜16世紀と推測される[67]。

63　ホイアン沖引揚げ品 Butterfield 2000（以下、ホイアン沖引揚げ品）-164頁 No.1421 などに類似している。

64　類例はホイアン沖引揚げ品 No.1353。町田市立博物館 1993 図178 にもあり、16世紀とする。

65　類例は東京国立博物館蔵品（15〜16世紀とする）（町田市立博物館 1993 の図152）があり、写真で見る限り、本例に似通っている。

66　類例は NMVH2005-Fig.218 などがある。15世紀とするが、下部の蓮弁文に複弁を描くので、15世紀後半と推測される。

67　黒土で龍文を盛り上げ装飾した類例は NMVH1995-Fig.14 にあり、15〜16世紀とする。

ソンバ・オプー城

（1）中国の陶磁器

〈青花〉

●景徳鎮窯

　Fig.28-159, 160 などは口縁部が外反に作られた青花碗。Fig.28-159 は見込に十字花文、口縁内側に梵字文、外面は花唐草文を描く。Fig.28-160 は見込に「福」字をコバルトで書いた碗。外面は蓮華唐草文を描く[68]。

　Fig.28-161 は内面に宝相華、地に点描を施す。外面に亀甲繋ぎ文、腰部に蓮弁繋ぎ文

Fig.28　ソンバ・オプー城跡
Somba Opu Fort, Ⅲ-2 period, 中国陶磁 Chinese ceramics

68　類例は山梨県一宮町荒巻本村出土品（東京国立博物館 1975 の図 195、大橋 1981 の 53 頁）がある。

165　　166

Fig.29　ソンバ・オプー城跡
Somba Opu Fort, Ⅲ-2 period, 中国陶磁 Chinese ceramics

を描く[69]。

　以上の青花碗は器形・文様から、レナ・カーゴ[70]引揚げ品に似通っているが、より崩れた表現であることから、15世紀末〜16世紀初と推測される。

　Fig.28-162は皿であり、見込の龍唐草や内外側面の花唐草文はレナ・カーゴの皿[71]の見込文様などに近いので、弘治（1488-1505）頃と推測される。

　Fig.28-163は口縁外反の皿。見込に唐草文、内外側面に花唐草文を描く[72]。

　Fig.28-164は丸皿。見込に岩と菊唐草文を描き、外側面に花唐草を配す[73]。

　Fig.29-165も丸皿であり、見込に麒麟文を描き、内外側面に花唐草文を配す[74]。

　Fig.29-166は皿。これも外側面に描かれた花唐草文などはレナ・カーゴ引揚げ品の中に見ることができるため、同様の時期と考えられる。

(2) ベトナムの陶磁器
〈青花ほか〉

　Fig.30-167は甲の中央に7弁の花を配した青花合子の蓋。型で8弁の花形に成形し、各弁に如意頭文を表す。類例はトロウラン遺跡の蓋があるが、周囲の文様は異なる。15世紀。

69　類例はレナ・カーゴ引揚げ品（Goddio et al. 2002）Fig.228。

70　フィリピンのパラワン島沖で引揚げられた沈没船。弘治（1488-1505）頃の沈没と推測されている。

71　文様などはレナ・カーゴ引揚げ品 Fig.67・115に似通っている。

72　これも文様などはレナ・カーゴ引揚げ品 Fig.188の碗外面の唐草に近い。

73　こうした意匠もレナ・カーゴ引揚げ品 Fig.183によりラフな表現のものが見られる。

74　こうした見込の意匠もレナ・カーゴ引揚げ品によりラフな表現のものが見られ、トプカプ宮殿蔵品 Fig.720（以下、トプカプ宮殿蔵品の番号は全て Krahl & Ayers 1986に基づく）にある。15世紀後半〜16世紀初とする。

167a

167b

168

169

170

171

172

Fig.30　ソンバ・オプー城跡
Somba Opu Fort, Ⅲ-2 period, ベトナム・タイ陶磁 Vietnamese & Thailand ceramics

　Fig.30-168 は蓋物の身。細い線描で唐草を表しており、トロウラン遺跡の盤（Fig.17-154）
内側面の唐草文の表現に似ることなどから、15 世紀でも中葉〜末と推測される。

⑶　タイの陶磁器
　〈鉄絵ほか〉
　Fig.30-169 は鉄絵合子。15 〜 16 世紀。
　Fig.30-170 は鉄絵合子[75]。
　Fig.30-171 は鉄絵合子の蓋。
　Fig.30-172左は合子の蓋。線彫で文様の輪郭を表す。15 世紀。シーサッチャナライ窯。
右は瓶と思われる[76]。

75　小学館 1984 図 330 の根津美術館蔵品「鉄絵柿香合」に近い。シーサッチャナライ窯とする。
76　これは小学館 1984 図 64 のような瓶（白濁釉褐彩鉄絵草花文瓢形、出光美術館蔵品）の胴部片であろうか。

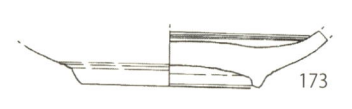

Fig.31　バンテン・ラーマ遺跡　Banten Lama Site, Ⅲ-2 period, タイ陶磁 Thailand ceramics

バンテン・ラーマ遺跡

（1）タイの陶磁器

〈青磁〉

Fig.31-173 は青磁大皿、見込に線彫で蓮花文を表し、その周囲に圏線を線彫で陰刻する。見込に三叉状の窯道具、高台内に輪状の窯道具の熔着痕が見られる。高台内は無釉。24 個体。シーサッチャナライ窯。15 世紀。

7. Ⅳ-1 期（15 世紀末～16 世紀中葉）

ソンバ・オプー城

（1）中国の陶磁器

〈青花ほか〉

●景徳鎮窯

Fig.32-174 は蓮子（レンツー）形と呼ばれる器形の碗。底部が下方に垂れた形が特徴で

Fig.32　ソンバ・オプー城跡
Somba Opu Fort, Ⅳ-1 period, 中国景徳鎮陶磁 Chinese Jingdezhen ceramics

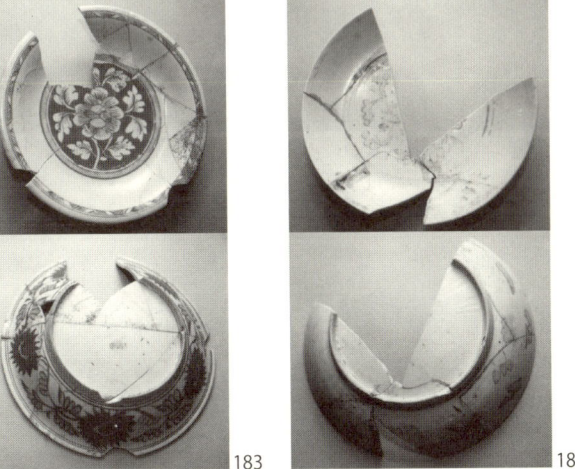

Fig.33　ソンバ・オプー城跡
Somba Opu Fort, Ⅳ-1 period, 中国景徳鎮陶磁 Chinese Jingdezhen ceramics

185　186

Fig.34　ソンバ・オプー城跡
Somba Opu Fort, IV-1 period, 中国景徳鎮陶磁 Chinese Jingdezhen ceramics

ある。見込は巻貝を描き、地を線条で埋める。右の外面腰部に略化した蓮弁と思われる文様を描く。

　Fig.32-175 は口縁部端を小さく折るように外反させた碗。よって口縁内側に文様帯を配するものは見ない。外側面に梵字を描き、腰部に蓮弁繋ぎ文を描く。見込にも梵字文を描く。梵字文の碗片と見られるものは、カンボジア王都ロンヴェークなどで細片が採集されている。

　Fig.32-176 は Fig.31-175 同様に口縁部を小さく外に折る。見込に花文、外面にも草花らしいが、おおらかな筆致で描く。

　Fig.33-177 は五彩の端反り碗。見込を蛇の目釉剝ぎした素地に内外に蓮弁を赤と緑で描くが、かなり剝落したもの。

　Fig.33-178 は口縁部を折縁とし、稜花形に刻んだ大きい皿。外側面にヘラ彫りで鎬文を彫る。右の見込中心に龍と雲を描き、次の区画帯に唐草文、内側面は型で鎬文を表し、左の口縁部には如意頭繋ぎ文を描く。口縁外側にも渦状の小さいまとまりの唐草を描く。バンテン・ラーマ遺跡では外側面を鎬ではない皿が見られる。

　Fig.33-179 も稜花形に刻んだ折縁皿。見込には竹が描かれ、岩で太湖石かと思われる文様を表す。内側面には連続の唐草文が描かれる。口縁の文様は四方襷かと思われる崩れた文様が描かれ、外面には渦繋ぎ文を配す。高台内中央に「大明年造」銘。

　Fig.33-180, 181 は稜花形の折縁皿。型成形で内側面の鎬文や口縁部を稜花形に作る。Fig.33-180 は口縁部に窓状の区画内に「金」「玉」「地」などの文字を描く。Fig.33-181 も同様の文様らしいが読めない。見込に麒麟文を描く。2点とも外側にはヘラ彫りの鎬文、口縁外側には渦繋ぎ文帯をめぐらす。

　Fig.33-182 は見込に Fig.28-164 のような太湖石に菊文の崩れた文様を描き、外側面も同様に崩れた花唐草を表現し、Fig.28-164 より後出と考えられる。

　Fig.33-183 は日本では「古赤絵」と呼ぶ、赤・緑絵具で文様を描いた五彩皿。口縁部を外反させた皿の見込に牡丹文、外側面に蓮華唐草文を描く。ブトン・ウォリオ城でも出土。16 世紀前半〜中葉。

　Fig.33-184 は丸形の皿に赤・緑絵具で文様を内外に施したものであるが、ほとんど剥落している。

　Fig.34-185 は白磁の端反り形皿。日本でも 16 世紀に多く出土する。

　Fig.34-186 は青花の小壺。外面に蓮華唐草文をコバルトで描く。内面に胴継ぎの痕が見られる。

ブトン・ウォリオ城

　Ⅳ-1 期には景徳鎮窯磁器が主となる。

(1) 中国の陶磁器

〈青花ほか〉

●景徳鎮窯

　Fig.35-187 は口縁部外反りの青花皿であり、見込に玉取獅子文を描く。

　Fig.35-188/191 の青花皿も 16 世紀前半〜中葉。Fig.35-188, 189 は口縁外反りの皿。Fig.35-190, 191 は丸形の皿。Fig.35-190 はレナ・カーゴ引揚げ品に似通っており、15 世紀末〜16 世紀初の可能性が高い。

　Fig.35-192 は五彩皿。赤・緑・黄色の 3 色を用い、輪郭線も赤線で引く「古赤絵」のタイプ。こうした特徴を持つ五彩は、日本で「天文年造」（1532-55）銘の小皿も伝世しているように 16 世紀前半〜中葉頃に多く作られたと推測される。

　Fig.35-193 は見込に梅樹文を描いた青花碁笥底皿。

　Fig.35-194 は法花の壺の肩部片。如意頭形の枠と間の瓔珞が堆花で表される[77]。

バンテン・ラーマ遺跡

(1) 中国の陶磁器

〈青花〉

●景徳鎮窯

　Fig.36-195, 196 は青花碗。底面が下方に垂れたいわゆる蓮子形碗である。Fig.36-195 は見込と外面に小さな花文かと思われる文様を描く。同類品は 23 個体（以下個体数のみを

77　類例は小学館 1976b 図 243 の三彩獅子牡丹文壺。

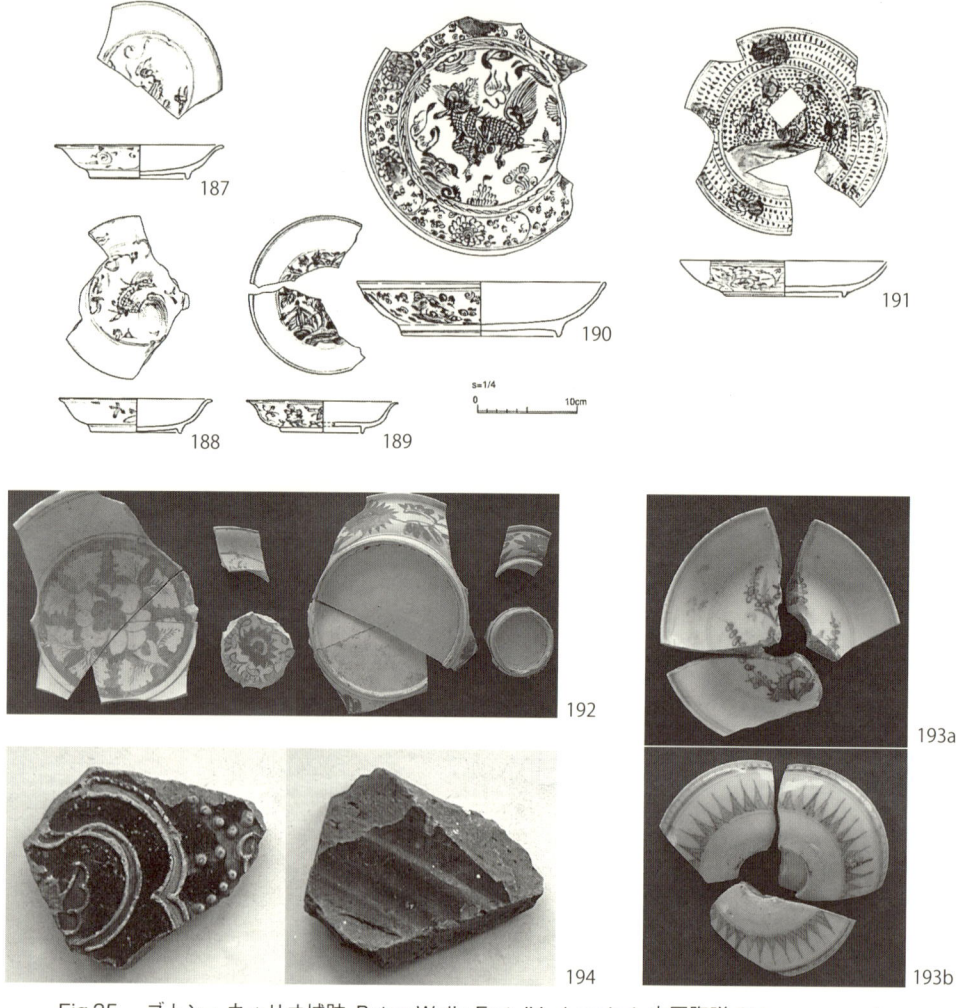

Fig.35　ブトン・ウォリオ城跡 Buton Wolio Fort, Ⅳ-1 period, 中国陶磁 Chinese ceramics

記す）。Fig.36-196 は見込に巻貝文、外面腰部に蕉葉文、口縁部に花かと思われる文様を描く。8 個体。両種の碗はともに日本でも一般的に出土している。16 世紀前半～中葉。

　Fig.36-197 は青花小皿。底部は碁笥底に削るのが特徴である。見込に花卉文、外面腰部に蕉葉文を描く。9 個体。これも日本でしばしば見られる。16 世紀前半～中葉。

　Fig.36-198, 199 は青花皿。198 は口径 30.6 cm の大皿であり、口縁部を折縁に作り、見込に花を中心に蓮弁文帯と唐草文帯が二重にめぐる。口縁部には四方襷文帯、外側面に唐草文帯を配す。同じような皿197 個体。日本ではあまり見られない意匠の大皿である[78]。Fig.36-199 は口径 23 cm の中皿であり、折縁に作る口縁部を稜花形に刻む。見込に玉取獅子文を描き、口縁部に渦文帯をめぐらす。外側面に篦彫りによる縦筋（本来、蓮弁を表したものか）を刻む。9 個体。この種の皿は日本でもいくらか出土例がある。これらの年代も

78　類例はトルコ・トプカプ宮殿蔵の Fig.781・782 にあり、16 世紀初とする。見込の蓮弁に花文もトプカプの Fig.682 の見込文様を崩した表現と推測される。

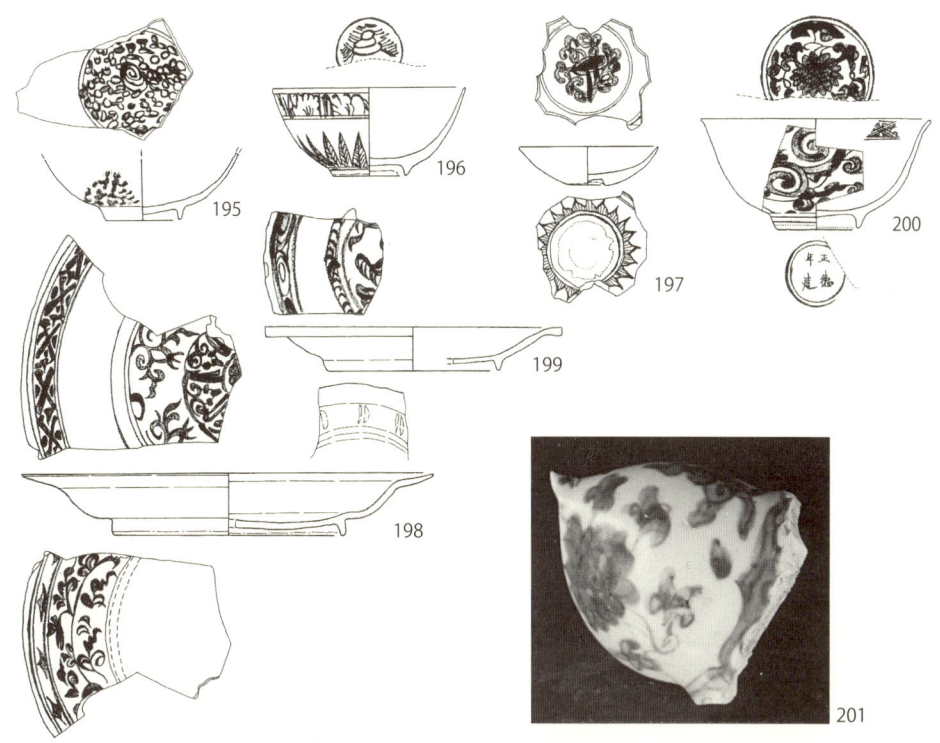

Fig.36 バンテン・ラーマ遺跡 Banten Lama Site, Ⅳ-1 period, 中国陶磁 Chinese ceramics

16 世紀前半〜中葉。

　Fig.36-200 は青花鉢。見込に菊唐草文・外面に龍唐草文・内面口縁部に四方襷文帯・高台内に「正徳年造」銘を染付する。42 個体。「正徳」は 1506〜21 年であり、「正徳年造」銘は製品の年代と考えてよかろう[79]。こうした鉢は日本での出土は少ない。

　Fig.36-201 は青花水注（クンディ）。乳首形の注口部分の破片であり、花唐草文が染付されている。1 個体。クンディの出土は、日本では長崎・万才町遺跡など極めて少なく、比較的似通った注口部の例はジャカルタ国立博物館所蔵品にある。16 世紀前半〜中葉。

（2）ベトナムの陶磁器

〈褐釉〉

　Fig.37-202 は褐釉瓶。いわゆる「南蛮粽花入れ」である。内面下部には巻上げ後の顕著なロクロ成形痕が残る。外面から内面上部に褐釉を施す。日本には花入れとして伝世したものが少なくないし、堺環濠都市遺跡・長崎市栄町遺跡などで出土している。5 個体。15 世紀〜16 世紀か。

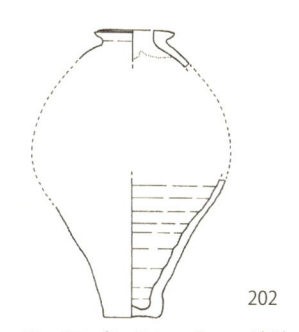

Fig.37 バンテン・ラーマ遺跡
Banten Lama Site, Ⅳ-1 period, ベトナム陶磁 Vietnamese ceramics

79　似たような龍唐草を描いた皿がトプカプ宮殿蔵の皿（Fig.785/787/788）にあり、16 世紀初とする。

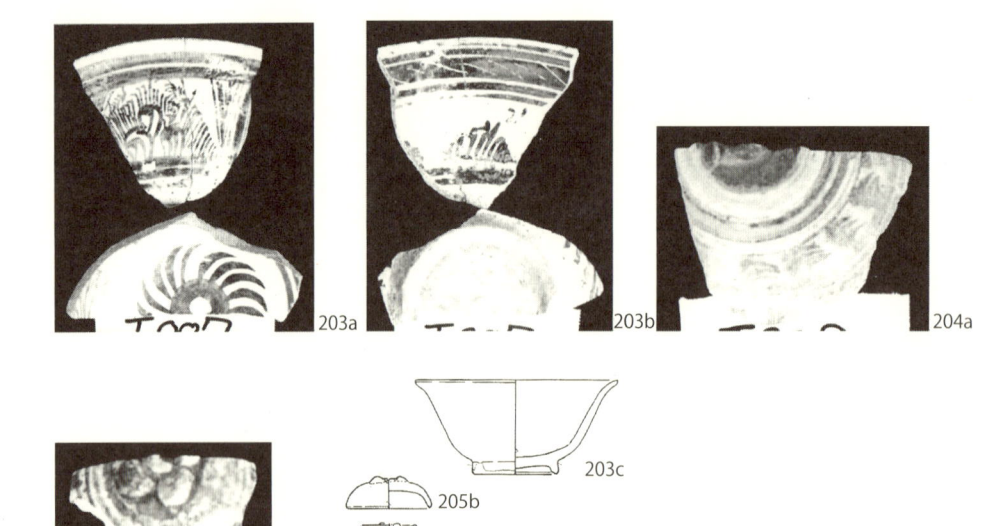

Fig.38 バンテン・ラーマ遺跡 Banten Lama Site, IV-1 period, タイ陶磁 Thailand ceramics

（3）タイの陶磁器

　本時期であげたが、15世紀のものも少なくないと思われる。

〈鉄絵〉

　Fig.38-203は鉄絵碗。見込に足付窯道具の熔着痕がある。6個体。15世紀。スコータイ窯。

　Fig.38-204, 205は鉄絵合子蓋。内面無釉。合計15個体。15～16世紀。

8. IV-2期（16世紀後半～17世紀初）

ソンバ・オプー城

（1）中国の陶磁器

〈青花ほか〉

●景徳鎮窯

　Fig.39-206は見込に牡丹かと思われる草花文様を描き、トプカプ宮殿博物館No.1531を見ると、内側面に葡萄蔓文で埋める。外面には簡略化しているが、トプカプ宮殿例を見ると松梅文を描く。類例はバンテン・ラーマ遺跡のほか、カンボジアの王都ロンヴェークやポニェルー[80]採集品の中にある。

　Fig.39-207は五彩碗。左下は饅頭心形碗であり、見込に蓮鷺文を染付。高台内に「萬福修同」銘を染付。外側面に色絵具で文様が描かれる。

80　ロンヴェークは15世紀中葉のアンコール放棄以後のカンボジア王都で、トンレサップ川に面したポニェルーは外港。

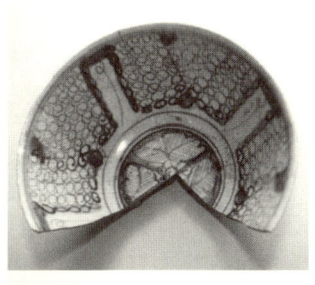

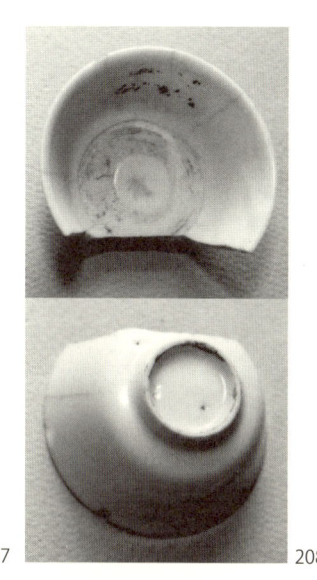

206

207

208

210

211

Fig.39 ソンバ・オプー城跡
Somba Opu Fort, Ⅳ-2 period, 中国景徳鎮陶磁 Chinese
Jingdezhen ceramics

209

Fig.39-208 は白磁小碗であり、見込は蛇の目釉剥ぎされる。16世紀後半頃。

Fig.39-209 は青花壺で、胴部下半を絞った器形であり、裾には蓮弁文をコバルトで描く[81]。肩部には圏線で区画した中を如意頭形の枠取し、その中に蓮華唐草文を配す。頸の付け根に如意頭繋ぎ文帯をめぐらす。頸部にはトプカプ宮殿の例を見ると如意雲文を描く。

Fig.39-210 は五彩の壺。

Fig.39-211 の上は鳥形と思われる瓶であろう。

Fig.40-212 は青花小壺。外面に折枝文、肩部に鋸歯状蓮弁文を描く。底部は平底。

81　類例はトプカプ宮殿蔵 Fig.824 がある。高さ 29～30cmとあり、16世紀前半～中葉とする。

212　　　　　　　　　　　　213

Fig.40 ソンバ・オプー城跡
Somba Opu Fort, IV-2 period, 中国景徳鎮陶磁 Chinese Jingdezhen ceramics

　Fig.40-213 は法花の壺。胴下部を絞り、蓮弁文を表す。頸部や肩の文様などは Fig.39-209 の青花壺に類似しており[82]、同じ遺跡に景徳鎮の青花と法花の異なる装飾の壺が 16 世紀に入ったことを示唆する。

〈青花〉

●漳州窯

　Fig.41-214 は列点文碗。この文様の元は景徳鎮窯の 16 世紀前半頃に小花で埋めた蓮子形碗があり、それを簡略化したものと推測される[83]。

　Fig.41-215 は見込に花卉文、外面にも草花と思われる文様を太い筆致で勢いよく描いた碗[84]。

　Fig.41-216 は見込に略化が著しいが、「善」の字の可能性がある文様を描いた碗。

　Fig.41-217 は見込に「福」字を太い筆致で描いた碗[85]。

　Fig.41-218 は見込に玉取の獅子か麒麟と思われる文様を太い筆致で勢いよく描いた皿。

　Fig.41-219 は見込に花卉文を描いた皿。

　Fig.41-220 は見込に花卉文、外に小さく折った口縁部に唐草文を描く[86]。

　Fig.41-221 は見込を円圏線で 2 つに区画し、それぞれに花卉文と思われる略化した草花を太い筆致で描く。内側面にも四方に草花を表す[87]。

　Fig.42-222, 223 は折縁の大皿。口縁部には花卉文を表す窓絵を 6 ヶ所所配し、地を鱗

82　伝世例では談雪慧他 1998-195 頁上段左にあるが、トプカプ宮殿蔵品 Fig.824 に似通っている。
83　類例は福建省安渓魁斗窯（曽 2001 の 77 頁）で見られる。
84　類例は福建省平和南勝花仔楼窯（曽 2001 の 61 頁）で見られる。
85　福建省安渓魁斗窯で見られる。
86　類例は Adhyatman1999-Fig.1 がある。
87　類例は Adhyatman1999-Fig.7 がある。

Fig.41 ソンバ・オプー城跡
Somba Opu Fort, Ⅳ-2 period, 中国漳州陶磁 Chinese Zhangzhou ceramics

Fig.42 ソンバ・オプー城跡
Somba Opu Fort, IV-2 period, 中国漳州陶磁 Chinese Zhangzhou ceramics

状文で埋める。Fig.42-222 は見込に鳥と草花などを表し、Fig.42-223 は見込に鳳凰と草花などを描く[88]。この種の大皿は日本でも出土する。

ブトン・ウォリオ城

(1) 中国の陶磁器
〈青花ほか〉
●景徳鎮窯

Fig.43-224 のような青花饅頭心形碗が多く見られる。

Fig.43-225, 226 のような青花素地に赤などの色絵具で文様を加えたものがある。Fig.43-226 は高台内に「萬福修同」と見られる銘を染付する。類例はソンバ・オプー城（Fig.39-207 左下）。

バンテン・ラーマ遺跡

(1) 中国の陶磁器
〈青花ほか〉
●景徳鎮窯

Fig.44-227 は青花小坏。見込に海上に浮かぶ三神山文を描く。外面腰部に波濤文、高台内に「大明年造」銘を染付する[89]。3 個体。16 世紀後半頃。

Fig.44-228 は五彩皿か鉢。見込には 227 と同様の文様を赤中心に表す。外面腰部に蓮弁文?、高台内に「□□年造」銘を染付で二重圏線内に記す。8 個体。年代も 227 と同じ。

88　類例は Fig.42-222 が Adhyatman1999-Fig.50、Fig.42-223 が Adhyatman1999-Fig.46 にある。

89　長崎県平戸和蘭商館跡（平戸市教育委員会1988の第20図27）で銘が異なる類品が出土しているが、日本では少ない。

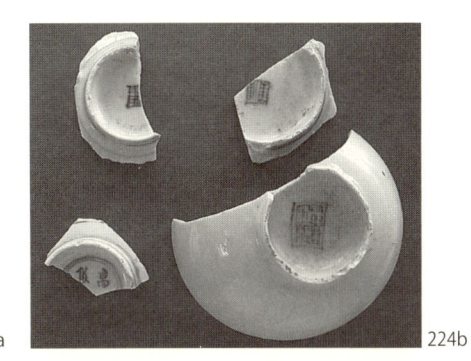

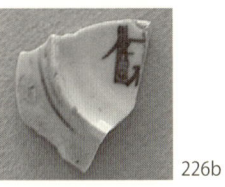

Fig.43 ブトン・ウォリ城跡
Buton Wolio Fort, Ⅳ-2 period, 中国景徳鎮陶磁 Chinese Jingdezhen ceramics

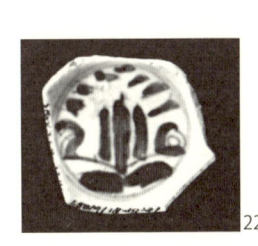
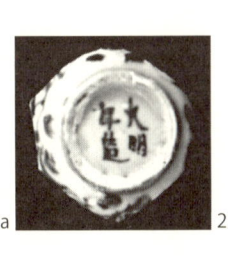
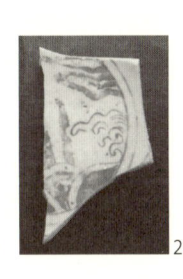

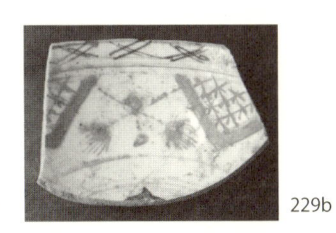
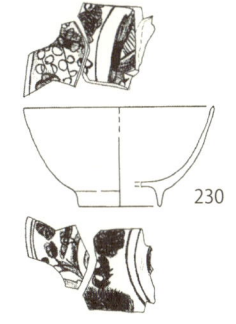

Fig.44 バンテン・ラーマ遺跡
Banten Lama Site, Ⅳ-2 period, 中国景徳鎮陶磁 Chinese Jingdezhen ceramics

日本での出土例は知らない。

　Fig.44-229 は五彩碗。文様の一部をコバルトで描いた青花素地に赤・緑・黄などの色絵具で加彩したもの。外面は窓絵と花卉文、内側面に瓔珞文、口縁部に四方襷文帯を表す。20 個体。16 世紀後半。日本ではあまり見ないタイプである。

　Fig.44-230 は青花碗。1590～1610 年代。見込に花卉文、内側面に葡萄文、外面松梅文を描く[90]。31 個体。

〈中国陶器〉

　Fig.45-231 は三彩耳付壺。低火度釉の陶器であり，外面に唐草文を貼り付ける。いわゆるトラディスカントの壺。日本でも少量出土例がある。1 個体。16 世紀～17 世紀初。

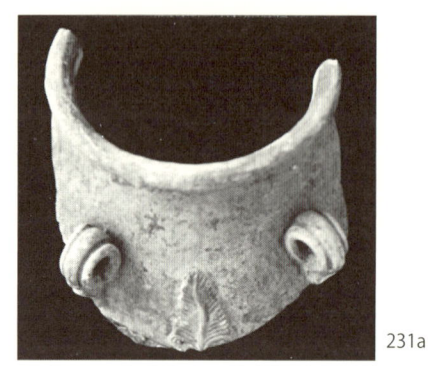
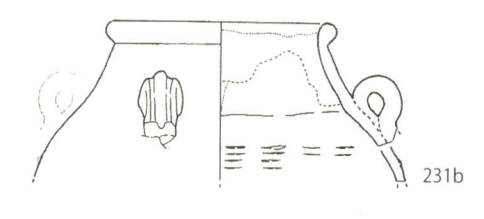

231a　　　　　　　　　231b

Fig.45 バンテン・ラーマ遺跡
Banten Lama Site, Ⅳ-2 period, 中国陶磁 Chinese ceramics

（2）ミャンマー陶器

　Fig.46-232 は錫釉と見られる白濁釉を施した大皿であり 2 個体以上出土している[91]。Fig.46-232 下は白濁釉に緑彩を施した大皿。

232

Fig.46 バンテン・ラーマ遺跡
Banten Lama Site, Ⅳ-2 period, ミャンマー陶磁 Myanmar ceramics

90　長崎市栄町遺跡（長崎市埋蔵文化財調査協議会 1993 の第 36 図 51）で出土している。また伝世品はトプカプ宮殿蔵 Fig.1531 にあり、17 世紀初とする。

91　日本では平戸和蘭商館跡出土例（平戸市教育委員会 1988 の第 21 図 35）があり、特徴は佐々木他 2004 の Fig.117 上左や Fig.120-2 に似通っている。Fig.46-232 下の白濁釉緑彩皿についてはミャンマー産かどうか疑問とされるが、筆者は前掲論文 Fig.113 のように白濁釉緑彩の中では底部の作りが粗く、無釉であることなどから、年代が後出と推測する。

9. Ⅴ-1期（17世紀前半頃）

ソンバ・オプー城

（1）中国の陶磁器

〈青花ほか〉

● 景徳鎮

Fig.47-233 は青花小坏。

Fig.47-234 は青花小坏。17 世紀であろうが、前半か後半か明確でない。

Fig.47-235 は青花芙蓉手の小鉢。型成形で輪花に作る[92]。17 世紀第 1 四半期頃であろう。

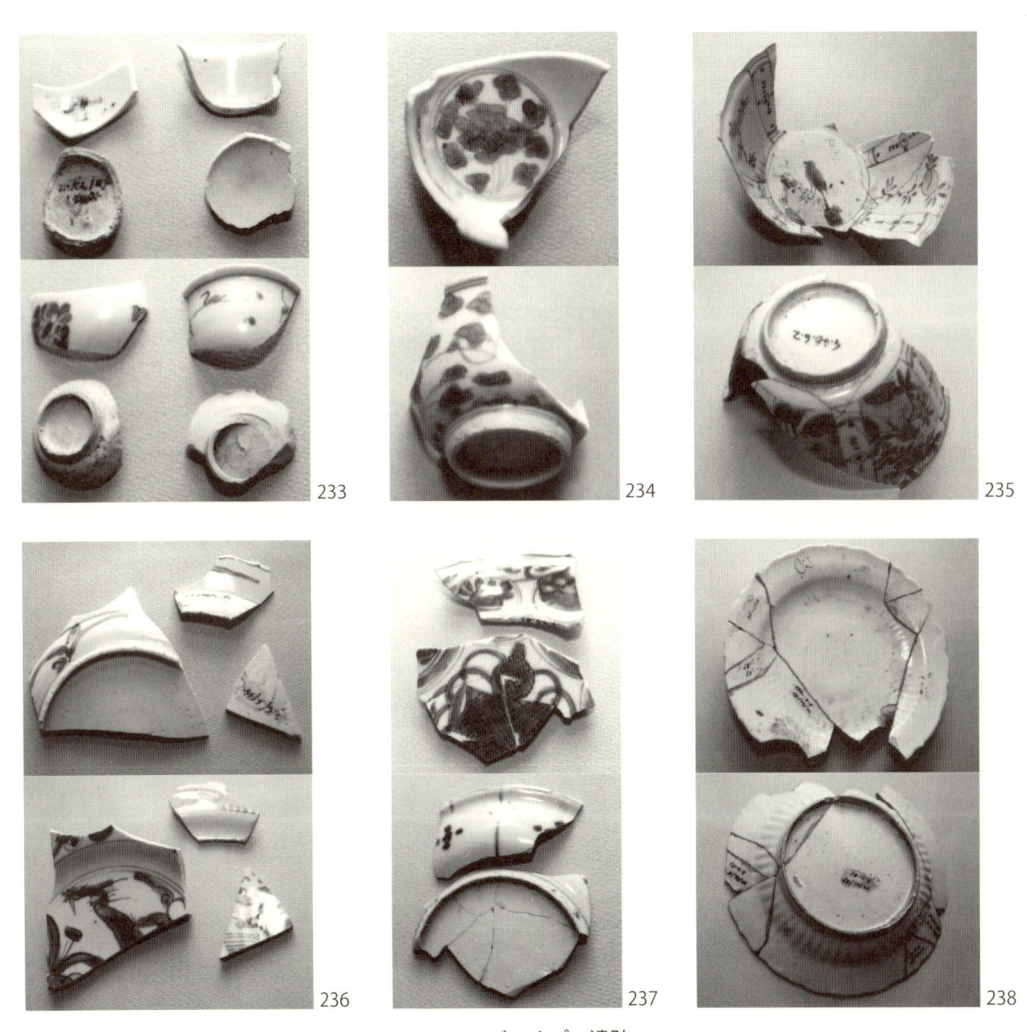

233 234 235

236 237 238

Fig.47 ソンバ・オプー遺跡
Somba Opu Fort, V-1 period, 中国景徳鎮陶磁 Chinese Jingdezhen ceramics

---

92 外面の区画間の瓔珞などは、1613 年セントヘレナ島沖で沈んだオランダ船ヴィッテレーウ号引揚げ品 Pijl-Ketel 1982-Fig.8852 に似通っているが、内面文様はトプカプ宮殿蔵 Fig.1495 に近い。

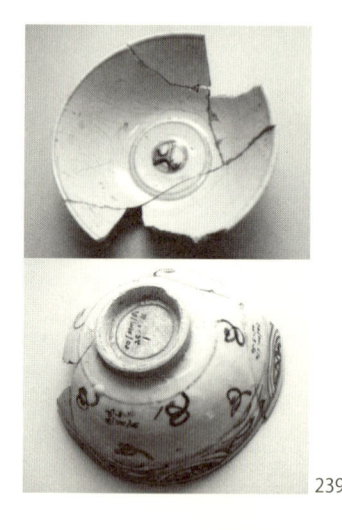

239　　240　　241

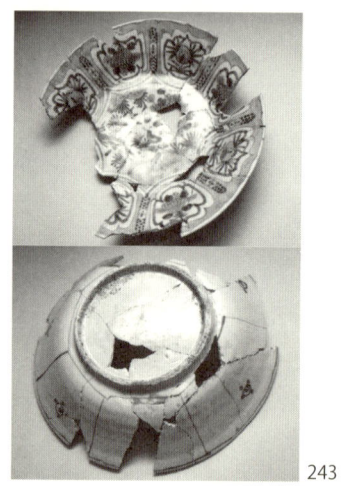

242　　243

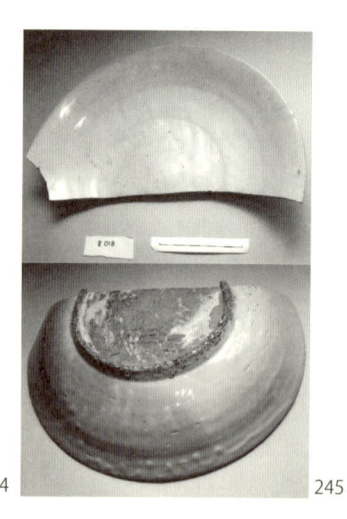

244　　245　　246

Fig.48 ソンバ・オプー遺跡
Somba Opu Fort, Ⅴ-1 period, 中国漳州陶磁 Chinese Zhangzhou ceramics

Fig.47-236の左2点は青花折縁皿。見込に鳳凰と草花を描く[93]。

Fig.47-237は芙蓉手の一種である名山手の青花小皿。型成形で輪花とし、見込は宝文、内側面の宝珠形の窓内に花卉文などを描く。外面も区画線を縦に引き、間に宝文を描く[94]。

Fig.47-238は白磁で型打ち成形による折縁の輪花皿。

● 漳州窯

Fig.48-239は青花碗[95]。

Fig.48-240は見込に蓮鷺文、外側面も蓮を描いた青花碗[96]。

Fig.48-241は青花皿であり、二重線で2つに区画した見込に草花文を文様化した意匠[97]。

Fig.48-242は日本でも多く見られる大きい青花皿。見込に鳳凰文と竹などを描き、内側面に窓絵を四方に配し、間に算木文が崩れて「三」のような文様を描く。口縁部に雷文帯を表す[98]。

Fig.48-243は芙蓉手の1種であるが、見込は名山手のように表す青花皿[99]。

Fig.48-244は五彩の大皿。色の剝落が著しく文様が判然としないが、見込に対称的に鳳凰と牡丹を描き、折縁口縁の四方の窓絵に花、その間の窓絵に花卉文のような草花を描き、地を鱗状文で埋めた例と類似と思われる[100]。

Fig.48-245は青磁大皿。

Fig.48-246は白磁稜花形小皿。この種の稜花形小皿は福建省徳化窯の小皿があるが、それは型作りで見込や高台に胎土目跡を残すのがふつうである。おそらく本例は近い時期に他の福建省の窯で作られたものと思われる。

ブトン・ウォリオ城

(1) 中国の陶磁器

1590年代から17世紀前半のものとして、景徳鎮窯と漳州窯製品が多量に出土している。

〈青花ほか〉

● 景徳鎮窯

Fig.49-247は高台内に「貴」字を染付した白磁碗である。

Fig.49-248は青花碗などであり、左下は青花芙蓉手小鉢。

93　類例はヴィッテレーウ号引揚げ品（Pijl-Ketel 1982の187頁）。

94　ヴィッテレーウ号引揚げ品 Pijl-Ketel 1982 95頁 No.5175に似る。

95　日本でも出土例が多い。類例は福建省漳浦坪水窯で見られる。

96　類例は福建省平和南勝花仔楼窯にあり、Adhyatman1999-Fig.115やヴィッテレーウ号引揚げ品 Pijl-Ketel 1982 208頁に見られる。

97　この青花文様は Adhyatman1999-Fig.180の五彩皿の見込文様に似通っている。

98　類例はヴィッテレーウ号引揚げ品 Pijl-Ketel 1982　201頁、Adhyatman1999-Fig.71にある。

99　名山手は宝珠形の窓と、見込周囲にまりばさみ文様を描く芙蓉手の一種であり、小皿中心に作られ日本でも出土例は多い。類例は佐賀県立九州陶磁文化館 2003-No.341にあり、口径26.8cmがある。

100 Adhyatman1999-Fig.197

Fig.49-249 は青花赤壁賦文の鉢であり、見込周囲に花文帯をめぐらす。外面には赤壁賦と思われる漢詩が描かれ、一方に舟人物文が描かれる。高台畳付は幅広く削り出され、底部無釉である。1620～40 年代と考えられる。

Fig.49-250／Fig.50-252 の青花皿は、側面を区画した芙蓉手意匠であり、ヨーロッパ向けの代表的意匠である。Fig.50-252 の右上は名山手意匠の皿。Fig.50-252 左上はモンス

247　　248a　　248b　　249a　　249b　　250a　　250b　　251a

Fig.49 ブトン・ウォリオ城跡
Buton Wolio Fort, Ⅴ-1 period, 中国景徳鎮陶磁 Chinese Jingdezhen ceramics

ターマスクと呼ばれる芙蓉手の鉢。

　Fig.50-253 も様々な意匠の青花皿であり、より簡素化された芙蓉手を含む。

　Fig.50-254 は釉裏紅青花。Fig.49-249 と同様、蛇の目高台であり、底部無釉。1620～40 年代と考えられる。

　Fig.50-255 外側面は褐釉地に白花とコバルトで鷺と水草などの文様を表した餅花手と

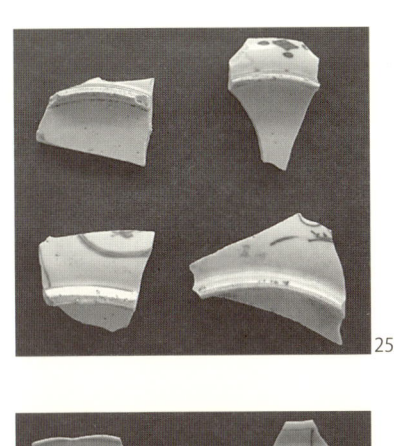
251b

252a

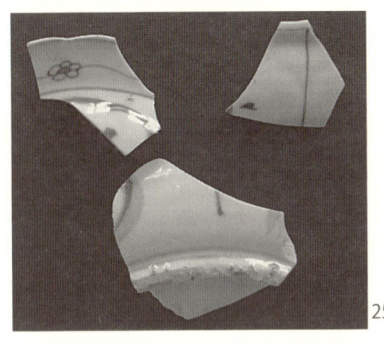
252b

253a

253b

254a

254b

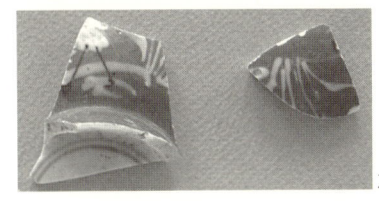
255

256

Fig.50 ブトン・ウォリオ城跡
Buton Wolio Fort, V-1 period, 中国景徳鎮陶磁 Chinese Jingdezhen ceramics

呼ばれるもの。

Fig.50-256 は青花合子。16 世紀後半～17 世紀であろう。

●漳州窯

Fig.51-257 の青花皿は 17 世紀前半と考えられる。上の 1 点は見込に鳳凰文を描き、口縁部に雷文帯を染付した皿であり、日本でも出土例は多い。

Fig.51-258 は青磁大皿であり、内側面にヘラ彫りの菊弁文を表す。

Fig.51-259 は瑠璃釉白花の餅花手大皿。

Fig.51-260 は五彩合子の身。

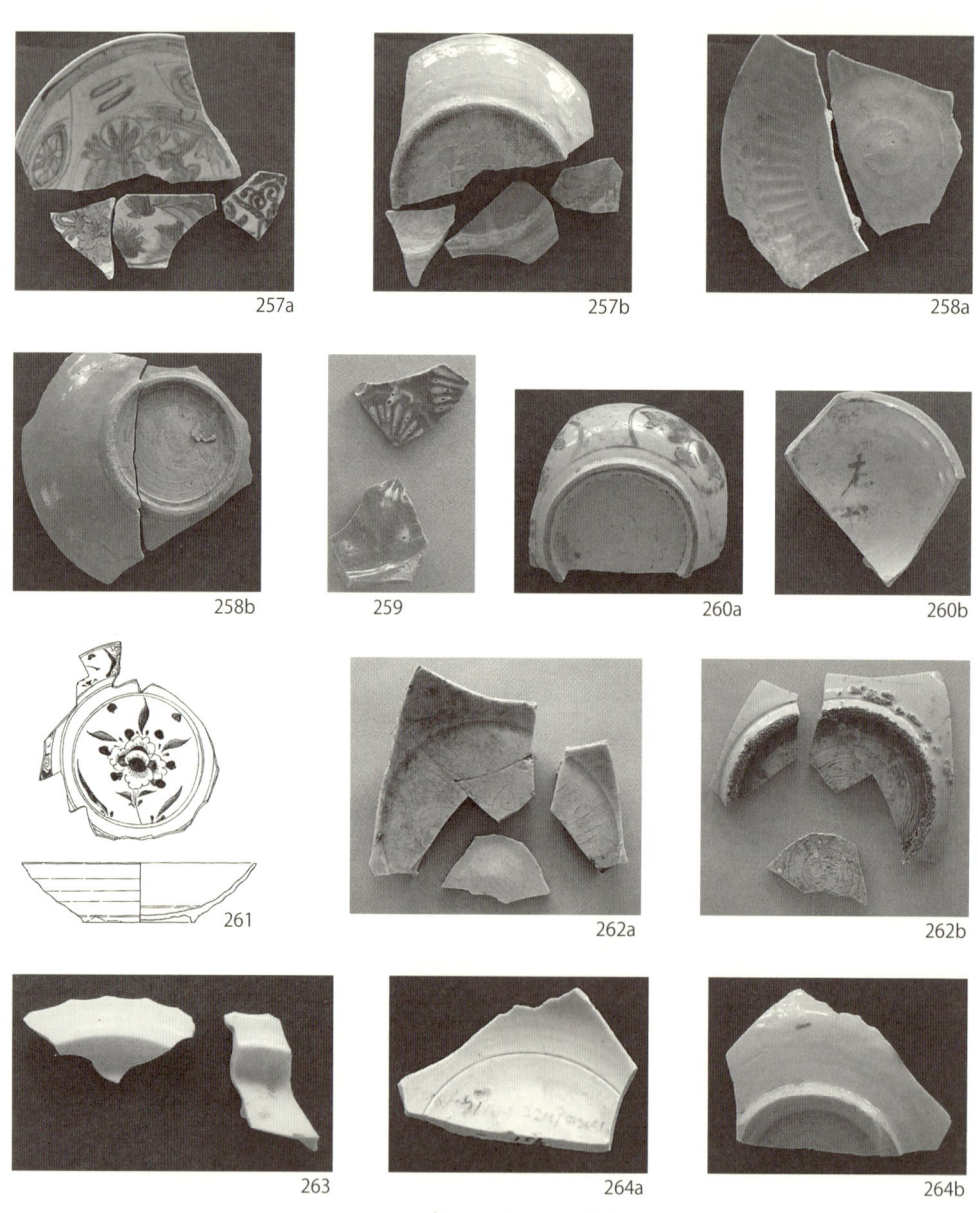

257a　　257b　　258a

258b　　259　　260a　　260b

261　　262a　　262b

263　　264a　　264b

Fig.51 ブトン・ウォリオ城跡
Buton Wolio Fort, V-1 period, 中国漳州・徳化陶磁 Chinese Zhangzhou & Dehua ceramics

Fig.51-261 の五彩大皿は素地の釉調や底部の作りなどの特徴から、漳州窯の大皿とし
ては末期の 17 世紀中葉と思われる。Fig.51-262 の青磁大皿も同様と考えられる。

Fig.51-262 の青磁大皿は内面に線彫り文が施される。

● 福建・徳化窯

徳化窯は独特の白磁の生産地である。

Fig.51-263 は型成形で作られた白磁稜花形小皿。16 世紀末〜 17 世紀前半。

Fig.51-264 は白磁皿であり、型成形で作られ、見込と高台畳付に胎土目痕が見られる
のが特徴。釉調も象牙白と呼ばれる独特の白色を呈す。17 世紀。

バンテン・ラーマ遺跡

（1）中国の陶磁器

〈青花ほか〉

● 景徳鎮窯

Fig.52-265, 266 は青花折縁中皿。Fig.52-265 は口縁部に唐草文、外面にも花唐草文を
描く。6 個体。1590 〜 1630 年代。Fig.52-266 は見込に樹下鹿文、折縁口縁部に水鳥に草
花文を描く[101]。32 個体。1590 〜 1610 年代。

Fig.52-267 は青花中皿。丸形であり，見込に跳魚図、内側面に宝文、外側面にも宝文
を描く。93 個体。日本での出土例は知らない。1590 〜 1630 年代。

Fig.52-268 は青花大皿。内面に山水風景を表し、外面には樹木を表す。6 個体。このよ
うに大きなサイズの大皿は日本では元青花を除くと、芙蓉手大皿が江戸初期に平戸和蘭商
館跡などで少量出土する程度で少ない。しかもこのように芙蓉手以外の意匠となるとさら
に出土例は希である。1590 〜 1630 年代。

Fig.52-269 は青花皿。口径はおよそ 14.6cm であり、型に当てて側面の窓枠などを陽刻
で表す。34 個体。芙蓉手の一種の「名山手」。見込は花鳥文、側面の窓内に花卉と宝を交
互に描く。外面も区画し宝文を染付する。1590 〜 1630 年代。

Fig.52-270 は青花芙蓉手皿。同様の皿は中・大皿の破片であり、精粗が見られる。本
例は精緻な作行きである。内側面は芙蓉手の特徴である区画内に花卉と宝文を描き、見込
周囲には紗綾形と三角？地文を伴うまりばさみ文を配す。外側面も区画内に宝文を表す。
これら芙蓉手皿も側面の区画文は型を当てて陽刻した素地に染付する。Fig.52-270 は 41
個体。こうした芙蓉手皿はヨーロッパで好評を博したため、注文で長期にわたって製作さ
れたと考えられる[102]。Fig.52-270 の年代は 1590 〜 1630 年代。

---

101 類例は長崎市栄町遺跡 2 区 12 号土坑出土品がある。伝世品では、ポルトガル・リスボンの ANASTACIO
　　GONCALVES 博物館蔵品（Pinto 1996 の 83 頁）にある。これらを見ると口縁部は稜花形に刻む。

102 輸出品のためか中国国内での出土例はあまり見ないが、江西省広昌県の墓（姚他 1990 の 86 〜 89 頁）などから
　　出土することが報告されている。生産地に近いことなど特殊な例かもしれない。紀年墓出土例であり、主に万暦
　　36 年（1608）から南明弘光元年（1645）にかけての芙蓉手皿が示されている。

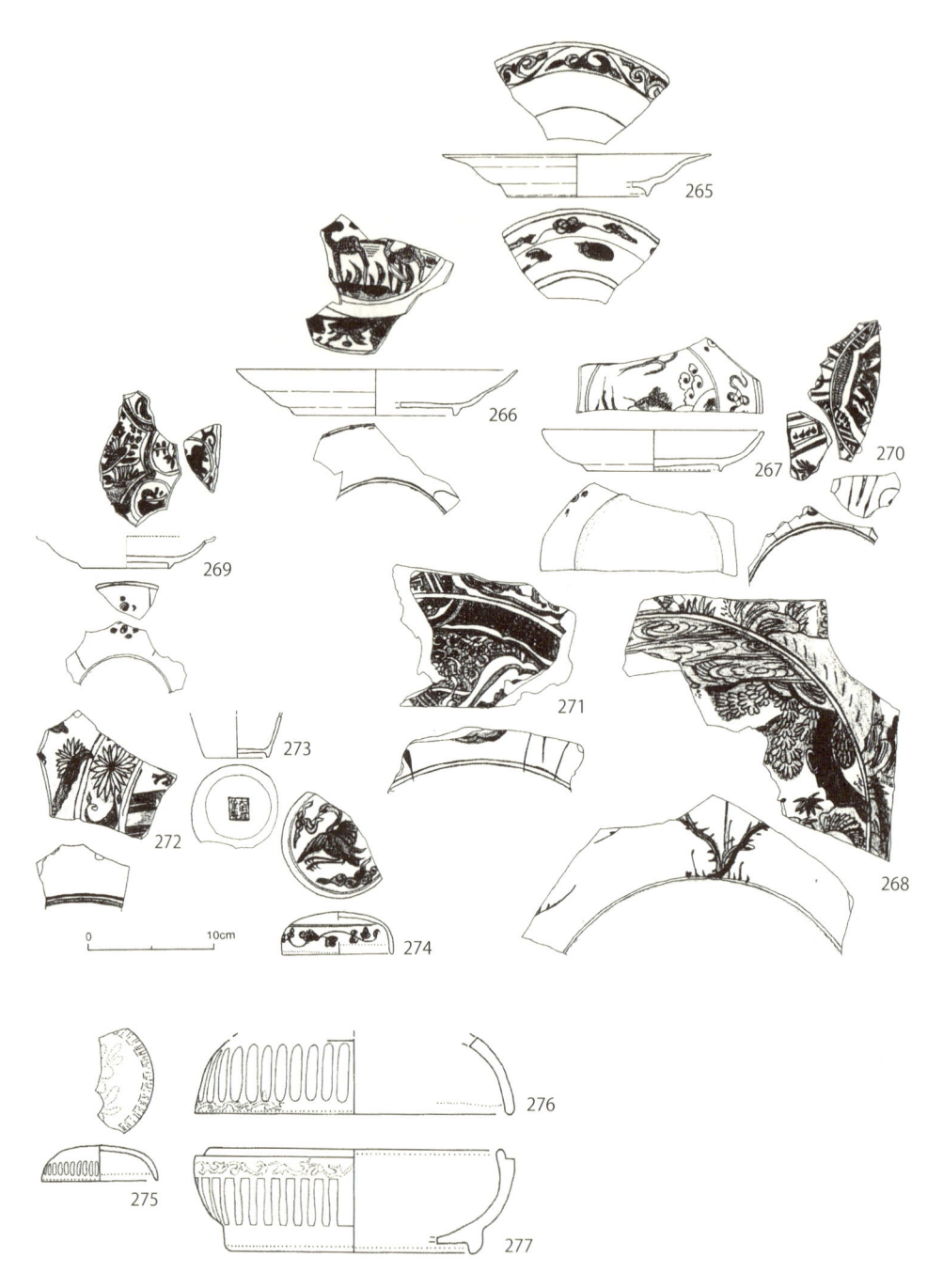

Fig.52 バンテン・ラーマ遺跡
Banten Lama Site, Ⅴ-1 period, 中国景徳鎮陶磁 Chinese Jingdezhen ceramics

　Fig.52-271 は口径 40cm を越すような芙蓉手大皿片。見込にも緻密な文様を埋め、周囲にまりばさみ文をめぐらす。内側面は区画に窓絵を配す。外側面も区画に窓枠を表す[103]。17個体。1590～1610年代。

　Fig.52-272 は青花大皿。芙蓉手の一種で内側面の区画内にチューリップデザインを施すタイプと見られる。特徴の一つは見込周囲に文様帯を設け、菊文を独特の表現の葉と共に描く。側面の文様はチューリップ文の区画部分は残らないが、それと交互に配した唐人風景図の区画の一部と推測され、土坡に草を描く。見込部は欄干など建造物の一部と推測され、これもチューリップデザインの芙蓉手大皿に一般的な構成文様である[104]。3個体。17世紀第2四半期。

　Fig.52-273 は白磁猪口。高台内に二重方形枠内に「大明成化年製」の二行6字銘を染付する[105]。1個体。1600～10年代と考えられる。

　Fig.52-274 は青花合子の蓋。上面に雲鶴文、側面につる草文を描く。1個体。16世紀後半～17世紀前半。

　Fig.52-275 / 277 は褐釉白花合子。Fig.52-275 は小型の合子の蓋であり、上面に褐釉の上に白土で花卉文を描き、側面には縦筋を箆彫で陰刻する。3個体。Fig.52-276, 277 は大型の合子の蓋と身であり、側面に縦筋を箆彫した素地に褐釉をかけ、口縁下に唐草文を白花で表す。Fig.52-276 は6個体、Fig.52 277 は3個体。16世紀末～17世紀前半。

　●福建

　福建省南部の徳化・安渓・漳州地方に窯が分布する。徳化窯の白磁を除けば主に景徳鎮窯系磁器より粗製の磁器生産を行なった。その流れで広東省北部にも粗製磁器生産の窯がいくらか分布している。この地域の青花生産は景徳鎮窯の青花が磁器の主流となっていく中で、16世紀後半から本格的に始まった。そのためバンテン・ラーマではⅣ-2期以降に現れる。

　Fig.53-278 は青花碗。比較的白い土であり、全面に施釉され、高台畳付にボソボソとした敷き砂（モミガラ）の熔着が見られる。外面に花唐草、見込に花卉を描く[106]。197個体。1590～1630年代。漳州窯。

　Fig.53-279 は五彩鉢。日本で「呉州赤絵」と呼んだもの。化粧掛けした素地であり、高台付近の施釉は雑であり、粗い敷き砂が熔着する場合もある。そうした粗放な素地に赤中心の色絵具で蓮文などを描く。口縁部には地文と窓絵の文様帯を表す。1個体。1590～

---

103 日本での類例は平戸和蘭商館跡など少ない。

104 チューリップデザインの大皿の意匠はかなりの種類があり、この陶片にもっとも似通っているのはトルコ・トプカプ宮殿蔵 Fig.1609 の大皿（口径48cm）である。日本での出土例は別のタイプのチューリップデサイン大皿片であり、長崎・出島和蘭商館跡（長崎市教育委員会 1986 の Fig.37-3）などに少量見られる。

105 類品は長崎・平戸和蘭商館跡の1616年頃の海岸石垣築造に伴う造成土から出土している。二重方形枠内の「大明成化年製」銘は大阪市住友銅吹所跡出土品（大阪市文化財協会 1998 の図 24-341～343）にもあり、伝世品では永青文庫蔵「豆彩団龍文杯」に見られ、清・雍正期とされる。

106 日本でも出土例は多く、肥前の胎土目積み段階（1590～1610年代）の陶器と共伴する例が多い。

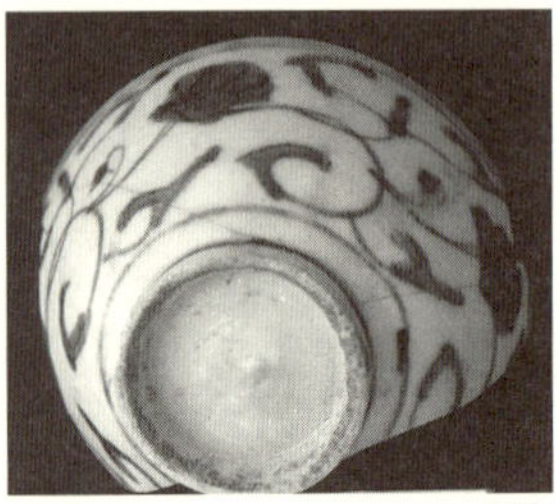
278

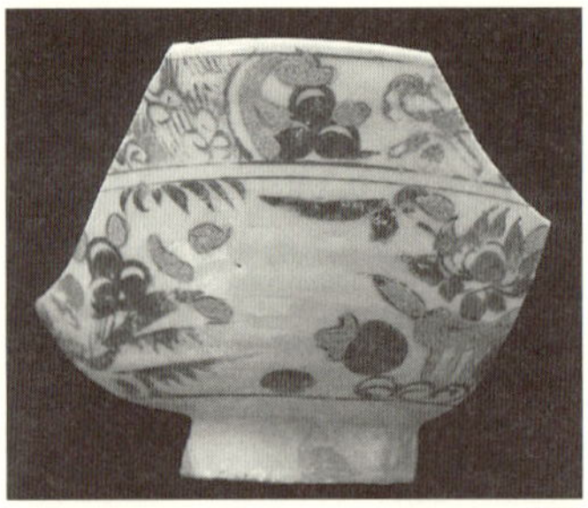
279

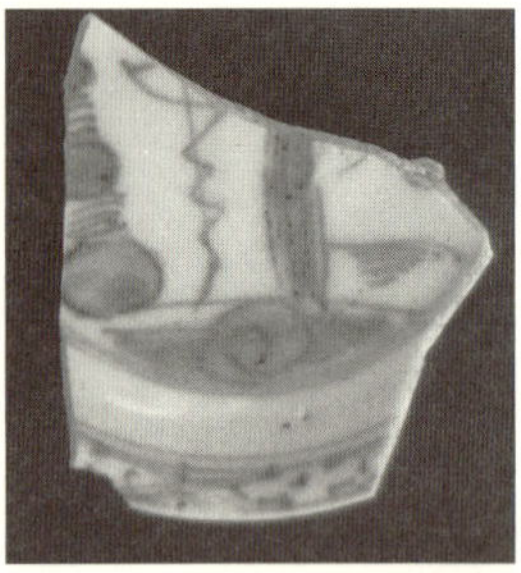
280

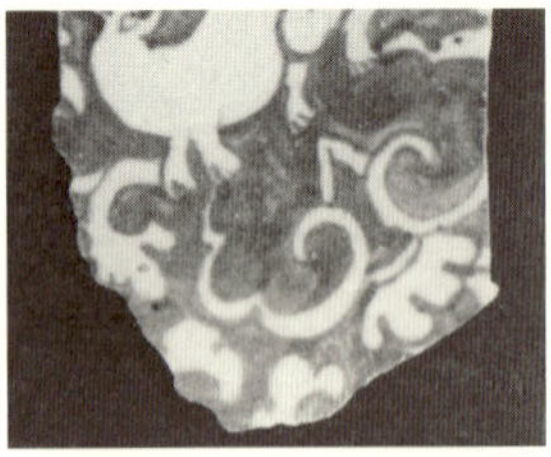
281

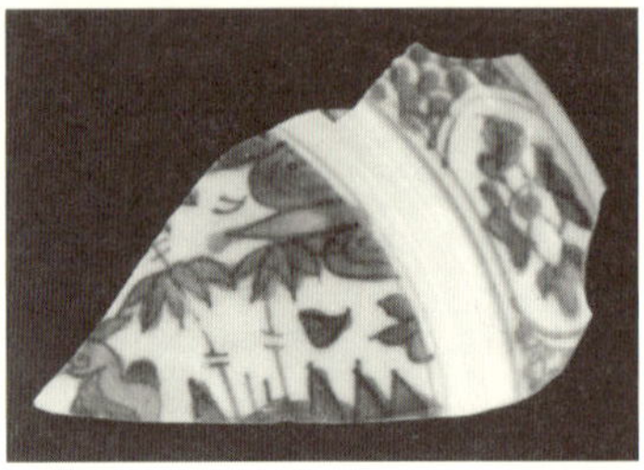
282

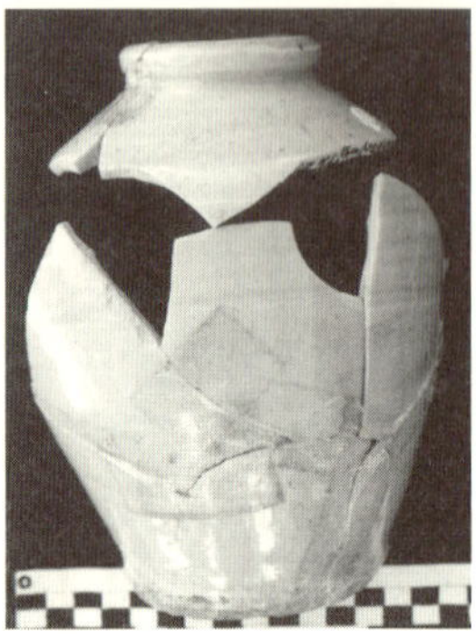
283

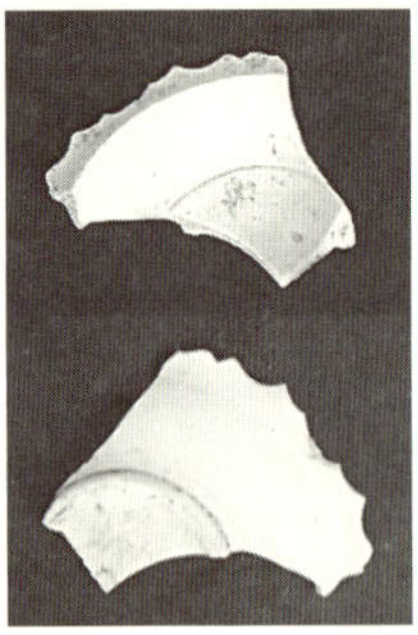
284

Fig.53 バンテン・ラーマ遺跡
Banten Lama Site, V-1 period, 中国漳州・徳化陶磁
Chinese Zhangzhou & Dehua ceramics

1630年代。漳州窯。

Fig.53-280は青花小皿。素地の状態や高台の状態はFig.53-278の碗に近い。見込に旗や塔を描き、緩く折った口縁部内側に四方襷文帯をめぐらす[107]。1個体。1590～1630年代。漳州窯。

Fig.53-281は青花皿。見込には麒麟かと思われる文様を表す。1個体。1590～1630年代。漳州窯。

Fig.53-282は青花折縁大皿。日本で呉州手（呉須手）、ヨーロッパでスワトウウェアと呼んだもの。見込に鳳凰や竹を描き、口縁部に青海波地に窓絵を配し、窓内に花文を表す。この意匠の皿は日本でも出土例は多い。またベトナム・ホイアン[108]でもかなり出土している。この種のものは化粧掛けした上にコバルトで文様を描き、透明釉を施す。371個体。1590～1630年代。漳州窯。

107 日本の出土例も少なくないが、ベトナム・ホイアンでも出土している。類品は漳州・詔安県窯（福建省博物館1997）で見られる。

108 中部ベトナム、クアンナム・グエン氏政権の港市。

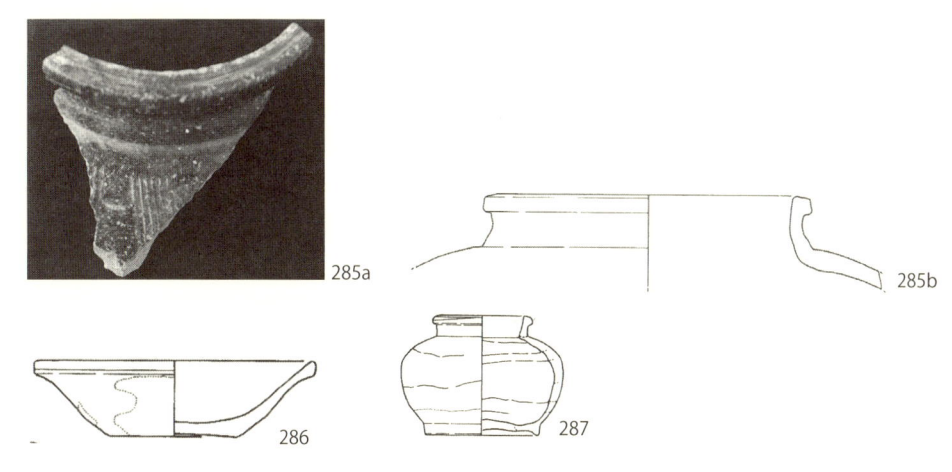

Fig.54 バンテン・ラーマ遺跡
Banten Lama Site, Ⅴ-1 period, 中国陶器 Chinese Stonewares

Fig.53-283 は白磁長胴瓶。いわゆる安平壺である。器形は口縁部、底部などを細かく見ればいくつかに分けられるが、ここでは一括して報告する[109]。31 個体。福建産。

● 徳化窯

Fig.53-284 は白磁稜花形皿。型押し成形によって高台まで作り出したため、底部に粘土皺が見られるのが特徴。見込と高台に胎土目積みの痕が見られる[110]。同様の胎土目積み、型成形の白磁碗が 14 個体分ほど出土。16 世紀末〜17 世紀前半。徳化窯。

〈中国陶器〉

Fig.54-285 は褐釉壺。肩に叩き痕が見られる。1 個体出土。17〜18 世紀。

Fig.54-286 は褐釉皿。灯明皿と推測される。底部には右巻の糸切痕が残る。内面に鉄漿をかける。27 個体。17〜18 世紀。

Fig.54-287 は黒釉小壺。輪積み成形の痕を顕著に残し、高台を作り出す。底部を除き黒釉を施す。口唇部は二次的に擦って露胎としている[111]。1 個体。17 世紀。

（2）ベトナムの陶磁器

〈鉄絵〉

Fig.55-288 は鉄絵碗。見込は蛇の目釉剝ぎであり、底部は無釉。見込に鉄絵文様を施す。ブトン・ウォリオ城例（Fig.67-343）より胎土が緻密であり、古式と考えられる。1 個体。

---

109 台湾の安平（ゼーランディア）城に因む名であるが、16 世紀末から 17 世紀にかけて日本から東南アジアにかけて多量に流通したものと考えられる。古い例は平戸和蘭商館跡出土品があるが、新しい例は 1690 年代頃の沈船ブンタウ・カーゴ引揚げ品がある。

110 口縁部を稜花形に刻むが、この種の素地に赤などで五彩を施したものが、大阪市（森 1992、五彩皿はベトナムではなく徳化窯産）で出土している。また、同様の胎土目積み、型成形の白磁碗が長崎（長崎市教育委員会 1997 の第 18 図 8）、沖縄などで出土している（大橋 1999a）。

111 類例は根津美術館 1993-116 頁にあり、『大正名器鑑』第 2 巻の「霊亀」茶入れに類似と言う。これは小堀遠州よりの伝来経緯がある。

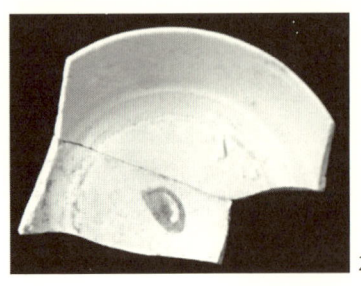

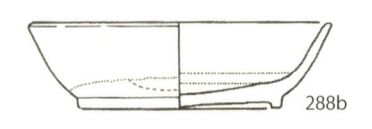

288a

288b

Fig.55 バンテン・ラーマ遺跡
Banten Lama Site, V-1 period, ベトナム陶磁 Vietnamese ceramics

17 世紀。

(3) 肥前の陶磁器

●肥前磁器

現在の佐賀・長崎両県にまたがる肥前地方では近世に陶器、磁器が盛んに焼造された。普通、出荷港の名に因んでそれぞれ「唐津焼」「伊万里焼」と呼ばれた。しかし本論では生産地の実態に近い地域名を冠した「肥前陶器」「肥前磁器」と称する。

Fig.56-289 は染付手塩皿。中国で言う「青花」を日本では「染付」と称す。口縁部を菊花形に刻み、内側面に菊弁を染付する。同様の手塩皿は佐賀県山内町窯ノ辻窯で見られる。国内向けの磁器であり、日本以外ではバンテン・ラーマの出土例のみである[112]。2 個体。1630 ～ 40 年代。

Fig.56-290, 291 は染付皿。Fig.56-290 は口縁部上面を曲面に作り、そこに木目状の文様を表す。内側面に四方襷文を描く[113]。1 個体。Fig.56-291 は見込に岩牡丹文を描き、周囲に如意頭繋ぎ文を染付する。2 個体。1640 年代頃。

●肥前陶器

Fig.56-292 は砂目積み陶器皿。白色精土を用いた玉子色の陶器であり、嬉野市内野山窯産と推測される。1 個体。1610 ～ 40 年代。

Fig.56-293 は鉄釉皿。内側面に線彫で唐草文を陰刻し鉄釉をかける。外面下部は畳付を除き鉄漿を塗る。見込と畳付に陶石かすのような白い目跡が見られる。17 世紀第 2 四半期。この他、三島手、刷毛目陶器もあり、合計で 7 個体。

---

112 1989 年の調査でこの出土品を発見したが、これにより肥前磁器の海外輸出は 1640 年代に遡る可能性が確定的となった。

113 Fig.56-290 のような曲面状の口縁部に木目状文様を描く中皿は、1640 年代頃に山辺田 3 号窯、猿川窯（大橋他 1988 の第 74 図 1 ～ 4）などいくつかの窯で出土している。やはり輸出用ではなく、海外ではバンテン・ラーマのみで出土している。

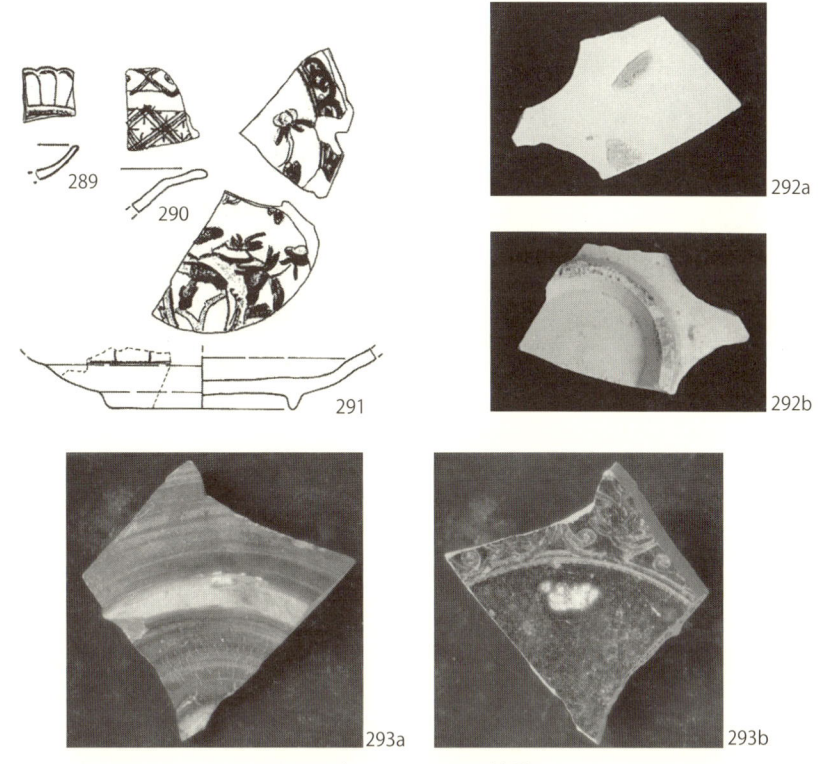

Fig.56 バンテン・ラーマ遺跡
Banten Lama Site, Ⅴ-1 period, 肥前陶磁 Japanese Hizen ceramics

（4） イスラームの陶器

中近東産のイスラーム陶器と思われるものが少量出土している。

Fig.57-294 は染付を施した碗。白化粧を施した素地に花唐草文を染付する。高台内外無釉。1個体。16～17世紀。

（5） ヨーロッパの陶器

Fig.57-295/297 はアルバレロ形壺。錫釉を施した軟質陶器であり、Fig.57-295 は錫釉に藍彩で胴部に煙草葉と思われる文様を表す。Fig.57-296, 297 は錫白釉を施したものであり、大小様々な器形がある。藍彩壺は17個体。Fig.57-296 のような中型品は14個体。Fig.57-297 のような長胴壺は14個体。他に大型品5個体、小型品12個体がある。オランダ・デルフト窯。17世紀頃。

Fig.57-298 は塩釉炻器の手付水注であり、いわゆる髭徳利[114]。40個体。16世紀後半～17世紀。

---

114 日本でも長崎（長崎市教育委員会 1986 の Fig.37-19）や平戸（平戸市教育委員会 1988 の 97 頁 36）などで出土例がある。

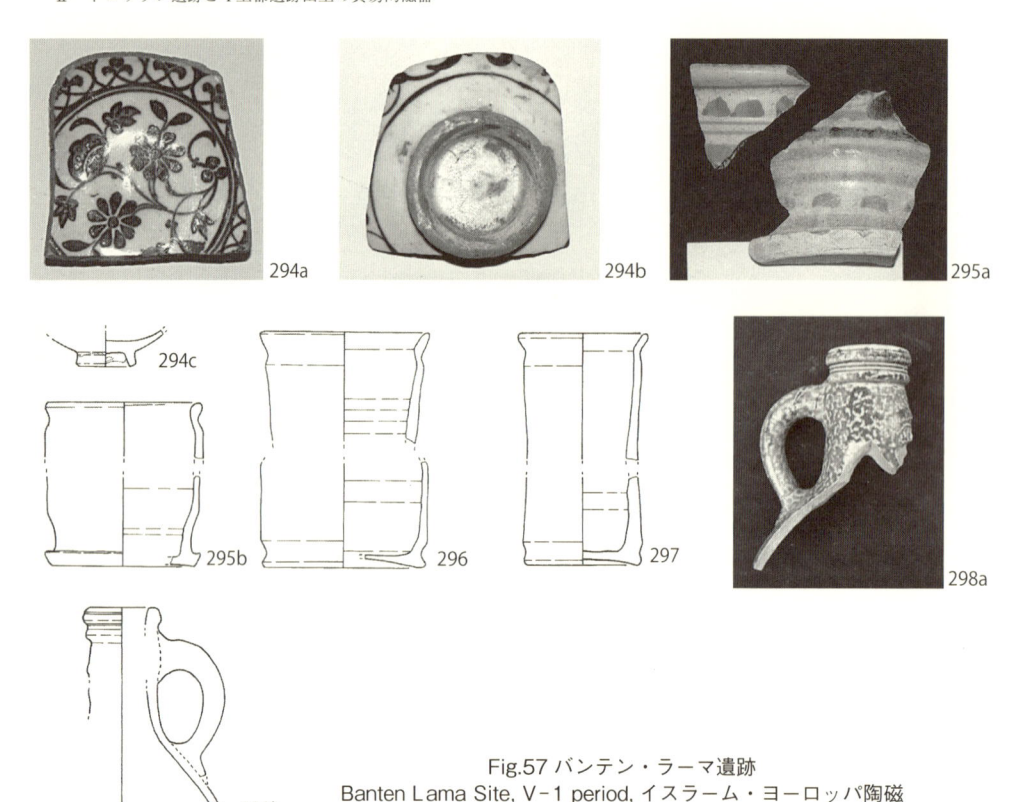

Fig.57 バンテン・ラーマ遺跡
Banten Lama Site, V-1 period, イスラーム・ヨーロッパ陶磁
Islamic & European ceramics

ティルタヤサ遺跡

(1) 中国の陶磁器

〈青花ほか〉

●景徳鎮窯

Fig.58-299 は青花鉢であり、口縁部を小さく折り返している。外面に菊を描いたものと、鳥が描かれた部分の破片が出土している。17 世紀前半。

Fig.58-300 は青花鉢。見込は二重圏線内に唐草文か。高台内は二重圏線内に「玉堂佳器」銘。崇禎期（1628-44）と思われる。

Fig.58-301 左は青花角皿。折縁に作り、見込には文様の中に「……天……」の詩句を記す。高台は厚く削り出す。崇禎期。

Fig.58-301 右は褐地白花の小碗か小坏。口縁部片。外面に褐釉、内面透明釉をかけ分け、外面の褐釉の上に白土で文様を表す。日本では餅花手とも言う。17 世紀前半。

Fig.58-302 は青花大皿の底部片と口縁部及び側面の破片である。底部片は見込に鹿や草花、岩を描き、外底面は無釉である。口縁部と側面の破片は同一個体と推測され、口縁部を稜花に作り、水を表す横線を引いた中に草花を描く。17 世紀前半。

●漳州窯

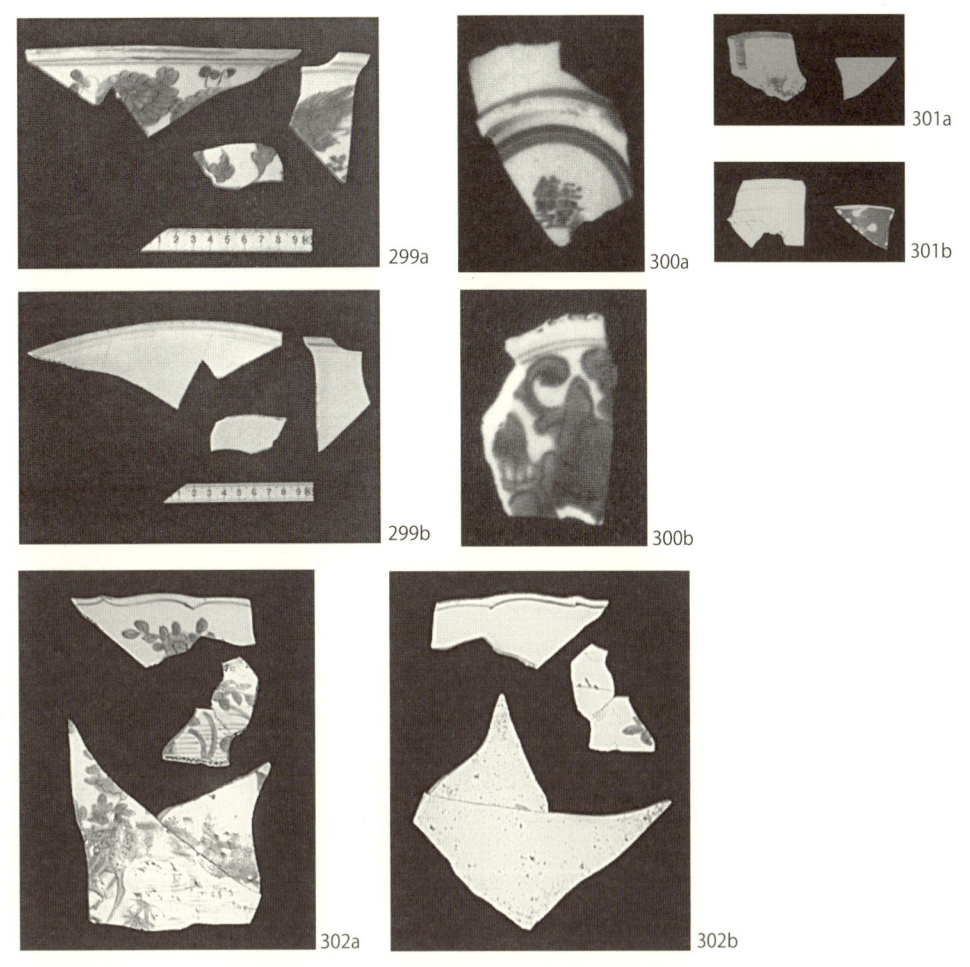

299a 300a 301a 301b 299b 300b 302a 302b

Fig.58 ティルタヤサ遺跡
Tirtayasa Site, V-1 period, 中国景徳鎮陶磁 Chinese Jingdezhen ceramics

Fig.59-303 は青花碗の底部片。見込に花卉文、外面に唐草文を描く。17世紀前半。

Fig.59-304 は白磁大皿。内面は化粧掛けし、線彫で文様を描く。畳付から高台内は無釉。畳付に粗い砂が熔着。焼成不良で釉は白濁色を呈する[115]。17世紀前半。

Fig.59-305 は青花角小皿。四方入隅に作り、高台は平面方形に作る。側面は竹文か[116]。17世紀前半。

Fig.59-306 は青花大皿の側面の破片。内側面に独特の花鳥文が描かれている[117]。見込文様の一部から見ると航海図の可能性が高い。17世紀前半。

以上のように明末の磁器は僅かであり、産地は景徳鎮窯と漳州窯であるが、後者の方が多い。以上の他、この時期と推測される陶器はタイの壺類の細片がいくつか見られる。

---

115 類品は有楽町1丁目遺跡（武蔵文化財研究所 2015）の明暦大火被災資料中に見られる。
116 漳州窯・花仔楼窯に類品が見られる。
117 類品は Harrisson1979-Fig.150 の航海図大皿と Adhyatman1999-Fig.87 がある。

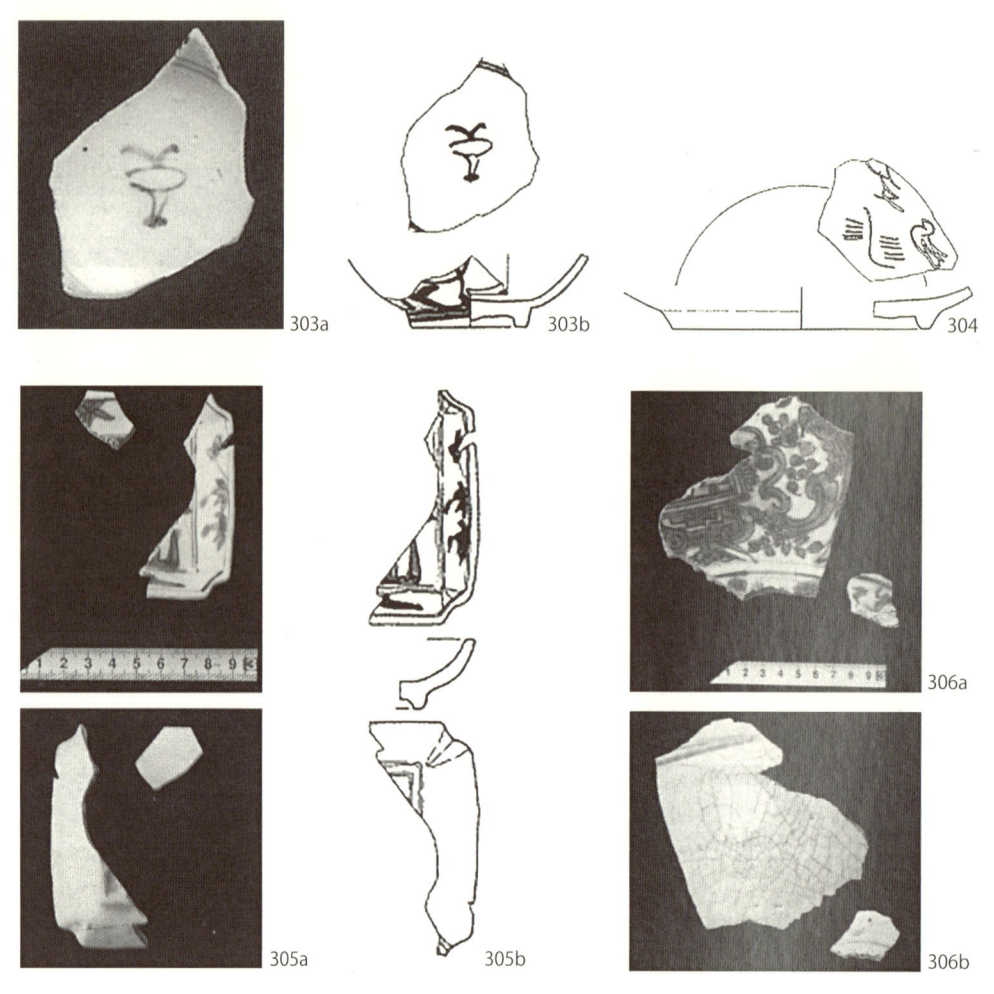

Fig.59 ティルタヤサ遺跡
Tirtayasa Site, Ⅴ-1 period, 中国漳州陶磁 Chinese Zhangzhou ceramics

10.　Ⅴ-2期（17世紀後半〜18世紀初）

トロウラン遺跡

(1) 肥前の陶磁器

●肥前磁器

Fig.20-307は白磁の碗であり、肥前・有田産である。1650〜80年代の特徴を持つ。

Fig.20-308は染付蓋付小鉢の蓋。文様はラフに表現されているので不明瞭であるが、おそらく雲龍文と思われる。1655〜80年代と推測される。肥前・有田産。

Fig.20-309・310は色絵の合子の蓋である。Fig.20-309は成形後、外側面にヘラ彫りで菊弁状の刻線を施す。この白磁素地の上面に黒線で牡丹折枝文を描き、青色絵具で塗りだむ。黒線が取れた部分は白抜き線のようになっている。Fig.20-310は白磁素地の上面を

赤の二重圏線を引いて区画し、甲部に赤で窓絵状の枠取をする。その中心に赤い花を表し、周囲の色はかなり剥落しているが、緑か黄で葉を表現。側面にも赤・緑・黄などで花を表すが色の剥落は著しい。

　肥前磁器は合子が2点と目立つ点はインドネシア地域の特色でもある。蓋付小鉢はカンボジア・タイなどに多い傾向がある。いずれにせよ、碗以外は日本国内向けではなく、17世紀後半の東南アジア向けの肥前磁器である。

　そして、本遺跡ではバンテン・ラーマやジャカルタの遺跡、スラウェシのブトン・ウォリオ城などで出土する18世紀前半の肥前磁器が出土していないことは、18世紀のこの地域にはオランダ東インド会社が関わらなかったことが推測される。

　その200年後の明治に肥前磁器の日常品が少量ながら入る。明治の型紙摺りの染付碗類が出土する例は東南アジアではカンボジア・ラオスなどでも確認されている。しかし、日用品の碗は型紙摺りまでであり、その後の銅版転写は肥前産のものは見られない。カンボジア・ラオスでは瀬戸美濃の銅版転写の磁器が主となるようである。

ソンバ・オプー城

(1) 中国の陶磁器

〈青花ほか〉

●漳州窯

　Fig.60-311の左は青花百寿文碗。外面に「寿」字を書き連ね、口縁内側に花状の文様を描き連ねる。17世紀後半の中で多く作られるが、1650年代頃の初期のタイプより、1660年代以降の新しいものは崩れが進む。本例は比較的古式なので1650年代と推測される。

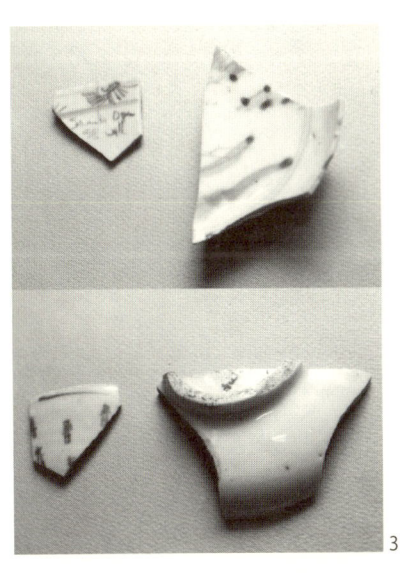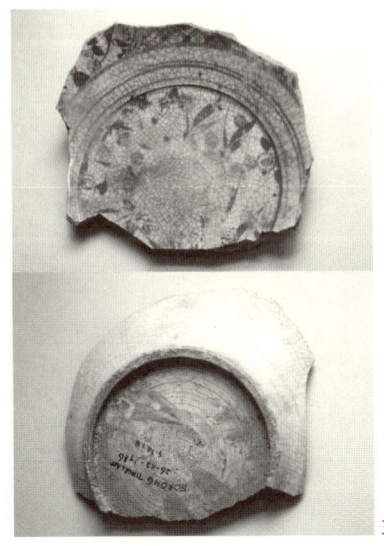

311　　312

Fig.60 ソンバ・オプー城跡
Somba Opu Fort, Ⅴ-2 period, 中国漳州陶磁 Chinese Zhangzhou ceramics

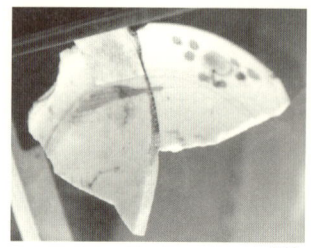
313

314

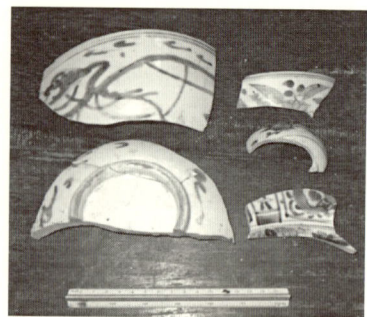
315a

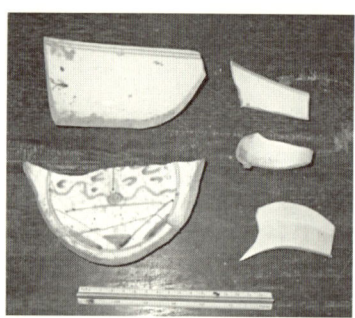
315b

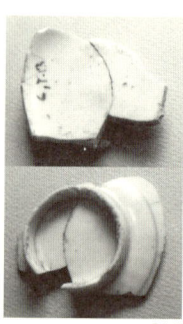
316

317

318

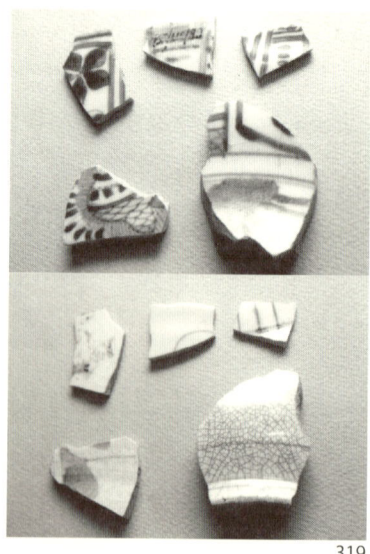
319

Fig.61 ソンバ・オプー城跡
Somba Opu Fort, Ⅴ-2 period, 肥前陶磁 Japanese Hizen ceramics

　Fig.60-311 右は小皿。17世紀後半。

　Fig.60-312 は細かい貫入が入り、高台内にはほとんど釉がかかっていないのが特徴の五彩大皿。こうした特徴の皿は17世紀後半に見られ、福建南部産と考えられる。不明瞭であるが、見込に牡丹のような草花を描く。類例はブトン・ウォリオ城（Fig.51-261）出土品。

（2）肥前の陶磁器

　●肥前磁器

　Fig.61-313 は内側面に花卉文を描く皿。1640年代頃。

　Fig.61-314 は見込に「日」字を染付し、蛇の目状に釉剥ぎした皿[118]。

　Fig.61-315 の左2点は同類であり、見込に荒磯文を描く大碗。これらは1660～70年代と推測される。

　Fig.61-315 右下は芙蓉手皿。1660年代前後。

　Fig.61-316 は染付碗。

　Fig.61-317 左側2列の下段を除く5片は鉢であり、口縁部内側に雷文帯を描く。1660～70年代前後と推測される。右上は小さく折縁とした鉢であり、1660年代前後。

　Fig.61-318 は皿。右上は粗製の芙蓉手皿。

　Fig.61-319 は芙蓉手皿であり、1660～70年代前後と考えられる。

　Fig.62-320 の左は蓋。右はアルバレロ形壺であり、1650～70年代と考えられる。

　Fig.62-321 は色絵小皿。色はかなり剥落しているが、桜のような樹に飛鳥と思われる文様が描かれる。広義の柿右衛門様式と思われる。1670～90年代と推測され、インドネシアでは珍しい出土例である。

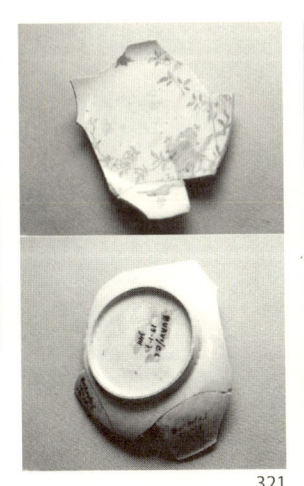

320

321

322

Fig.62 ソンバ・オプー城跡 Somba Opu Fort, Ⅴ-2 period, 肥前陶磁 Japanese Hizen ceramics

118 類例はスペイン時代のマニラのイントラムロス内のベテリオ・デ・ラ・コンパーニャ・デ・ヘスス（Beaterio de la Compania de Jeesusu）遺跡出土品にある（野上他 2005）。

Fig.63 ソンバ・オプー城跡 Somba Opu Fort, V-2 period, 肥前陶磁 Japanese Hizen ceramics

　　Fig.62-322 は染付の皿。17 世紀後半であり、おそらくすべて有田産と考えられる。下段の大きい底部片は見込に描いた如意頭に草花を加えたような文様を内側面に描いた皿片がバンテン・ラーマ遺跡出土品にある[119]。年代は 1650〜80 年代とする。

　　Fig.63-323 の右下の大きい破片は染付皿であり、1680〜1700 年代と考えられる[120]。

　　Fig.63-324 の左は瓶。右上は芙蓉手皿。

ブトン・ウォリオ城

(1) 中国の陶磁器

〈青花ほか〉

●景徳鎮窯

　Fig.64-325 は景徳鎮の可能性があるやや粗製の青花碗。

　Fig.64-326 は青花碗。17 世紀末〜18 世紀初。

　Fig.64-327 は内面にヘラ彫り文様を施し口縁部に四方襷文を染付した青花皿。類例はバンテン・ラーマ遺跡例（Fig.70-358）などがある。17 世紀末〜18 世紀前半。

　Fig.64-328 は大皿。高台が二重に作られているのが特徴。17 世紀末〜18 世紀初。

　Fig.64-329 は五彩大皿であり、青花同様、高台が二重に作られているのが特徴。17 世紀末〜18 世紀初。

　Fig.64-330 は三彩皿。

　Fig.65-331 は外面褐釉、内面と高台内を染付とかけ分けた碗・鉢類。左上は小振りで

---

119 佐賀県立九州陶磁文化館 1990 図 288

120 ジャカルタのオランダ東インド会社倉庫跡のパサール・イカン遺跡（佐賀県立九州陶磁文化館 1990 図 217）出
　　土品にあり、佐賀県立九州陶磁文化館 1991-図 399 も同類。

325 325b 326a

326b 327

328a 328b

329a 329b

330a 330b

Fig.64 ブトン・ウォリオ城跡 Buton Wolio Fort, Ⅴ-2 period,
中国景徳鎮陶磁 Chinese Jingdezhen ceramics

331a 331b 332a

332b 333a 333b

334 335

Fig.65 ブトン・ウォリオ城跡 Buton Wolio Fort, V-2 period,
中国景徳鎮陶磁 Chinese Jingdezhen ceramics

あり、ヨーロッパ向けのコーヒー・紅茶用カップと思われる。こうした褐釉をかけた磁器
はヨーロッパでは普通バタヴィアンウェアと呼ばれる。

　Fig.65-332 は 331 と同様の皿類。

　Fig.65-333 も褐釉かけ分けの青花や五彩などの皿である。

　Fig.65-334 は瑠璃釉地に窓絵を施した大型の壺。窓絵内にはコバルトと釉裏紅で文様
を施す。

　Fig.65-335 は五彩の大型の壺。これらの大型壺は V-2 期の中でも 17 世紀末〜18 世
紀初と推測される。1690〜1730 年代頃には有田の色絵と染付大壺が多いのが本遺跡の特
色であるが、それと重なる時期の景徳鎮の大型壺が多いのも注意しなければならないで
あろう。

Fig.66 ブトン・ウォリオ城跡 Buton Wolio Fort, V－2 period,
中国福建・広東陶磁 Chinese Fujian/Guangdong ceramics

● 福建・広東

　Fig.66-336 は印青花[121] が主。これらの年代は 1680 年代から 18 世紀前半までを考える
必要がある。

---

121 外面にハンコで青花文様を施す装飾法を中国では「印青花」と呼び、福建・広東地方の窯で行われた。日本でも
　沖縄や長崎でかなり出土しているが、大阪・道修町遺跡（享保 8 年〈1723〉の大火による火事場整理土坑（森
　1993））で出土している。台湾・左営鳳山県旧城遺跡（臧他 1993 の 835 頁、図版 56）でも出土。

343a 343b

Fig.67 ブトン・ウォリオ城跡
Buton Wolio Fort, V-2 period, ベトナム陶磁 Vietnamese ceramics

　Fig.66-337 は印青花碗。外面に寿字と思われる文字文を連ね、見込に花文をハンコで表す。口縁部を小さく折り、如意頭と思われる連続文を描く。印青花碗としては上質であり、見込も釉剥ぎしていない。日本などでもあまり見ないタイプであり、位置付けについては今後の課題でもある。

　Fig.66-338 などの青花皿がある。左の皿は木葉と詩句を表現する皿。

　Fig.66-339 は青花大皿。見込を蛇の目釉剥ぎしている。

　Fig.66-340 は粗製の印青花の皿。見込は蛇の目釉剥ぎし、重ね積み焼成したもの。内側面に梵字文を押捺して染付。こうした印青花の粗製の皿は福建・広東地方の窯で 17 世紀末から 18 世紀前半に多く作られ、一部の窯ではその後も続いたと考えられる。バンテン・ラーマ遺跡でも出土している（Fig.72-376）。

　Fig.66-341 は印青花の碗・鉢類。右上は梵字文をハンコで繰り返し押捺したもの。左上は「寿」字と花のような文様を交互にハンコで押捺する。日本でも沖縄などで見られる。

　Fig.66-342 は徳化窯産と考えられる白磁合子の身。

(2) ベトナムの陶磁器
〈鉄絵〉

　Fig.67-343 は鉄絵印判手碗。外底は無釉であり、見込は蛇の目釉剥ぎ。類例はソンバ・オプー城、バンテン・ラーマ遺跡（Fig.55-288）など多く見られる。日本でも出土例は多い。

(3) 肥前の陶磁器
●肥前磁器

　Fig.68-344 は染付碗類。右下の荒磯文碗は 1 点と少ない。すべて 1655 ～ 80 年代の中におさまると考えられる。

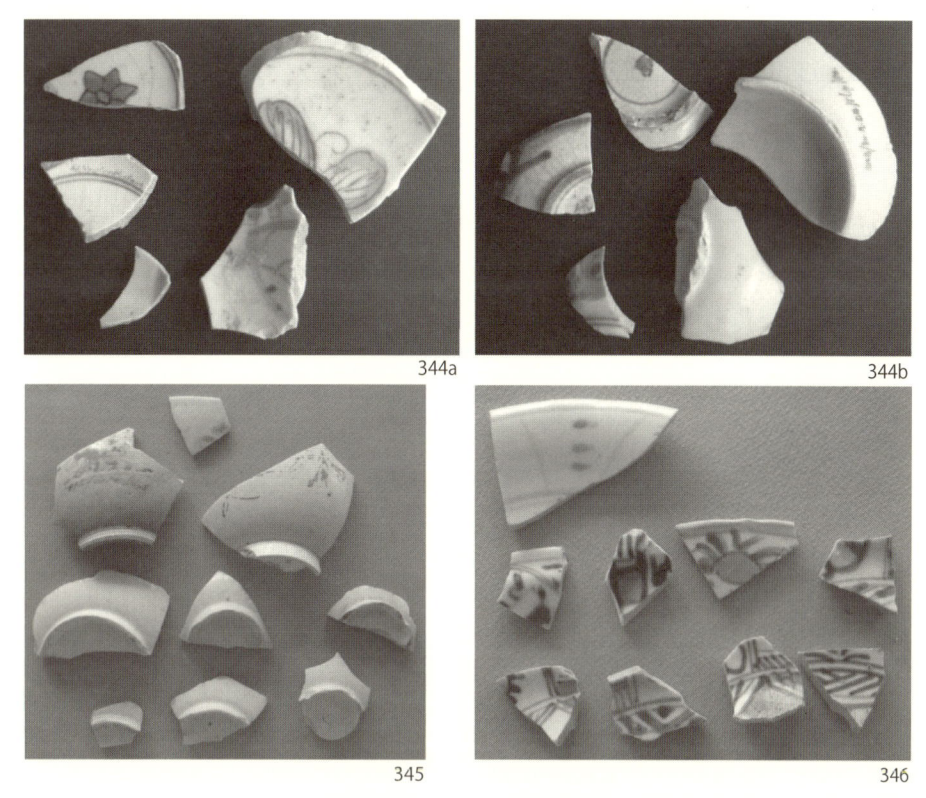

344a

344b

345

346

Fig.68 ブトン・ウォリオ城跡
Buton Wolio Fort, Ⅴ-2 period, 肥前陶磁 Japanese Hizen ceramics

　Fig.68-345 は色絵の碗である。色絵の皿が堀試掘出土品にある。1680〜90 年代頃と考えられる。

　Fig.68-346・Fig.69-347 は染付芙蓉手皿。Fig.68-346 左上は粗製の芙蓉手皿。1650 年代頃。中段左 1 点、Fig.69-347 上段左から 3 番目の小皿は芙蓉手の一種である名山手意匠。

　Fig.69-348 は染付皿。右列中は内側面に鳳凰文と思われる文様が描かれ、おそらく寿字鳳凰文皿と考えられる。

　Fig.69-349 は青磁大皿。高台内蛇の目釉剥ぎして鉄泥を塗っているのが特徴。肥前でも有田産と考えられる。1650〜70 年代。

　Fig.69-350 は蓋が付く染付大深鉢であり、1660〜80 年代。類例はオランダ[122]、イギリスなどにある。

　Fig.69-351 の左は見込に「VOC」マークを施した鉢。1690〜1700 年代と考えられる。こうした見込に「VOC」を染付した鉢の類例は僅かにある。

　Fig.69-352 は染付のクンディや合子など。

122　Jörg 2003 の図 204

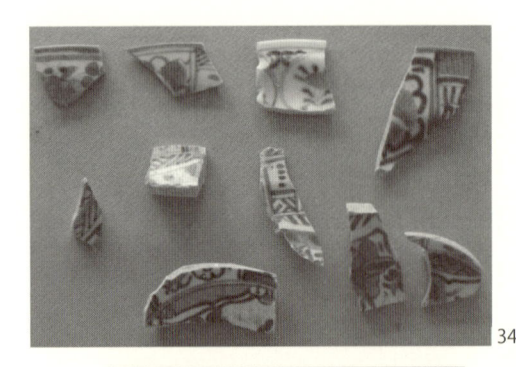
347

348

349a

349b

350a

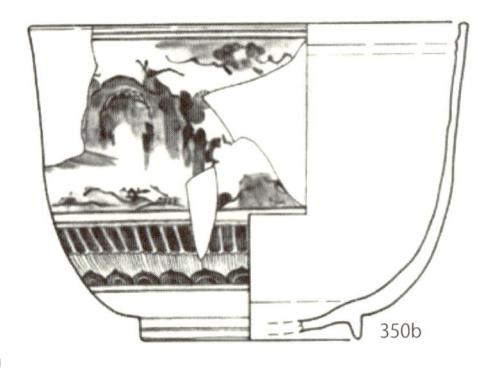
350b

351

352

Fig.69 ブトン・ウォリオ城跡
Buton Wolio Fort ,Ⅴ-2 period, 肥前陶磁 Japanese Hizen ceramics

バンテン・ラーマ遺跡

(1) 中国の陶磁器

〈青花ほか〉

● 景徳鎮窯

Fig.70-353 は三彩青花碗。外面に緑・黄・紫・白の釉をかけ分け、内面は如意頭を連ねた唐花文を見込に描く。内側面は唐草文と思われる。高台内は透明釉をかける。79 個体。17 世紀後半～18 世紀初。

Fig.70-354 は三彩碗。高台内以外に緑・黄・紫・白に塗り分けた三彩。高台内はコバルトで二重圏線を施す。94 個体。17 世紀後半～18 世紀前半。

Fig.70-355 は緑釉陰刻文鉢。外面に Fig.71-365 と同様の花文をヘラ彫りした素地に緑釉を施す。1 個体。17 世紀後半～18 世紀初。

Fig.70-356 は三彩鉢？。線彫を施した素地に紫釉を主とし、線彫部分に緑・黄を塗り分ける。高台内はコバルトで二重圏線を施す。3 個体。17 世紀後半～18 世紀前半。

Fig.70-357 は五彩大皿。高台を二重に作るのが特徴である。内面に明るい緑や黄などの色絵具で花文様を描く。7 個体。同類がティルタヤサ遺跡で出土しており、17 世紀後半と推測される。

Fig.70-358 は青花陰刻文皿。内面にヘラ彫り文を施した素地に見込周囲と口縁部に四方襷文帯、窓絵草花文を染付する。84 個体。こうした装飾の景徳鎮磁器は康熙頃（1662-1722）に皿鉢類や壺瓶類に多く見られる。17 世紀第 4 四半期～18 世紀第 1 四半期。

Fig.70-359 は三彩合子。蓋と身であり、緑・黄・紫・白に塗り分けた三彩。蓋が 7 個体、身が 5 個体。17 世紀後半～18 世紀前半。

Fig.70-360 は色釉を施した人形類。瑠璃釉、錆釉の人物像、緑釉の鳥形？、置物などがある。この種の人形は康熙頃（1662-1722）に多く見られる。こうした人形類は 6 個体。

Fig.70-361 は褐釉青花小皿。内面は波涛の中に梅花状の小花を散らす。高台内中央に Fig.71-363 の碗と同じ四弁花を染付する。

Fig.71-362 は青花碗。見込と外面に菊唐草文を描く。外面腰部に蓮弁文帯をめぐらす。144 個体。類品はティルタヤサ遺跡出土品に見られる。

Fig.71-363 は褐釉青花碗。見込と内側面には花唐草を染付する。外側面に褐釉をかける。高台内には Fig.70-361 同様の四弁花銘を染付する。

Fig.71-364 は青花小碗。見込に花卉文、高台内に宝文の一種のような銘を染付する。

Fig.71-365 は Fig.70-358 と同様の装飾を施した鉢。見込に花文、外側面にヘラ彫りで花文様を陰刻する。口縁部内外と見込周囲に七宝繋ぎ文帯を染付する。10 個体。17 世紀第 4 四半期～18 世紀第 1 四半期。

Fig.71-366 は青花合子の蓋。上面に玉取獅子文を描く。4 個体出土。この時期ではなく

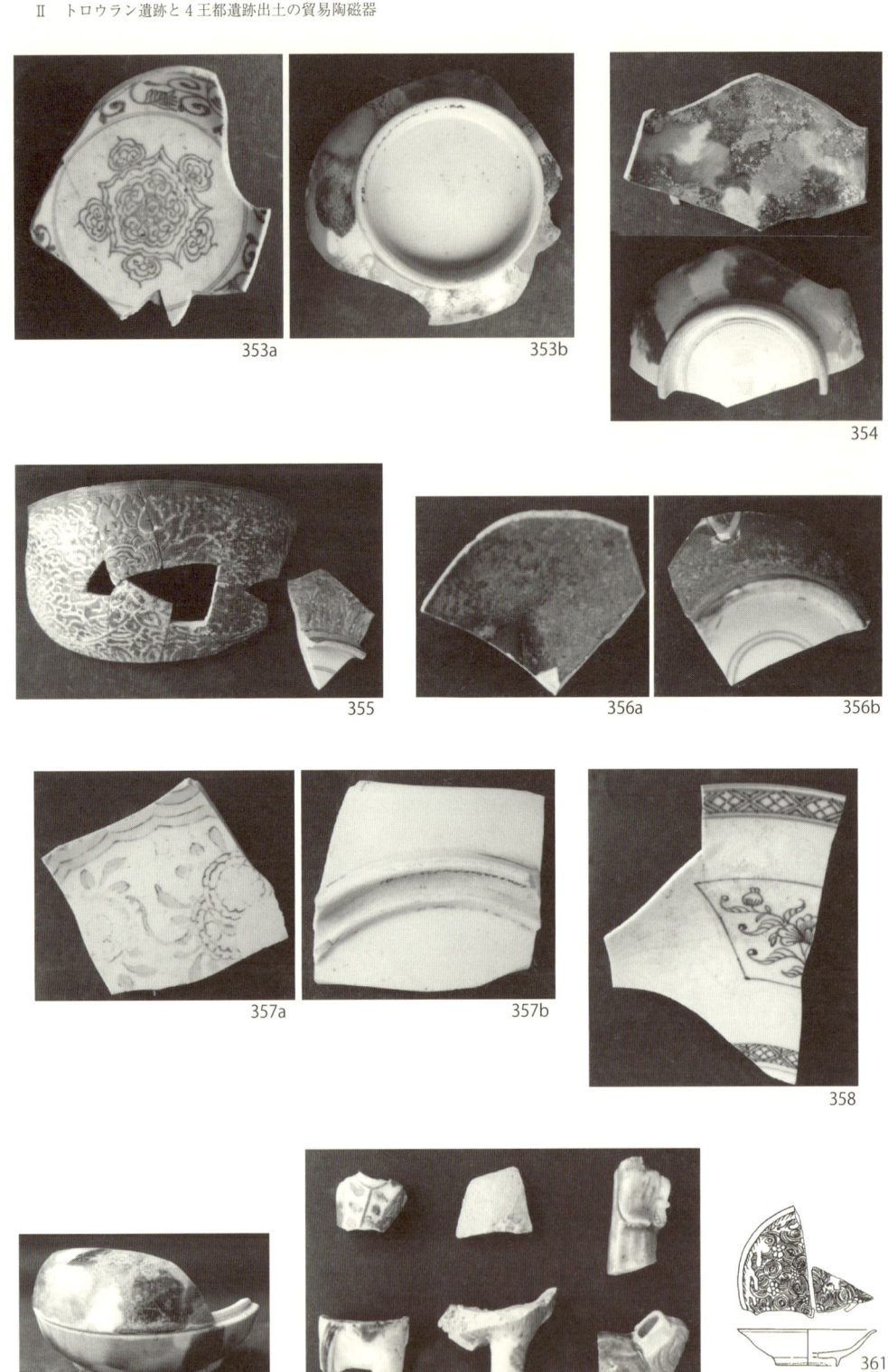

353a　353b

354

355　356a　356b

357a　357b

358

359　360　361

Fig.70 バンテン・ラーマ遺跡 Banten Lama Site, V-2 period,
中国景徳鎮陶磁 Chinese Jingdezhen ceramics

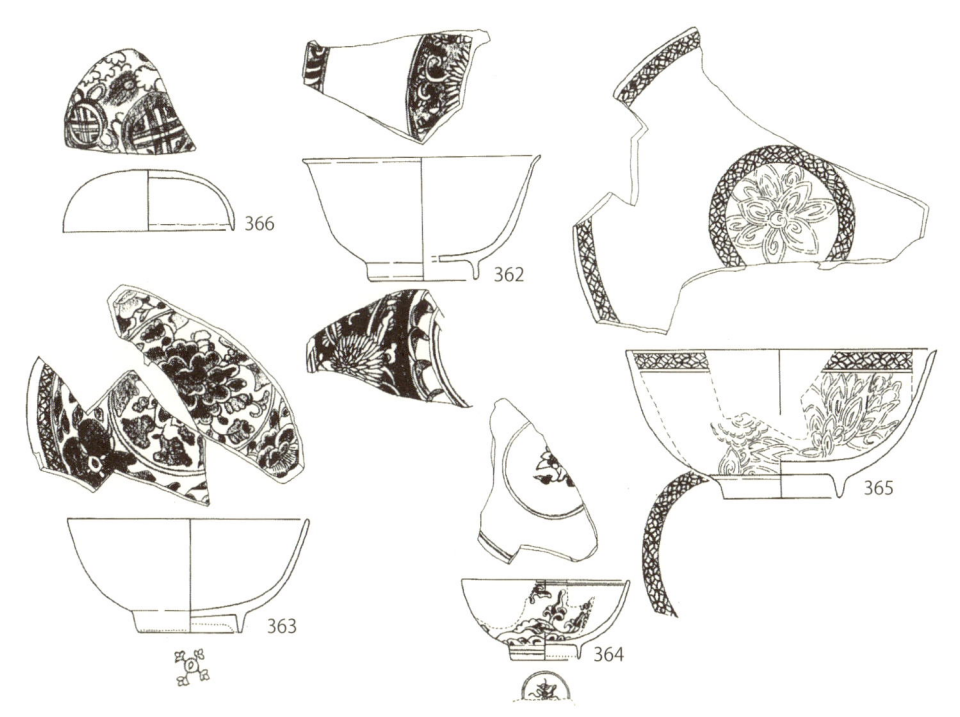

Fig.71 バンテン・ラーマ遺跡 Banten Lama Site, Ⅴ-2 period,
中国景徳鎮陶磁 Chinese Jingdezhen ceramics

17 世紀前半頃の可能性が高い。

● 福建広東系

Fig.72-367 は青花皿。見込に木の葉と詩句文を描く[123]。57 個体。17 世紀後半。

Fig.72-368 は青花小皿。成形や施文状態が初期伊万里に似通っていることからしばしば誤認された。兎山水を描き全釉で高台畳付にモミガラが熔着[124]。同類品は 13 個体。

Fig.72-369 は青花皿。作行は Fig.72-368、Fig.72-377 と同様であり、底部にモミガラの熔着が見られる。内面に柳下で拳をしながら酒を飲む中国の民の様子が描かれる[125]。14 個体。17 世紀後半〜18 世紀初。

Fig.72-370 は青磁大皿。明末の大皿に比べ化粧掛けもせず、高台の作りも異なり、高台周辺は無釉が普通となる。内面に線彫の文様を施す[126]。133 個体。17 世紀中葉〜末。漳州窯系。

---

123 類品は 1661 年に鄭氏が入って築かれた台湾南部西海岸の左営鳳山県旧城遺跡出土品にあり、漳州朱厝窯や安渓県安渓窯（葉 1990 の図版 3-5）などで見られる。鳳山県旧城例は木の葉に「太平年興」の文字を入れるが、「乙卯冬記」を加えた出土例があり、1675 年と推測されている。木の葉にこの文字を入れた皿は広東・大埔県水尾窯（楊 1990 の 4 頁）に見られ、報文には「太平年己未□」「太平年庚申□」の文字の記された陶片もあると言う。己未は 1679 年、庚申は 1680 年の可能性が高い。

124 左営鳳山県旧城に類品がある。

125 このジャンケン遊びで負けると酒を飲む風俗は、景徳鎮磁器にも康熙頃（1662-1722）の大皿に描かれた例がトプカプ宮殿蔵品 No.3248, 3249 にあり、また有田磁器でも 18 世紀初頭の色絵磁器に似通った風俗を描いた例がある。日本では出土例を見ない。

126 日本ではほとんど出土しないが、東南アジアやトルコ・トプカプ宮殿蔵品に見られる。

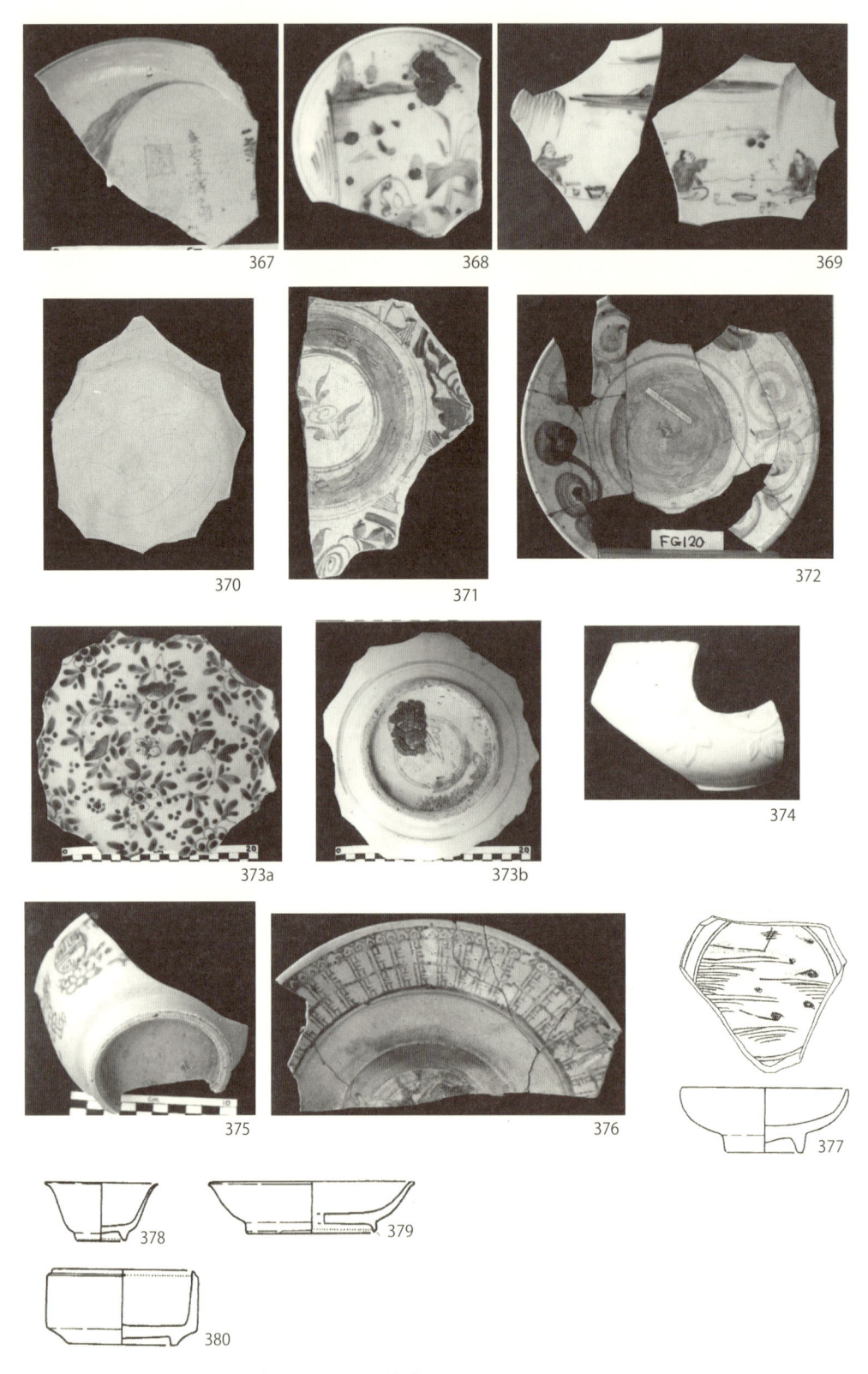

Fig.72 バンテン・ラーマ遺跡 Banten Lama Site, V-2 period,
中国福建・広東陶磁 Chinese Fujian/Guangdong ceramics

Fig.72-371 は五彩大皿。見込を蛇の目釉剥ぎした粗製の素地に赤・緑・黄で絵付けする。見込に花卉を描き、蛇の目釉剥ぎ部分は緑で塗りつぶし、内側面は区画し草花などを描く。210 個体。17 世紀中葉～末。漳州窯系。

Fig.72-372 は青花大皿。口縁部先端を小さく外に折る。見込を無釉にし、内側面に簡略化した唐草文を軽妙な筆致で描く[127]。2 個体。17 世紀後半～18 世紀初。

Fig.72-373 は青花皿。内面を草花で埋める。高台内に二重圏線と銘を染付する。内面の文様は有田・長吉谷窯の例に通じるものがある。長吉谷例は 1660 年代頃の年代が推測でき、本例も近い年代と考えられる。106 個体。17 世紀後半。

Fig.72-374 は白磁合子の蓋。徳化窯白磁の特徴とされる象牙白に属するものと、白色のものがある。型を使い、外面に陽刻文様を施す。597 個体。17 世紀後半～18 世紀前半。

Fig.72-375 は印青花碗。53 個体。17 世紀末～18 世紀中葉。

Fig.72-376 は印青花皿。見込を蛇の目釉剥ぎし、内面に梵字文などをハンコで表す[128]。50 個体。17 世紀末～18 世紀中葉。

Fig.72-377 は見込に山水文を描く[129]。57 個体。17 世紀後半。

Fig.72-378・379 は緑釉かけ分けの小坏と小皿。緑釉小坏は低火度緑釉を施したものであるが、本来、磁器の可能性がある。Fig.72-379 は焼成不良のため、内面は白いが透明釉であろう[130]。22 個体。17 世紀～18 世紀前半。福建省南部産か。Fig.72-379 は内面から外側面に緑釉、高台内は透明釉を施す。25 個体。17～18 世紀前半。

Fig.72-380 は緑釉合子、内面透明釉で磁器である。16 個体。17～18 世紀。

〈中国陶器〉

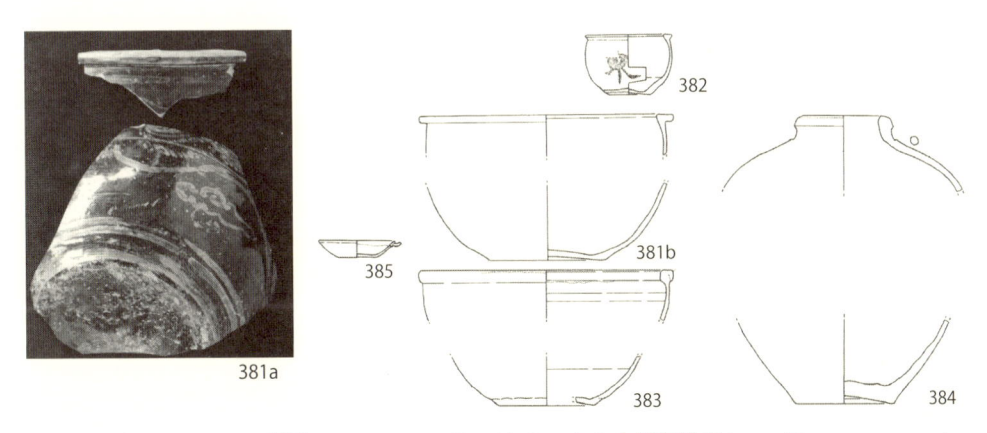

Fig.73 バンテン・ラーマ遺跡 Banten Lama Site, Ⅴ-2 period, 中国陶器 Chinese Stoneware ceramics

127 日本では見られないが、左営鳳山県旧城やタイ中部の離宮跡ロブブリ遺跡（Chandavij 1989）でも類品が出土している。
128 こうした中・大皿は日本ではほとんど出土しないが、タイ・ロブブリ遺跡など東南アジアで見られる。
129 ベトナム南部コンダオ島沖で 1690 年頃沈没のブンタウ・カーゴ引揚げ品にある（Jörg & Flecker 2001）。
130 焼成不良で軟質に見える緑釉などの合子類は、商業サルベージの商品「ハッチャー・ジャンク」（1643-46 頃）（Sheaf 1988）にある。

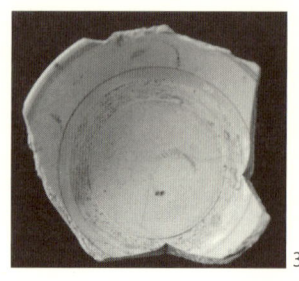
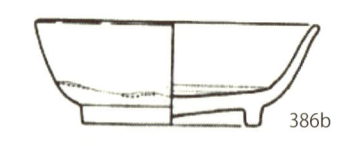

386a

386b

Fig.74 バンテン・ラーマ遺跡
Banten Lama Site, Ⅴ-2 period, ベトナム陶磁 Vietnamese ceramics

　Fig.73-381 と 383 は褐釉鉄絵鉢。素地は淡褐色の精土であり、光沢の強い褐釉に黒褐色を呈する絵文様を表す。日本では見ない。口縁部は無釉。7 個体。

　Fig.73-382 も褐釉鉄絵鉢であり、1 個体。17 ～ 18 世紀。

　Fig.73-383 は褐釉鉢。内面のみ褐釉を施し、外は露胎で淡褐色を呈す。甕の蓋として作られた可能性がある。底部に砂目痕が見られる[131]。14 個体。17 世紀。

　Fig.73-384 は褐釉の壺。

　Fig.73-385 は褐釉小皿。内面のみ褐釉をかけ、口縁部は無釉である。口縁外側の一方に小さな舌状の把手を貼り付ける。灯明皿と推測される[132]。300 個体。17 世紀～ 18 世紀前半。

(2) ベトナムの陶磁器
〈鉄絵〉

　Fig.74-386 は鉄絵碗。見込は蛇の目釉剝ぎであり、底部は無釉。内面に圏線を引き、見込と内側面、外側面に菊花と思われる文様をハンコで押す。66 個体。17 世紀後半。

(3) 肥前の陶磁器
●肥前磁器

　Fig.75-387、Fig.76-387c は色絵大皿。白磁素地の見込に菊を描く。区画文を表した口縁部の陶片が同一個体の確証はないが、素地の状態などからその可能性が高いので一緒に図示した。外側面に唐草文、高台内に二重方形枠内の銘（「福」字であろう）を色絵で表す。色絵は緑・黄・紫・黒線などを用い、赤は使わない。外面文様の特徴からも「初期色絵」の中期（1650 年代、特に前半頃）に属する大皿と考えられる。2 個体かと推定される。

　Fig.75-388 は染付碗。見込に波間に鯉が跳ねる荒磯文を表す。このタイプは外面に雲龍もしくは雲龍鳳を描き、内側面に魚文を三方に配すものが基本である。より大振りの鉢

---

131 類品は左営鳳山県旧城遺跡で見られる。

132 ブンタウ・カーゴ引揚げ品に見られるが、これは把手が口縁部内側から貼り付ける点で異なる。左営鳳山県旧城でも出土しているが、これも内側から貼り付けている。

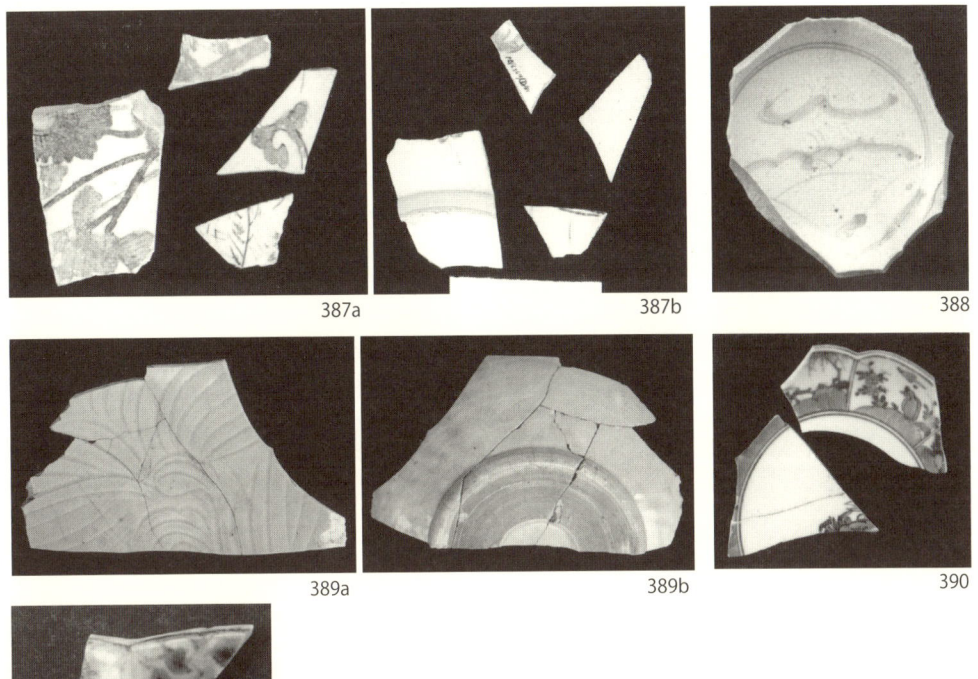

387a   387b   388

389a   389b   390

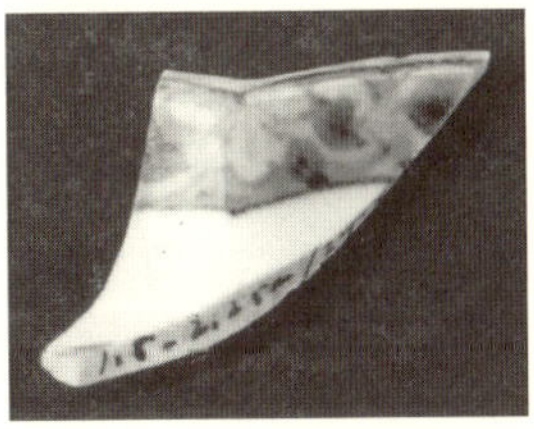

391

Fig.75 バンテン・ラーマ遺跡 Banten Lama Site, Ⅴ-2 period,
肥前陶磁 Japanese Hizen ceramics

形の場合、口縁部内側に雷文帯などの文様帯を描くのが普通である。見込の荒磯文が、鯉の代わりに龍頭を描くものなどもある。この荒磯文碗は明末の中国磁器を手本に作られ、主に東南アジア向けに一時期、肥前一帯で大量生産された。

　Fig.75-389 は青磁皿。高台内を蛇の目釉剝ぎし、鉄漿を塗る。この部分にチャツの熔着痕が見られる。内面にヘラ彫りで植物文様？を施す[133]。10 個体。17 世紀後半。長崎県波佐見窯産。

　Fig.75-390, 391 は型打成形によって輪花に作る染付皿。Fig.75-309 は口銹を施し、見込に蟹を描き、内側面は区画内に花鳥文などを描く。外側面に唐草文、高台内に渦福字銘を染付する。銘の周囲にハリ支え跡が 2 ヶ所以上ある。有田町南川原窯ノ辻窯産と考えられる。蟹文を主文に描くことは肥前磁器では稀であるが、バンテン・ラーマでは明末の景徳鎮磁器にも見られ、注文もしくは意図的に選んで輸入した可能性もある。6 個体。1680 ～ 1700 年代。Fig.75-391 は口縁部の小片であるが、特徴的な意匠であり、ヨーロッパから意匠まで注文を受けて有田で作ったと見られる[134]。1 個体。1690 年代頃。

---

133 こうした青磁大皿は日本以外ではインドネシアで出土するほか、トルコで伝世品（大橋 1998）が 2 点確認される。

134 類品はオランダ・ハーグ市立美術館蔵「染付帆船図変形皿」（長径 16cm（有田ポーセリンパーク 1993 の図 28））やフロニンゲン博物館蔵品（佐賀県立九州陶磁文化館 2000 の図 68）であり、イギリスのバーレイハウス蔵品（Burghley House 1983 の Fig.44）にもある。ハーグの伝世品を見ると、見込にオランダの陶画家ファン・フライトムの作品に見られるような様式の図が描かれる。

　Fig.76-392 は色絵小皿。型打成形によって輪花に作る白磁素地の内面に草花を赤・緑などで表し、外面は赤で圏線を引く。1 個体。1660 ～ 90 年代。有田産。

　Fig.76-393 は色絵折縁皿。白磁素地の見込周囲に赤で二重圏線を引き、内側面に花唐草を赤・緑？で表し、口縁部に蓮弁文帯を赤で描く。外面は赤で圏録を引く。5 個体。1655 ～ 80 年代。有田産。

　Fig.76-394 は白磁三足皿。型を使い、口縁部を花弁か葉をかたどった形状に作る。底部は円形に無釉とし、磁製のチャツのような窯道具を当てて窯詰めする。足は猿面のようである。型押しで表し、それを貼り付ける[135]。1 個体。17 世紀後半。有田産。

　Fig.76-395 は染付芙蓉手皿。見込周囲にまりばさみ文を描く。明末の中国磁器を手本としたものであり、輸出向けに肥前で大量生産された。48 個体。1660 ～ 80 年代。

　Fig.76-396 は染付芙蓉手大皿。見込に花鳥文を描く。3 個体。1660 ～ 80 年代。

　Fig.76-397 は色絵芙蓉手大皿。白磁素地の見込周囲にまりばさみ文、外面には折枝文を赤・緑・黄・黒線などで描くが、赤以外は変色している。1 個体。1660 ～ 70 年代。有田産。

　Fig.76-400, 401 は染付大皿。Fig.76-400 は口縁部を輪花に刻んだ素地の見込に花盆文、内側面に草などを描く。外側面に唐草文を染付。高台内にハリ支え痕が残る。こうした花盆文は輸出向けに盛んに描かれた。3 個体。1680 ～ 90 年代。Fig.76-401 は型打成形によって口縁部を輪花に作る。見込に岩に梅樹、内側面を区画し、梅や草花を表す。外側面に折枝文を染付。口唇部にコバルトを塗るのも特徴。55 個体。1670 ～ 90 年代。有田産。

　Fig.76-402 は染付髭皿と見られる。口縁部端部を小さく上方に折り返すのが髭皿の特徴。内側面に花鳥文を描く。

　Fig.76-403 は染付碗。見込に初期的な五弁花文、外面に山水文、高台内に「大明年製」銘を染付する。1 個体。1670 ～ 80 年代。有田産。

　Fig.76-404 ／ 406 は色絵合子。Fig.76-404 は蓋であり、白磁素地の上面に草花、側面につる草などを赤・緑・黄？などで描く。14 個体。Fig.76-405 は身であり、文様の有無は不明。35 個体。Fig.76-406 も身であり、外面に文様を施すが不鮮明[136]。34 個体。1655 ～ 80 年代。有田産。

　Fig.76-407 は染付八角蓋付鉢。型押成形によって八角に作られ、外面に陰刻文様を施す。文様は紗綾形地文と柴束文を交互の面に陰刻し、その上から濃み筆でコバルトを塗って文様を浮かび上がらせる。元禄（1688 ～ 1704）頃に有田で多く行われた装飾法である。2 個体。1690 ～ 1700 年代。有田産。

　Fig.76-408 は染付蓋付大鉢の蓋。外面を区画して上部は牡丹唐草、側面は岩梅・菊などを描く。こうした大型の蓋付鉢は輸出向けに作られたものと考えられ、ヨーロッパに伝

---

135 類例は見ないが猿面の足は青磁三足皿の足として 17 世紀中葉に見られるものに近い。

136 こうした合子は日本でも出土するが、インドネシアでの出土の割合は多い。中国磁器、ベトナム陶器なども加えると多量である。これは主にこの地域で流行ったビンロウ噛みの石灰入れとして需要が多かったと言う。

Fig.76 バンテン・ラーマ遺跡
Banten Lama Site, Ⅴ-2 period, 肥前陶磁 Japanese Hizen ceramics

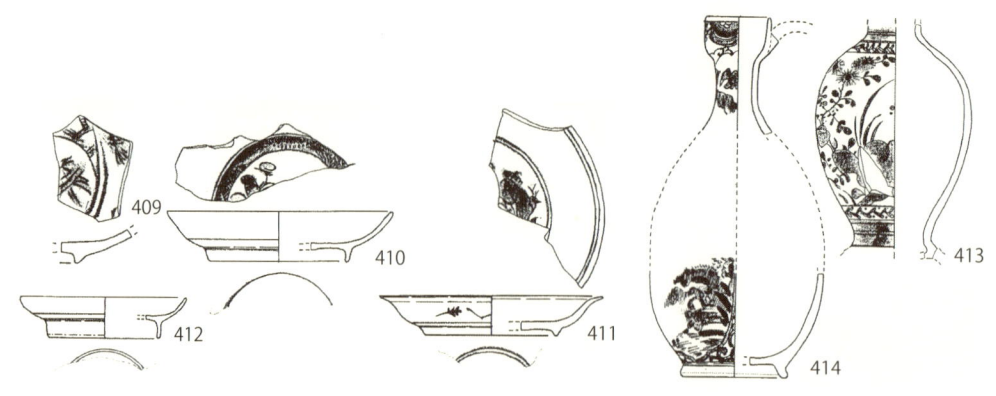

Fig.77 バンテン・ラーマ遺跡
Banten Lama Site, V-2 period, 肥前陶磁 Japanese Hizen ceramics

世品が少なくない。蓋付鉢という意味での同類品は92個体。1660〜18世紀初。有田産。

　Fig.77-409は色絵中・大皿。赤の圏線で区画した見込に緑・黒線などで仙境図を描き、内側面に赤の印判文と緑の円形内に山水文（仙境図か）を描く。素地の釉は充分溶けておらず、有田との違いが認められる。意匠は印判手仙境図という中国の漳州窯五彩（呉州赤絵）に見られるものであり、17世紀には佐賀県嬉野市吉田窯で主に見られる意匠である[137]。18個体。1650〜60年代。

　Fig.77-410, 412は染付皿。Fig.77-410は見込に牡丹と思われる草花を描き、周囲に墨弾きによる花文を配した帯文をめぐらす。こうした装飾、器形の特徴は有田の長吉谷窯、柿右衛門窯出土品に共通するものがあり、同時期の有田産と推測される。1個体。1655〜70年代。Fig.77-412は高台を高く削り出した皿であり、高台内に染付二重圏線を施す。この破片では内面部分に文様はないが、他の内面部分に文様を施している可能性が高い。1個体。1660〜90年代。有田産。

　Fig.76-398, 399, Fig.77-411は染付端反皿。Fig.77-411は見込に岩などを描き外側面に折枝文、高台内に二重圏線を染付する。44個体。1670〜90年代。Fig.76-399は口縁部を輪花に刻む。見込に五弁花、内側面に唐草文、外側面に唐草文を染付する。五弁花文は、1690年代以降画一化し流行する五弁花の表現とは異なるので、五弁花の出現期の一つと見られる。2個体。1680〜90年代。Fig.76-398は見込に草花と思われる文様を描き、内側面に渦に梅花、外側面に唐草文を染付する。1個体。1680〜1700年代。以上は有田産。

　Fig.77-413は染付手付水注。この種の器形の水注は1660〜80年代にかけてヨーロッパ向けに作られた。ヨーロッパでは金属のワンタッチ開閉式蓋を取り付けて用いた。胴部に草花、その上下に月桂樹の帯と濃みの帯をめぐらす。1個体。1660〜70年代。有田産。

---

137 ジャカルタのパサール・イカン遺跡出土品（佐賀県立九州陶磁文化館1990の図148・149）のなかに初めて発見したが、バンテン・ラーマ（佐賀県立九州陶磁文化館1990の図290）でもかなり見られ、インドネシアで多く出土している。日本でも少量出土例が見られるが、現在のところインドネシアで一番多く見られるため、輸出向けに作られたものと推測される。

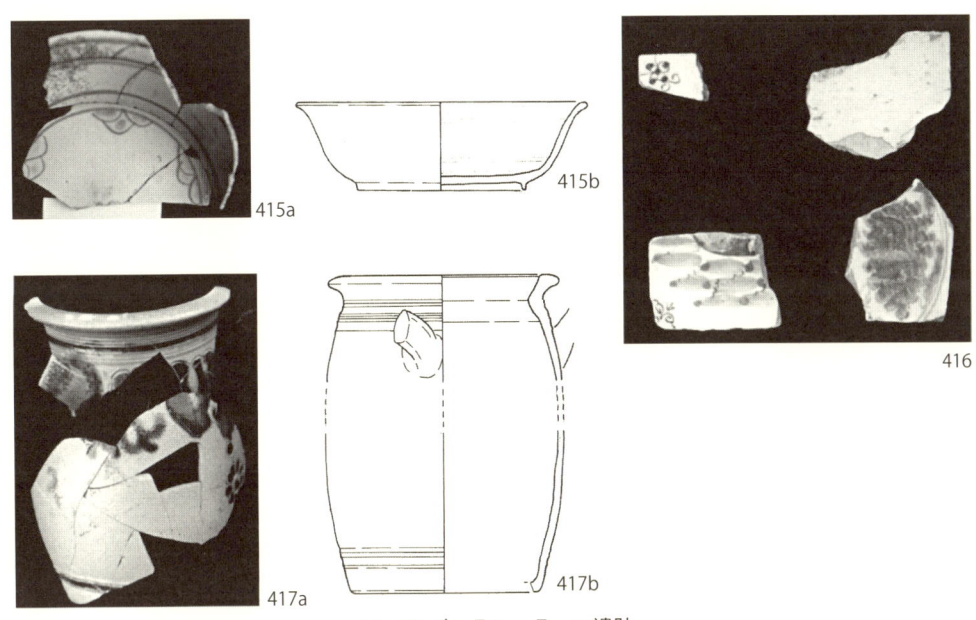

Fig.78 バンテン・ラーマ遺跡
Banten Lama Site, V-2 period, ヨーロッパ陶磁 European ceramics

　Fig.77-414 も染付手付水注。胴部主文は三方の区画内に山水文を描き、口縁部には如意頭文をめぐらす[138]。1個休。1670〜80年代。有田産。

（4）ヨーロッパの陶器

　Fig.78-415 は藍絵鉢。錫釉に青で線書きし、より薄い水色の顔料で濃みを施す。外面口縁部に窯詰めの目跡が1ケ所残る。2個体。18世紀。オランダ。

　Fig.78-416 は藍絵タイル。左上は隅の部分であり、タイルの隅文様として多く用いられた花文を描く。左下は帆船を描いた意匠と推測される。17世紀後半か。右下は二重円圏内に風景を描いたもの。17世紀後半か。全てデルフト陶器。

　Fig.78-417 は塩釉炻器の耳付壺。青顔料で彩色。13個体。17世紀。

ティルタヤサ遺跡

（1）中国の陶磁器

〈青花ほか〉

●景徳鎮窯

　Fig.79-418 は青花鉢。見込文様は不明だが、内外側面に花唐草、口縁部内側に蓮弁か。口縁部外面は雷文帯。腰部は剣先形蓮弁文、高台側面には波濤？を描く。17世紀後半。

　Fig.79-419 は口縁外反りの青花碗か鉢の口縁部片。Fig.80-420 より文様を丁寧に描く。

---

138 類品はヨーロッパで 1689 年銘の銀蓋が付く（永渕 1997）。伝世品は少なくない。

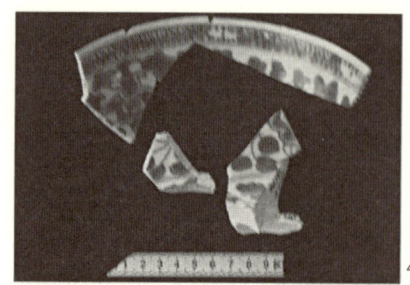

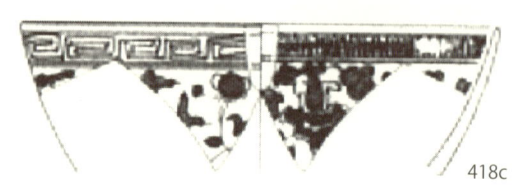

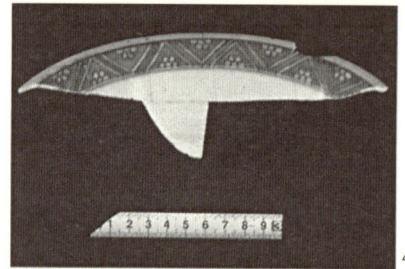

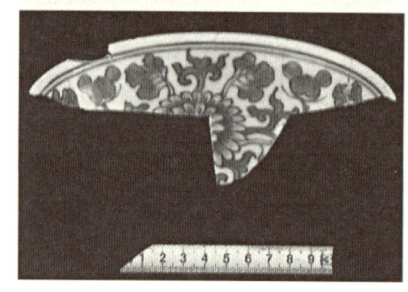

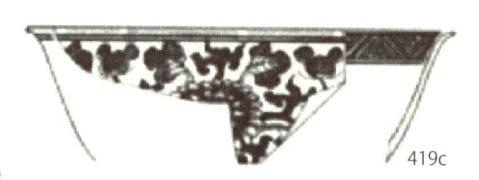

Fig.79 ティルタヤサ遺跡 Tirtayasa Site, Ⅴ-2 period, 中国景徳鎮陶磁 Chinese Jingdezhen ceramics

外面に菊唐草、口縁内側に花菱文を染付する[139]。17 世紀後半。

　Fig.80-420 は青花碗。見込と外側面に菊唐草を描く。腰部に蓮弁と思われる連続文を配す。高台畳付は平らに削る。17 世紀後半。

　Fig.80-421 は青花鉢。見込に花木と虫、外面も花木・岩などを描く。高台内には「大清康熙年製」銘が染付される。1660 〜 80 年代。

　Fig.81-422 は青花碗。外面と口縁部内側に線描きのみの菊唐草文を染付する。見込に

---

139 トプカプ宮殿蔵品No.2029 に類品がある。

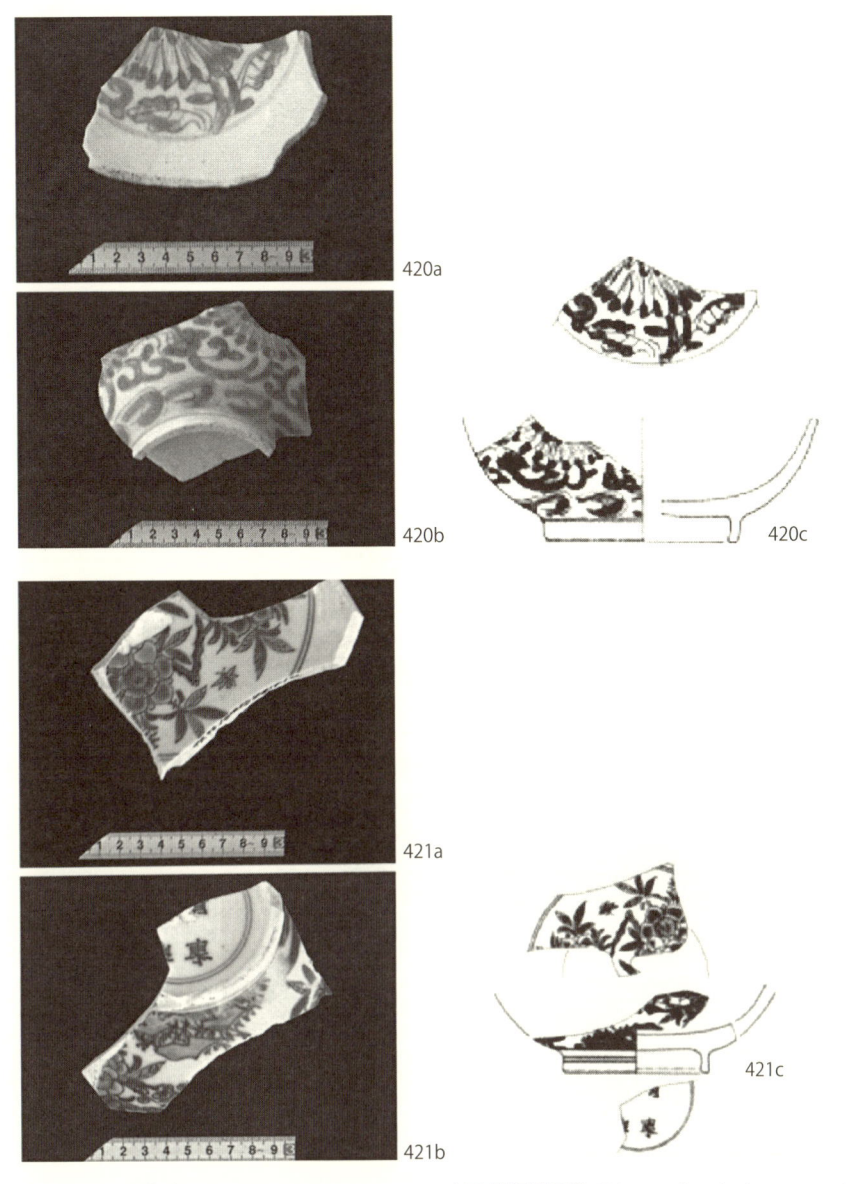

Fig.80 ティルタヤサ遺跡 Tirtayasa Site, Ⅴ-2 period, 中国景徳鎮陶磁 Chinese Jingdezhen ceramics

も文様が描かれる。いわゆるペンシルドローイング。17世紀後半。

　Fig.81-423, 424 が Fig.79-419 と似通った青花碗。

　Fig.81-425 は青花碗の底部。見込は区画内に蓮唐草、外側面唐草、腰部に蓮弁文を描く。17世紀後半。

　Fig.81-426 は青花鉢。外面にパルメット文に似た花様の文様を描き、内側面にも明らかでないが花唐草と見られる文様を染付。高台畳付を平らに削る。17世紀後半。

　Fig.82-427 は青花鉢の底部。見込に如意頭唐草文を表しており、Fig.82-428 と同類の可能性がある。

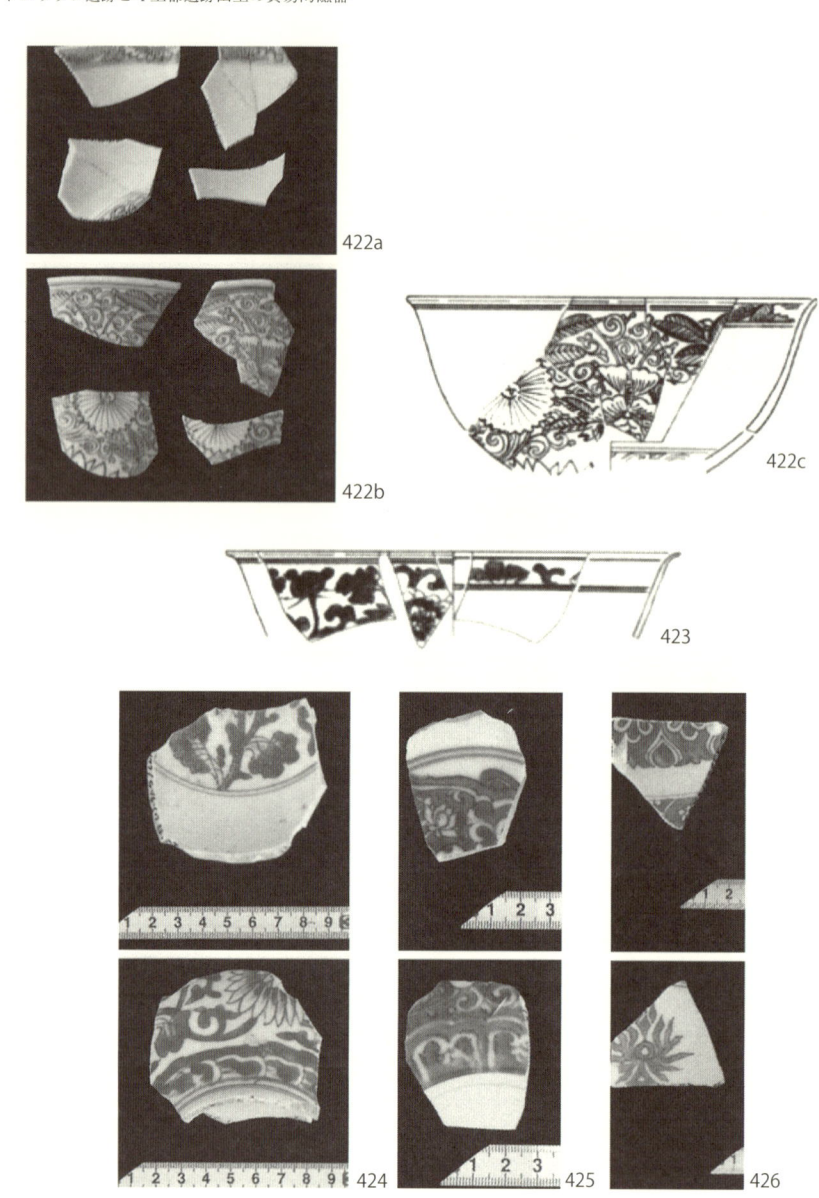

Fig.81 ティルタヤサ遺跡 Tirtayasa Site, Ⅴ-2 period, 中国景徳鎮陶磁 Chinese Jingdezhen ceramics

　　Fig.82-428 は青花鉢の底部。見込に火焔宝珠内に寿字を白抜きで表す。外面は如意頭
唐草を描く。高台畳付は平らに削る。17 世紀後半。

　　Fig.82-429 は青花小碗。見込に蓮文、外側面に蓮唐草文、腰部に蓮弁文、高台内に方
形枠内の幾何文様銘を染付する[140]。17 世紀後半。

　　Fig.82-430, Fig.83-431 は青花大皿。見込に花唐草文、内側面に如意頭繋ぎ文、口縁部
に唐草文をめぐらす。外側面に宝文を描く。高台は二重に作る[141]。17 世紀後半。

---

140 トプカプ宮殿蔵品No.2051 に類品がある。

141 トプカプ宮殿蔵品No.2099 に類品がある。

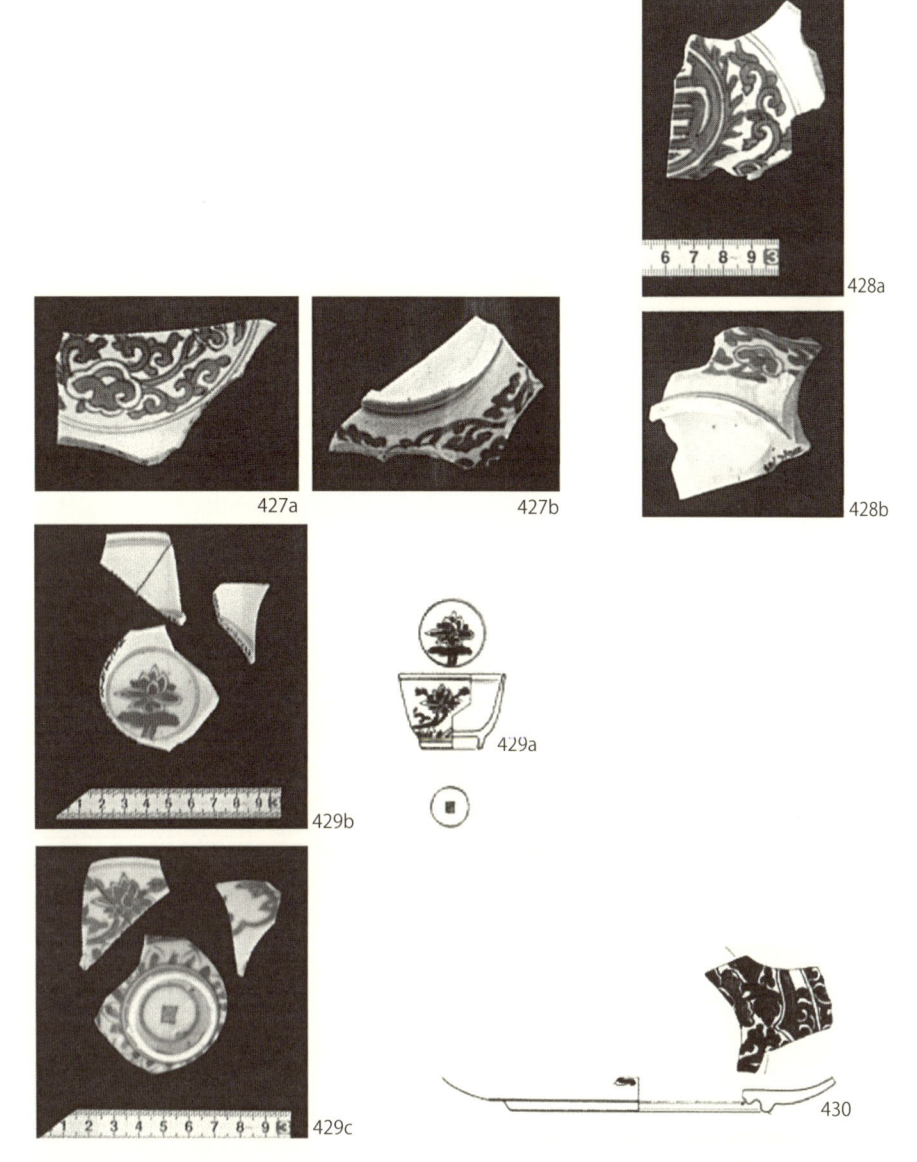

Fig.82 ティルタヤサ遺跡 Tirtayasa Site, V-2 period, 中国景徳鎮陶磁 Chinese Jingdezhen ceramics

　Fig.83-432は五彩大皿。内面から外側面にかけて、独特の唐草を明るい緑絵具中心に表す。高台は二重に作るのが康熙（1662～1722）頃の大皿に多い特徴。17世紀後半。バンテン・ラーマ遺跡で類例がある。

　Fig.83-433も五彩大皿。やはり高台は二重高台に作る。

　Fig.83-434は緑釉碗。畳付以外に施釉。17世紀後半。他に単彩は黄釉碗がある。

　Fig.83-435は三彩の碗。内外に紫・緑・黄・白（透明）の釉を塗り分ける。見込に窯詰め時と考えられる茶色の目跡が見られる。17世紀後半。

　Fig.83-436, Fig.84-437は三彩皿。内面と外側面に緑・黄・紫・白（透明）で塗り分け

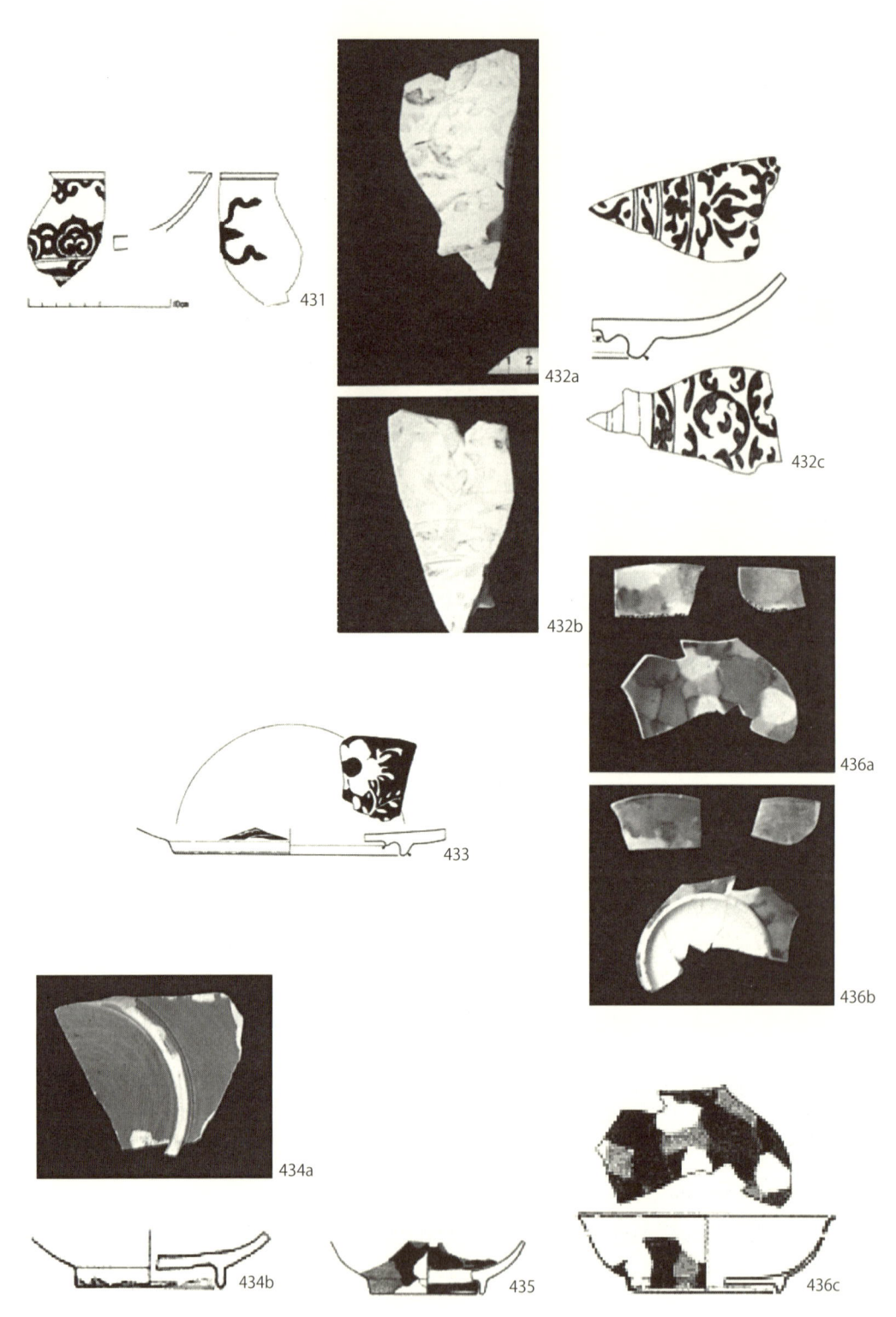

Fig.83 ティルタヤサ遺跡
Tirtayasa Site, Ⅴ-2 period, 中国景徳鎮陶磁 Chinese Jingdezhen ceramics

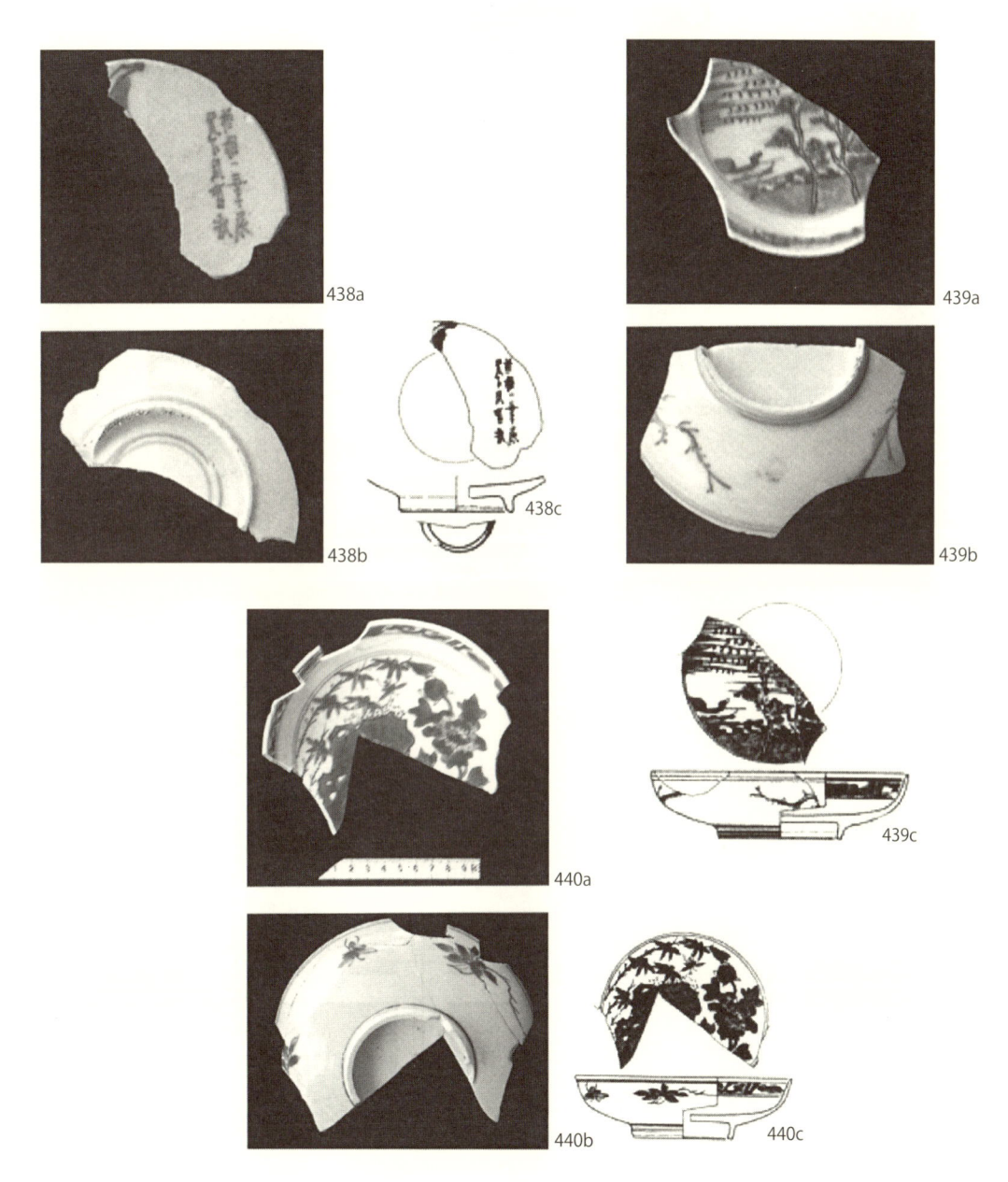

Fig.84 ティルタヤサ遺跡
Tirtayasa Site, Ⅴ-2 period, 中国景徳鎮陶磁 Chinese Jingdezhen ceramics

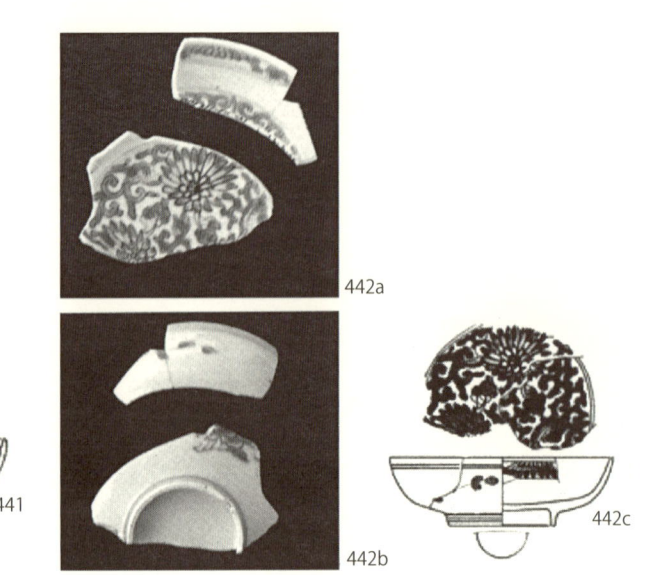

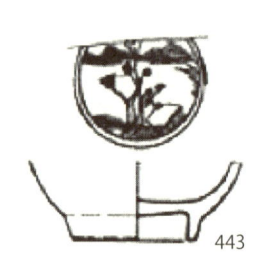

Fig.85 ティルタヤサ遺跡
Tirtayasa Site, Ⅴ-2 period, 中国景徳鎮陶磁 Chinese Jingdezhen ceramics

る。高台内は本焼時に透明釉を施す。数個体分出土している。17世紀後半。

　Fig.84-438は青花皿。見込に桐葉に「梧桐一葉落、天下尽皆秋」の漢詩を染付する。17世紀後半。

　Fig.84-439は青花皿。見込に釣人山水文を描く。口縁文様は不明。外側面は樹木を染付。17世紀後半。

　Fig.84-440は青花皿。見込に太湖石に牡丹竹虫文、口縁部に花唐草文を描く。外側面は折枝花文と虫を描く。高台畳付は平らにカットする。17世紀後半。

　Fig.85-441は青花皿。見込に龍唐草？、口縁部に花菱？を描く。外側面は折枝文？を染付する。17世紀後半。

　Fig.85-442は青花皿。見込に菊唐草文、口縁部にも半菊唐草文を描く。外面は折枝花文を染付[142]。17世紀後半。

　Fig.85-443は褐釉青花小坏。見込に山水文を染付。外面は褐釉をかけ分ける。17世紀

---

142 トプカプ宮殿蔵品Fig.2030に類品がある。

444

445a

446a

446b 445b
446c 445c

447

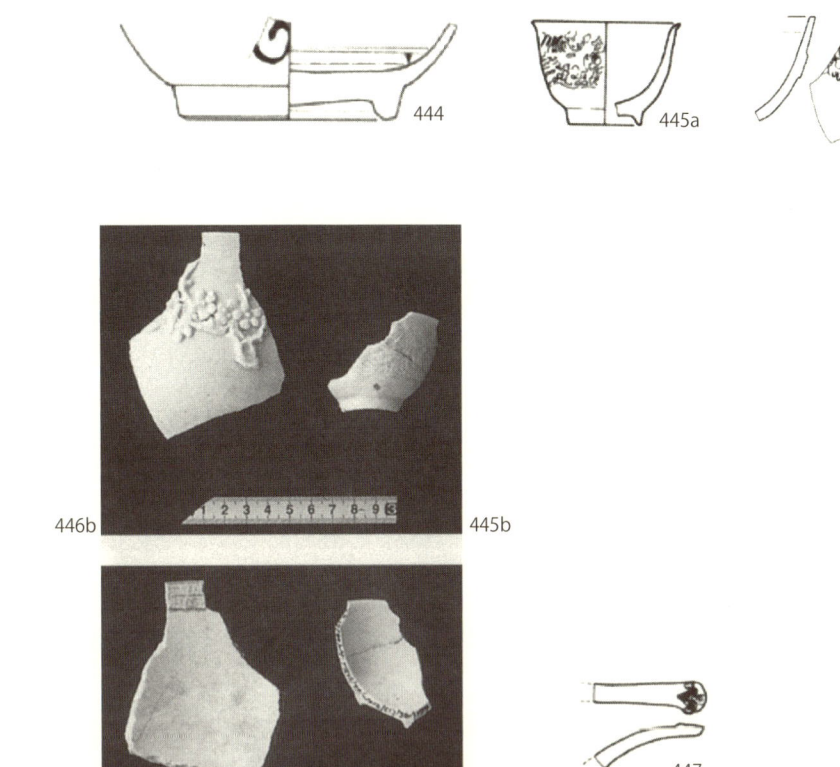

Fig.86 ティルタヤサ遺跡 Tirtayasa Site, V-2 period,
中国福建・広東陶磁 Chinese Fujian/Guangdong ceramics

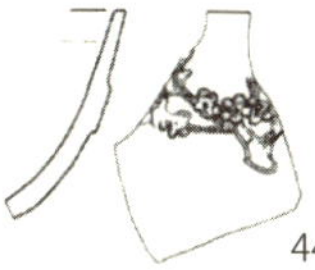

後半。

●福建・広東

Fig.86-444 は青花碗。見込に二重圏線、外側面にも文様を染付。見込は無釉。外底部も無釉。17 世紀後半か。

●徳化窯

Fig.86-445 は白磁小坏。端反形であり、型押し成形で外側面に陽刻文様を表す。焼成状態は悪い。徳化窯産であろう。17 世紀後半か。

Fig.86-446 は白磁蓋物身。型押し成形で外面に梅かと思われる貼付文様を施す。内面口縁部は無釉。17 世紀後半。

Fig.86-447 は白磁散蓮華。型押し成形で把手先端に文様陽刻[143]。17 世紀後半。

143 ブンタウ・カーゴの類例（Jörg & Flecker 2001）は先端の尖るスプーン部がつく。

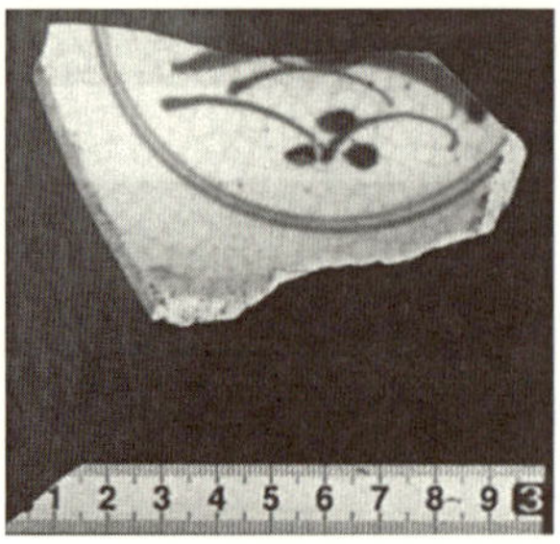

Fig.87 ティルタヤサ遺跡
Tirtayasa Site, Ⅴ-2 period, 肥前陶磁 Japanese Hizen ceramics

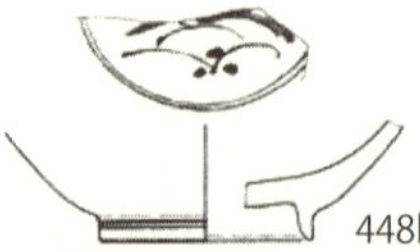

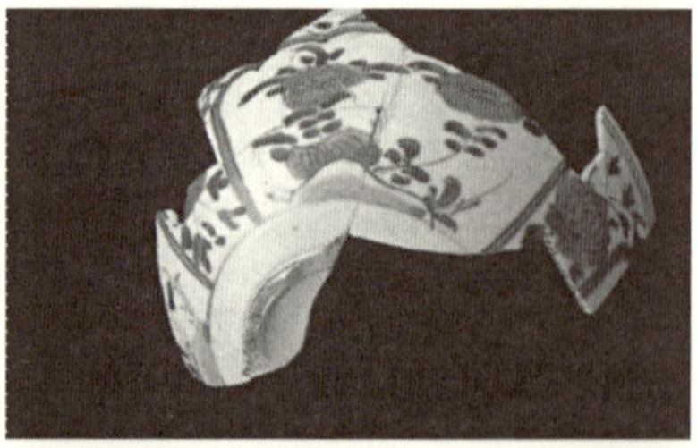

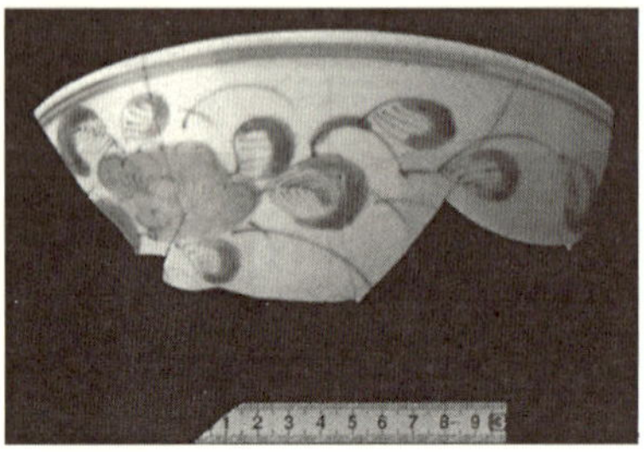

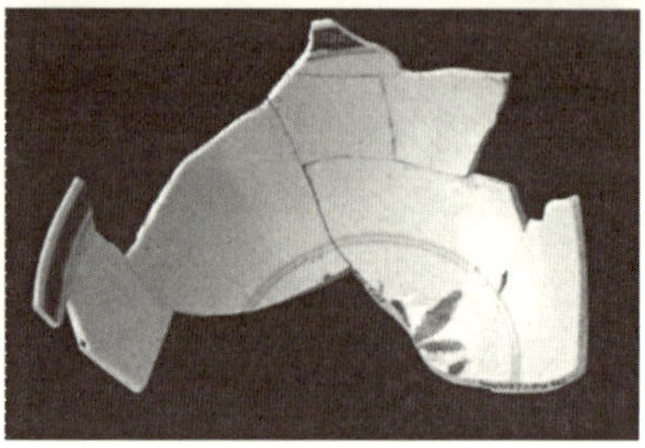

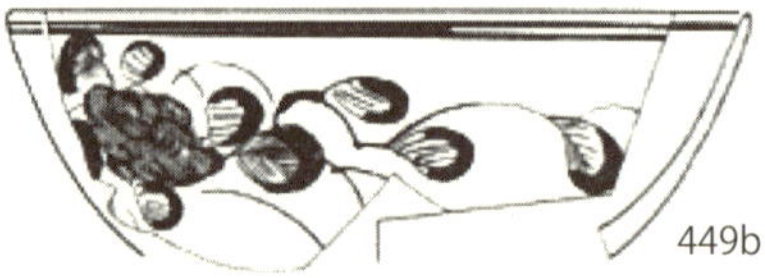

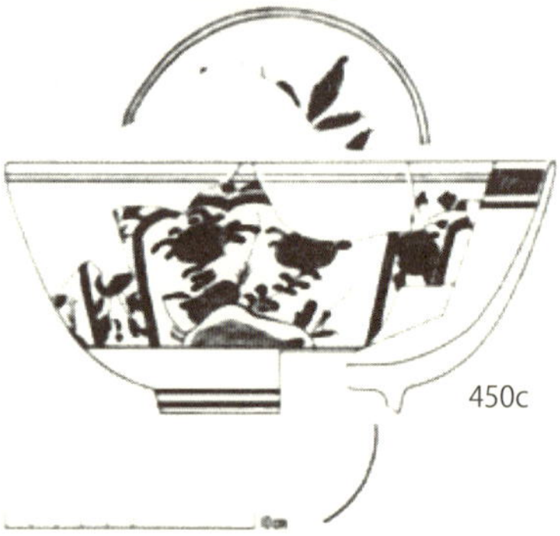

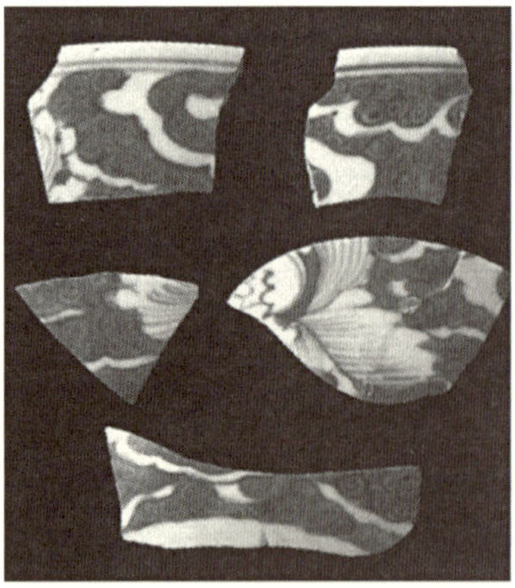

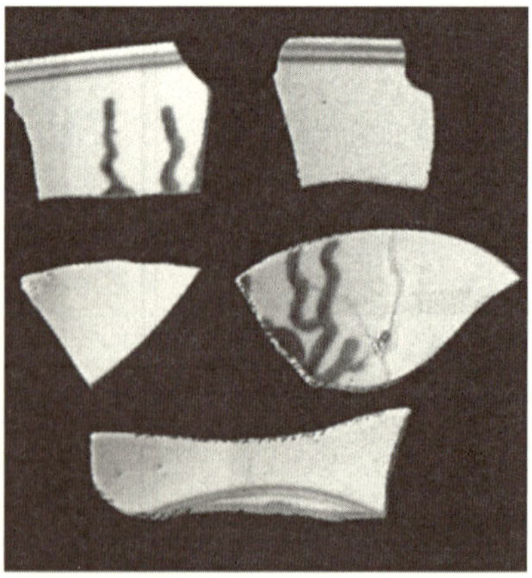

（2）肥前の陶磁器

●肥前磁器

Fig.87-448 は染付見込荒磯文碗の底部である。見込の荒磯文の波の部分はかなり崩れた表現であり、荒磯文碗の製作年代、1655～80 年代の中では後出と考えられる。

Fig.87-449 は染付牡丹文鉢。外面に牡丹文を描く。より硬直化が進んだ牡丹の表現で、見込に VOC の文字を染付した鉢の例があり、1690～18 世紀初と推測されるが、それより古式である。1660～80 年代。

Fig.87-450 は染付窓絵草花文鉢。外面に窓絵を三方に配し、窓内に草花文を描く。口縁部内側に雷文帯を配し、見込に草花文を描く。1660～70 年代。

Fig.87-451 は染付牡丹文鉢。外面に渦地文の中に牡丹花と雲を表す。内側面には火焔宝珠と思われる文様を描く。1660～80 年代。

Fig.88-452 は染付鉢。内側面に草花文を描き、見込にも二重圏線内に文様がある。外面は円弧を描く花唐草文。1660～80 年代。

Fig.88-454 は色絵小皿。口縁部は輪花状。見込には色絵（黄色他。絵具は大部分剝落）で秋草文。1660～80 年代。

Fig.88-453, 455 は染付小皿。455 は見込に山水文を描く。焼成は甘く細かい貫入が見られる。1660～70 年代。Fig.88-453 は見込に鳥と草、水を表す。1660～80 年代。これらも国内向け製品であろうが、Fig.88-455 は輸出用カップ＆ソーサーの受皿の可能性もある。

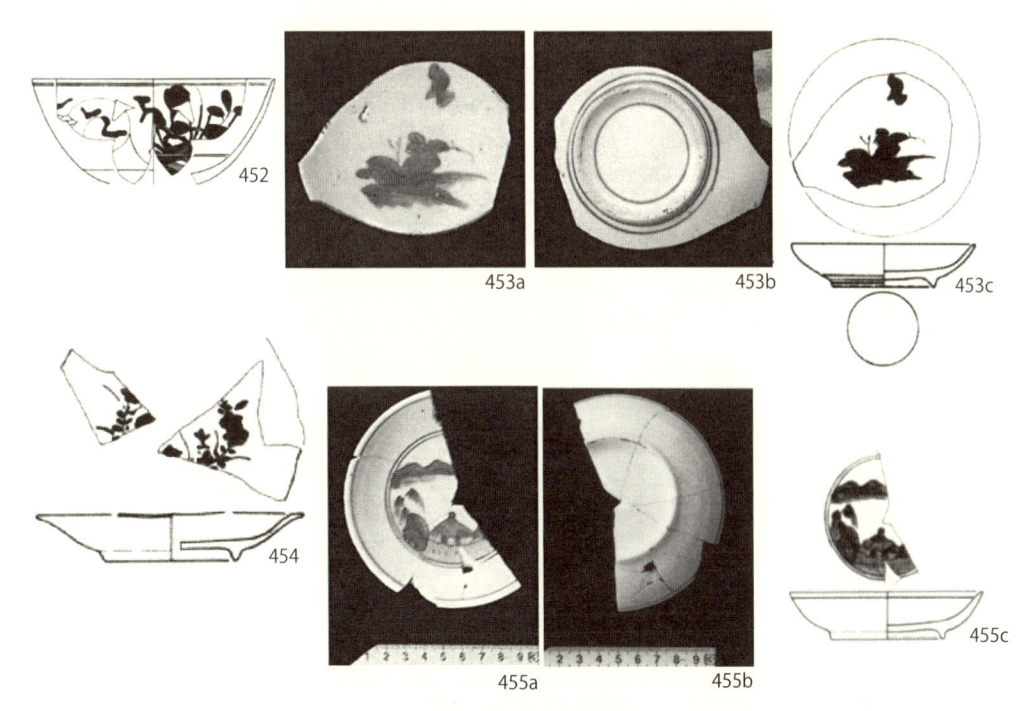

Fig.88 ティルタヤサ遺跡
Tirtayasa Site, Ⅴ-2 period, 肥前陶磁 Japanese Hizen ceramics

　Fig.89-456, 458 は色絵折縁皿。Fig.89-456 は内側面に花唐草文、口縁部に蓮弁文を描く。見込と側面に草花を赤の圏線と青・黄などの色絵具で表す（写真は剥落部を鉛筆で塗る）。素地の焼成は少し甘く貫入が多い。1660～80年代。これは輸出向けの可能性がある。

　Fig.89-457, Fig.90-462 は染付皿。Fig.89-457 は内側面に草花を描き、外面に草文かと思われる文様を染付する。1660～80年代。Fig.90-462 は見込に草花、内側面に桐を散らした意匠を染付。外側面に折枝文か。高台内に「製」字が見られ、一字銘の可能性がある。1660～80年代。これらは日本国内向け製品と考えられる。

　Fig.89-459 は染付芙蓉手皿であるが、Fig.90-460 とは意匠的にかなり異なる。つまり見込の草花文、内側面の花卉文、区画間の瓔珞文などが異なる。しかし、有田の長吉谷窯など窯跡でもこれらは一緒に出土しており、併存した時期もあると考えられる。1660～70年代。

　この他図示しなかったが、芙蓉手の皿は大皿の破片も出土しており、大・中・小の組み合わせで使われていた可能性がある。

　Fig.90-460 は染付芙蓉手皿。見込に草花を描き、側面に区画内に宝と花卉文を配す。外側面にも簡略化した区画文様を粗放な表現で描く。芙蓉手皿はサイズに大中小あるが、これは小さいタイプ。1660～80年代。

　Fig.90-461 は染付大皿。内側面は区画して花卉文を描く。外面に折枝か。外底面にハリ支え跡が見られる。これも意匠的に輸出向けと考えられる。1670～80年代。

　Fig.90-463, 464 は染付中皿。Fig.90-463 の見込文様は不明だが、内側面には墨弾きで捻花文を表す。外側面に折枝文を描く。1660～80年代。Fig.90-464 は見込に五弁花か四弁花文、内側面に墨弾きによる流水文を表す。外側面は折枝文か。1670～80年代。これらは国内向けに作られたと考えられる。

　Fig.91-465 は青磁大皿。見込にヘラ彫りと櫛描きにより草花を陰刻し、周囲に雷文帯をヘラ彫り。底部は高台内を蛇の目釉剥ぎし、鉄漿を塗る。その内方は一段深く削り込んでいる。蛇の目釉剥ぎ部分には窯詰め時のチャツの熔着痕があり、チャツは共土である。波佐見窯産。1660～80年代。

　Fig.91-466 は染付大合子の蓋。外面甲部に花鳥文、周囲に渦文帯をめぐらせ、側面に牡丹唐草文を染付する。こうした大合子は国内遺跡では見られず、バンテン・ラーマ遺跡[144] では出土しているから、輸出向けに作られたものと考えられる。1660～70年代。

　Fig.91-467 は染付大合子の身。外面に牡丹唐草文を染付する。1670～80年代。これも輸出向けであろう。

　Fig.91-468 は白磁合子身。型押し成形で受けがつく。外面体部は陽刻の斜線で区画し

144 佐賀県立九州陶磁文化館 1990 図 309～311

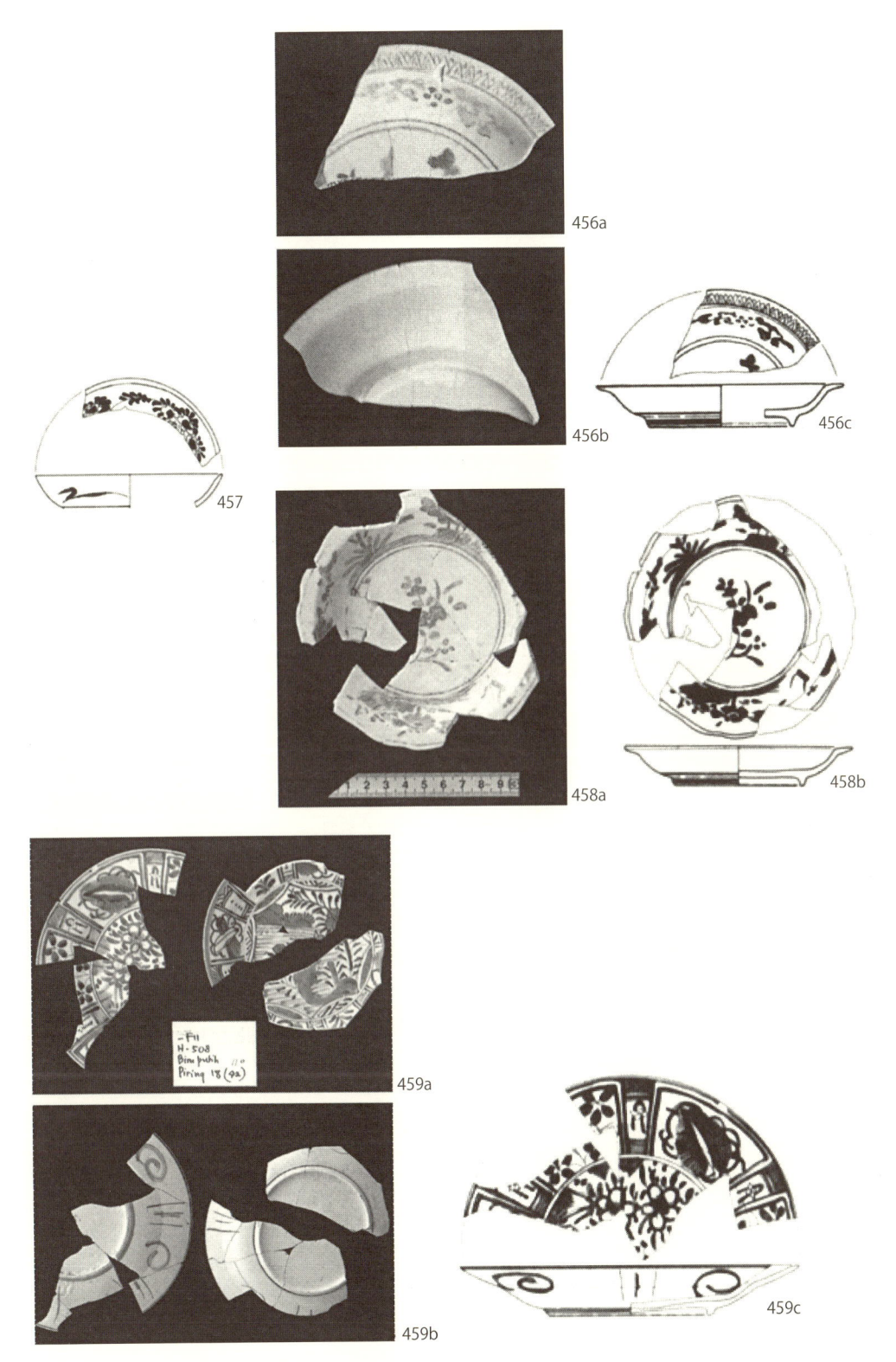

Fig.89 ティルタヤサ遺跡
Tirtayasa Site, Ⅴ−2 period, 肥前陶磁 Japanese Hizen ceramics

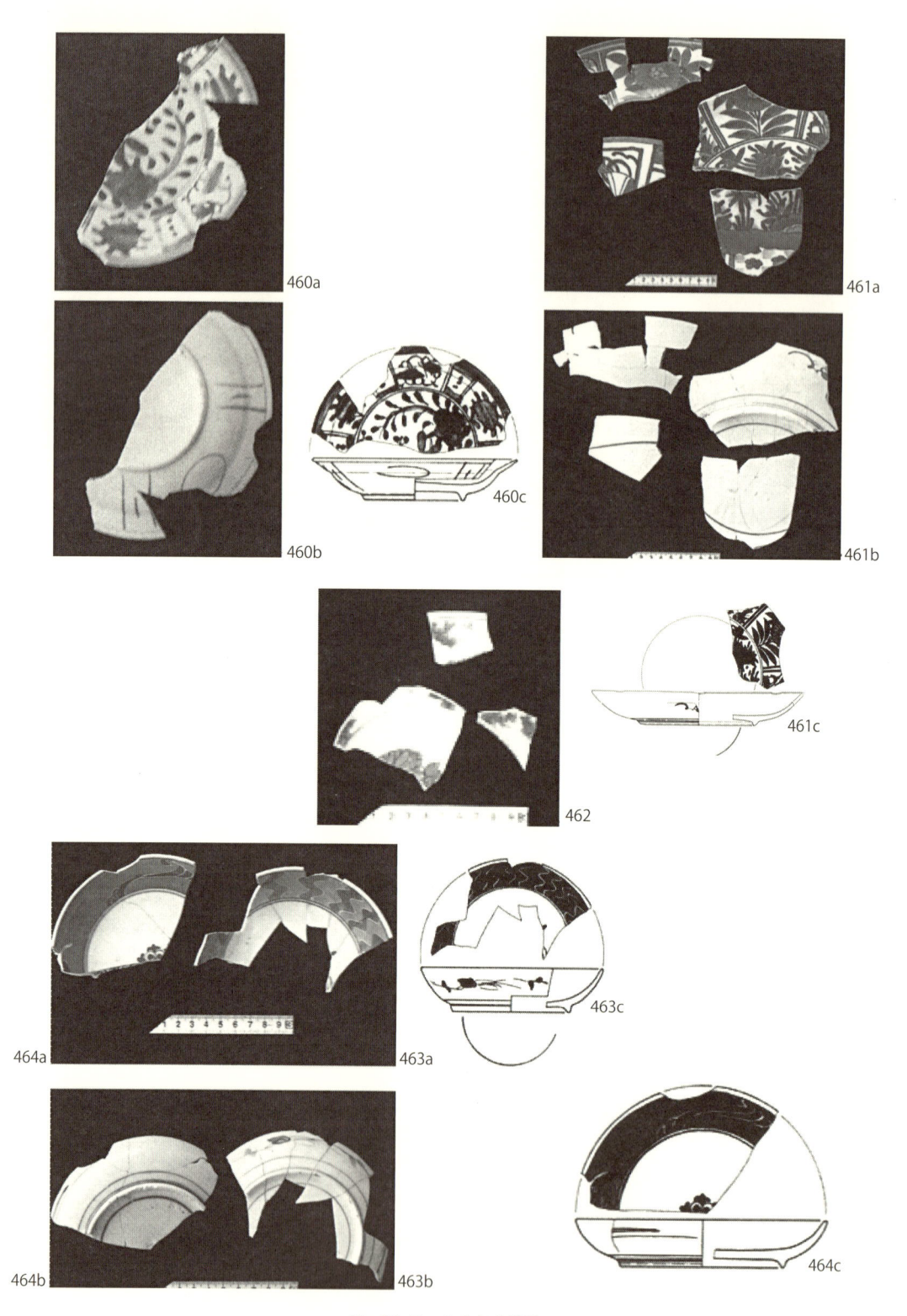

Fig.90 ティルタヤサ遺跡
Tirtayasa Site, Ⅴ-2 period, 肥前陶磁 Japanese Hizen ceramics

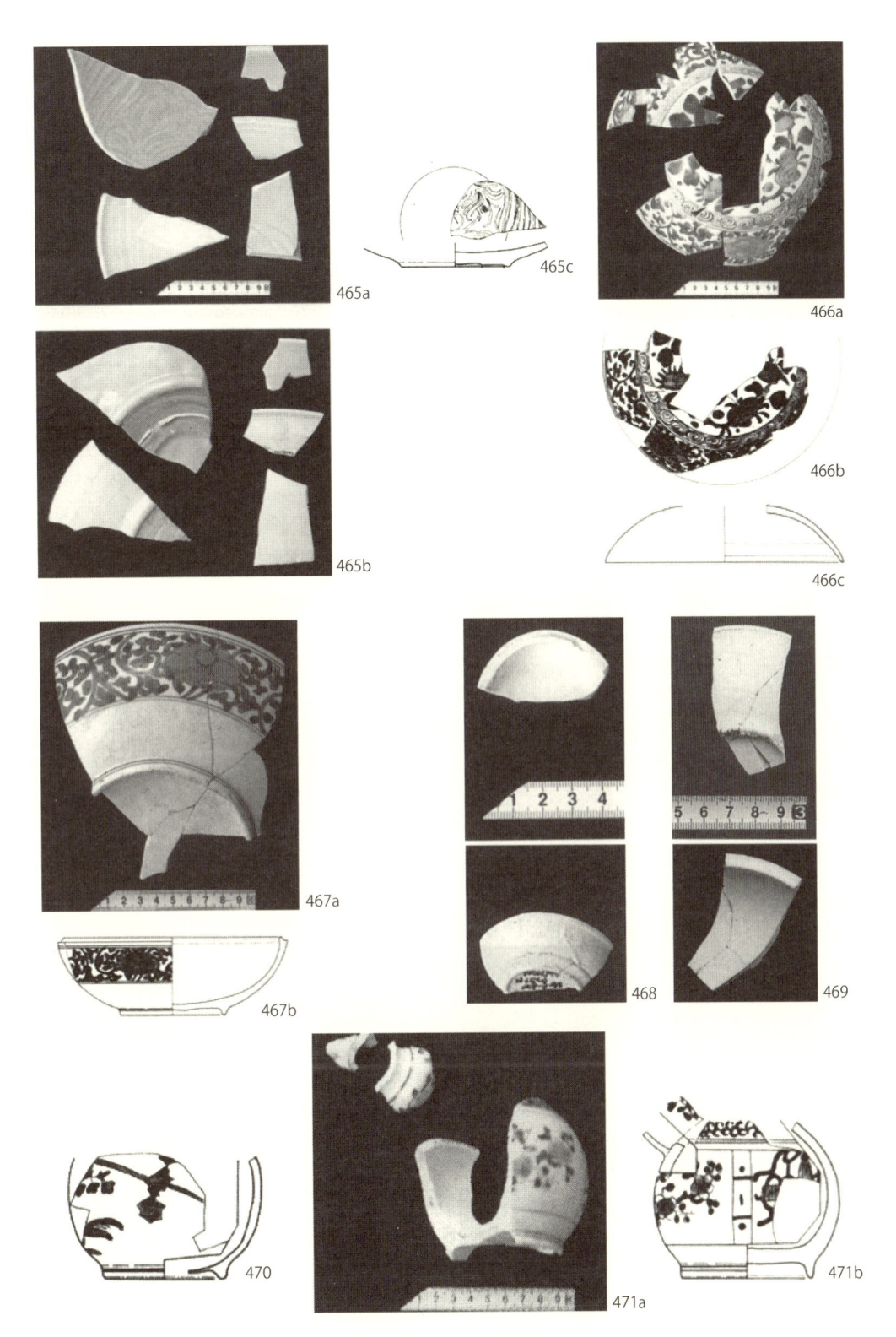

Fig.91 ティルタヤサ遺跡
Tirtayasa Site, Ⅴ-2 period, 肥前陶磁 Japanese Hizen ceramics

た中に円形文を充填。高台部周囲と受部は無釉。肥前か。17世紀後半。

　　Fig.91-469は色絵合子身。受けがつく。外面の口縁部に赤色の圏線が引かれる。17世紀後半。

Fig.92 ティルタヤサ遺跡 Tirtayasa Site, V-2 period, ベトナム陶磁 Vietnamese ceramics

　Fig.91-470は染付瓶。外面に草花を描く。1660～80年代。

　Fig.91-471は染付クンディ。外面は芙蓉手意匠とし、区画した中に宝文と梅樹文を描く。1660～80年代。

（3）ベトナムの陶磁器

〈鉄絵〉

　Fig.92-472は鉄絵印判手菊花文碗。見込と外側面にスタンプで菊花文を押す。見込は蛇の目釉剥ぎし、外底は無釉とする。ベトナム産。17世紀後半。類例はバンテン・ラーマ（Fig.74-386）などで出土。

11.　Ⅵ-1期（18世紀前半頃）

ブトン・ウォリオ城

（1）中国陶磁

〈青花ほか〉

●景徳鎮窯

　Fig.93-473は、この時期の青花芙蓉手皿。17世紀末～18世紀第1四半期。

　Fig.93-474は皿。見込に渦状文と花を表す。内外側面に独特の草花文を表す。バンテン・ラーマ遺跡でも出土し（Fig.99-505）、ヨーロッパ向けに作られたものと思われる。バンテン・ラーマ遺跡では同様の文様の蓋付鉢（Fig.102-538）も出土している。

　Fig.93-475は氷裂梅花文から変化した意匠を見込に描いた皿。

　Fig.93-476は青花に五彩を加えた皿。いわゆるチャイニーズイマリが主。

　Fig.94-478は褐釉五彩の皿。

　Fig.94-479は褐釉五彩の蓋物。

　Fig.94-480は五彩の合子や蓋物。

●福建

　Fig.93-477は独特の花唐草文を内面全体に表した皿。バンテン・ラーマ遺跡では似通った文様の景徳鎮産の皿が出土（Fig.101-531）。景徳鎮のものはヨーロッパでも伝世例は少なくない（ドイツ・ヘッセン州立博物館蔵）。

　Fig.95-481は折縁の扁平な皿。口縁部は濃み塗りする。左2点は粗製であり、明らかに

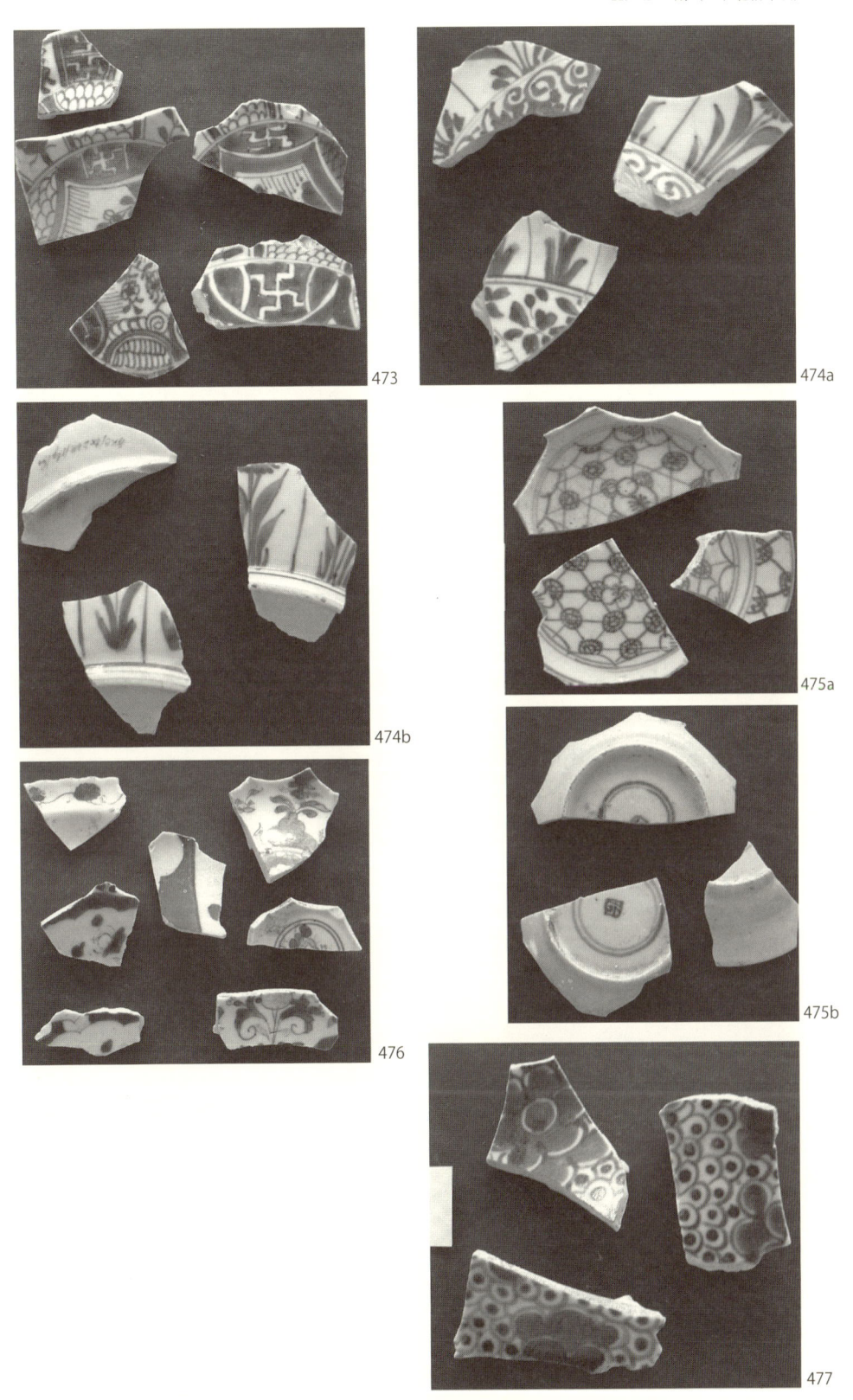

473
474a
474b
475a
475b
476
477

Fig.93 ブトン・ウォリオ城跡
Buton Wolio Fort, Ⅵ−1 period, 中国景徳鎮・福建陶磁 Chinese Jingdezhen/Fujian ceramics

478a　478b

479　480

Fig.94 ブトン・ウォリオ城跡
Buton Wolio Fort, VI-1 period, 中国景徳鎮陶磁 Chinese Jingdezhen ceramics

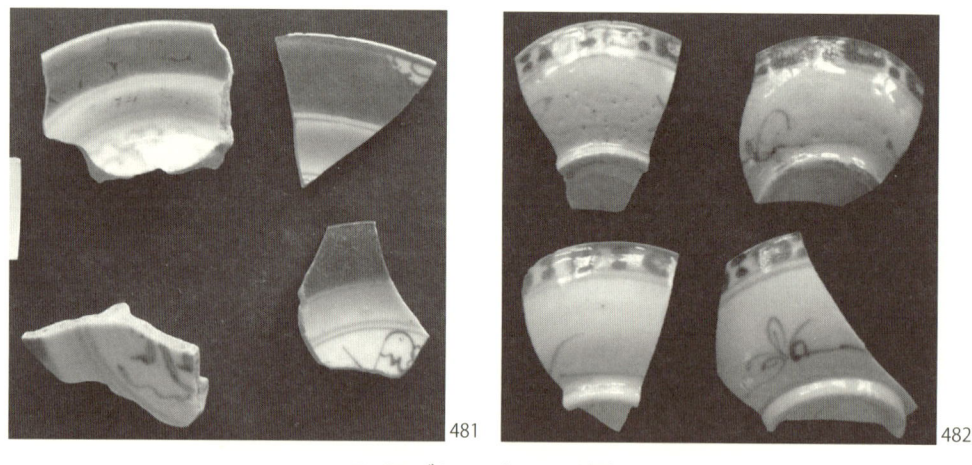

481　482

Fig.95 ブトン・ウォリオ城跡
Buton Wolio Fort, VI-1 period, 中国福建陶磁 Chinese Fujian ceramics

　福建産と考えられる。右 2 点の類品はバンテン・ラーマで出土（Fig.102-540・541）し、景徳鎮産として扱う[145]。17 世紀末〜 18 世紀前半。

　Fig.95-482 は青花碗類。主に丸形の小碗が多い。型作りで口端の釉を剝いだ、いわゆる口禿に作る。徳化窯産。18 世紀前半から中葉のものと思われる。

---

145 このような折縁でダミ塗りした皿は、見込文は違うがトプカプ宮殿蔵品 Fig.2610 にもある。

（2）肥前の陶磁器

●肥前磁器

Fig.96-483 は牡丹唐草文大皿、輸出向けである[146]。

Fig.96-484 の左3点は色絵壺の蓋。右1点は Fig.97-491 と同様の染付八角大壺の蓋。胴部の窓絵内に鳳凰文を描いており、地文に独特のムカデ様の唐草文を描く。

Fig.96, 98-485 は色絵大壺の蓋。

Fig.97-486／488, 492 は色絵金襴手大壺。Fig.97-486, 487 や Fig.97-492 右上は胴部に牛と石垣をもつ屋敷塀、門や邸宅、花樹を描く。頸部には花菱文を窓間に描く。肩には松皮菱の窓枠を配す[147]。Fig.97-487, 488 は外面を八角に面取している大壺[148]。

Fig.97, 98-489 も外面を八角に面取した染付八角壺の蓋。窓間に兎を主題とした文様を描く。この蓋は意匠から見ても堀試掘出土の鯉滝登り文大壺片 Fig.97-490 と同類と考えられる[149]。Fig.97-492 の下右の底部片もこの類の破片と思われる。Fig.97-494 の染付大壺片も鯉滝登り文を描き、Fig.97-490 と同類。

Fig.97-491 の八角大壺はムカデ様の唐草文を染付している。口縁部には独特の蓮弁文

483a   483b

484   485a

Fig.96 ブトン・ウォリオ城跡 Buton Wolio Fort, Ⅵ-1 period, 肥前陶磁 Japanese Hizen ceramics

---

146 佐賀県立九州陶磁文化館 1995-132 に近い意匠である。

147 こうした意匠の大壺の例は USUI コレクション（日本経済新聞社 2009 の図143）にある。佐賀県立九州陶磁文化館 2000 の図190 にもあるが面取ではない。

148 面取大壺の類品として蒲原コレクション（有田町教育委員会 2008 の図5）があり、六角大壺で蓋付総高 78.9cm である。

149 類品は戸栗美術館蔵品（身の高さ 58.2cm、戸栗美術館 1998 の図218）や古伊万里調査委員会編 1959 の第33図（身の高さ 59.2cm）のような、染付鯉滝登り松竹文八角壺と考えられる。

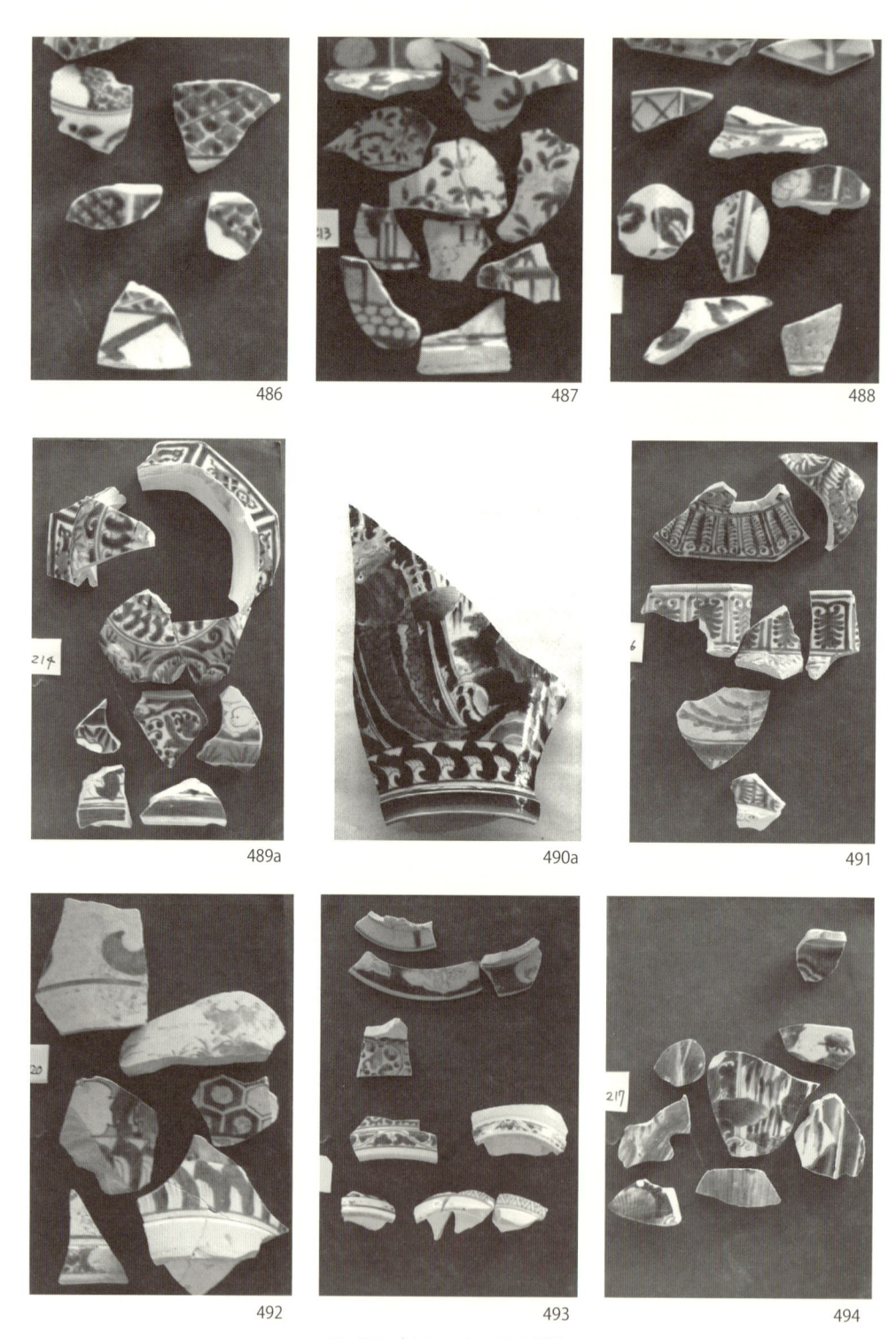

486　487　488

489a　490a　491

492　493　494

Fig.97 ブトン・ウォリオ城跡
Buton Wolio Fort, VI-1 period, 肥前陶磁 Japanese Hizen ceramics

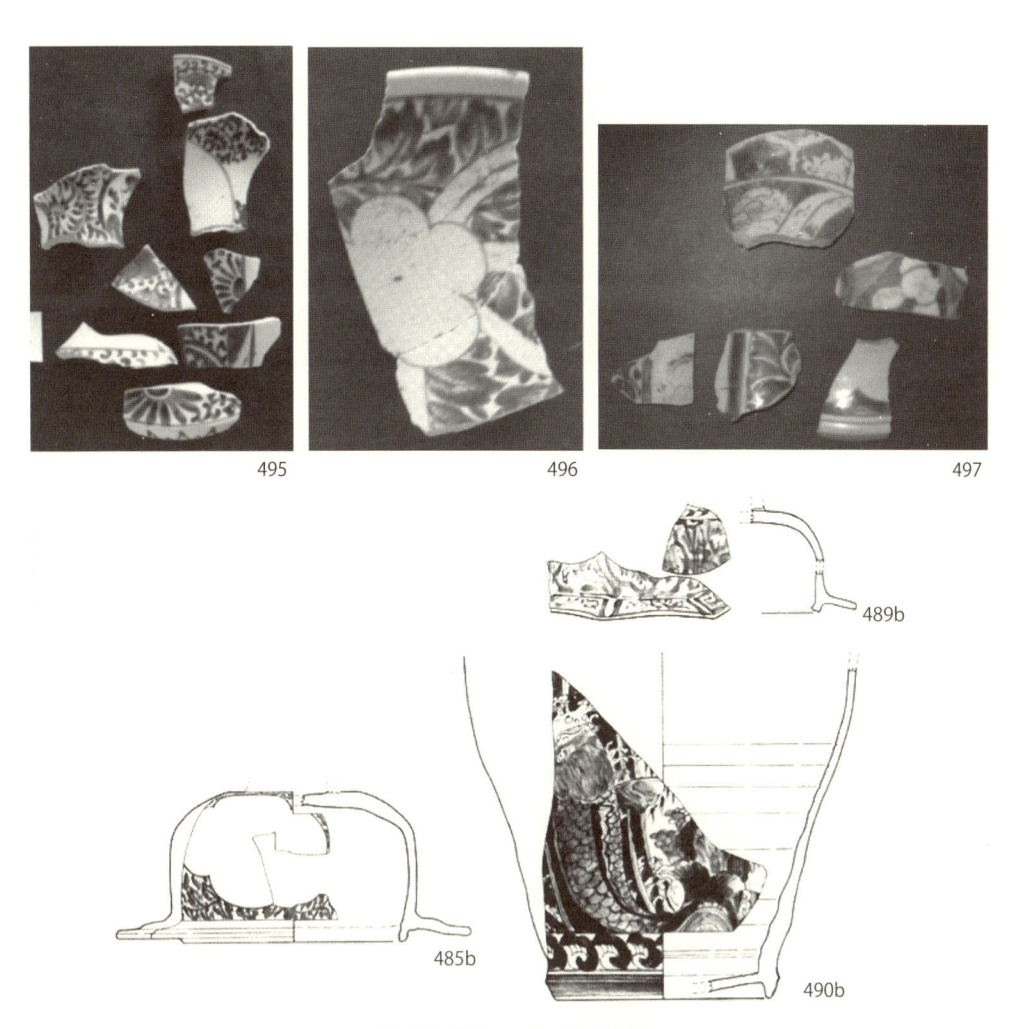

Fig.98 ブトン・ウォリオ城跡
Buton Wolio Fort, VI-1 period, 肥前陶磁 Japanese Hizen ceramics

を染付する。

　Fig.98-495 は染付大瓶であり、2 種以上ある。左上の窓間にムカデ様の唐草文を染付し
た瓶は、Fig.97-491 の八角大壺とセットの瓶の可能性がある。他の破片は色絵が見られ
ないが、色絵素地の可能性がある。

　Fig.98-496 は色絵金襴手瓢形大瓶[150]。こうした瓶は同意匠の壺とのセットで作られたの
が普通であるから、Fig.98-496 は色絵松鶴文大壺のような意匠の壺とセットで作られた
可能性が推測できる。

　Fig.98-497 も色絵の大瓶。

---

150 染付の唐草地に紐で結んだ意匠は九州陶磁文化館蔵の色絵松鶴文大壺（総高 68.5cm、大橋 2011 の図 150・151）
　　に近い。

バンテン・ラーマ遺跡

(1) 中国の陶磁器

〈青花ほか〉

● 景徳鎮窯

Fig.99-498 は褐釉青花小坏。外面に褐釉をかけ、見込にコバルトで花籠文を表す。高台内に「聚玉堂製」銘を染付する。6 個体。少し違うが同類と思われる「聚慶堂製」銘は中国にあるが一般的でない。見込花籠文の褐釉青花小坏はこの時期の輸出用に多く、見込花籠文を施した小坏はこの時期の肥前磁器で写した例が見られる。

Fig.99-499 は青花小鉢。型で捻花に作り、それに合わせてコバルトによる線で区画をし、草花などを描き込む、見込には花文を配す。高台内にも小花文を染付する。12 個体。17 世紀末〜18 世紀第 1 四半期。

Fig.99-500/502 は青花芙蓉手皿。明末の芙蓉手皿に倣ったもの。見込はまりばさみ文のなかに花などを描く。内側面は区画内に花卉文、宝文を交互に描く。Fig.99-501 は高台内に二重方形枠銘を染付する。Fig.99-502 は高台内に二重圏線を染付する。25 個体。17 世紀末〜 18 世紀初。

Fig.99-503 は青花素地に色絵を施した大皿。内面にコバルトで松と竹を描き、その素地に赤で加彩したもの。6 個体。17 世紀後半〜18 世紀初。

Fig.99-504 は青花双耳付蓋付鉢。ヨーロッパからの注文による器形であろう[151]。外面に松などを描いた中国の庭園を表す。17 個体。17 世紀末〜18 世紀前半。

Fig.99-505 は青花皿。見込に花つる草文、内側面の区画内に草花を描く[152]。74 個体。17 世紀末〜18 世紀中葉。

Fig.99-506 は褐釉青花小皿。外側面に褐釉を施す。内面は花、如意頭繋ぎ文帯を中心に花卉文を染付する。2 個体。17 世紀末〜18 世紀前半。

Fig.100-507 は青花皿か鉢。見込は饅頭心状にふくらみ、底部は碁笥底形に作る。見込は十字花文、周囲に如意頭繋ぎ文帯などをめぐらす[153]。1 個体。18 世紀。

Fig.100-508 は青花皿。見込には文字の周りに如意頭繋ぎ文をめぐらし、内側面には寿字文を二段に連ねる。外側面にも寿字文をめぐらす、高台内には二重方形枠内に渦状文を表した銘を記す。1 個体。18 世紀前半頃。

Fig.100-509 は五彩碗。外面にコバルトによる文様を施した素地に赤で加彩している。ヨーロッパへの輸出向けの装飾であり、ヨーロッパではチャイニーズイマリと呼ばれる。61 個体。18 世紀前半頃。

---

151 同様の器形の五彩の例はポルトガル（Pinto 1996 の 226 頁）にある。ヨーロッパ陶器にも見られる。
152 類品はロブブリ遺跡で出土しており、トプカプ宮殿蔵品Fig.2208 のカップとソーサーがある。
153 この意匠の崩れたタイプはロブブリ遺跡や長崎唐人屋敷跡出土品に見られる。

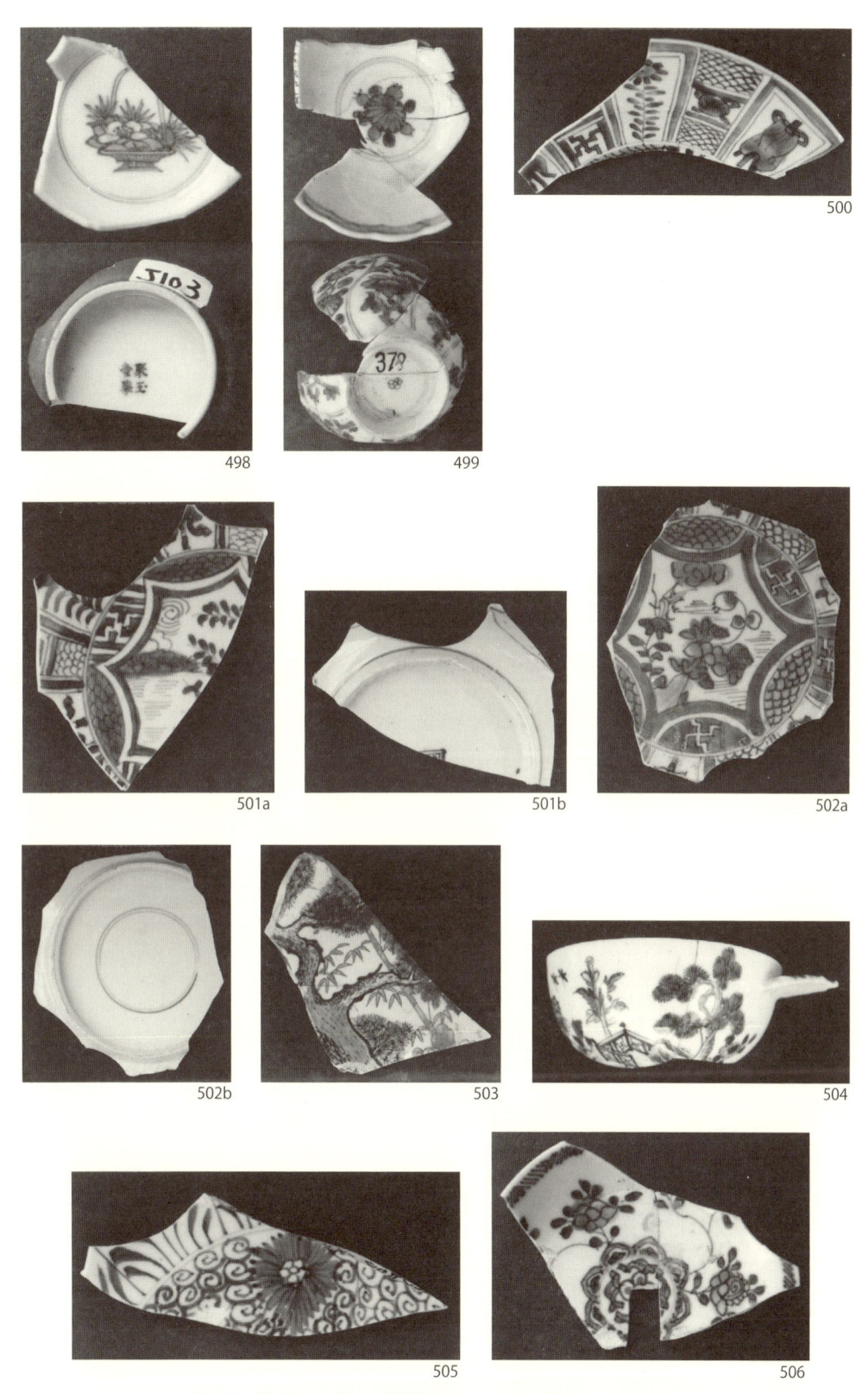

Fig.99 バンテン・ラーマ遺跡 Banten Lama Site, Ⅵ-1 period,
中国景徳鎮陶磁 Chinese Jingdezhen ceramics

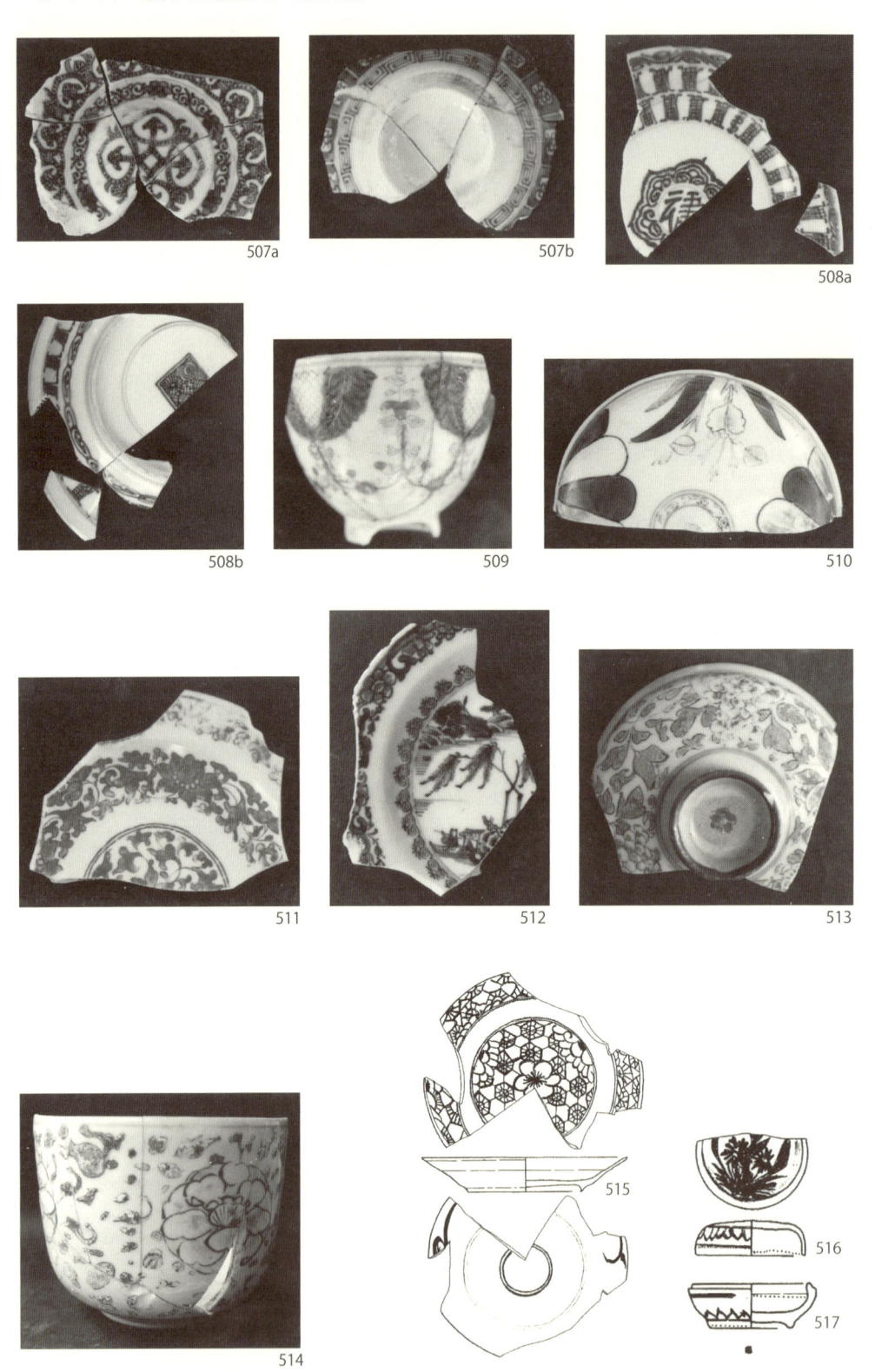

507a

507b

508a

508b

509

510

511

512

513

514

515

516

517

Fig.100 バンテン・ラーマ遺跡
Banten Lama Site, Ⅵ-1 period, 中国景徳鎮陶磁 Chinese Jingdezhen ceramics

　Fig.100-510 は五彩蓋。外面に菊花と草花を染付に赤・緑・黄で表す[154]。こうした菊花を描いたチャイニーズイマリは鉢や皿など少なくない。有田の金襴手様式にあるので、有田磁器が本歌となったものと思われる。1 個体。18 世紀前半。

　Fig.100-511 は五彩皿。内面に赤のみで花唐草を描く。50 個体。18 世紀。

　Fig.100-512 は青花皿。見込に柳山水文を描く。172 個体。17 世紀末〜18 世紀前半。

　Fig.100-513, 514 は五彩蓋付鉢の蓋と身。文様が違うのでセットではないが、外面に花唐草を色絵具で表す[155]。Fig.100-514 は 21 個体。これらは 18 世紀前半〜中葉。

　Fig.100-515 は青花折縁皿。口銹を施し、内面に氷裂梅花文を描く。46 個体。18 世紀前半〜中葉。産地は景徳鎮であろう。類例はブトン・ウォリオ城（Fig.93-475）がある。

　Fig.100-516, 517 は青花合子。Fig.100-516 は蓋であり、草花を描く。同類品は 128 個体。Fig.100-517 は腰部に蓮弁文帯を染付。85 個体。17 世紀後半〜18 世紀。

　Fig.101-518, 519 は青花小坏。Fig.101-518 は見込に花文、Fig.101-519 は外面に魚文などを染付する。高台内に方形枠内銘を染付する。Fig.101-518 が 6 個体、Fig.101-519 が 130 個体。17 世紀後半〜18 世紀前半。

　Fig.101-520 は青花小坏。外面に菊文、見込水鳥文を染付する。1 個体。17 世紀中葉〜末。

　Fig.101-521 は青花小坏。内外に不明瞭な文様が染付される[156]。外面には三星のような文様と馬を描いている。32 個体。17 世紀後半〜18 世紀前半。

　Fig.101-522 は褐釉青花小坏。外面に褐釉を施し、内面は青花文様を描く。見込と内側面に草花、口縁部に波濤文から変化したと考えられる文様を配す[157]。1 個体。17 世紀第 4 四半期〜18 世紀初。

　Fig.101-523 は青花小坏。側面に型成形で蓮弁形の陽刻を施す。それに合わせて外面に蓮弁形の区画を描き、中に草花を染付する。上部に花唐草文をめぐらす。見込に松文、内面口縁部に Fig.101-522 と同様の波濤文から変化したと考えられる文様を描く[158]。口銹を施す。9 個体。17 世紀末〜18 世紀第 1 四半期。

　Fig.101-524 は褐釉五彩の小坏。外面に褐釉を施し、口銹を塗った素地に、内面に赤で牡丹と思われる草花を描く。86 個体。17 世紀第 4 四半期〜18 世紀前半。

　Fig.101-525 は深めの青花皿。見込に花？文、内側面に折枝文を描く。高台内に方形枠の銘が染付される。2 個体。17 世紀後半。

---

154 トプカプ宮殿蔵品 Fig.2977 の砂糖入れの蓋に比較的似ている。1700〜25 年頃とする。

155 Fig.100-513 はトプカプ宮殿蔵品 Fig.2871 に類似。1710〜40 年頃とする。

156 ブンタウ・カーゴ引揚げ品 Jörg & Flecker 2001 に類品があり、それを見ると見込文は崩れているが、跳魚図と思われる。

157 こうした文様と内側面の草花の組み合わせはブンタウ・カーゴ引揚げ品と似通っている。

158 このように陽刻で蓮弁形を表し、それに従って青花で枠を描くのはブンタウ・カーゴ引揚げ品にも見られる。ブンタウ・カーゴ引揚げ品では亀甲繋ぎ文になっており、本例も下を切った状態だが亀甲繋ぎ文様の変化したものかもしれない。

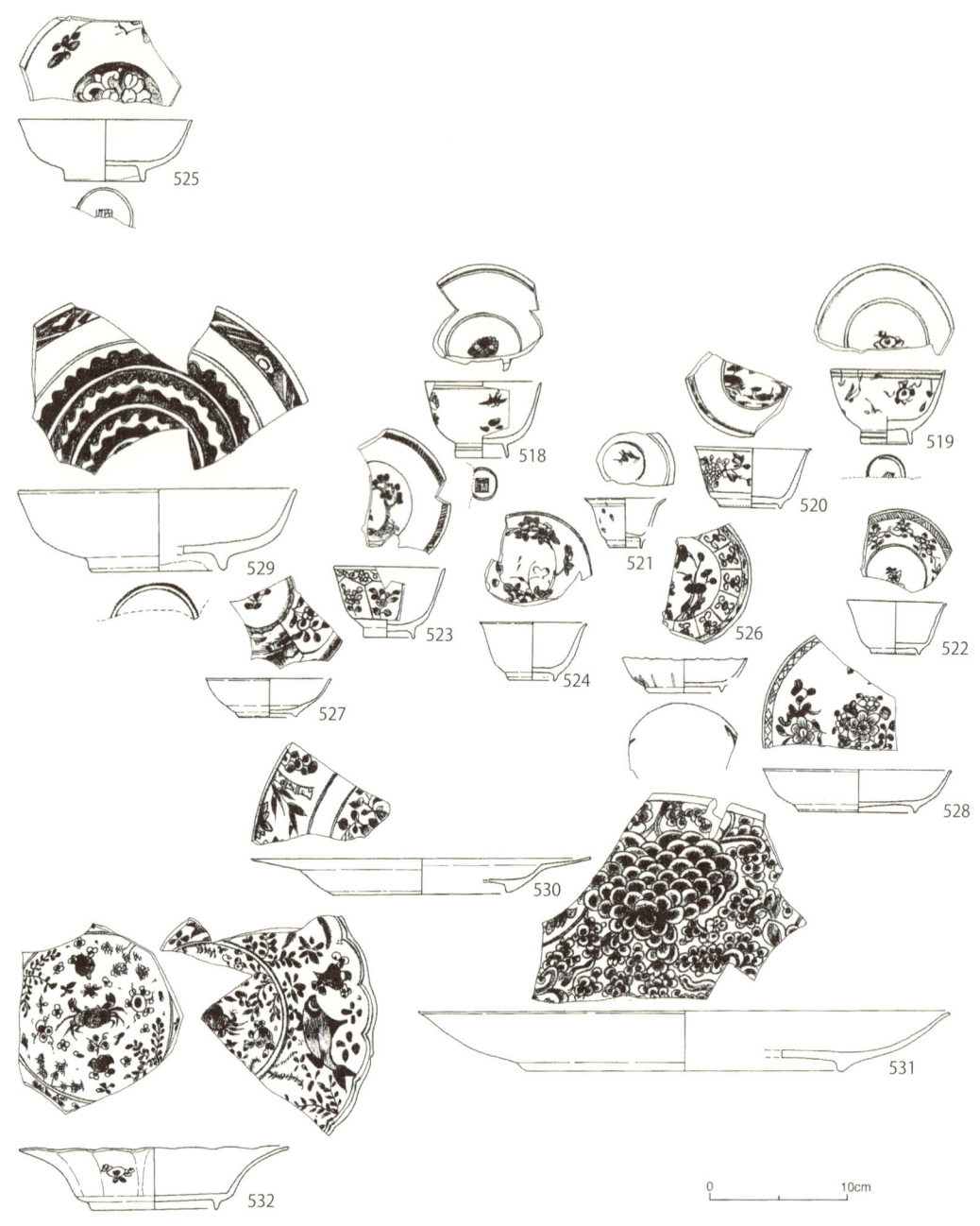

Fig.101 バンテン・ラーマ遺跡 Banten Lama Site, VI-1 period,
中国景徳鎮陶磁 Chinese Jingdezhen ceramics

　　Fig.101-526 は青花小皿。外側面に縦筋を陰刻し、見込に梅樹、内側面に簡略化した花
唐草を区画内に描く。Fig.101-523 のソーサーの可能性がある。12 個体。17 世紀第 4 四
半期〜18 世紀第 1 四半期。

　　Fig.101-527 は褐釉青花小皿。外面に褐釉を施し、見込に花卉、内側面は区画内に山水
と花卉を交互に描く。463 個体。17 世紀第 4 四半期〜18 世紀前半。

　　Fig.101-528 は褐釉青花皿。外面に褐釉を施し、内面にいくつかの草花文を描き、口縁部に四方襷文の崩れと推測される斜格子文を染付する。33 個体。17 世紀第 4 四半期〜18 世紀前半。

　　Fig.101-529 は深めの褐釉青花皿。見込は鳳凰文か。12 個体。17 世紀後半〜18 世紀前半。

　　Fig.101-530 は青花折縁皿。底部は碁笥底状に内側のみ削り込む。こうした底部はオランダのプロンクが磁器注文のために 1743 年に製作した原画にもあるようにヨーロッパからの注文によるのであろう。輸出向けに多く見られる。折縁の平たいプレートはヨーロッパの食卓の器として主要なものであったと見られる。口錆を施す。口縁部に竹と葡萄文を描く[159]。69 個体。18 世紀前半。

　　Fig.101-531 は青花大皿。口錆を施し、内面に花唐草文を描く[160]。184 個体。17 世紀後半〜18 世紀初。

　　Fig.101-532 は青花鉢。型に当てて輪花に作る。見込中央に蟹を配し、周囲に水草を描き、内側面は水草の中に魚を描く[161]。9 個体。17 世紀後半〜18 世紀初。

　　Fig.102-533 は褐釉青花鉢。外面に褐釉を施す。見込に葦雁文、内側面は花卉文で埋める。16 個体。17 世紀後半〜18 世紀第 1 四半期。

　　Fig.102-534 は青花鉢。外面下部に蓮弁文帯、口縁部に渦文帯などをめぐらす。見込は花か葉をデフォルメした文様を描き、口縁部にも蓮弁の変化した文様帯をめぐらす[162]。61 個体。17 世紀末〜18 世紀中葉。

　　Fig.102-535 は褐釉五彩小碗。褐釉を内外に施し、外面に葡萄の葉とされる葉形の窓を透明釉で表した素地に色絵を施す[163]。64 個体。18 世紀。

　　Fig.102-536 は青花皿。見込に太湖石に牡丹や樹木・欄干など中国の庭園を表し、内側面は四方襷文帯をめぐらし、口縁部にも幾何学文様などでヨーロッパ向けに作られたボーダーを描く。92 個体。17 世紀末〜18 世紀中葉。

　　Fig.102-537 は青花折縁皿。底部は内側だけを削り込む。見込と内側面に花卉文を散らし、見込周囲と口縁部に斜格子文帯をめぐらす。337 個体。18 世紀前半〜中葉。

　　Fig.102-538 は Fig.99-505 内側面と同様の意匠の蓋付鉢。外面に区画内に独特の草花を描く[164]。4 個体。17 世紀末〜18 世紀中葉。

---

159 トプカプ宮殿蔵品 Fig.2439 の皿に類似している。

160 独特の花文であり、類品はトプカプ宮殿蔵品 Fig.2054 にある。

161 類品はトプカプ宮殿蔵品 Fig.2203 にある。

162 ロプブリ遺跡で同様の鉢が出土しており、インドネシアでも類似のものが見られる。

163 色は剥落したり変色しているため原状は明らかでないが、トプカプ宮殿蔵品 Fig.3313 などを見ると、窓の部分には粉彩で草花などを表したものと考えられる。トプカプ例は褐釉地に金彩を施す。類品はロプブリ遺跡出土品にある。

164 類品はトプカプ宮殿蔵品 Fig.2193 がある。

Fig.102 バンテン・ラーマ遺跡 Banten Lama Site,Ⅵ-1 period,
中国景徳鎮陶磁 Chinese Jingdezhen ceramics

　　Fig.102-539 は青花蓋付鉢。外面に菊唐草を描く。口唇部は無釉[165]。151 個体。17 世紀
末〜18 世紀前半。
　　Fig.102-540, 541 は青花折縁皿。Fig.102-540 は口銹を施し、見込に花籠文を描く。Fig.102-
541 は見込に仏手柑を描く。Fig.102-540 は 37 個体。Fig.102-541 は 3 個体。17 世紀末〜

165 この種の文様の蓋がトプカプ宮殿蔵品Fig.2198 などにある。

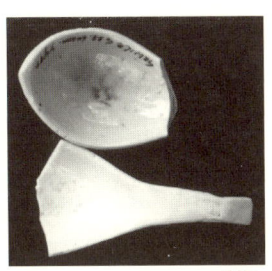

543　　　　　　　544　　　　　　　545a

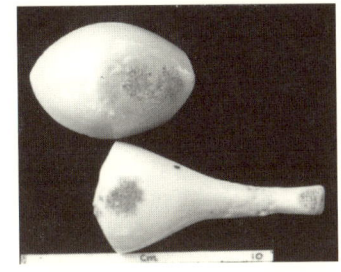
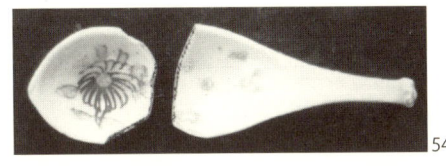

545b　　　　546

Fig.103 バンテン・ラーマ遺跡
Banten Lama Site, Ⅵ-1 period, 中国福建広東陶磁 Chinese Fujian/Guangdong ceramics

18 世紀前半。

　Fig.102-542 は青花芙蓉手皿。233 個体。18 世紀前半。この時期の中でも Fig.99-502 より後出の芙蓉手と思われる。

　●福建・広東

　Fig.103-543 は五彩碗。

　Fig.103-544 は五彩碗。型押しによって成形し、口禿であるがこれは焼成時に合わせ口で窯詰めしたためである。外面に花唐草文を赤・緑・黄で表す[166]。2 個体。17 世紀後半〜18 世紀。徳化窯系。

　Fig.103-545, 546 は散り蓮華。型押しによって成形し、全釉のため、底面には焼成時に敷いたモミガラが熔着。Fig.103-545 は白磁であり、Fig.103-546 は五彩で花文を描く。17 世紀末頃から作った可能性がある[167]。Fig.103-545 は 124 個体、Fig.103-546 は 22 個体。18 世紀頃を中心とする年代が推定される。徳化窯系。

　〈中国陶器〉

　Fig.104-547 は三彩折縁皿。口縁部は輪花に作り、内面に刻線と色釉により草花を表す。色釉は赤・緑・黄・紫である。陶器であるが高火度の色釉である[168]。3 個体出土。

　Fig.104-548 は褐釉耳付鉢。淡褐色の素地であり、型で成形し、外面に陽刻文様、内面

---

166 類品はロプブリ遺跡で見られる。

167 1690 年頃沈没のブンタウ・カーゴ引揚げ品 Jörg & Flecker 2001 にも類似のものが見られる。

168 この種の三彩は日本では見ないが、ジャカルタ国立博物館展示品にあり、また輪花ではないものがベトナム陶器として紹介されている（愛知県陶磁資料館 1987）。年代を 16〜17 世紀とするが、技法から見ると 18 世紀頃ではあるまいか。産地についてもベトナムで確認できておらず、中国南部の可能性を考えておきたい。類例はベトナム南端カマウ岬沖沈没船引揚げ品 Fig.145 にある。「雍正」銘の景徳鎮磁器が共伴している。

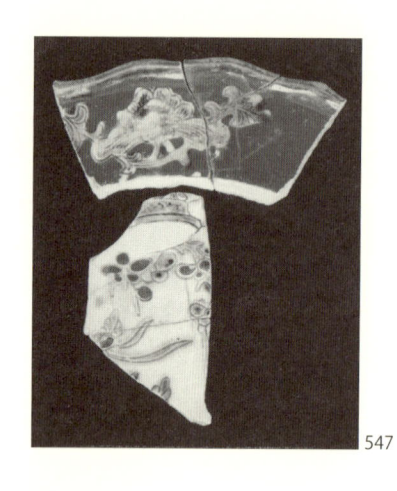

547

548a

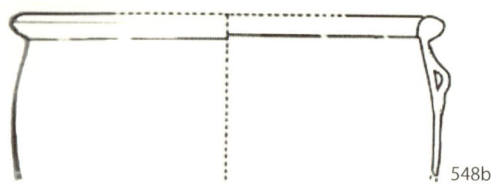
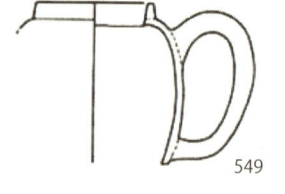

548b

549

Fig.104 バンテン・ラーマ遺跡
Banten Lama Site, VI-1 period, 中国陶器 Chinese Stoneware ceramics

に粒状の圧痕が見られる。内外に褐釉を施し、口縁部のみ無釉とする。日本では長崎で出土している程度である。70 個体。17 ～ 18 世紀。

　Fig.104-549 は無釉炻器の手付水注。橙褐色の精土を用いて型で成形するのが普通であり、江蘇省の宜興窯で焼造された。本来蓋が付き、飲茶用として作られた[169]。いわゆる朱泥であり、この種の宜興窯のティーポットはヨーロッパにも多く渡っており、ドイツのマイセン窯などで模倣された。日本でもこの影響で万古焼などが生れた。10 個体。17 ～ 19 世紀。

（2）肥前の陶磁器

●肥前磁器

　Fig.105-550 は色絵髭皿。型打成形によって口縁部は輪花に作る。見込に花盆文を赤・緑などで表す。18 世紀第 2 四半期～第 3 四半期。

　Fig.105-551, 552 は色絵金襴手様式小皿。輸出用のカップの受け皿（ソーサー）である。一部染付を施した素地に赤・金などの色絵具で描く。Fig.105-551 は見込に花卉、内側面に草花を表す。Fig.105-552 は見込蛇の目釉剝ぎした素地であり、蛇の目釉剝ぎ部分を色

---

169 日本では長崎・岩下遺跡（長崎県教育委員会 1984 の 113 頁 Fig.31・32）で 17 世紀後半～ 18 世紀初頭の肥前陶磁器と共に出土している。商業サルベージ商品「ナンキンカーゴ」（推定 1752 年沈没のヘルダーマルセン号引揚げ品）にあり、1750 年頃とする。左営鳳山県旧城にも見られる。

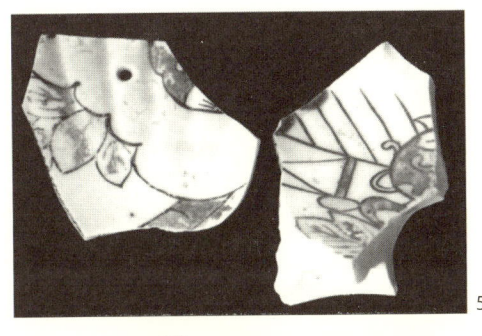
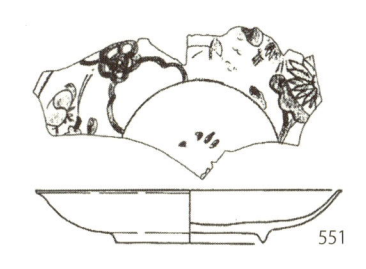
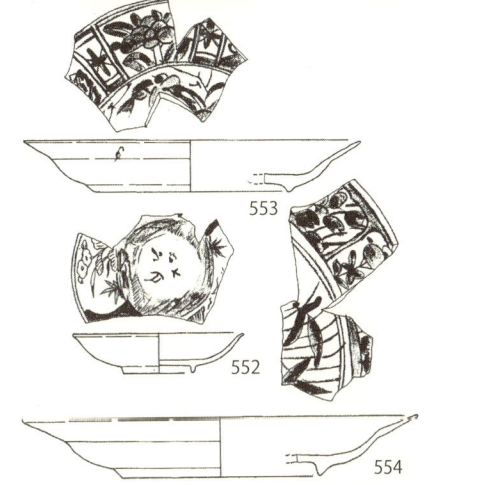
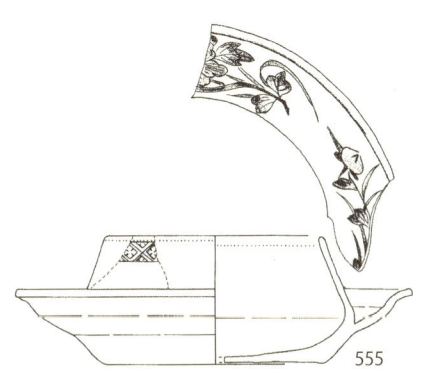

Fig.105 バンテン・ラーマ遺跡
Banten Lama Site, Ⅵ-1 period, 肥前陶磁 Japanese Hizen ceramics

絵具で塗りつぶして隠す。中央に花卉、内側面の窓内に草花を描く[170]。Fig.105-551 は 284 個体。Fig.105-552 は 41 個体。1690〜18 世紀前半。有田産。

　Fig.105-553 は染付芙蓉手皿。口銹を施し、見込に果木文を描き、内側面は区画内に花卉文と宝文を描き込む。区画内や区画間の文様表現も中国磁器を手本とした芙蓉手意匠からは変化している[171]。7 個体。1690〜1740 年代。

　Fig.105-554 は染付芙蓉手皿。芙蓉手の特徴である内側面文様は中国の芙蓉手意匠とは著しく異なる。内側面の大きい区画内には牡丹、菊、果木を 6 方に配す。その区画間には花卉文を描く。見込は花盆文と思われる文様が描かれる[172]。4 個体。1700〜40 年代。有田産。

　Fig.105-555 は染付鍔付鉢。本来、蓋付であり、鍔部上面に牡丹折枝を描き、口縁部に四方襷文帯をめぐらす。平底の底部は無釉。3 個体。18 世紀前半。有田産。

---

170 こうした色絵のソーサーは日本国内では長崎や山口県萩城下町遺跡（山口県埋蔵文化財センター 2002 の 93 頁図 56 は色絵素地）などで少量出土している。日本以外ではインドネシアで出土しているほか、オランダ・アムステルダムで出土例（佐賀県立九州陶磁文化館 2000 の図 267〜272）がある。ヨーロッパにおける伝世品は多い。

171 類例はパサール・イカン遺跡（佐賀県立九州陶磁文化館 1990 の図 222）やジャカルタの進藤コレクション（佐賀県立九州陶磁文化館 1990 の図 53〜56）にあり、日本国内では長崎出島（長崎市教育委員会 1986 の Fig.37-3）で出土している。有田・稗古場窯（大橋 1995 の第 2 図 I-イ）などで見られる。

172 類品は進藤コレクションにある。

12. Ⅵ-2期（18世紀後半頃）

ブトン・ウォリオ城

（1）中国の陶磁器

〈青花ほか〉

●景徳鎮窯

Fig.106-556は青花梵字文皿。バンテン・ラーマでも出土（Fig.108-578）。

Fig.106-557はヨーロッパ輸出向けの青花皿。いわゆるウィロウパターンのような意匠の可能性がある。

Fig.106-558はヨーロッパ輸出向けの青花皿。バンテン・ラーマでも出土（Fig.109-586）しているような、いわゆるウィロウパターンのような意匠である。

Fig.106-559は変形の五彩皿。色絵具は変質しているが、おそらく粉彩タイプと思われる。18世紀後半〜19世紀前半。

Fig.106-560は青花合子。

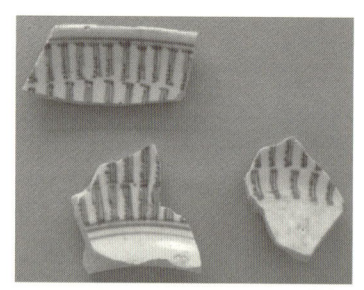
556a

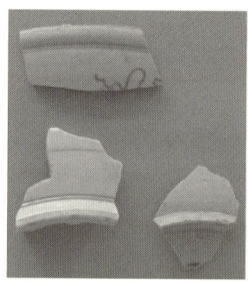
556b

557

558

559a

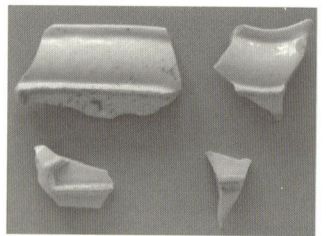
559b

560

Fig.106 ブトン・ウォリオ城跡
Buton Wolio Fort, Ⅵ-2 period, 中国景徳鎮陶磁
Chinese Jingdezhen ceramics

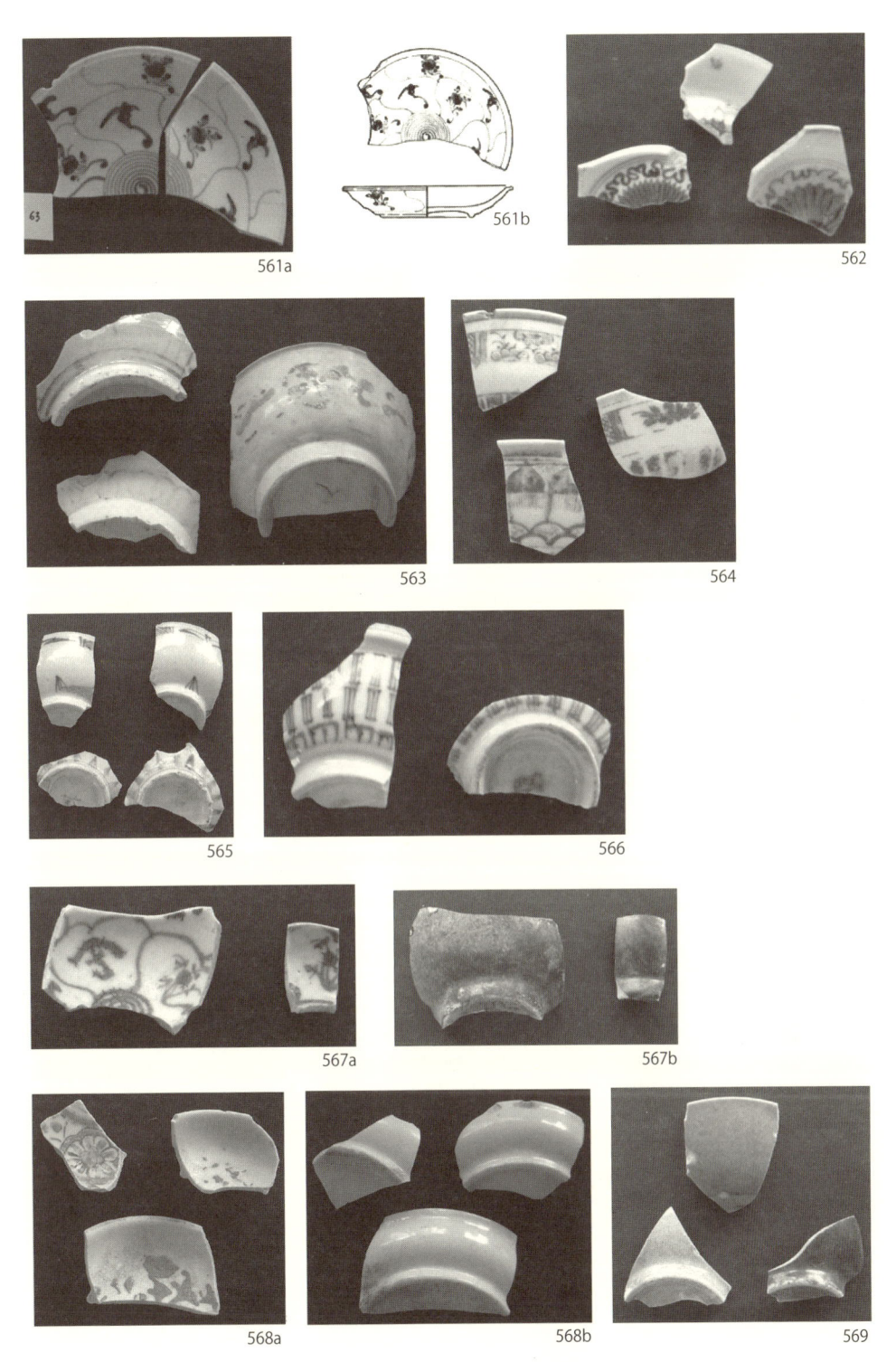

Fig.107 ブトン・ウォリオ城跡
Buton Wolio Fort, Ⅵ-2 period, 中国福建陶磁 Chinese Fujian ceramics

●福建

Fig.107-561 は青花仙芝祝寿文皿。バンテン・ラーマでは景徳鎮産と考えられるものも出土（Fig.108-575）[173]。仙芝祝寿文の意匠は 18 世紀に多く作られ、肥前磁器にも影響を与えた。日本では 18 世紀後半から幕末にかけて肥前や瀬戸・美濃で碗・皿などが作られた。

Fig.107-562 は外反りの器形の青花皿。見込に菊花と波状の唐草文様を表す。バンテン・ラーマでは外反りでなく丸形の皿が出土している（Fig.110-597）。

Fig.107-563 は五彩碗。左上 1 点は見込蛇の目釉剥ぎした素地。

Fig.107-564 は五彩碗の口縁部であり、口縁端を小さく外に折る。以上のような碗は 18 世紀。

●徳化窯

この時期の徳化窯製品の特徴は、型成形と口禿であること。徳化窯は 17 世紀まで白磁中心であり青花の例はほとんどなかったが、18 世紀には青花の粗製品が沢山作られ広く流通した。

Fig.107-565, 566 は青花碗類。主に丸形の小碗が多いが、Fig.107-566 の左上 1 点は口縁部を折り返した器形であり、用途的にも他と異なり、蓋付碗の使い方が推測される。

Fig.107-567 は褐釉青花小碗であり、内面にコバルトで仙芝祝寿文を描く。

Fig.107-568 は五彩の小皿。

Fig.107-569 は外面に瑠璃釉、内面に透明釉をかけ分けた碗。

バンテン・ラーマ遺跡

（1）中国の陶磁器

〈青花ほか〉

●景徳鎮窯

Fig.108-570 は五彩手付碗。こうした手付のカップはソーサー付のチョコレートカップと考えられる。外面に五彩が施される。1 個体。18 世紀。

Fig.108-571 は五彩碗。コーヒーなどの飲用のカップであろう。外面に帆船を黒絵具中心に表す。帆船文もヨーロッパからの注文で 18 世紀に多く描かれた。1 個体。18 世紀。

Fig.108-572 は五彩碗。外面に赤を吹き付けた地に白抜きの窓絵を粉彩で飾り、高台内に「大清乾隆年製」銘を染付する[174]。12 個体。18 世紀後半〜 19 世紀初。

Fig.108-573 は五彩蓋。鉢の蓋と思われるが、外面に粉彩で草花を表し、高台内に赤で蘭花を描く。53 個体。18 世紀中葉〜 19 世紀初。

Fig.108-574 は五彩鉢の蓋。黒絵具で輪宝文や文字？を描く。1 個体。18 世紀中葉〜 19 世紀初。

---

173 トプカプ宮殿でも景徳鎮のものがある（トプカプ宮殿蔵品 Fig.2543）。
174 この種の碗は日本でも長崎のほか、各地で時折出土する。

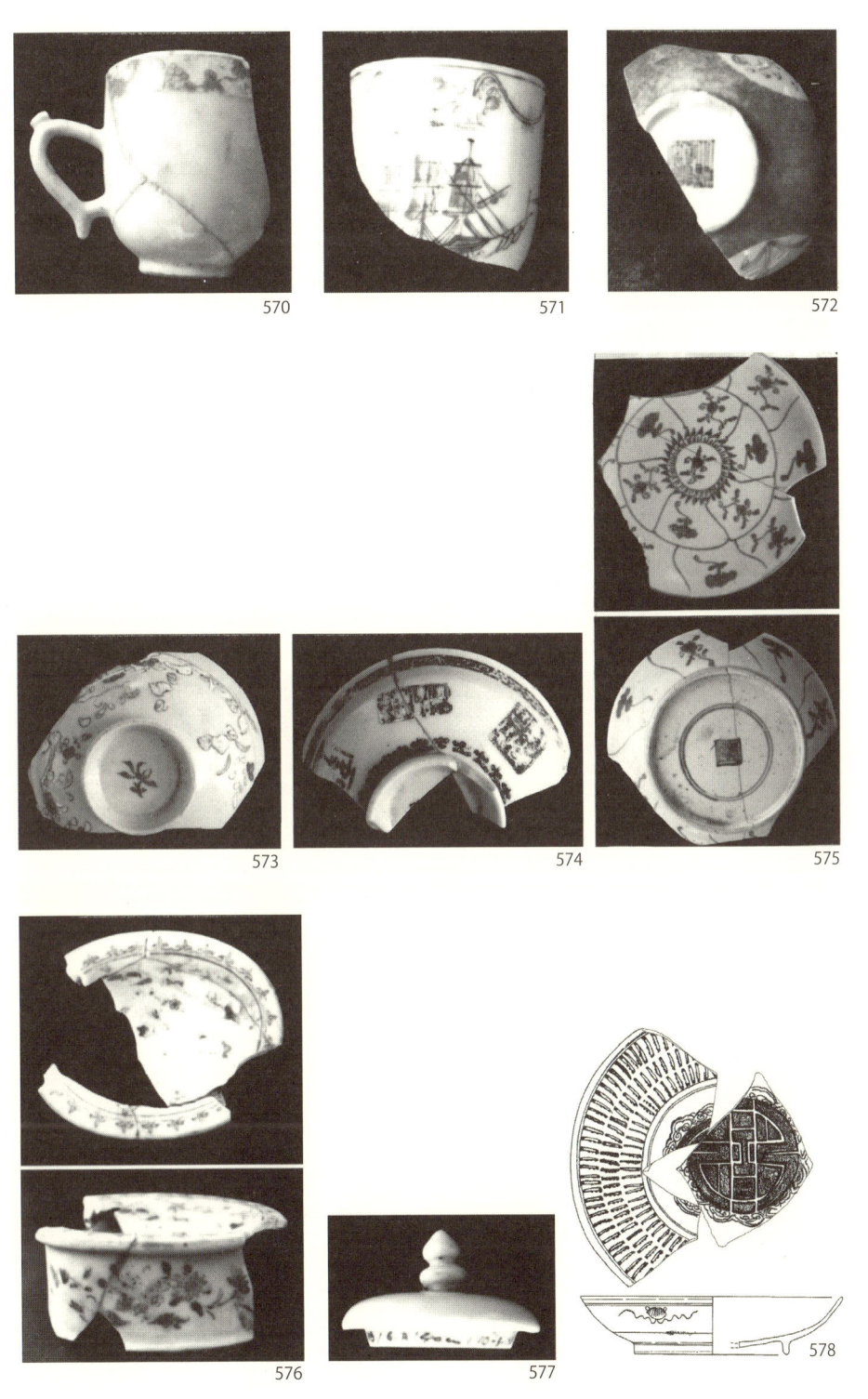

Fig.108 バンテン・ラーマ遺跡
Banten Lama Site, Ⅵ-2 period, 中国景徳鎮陶磁 Chinese Jingdezhen ceramics

　Fig.108-575は青花皿。内外に仙芝祝寿文を描き、高台内に二重方形枠内に渦状？の銘を染付する。福建地方の製品の可能性も若干残る。7個体。18世紀。有田でもこの種の文様の皿を18世紀後半から作り出す。

　Fig.108-576は五彩塩入れ。粉彩？で内外に花文様を施す。こうした塩入れはヨーロッパのサービスセットの一つであり、18世紀に見られる器種である。2個体。18世紀。

　Fig.108-577は白磁蓋[175]。12個体。18世紀。

　Fig.108-578は青花皿。産地が景徳鎮か福建かは明確ではないタイプ。見込に寿字？、内側面に梵字文を連ねる。80個体。18世紀。類例はブトン・ウォリオ城（Fig.106-556）にあるが、口縁形や材料などに微妙な違いがある。本例はFig.106-556より後出と推測される。

　Fig.109-579は青花小坏。外面に山水、見込に水に岩と思われる文様を染付する。86個体。18世紀。

　Fig.109-580は青花小坏。Fig.109-584と同様の意匠を外面に描く。高台内には「若深珍蔵」銘を染付する。42個体。18世紀中葉～末。

　Fig.109-581は青花小坏。外面と見込には花唐草を描く[176]。9個体。

　Fig.109-582は青花小坏。内外に仙芝祝寿文を描く[177]。高台内に青花銘を施す。25個体。18世紀後半～19世紀初。

　Fig.109-583は青花小坏。底部を碁笥底状に削る。外面に花唐草を描く。極めて小さく、日本では沖縄で比較的多く見られ、沖縄の壺屋焼がそれを模した陶器を18世紀から19世紀頃に作っている。おそらく泡盛など強い酒を飲むのに使ったと考えられる。バンテン・ラーマでの用法はわからないが出土量は多くはない。2個体。18世紀後半～19世紀前半。

　Fig.109-584は青花皿。見込と内側面に青銅器の意匠から取ったと思われる文様を描く。61個体。18世紀中葉～末。

　Fig.109-585は青花皿。見込に花卉文を散らし、見込周囲に如意頭もしくは日本で輪宝文と呼ぶ文様の連続文をめぐらし、口縁部にはヨーロッパで好まれるボーダーを細かく描く[178]。1個体。18世紀。

　Fig.109-586は青花折縁皿。いわゆるウィロウパターンの意匠である。見込は柳を中央に配した中国風景を描き、周囲に青海波文帯、内側面に波涛文帯、口縁部に幾何学文帯を描き込む。この意匠もヨーロッパ向けの代表的な意匠の一つである。底部にハリ支えの痕が見られるが、肥前・有田磁器に見られるハリ支え痕に倣ったものと思われ、中国磁器でもヨーロッパ向けの中にいくらか見られるものである。149個体。18世紀中葉～末。

175　この宝珠形のつまみをもつ独特の器形はタイ向け磁器に多く見られ、ポルトガル例は五彩だが、同様の形状の蓋をもつ。

176　類品はロプブリ遺跡出土品（Chandavij 1989）にあり、また1763年没の伝売茶翁用品（佐賀県立博物館1983の22頁）にある。日本でも遺跡出土例は沖縄や長崎中心に少なくない。

177　この意匠の小坏や小碗などは沖縄や長崎などを中心に比較的多く出土している。そのため肥前磁器も18世紀後半からこの意匠の碗皿を作ったし、瀬戸美濃系の磁器なども19世紀にこの意匠の染付をたくさん作る。

178　似通ったデザインの例はトプカプ宮殿蔵品Fig.2595があり、1750～70年代とする。

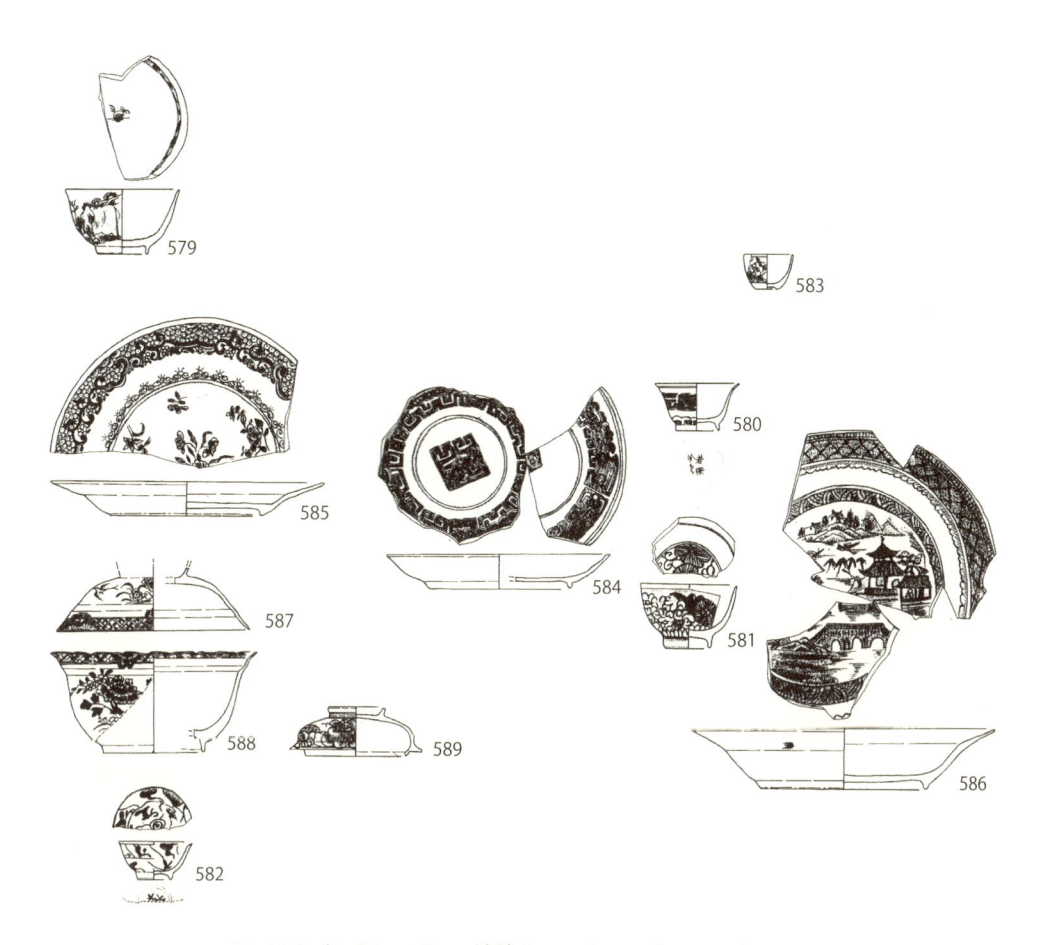

Fig.109 バンテン・ラーマ遺跡 Banten Lama Site, Ⅵ-2 period,
中国景徳鎮陶磁 Chinese Jingdezhen ceramics

　Fig.109-587, 588 は青花蓋付鉢。Fig.109-587 は蓋であり、外面主文は草花と鳥を描く。
口縁部に四方襷文帯の中に花かと思われる文様を配す。この口縁部文様は Fig.102-536 の
皿と同様と考えられる。同類品は 25 個体。Fig.109-588 は身であり、外面主文は草花を
描く。口縁部外面は蓋と同様であるが、内面にも四方襷文帯を描く[179]。14 個体。18 世紀。

　Fig.109-589 は青花蓋。外面に花唐草を線書きのみで描く[180]。15 個体。18 世紀後半頃。

　●福建

　Fig.110-590 は青花碗。外面に寿字と牡丹唐草文を描く。こうした鉢と呼んでもよい大
振りの碗は文様の種類が多い[181]。36 個体。18 世紀。福建南部地方。

　Fig.110-591, 592 は青花小碗。型押しによって成形し、口禿が特徴。Fig.110-591 は口

179 類似器形の小さいものはトプカプ宮殿蔵品 Fig.2641 にあり、1750〜80 年代とする。
180 類品はロプブリ遺跡で出土し、トプカプ宮殿蔵品 Fig.2394 にあり、1720〜50 年代とする。
181 日本でも沖縄で多量に見られるほか、長崎などで少量の出土例がある。左営鳳山県旧城をはじめ東南アジアには多い。

Fig.110 バンテン・ラーマ遺跡
Banten Lama Site, Ⅵ-2 period, 中国福建陶磁 Chinese Fujian ceramics

縁部に丸と点の文様帯、Fig.110-592は窓絵と斜格子地文帯を描く[182]。Fig.110-592は215個体。18世紀。徳化窯系。

Fig.110-593は白磁小碗。型押し成形と口禿が特徴[183]。この素地に青絵具中心の簡単な色絵付したものもある。588個体。18世紀後半〜19世紀前半。徳化窯系。

Fig.110-594は青花皿。見込に唐人文を描き、高台内に「和美」銘を染付する[184]。30個体。18世紀。

Fig.110-595, 596は青花皿。Fig.110-595は見込に鶴を描き、高台内に「源裕」銘を染付する。103個体。18世紀。Fig.110-596は見込を花文で埋める。19個体。18世紀。

Fig.110-597は青花皿。見込に花唐草文を描き、高台内に「□興」銘を染付する[185]。265個体。18世紀。

Fig.110-598は青花皿。見込に龍を描き、高台内に銘を記す。同類品は43個体。18世紀。

Fig.110-599は青花皿。内面から外側面にかけて雲龍文を表し、高台内に銘を記す[186]。12個体。18世紀中葉〜末。これらは福建南部地方産。

Fig.110-600は青花皿。型押しによる成形と口禿が特徴。見込に龍と思われる文様を染付する[187]。245個体。18世紀。徳化窯系。

〈中国陶器〉

Fig.111-601は緑釉植木鉢。素地は精土を用い薄く作る。写真右は丸形であり、型を使って成形する。外面に緑釉を施す。16個体。写真左は角形であり、粘土板を貼り合わせて成形し外面に緑釉を施す[188]。11個体。17世紀後半〜18世紀。

Fig.111-602は無釉焼締陶器水注。急須の把手であり、注口は把手と直角の位置に付く[189]。10個体。17〜18世紀。

(2) 肥前の陶磁器ほか

●肥前陶器ほか

Fig.112-603は陶器耳付鍋。外に折った口縁部に耳を貼り付ける。無釉の底部脇に小さな角状の足を貼り付ける。淡褐色の素地に透明釉を施すものと、鉄釉を施すものがある。

---

182 両者とも、沖縄でたくさん出土するし、東南アジアでは普通に見られる。Fig.110-592は左営鳳山県旧城出土品やトプカプ宮殿蔵品Fig.2647にある。

183 日本では沖縄でもっとも多く出土しているが、他地域でも時折出土している。左営鳳山県旧城でも出土しており、東南アジアにかけて多量に流通したものと見られる。

184 この種の皿は、日本では沖縄（沖縄県立埋蔵文化財センター 2001bの第26図13）で出土例が多い。

185 類品は徳化窯にある（徐 1990の88〜97頁）。

186 類品はトプカプ宮殿蔵品Fig.2611にあり、こうした雑器がトプカプに渡ったことは興味深い。

187 日本では沖縄、長崎で出土するほかは少ないが、左営鳳山県旧城をはじめ東南アジアでは多い。商業サルベージ商品「ナンキンカーゴ」（推定1752年沈没のヘルダーマルセン引揚げ品）（Jörg 1986の図88）にあり、1750年頃とする。

188 こうした緑釉陶器は日本では長崎で出土しているが少ない。

189 類品はブンタウ・カーゴや左営鳳山県旧城出土品に見られる。日本では売茶翁（1763年没）が用いたと伝えられる伝世品がある。

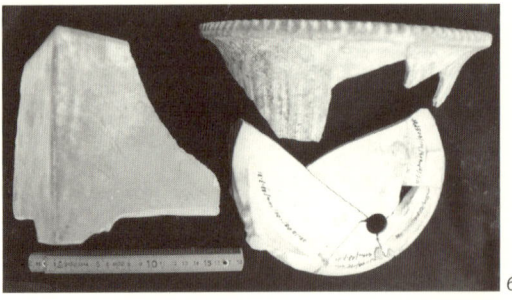

Fig.111 バンテン・ラーマ遺跡
Banten Lama Site, Ⅵ-2 period, 中国陶器 Chinese Stoneware ceramics

Fig.112 バンテン・ラーマ遺跡
Banten Lama Site, Ⅵ-2 period, 肥前陶磁 Japanese Hizen ceramics

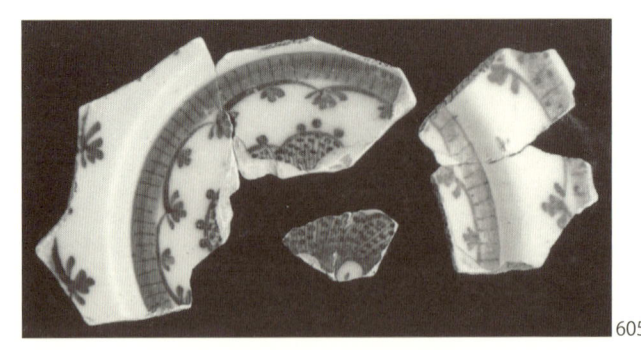

Fig.113 バンテン・ラーマ遺跡
Banten Lama Site, Ⅵ-2 period, ヨーロッパ陶磁 European ceramics

こうした耳付鍋は関西系の窯で 18 世紀に作られ、日本では一般的である[190]。16 個体。

　Fig.112-604 は褐釉甕。甕の肩部と底部（写真右）の破片。内面に叩き成形による格子目状の当て具痕が見られる。内外に鉄釉に近いものを施す[191]。肥前の壺・甕類は初期には青海波状の当て具痕であった。バンテン・ラーマで細片であるが 1 点青海波状の叩き痕をもつものがあり、肥前陶器の輸出の年代が遡る可能性も残る。1 個体。18 世紀か。

（3）ヨーロッパ陶磁

　Fig.113-605 は藍絵皿。白釉の上に青顔料で見込に孔雀？などを描く。胎土は粗い軟質陶器。畳付の釉は使用によって剝がれている。6 個体。18 世紀か。オランダ。

13. Ⅶ−1 期（19 世紀前半頃）

ブトン・ウォリオ城

（1）中国の陶磁器
〈青花〉
●景徳鎮窯
　Fig.114-606 は青花碗。19 世紀初～中葉。

　Fig.114-607 は青花碗。外反りに作る碗に花唐草文を描く。見込にも花卉文を描く。日本でも多く見られ、幕末の薩摩南京皿山などの磁器に影響が見られる。

　Fig.114-608 は青花であり、花唐草文を描いた皿。このタイプは景徳鎮か福建産か明確ではない。

　Fig.114-609 はいわゆるペンシルドローイングで花唐草文を染付した青花蓋付鉢。18 世紀末～ 19 世紀中葉。

バンテン・ラーマ遺跡

（1）中国の陶磁器
〈青花〉
●景徳鎮窯
　Fig.115-610 は青花碗。外面腰部に蓮弁文、見込に花卉文を描き、高台内に方形枠内に「大清嘉慶年製」銘を染付する[192]。4 個体。19 世紀前半。

●福建

---

190 日本以外では南アフリカのケープタウンで出土しており、2 ケ所に共通するのはオランダ勢力が強い点である。

191 こうした叩き成形による肥前の甕が日本以外で初めて確認されたのが本例であるが、その後オランダでも出土例（未報告、アムステルダム考古局で筆者実見）が加わっている。

192 この意匠の碗も日本でしばしば見られる。出土例はとくに沖縄（沖縄県立埋蔵文化財センター 2001c の第 28 図 31、皿形は沖縄県教育委員会 1999 の第 29 図 25）に多いが、バンテン・ラーマでは比較的少ない。

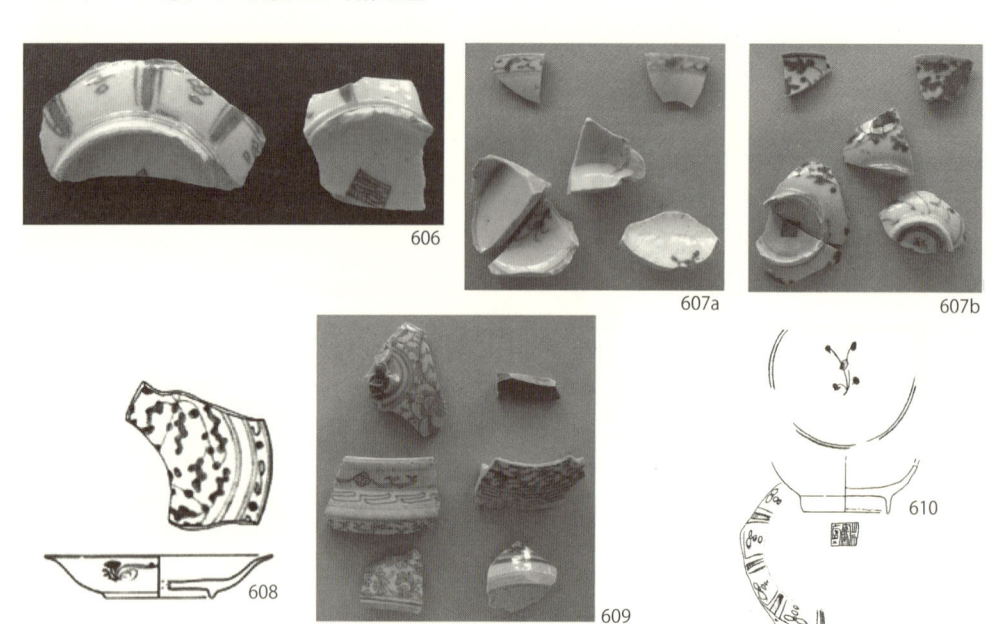

606

607a

607b

608

609

610

Fig.114 ブトン・ウォリオ城跡 Buton Wolio Fort,
Ⅶ−1 period, 中国景徳鎮陶磁 Chinese Jingdezhen ceramics

Fig.115 バンテン・ラーマ遺跡
Banten Lama Site,
Ⅶ−1 period, 中国景徳鎮陶磁
Chinese Jingdezhen ceramics

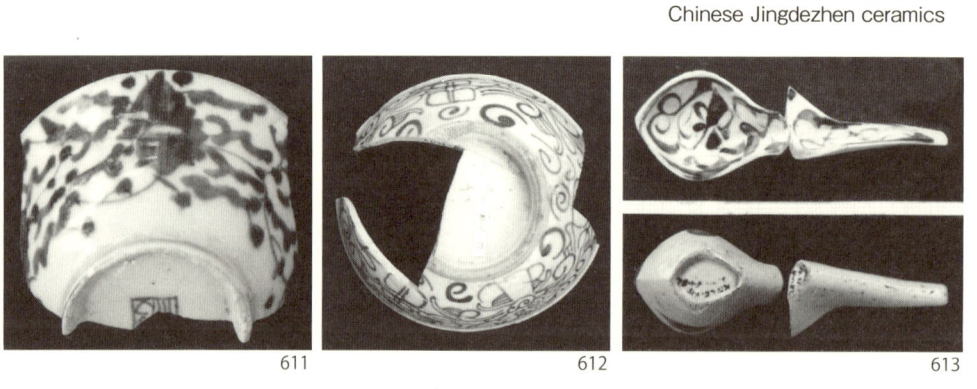

611

612

613

Fig.116 バンテン・ラーマ遺跡
Banten Lama Site, Ⅶ−1 period, 中国福建陶磁 Chinese Fujian ceramics

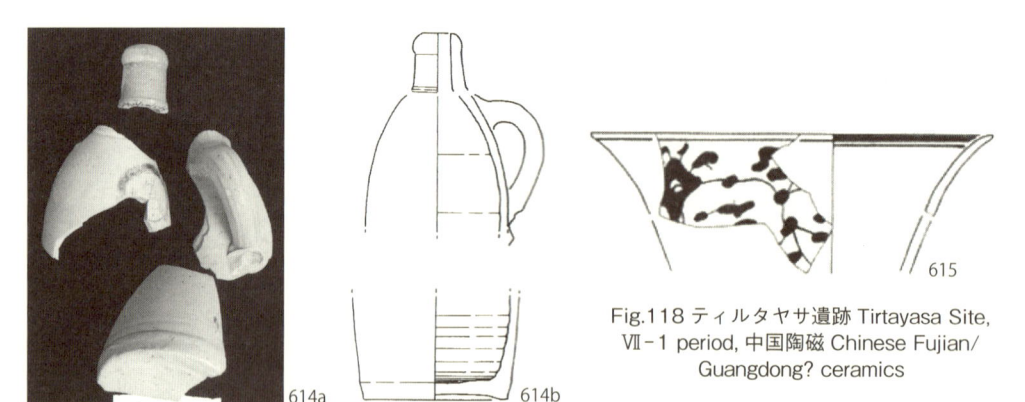

614a

614b

615

Fig.118 ティルタヤサ遺跡 Tirtayasa Site,
Ⅶ−1 period, 中国陶磁 Chinese Fujian/
Guangdong? ceramics

Fig.117 バンテン・ラーマ遺跡 Banten Lama Site,
Ⅶ−1 period, ヨーロッパ陶磁 European ceramics

Fig.116-611 は青花碗。このタイプは景徳鎮か福建産かが明確でない。外面に花唐草を描く。高台内にも銘を染付する。日本では沖縄にもっとも多いが、他にも少量出土例はある。2 個体。19 世紀前半〜中葉。

Fig.116-612 は青花鉢。外面に花唐草を描く[193]。20 個体。福建系。18 世紀中葉〜 19 世紀初。

Fig.116-613 は青花散蓮華。内面に唐草状の文様を描く[194]。38 個体。18 世紀後半〜 19 世紀前半。

（2）ヨーロッパ陶磁

Fig.117-614 は塩釉炻器の手付瓶。肩に刻印を施す。29 個体。18 世紀〜 19 世紀中葉。

ティルタヤサ遺跡

（1）中国の陶磁器

〈青花〉

●福建か

Fig.118-615 は青花碗。外反形であり、口縁内側を帯状にコバルトで塗る。外面にラフな花唐草文を描く。景徳鎮か福建産か明確ではない。19 世紀前半 - 中葉。

14. Ⅶ–2 期（19 世紀後半頃）

ブトン・ウォリオ城

（1）肥前系の磁器

Fig.119-616 のように肥前系の明治〜大正の型紙摺による染付碗がわずかに出土している。これは腰部の文様などから愛媛の砥部焼と推測される。

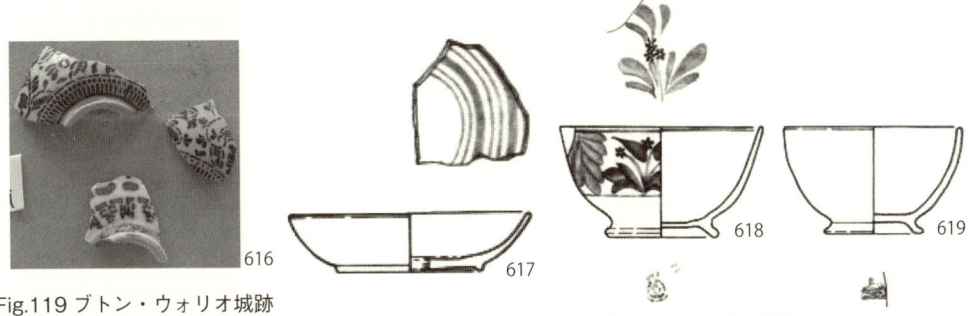

Fig.119 ブトン・ウォリオ城跡
Buton Wolio Fort, Ⅶ–2 period,
肥前系陶磁 Japanese Hizen
ceramics

Fig.120 ブトン・ウォリオ城跡
Buton Wolio Fort, Ⅶ–2 period, ヨーロッパ陶磁
European ceramics

193 日本ではあまり見ないが、左営鳳山県旧城、ホイアン、ロプブリ遺跡などで多く見られる。
194 日本では沖縄、長崎などで少量出土しており、ロプブリ遺跡でも見られる。

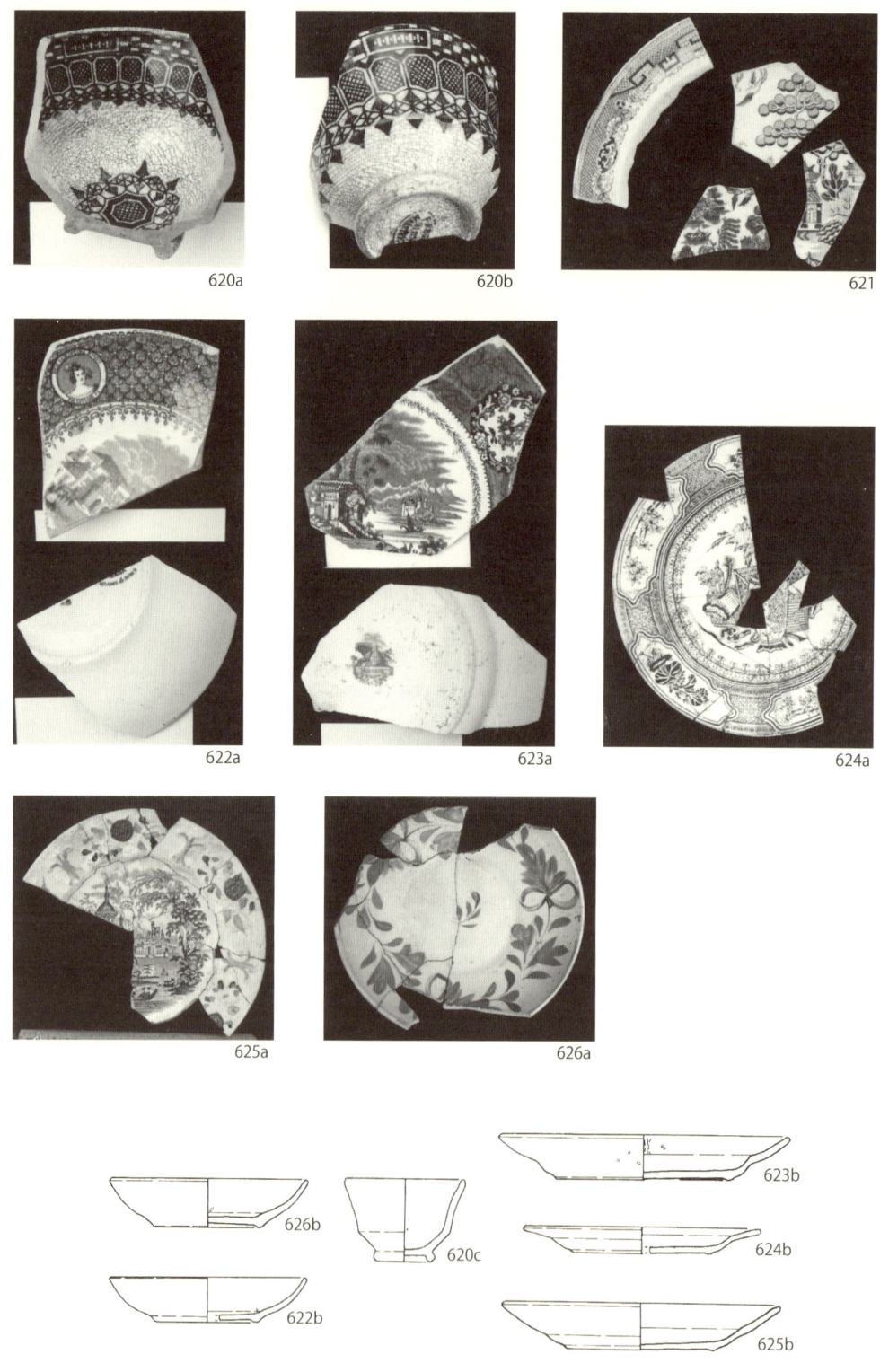

Fig.121 バンテン・ラーマ遺跡
Banten Lama Site, Ⅶ-2 period, ヨーロッパ陶磁 European ceramics

(2) ヨーロッパの陶器

Fig.120-617／619 はヨーロッパの陶器。19 世紀後半以降は中国陶磁が激減し、食器はヨーロッパの陶器が主となる。

バンテン・ラーマ遺跡

(1) ヨーロッパの陶器

Fig.121-620 はカップ。青顔料で Alpine パターンを銅版転写したもの。高台内に Fig.121-622 と同様のマークが転写される。

Fig.121-621 は銅版転写皿、ウィロウパターン。写真下はオランダ・ペトゥルス・レグゥート窯。他はイギリス産。19 世紀中葉。

Fig.121-622 はソーサー。青顔料による銅版転写皿。底部に「ADAMS ＆ SONS」の銘が見られる。イギリス・アダムス＆サーンズ窯。

Fig.121-623 は銅版転写青花皿。オリエンタルパターンの意匠を青顔料で表す。他に見込文様が異なり、緑顔料で表したものもあり、高台内に「ORIENTAL」のマークを転写。29 個体。オランダ・マーストリヒトのペトゥルス・レグゥート窯。

Fig.121-624 は銅版転写皿。黒絵具による釉下彩。高台内に「□ADAMS」のマークが記される。イギリス産。19 世紀後半。

Fig.121-625 は側面に陽刻文を施した銅版転写皿。側面は陽刻による草花文の上から紫（赤か）・黄・黄緑・水色で彩絵を施す。10 個体。同型の白磁皿が別にある。11 個体。イギリス産か。19 世紀中葉〜末。

Fig.121-626 は色絵皿。内面に緑・青・赤で草花を表す[195]。カップ＆ソーサーのソーサー。47 個体。

---

195 類例は長崎市上町遺跡出土品（永松 1993）にあり、イギリス・アダムス＆サーンズ窯とされる。

Ⅲ　陶磁器の編年と特色

　インドネシアにおいて 1989 年以来、繰り返し行った出土陶磁調査によりおびただしい陶磁器資料を分類整理してきた。調査の開始の早いものからあげると、バンテン・ラーマ遺跡、ティルタヤサ遺跡、ソンバ・オプー城、ブトン・ウォリオ城、トロウラン遺跡である。

　その分類整理の結果は、主なものを逐次報告してきたが、今回、その全体を Ⅰ-1 期 ～ Ⅶ-2 期までの 14 の時期に分け、種類や産地を考慮しながら解説を加えた。

　これを通覧するとインドネシアにおける土器を除く、貿易陶磁器の各時期の様相を概観できるが、広域にわたるため、5 遺跡をまたがった特徴について、ここで述べてみたい。

1. 遺跡の盛衰

　まずは、貿易陶磁器の年代観により、取り上げた各遺跡がいつ頃始まり、どのような時期に盛んであり、いつ頃衰退していったかを知ることができる。

〈トロウラン遺跡〉

　5 遺跡のうちでもっとも古い時期に繁栄期があったトロウラン遺跡は、マジャパイト王国時代以前と王国時代の、中国・ベトナム・タイの陶磁器を分類整理してきた。王国以後の陶磁器も、16 世紀後半～17 世紀前半の明末期の中国陶磁器も少量出土し、17 世紀後半の肥前磁器合子など 9 点、17 世紀後半～18 世紀の中国磁器なども少量ある。19 世紀の中国磁器や西洋陶器も少量ある。このように王国が滅亡した後も、人々の生活が営まれた地域であろうから、少量の貿易陶磁器の出土が継続して見られる。しかし、それは王国時代の出土傾向とは量的・質的に著しく後退するのである。そうした時期の貿易陶磁は肥前磁器以外、本稿では割愛した。

　中国、ベトナム、タイの陶磁器の質量がⅡ期（13 世紀末～14 世紀）、Ⅲ期（15 世紀～16 世紀初）に集中していることで、マジャパイト王国が 14、15 世紀に栄えた国であることを裏付けるものである。13 世紀末に始まるというのは妥当であるし、王国の滅亡については 15 世紀末～16 世紀初の少量の中国磁器やわずかながらもベトナム青花が出土している点から、16 世紀初の滅亡説を裏付けている。

　この豊富な内容のベトナム陶磁器は、15 世紀後半～16 世紀初の沈没船資料として知られるホイアン沖引揚げ品[1]との比較により、この資料に類似するものが、本遺跡出土のベ

1　Ⅱ章註 29

トナム陶磁器の最も新しいグループであり、多くはこれより古式のタイプである。ベトナム陶磁器の年代の重要な基準資料として知られる、トルコ・トプカプ宮殿博物館蔵の大和8年（1450）銘の天球瓶より古いタイプが多いのである。青花であれば15世紀前半頃のものが多いようであり、他の白磁・青磁・鉄絵などは14世紀のものが少なくない。15世紀には、ベトナム青花に加え、タイの青磁と鉄絵陶器が多くなる。もちろん中国龍泉窯の青磁も多量に出土しているが、このような東南アジアの青花・青磁・鉄絵も多くなることがトロウラン遺跡の特色である。

　マジャパイト王国時代に当たる貿易陶磁器は内容を見ると、13世紀末から14世紀には龍泉窯の青磁も酒海壺を始め、盤・鉢・瓶など高級な青磁が少なくない。そして14世紀後半の元末・明初でも景徳鎮の青花大壺類など高級磁器が多い。磁州窯の翡翠釉や鉄絵陶器大壺も14世紀に当たる。15世紀に比べ、14世紀には中国の青磁・青花・紅釉・釉裏紅・白磁・翡翠釉・鉄絵などの高級な大壺・瓶類が多いことが特徴として挙げられる。それは明・洪武（1368〜98）期の大壺まで見られる。明に入ると洪武期の後は、瓶などで、いわゆる威信財的なものは永楽（1403〜24）期の天球瓶や梅瓶などが官窯クラスのもので見られる。青花碗も官窯クラスのものが出土しているが、永楽頃までである。そして本遺跡出土の14世紀後半から15世紀初めにかけてと推測される青花を中心に被熱痕が多い。大火が想定されるのである。記録からは14世紀後半のハヤム・ウルク王（在位1350−89）が名君とされるが、15世紀初には国内で対立が生じていると考えられ、鄭和の第1回航海の際にジャワに寄航したが、東王と西王の抗争が記録される。陶磁器から推定される火災がこのような抗争時に起きた可能性が高いのである。この点については深見純生氏の研究[2]によると、鄭和の第1回航海（1405−07）の際、マジャパイトの都で内戦に巻き込まれ170人の死者が出た（51頁）。この内戦により王都の中に東西2つの王宮があり、その間の対立と内戦であったと明らかになった。記録などから見ると、この内戦時に王宮、あるいはこうした威信財的な磁器の保管場所が焼けたことの表れかと推測される。

　王国自体はそれで弱体化したとは言えないと深見氏は述べる。過去の歴史家は史料の誤読があり、実際は中国への朝貢が1450年代まで多いとする。中国ではマジャパイトを「爪哇」と記すが、15世紀のジャワの朝貢は1400年代11回、1410年代7回、1420年代14回、1430年代7回［実は8回］、1440年代8回、1450年代3回、1460年代2回、1470・80年代0回、1490年代2回とする。よって、マジャパイトの対明朝貢貿易は1450年代前半まで持続的に行われていたと言える。このように15世紀と言っても朝貢貿易は1460年代までであり、15世紀後半には行われない時期が20年以上あったことがわかる。これは中国明の朝貢体制の中で、琉球も1440年代に朝貢回数減少に転じるので、1450年代以降の朝貢回数減少の原因は明朝側の制限、つまり消極姿勢にあった。この原因は明の

2　深見 2014

財政悪化であったとする。

　とはいえ、1465 年から 30 年間爪哇の朝貢がないのは爪哇側に何らかの原因があったと考えるべきであろうとする。15 世紀後半、特に 1460 年代以後、その地位はムラカ（マラッカ）やアユタヤに移っていったとする。トロウランをはじめインドネシアではほとんど見ないベトナム・タイの陶磁器がラオス[3]で多く見られることはその表れかもしれない。1460 年代以前まで朝貢が続いたことをトロウラン遺跡出土の多量の中国龍泉窯青磁が示している。つまり、青磁の碗皿が 15 世紀中葉頃までのものがほとんどであり、後半のタイプの青磁は少量となること、景徳鎮の青花も 15 世紀初頃の後は 15 世紀末〜16 世紀初のレナ・カーゴ引揚げ品[4]に近いものが少量出土しているが、明らかなその間のものは見ないのである。まさに、朝貢回数の変化に比例するような中国青磁、青花の出土量である。15 世紀後半頃の割合に絞ってみるとトロウラン遺跡出土の龍泉窯青磁の碗皿は 15 世紀としてあげた 1,120 個体中 1% 弱であるし、景徳鎮青花は 263 個体中 44% 位であるが、多いのはレナ・カーゴ引揚げ品に近い。つまり、弘治（1488 – 1505）頃と推測される青花磁器である。

〈ソンバ・オプー城〉

　次にゴワ王国の居城ソンバ・オプー城は、15 世紀前半頃の中国・景徳鎮青花が少量とタイの青磁や鉄絵陶器が出土しており、王国の居城としての機能は 15 世紀前半頃に始まると考えられる。それがⅢ-2 期（15 世紀後半〜16 世紀初）に景徳鎮磁器も多くなり、ベトナム青花も加わり、タイの陶磁器もあるなどにより、盛んになることが分かる。さらにⅣ期（15 世紀末〜16 世紀）には景徳鎮磁器が多く出土し、ラオスのヴィエンチャンで多く見られるようなベトナム、タイ陶磁器はほとんど見られなくなる。マジャパイト王国滅亡により、ベトナム、タイ陶磁器が 16 世紀のインドネシア群島部に流通しなくなるのであろうか。今後も注意する必要がある。

　V-1 期（17 世紀前半）には景徳鎮磁器に加えて、というより漳州磁器の方が多く出土する。

　V-2 期（17 世紀後半）に福建南部産の粗放な磁器が少し見られるが、肥前磁器が多くなる。生田滋氏によると、ゴワ王国は 1530 年頃からマカッサル人がゴワ（マカッサル）を中心として国家を形成した[5]というが、出土陶磁器の内容からは 15 世紀には一定の勢力がこの地域に拠点的なものを作り始めていた可能性が考えられる。16 世紀から中国磁器が増えていくのは、生田氏が言うように、ゴワ王国は半島を統一すると、貿易と海賊活動に進出するようになった。特に 17 世紀に入ると、ゴワ王国はカリマンタン南岸、スンバワ島、

3　ベトナム陶磁については清水 2014。このうち、PL.15-18、20-28 などが、トロウラン遺跡に見られず、16 世紀頃と推測されるベトナム陶磁である。

4　Ⅱ章註 70

5　石澤・生田 2009

ロンボク島などを攻撃した。17世紀に入ると、ポルトガル人のほかに、イギリス、デンマーク両東インド会社、それにフランスもオランダ東インド会社に対抗してゴワに進出したと言う。さらに、オランダも商館を開設したことがあるが、王国は会社の貿易独占政策を拒否し、会社とは敵対関係に立つようになったとする。そして1641年にオランダがムラカを占領すると、ムラカに住むポルトガル人の多くがゴワに移動し、ここを基地として活動するようになった。オランダ東インド会社は1660年ブギス人の指導者アルン・パラッカがゴワ王国に対して反乱を起こしたのにつけ込み、1666年、ブギス人と同盟を結んでゴワを攻撃し、激しい戦闘の後、ゴワ王国のスルタン・ハサヌッディン（在位1653-69）を屈服させた。ハサヌッディンはもう一度抵抗したが、1669年には退位を余儀なくされ、要塞は会社のものとなり、すべてのヨーロッパ人・マレー人はゴワから追放されたとある。このように、1669年でゴワ王国は終わるが、出土陶磁器も1660年代前後の肥前磁器で基本的には終わることが、その歴史を物語っていると言える。

　ティルタヤサ遺跡のように1682年にオランダ軍に攻められ陥落して終わる場合には、1670～80年代の中国景徳鎮磁器などがかなり入ってくるのであるが、ゴワ王国ソンバ・オプー城の場合、1684年の展海令の前の1670～80年代初の中国磁器が少しずつ輸出が始まる段階に至る前で、オランダに滅ぼされ終わったために肥前磁器だけの段階で終わったと言える。

〈ブトン・ウォリオ城〉

　次はスラウェシの南東部に位置するブトン王国の居城ウォリオ城の出土陶磁である。ブトンは1542年にイスラーム化し、スルタンを君主とするイスラーム教国として現代まで続いたと言う。

　調査した陶磁資料では、16世紀以降の多量の陶磁器が1542年以降の王国の歴史を裏付けている形であるが、陶磁資料の中にそれ以前の13世紀から15世紀前半頃の間の中国龍泉窯の上質の青磁などが少量含まれていた（Fig.23-99左）。また15世紀前半頃、Ⅲ-1期のベトナム青花が少量出土している（Fig.27-150）。

　14世紀に遡る上質の龍泉窯青磁が何を意味するかであるが、ブトンが記録上の初見である、マジャパイト王国ハヤム・ウルク王時代の仏教宮廷詩人プラパンチャ作の宮廷年代記『ナーガラクルターガマ』（1365年）によると、ブトンがバンタユン（バンタエン）、ルゥック、ウダマカトラヤ（タラウド諸島）、マカッサル、バンガイ、スラヤルとともに属領として掲げられているという[6]。中国磁器を入手できるような勢力圏の中にブトンがいたことを推測できる。

　しかし隣接するゴア王国のソンバ・オプー城で見られたようにゴワ王国が栄え始めた

6　石井監修1991の241頁

15世紀後半〜16世紀初めの中国景徳鎮の青花は、ウォリオ城では出土していないから、ゴワ王国の方が早く栄え始めたと推測される。15世紀後半の確実な陶磁器は見られないから、イスラーム教国の成立に至るまでブトンに中国陶磁の流通が途絶するような状況があったと推測される。ブトンで1542年頃にはイスラーム教を奉じる王国の成立が伝えられるのを、中国磁器も裏付けている。以来、現代に至るまで、スルタンを君主とする王国が続いたのであるが、記録があまりないから詳しい歴史が分かるわけではない。しかし、豊富な質量の輸入磁器によって王国の力が17世紀、18世紀に頂点があったことが分かる。豊富な中国磁器は日本の江戸時代の遺跡では見られないものがほとんどであるが、ジャワ島のバンテン・ラーマ遺跡の内容と最も似通っている。オランダ東インド会社が双方に中国磁器をもたらしたためであろう。

ブトン・ウォリオ城Ⅱ−2期（14世紀）

中国の龍泉窯の青磁が少量出土している。青磁酒会壺か大瓶（Fig.23-99左）と思われるものは外面に鎬蓮弁文をヘラ彫りで表している。Fig.23-99右は磁州窯の鉄絵壺である。トロウラン遺跡のFig.6-56と同類と考えられる。14世紀のものであり、当時の高級品であり、通常の交易品である碗・皿に比べて、威信財的性格を持つ。

以上のように、この時期の輸入陶磁器は後の碗・皿のような食器類と違い、特殊なものが多い。上述のようにブトンが記録上の初見である、マジャパイト王国ハヤム・ウルク王時代の『ナーガラクルターガマ』には、属領としてあげられ、ブトンでは14世紀後半〜15世紀初の上質の青磁や磁州窯鉄絵が出土しているが、それ以後の中国磁器がないのは、マジャパイトのトロウラン遺跡で15世紀初の永楽期まで上質の中国磁器が見られるが、その後はそうした中国磁器が見られなくなる変化と何か関係があるのであろうか。トロウラン遺跡の場合、中国磁器に代わってベトナム陶磁に陶板をはじめ特別なものが多く見られるが、ブトンではそれはない。つまり、マジャパイト王国のトロウランと同様に威信財的な中国陶磁器が、15世紀になると見られなくなるのは中国側の事情によるのかもしれない。

ブトン・ウォリオ城Ⅳ期（15世紀末〜17世紀初）

Ⅳ−1期（16世紀前半頃）は中国・景徳鎮窯の青花の碗皿が主であり、五彩も少なからず見られる。

Ⅳ−2期（16世紀後半頃）になると、引き続き景徳鎮窯の青花碗皿が主であるが、福建・漳州窯の青花がわずかに加わり始める。

このほかタイの黒釉耳付壺なども出土している。

そうした広域流通した一般的なもののほか、法花の広口壺（Fig.35-194）かと思われる特殊な威信財的役割のものがある。肩部の破片であるが、産地は赤い土の特徴から中国北部の山西省あたりの可能性が高いと思われる。法花の産地についてはいまだ明確でないものが多い。如意頭文かと思われる枠の中に花束らしき文様を配し如意頭間に瓔珞文を表す

が、類似の如意頭、瓔珞の組み合わせの文様例は管見の限りでは瓶子形が多く、壺の例としてはジャカルタ国立博物館蔵の東カリマンタン発見とされる口の狭い壺が1例ある[7]。しかもこれほど複雑な瓔珞文様ではない。内面の状態からも広口壺の可能性を推測するのだが、いずれにせよこの種の法花としては、伝世の遺例に比べても、優れた水準の文様構成と言える。その意味でも法花の最盛期に達した時期とされる、15〜16世紀の中で作られたと推測される。

他にタイやミャンマー、中国の陶器が出土している。

ブトン・ウォリオ城Ⅴ-1期 （17世紀前半頃）

陶磁器の出土量は増大する。とくに景徳鎮窯と漳州窯の磁器が多量に出土する。碗皿だけでなく、大皿・小坏・合子・瓶など器種も豊かになる。また福建・徳化窯の白磁碗皿（Fig.51-263, 264）・合子や福建のいわゆる安平壺が見られる。他に1点ずつではあるが、肥前の染付手塩皿とヨーロッパのデルフトの白釉アルバレロ形壺が出土している。肥前の手塩皿は輸出用ではなく、日本以外での出土はバンテン・ラーマ遺跡（Fig.56-289）に次いで2例目である。

他にトラディスカント壺と呼ばれる三彩壺などはⅣ期、16世紀に含めたほうが良いものである。中国南部で作られたと考えられる。

この16〜17世紀の一般的な陶器として、中国南部の褐釉壺とタイの焼締め壺がある。詳細な年代は明らかでないが、明末頃の可能性が高いものである。

もう一つはタイのシンブリ窯の焼締め壺である。厚手であり、大阪府堺の遺跡出土品は硫黄が入っていた例があり、硝石・硫黄などの火薬原料などを入れるために16世紀後半〜17世紀に多く流通したものと推測される[8]。

ミャンマー産の陶器として、白濁釉大皿などと黒釉白彩大壺の胴部片がある。ミャンマーの陶器はインドネシアでも日本でも出土例は少ない。前者は日本でも平戸、長崎などで少し見られる程度であるし、後者も近年、大分県大友氏の中世府内町で出土した程度である。

17世紀中葉と明らかなものとして、肥前陶器の緑釉皿が1点ある。砂目積であり、インドネシアなど東南アジアでしばしば見られる17世紀後半の二彩手の大皿より古い。この時期の肥前陶器はバンテン・ラーマ遺跡などでもわずかに出土している。この17世紀がもっとも出土品が多いが、18世紀も引き続き多い。

ブトン・ウォリオ城Ⅴ-2期 （17世紀後半頃）

この時期は、景徳鎮磁器や漳州窯の磁器が激減し、代わって肥前磁器が多量に出土する。1644年以降、中国の内乱による中国磁器輸出激減のため、中国磁器の出土が1670年代まで減退したことが理由と考えられる。

7　Adhyatman 1981の図270、高さ20cm、15世紀とする。

8　大橋2004

　清王朝に抵抗を続けた鄭氏一派が貿易活動を活発に行なう中で、彼らとの関わりの強かったであろう福建広東地方の粗製品がかなり出土している（Fig.66-338 など）。密貿易によるものであろう。日本などではふつう見られないタイプの青花である。

　肥前磁器は 1660 年代以降のものがほとんどである。バンテン・ラーマやパサール・イカン遺跡で見られたような嬉野市吉田窯などの粗製品は見られない。つまり 1650 年代と推測されるような粗製品は Fig.68-346 左上程度で少なく、したがってバンテン・ラーマで見られた 1650 年代の初期色絵大皿も見られない。青磁大皿は長崎県波佐見産より有田窯のものが多い。肥前の中でも有田窯のものがほとんどであるように思われる。つまり高級品が多いのである。その点ではティルタヤサ遺跡[9]に似通っている。しかし、肥前磁器にティルタヤサ遺跡で出土した 1670 年代末〜80 年代初の五弁花文の皿（Fig.90-464）のようなものはなく、その前に位置付けられる見込荒磯文碗も Fig.68-344 右下はティルタヤサ遺跡の Fig.87-448 ほど文様表現が崩れていないため、より古式と言える。よって、ウォリオ城では次のVI-1 期、18 世紀前半の有田の大壺、瓶が多数出土しているが、バンテン・ラーマのように食器が引き続き 18 世紀まで見られるのとは少し異なる。つまり、ウォリオ城では 1660〜70 年代の有田磁器が多く、1680 年代からは中国磁器が多くなる。有田の磁器は 1680〜90 年代のものは Fig.69-347 下 1 点以外ほとんど見られなくなり、1690 年代以降の 18 世紀第 1 四半期の大壺・大瓶が 90 個体以上出土するという特異な出土状況を見せる。大壺・大瓶以外では Fig.96-483 の染付大皿程度であり、これも威信財的なものであるので、通常の流通ではなく、オランダからの贈り物の可能性がある。食器は景徳鎮や福建産の磁器に代わっている。

ブトン・ウォリオ城VI期（18 世紀頃）

　VI-1 期は再び景徳鎮磁器が大量に出土する。これは 1684 年に中国の展海令によって、中国磁器の輸出が本格的に再開されたためであろう。つまり、この時期の景徳鎮製品は 1680 年代から 18 世紀前半にかけてと推測されるものである。本遺跡の全期を通じてもっとも多種多様な磁器が出土している。また大型の壺などが目立つ。

　次に多い肥前磁器もV-2 期に比べてヨーロッパ向けと考えられるものばかりであり、大壺・大瓶が肥前磁器 111 個体中、90 個体を占めるという多さである。1690 年代以降、18 世紀前半にかけての有田で大きな壺が作られる。総高 50cm を越す壺であり、しかも壺と花瓶のセットで作られるのである。この壺・瓶の 5 点セットが有田に注文され始めた理由は、次のことが考えられる。

　1685 年の幕府の長崎貿易制限令で、オランダ船による公式貿易での磁器輸出が減退する。それに対し脇荷と呼ばれる私貿易の額も決められたが、オランダはこの私貿易で磁器輸出を主に行なう。オランダ東インド会社は幕府によって貿易額が制限されたので、収益

9　坂井編 2000、同 2004、同 2007

率の良い商品を重点的に輸出せざるをえなくなり、収益率が比較的少ない商品は私貿易に受け継がれたと考えられると言う[10]。

そして、それまでオランダ東インド会社は私貿易を制限する傾向があり、1667年にも「私貿易品は、船腹に余裕がある場合には積み入れて送ることを許す。ただしその貨物の嵩（体積）に応じて最低20％、最高30％の運賃および関税を支払わねばならない」という[11]。つまり、1685年で私貿易が決まった貿易額になったために体積での制限意識が薄くなったことも一因かもしれない。

ヨーロッパの需要と絡み合いながら、この頃から大型の壺・瓶5点セットの輸出が始まったのであろう。脇荷輸出で壺・瓶の5点セットが輸出されたことは、1709年、壺2,256個、花生1,286個、1711年、壺9,619個、花生4,076個、1712年、壺2,180個、花生1,490個と、それぞれ壺・花生がたくさん入っているし、常に壺の方が多く、1709年、1712年の壺と花生の割合はほぼ壺3対瓶2の数量関係にある。つまり5点セットと同様であることから、この記録の壺・瓶は5点セットとして売ることができるような壺・瓶の数量関係で調達されたものが多いことが推測できる。

私貿易が盛んになったため、幕府は1696年、出島に脇荷専用蔵を二軒建てるほどであり、1723年までは脇荷輸出が盛んであったと推測される。まさにドイツ・ドレスデンのザクセン選帝侯アウグスト強王が盛んに日本の磁器を収集していた時期が、この私貿易が盛んであった時期の中に入る。このように壺・瓶の5点セットの注文・製作が始まったのは、1685年の幕府の長崎貿易制限令で定額の私貿易に磁器貿易の中心が移る中で、大型品の注文も会社として認めるようになったことと、当時のヨーロッパにおける東洋趣味の元で、室内装飾用の大型磁器の需要が高まり、他者が所有しているものより大きな磁器を求める空気とが理由であろうし、あわせて壺・瓶の大型化も進んだものと推測される[12]。

肥前磁器では他に大皿やヨーロッパ向けの受皿付碗（コーヒー、紅茶飲用）が少量見られる。中国磁器では福建・広東の粗製青花、特に特徴的なものとして「印青花」が多く見られる。

Ⅵ-2期は肥前磁器1例を除いて消え、景徳鎮磁器が減少し、より安価な福建・広東の碗皿と徳化窯の型作りの小碗（Fig.107-565〜569）などが多量に出土する。つまり、ヨーロッパ向けの高級磁器はほとんど見られなくなる。

ブトン・ウォリオ城Ⅶ期（19世紀）

Ⅶ-1期になると、さらに磁器の出土は減る。しかしバンテン・ラーマに比べれば出土しているので、1809年にオランダによって破壊されたバンテン・ラーマとは異なり、少量の出土が見られる。かえってオランダ東インド会社が1799年に解散するなどによりオ

10　山脇1988の385〜391頁

11　山脇1988の389頁

12　大橋2004、同2011の10頁

ランダの陶磁貿易がほとんど絶えるための激減と推測される。

19世紀後半頃の陶磁器は中国磁器が減退し代わってヨーロッパの陶器の流通が盛んになる時期である。ウォリオ城出土陶磁も中国磁器の確実な例は消え、代わってヨーロッパ陶器や肥前の型紙摺りによる染付碗が少量出土している。全体に陶磁器の出土が激減していく時期である。

以上のようにウォリオ城出土の多量の陶磁器の年代は17〜18世紀に中心があり、その種類の豊富さから見てもバンテン・ラーマ遺跡に近いものである。もちろんバンテン・ラーマ遺跡に比べれば種類は少ない。

17〜18世紀に陶磁器が多いのも、オランダ東インド会社の活動時期に合致するため、オランダ東インド会社がもたらした可能性が高いと考えられる。このようにスラウェシの中でも、ゴワ王国のソンバ・オプー城との歴史の違いを、陶磁器が物語っている。

〈バンテン・ラーマ遺跡〉

15世紀以前の陶磁器はほとんどなく、あっても中国陶磁とタイ・ベトナムの陶磁であった。

バンテン・ラーマⅣ期（16世紀頃）〜Ⅴ-1期（17世紀前半頃）

Ⅳ-1期になると、中国・景徳鎮磁器が少量出土するが、全体に占める割合は1%と少ない。Ⅴ-1期（16世紀末〜17世紀前半）からⅥ期（18世紀頃）の陶磁器が全体の89%を占め、バンテン王国の歴史を裏付けている。Ⅴ-1期の中でも1590年代以降の中国磁器が多く、この時期には景徳鎮（35%）のほかに福建省南部の漳州窯磁器が加わり、45%を占めることになる。この頃、オランダに続いてイギリスもアジア貿易に参入した。景徳鎮と漳州の磁器は品質的に上質と粗製品の差があり、つまり価格的に高価と安価の差があったと推測される。すなわち需要者側にもそれまで景徳鎮の青花を買って使えなかった階層に、この福建地方の粗製青花が普及していったこと、青花の需要層の幅を拡大したと考えられる。碗・小皿や福建・漳州地方の粗製中・大皿の流通に関しては東南アジアから日本で大きな差のない流通を見せている。景徳鎮でヨーロッパ向けに多量に作られたと考えられる芙蓉手大皿や鉢・瓶などは日本と同様、ヨーロッパなどに比べて少ない。

バンテン・ラーマⅤ-2期（17世紀後半〜18世紀初）

この時期に日本の肥前磁器が1,017個体と多量に出土することになるのは、1644年以降の明清の王朝交替に伴う内乱が主因である。1683年に台湾鄭氏が降伏して終わるまで、清朝が海上の鄭氏一派に対する経済封鎖のために貿易を禁じたからである。中国磁器の代わりに肥前磁器が東南アジアからヨーロッパにまで運ばれた。1644〜84年の間も中国磁器が全く輸出されなかったわけではなく、密貿易によって福建・広東地方などで作られた磁器がわずかな景徳鎮磁器と共に東南アジアには流通したものと考えられる。しかし、現段階では康熙様式の中で1684年以前のものだけを限定・抽出することは困難である。

よって康熙様式の磁器をこの時期のものとしてあげたために、中国磁器の割合が高い比率になっている。

　ところが実際は 1684 年以前、特に 1670 年代以前には中国磁器の割合は肥前磁器より少なかったと考えられ、1669 年滅亡のゴワ王国のソンバ・オプー城では、この時期の磁器は肥前磁器がほとんどである。1682 年廃絶のティルタヤサ遺跡では 1670 年代頃から中国磁器が多く入り始めたようであるが、なお肥前磁器の割合の方が多い。つまり 1684 年の展海令以降、待っていたとばかりに中国磁器の輸出が再開されたと想像できる。ケープタウンの 1697 年沈没のオランダ船オースターランド号引揚げ品なども中国景徳鎮磁器が主体であり、有田磁器はわずかである。1690 年代頃のブンタウ・カーゴ引揚げ品[13] も中国磁器輸出再開後の好資料である。1684 〜 18 世紀初頭におけるバンテン・ラーマ遺跡出土品を見ると景徳鎮のヨーロッパ向け磁器が増える。その点は肥前磁器も共通である。

　つまり景徳鎮や肥前磁器の場合、東南アジア向けというのが消える。東南アジア向けの磁器生産は主に福建・広東地方が受け持つことになる。景徳鎮と有田はヨーロッパ向け磁器を作り、その一部がバンテン・ラーマでたくさん出土している。

バンテン・ラーマⅥ期（18 世紀）

　この時期になると肥前磁器の割合は 3% と大幅に減少するが、Ⅵ-1 期（18 世紀前半）までは相当量の出土が見られる。特徴としては東南アジア向けの磁器は基本的に見られず、ヨーロッパ向けの磁器がオランダ船によって運ばれたものと推測される。景徳鎮磁器もそうしたものが主体であり、有田磁器と競争する中でヨーロッパ向けに作られたと考えられる、いわゆるチャイニーズイマリの五彩（Fig.100-509, 510）もアジアでは他にブトン・ウォリオ城（Fig.93-476）などオランダとの関わりが推測できる遺跡のみで見られる。景徳鎮の特徴的な製品として、褐釉を透明釉などとかけ分けた、褐釉青花（Fig.99-498）や褐釉五彩のカップ＆ソーサーなどがある。褐釉地に透明釉で窓を表し、五彩を施したりするものも多い。これらはヨーロッパでバタヴィアンウェアと呼ばれるのであるが、トプカプ宮殿蔵品にも多いし、ヨーロッパでも多く見られる。いずれにせよ 18 世紀前半頃に多く、ブトン・ウォリオ城でも出土している（Fig.94-478, 479）。ブトン・ウォリオ城でも出土している器種では、有田や景徳鎮がこの時期ヨーロッパなどに多く輸出した大小の壺・瓶セットなどはバンテン・ラーマではほとんど見られない。やはり、建物内の壁面を磁器で飾るような趣味は日本同様になかったのであろう。ヨーロッパの天井の高い建築との違いが現れているように思われる。

　一方、東南アジア向けと考えられる磁器はⅤ-2 期に引き続き福建・広東系の磁器であり、36% を占める。この主体は福建南部産の磁器であり、とくに徳化窯を中心とする。徳化窯の特徴的な磁器としては型押成形によって作られ、口禿にして窯詰め焼成した碗皿

13　Jörg 2001

（Fig.110-591／593, 600）である。青花・白磁・五彩・褐釉・瑠璃釉などがある。大量生産によって価格も安かったに違いない。広く東南アジアから台湾、日本に見られ、日本では沖縄や長崎で相当量出土している。V-2期までの福建・広東系磁器は比較的素地が悪く、焼成不良もあって淡褐色や灰色を帯びたものが主であった。それがⅥ期になると素地は景徳鎮並みに白いものが普通となる。

バンテン・ラーマⅦ期（18世紀末〜19世紀）

この時期の中で王宮がオランダによって破壊されたように、バンテン・ラーマの終末期のために、出土割合はバンテン・ラーマ全体の9％と激減する。景徳鎮磁器はほとんどなく、主に福建・広東系磁器であるが、19世紀後半になるとヨーロッパ陶器の食器が中心になることは注意しなければならない。この傾向はバンテン・ラーマだけでなく、ブトンやトロウランでも見られるので、インドネシア全体にヨーロッパ陶器が多く流入することになったのであろう。

〈ティルタヤサ遺跡〉

ティルタヤサ遺跡出土の陶磁器を見ると、磁器に関しては17世紀後半（V-2期）のものがほとんどであり、それより古い明末の磁器が少し混じっている程度であり、また18世紀以降の磁器も微量に見られるが、粗製品であり、離宮とは関係ない後世の人々の生活によるものと考えてよい。17世紀後半の磁器を産地別に見ると肥前と景徳鎮産のものがほとんどであり、福建・広東系の磁器はほとんど見られない。またベトナム産の印判手碗もわずかである。バンテン・ラーマ遺跡ではこの時期には福建・広東系の磁器の割合が高かったが[14]、この相違についてはバンテン・ラーマ遺跡の方が長い期間王都であり、またそこで生活する人々の階層に比較的幅があったことが理由として考えられる。ティルタヤサは一時的な離宮のため、王と王を取り巻く人々が主であったことを物語るのかもしれない。当時の磁器に対する評価が、景徳鎮磁器と肥前磁器に対し、福建・広東系やベトナムの鉄絵碗は相対的に低品質の―言い換えれば安価な―磁器として需要層も異なっていたことを物語る。

肥前磁器の製作年代はほとんどが1660〜80年代に収まるものである。この中でも五弁花文を表した皿などは上限が1670年代末と推測され、1680年代の可能性が高い。ティルタヤサ離宮がオランダによって攻略された1682年12月に近い年代が推測される。中国・景徳鎮磁器についても1684年の展海令によって本格的な輸出を再開する前の康熙年間の製品が主と思われる。

Fig.84-438の桐一葉の青花皿などは福建・漳州窯系の紀年銘の例が1675、1679、1680年と見られることなどから考えると、1660〜70年代まで遡るのではなかろうか[15]。この時

14　大橋・坂井 1999
15　大橋 1999 の50〜53頁

期は 1661 年の遷界令によって清朝が貿易を禁止した時期にあたり、わが国にもほとんど中国磁器が入らなかったし、輸出された磁器は少ないと考えられ、この時期に特定できる中国磁器の例は少ないのが実態であった。

肥前磁器については佐賀県有田磁器が中心であるが、他に長崎県波佐見産の青磁皿もある。

また 1660〜80 年代の磁器、とくに碗皿については、肥前、中国ともに同意匠、同器形が複数個体出土しているものが多く、セットで所有し、使われていたことが考えられる。食器のためであろう。

肥前磁器を見ると輸出用に作られたものとそうでないものがある。その点はバンテン・ラーマ遺跡やパサール・イカン遺跡[16] などでも同様であるが、17 世紀後半の肥前磁器に共通の特徴と言える。このことは運んだ主が中国かオランダかは特定できないが、輸出用磁器を注文して作らせるだけでなく、肥前・有田窯が日本国内向けに作った磁器の中から適宜選定して購入することも盛んに行われたことを物語っている。このようなケースは、1684 年の展海令で中国磁器輸出が本格化すると、ほとんど見られなくなる。

もう 1 つ考えられることは、オランダに対抗したティルタヤサ大スルタンの離宮ということを勘案すれば、オランダ船より中国船が運んだ可能性が強く、そのためオランダがヨーロッパ向けに注文した輸出用磁器は少なく、日本国内向け肥前磁器が多いのかもしれない。

いずれにせよ本遺跡の陶磁器資料は、ティルタヤサ離宮の年代推定に重要な役割を果たすだけでなく、東南アジアにおける 17 世紀の陶磁貿易の実態解明に貴重な資料を提供したと言えよう。

2. インドネシア出土の貿易陶磁器の要点

次に、インドネシアにおける出土陶磁器内容の特質を見てみよう。

まず中国陶磁器の中で、いくつかの注目されることを述べる。

2-1. トロウラン遺跡の陶磁器

トロウラン遺跡の中国陶磁器ではマジャパイト王国成立以前のものも少なからず出土していることである。

越州窯青磁碗や長沙窯皿（Fig.1-11）などのように 9〜10 世紀頃のものも出土している。さらに Fig.1-1 のように、これより年代が遡る可能性があるものも見られる。記録から 640 年にはジャワの訶陵国が初めて中国に入貢したとある。さらに隋唐時代に東南アジ

16　佐賀県立九州陶磁文化館 1990 の図 108〜264

ア群島部からの朝貢が断続的に記録されていることなどに関わる可能性を今後検討しなければならないであろう。宋時代（960–1279）には三仏斉国が朝貢を始めているし、東部ジャワで古マタラム国の有力者シンドク（在位 927–947）が王となり、11 世紀初にはアイルランガ王が現れ、クディリ王国を建てた。この頃の越州窯青磁には碗鉢だけでなく、Fig.1–05, 06 のような珍しい耳付壺が出土しており、Fig.1–07/10 の白磁もある。中国との交易が盛んになり始めた証しと考えられ、いわゆる威信財的なものが入り始めたことが分かる。この地域がマジャパイト王国以前にも、ある程度の政治・経済力があったことを物語る。

トロウラン遺跡出土の Fig.6–52 は青花紅釉蓋付壺の細片である。これまで出土例は、中国河北省保定市で 1 対が出土しているほか、モンゴル・オロンスム遺跡で本遺跡のものと同様の細片が 1 点出土しているにすぎない。これが中国大陸でなく、海を渡ったインドネシアで発見されたことは重要である。14 世紀のいわゆる元様式の青花は多くの器種が出土しており、粗放な Fig.5–39, 40 のような碗・鉢類や小瓶などもあるが、大型の鉢・皿・盤（Fig.5–43）も多く、高水準の磁器は釉裏紅（Fig.6–53）や白磁も加えると、1 つの遺跡としては世界的に見ても例を見ないほどの豊富な内容と言える。この時期は宰相ガジャ・マダ（1364 年死去）が政治の実務をとった時代である。

トロウラン遺跡では枢府手の白磁碗・鉢・皿（Fig.3–23, 24, Fig.5–36, 37）も多く出土しているが、類似の白磁素地に緑色絵具で文様を描いた鉢（Fig.11–108）が出土している。

従来、景徳鎮の五彩は青花豆彩などが有名であり、景徳鎮市珠山で成化（1465-87）期の官窯跡が発掘調査され豆彩が出土している [17]。しかし、それ以外の 15 世紀前半の五彩は明らかでない。このように緑色絵具だけで絵付けした例は「大明弘治年製」（1488–1505）の龍文鉢 [18] があるが、解説文に「成化在銘のものもあるようだが」と記される。本例はこうした官窯クラスのものとは異なり、類例を知らない。景徳鎮の五彩磁器の始まりを考える時に重要な資料と考えられる。

2-2. トロウラン遺跡の鉄絵陶板

トロウラン遺跡で出土した鉄絵陶板であり、本報告では中国・磁州窯と判断したが、これまで長くベトナム産の陶板とされてきたものである。

2012 年 1 月の第 1 回調査の際、これが中国・磁州窯と気付いたのは、その文様がベトナム青花とは著しく異なり、一般に知られる磁州窯の壺瓶などの文様に似通っていたからである。本遺跡で磁州窯の他器種の製品が出土していないならば注意を要したが、第 2 回の調査で、磁州窯の鉄絵と翡翠釉の壺・鉢が少なからず出土していることが分かった。これらの年代は 14 世紀であり、鉄絵陶板も文様などから同時期と推測される。とすれば、

17　景徳鎮市 1993

18　小学館 1976b–63・64

ベトナムの青花陶板の多くは、15 世紀前半頃のものと考えられるのとは差違がある。平面的形状も鉄絵陶板の方が方形のものがあるなど、より中国の方形磚に近い形状であり、ベトナム青花陶板は複雑な形が多く、中国の磚や瓦などの形状とはずいぶん違って見える。14〜15 世紀と言える陶磚の遺例がほとんどないが、大英博物館蔵品に青花磁器の景徳鎮の磚が 2 点ある[19]。2 点は同意匠であり、形状は方形であり、ベトナム青花陶板の多様な形状とは異なる。極めて東洋の一般的な磚の形状であり、製作年代は 15 世紀前半と考えられている。それに青花文様が施されているが、その文様表現がぼかしを加えており、同様の文様表現はベトナム青花陶板に見られる。また、そのぼかしを加えたベトナム陶板の文様は景徳鎮陶磚の文様の一部に近い。このことから、ベトナム陶板の一部には 15 世紀初頃の景徳鎮陶磚の影響を受けたものがあると推測できる。つまり、15 世紀前半の多様なベトナム青花陶板の製作は、14 世紀の磁州窯鉄絵陶板をもとに、作りなどの見本として注文させ、その青花文様などは景徳鎮青花の文様や陶磚の文様・文様表現などを手本に作られ、平面の形状は地元の建築装飾の考え方に従って注文されたのであろう。

　このベトナム青花陶板の注文のきっかけも、15 世紀初のマジャパイトの内戦による王宮の火災・焼亡などが原因となった可能性が高いように思われる。

　ベトナム産の陶板も出土例は稀のようであるが、磁州窯にしても、インドネシアの東ジャワ・トロウラン遺跡以外では類例を知らない。一方、本遺跡では少量のイスラーム陶器の白釉藍彩タイル（Fig.10-93/95）と青釉タイル（Fig.10-96/98）が出土している。イスラーム陶器でのタイルはすでに 14 世紀以前の例がある。このイスラーム陶器タイルは、13〜14 世紀のモンゴル帝国時代に交易を中心的に担ったムスリム商人が運んだ可能性が推測できる。出土しているのはベトナム青花陶板同様に縁を作り出すタイプと板状の方形陶磚で青釉をかけただけの 2 群に分けられる。この 2 群の使い方は不明であるが、中近東では藍彩タイルの間に青釉タイルを配した例がある。今後の研究課題かもしれないが、これをヒントにして、14 世紀の中で中国・磁州窯に注文したのかもしれない。鉄絵の縁を作り出した陶板（Fig.7-58/63）と、板状の鉄釉陶磚（Fig.7-64/67）である。陶板と陶磚には建材としての使い分けがあったのであろう。陶磚の方は床に敷き詰めた可能性も考えられるが、中近東の例からは一緒に壁面装飾した可能性もある[20]。陶板は側面まで施釉されており、ドゥマッ大モスクなどの例のように壁面装飾などの可能性がある。この 2 群があるのも磁州窯陶器とイスラーム陶器と推測したものに共通である。

　磁州窯の陶板は方形が基本であるのに対し、15 世紀前半のベトナムの陶板は様々な形状となる点でも異なる。Ⅲ-1 期（15 世紀前半）に中国に代わりベトナムに注文されるようになったものと推測される。理由は未解明であるが、本遺跡でもベトナム青花が増大

19　The Trustees of British Museum 1995
20　Carswell 1998 の fig.7 は 1435 年頃とするエディルネのオスマン・トルコ 6 代ムラト 2 世モスク壁面である。

していく時期であり、より変化に富んだ形状の青花陶板があり、15世紀に入ると少量の
五彩陶板（Fig.15-137）も加わったことが出土品から読み取れる。文様などから15世紀前
半、下っても中ごろまでが中心であり、ドゥマッ大モスク建立（1466～1506年の間の4説
がある）の15世紀後半頃の前までにトロウランに入ったことが推測される。ただし、「デ
マク（ドゥマッ）はすでに14世紀後半にはマジャパイト王国内における唯一の回教藩王
が統括する領国であった」[21] ことは、ムスリム商人の貿易活動ともつながり、14世紀にイ
スラームの陶板・磚が取り入れられ、それを消化・発展させることがマジャパイト王国内
で進んだ様子が想像される。その終焉もドゥマッ大モスクの創建者であるラデン・パタの
父に当たるブラウィジャヤ五世王の1478年、王朝が終わる時期を考慮すると、15世紀中
葉まででベトナム青花陶板の注文が終わることは妥当と考えられる。繭山氏はベトナム青
花陶板（氏は陶塼という）がジャワ北部および東部に限られていることについて、マジャ
パイト王国とチャンパ王国との交流、とくにチャンパ公主ダラワティ（回教徒）を妃とし
たマジャパイト七代クルタウィジャヤ王（在位1447-51）や、マジャパイト朝最後の王ブ
ラウィジャヤ五世（在位1466-78）の時代に両国関係の緊密を指摘される。ただし、ベト
ナム青花陶板を見ると多様であり、15世紀中葉というよりも、もう少し早い時期と推定
できるものもあり、15世紀中葉はあくまでも製作の下限年代と推測される。

　マジャパイト王朝が滅び、ラデン・パタはドゥマッのスルタンとしてドゥマッの繁栄を
築く時、ドゥマッ大モスクを建設する。その時、旧マジャパイト王宮から建築材の一部を
運び、その中にトロウラン遺跡出土の陶板と同じようなベトナム青花陶板が含まれる結果
となったのであろう。ここには、より古い14世紀のイスラーム陶器陶板や磁州窯の鉄絵
陶板は見られないのは当然と言える。すでに15世紀のマジャパイト王宮などからは消え
ていた可能性が高いからである。しかし、ドゥマッの北東のクドゥスのミナレット・モス
クに磁州窯の鉄絵陶板と考えられるものが門の装飾に取り付けられている例を坂井氏が紹
介している[22]。平面形状は長方形である。やはりベトナム青花陶板の複雑・多彩な形状と
は異なる。

　多彩なベトナム陶板の中には装飾にぼかしダミや、文様に景徳鎮の15世紀前半と推
測される青花陶磚（大英博物館蔵）に共通する特徴が看取されるものがある。坂井・大橋
2014 Fig.262などであるが、Fig.15-135も唐草の中の塗りつぶしに似通ったダミを行なっ
ている[23]。これらはFig.15-136などの陶板意匠がベトナム青花の大皿などに近いのに比べ
て、景徳鎮の青花陶磚に近い表現と言える。

21　繭山 1977
22　坂井 2015
23　坂井 2009 の写真 11, 12 も同類か

2-3.　15 世紀以降の変遷

　トロウラン遺跡では永楽（在位 1403－24）以降の中国磁器には官窯クラスの水準の磁器は見られなくなる。中国にとってのインドネシアの位置付けが変化するのかもしれない。かえって、ベトナム、タイの陶磁器のウェートが高まる時期と言えよう。ベトナムの陶磁器も 14 世紀にある程度の流通がトロウランなどで見られたが、15 世紀に主があり、15 世紀前半にはタイの陶磁器も加わる。

　しかし、16 世紀になると、ラオスでは多く出土している明らかなベトナムの青花や五彩大皿もインドネシアの 16 世紀のソンバ・オプー城、ブトン・ウォリオ城などで見られない。タイの鉄絵もラオスなどで多いものは、バンテン・ラーマなどにわずかに見られる程度である。そこに東南アジアでの陶磁流通に 15 世紀とは異なる状況があったと考えられる。ラオスの場合、16 世紀に国力が高まったというのに符合するかもしれない。バンテン・ラーマでは 16 世紀後半にタイのシンブリの焼締め四耳壺やミャンマーの錫釉陶器大皿などが出土するが、他ではあまり見ないので、西部ジャワで栄え始めたイスラーム教国バンテンの貿易相手の関係かもしれない。この 2 つは日本でも少量ながら出土例が見られる。

　16 世紀では、景徳鎮の青花と五彩の碗鉢と皿がスラウェシのゴワ王国のソンバ・オプー城とブトン王国のウォリオ城で出土する両者の内容には共通点が多い。これらはインドシナ半島のカンボジア、ラオスで見られるものと共通点が多い。逆に日本では少ないものがある。日本ではより小さい小皿と碗が主要である傾向がある。これは食生活に関係するのであろう。

　15 世紀、永楽以後に引き続き中国磁器での特別な官窯クラスのものはほとんどインドネシアでは出土していない。カンボジア、ラオスで少量見られる「陳守劉造」銘の古赤絵のような上質の五彩も見ない。しかし、それに準ずる古赤絵や五彩の碗皿は出土している。16 世紀後半の嘉靖金襴手に近い碗もラオスなどでは見られるが、インドネシアではほとんど見られない。16 世紀後半から加わる漳州窯の青花も、古いタイプはラオスほど多くはない。多くなるのは 17 世紀前半である。17 世紀前半はオランダ東インド会社が景徳鎮の芙蓉手意匠の青花皿や鉢・小鉢・瓶などを盛んに運ぶ。インドネシアでも少なからず出土する。芙蓉手の中でも崇禎期（1628－44）に始まるチューリップデザインの皿がバンテン・ラーマで出土している。崇禎期には日本やインドシナ半島でも見られる赤壁賦文鉢はブトン・ウォリオ城で出土している（Fig.49-249）。一方で、崇禎期頃に日本などで多い高台部を蛇の目高台で無釉とするもの、あるいは無釉の底部の端反り小皿はインドネシアではあまり見ない。ベトナム、ラオスでは見られる。

　もちろん、日本の茶人が注文したと考えられる「古染付」、「祥瑞」の典型的な青花や五彩はインドネシアをはじめ東南アジアというより、日本以外では出土していない。

2-4. 肥前陶磁器

　東南アジアに海外輸出された肥前陶磁器の特質については、すでに1990年の『海を渡った肥前のやきもの展：図録』で詳細に述べたが、その後の整理で明らかになったことも加えて概略をまとめると次のとおりである。

　インドネシアで肥前の陶器がわずかではあるが出土し、肥前の磁器の方は、1640年代頃の手塩皿（Fig.56-289）や中皿などがわずかに出土している。オランダ東インド会社の記録に1647年、シャム経由カンボジア行きの中国船が長崎から粗製の磁器を輸出したとあることを裏付ける。この時期の肥前磁器の特徴は輸出向けに作られたものではなく、国内向けの中から選ばれて輸出されたと考えられるものばかりである。肥前陶器もそうであるが、今確認されるのは、白っぽい陶器で嬉野市内野山窯産の可能性が高い砂目の中皿（Fig.56-292）などである。これらの上限は1610年代であり、1647年の磁器輸出より早い可能性もあり、鎖国に入る以前の朱印船貿易時代の可能性も考えておかねばならない。

　1644年の中国の王朝交替に伴う内乱が、東南アジアの貿易陶磁器流通にも大きな影響を及ぼす。日本同様に1644年以降、中国磁器の流通が激減するのであり、早くも1647年頃から反清勢力の中国船がインドシナ半島とともにインドネシアにも肥前磁器を運び始めたものと推測される。

　肥前磁器の出土量が増加するのは1650年代である。粗製芙蓉手皿、日字鳳凰文皿、有田の色絵大皿（Fig.75-387）、吉田の色絵大皿（Fig.77-409）などが明らかに1650年代と言える肥前磁器である。特に50年代前半かもしれない。有田の色絵大皿を除くと輸出向けと言えるものである。こうした輸出用磁器が1650年代に入ると作られ始める。日字鳳凰文皿はインドネシアでは少なく、多いのはベトナムである。しかもFig.61-314は見込蛇の目釉剥ぎしており、これは有田でなく波佐見の可能性が高い。ベトナムでは普通の有田などで作られた日字鳳凰文皿が多い。蛇の目釉剥ぎされた日字鳳凰文皿もホイアンで1点出土しているし、フィリピンでも1点あるが、鳳凰文か否かは不明。

　1650年代後半の中で中国の海禁令以後、中国磁器の輸出再開の見通しがなくなり、オランダ東インド会社も肥前磁器の本格的輸出に踏み出していく。この代表的製品が東南アジア向けの雲龍（龍鳳）見込荒磯文碗鉢である。ベトナム、タイ、カンボジア、ラオス、マレーシアなど東南アジア諸国で出土しているが、インドネシアでもソンバ・オプー城、ブトン・ウォリオ城、バンテン・ラーマ、ティルタヤサ遺跡でも少量ながら出土している。荒磯文碗の中でも新旧があるが、4遺跡の中ではティルタヤサ遺跡出土のFig.87-448が文様の崩れが進んでおり、新しいと考えられる。このグループの碗鉢は見込に荒磯文と呼ばれる鯉が飛び跳ねる図、中国で「跳魚図」という文様を描くのが基本である。しかし、これをアレンジしたもので、波の上に龍頭を描くもの、もしくは龍を描くものが肥前で作られ、ベトナムでは出土例が少なくないし、タイ・アユタヤなどで見られる。イン

ドネシアでは今のところ跳魚図のみで龍頭の例は見ない。また、1650年代末〜60年代頃に荒磯文以外の意匠の鉢が東南アジア向けに盛んに作られ、東南アジア諸国で出土している。インドネシアではブトン・ウォリオ城（Fig.68-344, 345）で少量見られるが、多く出土したのは、ティルタヤサ遺跡である（Fig.87-449/Fig.88-452）。次に、輸出向けの代表的なものに芙蓉手皿がある。これは東南アジア向けというより、オランダ東インド会社が主に求め、広く欧州まで運ばれた。この中でも粗製の簡略化した芙蓉手皿は今のところ東南アジア中心と考えられているが、インドネシアでの出土例はソンバ・オプー城（Fig.61-318右上）、ブトン・ウォリオ城（Fig.68-346左上）のほか、パサール・イカン遺跡、バンテン・ラーマ遺跡でも出土している[24]が、ティルタヤサ遺跡では出土していない。

　1650年代末からオランダ東インド会社が本格的な欧州までの輸出のために肥前に作らせた芙蓉手皿はより景徳鎮の明末の芙蓉手に近い。ソンバ・オプー城（Fig.61-319）、ブトン・ウォリオ城（Fig.68-346〈中段左は名山手〉・Fig.69-347〈上段右から2列目は名山手、下段の1点は年代が17世紀末〉）、バンテン・ラーマ（Fig.76-395/397）、ティルタヤサ離宮（Fig.89-459, Fig.90-460）などがあるが、ティルタヤサ遺跡の芙蓉手は略化が進んでおり、年代的に後出と言えるものが中心であり1650年代にかかるものはない。

　1651年に即位したティルタヤサ大王は1663年からの大規模灌漑によるティルタヤサ地方周辺の開発を行った。1677年再びオランダと戦争状態になり、さらに内戦が勃発したという。ティルタヤサ大王は1678年に息子のハジ王に譲位してティルタヤサ離宮に移った。ハジ王がオランダ側に付いたので1682年2月ティルタヤサ大王はバンテン・スロソワン王宮を攻略し、ハジ王は逃走。同年3月オランダ軍が攻略し、1682年末にはオランダ軍の攻撃でティルタヤサ離宮は陥落したと推測される。1683年3月大王はハジ王に降伏した[25]。

　このように1663年から1682年の間の可能性が高いティルタヤサの離宮としての年代を裏付けるような肥前磁器である。この1660〜70年代頃バンテン・ラーマとティルタヤサ遺跡にだけ多いものとして、小皿がある。バンテンではFig.76-392/394、Fig.77-410/412があり、ティルタヤサではFig.88-453/455、Fig.89-456/458がある。これらの小皿には特別東南アジア向けと言えるものはないし、輸出向けという明確な特徴もない。しいて言えば、Fig.89-456, 458のような折縁皿は輸出向けかもしれない。Fig.89-456とバンテン・ラーマのFig.76-393は同類。Fig.88-454もバンテン・ラーマのFig.76-392と同類のようであるし、Fig.90-463, 464は内側面に墨弾きで文様が表される。東南アジアでは珍しいが、両者のうちでは相対的にはFig.90-464の方が見込四弁花か五弁花なので新しいと思われる。こうした意匠も日本国内向けと思われる。見込に五弁花文は海外で出土する例は、バンテン・ラーマ遺跡Fig.76-399, 403以外はメキシコ・テンプロ・マ

24　佐賀県立九州陶磁文化館 1990 の97頁、129頁

25　Halwany 1993

ヨール周辺遺跡出土の染付小碗2点[26]などで見られるが少ない。伝世例も比較的少ない。さらに大皿でもティルタヤサ遺跡 Fig.90-461 とバンテン・ラーマの Fig.76-401 は比較的近い。Fig.91-465 の青磁大皿は東南アジアの中ではインドネシアに多く、ブトン・ウォリオ城 Fig.69-349、バンテン・ラーマ Fig.75-389 がある。バンテン・ラーマの Fig.75-389 とティルタヤサ遺跡 Fig.91-465 は高台内の蛇の目釉剥ぎの中央が1段くぼんでおり、見込の彫文様、釉調なども似通っており、長崎県波佐見窯の青磁であり、1660～70年代、しいて言えば1670年代頃と考えられる。

インドネシアでは先述の色絵大皿だけでなく、17世紀後半の青磁大皿・染付芙蓉手大皿・肥前陶器大皿など大皿がベトナム、タイ、カンボジア、ラオスに比べて多いことである。ベトナムでは碗・鉢と小皿が主たる器種であるから明らかに違いが認められる。それぞれの食生活の違いに基づく可能性が強い。

ティルタヤサ遺跡の染付大合子の蓋（Fig.91-466, 467）は東南アジアではインドネシアでのみ確認されており、バンテン・ラーマ遺跡で出土している[27]。

合子は小合子がインドネシアでは一般的であり、トロウラン遺跡、バンテン・ラーマ遺跡（Fig.76-404～406）、ティルタヤサ遺跡（Fig.91-468, 469）などに見られる。タイやカンボジアなどでも見られるが、これらの地域ではどちらかと言えば蓋付小鉢や小瓶の方が多いように思われる。

以上のように、バンテン・ラーマ、ティルタヤサ遺跡出土の肥前磁器には共通点が多い。バンテン・ラーマからティルタヤサ離宮に分かれた歴史を裏付けるものと言える。

これらとともに中国磁器、とくに景徳鎮の磁器が多く出土している。康熙時代（1662-1722）の特徴をもつ景徳鎮磁器が多い。これらが、ティルタヤサ遺跡の下限は1682年として、上限はいつかである。「大清康熙年製」銘の鉢が1点（Fig.80-421）あるので、1662年以降であろうが、Fig.80-420 の鉢などは長崎唐人屋敷跡の4層出土品に類似品がある（扇浦2013の第12図54・55）。この多量の中国磁器は唐人屋敷建設前の整地層の下層出土と言い、年代は1685～88年にかけてのものが主と推測される。そうした中国磁器の中に類似品があるということは、1682年に極めて近い年代の可能性が高いように思われる。唐人屋敷建設前の土層でこの中国磁器と一緒に出土する肥前磁器の中で多く出土する染付見込荒磯文碗の文様がかなり崩れており、やはり1670～80年代と考えられるものが多いこと、型紙摺りの碗があるなど荒磯文碗以外も1670年代以降と考えられる特徴がある。1点青磁染付碗の見込に五弁花文を染付しており、五弁花文も1680年代から用いられると思われる点からも、1685～88年にかけてのものが主という推測[28]を否定する証左はない。皿で西洋風景画を描いたものが複数出土しているが、これも1680年代以降と考えられる。

26　野上 2013 Fig.19-12, Fig.20-9

27　佐賀県立九州陶磁文化館 1990 図310・311

28　扇浦 2013

若干、古い様相をもつ小坏などがあるが、主体はやはり 1688 年を下限とする 1680 年代の可能性が高い。

　ティルタヤサ遺跡の中国磁器には唐人屋敷跡のこの資料と共通する Fig.80-420 なども あるが、それ以外のものはより上質であり異なる。そうした点から 1682 年以前をそれほ ど遡らないものと考えられる。品質が高いのは離宮という遺跡の性格によるのであろう。 三彩皿・碗も多く出土したが（Fig.83-435, 436, Fig.84-437）、ブトン・ウォリオ城（Fig.64- 330）、バンテン・ラーマ（Fig.70-353, 354, 359）で出土している。もう 1 つは二重高台の大 皿（Fig.82-430, Fig.83-432, 433）であり、ブトン・ウォリオ城（Fig.64-328, 329）、バンテ ン・ラーマ（Fig.70-357）でも出土している。これらがインドネシアにおけるこの時期共 通の特徴と言える。

　Ⅴ-2 期の遺跡出土陶磁の特徴として、もう 1 つはベトナムの印判の碗が出土している。 ブトン・ウォリオ城（Fig.67-343）、バンテン・ラーマ（Fig.74-386）、ティルタヤサ遺跡 （Fig.92-472）のように少ないながらも多くの遺跡で出土する。Ⅴ-2 期の中で肥前磁器中 心の 1650～70 年代頃に流通した中国磁器の可能性があるものとして、福建地方の磁器で あるソンバ・オプー城の Fig.60-311 の青花百寿文碗と小皿がある。百寿文碗は口縁内側 に花文帯を配し、外面に寿字を連ねる。このように口縁内側に文様を描く点、そして寿字 も唐人屋敷跡出土の寿字文碗に比べて明らかに古い。1660 年代頃の遭難船資料である鹿 児島県吹上浜採集品よりも古いかもしれない。江戸城の明暦大火（1657 年）被災資料の百 寿文碗は被熱をしていて口縁内側の文様は明確でない。口縁部が端反りでない点、口縁内 側の花文帯などの点でも、ラオス・ヴィエンチャン出土品に酷似している。ヴィエンチャ ンの百寿文碗は底部もあり、見込に「玉堂佳器」の文字を記す（大橋 2016）。よって、ソ ンバ・オプー城の百寿文碗の年代は明暦大火（1657）以前で上限は 1640 年代と推測され る。

　1650～70 年代の肥前磁器中心の時代の中国磁器に近いと思われるものとして、福建の 木葉文皿がある。木葉に木蓮が描き加えられた皿はブトン・ウォリオ城の Fig.66-338 左 とバンテン・ラーマ Fig.72-367 である。古式のタイプは台湾の左営鳳山県旧城遺跡で出 土し、木葉の文様と共に「太平年興、乙卯冬記」（1675 年と推測）の題記をもつものであ る。同遺跡では「太平年興」の題記の小皿も出土している。一般にこれと関連付けている ものが、1690 年代頃の沈船と推測されているブンタウ・カーゴ引揚げ資料にある。意匠 が少し異なり、「一葉約秋気、新春再芳菲」の詩句と玉蘭（木蓮）が木葉に加えて描かれ る。インドネシアでは、ブトン・ウォリオ城とバンテン・ラーマで出土したものはこの木 蓮を描き加えたものばかりである。これらは 1670 年代に遡ることはなく、1680～90 年代 のものと推測される。

　以上のように、明らかに 1670 年代以前、しいて言えば 1660 年代以前に遡る、つまり 1644 年以降 1660 年代にはほとんど新たに作られた中国磁器は流通しなかったものと推測

される。

　また東南アジアの中ではインドネシアのみで、18世紀前半に入ってもなお肥前（有田）磁器が出土する。内容的にはインドネシア向けのものというより、ヨーロッパ向けの磁器である。オランダ船がヨーロッパへ肥前磁器を運ぶ際に、必ずアジア貿易の根拠地バタヴィア（現ジャカルタ）を経由したからであろう。この時期の肥前磁器が出土するのは、次の重要な中継地ケープタウン（南アフリカ）である。

　このようにインドネシアの5つの遺跡から出土した膨大な量の陶磁器を見ると、13〜19世紀におけるこの地域の陶磁器流通の変遷がわかると共に、日本のこの時期における陶磁器流通内容との異同も明らかとなる。

IV　陶磁貿易と歴史

　本書の末尾として陶磁貿易史の観点で、トロウラン遺跡と4王都遺跡での陶磁片調査成果を4要素から見直してみたい。

1. 遡る各王都の歴史

　5遺跡に関わる王国は、マジャパイト王国（トロウラン）・バンテン王国（バンテン・ラーマとティルタヤサ）・ゴワ王国（ソンバ・オプー）そしてブトン王国（ウォリオ城）である。これらの中でブトン王国はほとんど無名で、起源はもちろん終末の状況も地元以外では知られていない。しかし他の3王国はインドネシアあるいは東南アジア群島部の歴史では有名であり、おおまかな時代観と流れは一般常識に近い[1]。

　中でも人口が集中し記録や関連遺跡が比較的良く残っているジャワ島のマジャパイト王国とバンテン王国は、それぞれの年代観についても難しい知識ではなくなっている。マジャパイトの起源は「元寇を利用したラデン・ウィジャヤ」の建国であり、工都として選んだトロウランは産物のマジャの実が苦かったので名付けられた[2]、との説話も良く知られている。また先イスラーム時代の古典ジャワ文化（ヒンドゥ・ジャワ）は中部ジャワ期と東部ジャワ期に分かれ、ボロブドゥールなどに代表される前者が10世紀にムラピ山の大噴火で壊滅して後者が始まったということも、ジャワ史あるいはインドネシア史の基本常識である。実際、大部分の寺院跡などの遺跡はきれいに両地域に分かれて残っている。

　バンテンの創建に近い年代1527年は、スンダ・クラパ港がイスラーム教徒によって占領されていることをポルトガル人が確認した年である。そのためバンテン・イスラーム王国の創建はその年より少し早いと考えられている。この年は現在ジャカルタ市の建市年として知られており、16世紀初めのバンテン建国は創建者ファタヒラと同一視されるイスラーム聖人スナン・グヌンジャティの名と共にやはり一般常識である。

　そのような一般的な時代観から考えると、今回まとめたI-1期（9-13世紀）はかなりかけ離れている。トロウランでは越州窯青磁・長沙窯黄釉鉄彩・景徳鎮窯青白磁などこの時期の陶磁は比較的多く、なおかつ高級製品が少なからず含まれていた。明らかにトロウランには「ラデン・ウィジャヤが苦いマジャの実を口にする」はるか以前から、輸入されていた上質の中国陶磁が運ばれていた。その量や連綿と続く各時代の陶磁器の状態を見れ

1　マジャパイトのガジャ・マダ、バンテンのティルタヤサそしてゴワのハサヌディンはインドネシア政府公認の民族英雄であり、それぞれ大学名や主要道路名など様々に使われている。

2　この説話の意味するところは苦いことが何の象徴なのかなど厳密には単純ではないと思われるが、「パイト」は苦いを意味するので一般にはマジャパイトは単に「苦いマジャ」の意味だけだと理解されている。

ば、少なくとも聖山プナングンガン山に最初の水浴場遺構が築かれる 11 世紀には何らかの重要な意味がある場所であったことは確実だと考えられる。

　さらに問題にすべきは、越州窯青磁の少なくない部分や長沙窯陶磁は唐代の製品であることである。前述のように東部ジャワ期は基本的に 10 世紀のムラピ山大噴火で中部ジャワが被災したことを契機にして始まったのに、これらの陶磁器の年代はそれより古い。もちろん少ない例だが中部ジャワ期の遺跡は、トロウランの比較的近くにも存在する[3]。そのため 10 世紀以前の中部ジャワ期にも、ヒンドゥ・ジャワ文化は東部ジャワにも広まっていたことは知られていた。しかし陶磁片資料は、その拠点の一つとしてトロウランが機能していた可能性を物語っている。トロウランのマジャの実は、ラデン・ウィジャヤが食べるはるか以前から苦かったことになる。

　また越州窯青磁と長沙窯陶磁は、一般に 9 世紀に始まった陶磁貿易の主要 3 種類に含まれる。その他の重要な中国陶磁としては邢窯白磁があり、さらにイスラーム青釉陶器も重要な要素である。これらに鞏県窯陶磁を加えた陶磁器群が、スマトラ南部東海岸のビリトゥン島沖で沈んだ船より発見されている[4]。私たちが調査した陶磁片ではそれらを確認することはなかったが、今後東部ジャワで発見されることも期待できる。ただし最初に中部ジャワに輸入されて伝世されたものが運ばれたとするのは、大噴火が移動の契機であるなら考えにくい。

　バンテン・ラーマでも、長沙窯陶磁が発見されている。先イスラーム時代の拠点であるバンテン・ギラン（上バンテン）遺跡は、バンテン川の 10 km 上流に位置する。当然、そこに運ばれた貿易陶磁は全て河口のラーマを経由したはずである。ギランでは初期貿易陶磁にも含まれる広東系青釉陶器も出ているため、ジャワ島西端のスンダ海峡地域がこの時代の貿易ネットワークに入っていたことが明瞭である。トロウランと異なって拠点そのものは短距離ながら移動しているが、地域としては 9 世紀と 16 世紀以降が決して別れてはいなかったことを意味している[5]。

　それ以外にスラウェシのソンバ・オプーではⅡ-1 期（13 世紀末～14 世紀）、ウォリオではⅡ-2 期（14 世紀後半）からの陶磁器が見られたことも重要である。

　ゴワ王国の伝承では 17 世紀第 2 四半期にイスラームに改宗した王は第 14 代と数えられており、1 代 20 年で計算すれば初代王トゥマヌルンの年代は 14 世紀中葉頃と推定される。個々の王たちの実在性はともかく、伝承された建国年代は陶磁器の輸入開始とそれほど大きな離齬がない。確認された福建南部産の白磁合子（Fig.22-29）が、トロウラン出土資料と類似していたことに注意する必要がある。

3　760 年紀年のディノヨ碑文発見地はトロウラン南東 50 km のマラン高原にあり、近くには中部ジャワ様式のバドゥッ寺院も残っている。

4　バトゥ・イタム（黒石）号として知られるダウ船で、引揚げ地のビリトゥン島の位置からジャワが当面の目的地だった可能性が高い（Krahl 2011）。

5　バンテン・ラーマではⅠ-2 期（13～14 世紀前半）・Ⅱ-1 期（13 世紀末～14 世紀）・Ⅲ-2 期（15 世紀後半～16 世紀初）が抜けているが、それらの時期の陶磁片はバンテン・ギランで見られる（Guillot *et.al.* 1994）。

　ウォリオでは前述のように、ヒンドゥ・ジャワ文化と似た先イスラーム時代の王名が伝承されていた。ここで発見された龍泉窯青磁と磁州窯鉄絵も、トロウラン出土の陶磁片に近い。ただしウォリオの場合、続くⅢ-2期（15世紀後半〜16世紀初）の陶磁器が欠落している。同じ時期にソンバ・オプーには、景徳鎮やベトナムの青花そしてタイ・シーサッチャナライの鉄絵陶器などが運ばれていた。この大きな違いの理由を考えると、ウォリオはトロウランの衰退と同一傾向にあるが、ソンバ・オプーは逆にこの時期の陶磁貿易と深く関わっていたことになる。またブトンと異なって、先イスラーム時代ゴワの13代の王名にはヒンドゥ・ジャワ文化的な要素はかなり乏しい。そのためソンバ・オプーはトロウランやバンテン・ラーマと似た古い時代からの一貫した連続性があるが、ウォリオはこの時期に陶磁貿易との接点を欠いたことになる。その理由は、マジャパイトとのより深い直接的な関係の有無だったのかもしれない。

　いずれにしてもトロウランと4王都遺跡の陶磁片は、通常の理解とは異なる古い時代からの歴史の存在を示したことは明らかである。そのような早期の陶磁貿易を可能にした政治的社会的背景はほとんど記録されず、また曖昧模糊とした伝承のみが伝えられただけだった。だが陶磁片から、そのような古い時代から続く連続性が明らかになった。それは拠点的な港市が長い時代に利用され続けたという、この地域の歴史の一般的な姿を語っていると見ることもできる。

2. 西方イスラーム世界との関係

　4王都遺跡はイスラーム王国の王都であり、聖地メッカのある西方イスラーム世界と密接な関係があるのは当然である[6]。またトロウランを都としたマジャパイト王国はヒンドゥ教を奉じた国家だが、マジャパイト成立直後の1297年までには東南アジア最古のイスラーム王国サムドゥラ・パサイがスマトラ北端のアチェ地方に誕生している。そしてハヤム・ウルク王時代の1368年までには、トロウランにはムスリムの共同体が存在していた[7]。そのような状況を、陶磁貿易史の観点から確認してみよう。

　西方イスラーム世界には、陶磁文化としてイスラーム陶器がある。メソポタミアやエジプト文明に起源を持つスズ釉を使った陶器だが、低火度焼成で軟質のため基本的に中国陶磁と競合する他のアジア地域へは運ばれていない。むしろ西方イスラーム世界自体が中国など東方陶磁の消費地であった。

　それはペルシャ人やアラビア人など西方イスラーム世界の商人たちがダウ船で東南アジアから東アジアへやってきていた、初期陶磁貿易の時代（9〜10世紀）からの傾向であっ

6　ティルタヤサ遺跡と深い関係のあるバンテン王国の内乱で大スルタンと争った息子のハジ・スルタンとは、メッカへの巡礼を済ませたムスリム（「ハジ」）なので通称がそのようになっている。

7　南部のトロロヨに、この年を最古の紀年銘とするイスラーム墓地が成立している。

た。ターコイズあるいはコバルト青釉がかけられた貼り付け文壺やアンフォラ壺の破片は広くこの時代の東アジアを含むアジア各地の港市遺跡で普遍的に発見されており、前述のようにビリトゥン島沖で沈んだダウ船の積荷にも含まれていた。ジャワにも運ばれていた可能性は極めて高いが、残念ながら私たちが調査した分のトロウランと4王都遺跡の陶磁片には含まれていなかった。なお越州窯青磁とともに、イスラーム青釉片そして多彩刻線文陶器（イスラーム三彩）片が、北スマトラ西海岸バルースのロブー・トゥア遺跡で発見されている[8]。

　続く中期陶磁貿易時代（11～13世紀）には、西方イスラーム世界は龍泉窯青磁を受容しつつ独自の陶器文化を発展させた。その一つは金属の光沢を模したラスター彩陶器であり、別の一つは建築物装飾として進展を遂げる施釉タイルである。共に同時代に確実に東方へ運ばれた証拠は、まだ確認できない。

　後期陶磁貿易時代（14～18世紀）には特に環インド洋世界の文化接触が恒常的になり、イスラーム陶器とアジア東部陶磁器の技術的交流が顕著になる。その端緒としての記念碑的な存在が、中国の白磁技術にイスラーム陶器の釉下コバルト彩装飾を融合させた青花の誕生である。その完成形とされる元時代の至正様式青花の優品が、数多く西方イスラーム世界に運ばれたことは良く知られている。

　トルコ・イスタンブールのトプカプ宮殿とイラン・アルダビールのシェイフ・サフィ廟のコレクションが有名だが、いずれもそれらへの搬入は生産から数世紀後である。それに対しインド・デリーのイスラーム王朝トゥグルク朝宮殿跡のフィルーズシャー・コトラで発見された至正様式青花の厖大な破片[9]は、より重要な意味を持つ。なぜなら発見地の宮殿は創建が1354年で、1398年には破壊されたからである。青花磁器が生産された至正年間（1341-67）前後とほぼ同時代となり、別の場所での伝世は考えにくい。そしてここでは至正様式の優品とともに、同時代の略描様式の青花片も発見されている。略描様式の元青花の発見地はフィリピンなどの東南アジアが多く、至正様式と共伴することはない。そのため両様式の元青花は、同時代製品ながら異なった供給先が想定されていたと思われていた。デリーでの両者の混在状況は極めて珍しいが、トロウランでも本書で紹介した至正様式の他に多数の略描様式元青花を私たちは確認している[10]。つまりデリーのフィルーズシャー・コトラで発見された元青花とトロウランの元青花は基本的な組み合わせが極めて似ており、なおかつトロウランの破片が後代に持ち込まれた可能性はありえないため、時代的にも共通することになる。

　そのようなトロウラン出土陶磁片の西方イスラーム世界との繋がりは、別の面にも表れている。それは青花に似た白地藍彩タイル（Fig.10-93/95）とターコイズ青釉方形タイル

8　Guillot *et.al*.1998（抄訳は森本 2006）

9　Smart 1975 及び三杉 1987

10　坂井・大橋 2014、p.16 の陶磁器種類 44～46

（Fig.10-96/98）である。共にトロウランに持ち込まれたのは14世紀頃と想定されるが、前者の製作年代は元青花と前後するか少し遅い時期が考えられるのに対し、単色釉の後者は13世紀までには西方イスラーム世界で誕生している。共にトロウラン出土陶磁片の中では極めて微量でしかないが、産地が西方であることは間違いない。なおかつこれらは、15世紀前半にかなりの量が発注された北部ベトナム産タイルの原型をなしている。そのような状況は、マジャパイト最盛期の14世紀後半にすでに成立していたトロウランのムスリム社会との関係を十分に示唆すると言える[11]。

　トロウランのあり方を引き継ぐものとして、バンテン・ラーマで出土した白地藍彩陶器皿（Fig.57-294）は重要である。この皿片は内側面に独特の連続葉文が描かれており、筆者はサッファビィ朝の製品と考えている[12]。17世紀後半にオランダ東インド会社は中国青花の代替品として当時のサッファビィ朝に中国青花を模した陶磁器を発注しており、そのような製品は東アジアでも発見されている。しかしバンテン・ラーマ出土のこの皿は、文様が中国青花との類似性は乏しくコバルトの発色も異なった感じを受けるため、16世紀代の製品ではないだろうか。

　前述したように1596年にオランダ人はバンテンに多くのアジア商人がいたことを記録しており、そこにはペルシャ人も含まれている。ペルシャ人が全てサッファビィ朝と直接関係があったとは限らないが、17世紀代にはペルシャ人のイスラーム学者がタイのアユタヤに定着している[13]。そのため16-17世紀に東南アジアに来たペルシャ人の数は、決して少なくないと考えられる。なぜなら当時インド亜大陸の覇権を握ったムガール帝国の公用語はペルシャ語であり、数多くのペルシャ人がインドへ移住していた。インドのイスラーム文化は東南アジアの初期イスラーム文化と深い関係にあり、ペルシャ的価値観の受け入れはシーア派という宗派を除けば東南アジアでは自然だったと言える[14]。

　バンテン王国はイスラーム国家であり、建国者のファタヒラはメッカ巡礼を果たしたイスラーム学者であった。そのようなバンテンの都へ、16世紀初頭に建国し17世紀前半に最盛期を迎えるサッファビィ朝の文物が持ち込まれることに何ら不思議はない。おそらく同様のことは、直接インド洋に面するアチェ・イスラーム王国でも起きていたに違いない。陶磁器特に食器形態のイスラーム陶器は質の点で中国陶磁には全く及ばないが、その背景にあるイスラーム文化とムスリムの貿易活動は深く東南アジア群島部に及んできたと言える。

11　西方イスラーム世界のタイルの起源はもちろんペルシャ文化地域だが、筆者はインド北西のイスラーム文化地域を経由してもたらされたと考えている（坂井2015）。
12　テヘランのレザー・アッバシー博物館が所蔵する白地藍彩陶器碗の内面に、ほとんど同じ文様が確認できる。
13　1631年にアユタヤに渡来したシェイフ・アフマッド・コミ。
14　例えば15世紀のマラッカのスルタンは歴代「シャー」というペルシャ語の称号を使用したが、直接の起源はインドのイスラーム諸王朝からきている。

3. 肥前陶磁を受容したインドネシア社会

　私たちが最初にインドネシア出土の陶磁片に関心を持ったのは、記録にないバンテン・ラーマでのおびただしい肥前陶磁の出土を知ったからである。そしてインドネシアの17・18世紀を含む遺跡では、どこでも肥前陶磁の存在を確認できた。それはジャワの遺跡にとどまらず、スラウェシのソンバ・オプーやブトンのウォリオでも同様であった。また本書では対象にしていないが、スマトラ北端のアチェでも肥前陶磁の存在は少なからず知られ、そこには特徴的な肥前陶器二彩手刷毛目鉢の度重なる発見も含まれている。

　ここでは前章との重複を避ける意味も込めて、トロウランでの肥前陶磁の存在について考えてみたい。

　トロウランでは、肥前の白磁碗（Fig.20-307）・染付蓋付小鉢（Fig.20-308）そして色絵合子（Fig.20-309, 310）を確認した。厖大な陶磁片全体の中では極めて微量であり、17世紀後半というそれらの年代はトロウラン全体の基本的な流れとはほとんど無関係である。それにも関わらず、ここに持ち込まれた事実は否定できない。

　マジャパイト王国の最後の状態は、他の多くのインドネシアの古い王国と同様にほとんど明らかではない。海岸部で力を持った中部ジャワのドゥマッなどの新興イスラーム港市が連合してトロウランを攻略したとも言われるが、1520年代であるとの時期が推定されるものの実情は不明である。鄭和来航時の内乱を思わせる二次焼成痕が14世紀後半の陶磁片には少なからず認められたが、16世紀初頭の時期の陶磁片にはそのような痕は見出せなかった。またドゥマッ大モスクに現存するベトナム産タイルはトロウランに最初運ばれた可能性があるが、それも決して火災にあったような痕跡を見せてはいない。何よりも後のジャワのムスリムは、ドゥマッの初代スルタンのラデン・パタをマジャパイト王の血統を引くと考えていた。現状では陶磁片の状態が示すように、1520年代以降トロウランでは何となく権力が消え去ってしまったと推測するしかない。

　ドゥマッはジャワのイスラーム港市国家の盟主であったが、マジャパイトに代わってジャワの支配圏を確立する以前の16世紀中葉に内訌で衰退してしまう。その後継をめぐって中部ジャワ内陸のパジャンとマタラムが抗争を続けるが、最終的に16世紀末にはマタラムが勝利し、1620年代までに中部ジャワと東部ジャワを統一する。この間、トロウラン地域はイスラーム港市の1つであるスラバヤの影響下にあった可能性が高いが、特別の役割はなかったと思われる。スラバヤが1625年にマタラムに統合された前後も同様だったようで、16世紀初頭以後トロウランにはほとんど特筆すべき陶磁器の搬入は認められない。マタラムは17世紀前半に全盛期を迎え、1620年代にバタヴィアを2回攻撃したりする。以後しばらくマタラムは勢威を保ったが、1674年にマカッサル戦争に関連したトルノジョヨの反乱が東部ジャワのマドゥラ島で発生し、翌年スラバヤは反乱軍に支配

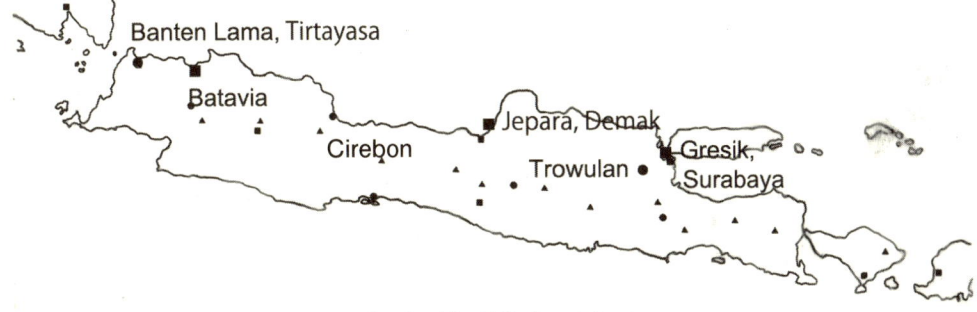

Map 2　ジャワ島 Java Island

される。この時マタラムのスルタンはオランダ東インド会社に援助を求め、77 年オランダ軍はスラバヤを奪回した。そしてそれ以降、マタラム王国はスラバヤを含むジャワ島の北海岸地域をオランダに割譲してしまう。

　肥前陶磁がトロウランに持ち込まれたのが 1655-80 年代なら、広義のスラバヤ地域に含まれるトロウランはマタラム支配下の安定状態から戦乱を経て支配者の交替が起きた状態だったと言える。そのような時期の肥前陶磁の、販売者と購買者を考えてみよう。

　この時代に肥前陶磁のインドネシアでの主な輸入港は、バタヴィアとバンテンである。前者はもちろんオランダが長崎から台湾のゼーランディアを経て運んだが、鄭成功の攻撃でそこを喪失した 61 年以降は直接バタヴィアまで持ってきている。バンテンへは基本的に台湾鄭氏関連の船が運び、一部はバンテン船やイギリス船が安平（旧ゼーランディア）またはアモイから輸入した。

　内陸のトロウラン地域へ来るルートは、ブランタス川で直接つながるスラバヤからの可能性が最も大きい。しかしマジャパイト時代と同様に、トゥバンなどジャワ北海岸の港からもありえるだろう。問題はバタヴィア・バンテンからそれらの港への移送だが、これについてオランダ史料をもとにした久礼克季の最近の研究[15] で興味深い事実が明らかになった。

　まずバタヴィアからオランダは、磁器を中部ジャワの港ジュパラへ 1636 年から、また翌年からはスラバヤ近郊のグルシッへ運んだ。金額が判明するのは肥前陶磁が大部分を占める 61 年以降になるが、60 年代ではジュパラ分が多いのに対し 70 年代以降はグルシッが増える（グラフ 1）。結果的に 81 年までの総額では、グルシッへの移送額は 2 割以上の高額になった。同時期に両港へ運んだ銅（やはり日本産）を見ると、ジュパラへの分は総額で 3 倍に近い。ジュパラはマタラム王宮の外港であり、ここでの販路はマタラムの中枢部に対してである。そこでの銅の需要は王宮から離れたグルシッよりもはるかに大きかったが、磁器の場合は特に 70 年代以降東部ジャワで大きな市場ができたことになる。

　一方ジャワ島北岸の諸港では、1670 年以降鄭氏船の活動が頻繁にオランダによって目

15　久礼 2016

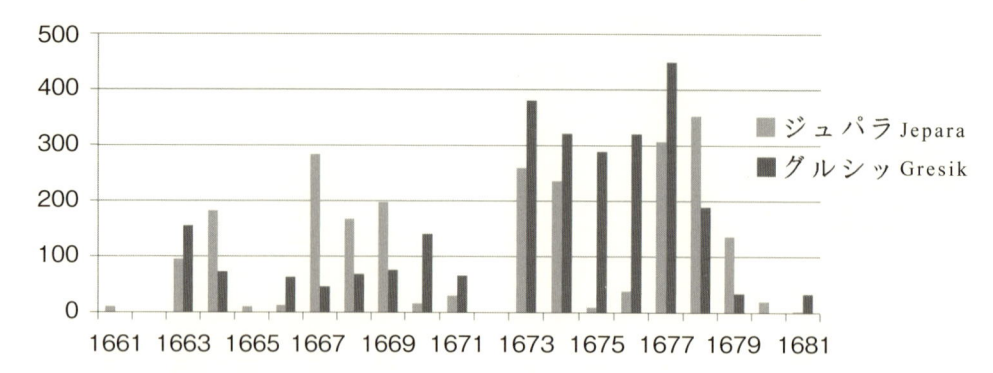

グラフ1　オランダ船によるバタヴィアからの磁器搬送金額（久礼2016より筆者作成）
単位：レイクスダールデル
Graph 1 Transportation Amount of Porcelains from Batavia by Dutch ships,
Based Kure 2016 in Reiksdaalder

撃されている。それは例えば71年に中部ジャワ東端の港レンバンでバンテンの港務長官の注文で建造されていた船が鄭氏に売却されたとか、あるいは72年に鄭氏の注文によりグルシッで船が建造された、などの事実である。またこれらの港での協力者の華人たちは、台湾出身者が多かったとも記されている。

　当時バンテンのティルタヤサ大スルタンが、オランダと対抗してこの地域での活動を広げていたことは間違いない。その契機はマカッサル戦争でのゴワの敗北で、娘婿にゴワの王族出身のイスラーム学者シェイフ・ユスフがいた大スルタンにとっては巻き返しを図る意味があったはずである。つまりオランダが肥前の可能性が高い磁器を東部ジャワに運んだのは間違いないが、バンテンあるいは鄭氏もその可能性を十分に持っていたことに注目する必要がある。

　では東部ジャワでの購買者は誰だったのか。まず重要なのは、グルシッ及びスラバヤは単に東部ジャワ市場の窓口だっただけでなく、ジャワとスラウェシやマルク諸島（香料群島）などの東部インドネシアを結ぶ交易の結節点だったことである。ジャワからのコメの輸出と東部インドネシアからの香料・海産物の輸入は、これらの港での伝統的な取引だった。ソンバ・オプーやブトン・ウォリオでの17世紀の陶磁器は、スラバヤとグルシッカら運ばれたものがかなり含まれていた可能性が高い。トルノジョヨ反乱は、マドゥラ島貴族の彼がスラバヤの貴族そして亡命してきたゴワ貴族たちと共に起こしたものである。その背景には当時のマタラムのスルタンの親オランダ政策に対する反発と共に、中部ジャワ内陸政権マタラムに対する伝統的な海上交易圏を形成していたマドゥラ・スラバヤ・ゴワの反発があったことは間違いない。

　そのような状況を考えると、この地域の交易を基盤に置いた貴族や商人たちが磁器の購入者であった可能性は高いはずである。しかし彼らがいたのはグルシッやスラバヤという港町であり、60km以上内陸のトロウランとは直接の関係は考えにくい。トロウラン近郊

のモジョクルトの町には貴族がいたはずだが、当時農村になっていたトロウランに住んでいたわけではない。

　再度、発見された肥前磁器の状態を見ると、碗・小鉢・合子といずれも小型製品であり、数量は微々たるものである。またⅢ章で述べられているように後の時代の製品は全く含まれていない。つまり例外的に少量が持ち込まれただけで、大きさからは簡単に運べるものである。とするなら例えばモジョクルトの貴族のような外部の所有者が、特別な事情で来訪した時に持参したものと考えるのが妥当だろう。特別な事情とは、チャンパ王女の墓[16]のようなトロウランに残る初期イスラーム墓への巡礼墓参などが想定される。そうであってもジャワ島ではこの時期の肥前陶磁は、少なくとも内陸の農村地帯へも運ばれるほどの供給がなされていたことは間違いない。

4. 大量生産雑器と華人

　トロウランとティルタヤサ及びソンバ・オプーは、17世紀末以前には基本的な役割を終えている。ところが長い期間利用されたバンテン・ラーマとブトン・ウォリオの出土陶磁片を見ると、最大量を示すのはいずれもⅥ-2期（18世紀後半頃）である。

　バンテン王国はティルタヤサ大スルタンの時代が最盛期だが、内乱後の1683年以降オランダに従属する。またブトン王国はマカッサル戦争の際にゴワとオランダのどちらに付くかが問題になったように重要な存在だったが、以後ほとんど普通の歴史書には登場しない。陶磁片の出土量とそれぞれ王国の活発な時代には、大きなズレが見られる。これは両国に限ったことではなく、東南アジア群島部の大部分の王国（ほとんどがイスラーム王国）の活発な時代は同じように17世紀後半を終末としている。そのためヨーロッパ系の歴史家は、1680年代までにこの地域は「交易の時代」が終わって「開発の時代」という新しい時代に入ったと考えている[17]。

　しかし18世紀、特に後半に大量の陶磁片が出土するのは、バンテン・ラーマとブトン・ウォリオに特異な現象ではない。例えばスマトラ北端のアチェ王国関連の港市遺跡、あるいはマレー半島南端のジョホール王国関連遺跡などどこでも似た状況があり、それは群島部にとどまらずⅡ章で紹介したタイのロプブリ・台湾の左営鳳山県旧城さらにベトナムのフォーヒエン[18]など多くの港市遺跡でも同じである。それらの遺跡で出土する陶磁片の大部分は決して地元の製品ではなく、中国福建の陶磁器である。つまり貿易陶磁であり、そのため「交易の時代」は18世紀にこそ活発になったとさえ見ることができる。

16　トロウランに残る1448年の紀年銘を持つイスラーム墓。マジャパイト王とドゥマッなどの新興ムスリム王権を結びつける存在であるチャンパ王女の墓として信じられているが、その証拠はない。

17　Reid 1988 など

18　北部ベトナムの港市遺跡。17・18世紀に北部ベトナムを支配したチン氏政権の外港で、オランダ東インド会社の商館も置かれていた。

　ここで注意を要するのは、18 世紀後半の福建産の陶磁器にはそれまでとは異なった大きな特徴があることである。まず大量の個数が運ばれたにも関わらず、種類は少なく大部分は碗皿類の食器である。そして決まり切った簡単な装飾が多く、型作りなどが多用されている。つまり大量生産の雑器であり、普通の博物館で展示されるような骨董価値のある陶磁器とは全く異なっている。

　福建のいくつかの産地では、17 世紀からそのような陶磁器を生産して輸出していた。例えば粗製白磁の安平壺（Fig.53-283）は液体容器で上下半分ずつを別に作って接合する方法で製作され、印青花（Fig.66-336・340 など）は文様をハンコで表している。ただこの時代にはそれらは特別のもので、決して大多数を占めていたわけではない。しかし 18 世紀後半に東南アジアで輸入された陶磁器の大部分はそのような大量生産雑器になってしまった。全くの農村地帯になって久しいトロウランでも 55 推定個体数が出土しているが、それはトロウランの全陶磁片の 7,754 推定個体数の 0.7% 程度になる。

　そのような福建産の粗製陶磁器の意味を考えてみよう。

　陶磁器にはさまざまな形状があるが、単純に分けると碗と皿、そしてその他になる（Ⅲ章末尾折込「表 1 トロウラン遺跡出土陶磁器集計表」参照）。碗と皿は普通の分類では食器であり、その他は食器以外の全ての種類である。トロウラン出土の全陶磁片は、碗 41.9%・皿 38.0% そしてその他 20.1% に分かれる。碗と皿の割合はかなり近いが、これを全体の94% に当たる中心時期（13 世紀末〜16 世紀初頭）で見ると、最初の 14 世紀前半を除く時期は皿が最大の割合である。

　陶磁器に限ることなく、食器として考えた時、ベトナムを除く大部分の現代の東南アジアでは皿類（中皿と大皿）が最も重要な形態で、主食の米飯も基本的に皿に盛られる。碗の用途はカレーを含むスープ類と麺の容器で、二次的な形態である。トロウランで全体に皿が多いことは、そのような食器として使った場合の区分を表している。しかし碗でも皿でも、日常的な食器として実際に使われた可能性は低い。伝統的な食事、特にマジャパイト時代はヒンドゥ教の浄不浄観の影響もあって、現在の南インドのように一回ごとに廃棄するバナナの葉などが使われていたはずである。陶磁器の実際の用途は、儀礼などの特別の食事に使われる以外は宝物的なものとして調度品に似た扱いをされていたと思われる。その場合でも、装飾と文様が目立つ皿が優位にあっただろう。上記の割合は、そのような使い分けであったことを反映している。

　ここで 18 世紀の陶磁器の雑器に戻ると、トロウランのこの時代では碗 47.1%・皿 32.9%そしてその他 20.0% となる。全体の区分に比べて、明らかに碗が増え半数近くに達している。マジャパイト時代と 18 世紀で同じ地域の住民の食生活が根本的に変化したことは考えにくいので、この変化は別の要因があるはずである。バンテン・ラーマでは 17 世紀後

半以降になると皿類の割合が過半数を占め、その傾向は終焉時まで続いている[19]。ブトン・ウォリオでも 18 世紀後半の雑器は同様に碗の割合が高くなっている傾向が認められる。

このことを合理的に解釈しようとすると、別の食文化の混入が想定できる。碗を重視する食文化を現す現象として最も考えやすい理由は、華人の移住である。東南アジアへの華人の大規模な移住は、17 世紀中葉の明清交替期が最初の大きな波だが、18 世紀後半により大規模な次の波が起きている。群島部の場合、彼らの出身地の大部分は福建南部である。もちろん最初の移住先は基本的に港町で、この地域ではスラバヤになる。そこから内陸の町に移り始め、18 世紀後半にはそのような状態に進んだ可能性が大きい。

華人は自身の食器を持ち込むと共に、彼らの食文化も地元民に影響を与えた。そのため碗中心の食器が、皿中心の地元民の一部に新たに受け入れられた[20]。ただしそれは基本的に都市の状況であって、トロウランの農村社会までそのようになった可能性は低い。ごく一部を除いて大部分の農村居住者の食生活は、一家族で皿が数枚のみという伝統的な食生活を続けていたはずである[21]。

それでは出土した 18 世紀後半の雑器の存在は、どのように考えられるのか。トロウラン在住の地元民自身の使用がほぼ限られる以上、外来者が持ち込んだとしか考えられない。それは前項で述べた肥前磁器の搬入と似たような、モジョクルトなど近くの都市居住者がイスラーム墓巡礼などのためにやってきた際に持ち込んだもの以外には想定しにくい。前世紀同様に 18 世紀のトロウランに港町と特別な繋がりのある人々が居住していたのでない限り、そのような状況でしか可能性はないだろう。

18 世紀後半の福建南部からの華人の移住は、ジャワ社会のみならず他の島々でも見られた大きな社会的変動である。それは陶磁貿易の視点でも、彪大な福建系粗製磁器の搬入という現象で目に見える状態になっている。ただトロウランの持つイスラーム文化の早期受容地というような特殊な条件を持つ場合に限って、農村部にまで大きな影響を及ぼしたのではないだろうか。似た状態はブトン・ウォリオでも見られる。ウォリオ城内はブトン王国の中枢で、王族と貴族しか住んでいない。しかし城外のバウバウ港市はナマコなどの海産物取引で賑わい、それらを扱う華人の居住が増え始めていた。その関係の中で、福建系雑器が城内へも大量にもたらされた。

華人移住は 19 世紀中葉頃から、さらに大きな規模になる。この時代の彼らと関係する陶磁器を考えるには、バンテン・ラーマとブトン・ウォリオでの状態が分かりやすい。後者ではほとんど陶磁片そのものが極めて減少してしまうのに対し、バンテン・ラーマでは

---

19 坂井 2002 の 90-91 頁　バンテン・ラーマには 17 世紀中葉までに華人がすでに多く移住している。

20 例えば麺食は地元民に受け入れられた華人食文化の一つである。ただし熱帯気候に合わせて、インドネシアでは麺とスープを分けて食べるのが一般的になっている。その場合、共に碗を使用する。なお大陸部では碗を使う麺食の比率がインドネシアより高いが、米飯の容器は基本的に皿であり、またタイ東北やラオスでの主食もち米は竹製の筒型容器に盛っている。

21 現在は農村でも一般的なコーヒーは、18 世紀には輸出商品として一部で栽培が強制され始めたばかりで、一般の農民が飲用した可能性はないだろう。

ヨーロッパの陶磁器が主体を占める状態で一定の量が出土している。19世紀初頭にバンテンの王宮は破壊され王国は消滅するが、バンテン・ラーマは依然として少ないながら華人が住み続けた小港市としての役割を19世紀末まで維持した。この時に華人たちが使っていた陶磁器は、さらに劣悪になっていた福建産雑器ではなく、ヨーロッパ陶磁に変わっていたのである。バウバウの華人たちも同様に使用陶磁器を変えた可能性があるが、それが城内にあまりもたらされなかったのは、ヨーロッパ陶磁の流通拠点であるバタヴィア・スラバヤからの遠さと共に、この時代には城内の貴族たちとの関係がかなり弱くなったからではないだろうか。

　ヨーロッパ人の植民地に移住した華人たちの生活がそれぞれの場所の条件に合わせて変化していくことを、これらの遺跡で出土した陶磁片は伝えてくれると言える。

参考文献

愛知県陶磁資料館 1987『企画展　東南アジアのやきもの』

有田町教育委員会　2008『欧州貴族を魅了した古伊万里―蒲原コレクション―』

有田ポーセリンパーク　1993『陶磁の東西交流展』

石井米雄監修　1991『インドネシアの事典』、同朋舎出版

石澤良昭・生田滋　2009『世界の歴史13　東南アジアの伝統と発展』、中公文庫

出光美術館　1982『近年発見の窯址出土中国陶磁展』

扇浦正義　2013『唐人屋敷跡』、長崎市教育委員会

大阪市文化財協会　1998『住友銅吹所跡発掘調査報告』

大橋康二　1981「15・16世紀における日本出土の青花碗に関する編年試案(1)」『白水』8号

大橋康二　1995「海外輸出された肥前磁器の特質について」『王朝の考古学』、雄山閣

大橋康二　1998「トルコで発見した肥前の青磁」『目の眼』259、里文出版

大橋康二　1999a「明末・清代における中国福建省徳化窯系磁器について」『大阪市文化財
　　協会研究紀要』2号、pp.241-248

大橋康二　1999b「秋二題」『目の眼』279

大橋康二　2004a『海を渡った陶磁器』、吉川弘文館

大橋康二　2004b「日本磁器―徳川将軍と欧州土侯の伊万里―」『JIKI』、イタリア・ファ
　　エンツァ市、国際交流基金

大橋康二　2016「17世紀後半、中国磁器の量を超えた肥前磁器の流通」『中近世陶磁器の
　　考古学　第四巻』雄山閣、pp.63-84

大橋康二監修　2011『海を渡った古伊万里―セラミックロード―』、青幻舎

大橋康二・坂井隆　1999「インドネシア・バンテン・ラーマ遺跡出土の陶片」『国立歴史
　　民俗博物館研究報告』82、pp.47-94

大橋康二ほか　1988『有田町史　古窯編』、有田町

沖縄県教育委員会　1999『喜友名貝塚・喜友名グスク』

沖縄県立埋蔵文化財センター　2001a『首里城―下之御庭跡・用物座跡・瑞泉門跡・漏刻
　　門跡・廣福門跡・木曳門跡発掘調査報告書―』

沖縄県立埋蔵文化財センター　2001b『首里城跡―管理用道路地区発掘調査報告書―』

沖縄県立埋蔵文化財センター　2001c『天界寺跡(I)』

亀井明徳ほか　2005『亜州古陶瓷研究II』、亜州古陶瓷学会

亀井明徳ほか　2008『亜州古陶瓷研究III』、亜州古陶瓷学会

亀井明徳ほか　2009『カラコルム遺跡出土陶瓷調査報告書II』、専修大学文学部アジア考
　　古学研究室

亀井明徳、ジョン・ミクシック　2010『インドネシア・トローラン遺跡発見陶瓷の研究―
　　シンガポール大学東南アジア研究室保管資料―』、専修大学アジア考古学チーム

京都国立博物館　1991『日本人が好んだ中国陶磁』

久礼克季　2016「台湾鄭氏―中国南部―東南アジアを結ぶ諸条件とオランダ東インド会社」『貿易陶磁と文献史料から東アジア・東南アジアの歴史を考える―16 世紀・17 世紀を中心とした海域におけるヒト・モノの流れ―』、立教大学アジア地域研究所

古伊万里調査委員会編　1959『古伊万里』

坂井隆　2002『港市国家バンテンと陶磁貿易』、同成社

坂井隆　2009「インドネシア、トロウラン遺跡とベトナムタイル Preliminary Study of Vietnamese Decorated Tile Found In Java, Indonesia (2)」『金沢大学考古学紀要』30、pp.28-41、金沢大学文学部考古学講座

坂井隆　2015「インドネシア、トロウラン遺跡出土のタイル」『東洋陶磁』44、pp.63-83

坂井隆編　2000『バンテン・ティルタヤサ遺跡発掘調査報告書』、上智大学アジア文化研究所・インドネシア国立考古学研究センター

坂井隆編　2004『海のシルクロードの拠点バンテン・ティルタヤサ遺跡の陶磁貿易の研究』、㈶なら・シルクロード博記念国際交流財団シルクロード学研究センター

坂井隆編　2007『バンテン・ティルタヤサ遺跡　ブトン・ウォリオ城跡発掘調査報告書』、NPO 法人アジア文化財協力協会

坂井隆・大橋康二　2014『インドネシア、トロウラン遺跡出土の陶磁器』、モノグラフシリーズ 15、上智大学アジア文化研究所

佐賀県立九州陶磁文化館　1990『海を渡った肥前のやきもの展』

佐賀県立九州陶磁文化館　1991『柴田コレクションⅡ』

佐賀県立九州陶磁文化館　1995『柴田コレクションⅣ』

佐賀県立九州陶磁文化館　2000『古伊万里の道』

佐賀県立九州陶磁文化館　2003『白雨コレクション 100 選』

佐賀県立博物館　1983『売茶翁』

佐々木達夫・野上建紀・佐々木花江　2004「ミャンマー窯跡踏査と採集陶磁器」『金沢大学考古学紀要』Vol.27、pp.147-246

清水菜穂　2010「ヴィエンチャン旧市街地内出土の肥前陶磁器」『世界に輸出された肥前陶磁』、九州近世陶磁学会

清水菜穂　2014「ラオス出土のヴェトナム陶磁」『14・15 世紀海域アジアにおけるベトナム陶磁の動き―ベトナム・琉球・マジャパヒト―』、昭和女子大学国際文化研究所紀要 Vol.21、pp.109-124

清水菜穂・ラオス国立博物館　2014「ラオス・シェンクワン県内仏教寺院における発掘調査」『東南アジア考古学』34、東南アジア考古学会

小学館　1976a『世界陶磁全集 11　隋・唐』

小学館　1976b『世界陶磁全集 14　明』

小学館　1981『世界陶磁全集13　遼・金・元』

小学館　1984『世界陶磁全集16　南海』

昭和女子大学国際文化研究所　2002『ベトナム・ホイアン地域の考古学的研究』

髙島裕之　2013「(5)無釉印花文壺」『鹿児島神宮所蔵陶瓷器の研究』、pp.64-66、鹿児島
　　神宮所蔵陶瓷器調査団

千代田区教育委員会　2011『江戸城の考古学Ⅱ　第Ⅱ分冊』

東京国立博物館　1975『日本出土の中国陶磁』

戸栗美術館　1998『日本陶磁名品図録』

長崎県教育委員会　1984『九州横断自動車道建設に伴う埋蔵文化財緊急発掘調査報告書』

長崎市教育委員会　1986『出島和蘭商館跡範図確認調査報告書』

長崎市教育委員会　1997『築町遺跡』

長崎市埋蔵文化財調査協議会　1993『栄町遺跡』

永渕友子　1997「輸出された肥前陶磁器の流れ（手付瓶・壺類）」『柴田コレクション(V)』
　　佐賀県立九州陶磁文化館

永松実　1993「発掘された食文化の洋風化について」『長崎出島の食文化』親和銀行

日本経済新聞社　1980『英国デヴィッド・コレクション中国陶磁展』

日本経済新聞社　2009『パリに咲いた古伊万里の華』

根津美術館　1993『南蛮・島物』

野上建紀　2013「ガレオン貿易と肥前磁器」『東洋陶磁』42、東洋陶磁学会、pp.141-176

野上建紀・Alfredo B. Orogo・Nida T. Cuevas・田中和彦・洪曉純 2005「ガレオン船で運
　　ばれた肥前磁器」『水中考古学研究』1

平戸市教育委員会　1988『平戸和蘭商館跡』

深見純生　2014「15世紀のマジャパヒト」『14・15世紀海域アジアにおけるベトナム陶
　　磁の動き―ベトナム・琉球・マジャパヒト―』昭和女子大学国際文化研究所紀要
　　Vol.21、pp.43-57

平凡社　1978『陶磁大系47　タイ・ベトナムの陶磁』

平凡社　1995『中国の陶磁8　元・明の青花』

平凡社　1997『中国の陶磁4　青磁』

町田市立博物館　1993『ベトナム陶磁』

町田市立博物館　2013『舛田コレクション　ヴェトナム陶磁の二千年』

繭山康彦　1977「デマク回教寺院の安南青花陶塼について」『東洋陶磁』4、pp.41-57

繭山康彦　1985「マジャパヒト王都址出土の元代青花磁片」『元の染付展―14世紀の景徳
　　鎮窯―』、pp.27-29、大阪市立東洋陶磁美術館

三杉隆敏　1987『世界の染付(4)』、同朋社

向井亙　2012『金沢大学文化資源学研究第5号　タイ陶磁器の編年研究』、金沢大学国際

　　　　文化資源学研究センター

武蔵文化財研究所　2015『有楽町一丁目遺跡』

森毅　1992「大阪で使われたベトナム製陶磁器」『葦火』40号、大阪市文化財協会

森毅　1993「江戸時代の唐物と和物」『葦火』43号、大阪市文化財協会

森本朝子　2006「スマトラ西海岸バルースのロブテュア遺跡」『金大考古』55、pp.1-11、金沢大学考古学研究室

矢部良明　1978『陶磁大系47　タイ・ベトナムの陶磁』、平凡社

山口県埋蔵文化財センター　2002『萩城跡（外堀地区）Ⅰ』

山脇悌二郎　1988「貿易篇―唐・蘭船の伊万里焼輸出―」『有田町史商業編Ⅰ』、佐賀県有田町

景徳鎮市陶瓷考古研究所・徐氏芸術館　1993『成窯遺珍―景徳鎮珠山出土成化官窯瓷器』

国立故宮博物院　1990『明代初年瓷器特展図録』、台北

国立歴史博物館　1992『中国名陶展』、台北

国立中央博物館　1977『新安海底文物』、Seoul

慈渓市博物館編　2002『上林湖越窯』、文物出版社

上海人民美術出版社　1981『中国陶瓷全集4　越窯』

徐本章　1990「試談徳化窯青花瓷装飾芸術及其影響」Ho Chuimei(ed.) *"Ancient Ceramic Kiln Technology in Asia"*

浙江省文物考古研究所・北京大学考古文博学院・慈渓市文物管理委員会　2002『寺龍口越窯址』、文物出版社

臧振華・高有徳・劉益昌　1993「左営清代鳳山県旧城聚落的試掘」『中央研究院歴史語言研究所集刊』

曽凡　2001『福建陶瓷考古概論』、福建省地図出版社

談雪慧他　1998『中国明代瓷器目録』

中国広西壮族自治区博物館・越南国家歴史博物館他　2009『越南出水陶瓷』

福建省博物館　1997『漳州窯』、福建人民出版社

香港大学馮平山博物館　1992『景徳鎮出土陶磁』

楊少祥　1990「広東青花瓷器初探」Ho Chuimei(ed.) *"Ancient Ceramic Kiln Technology in Asia"*

葉清琳　1990「安渓青花瓷器的初歩研究」Ho Chuimei(ed.) *"Ancient Ceramic Kiln Technology in Asia"*

姚澄清・孫敬民・姚連紅　1990「試談広昌紀年墓出土的青花瓷盤」『江西文物』2

Adhyatman, Sumarah. 1981. *"Antique Ceramics found in Indonesia"*, Jakarta: The

Ceramic Society of Indonesia.

Adhyatman, Sumarah. 1999. "*Zhangzhou (Swatow) Ceramics, Sixteenth To Seventeenth Centuries Found In Indonesia*", Jakarta: The Ceramic Society of Indonesia.

Adhyatman, S. & AbuRidho. 1984. "*Tempayandi Indonesia/Martavansin Indonesia*", 2nd ed., Jakarta: The Ceramic Society of Indonesia.

Burghley House. 1983. "*The Exhibition of Burghley House porcelain*".

Butterfield Auctioneers Corp. 2000. "*Treasures from The HoiAn Hoard*".

Carswell, John. 1998. "*Iznik Pottery*", The Trustees of The British Museum.

Chandavij, Natthapatra. 1989. "*Ceramics From Excavations Lop Buri 1986-1987*". Bangkok.

Christie's Limited. 1988. "*The Hatcher Porcelain Cargoes*".

Duppoizat, Marie-France & Naniek Harkantiningsih. 2007. "*Catalogue of the Chinese Style Ceramics of Majapahit, Tentative In ventory*". Cahierd' Archiple 36, Paris: Association Archipel.

Frankfurt. 1997. "*Chinesisches Porzellan*".

Goddio, Franck et al. 2002. "*Tresor De Porcelaines*".Periplus Publishing London Ltd.

Guillot, C. 1990. "*The Sultanate of Banten*". Jakarta: Gramedia.

Guillot, C., Lukman Nurhakim & Sonny Wibisono. 1994. "*Banten avant l'Islam: Etude archeologiquede Banten Girang (Java-Indonesie) 932?-1526*". Paris: Publicationsdel' Ecole Francaised' Extreme-Orient.

Guillot, C., Daniel Perret & Naniek H. Wibisono. 1998. "*Lobu Tua: Sejarah Awal Barus [Lobu Tua: The Early History of Barus]*", Jakarta: Yayasan Obor.

Guy, John. 1989a. 'The Vietnamese Wall Tiles of Majapahit', "*Transactionsofthe Oriental Ceramics Society 53 (1988-89)*".

Guy, John. 1989b "*Ceramic Tradition of Southeast Asia*", Singapore: Oxford University Press.

Harrison, Burbara. 1979. "*Swatow*".

Hasan M. Ambary, Hasan Djafar, Mundardjito. 1978. "*Laporan Penelitian Arkeologi Banten 1976 [Archaeological Study Report of Banten, 1976]*", Jakarta: Pusat Penelitian Purbakara dan Peninggalan Nasional.

Hasan M. Ambary, Halwany Michrob & John Miksic (ed.) 1988. "*Catalogue of Sites, Monuments and Artifacts of Banten*". Jakarta: Directorate for Protection and Development of Historicaland Archaeological Heritage.

Halway Michrob. 1993, "*Laporan Hasil Penelitian Arkeologi Situs Tirtayasa dan Situs Pagedongan [Arcaeological Stuty Report of Tirtayasa & Pagedongan Sites]*, Banten:

SPSP Jabar-DKI-Lampung".

Ho Chuimei 1990. "*Ancient Ceramic Kiln Technology in Asia*", Hong Kong Universtiy.

Jörg, C. J. A. 1986. "*The Geldermalsen History and Porcelain*", Groningen Kemper Publishers.

Jörg, C. J. A. 2003. "*Fine & Curious*".

Jörg, C. J. A. & Michael Flecker. 2001. "*Porcerain from The Vung Tau Wreck*".

Krahl, R. & J. Ayers. 1986. "*Chinese Ceramicsin The Topkapi Sarayi Museum Istanbul, A Complete Catalogue*", Sotheby's Publications.

Krahl, Regina, John Guy, J. Keith Wilson & Julian Raby. 2011. "*Shipwrecked Tang Treasuresand Monsoon Winds*", Washington: Smithsonian Books.

Miksic, John & Kamei Meitoku. 2010. "*Research on Ceramics Discovered at the Trowulan site in Indonesia*", Tokyo.

National Museum of Vietnamese History (NMVH). 1995. "*Bat Trang Ceramics 14th-19th Centuries*", Ha Noi.

National Museum of Vietnamese History (NMVH). 2005. "*2000 years of Vietnamese ceramics*", Ha Noi.

Pijl-Ketel, C.L. van der, 1982. "*The Ceramic load of The 'Witte Leeuw'*". Amsterdam: Rijksmuseum.

Pinto, Maria Antonia. 1996. "*Chinese Export Porcelain From The Museum of Anastacio Gong Alues*"

Reid, Anthony. 1988. "*Southeast Asia In The Age Of Commerce 1450-1680*". New haven: Yale Univ. Press.

Serrurier, L. 1902. 'Kaar Van Oud-Banten In Geroudheid, begracht door wijlen Mr. L. Serruirier (met eene in leiden gvan Dr. H. Brendes)'. TBG 45. Batavia.

Sheaf, Colin & Kilburn, Richard. 1988. "*The Hatcher Porcelain Cargoes, The Compete Record*", Oxford.

Smart, Ellen. 1975. 'Fourteenth Century Chinese Porcelain froma Tughlaq Palace in Delhi', "*Transactions of the Oriental Ceramic Society*", vol.51, 1975-7

The Trustees of The British Museum. 1995. "*Islamic Tiles-Venetia Porter-*", London.

Woodward. C. S. 1974. "*Oriental Ceramicsat The Cape of Good Hope 1652-1795*".

あとがき

　トロウラン遺跡の陶磁片調査を開始したのは 2012 年だが、その数年前に遺跡博物館の構内にあった陶磁片集積場を最初に見た時に驚かされた。さらにそれより 3・4 年前に故亀井明徳先生よりトロウランでの共同調査の打診があったのだが、インドネシア側の受け入れ体制が整わなかった。何とか実現の可能性が出来かけた時には、亀井先生は体調をくずされてしまった。

　膨大な陶磁片の調査に参加できたことは、まずインドネシア国立考古学研究センターのナニッ・ウィビソノさんのご好意のおかげである。私たちと彼女の共同研究は四半世紀前のバンテン・ラーマから始まっている。そのため本書はこの間の共同研究の総括であるとも言えるが、彼女は三上次男先生の訪問時にもバンテン・ラーマを案内している。

　亀井先生以外に三上先生を始め、ハッサン・アムバリー博士、ハルワニ・ミフラブ博士、アブー・リドさんなどバンテン・ラーマ以来お世話になった少なからぬ方々がすでに鬼籍に入られてしまった。それを思う時、まず本書の意味は方々の墓前に捧げるものである。同時に、これから陶磁貿易史、とりわけインドネシアのそれを学ぼうとする若い世代へ伝えるための、私たちの贈り物になれば幸いである。

　本書の執筆は、Ⅰ・Ⅳ章を坂井隆が、Ⅱ・Ⅲ章を大橋康二が担当した。英文訳はニコール・ルマニエールさんと内田ひろみさんの労をわずらわせ、またトロウラン遺跡出土陶磁片の図版作成は山本文子さんにお願いした。さらに調査に際しては、瀧本正志氏ほかアジア文化財協力協会の仲間たちの尽力を受けたことを末尾に記したい。

2018 年 1 月

坂井　隆

Hizen wares excavated from Royal Capital Sites in Indonesia
— Trowulan and other sites —

Sakai Takashi and Ôhashi Kôji

Translated by
Nicole Coolidge Rousmaniere

Preface

The author of *Passage of ceramics*, Professor Mikami Tsugio first visited the Towulan site, Indonesia in 1984. His itinerary included the remains of the Tikus Bath and the Brahu Temple, where restoration work had just been initiated. Professor Mikami exchanged ideas and thoughts on recently excavated ceramic sherds from those sites with Mr. Abu Ridho, guided him.

The first excavation of the Trowulan Site was conducted around 1920 by an Indonesian-born Dutch architect Maclaine Pont along with a local aristocrat, Kromojoyo Adinegoro. Mikami Tsugio was only in his late teens at this point. The Tikus Bath was the beginning of a program of works, and excavated by Adinegoro. Significant numbers of ceramic sherds were unearthed during the excavation and restoration of the site. Van Orsay de Flines, a friend of Pont, took a great interest in the archaeology and the excavated sherds. He deeply loved ceramics and built up enormous collection of them during his lifetime.

His collection was later donated to the National Museum of Indonesia, Jakarta to found the ceramic gallery in the museum. Abu Ridho who had guided Mikami through the sites was also his assistant. The ceramics sherds from the Trowulan Site have been for a long time the only sherds on permanent display in the Museum's ceramic gallery.

Around twenty years after Mikami's first visit to the site, we had the opportunity to research Trowulan ceramic sherds collection that had been assembled over the years. The Trowulan collection was important enough for us to go back and re-examine past research on the other four royal capital sites in Indonesia.

This publication is intended to honor the work of our predecessors as well as to open up avenues for new research. The research recorded here is meant as a summation of efforts made to understand the site during the past quarter of the century.

Finally, we would like to express our gratitude to the Idemitsu Foundation of Cultural and Social Welfare for their generous support towards this publication.

January, 2018

Sakai Takashi

Contents

I. Trowulan site and Four Royal Capital sites

1. Details of the research

The Trowulan archaeological site, in Trowulan, Mojokerto in the Eastern Java of the Republic of Indonesia, is located on the right bank of the lower reaches of the Brantas River, which is the second longest in Java. It is a flat land about sixty kilometres from the estuary port city Surabaya and overlooks the sacred Mt. Penanggungan towards about 25 kilometres east.

We cooperated with the National Archaeology Study Centre and classified the unsorted ceramic shards that had been stored in the Trowulan Museum. Three researches were led by the senior researcher Prof. Naniek Harkantiningsih Wibisono in January 2012, April 2013 and August 2015. Although the outlines of the first and second research was already reported in 2014 [I-1], it was limited to the key types which cover only about 15% of their entire shards collection. Therefore, some supplementary works were done at research in 2015 including making measured drawings to prepare this publication.

Under such circumstance, this publication should have been sufficient enough just as a formal report on the ceramic shards from the Trowulan Site. However, we came to recognise that the details of the Trowulan ceramics perfectly summarise our collaborative researches on the ceramic shards in Indonesia during the past 25 years [I-2]. This is a list of those past collaborative researches (Map 1):

1993 and 1997	Banten Lama Site, Java [I-3]
1997, 1999 and 2001-2006	Tirtayasa Site, Java [I-4]
2001	Somba Opu Fort ruins, Sulawesi [I-5]
2004-2006	Buton Wolio Fort ruins, Sulawesi [I-6]

Details will be described in the chapter II, but the most active periods of the ceramic trades at these four sites are from the sixteenth to eighteenth centuries. The original opportunity for our collaborative research in Indonesia was to confirm the export status of Japanese Hizen ware for which the four sites fit into appropriate periods. However, we actually identified ceramic shards made before the fifteenth century to no small extent in the three sites except the Tirtayasa, which only existed for a very short period.

The core of the Trowulan ceramic shards came from the end of the thirteenth to the beginning of the sixteenth century, although small number of the seventeenth century Hizen ware was also found together with a number of shards from well before the thirteenth century. This tells that the Trowulan Site is older than the other four sites, but the former is related to the latter rather than being completely separated. It became also clear that the Trowulan is the key to understand the early ceramic trade of the ninth and tenth centuries in Indonesia. This situation set a format of this publication that it would overlook the entire ceramic trade in Indonesia, rather than just focusing on the ceramics from the Trowulan Site.

Although some information is already given in the previous outline report, we will write again in this publication details of the Trowulan Site and progress of research because they are of importance. Four other sites will be given a simple introduction only since their details are already reported. The main aim of this publication is to provide the entire view of the wider ceramic trade of Indonesia, geographically stretching in the archipelago of the Southeast Asia.

2. The Trowulan Site

Trowulan is the major capital site of the Majapahit Kingdom.

The Majapahit is the last and largest kingdom of the Indianized Hindu Java royal authority, which had existed in Java since the fifth century. The kingdom was founded by Kertarajasa Jayawarddhana (r.1293-1309) in 1293 prompted by the Java expedition of the Mongol Empire. Under the kingship of Rajasanagara (r.1350-89) (Hayam Wuruk) in the late fourteenth century with a assistance from his great prime minister Gajah Mada, the kingdom extended its influences over wider territories, which corresponds to present-day Indonesia. The kingdom still maintained its influence in the beginning of the fifteenth century and received a visit by Zheng He from the Ming Empire. However, Majapahit was quickly losing its power in the latter half of the fifteenth century owing to the development of Islamic port cities along the north coast of Java. Finally, in ca.1527, the royal capital Trowulan fell to the attack from the rising Islamic power led by Demak.

The fall of Majapahit Kingdom meant the Islamisation of Java. This was significant to the Muslims in Indonesia, which now houses the largest Muslim population in the world. However, Majapahit is never received negatively in the tradition of Islamic worship in Java. It is said that Islamic sultanates in Java, which began with Demak share the lineage with the king of Majapahit [I-7].

Academic research of the Trowulan Site was launched by H. Maclaine Pont (1884-1971) and R.A.A. Kromojoyo Adinegoro around 1920 when Indonesia was the Dutch colony. For those nationalists aiming for independency, the Majapahit Kingdom was the ideal past glory. Trowulan became the key research subject in late 1950's after Indonesia gained independency, and the site was domestically listed as a candidate for a World Heritage Site in 2009.

Outline of the Trowulan Site

We are now going to see the details of the site.

The most significant discovery since the research was launched by the National Archaeology Study Centre in 1976 was the canal network running like a grid to cover the entire Trowulan, which was revealed in an aerial photograph. Although remains of city wall have not yet been found to this date, it is currently estimated that the site is within the area of 9 x 11 kilometres. The canal network was laid in the central area of the site (with a radius of four kilometres) is roughly divided into the following four archaeological features.

Kedaton district

This is positioned in the centre of the canal network. Various brick made architectural remains had been found in this district. Among them, a brick building standing next to the Kedaton Temple of which only foundation platform remains particularly draw our attention. This building went through many reconstructions. To the west remains a group of octagonal pillar foundation stones used for a long and large raised floor/stilt building. The Sentonorejo Residence site was excavated at the south side of the above-mentioned brick building. A floor covered with unglazed hexagonal tiles was discovered nearly intact at the Sentonorejo Residence site.

Kedaton sounds similar with *keraton*, the word meaning a palace in Javanese. This suggests a high possibility that this district might have served a pivotal function of Trowulan. Facing Kedaton in the south, there is Troloyo district housing the oldest Islam graves in Trowulan, which are inscribed the year 1368 in the Hijri calendar.

Segaran Pond district

The Segaran Pond district is located about 1.5 kilometres north from Kedaton, and is centred around the artificial reservoir Segaran (about 370 x 150m). Remains of two major residential buildings made in bricks were also excavated at the southwest shore of the reservoir. In addition, there remains a Muslim tomb with the year inscription of 1448 at the northeast side of the pond along the canal. This tomb is said to be of the Princess Champa. The Trowulan Museum was built in vicinity of the residential remains.

Temples district in the north

About two kilometres north-northwest from the Segaran Pond lies the Brahu Temple site, which is the largest existing brick made temple. With other temple sites scatter in vicinity, this area could be the religious district. At the point due east about two kilometres from the Brahu temple remains the brick made a *Candi Bentar* (split gate) Wringin Lawang Gate.

Temples district in the east

There is a brick Bajang Ratu Gate, thought to be a temple gate, in two kilometres from Kedaton. This gate was originally a main shrine of a temple built in the eastern Javanese style, but the wall opposite to the entrance was hollowed so visitors can go through the space. This style is older than the split gate. The Candi Tikus Bathing place is located less than one kilometre to the east. This bathing site, found in 1914 by R.A.A. Kromojoyo Adinegoro, overlooks the sacred mountain Penanggungan (1653m) to the east alongside the Arjuno mountains (3389m). Many ritual and temple sites had been found in and at the foot of the Penanggungan mountain including the Jolotundo (977) and Belahan (1042) Bathing places and Jawi Temple (1300) etc.

Studying ceramic shards

Study of the ceramic shards from Trowulan however progressed slowly. Since E.W.

van Orsay de Flines (1886-1964) took an interest in the 1920's, a long blank period followed. It was Mayuyama Yasuhiko who first approached in the 1970's and 80's to the Yuan under-glaze cobalt blue ceramics and Vietnamese tiles from Trowulan [I-8]. John Guy followed him up on the Vietnamese tiles [I-9], although their study was not based on the officially excavated materials, it certainly gave a strong impetus to the research of the day.

The National Archaeology Study Centre conducted a major distribution survey in the beginning of 1990's, it was not until 2007 when the first catalogue was published by Naniek Harkantiningsih Wibisono jointly with Marie-France Duppoizat [I-10]. Main subject of this publication was the ceramic shards found by the National Archaeology Study Centre, and not focused on the Trowulan Museum's collection. However, it was certainly the first academic report on the ceramic shards excavated from the Trowulan Site. Following this, Kamei Meitoku and John Miksic issued a detailed report on the under-glaze cobalt blue shards in the collection of the National University of Singapore which are thought to be from the Trowulan [I-11].

A provenance of the ceramic shards we studied is given below.

The Dutch architect H. Maclaine Pont for the first time excavated the Trowulan Site from 1921 to 1924. He tried to reconstruct the royal capital recorded in the *Nagarakertagama* [I-12] and even made an architectural reconstruction drawing. The Pont's residence built in Trowulan in 1924 with help from R.A.A. Kromojoyo Adinegoro worked as a museum and a number of finds including ceramic shards were gathered and stored there.

Pont did not have a deep knowledge in shards, but created a dedicated outdoor storage area in his garden. E.W. van Orsay de Flines selected those with particular importance from the collected shards [I-13]. At the beginning of 1960's after Indonesia's independence, survey of the Trowulan Site was positioned as one of the essential national projects, and the previous Pont's residence was made a branch office of the Agency of Archaeology of the time. The Pont estate subsequently became the Preservation of Cultural Properties Office for Eastern Java and function as a museum together with shards were transferred to the Trowulan Museum, which was founded in 1997.

These shards were stored in the former Pont's residence and also in the outdoor shards storage area (about W: 3.0 x L: 2.0 x H: 0.5m) both located on the museum premise. Some shards are inscribed with caption from the survey time and this suggests that they had been in the collection since the date. Shards found after the museum was built are packed in bags and stored inside of the museum. Because all of the no bagged shards in the storage area are glazed, it is certain that they were excavated from the Trowulan after the Pont's time although the majority was missing information about found spot.

3. The Four Royal Capital sites

The four royal capital sites refer to the Banten Lama, the capital of the Banten Sultanate located in Western Java, its royal villa in Tirtayasa, the Somba Opu Fort as the capital of Gowa Sultanate in the Southern part of Sulawesi, and the Wolio Fort as the capital of Buton Sultanate in the Southeastern Sulawesi. All of these four places are the pivotal authority of the Islamic sultanates and were eventually destroyed to ruins by the Dutch except the Wolio Fort.

We are now going to look at each sites briefly.

Banten Lama Site

The Banten Sultanate was found in the Sunda Strait laid between Java and Sumatera in the beginning of the sixteenth century. Its royal lineage is not always clear but it is said the sultanate traced back to Demak in the Central Java and its founder Fatahillah was a scholar of Islamic studies from Samudura-Pasai, Aceh in the northern edge of Sumatera. What we know is that even Sunda Kelapa (later became Batavia, and present-day Jakarta), the second important port city after the capital Banten was under their rule by 1527.

The area around the Sunda Strait had been long known for pepper production. Indianized culture took a root in this area from the early years. A little over ten kilometres away from the estuary of the Banten River lies the Banten Girang Site which is surrounded by moats. The Banten Girang was the stronghold during the pre-Islamic Period and a large volume of trade ceramics mainly from the twelveth and thirteenth centuries has been unearthed. After the Portuguese conquered on Malacca in 1511, the Muslim merchants avoided the Malacca Strait as the east-west trade route. Banten at the Sunda Strait became the essential alternative route. The Dutch who landed first time in Asia in 1596 came to Banten straight from South Africa and acquired peppers there [I-15].

The Dutch took advantage of the internal strife in Banten, in 1619 occupied Sunda Kelapa, which they later renamed as Batavia. For the following one and half centuries, with many twists and turns, Batavia and Banten co-existed by complementing each other as the largest port cities in the islands of Southeast Asia. The Dutch East India Company in Batavia gained dominant political power of the Banten Sultanate after 1682, but the Asian network, which Banten had been building up was maintained until the Dutch got involved with the second civil war in middle of the eighteenth century.

Despite that the sultan of Banten was mere puppet of the Dutch by the second half of the eighteenth century, its royal palace was destroyed in 1809 and the sultanate was completely vanished with an expulsion of the last sultan in 1832. In this sense, Banten was different from other sultanates in Java who were under the similar situation. It was rather unacceptable to the new Dutch colonial government, took it over from the Dutch East India Company.

The capital Banten, once housing 100,000 people in the latter half of the seventeenth century, changed to a farming village Banten Lama ('Old Banten') after the sultanate disappeared. The Great Mosque and the Klenteng/Chinese Temple Banten Lama were the only reminiscence of its former glory. The first study on Banten Lama was the recording of 36 remaining place names and was conducted by L. Serruriel in 1900 [I-16]. However, the first archaeological investigation had to be waited until 1968 for the joint surface survey done by the University of Indonesia and the National Archaeology Study Centre.

Eight years on in 1976, the reorganised National Archaeology Study Centre carried out the first excavation research of Banten Lama in cooperation with the University of Indonesia. The excavation was led by Hasan M. Ambary and became the first serious excavation research in the field of the Islamic cultural archaeology, a newly established field in the Indonesian archaeology. The research report published two years later in 1978 [I-17] set a future direction of not only Banten but also of the Islamic cultural archaeology.

While the excavation in Banten Lama continued annually, preservation activity was launched of the remains including the Surosowan Palace site, which was the main focus of the research. The first outcome of the excavation and preservation was edited by Hasan M. Ambary and Halwany Michrob with their colleagues and published in 1988 under the title of "Catalogue of Sites, Monuments and Artifacts of Banten" [I-18]. This publication provided for the first time research status, typical examples of structural remains and artifacts such as shards accompanied with photographs.

Outline of the site

The Banten Lama Site consists of three areas which are the palace area enclosed by the city walls, and the west with east outside of the wall, where a Chinese quarter and the great market once located respectively. The Banten River runs through the area within the wall from southeast to northwest. The left bank housed the royal palace and the Great Mosque of Banten while the right bank is facing the sea.

The inside of city wall - left bank

The Surosowan Palace was built in the centre of the palace area. Across the square, the north side is facing the Great Mosque of Banten which attracts many visitors still today. The wall we see today is an oblong shape (H: 3m, widest point 14m, east-west 282 x south-north 140m, inner area measures about 23,600㎡) with a star-shaped bastion in each of four corners. The wall was built by a refugee Dutch engineer in 1680. Excavation focused on the area around the main gate at the northwest side. Remaining of a brick made building for formal audience etc. bating place and waterworks had been found. Many building foundations had been found also in the north side of the wall, some of which predate the currently existing wall.

The inside of city wall - right bank

The Kaibon Palace site is located about 500 meters southeast from the site of the Surosowan Palace. The Kaibon was built in the beginning of the nineteenth century for the mother of the last sultan. Brick built walls arranged with split gates, ruins of a mosque and part of the main residence still can be seen today. However, ceramic shards dated to the seventeenth century had been excavated from this site to no small extent. In the seventeenth century, the site used to be at the point on the right bank where the Banten River was coming into the palace area. Some buildings might possibly have stood there.

The western outside of city wall

The Spilwijk Fort is located on the right bank at the estuary of the (old) Banten River. The fortress was constructed by the Dutch in 1685 and is made with coral limestone in an irregular square structure. A part of the fortress wall was used the city wall (width at the base about 1.5m, height about 4m). Pabean (the custom district) lies on the opposite side of the river, where the Klenteng Banten Lama, an Overseas Chinese Temple, stands since it was built after the second half of eighteenth century.

The site of Chinese quarter (Pacinan) is about 600 meters west of the Surosowan Palace. Ruins of a mosque and a Chinese tomb from the first half of nineteenth century remain today. It was after 1630's when this area developed as the Chinese district. The original Chinese district was enclosed in wooden fences and located around the Klenteng Banten Lama in the 1590's.

The eastern outside of city wall

There was once the great market in the location of about seven hundreds meters northeast of the Surosowan Palace. The area is the same place with the lively Karangantu port and its market today. The bronze cannon 'Ki Amuk' now on display in the Banten Lama Site Museum was here in the early twentieth century.

Study on ceramic shards

Numerous ceramic shards have been unearthed at this site since the first excavation in 1976. The Site Museum was opened in front of the Surosowan Palace in 1985, and such museum was a rare existence in Indonesia in those days. Preservation of Cultural Properties Office for the Western Java was set up within the museum and became the central point for protection of cultural property. Ceramic shards from the site were being stored outside the museum.

We studied and sorted out these shards which had been stored outside the museum. They were moved to the Banten Office of the National Archaeology Study Centre in neighbourhood just before we started. All of them were captioned with find spot and stratigraphic position. The majority of them was from the Surosowan Palace site but some were from other sites including the Spilwijk Fortress.

Tirtayasa Site

This is the site of a retirement palace for the Great Sultan Tirtayasa (ruled: 1651-1678). It is located 20 kilometres east of Banten Lama [I-19].

The Great Sultan was said the most clear-sighted among the sultans of Banten. He took a policy of strong army and wealthy nation in order to counter the Dutch East India Company. In particular, he introduced a positive measure on trade, which was the heart of the economy. For example, while previous sultans charged taxes to foreign merchants who came to Banten for peppers, the Great Sultan sent out own merchant ships to different parts of Asia. On foreign policy, he formed an alliance with other Islamic sultanates to encircle the Dutch East India Company.

As another economic policy, he launched a development of irrigation system in the Tirtayasa region in around 1663. The region had higher water level but the Great Sultan cultivated paddy fields on a large scale by building irrigation canals [I-20]. Tirtayasa means the great water in Javanese, and this exactly refers to the irrigation development by canals.

It was this region where the Great Sultan built a retirement royal villa after he abdicated the throne to his son Sultan Haji. However, the father and the son had a completely different policy against the Dutch and soon they found themselves seriously confronting each other. This led to a civil war broken in February 1682 and eventually turned to a war between the Great Sultan and the Dutch, who backed up the then disadvantageous Sultan Haji. The Dutch army took control of the Tirtayasa Villa in the same year and subsequently the Great Sultan was forced to surrender in March next year. The villa ended its short five years history.

Outline of the site

The site stretches over the east of the Tirtayasa village office. The mausoleum for the Great Sultan is located 100 meters north-northeast the village office. The long land from south to north (90 x 50m) on the south of the mausoleum is called the 'Sultan's land'. On the east side, across the low land also running south to north (width about 15m), there is another and larger oblong land (130 x 90m). Both lands are now used as communal burial grounds.

At the northwest corner of the larger Sultan's land, there is a rectangular area (50 x 25 meters) surrounded by small bank (bottom width 5 meters, height less than one meter). The Gunung Sewu hill, the highest in the neighbourhood stands west of the village office. A strategy map of the Tirtayasa Villa drawn by the Dutch shows a triangular pyramid shaped hill topped with a flag in the centre of the villa area. Judging from the current geography this has to be the Gunung Sewu.

Across a village road to south from the Sultan's land lies a polygon shaped space (about 120 x 120 meters), which used to be a rice mill. A winding stream makes west and south boundary of this land. An old road called 'Sultan's road' is running from the south edge of this land in direction of southeast. A great number of Chinese coins were found near the Sultan's road in the past.

A canal network constructed during the reign of the Great Sultan runs along the site and the Tirtayasa village from west to south, linking the Ujung River and the Durian River. The canal taken from the Ujung River branches off.

First rescue investigation and preservation in Tirtayasa Site were brought in by the Preservation of Cultural Properties Office in 1993 when they conducted an emergency research to confirm the area. Construction materials such as coral limestone and bricks with a large quantity of ceramic shards had been unearthed from the archaeological site, which is now used as communal cemeteries, through building new graves.

Study of ceramic shards

Six Japanese scholars participated in the International Seminar for Japanese ceramics found in Indonesia held in Banten Lama from 14 – 18 October 1992. They visited the Tirtayasa Site for the first time and confirmed many shards of Hizen ware had been scattered over the ground.

It was not until 1997 when the Study Group for Banten Site and the National Archaeology Study Centre carried out the first joint excavation research [I-21]. The second research, also aiming to classify the artifacts collected from the first excavation, had to be waited until July and August 1999 after the political situation in Indonesia had settled. Similar research of the Tirtayasa Site followed in August – September 2001, September 2002, October 2004, November 2005 and August – September 2006, making seven in total. First five researchs focused on the villa site but the canal locks were the main focus after the fifth.

It is certain that the villa once stood in the 'Sultan's land' as we had found a section of the outer wall. However, the land is a communal cemetery for residents today. The underground structural remains are destroyed and a large quantity of shards emerge over the land surface every day through constructing new graves. Confirming the original position of shards through excavation is getting difficult day by day [I-22]. Shards already unearthed and scattered over the ground could also be useful because of a very short life of the villa, but the current situation restricts to appreciate the precise condition of excavation.

Somba Opu Fort

The Sulawesi Island is located northeast of the Java Island across the Java Sea. It is a large, strange K-shaped island in the eastern part of Indonesia. The Bugis and Makassar people inhabiting in the southern part of the Sulawesi are well known as one of the prominent traditional trader in Indonesia. Both people founded several Islamic sultanates during the sixteenth to eighteenth century, which is around the same period and had a close relation with the Banten Sultanate. In particular, a Makassar Syekh Yusuf, a son-in-law of Great Sultan Tirtayasa of Banten is well known as the Muslim leader who continued to resist against the Dutch along with the Great Sultan.

Based in Makassar, the Gowa Sultanate was a marine power that took a great part in spice trade for the Maluku (Moluccas) Islands. Once dominated the south of the Sulawesi allied with the neighbouring Tallo Kingdom in the middle of the sixteenth century, Gowa extended its influences over the Maluku Islands. Then in 1605 as the King Alauddin converted to Islam it became the most powerful sultanate exercising major influence over the spice trade in the east part of the Southeast Asian islands.

Two generations after, the sixteenth king Sultan Hasanuddin (ruled: 1653-1669) spent most of his life on the battle against the Dutch East India Company. He is one of the great national heroes in Indonesia even today. The primary cause of the battle was the supremacy over the spice trade in the Maluku Islands and because he owned a powerful fleet, the last stage of the battle (1666-1669) is known as the Makassar War.

Outline of the site

The Somba Opu Fort remains stand about five kilometres south from the Ujung Pandang (Rotterdam) Fort, which is the centre of Makassar today. Makassar is close to the south edge of the west coast of South Sulawesi facing the Strait of Makassar.

The fort is on the right bank of the Jeneberang River. Although being about two kilometres away from the river, the outlet is running on the northeast side. The original stronghold of the Gowa Kingdom was the Gowa Citadel going upstream of the same river about four kilometres. The Somba Opu likely became the base port city before the beginning of the seventeenth century.

The citadel fenced by square walls with bastions had been already built in the centre of Somba Opu by 1630's. The citadel lost its function when Sultan Hasanuddin was defeated at the last of a series of battles with the Dutch in 1669. Only remaining structure today are the south wall (650 meters long) together with the south edge of the east and west walls linking to the south wall (each about 100 meters long), made by bricks. The walls are quite thick from a standard of Southeast Asian islands and the south wall is 3.7 to 4.1 meters thick. The west wall, which was clearly restored, measures 10.5 meters-width. A third in the middle of the south wall which is about 100 meters in length, is projected. There is a round bastion at a south-west corner and a defensible gate on the west wall.

Study of ceramic shards

Following an invitation to the joint project on the ceramic shards excavated from the Somba Opu Fort ruins from the Preservation of Cultural Properties Office for South & Southeast Sulawesi in 2001, we participated in the study in September of the same year. This became the first academic research on ceramics in Sulawesi for Japan to get involved. Illegal digging of ceramics from the ancient tombs around Makassar had been actively going on since pre-war period. The most popular destination of these ceramics is antiques markets in Japan to this day. The first academic research on ceramics was carried out under this circumstance as the joint research.

The ceramic shards were found during the maintenance of the Somba Opu Fort ruins and were kept in the Preservation of Cultural Properties Office. Besides those on display in a site museum, the majority was stored in the Office situated in the site of Ujung Pandang Fortress.

The South Sulawesi drawn attentions since the Dutch colonial days for a large quantity of ceramics being remained. The van Orsay de Flines Collection currently housed in the National Museum of Jakarta and the major part of the Mr. and Mrs. Shindo Collection, which collected Hizen ware inherited in Indonesia, came from the South Sulawesi. It is unfortunate that there has been little scientific studies made on ceramics found from Sulawesi.

Burton Wolio Fort

Only a little have known of the Wolio Fort in the Buton Island, the Southeast of Sulawesi. The Buton Sultanate was based in this citadel and active from the sixteenth to twentieth centuries, but this sultanate is not so well known among many other sultanates in Indonesia. The official publication of Indonesian history only briefly mentioned about Buton that it was attacked by and subordinated to the Gowa Sultanate in the 1630's and Buton became a battlefield several times during the war between the Gowa and Dutch started in the 1650's.

The early kingdom was born already in around the fourteenth century in the Buton Island. As tradition goes, king's names of pre-Islamic period show strong influence from the Hindu-Java culture. The Islamic influence reached the region in the sixteenth century. The sixth king La Kilaponto converted to Muslim in 1540 and this precedes more than half a century to Islamisation of the Gowa.

The ruling system as an Islamic state was established by the late sixteenth century and the Dutch recorded that the Wolio Fort was under construction in 1613. This growth owed to the fact that Buton was becoming strategically important being on the route to the Maluku Islands, as a result of competition over spice trade.

Subsequently forts were built one after another in Buton's territory. Externally this owed to spreading of the Makassar War but there was also an internal cause. That is, a sultan was to be selected from three lineages, which potentially lead to the internal conflict. As a result, sultan changed within short period of time and many forts were built as a showcase for power of aristocrats. Buton had a population of only 100,000 in the nineteenth century when the last fort was constructed. Even with such limited human recourse, those in power continued to be interested in reinforcing defence by building forts.

Buton maintained collaborative relationship with the Dutch and could keep the sultanate until after the Independence of Indonesia unlike the Gowa who was directly attacked by the Dutch, even if it was only for an appearance.

Outline of the site

More than a hundred fort sites are said to be in the whole territory of the old Buton Sultanate. The Wolio Fort site inside which descendants of nobles still reside was the main citadel for rulers below sultan.

The Wolio Fort stands on the raised coral cliff on the left bank of the Bau-bau River in the suburb of the Bau-bau port. The walls have irregular square shape with the longer north and east walls and shorter west wall (north: about 440 meters, east: about 390 meters, west: about 270 meters, south: about 1450 meters).

The northeast corner has an extremely sharp angle to accommodate the geographical feature that hill ridge is narrowing towards northeast. The wall is made by building up coral limestone in size of a human head. The north and east wall built on a rocky cliff and is 8-10 meters in height, while height of the west and south wall on flat land, surrounded by moat, is only 3-5 meters. The entire wall measures 2.6 kilometres and there are 14 gates as well as 18 bastions.

The eighteenth century Royal Mosque, tombs of successive sultans and the last sultan's residence still exist inside the Wolio Fort, which overlooks the Buton Strait.

Research on the ceramic shards

Through restoration of the walls that began in the 1980's, a significant number of shards and human bones were found and kept in the Fort Ruins Restoration Office located inside the fort site. The fort was used both as residence and burial place. Most of the empty lands except remaining buildings is thought to be burial places in the past, and many shards once buried in graves are dispersed on the ground.

We preliminarily studied shards at a survey in September 2002 and worked out the number of unit reached to 5,983 just for porcelains only (calculated on bottom parts). Judging from this number, it is speculated that unexpectedly large number of ceramics had been buried in each tomb [I-23]. While working on joint excavation with the National Archaeology Study Centre in November 2004, November to December 2005, and September 2006, we also classified the shards. This says that the majority of targeted shards had been found through the wall restoration works but there was a small number of excavated finds by us.

Chapter I Note

1 Sakai & Ōhashi 2014

2 The studies were conducted under a private organization the Study Group for Banten Site from 1991 to 2007, while Association for Asian Cultural Properties Cooperation from 2007 (Reference to the website of the Association).

3 Ōhashi & Sakai 1999

4 Sakai (ed.) 2000, 2004, 2007

5 Sakai (ed.) 2004

6 Sakai (ed.) 2007

7 According to the oral history, the name of all Majapahit kings was called *Brawijaya* from the first king. However, the contemporary inscriptions do not mention such name. The names of first king Raden Wijaya and the fifth king Hayam Wuruk also appear in the later legend.

8 Mayuyama 1977, 85

9 Guy 1989

10 Duppoizat & Naniek 2007. This catalogue listed thirty-five under-glaze cobalt blue or under-glaze copper red painting with decoration as Jingdezhen porcelains (twenty-five of which were identified as of the Yuan period). It is not certain how much the published photographs cover the actual excavated volumes, but mixture of the simplified style and the Zhizheng style are illustrated under the Yuan porcelain. The fragments introduced under the Vietnamese included celadon, iron brown glaze, iron oxide painting, iron glaze and raised white decoration, under-glaze cobalt blue, over-glaze polychrome enamels decoration and stoneware sculptures (celadon, under-glaze cobalt blue, white glaze, white and brown glaze) .

11 Miksic & Kamei 2010. Although the ceramic shards were highly probable to have been

found at Trowulan, the provenance cannot be certainly established because they were illegal digging items.

12 This Old Javanese eulogy recorded the status of the Majapahit Kingdom by a court poet Prapanca in 1365. It was found at Lombok in 1894, and the original name was called Desawarnana.

13 They included seven fragments of Yuan under-glaze cobalt blue large dishes in the Zhizhen style and a fragment of Cizhou ware bowl in turquoise blue glaze as Chinese ceramics, as well as Vietnamese under-glaze cobalt blue and polychrome tiles with Islamic tiles in Persian blue. Until recently, they had been the only fragments on display for a long time in the ceramics gallery of the National Museum of Indonesia in Jakarta.

14 A number of Islamic sultanates were founded in the modern day Indonesian territory after the late thirteenth century, but none competed with the Majapahit for its extensive influence. Although Islamic sultanates of all scale exist everyplace, there are not many Islamic royal palaces turned to ruin by the strife with the Dutch except the one of the Aceh Sultanate in the northern point of Sumatra.

15 The Dutch met trading merchants from all around Asia including the Overseas Chinese in Banten. One could see the liveliness and height of ceramic trade of this period through the situation in Banten.

16 Serruriel 1902

17 Hasan et al.1978

18 Hasan et al.1988

19 Guillot 1990

20 The brick made sluice gate was actually found within the canal network (Sakai (ed.) 2007, pp.42-45).

21 This became the first collaborative excavation research between Japan and Indonesia (Sakai (ed.) 2000).

22 The similar situation applies to Trowulan where major mining of brick clay has been taking place. Preserving archaeological sites in Indonesia closely relates to stabiliz action of local life.

23 Originally, the residence in the fort were descendent of aristocrats and it is highly possible that they possessed a certain volume of heirloom ceramics, although it could not been confirmed at the time of our research. It is assumed that a large volume was obtained through antique dealers at some point as a possibility.

II. Trade ceramics excavated from the Trowulan site and Four Royal Capital sites

The recording and analysis of artifacts from the Banten Lama site in 1993 was our first collaboration with the National Archaeological Study Centre of Indonesia. Further studies of artifacts followed in Tirtayasa Site, and also Somba Opu and Buton Wolio Forts in Sulawesi. The research that resulted allowed a technical understanding of ceramic trade in and from Indonesia after the fifteenth century but did not offer further insights to the prior period.

We then focused on the archaeological finds at Trowulan Site, which was thought the capital of the Majapahit Kingdom in East Java and analyzed the artifacts on three occasions after January 2012. From this site, we learned a great deal about the trade in ceramics in Indonesia from the thirteenth century, in particular their designs and forms.

To discuss this trend, we roughly divided the periods in the following charts, which indicate site and production areas. Please note that the centuries in parenthesis are given only as a reference. Under these periods, explanations were given by site and production area.

I-1 (9th – 13th centuries)
I-2 (13th – first half of 14th centuries)
II-1 (late 13th to 14th century, foundation of the Majapahit Kingdom)
II-2 (14th century, particularly focused on the second half)
III-1 (15th century, particularly focused on the first half)
III-2 (second half of the 15th to the beginning of the 16th century)
IV-1 (late 15th to middle of the 16th century)
IV-2 (second half of the 16th to early 17th century)
V-1 (around the first half of the 17th century)
V-2 (around the second half of the 17th century to the beginning of the 18th century)
VI-1 (around the first half of the 18th century)
VI-2 (around the second half of the 18th century)
VII-1 (around the first half of the 19th century)
VII-2 (around the second half of the 19th century)

The order of sites is arranged from older to more recent for the key period of each site, specifically those of the Trowulan Site, Somba Opu Fort, Buton Wolio Fort, Banten Lama Site and Tirtayasa Site.

1. Period I -1 (9th to 13th centuries)

Trowulan Site

Imported ceramics with rich contents were found at Trowulan Site. A significant volume of the fragments on which we worked was collected through excavation and collection of surface. They were classified according to production sites and types. Estimated total number of individual object/unit was worked out from the number of fragments by counting rims and bottoms. The total number comes to 7,754 units (Table 1).

(1) Chinese ceramics

The ceramics discussed below all likely date to the pre-Majapahit Kingdom period.

Besides celadon glaze porcelain, white porcelain, and Qingbai porcelain, there is one stoneware example with iron brown decoration in yellow glaze. The various Celadon porcelain are types from the Yue kilns in Zhejiang province, the Longquan kilns also in Zhejiang province, and the Tongan kilns in Fujian province. Much of the white porcelain appears to be of Fujian origin. Celadon and white porcelain fired at the Jingdezhen kilns in Jiangsi province are mixed in with wares from other kilns. Stoneware with iron-oxide decoration in yellow glaze was fired at the Changsha kiln in Hunan province.

Celadon ware

Yuezhou type ware

Fig.1-01: This celadon ware was made in a cup shape. The base is trimmed to serve as a stand and scooped out inside to create an arch. The base is unglazed and is unevenly fired leaving spots similar to spur marks. A celadon bowl with a similar base was excavated at the Xiaoshan kilns, Zejiang province [II-1], although the latter example has an exterior surface decorated with a comb pattern created from the bottom upwards and the interior is incised with a flower pattern. A celadon bowl with a similar design has been attributed to the Yuezhou Shanglinhu kiln [II-2].

Fig.1-02: This celadon bowl with a foot-ring has unique white circular spur marks around the inner bottom and traces of these marks continue on the base of the foot-ring. A similar piece was found in Western Java [II-3], and an example with this kind of spur marks was excavated at the Yuezhou Shanlinhu kiln (Pidaoshan) [II-4].

Fig.1-03, 04 are large dishes with an incised design of floral scroll on the interior, and carved lotus petals on the exterior. They have a plectrum-shaped foot-ring. Fig.1-04 is unglazed or glaze had been flaked off (around the tenth century) [II-5].

Fig.1-05 is a gourd-shaped jar with unique ears, which are pierced and applied on to the body. Another molded piece is pasted over the ears. There is an incised line around the shoulder and double lines are vertically carved in relief [II-6].

Fig.1-06 is a rim section of a jar that would have had a cover [II-7]. It seems two pieces of two kinds ears were attached.

White porcelain

Chinese wares

Fig.1-07, 08 were likely fired in regional kilns in Fujian province. Fig.1-07 is a bowl with a rounded rim and Fig.1-08 is a bowl ornamented with incised comb line pattern and a slightly inverted rim.

Qingbai porcelain

Jingdezhen ware

Fig.1-09, 10 are bowls but bottle shapes and covers are also found.

Iron-oxide decoration in yellow glaze

Changsha ware

Fig.1-11 is a dish decorated with lines in iron oxide and yellow glaze.

Other wares

Chinese ware

Fig.1-12 is a dish with matt white glaze. Small squares in the inner bottom are left unglazed to allow for the placing of spurs in the firing. The base is left unglazed and brown spur marks are visible on the base of foot-ring.

Banten Lama Site

(1) Chinese ceramics

Fig.21-13 is an ewer with iron brown decoration in yellow glaze applied on to the exterior [II-8]. This sherd dates to the ninth century and is the Changsha ware.

2. Period I-2 (13th – first half of the 14th centuries)

Trowulan Site

(1) Chinese ceramics

Celadon ware

Longquan ware

Fig.2-14 is a high-quality dish. The exterior is decorated with carved ribbed lotus petals and the base of foot-ring is left unglazed. The inner bottom has an applied fish decoration.

3. Period II-1 (late 13th to 14th century)

Trowulan Site

There is an increase in volume in the number of artifacts recovered. Fragments dating up to the first half of the fourteenth century are included in this section.

(1) Chinese ceramics

Celadon ware

Longquan ware

Fig.3-15 is a *jiu-hai* 酒海 jar with a distinct bulbous body decorated with a caved and ribbed lotus petal design. The rim and base of the foot-ring are left unglazed. The bottom slab had been shaped separately and then pasted with celadon glaze during the firing process (27 units). Similar types of celadon covers are also found [II-9].

Fig.3-16 is a drum-shaped large bowl with cover. The exterior is applied with peony arabesque pattern and small beads balls are pasted around the edge of foot-ring [II-10].

Fig.3-17 is a large bowl with a design of carved lotus flower petals [II-11]. This kind of bowl is often referred in China to as a *jing-shui-bo* 淨水鉢 .

Qingbai porcelain

Jingdezhen ware

Fig.3-18 is a cover of a container decorated with carved design (from the twelfth to the first half of the fourteenth century).

Fig.3-19 is a molded octagonal small cup carved in relief with characters *jin-yu-man-tang* 金玉満堂 on the exterior and lotus petals motif on the lower body. Section lines on the rim and interior are expressed with linked beads [II-12].

Fig.3-20 is a bottle with roundels formed in double beaded lines. An applied pattern is visible within a roundel of the right of the sherd. There is a similar example in metal bearing the coat of arms of Louis the Great (1342-82) of Hungary, which is dated to around 1325 [II-13]. A white porcelain Buddha figure with the year mark of Dade 2 or 3 (1298) in ink suggests that the linked bead line motif had appeared by the end of the thirteenth century. Many porcelain fragments with linked beads decoration were also excavated from Trowulan Site (from the fourteenth century).

White porcelain

Chinese wares

Fig.3-21, 22 are covered containers made in a mold and decorated with floral arabesque in relief. They are similar to the large covered box made in white porcelain (Fig.22-29) that was excavated in the Somba Opu Fort.

Jingdezhen ware

Fig.3-23, 24 are bowls. The interior is decorated with molded relief patterns and the bases are unglazed.

(2) Vietnamese ceramics

Celadon ware

Fig.4-25 is a small bowl decorated on the interior with multiple a chrysanthemum pattern. The glaze has yellow tint while the exterior of the bottom is unglazed. The foot-ring is planned and there are some small gaps inside its perimeter (probably the fourteenth century) [II-14].

Fig.4-26 was formed with a mold. The interior is decorated with impressed circles. A line is incised around the inner bottom and a small brown spur mark is left exposed remains is visible. The exterior of base is not glazed [II-15].

Fig.4-27 is a dish with a carved flower and grass pattern on the inner bottom and is encircled with an incised ring. The interior of the dish also has a carved motif. The inside of the foot-ring is painted in iron slip, and this style of decoration is termed *a chocolate bottom* [II-16].

White glaze ware

Fig.4-28 is a bowl decorated with ribbed lotus petals on the exterior. The inside foot-ring is painted in iron slip and it is entirely glazed in white except for the base of foot-ring. There is a small spur mark on the inner bottom [II-17].

Somba Opu Fort

(1) Chinese ceramics

Fujian ware

Fig.22-29 is a large qingbai glazed covered box from the southern part of Fujian province. It is formed in a mold and has a *Ru-i* head pattern with floral arabesque carved in relief on both the body and cover (from the late thirteenth to the first half of the fourteenth century) [II-18]. This example resembles covered box found at Trowulan Site (Fig.3-22).

Other Chinese wares

Fig.22-30 is a jar with four ears in iron brown glaze. The vertical ears are adhered to the shoulder.

4. Period II-2 (14th century, with particular focus on the second half)

Trowulan Site

Ceramic finds increased at this site specifically with the Jingdezhen under-glaze cobalt blue ware examples and celadon glaze ware from the Longquan kilns. Many of these pieces are dated to the late Yuan and early Ming periods.

(1) Chinese ceramics

Celadon ware

Longquan ware

Fig.5-31, 32 are the bottom fragments of large bowls. The centre of the bases was pierced with holes before glazing in celadon. A separately molded celadon disk in the shape of chrysanthemum was placed in the inner bottom, which was then pasted through firing. The inside is decorated with carved designs with lotus flower (s) on the interior (6 units). A similar piece was also excavated in Fustat, Egypt and copies were made in Islamic stoneware.

Fig.5-33 is a large foliated dish. Both interior and exterior are decorated with sharp ribbed lotus flower petals. There is a circular ring where the glaze was shaved off inside the foot-ring.

White porcelain

possibly Fujian ware

Fig.5-34 is a bowl with the glaze on the rim removed. Base wrinkles are visible on the external of the rim, which indicates that this bowl was first roughly shaped in a press mold and then the bottom half and foot-ring was trimmed on a wheel. The bowl was fired inverted or with another vessel joined at the mouth.

Fig.5-35 is a dish with a flat rim decorated with carved lotus or chrysanthemum petals. The design of the flowering plants is impressed in the inner bottom. This dish resembles a bowl with stamped designs called the Birosuku type in Japan and could be dated to the fourteenth century. We confirmed one Vietnamese white glaze dish in a similar shape and decorated was found with the same kind of design (Fig.8-77). The

Vietnamese ware would have been possibly influenced by this kind of Chinese porcelain.

Jingdezhen ware

Fig.5-36, 37 are small bowls with stamped flower pattern similar to Fig.3-23, 24. The foot-ring is unglazed. They appear to be made in relation to the Shu-fu style and dated to the fourteenth century. Fig.5-36 has stamped chrysanthemum petals on the lower half of the interior.

Fig.5-38 appears to be a cover of an ewer. The knob is made in a form of a *Cintamani* [II-19]. It is unknown if there were rings attached because a third of the cover has been lost.

Under-glaze cobalt blue ware

Jingdezhen ware

Fig.5-39, 40 are bowls with unglazed foot-ring and interesting designs in the inner bottom. Fig.5-39 is painted frog with the blown-glaze technique, and Fig.5-40 shows a design of fish.

Fig.5-41 is a bowl or large bowl decorated with a design in the inner bottom of water bird in a lotus pond. The foot-ring is unglazed and shaped thickly into a shape of *tokin/* projected entre. Fig.5-42, similar to Fig.5-41, also shows a design of a water bird in lotus pond. There is also a fragment of a rim decorated with floral arabesque pattern on both sides.

Fig.5-43 is a large dish. The interior ground is covered with in cobalt (a blue pigment of cobalt oxide is wrote as cobalt in this book) over which a design of phoenix, floral arabesque and probably peony appear in white. The bottom exterior is unglazed. The side of interior is also decorated with leaves, probably of peony, left in white [II-20]. Many fragments of a large dish were excavated but most of them are quite thin.

Fig.5-44 is an ewer with an unglazed flat bottom. The inner bottom is painted with a bird design while the exterior is decorated with a lotus petal pattern. The rim is unglazed. Base ridges are visible on the base, which suggests that this was made in a press mold. The spout is almost severed and only identified by its root. Other ewers have been excavated, but most of them are more finely manufactured.

Fig.5-45 is a cover of an octagonal jar. The lip was folded downwards in order to wrap around the rim of the body. This is a typical shape for covers of large jars during this period. The cover is octagonal and each facet is decorated with a lotus petal pattern. The edge of the brim is lost but the cover is painted with a design of a linked jewel pattern and a meander pattern circulating the joint of the knob [II-21].

Fig.5-46 is a rim of a large jar. The mouth is folded upwards with sharp angle [II-22].

Fig.5-47, 48 are covers for round jars formed in double structure to wrap around the rim of the jars. Fig.5-47 has a rim decorated with a key-fret pattern and a meander pattern runs around the rim, which is folded downwards. Fig.5-48 is in contrast painted with a arabesque and linked jewel patterns on the brim and rim [II-23].

Fig.6-49 is a cover of a jar in the shape of a lotus leaf with leaf veins painted in cobalt blue oxide. No other artifacts with the same design have been identified.

Fig.6-50 is a similar type of Fig.6-49, and also is a cover of a small jar in the shape of lotus leaf. The body to accompany this cover was not found. There is an example of a small jar excavated in the Jingdezhen with a design of flowers and grasses in under-glaze cobalt blue with a leaf-shaped painted cover with veins delineated in under-glaze copper brown. Fragments of this type of jar have been uncovered, and this may suggest a possibility that there were some examples of jars and covers with different designs.

Fig.6-51 is a rim of a jar. The shape is common and straight but the edge is slightly thicker at the edge.

Fig.6-52 is a fragment of the body of a large jar in under-glaze cobalt blue and copper red. The body has roundels shaped with double lines of linked beads. The roundels are indented and pasted with lattice pattern and applied copper red glaze [II-24].

Fig.6-53 is a shoulder fragment of a jar decorated in under-glaze copper red. A band of floral arabesque motif is painted between two lines in under-glaze copper red. Bands of linked jewel and lotus petal patterns are arranged above and beneath the floral scroll band. *Ru-i* head pattern is drawn at the lowest section [II-25].

Fig.6-54 is a bottle with octagonal faceted body decorated in three horizontal sections while the inside is unglazed. This was first made in separate parts on a wheel then joined at the body. The foot-ring is a faceted octagonal only on the external edge [II-26].

Iron-oxide painted stoneware
Cizhou ware

Fig.6-55, 56 are jars with iron-oxide painting. Fig.6-55 is a lower body of a vessel. The base of foot-ring is unglazed and broadly planed. The exterior was first treated with white slip, painted in iron-oxide, and finally covered in transparent glaze. Painted panels decorate the body. Fig.6-56 are the fragments of the mouth and upper body [II-27].

Fig.6-57 is a large bowl called *xi* 洗. The mouth is curved. The interior is decorated with wave-like lines [II-28]. In addition, a jar and large bowl in turquoise blue glaze were also excavated.

Fig.7-58/63 are ceramic slabs decorated with a black motif painted in iron glaze over a white slipped surface. The shape appears square. The reverse side has wide foots. Fig.7-58 to Fig.7-60 have a continuing diamond pattern running on the border. Fig.7-58 has white diamond pattern after painted all of the base. A shard to bellow has meander pattern at edge with thick belts at both sides. Fig.7-61 has a meander pattern on the border between thick outlines. The border of Fig.7-62 is painted with a continuing arabesque in white over black ground. Mayuyama (1977) and a reference published by Shogakukan (1984) have identified these ceramics as Vietnamese. However, patterns and square shape suggest that they were actually fired at the Cizhou type kilns in China prior to the production of Vietnamese under-glazed cobalt blue tiles. They are thought to be of the fourteenth century.

Fig.7-64/67 are ceramic tiles. Front surface is covered with iron-oxide black glaze. Application of white slip is not traced. They are in square shape with no wide foots on the reverse side. On the front surface, white raised line is drawn in a square.

The surface is glazed in iron brown and then a brown pattern, probably flower and grasses are painted within a foliated panel. They are thought to be made in China (the fourteenth century).

Stoneware with iron brown glaze

Fig.7-68 is a bottle with unglazed lower bodies both in and outside. Fig.7-68 is a fragment of a rim and shoulder.

Fig.7-69 is a jar.

(2) Vietnamese ceramics

White glaze ware

Fig.8-70 is a small bowl or dish with a pair of applied fish design in the inner bottom. The foot-ring is thin and finely made, and the base of foot-ring is also glazed. A visible cobalt splash suggests that this was made after production of under-glazed cobalt blue ware began (estimated from the second half of the fourteenth to early fifteenth centuries).

Fig.8-71 is a small cup whose or in which the interior is decorated with impressed relief design. A seven-petal flower pattern is arranged within double raised rings in the centre. Design of flowering plants or floral arabesque ornaments the interior. This is fine quality white porcelain with a creamy hue. This small cup is older than the salvaged cargo from off Hoi An [II-29] (from the second half of the fourteenth to the first half of the fifteenth centuries) [II-30].

Fig.8-72 is a stemmed dish in transparent glaze on the exterior [II-31].

Fig.8-73 is a jar decorated on the exterior with carved ribbed design. The exterior was treated in transparent glaze over white slip. Inside the foot-ring is painted with iron slip. The interior bottom has a raised periphery within which some spur marks are visible (around the fourteenth century) [II-32].

Fig.8-74 is a large bowl with a shallow and wide foot-ring. The body is flared upwards from the foot-ring. There are spur marks on the interior bottom [II-33].

Fig.8-75 is a large bowl with a swollen lower body. The base of the foot-ring is wide and the underside is unglazed. There is an unglazed circular ring in the centre of the interior, which presents visible traces of sand. This is possibly made in the Central Vietnam (the fourteenth century).

Fig.8-76 is a superior quality dish with a swollen body and a curved rim. The glaze on the rim is removed. Inside the foot-ring is painted with iron slip.

Fig.8-77 appears to be a celadon small dish in poor quality. Rough carved relief pattern ornaments the interior and exterior. The upper section on both sides was likely painted in white slip first, and covered with something like ash glaze. There is an unglazed circular ring in the central roundel over which white sand like spur marks are left. The rim shows incised lines on the interior (from the fourteenth to the first half of the fifteenth centuries) [II-34] and possibly made under the influence of Chinese white porcelain dish (Fig.5-35).

Stoneware in iron brown glaze

Fig.8-78 is a bowl decorated on the interior with a relief design of impressed flower and grasses. The exterior is differently coloured in iron brown glaze. A transparent glaze over the interior has a slight tint of yellow-green. There are spur marks in the inner bottom. The influence of Chinese tea bowl is possible [II-35].

Fig.8-79 is a large bowl decorated with a relief design of a flowering plant, which resembles the design of Fig.8-78. This bowls is also glazed differently on each side with a transparent glaze inside and iron brown glaze outside. Five small brown spur marks remain in the inner bottom. The base is unglazed. This bowl and Fig.8-78 are both assumed dated to the thirteenth to fourteenth centuries.

Sgraffito decoration on black ground

Fig.8-80, 81 - the foot-ring is faceted on its side similarly to Fig.8-74. The body is lifted upwards from the ridge. Inside, dented band runs around the bottom. White slip covers the body except for the base, over which iron glaze is painted. The pattern was expressed in sgraffito before the body was covered in transparent glaze.

Two shards in right and left have the area inside the foot-ring painted with iron slip and there are small spur marks in the inner bottom. Similar example of Vietnamese stoneware with sgraffito designs on a black ground have not been found. It is thought that this type of ware was influenced by decorative techniques used in Cizhou ware during the Yuan period (the fourteenth century).

White glaze with iron-oxide decoration

The exterior of Fig.9-82 is applied with transparent glaze. The design is made in sgraffito, which was then covered in iron blown glaze. The outlines of design are dotted. There are small base balls applied on the body fragment [II-36]. Splash of cobalt blue on the fragment leads us to date this ware to the periods of under-glazed cobalt blue production. A slight indent was made around the edge of the inside bottom and there are spur marks (from the second half of the fourteenth to the first half of the fifteenth centuries).

Green glaze ware

Fig.8-83 is a small bowl. The exterior is coloured in green glaze over carved ribbed design. The interior is treated with transparent glaze. One side of the foot-ring is painted in iron slip but the foot-ring itself is unglazed. The edge of the foot-ring was planned off to make it look like a low stem.

Fig.8-84 is a dish with a design of layers of chrysanthemums in green glaze. Chrysanthemums are press molded on the interior. The base is unglazed. The interior has an unglazed circular ring and there is a trace of stacking over other object directly.

Fig.8-85 is a dish decorated inside with carved design in green glaze. A circular ring around the centre is unglazed. Inside the foot-ring is painted in iron slip. There are traces that show that this dish had been burnt secondly.

Fig.8-86 appears to be a large dish with a gourd-like design in clear relief. The foot-ring is carefully planned to make a shape of a *yunzi* piece container. There is a deep cut caused by the shaving of the base. The inside of the foot-ring is painted in iron slip (from the fourteenth to the first half of the fifteenth centuries).

Celadon

Fig.9-87 is a large jar. The base is unglazed and inside the foot-ring is shallowly planed. At forming, an indent was made around the interior bottom and this is the same technique applied to under-glazed cobalt blue jars. The tone of the glaze is close to green but it is more likely celadon (from the fourteenth to the fifteenth centuries).

Iron-oxide painted stoneware

Fig.9-88 is a small bowl with a swollen lower body and a curved rim. The inner bottom shows an iron painting of a flowering plant similar to chrysanthemum. On the upper part of the exterior, a flowering arabesque design is painted between the two lines. The underside is unglazed.

Fig.9-89 is a bowl with swollen lower body and a curved rim. This bowl is larger than Fig.9-88 and inside of the rim is ornamented with roughly drawn floral arabesque design [II-37].

Fig.9-90 is a small dish molded into a chrysanthemum shape. The base of foot-ring is broadly planed. The interior has two double rings drawn in iron glaze. The centre of the dish is decorated with a flowering plant motif. Transparent glaze with a yellow-green tint covers the dish except for the underside. There are small spur marks in the inner bottom. The interior of the foot-ring is painted in iron slip [II-38].

Fig.9-91 is a mid-sized dish in shape of a basin with a flat rim. The base of foot-ring is broadly planed. White slip covers from the interior to the exterior rim. On the interior, iron paints of chrysanthemum like flower and loose floral arabesque pattern decorate the inner bottom and the rim. Small brown five spur marks are left in the inner bottom [II-39].

Fig.9-92 is a large dish. This dish is coarsely made compared to Fig.9-91. It has a basin shape and there are circular dents smaller than the pattern in the inner bottom. The unglazed base of the foot-ring is planed broad and shallow. On the exterior, an iron painting of flower and grasses roughly drawn is positioned inside a circle. The rim is decorated with simplified floral arabesque design. There are six brown spur marks left in the inner bottom and the base of foot-ring. This is thought to date later than Fig.9-91.

Ceramic sculptures

Fig.18: Thin fragments of large sculptures were excavated in a great quantity in Trowulan. The majority appears to be Vietnamese. One of the sculptures could be reconstructed to some degree. One fragment looks like a big dog made in white glaze with differently coloured sections in iron brown glaze. Joins to the head remain and a leash around the neck, dangling bells and ornaments were applied later. The brown sections over the white ground create a patchy effect. The remains of a front leg is left on the oval shape pedestal. This dog is assumed to be dated to the fourteenth to the first half of the fifteenth centuries.

(3) Islamic tiles

Fig.10-93/95 are made with coarse and sandy base. The surfaces are covered in white glaze, over which cobalt blue designs are painted. Those which still retain the original shape show that they were framed around the edge [II-40]. These Islamic stoneware tiles were imported to the kingdom around the fourteenth to the first half of the fifteenth centuries. There is a high possibility that Vietnamese under-glaze cobalt blue tiles were made to a special order under the influence of these Islamic tiles. Given a close look at the section, we understood that the base consists of two tiers. It is suspected that mortar was inserted inside when installing these tiles.

Fig.10-96/98 are ceramic tiles with a turquoise blue glaze. They are made of coarse base and given white slip before glazing only the surface. They are likely Islamic stoneware (from the fourteenth to the first half of the fifteenth centuries). There is a brown spur mark on the surface.

Buton Wolio Fort

(1) Chinese ceramics

Longquan and Cizhou wares

Fig.23-99 on the left appears to be a jar with ribbed lotus flower design. It is a Longquan ware (the fourteenth century).

Fig.23-99 on the right is a fragment of the shoulder of a jar with iron-oxide painting. It is from a kiln in the Cizhou area and dates to the fourteenth century.

Banten Lama Site

(1) Chinese stoneware

Fig.24-100 is a large jar in iron brown glaze. The exterior is decorated with incised phoenix pattern [II-41].

5. Period III-1 (15th century, particularly focused on the first half)

This period includes the ceramic obviously dated to the Ming period.

Trowulan Site

(1) Chinese ceramics

Celadon ware

Longquan ware

The interior of Fig.11-101 is decorated with lotus petal pattern that was drawn by spatula. Impressed flower pattern is applied in the inner bottom. The rim is pushed inwards following the shape of flower petals to create lobes. There is an unglazed circular ring area in the foot-ring, where melted trace of a kiln tool remains (1 unit).

Fig.11-102 is a small dish with a curved rim. Both sides are decorated with carved chrysanthemum petal pattern. The interior of foot-ring is unglazed. The production date is thought to be from the first half to the middle of the fifteenth century.

Under-glaze cobalt blue ware

Jingdezhen ware [II-42]

Fig.11-103 is a bowl decorated with a arabesque pattern in the inner bottom, meander pattern on the foot-ring and lotus petal motif on the side of foot-ring [II-43].

The base of the foot-ring was carefully removed of glaze.

Fig.11-104 is a large jar. The body is incised with vertical lines and decorated with flower pattern in cobalt. A band of meander pattern also in cobalt blue decorates the tapering foot. Heirloom examples inform us that a lotus petal motif was painted in cobalt blue on the upper part of the body. This is undoubtedly an under-glaze cobalt blue decorated ware [II-44].

Fig.11-105 is a large globular bottle called *Tianqiu*-bottle. The body is decorated with an under-glaze cobalt blue design of dragon and floral arabesque, and the straight mouth with a band of floral arabesque between the lines also in under-glaze cobalt blue. Other shard of dragon pattern was found, and it is possible two dragon shards at bellow are also the same unit [II-45].

Fig.11-106, 107 are fragments of a body part of a jar in under-glaze cobalt blue with copper-red painting. Panels are outlined in alternating blue lines of cobalt and red lines of copper. Indistinct patterns painted in under-glaze cobalt blue and copper-red decorate the insides of the panels (around the first half of the fifteenth century).

Over-glaze polychrome enamels decoration (Wucai)

Jingdezhen ware

Fig.11-108 is a fragment of the body of either a dish or large bowl. Patterns are painted in green enamel over white porcelain on the body of the Shu-fu type. The interior is molded and has a raised area around the inner bottom and impressed relief design over-pained with patterns in green enamel. Externally it is decorated with lotus petal style motif in green enamel.

(2)Vietnamese ceramics

Iron-oxide painted stoneware

Fig.12-109 is a large jar, and these fragments are from the lower part of the body including the bottom. The foot-ring is carved inside, and the exterior is painted in white slip. Transparent glaze covers this jar except for the base. This jar and Fig.9-88/92 share similarities with a group of older type under-glaze cobalt blue in terms of shape and patterns. Production dates are also similar and Fig.12-109 (the second half of the fourteenth century or the first half of the fifteenth century latest).

Under-glaze cobalt blue and polychrome over-glaze enamels

Fig.12-110 is a chrysanthemum shaped small dish made in a mold. A flower motif, probably chrysanthemum, is painted in the inner bottom in cobalt, which is circled with double rings. The base of foot-ring is broadly planed and the inside is painted in iron slip. A spur mark left on the inner bottom helps to date (from the second half of the fourteenth to the first half of the fifteenth centuries).

Fig.12-111, 112 are small dishes in a form of basin. Internally they were carved to form chrysanthemum petals. A single or double rings are painted in the inner bottoms within a design of floral spray. The rims are painted with a loose floral arabesque in cobalt blue. While the dish (Fig.12-111) has a particularly broad base of foot ring, which is unglazed, the small dish (Fig.12-112) has a space inside the foot-ring painted in iron.

They both have small spur marks in the inner bottoms (from the second half of the fourteenth to the first half of the fifteenth centuries).

Fig.12-113 is a bowl with a swollen body and a curved rim. Both sides of the bowl, except the base, are applied with white slip and patterns painted in cobalt blue. The circle in the inner bottom is darker blue, while the motifs – a spray of flower in the centre, as well as a simplified arabesque around the rim and on the exterior - are painted in lighter blue. Iron slip is painted inside the foot-ring (from the second half of the fourteenth to the first half of the fifteenth centuries) [II-46].

Fig.12-114 appears to be a cover of a large jar. It is formed to wrap the rim, characteristic of a rim for the Jingdezhen under-glaze cobalt blue of the fourteenth century. The external body is decorated with a band of arabesque in cobalt. It was not applied with white slip. There are no heirloom objects identified so far (from the second half of the fourteenth to the first half of the fifteenth centuries by judging from the dates of the Jingdezhen under-glaze cobalt blue).

Fig.12-115 is also a cover of a large jar. This type of cover is usually painted with a band of floral arabesque on the top. It is decorated with a distinctive meander pattern. This kind of meander pattern was often introduced in the Cizhou type ware with iron-oxide painting from the Yuan period, which presumably influenced this example. There are a few heirloom objects among a group of old style Vietnamese under-glaze cobalt blue [II-47]. The reverse side of these lids is painted in white slip but not on the brim.

Fig.12-116 is a cover of a jar. It is made in double structure similar to Fig.12-114. Lotus petals are painted on the exterior (from the second half of the fourteenth to the first half of the fifteenth centuries).

The central area of Fig.12-117 shows a circle line in relief. Although the centre is a bit warped by firing, it is presumed to be a stemmed stand. The base is unglazed and flat, but a little bit above at the border of the glazed area there is a trace of something attached at firing. This may suggest that Fig.12-117 was originally attached with a stem. It is decorated internally with a relief design made in mold and painted with three tired twisted flowers in cobalt over the relief design. The same kind of twisted flowers are also painted in cobalt on the exterior. This is a good quality ware and the type of cobalt suggests the date to be the second half of the fourteenth to the fifteenth centuries [II-48].

Fig.12-118 is a large dish decorated in cobalt blue with a wave motif around the inner bottom, floral scroll pattern on the interior, and arabesque pattern around the rim. The external is arranged with lotus petal motif but it is a single petal, which suggests that this dish is older than the salvaged cargo from off Hoi An. The mouth is removed of glaze. Space inside the foot-ring is painted in iron slip (from the second half of the fourteenth to the first half of the fifteenth centuries) [II-49].

Fig.13-119 is a jar similar to Fig.13-120, 121. The central body is decorated with motifs of peonies and lotus petals. Foliated panels are arranged around the shoulder and designs of a bird on a plum tree and bamboo leaves decorate the inside of the panels.

The ground between these panels is filled with wave patterns. The lower part of the body is painted with a continuing lotus petal motif and above that a horizontal band of floral arabesque. Underneath the lotus petals appears *Ru-i* head pattern (from the second half of the fourteenth to the first half of the fifteenth centuries) [II-50]. Its base is unglazed and planned to form a foot-ring. The outline of the internal bottom is slightly indented. White slip is painted over the exterior except the base, while the internal presents partially damaged glaze by secondly firing.

Fig.13-120, 121 are fragments of bodies from large jars. One is decorated with a design of a cloud and dragon, and another with a peony arabesque. The lotus petal pattern has no sub-petals (from the second half of the fourteenth to the first half of the fifteenth centuries).

Fig.13-122 is likely a bottom part of a jar. A floral arabesque pattern decorates the lower body. The foot-ring is planned and painted in iron slip inside. This is a type of jar decorated in two colours, as a line below the floral arabesque pattern is in brown. The internal centre is dented and there are small spur marks on this dented area. The exterior is painted in white slip but the interior is just treated with transparent glaze (from the second half of the fourteenth to the beginning of the fifteenth centuries).

Fig.13-123, 124 are fragments from a bottle. A similar example with this type of shape and pattern is a bottle with a dragon design (named *Byakue* 白衣). Fig.13-123 shows resemblance to the convex band decorated on the lower part of the neck of this dragon design bottle. Fig.13-124 is considered to be the lower part of the body. The above-mentioned bottle with dragon design has fixed rings carved in relief on both sides, and these fragments also have a carved relief pattern on its body. Judging from the patterns, they were possibly made later than the '*Byakue*' (from the second half of the fourteenth to the first half of the fifteenth centuries).

Fig.14-125 is a large size vessel stand with a reticulated design on the body (probably during the second half of the fourteenth to the first half of the fifteenth centuries) [II-51].

Fig.13-126 is a cover of a jar with curved brim. The exterior is painted with a wave pattern in cobalt. This wave pattern is very similar to that shown in the stem of the '*Byakue*' referenced earlier (made in the fourteenth century). Fig.13-126 is thought to be later (probably the fifteenth century).

Fig.14-127 is a cover of container with a molded flat top and foliated side. Although clouds and animal legs are still identified, the whole design is indistinct. The side has molded panels and remaining fragments show that Qilin and clouds, and deer and clouds are painted in each panel. There are smaller, vertical frames between these panels each of which shows bamboo flanked by three small-circled characters. It is recognized that they are three different characters repeatedly arranged in the same order between the frames but details are not legible. The ground under these circled characters is decorated with an indistinct geometric/*sayagata* pattern. Transparent glaze was applied over the white slipped body, but the glaze was removed from the area that touched the body. Influence of the Jingdezhen under-glaze cobalt blue is possible (from the second half of the fourteenth to the first half of the fifteenth centuries).

Fig.13-128 is a footed small bowl. The foot is formed through carving, with the same technique used for the bowl in green glaze (Fig.8-83). The side of the foot is painted in iron slip. The inner bottom shows a character *fu* 福 in cobalt blue within a circle and a cobalt blue pattern also appears on the external.

Fig.13-129 is a small bowl with a curved rim. The inner bottom is painted with a design of flowering plant, the rim with floral arabesque pattern, the lower body with lotus petal pattern and the upper body with arabesque, all in cobalt blue (the fifteenth century).

Fig.14-130 is a large dish in a basin shape. The interior is filled with a design of a stylized flower with six petals in cobalt blue. The rim is unglazed. The exterior is ornamented in lotus petals without sub-petal. The outlines of the patterns are thicker compared to Fig.17-155, and Fig.14-130 was likely fired during the second half of the fourteenth to the first half of the fifteenth centuries [II-52]. Iron slip is painted inside the foot-ring.

Fig.15-131 is a basin shaped large dish with a design of fish and algae in the inner bottom. The edge of the flat rim points slightly upright and indentations were made by fingers to give it a lobed shape. Examples of such pointy foliate dish are well known, including a large dish in the collection of the Matsuoka Museum of Art, but the Fig.15-131 takes an unusual lobed shape. The rim is unglazed. A wave pattern around the inner bottom shows little difference with the wave pattern painted on large dishes from the salvaged cargo of off Hoi An. The interior is decorated with a treasure motif, while arabesque pattern is arranged around the rim. Another arabesque pattern ornaments the external body and inside the foot-ring is painted in iron slip (the fifteenth century) [II-53].

Fig.14-132 is a cover of jar painted with lotus leaf arabesque in cobalt blue. After forming on a potter's wheel to a circle shape, the rim was shaped into a lotus leaf. The top was given white slip, then glazed in transparency except for the surface of brim that touches the body. A lotus stem shaped knob is attached (from the second half of the fourteenth to the first half of the fifteenth centuries). Because the Jingdezhen under-glaze cobalt blue covers with a similar pattern had been also excavated (Fig.6-50), this is likely to have been influenced by the Jingdezhen ware.

Fig.14-133 is a crab-shaped covered box. White slip covers the exterior (the fifteenth century) [II-54].

Ceramic-slabs

Fig.15-134 is an under-glaze cobalt blue ceramic-slab with a reticulated frame, which is associated with Fig.14-125. This has a convex circle band in-filled with treasures motif. The frame is carved in a *Ru-i* head shape and decorated with a chrysanthemum arabesque (over 15 units). This type of slab was not found in the Great Mosque of Demak and the ornamentation is also very different. The earlier mentioned stand was presumed to date from the second half of the fourteenth to the first half of the fifteenth centuries. While many other pieces artifacts share similarities with the slabs in the Great Mosque and given a possible date as the first half of the fifteenth century, Fig.15–134 is highly possibly older. Given that, we would date it to the second half of the fourteenth to the first half of the fifteenth centuries.

Fig.15–135 is a fragment of under-glaze cobalt blue ceramic-slab decorated with a floral arabesque design. The image on the left is shaped in six-petal *mokkou* 木瓜 (Mayuyama 1977, Fig.1–3). Other two pieces on the right are of a similar type but style of floral arabesque is slightly different and this suggests a possibility of different production date [II-55].

Fig.15–136 is an under-glaze cobalt blue ceramic-slab in a shape of cross with steps. The lower right appears to have a phoenix pattern (Mayuyama 1977, Fig.1–5, 6). This fragment shows the tail of a phoenix in the form of a floral arabesque. Others are thought to be of similar type, but the centre has a different design.

Fig.15–137 is a ceramic-slab with under-glaze cobalt blue lines and over-glaze polychrome enamels decoration in green and red enamels [II-56] (the fifteenth century).

(3) Thailand ceramics

Celadon ware

Fig.16–138 is a celadon porcelain cover with a knob in *Cintamani* shape. The inside of the cover is unglazed. The top has a carved ribbed design and a lotus petal pattern was carved and combed in double circles [II-57].

Fig.16–139 shows a flower – possibly a lotus – outlined in spatula in the inner bottom, which is circled by rings. The space beyond the rings is decorated with combed flower patterns [II-58]. The exterior is also ornamented with ribbed design and the base is unglazed. Inside the foot-ring, there remains a blackened mark of a relatively big kiln tool.

Iron-oxide painted stoneware

Fig.16–140 is a basin or large bowl with an iron-oxide painted fish design in the inner bottom. From the interior to exterior it was coated with white slip and then iron-oxide decoration was added before finally being covered with transparent glaze except for the base [II-59]. Some spur marks created by a kiln tool are left in the inner bottom of the dish.

Fish designs shown in Fig.16–141, 142 both have bottom outlines with a circle around them. They are either a large bowl or a dish. The style of these wares is later than Fig.16–140 [II-60].

Ash glazed ware

Fig.25–143/146 are unglazed high fired grey ceramic jars with stamped decoration on the exterior. Fig.25–143 is a fragment of a rim and Fig.25–144 is a shoulder. A small ear is attached to the lower left of Fig.25–144. On Fig.25–145 the body fragments and the one on right are processed into a disk shape. The body of both two shards was pressed the elephant pattern by seal. Fig.25–146 are fragments of a base.

Some examples with a design of stamped elephants on the body are known by different names in the Bangkok National Museum, the Tochinboku Collection and the Kagoshima Jingu Shrine [II-61]. The bottom of Fig.25-146 is closer to the piece in Kagoshima, but there were other pieces belonging to the Bangkok type also excavated. Regarding the elephant pattern, while the Kagoshima Jingu and Tochinboku Collections show an elephant with its trunk lifted upwards, the trunk in Fig.25-145 is clearly pointed downwards and curled inwards. Many pieces excavated at Trowulan are decorated with a convex band around the neck, as shown in Fig.25-143, but this kind of decoration is only known at Trowulan so far.

Somba Opu Fort
(1) Chinese ceramics
Under-glaze cobalt blue ware
Jingdezhen ware

Fig.26-147 is an under-glaze cobalt blue bowl with a slightly curved rim. A flower motif is arranged in the inner bottom and a floral arabesque design is painted on the exterior.

(2) Thailand ceramics

Fig.26-148 is a celadon cover with a sacred the *Cintamani* knob. The top of the cover is incised with a ribbed design. Finer example was found in Trowulan (Fig.16-138). It was probably a Si Satchanalai ware (the first half of the fifteenth century).

Fig.26-149 is a basin shaped large dish with iron-oxide painting. The glaze turned opaque owing to insufficient firing, but it might also be celadon. An unique motif of flowering plant is painted in the inner bottom, and successive patterns decorate its exterior. The pattern and form indicate that this is fired at a Si Satchanalai kiln (around the first half of the fifteenth century) [II-62].

Buton Wolio Fort
(1) Vietnamese ceramics
Under-glaze cobalt blue ware

Fig.27-150 shows a group of fragments including a large dish, covered box (upper right) and bowl (lower right). The large dish at the upper left has a thick design as well as single petal lotus on the exterior, which helps to date of this to around the first half of the fifteenth century. A bowl at the lower right looks similar to another example found at Trowulan Site (Fig.12-113). A similar type of the covered box at upper right is also presented at Trowulan.

6. Period III-2 (the second half of the 15th to the early 16th century)
Trowulan Site

Ceramics appear to fall into the final period of the Majapahit Kingdom.

(1) Chinese ceramics

Under-glaze cobalt blue ware

Jingdezhen ware

Fig.19-151 is a bowl decorated with a design of a seashell in the inner bottom. The rim would have been curved (from the end of the fifteenth to the beginning of the sixteenth centuries).

(2) Vietnamese ceramics

Under-glaze cobalt blue and other wares

Fig.17-152 is a bowl with a design of character *fu* 福 in cobalt blue in the centre. Around the character there is unglazed circular area. Lotus petals are arranged in lower part of the body. Considering the styles of the character and lotus petals (from the second half of the fifteenth to the beginning of the sixteenth centuries) [II-63].

Fig.17-153 is a bowl with a small character *zheng* 正 painted in cobalt blue within a circle line in the centre. Iron slip applied on inside foot-ring is faint, which is one of the features to indicate the sixteenth century is a highly likely date of this bowl [II-64].

Fig.17-154 is a large dish in a basin shape. It is decorated with a band of wave motif around the centre and its interior and rim are decorated with floral arabesque pattern. The exterior displays a motif of double petal lotus flower. The foot-ring has its interior filled in iron slip and the rim has no glaze (the middle to the second half of the fifteenth century).

Fig.17-155: The interior of this large dish in a basin shape is filled with a six-petal stylized flower in cobalt blue. The rim is unglazed. The pattern resembles closely to one illustrated in Fig.14-130, but Fig.17-155 has a finer cobalt blue outline and the lotus petals on exterior have sub-petals. The motif of additional petals between the main ones is also found in the globular bottle with the year writing of 1450 by under glaze cobalt blue in the Topkapi Palace Museum collection, and is much closer to the salvaged cargo from off Hoi An (from the second half of the fifteenth to the beginning of the sixteenth century) [II-65].

Fig.17-156 is a large bowl with small beads balls attached just beneath the outer rim. The body is decorated with a floral arabesque motif. A different arabesque motif is arranged between the beads balls, and the inner rim is also decorated with a floral arabesque in cobalt. The rim is unglazed. The patterns on this bowl are loosely painted (from the second half of the fifteenth to the beginning of the sixteenth century) [II-66].

Fig.17-157, 158 The body of this bottle has a dragon motif made with dark base. It is glazed in transparent glaze. The foot is painted in iron slip (presumably from the fifteenth to sixteenth century) [II-67].

Somba Opu Fort

(1) Chinese ceramics

Under-glaze cobalt blue ware

Jingdezhen ware

Fig.28-159, 160 are under-glaze cobalt blue bowls with curved rims. Fig.28-159 has a cross-shaped flower motif in the inner bottom, the Siddham script pattern around the inner rim and floral arabesque design on the exterior. Fig.28-160 shows an under-glaze cobalt blue character *fu* 福 in the centre. The exterior is ornamented with lotus scrolling vine pattern [II-68].

Fig.28-161 is decorated with *bao-xiang-hua* 寶相華 (stylized floral arabesque) pattern over a dotted ground. The upper two-third of the exterior is ornamented with linked tortoise shell pattern and the lower body with linked lotus petal pattern [II-69]. Although these under-glaze cobalt blue bowls resemble the salvaged items from the Lena Cargo [II-70] in terms of shape and pattern, the style is more simplified (from the end of the fifteenth to the beginning of the sixteenth centuries).

Fig.28-162 is a dish. The dragon and arabesque pattern in the centre as well as the floral arabesque design on both sides look close to the patterns appear on a dish from the Lena cargo [II-71] , so this example is likely made in the Hongzhi era.

Fig.28-163 is a dish with a slightly curved rim. The centre sports a arabesque design and both sides are painted with floral arabesque [II-72].

Fig.28-164 is a round dish. A design of rock, chrysanthemum and arabesque fills the inner bottom, and chrysanthemum arabesque pattern is distributed on both sides [II-73].

Fig.29-165 is also round dish with a Qilin painted in the central roundel. Both sides display a floral arabesque design [II-74].

Fig.29-166 is also a dish decorated with a floral arabesque design. The similar design can be found in the salvaged examples from the Lena Cargo, thus the date is also around the same period.

(2) Vietnamese ceramics

Under-glaze cobalt blue and other wares

Fig.30-167 is a cover of under-glaze cobalt blue covered box with a flower pattern with seven petals displayed in the centre of the top. It was molded in a shape of an eight-petal flower and each petal is painted with a *Ru-i* head motif. A similar cover was found in Trowulan but with a different pattern on the side (the fifteenth century).

Fig.30-168 is a container missing a cover. A floral arabesque design is manufactured in fine lines. Given that the style is analogous to the floral arabesque design painted in the interior of the basin from Trowulan (Fig.17-154), the dating of Fig.30-168 would be the fifteenth century, in particular the middle to the end.

(3) Thailand ceramics

Iron-oxide painted stoneware

Fig.30-169 is a covered box decorated with iron-oxide painting (the fifteenth to sixteenth century).

Fig.30-170 is a covered box decorated with iron-oxide painting [II-75].

Fig.30-171 is a cover of covered box ornamented with iron-oxide painting.

Fig.30-172 This fragment is a cover of covered box [II-76]. The outline of a pattern is incised (the fifteenth century, Si Satchanalai ware).

Banten Lama Site

(1) Thailand ceramics

Celadon ware

Fig.31-173 is a large celadon dish. A lotus flower motif in the centre and a double circle is incised around the rim or simply in the centre with an incised double circle. There remains attached traces of kiln tool, three-pronged kiln tool in the inner bottom and ring shaped kiln tool inside the foot-ring. The foot-ring is unglazed inside (24 units, the fifteenth century, Si Satchanalai ware).

7. Period IV-1 (from the end of 15th to the middle of 16th century)

Somba Opu Fort

(1) Chinese ceramics

Under-glaze cobalt blue and other wares

Jingdezhen ware

Fig.32-174 are bowls in a shape called *Lianzi*. Characteristic to this type of bowl, the base sags. The central area shows a seashell painted on the ground of line pattern. The fragment on the right is decorated with a simplified lotus flower.

Fig.32-175 is a bowl with a rim slightly folded outwards. There is decoration on the inner part of the rim. The exterior is painted with the Siddham scripts and a linked lotus petal motif on the lower part close to the bottom. The inner bottom also shows a Siddham scripts. Fragments with the Siddham script are known to be collected at Longvek, once the capital of Cambodia.

The rim of Fig.32-176 is also folded similarly to Fig.32-175. The centre of this bowl displays a flower in bloom and the exterior is also decorated with a motif of flower and grasses in a free, broad brushwork.

Fig.33-177 is a bowl with over-glaze polychrome enamels decoration and a curved rim. There is an unglazed circular ring in the centre. Lotus petal pattern is painted on both sides of the body in red and blue enamels, but most of the colours have been worn away.

Fig.33-178 are large lobed dishes with flat rims. A ribbed pattern is carved on the exterior body. The dish on the right has a cloud and dragon design in the central area surrounded by a section filled with a floral arabesque pattern. The interior side is molded to present a ribbed pattern. The rim of the dish on the left is painted with linked *Ru-i* head pattern and the revere side is decorated with swirl like arabesque. A similar dish was excavated in Banten Lama, but it is without the ribbed pattern on the exterior.

Fig.33-179 is also a lobed dish with a flat rim. The inner bottom shows a design of bamboo and rock (from Tai-Hu Lake in China) in under-glaze cobalt blue. A continuous arabesque motif is arranged around the central design. The rim is decorated with a continuous pattern, which could be a loose version of a geometric cord pattern. The exterior is ornamented with an under-glaze cobalt blue design of linked swirl. There is a reign mark in the centre of the foot-ring, which reads 'Made in the Great Ming dynasty'.

Fig.33-180, 181 are lobed dishes with flat rim. They were formed in mold to create a lobed rim and ribbed pattern inside. Fig.33-180 is painted with characters *jin* 金, *yu* 玉 and *di* 地 each within a small roundel around the inner rim. Fig.33-181 has a similar design but characters are illegible. Fig.33-181 sports a Qilin design in the inner bottom. Both dishes have their external body decorated with carved ribbed pattern and a linked swirl motif runs around the rim.

Fig.33-182 is decorated with a design of rock and chrysanthemum in the inner bottom, similar to the design on Fig.28-164, although the former is more loosely painted. Floral arabesque pattern, again loosely painted, is arranged on the exterior. This dish was thought to be made later than that of Fig.28-164.

Fig.33-183 is a dish with an over-glaze decoration in red and green enamels. This type of dish is decorated in the *Ko-akae* 古赤絵 style. The dish has a curved rim and designs of peonies or a peony in the inner bottom and a lotus flower with arabesque on the exterior surface. The same kind of dish was also excavated in Buton Wolio Fort (from the first half to the middle of the sixteenth century).

Fig.33-184 is a round dish with an over-glaze decoration in red and green enamel.

Fig.34-185 are white porcelain dishes with rims curved outwards. This type of dish dated to the sixteenth century is also found in Japan in large quantities.

Fig.34-186 is an under-glaze cobalt blue small jar. The body is decorated with design of lotus flower with a arabesque

Buton Wolio Fort

The Jingdezhen porcelain comprises the main portion of the finds from the period IV-1.

(1) Chinese ceramics

Under-glaze cobalt blue and other wares

Jingdezhen ware

Fig.35-187 is a under-glaze cobalt blue dish with a curved rim. A design of a lion holding a ball is painted in the inner bottom. A type of *Ko-akae*.

Fig.35-188/191 are under-glaze cobalt blue dishes (from the first half to the middle of the sixteenth century). Fig.35-188 and 189 have a curved rim. Fig.35-190 and 191 are in round shape. Fig.35-190 resembles the salvaged items from the Lena Cargo and highly likely to have been fired in the late fifteenth to the beginning of the sixteenth century.

Fig.35-192 is decorated with an over-glaze polychrome enamels decoration in two colours – red and green. The outline of the motif is also painted in red. This type of wares in over-glaze polychrome enamel decoration appeared to be made in large quantities from the first half to the middle of the sixteenth century in Japan, as we know of an heirloom object of small dish with a year mark 'Made in *Tenbun* 天文 era' (1532-55).

Fig.35-193 is a under-glaze cobalt blue dish with a plum tree design painted in the inner bottom. The base takes a shape of a *Yunzi* piece box.

Fig.35-194 is a fragment of a shoulder part of a jar. This jar is decorated with a technique, which allows to glaze in different colours within raised borders. An outline of a *Ru-i* head and jewel patterns between them are raised in relief [II-77].

Banten Lama Site

(1) Chinese ceramics

Under-glaze cobalt blue ware

Jingdezhen ware

Fig.36-195, 196 are under-glaze cobalt blue bowls. They are in *Lianzi* shape and have drooped base. Fig.36-195 is decorated with a pattern, probably of small flowers, in the inner bottom and also on the exterior (23 units). The inner bottom is painted with a seashell motif and a repeated banana leave pattern decorates the lower external space of Fig.36-196. The rim has a flower pattern (8 units). Both types of bowls are commonly found also in Japan (from the first half to the middle of the sixteenth century).

Fig.36-197 is a under-glaze cobalt blue small dish. Its base is characteristically planed in a shape of a *Yunzi* piece box. The centre is given a decoration of flower design and banana leaves motif runs around the lower part of the body (9 units, from the first half to the middle of the sixteenth century). This type is also often seen in Japan.

Fig.36-198, 199 are under-glaze cobalt blue dishes. Fig.36-198 is very large and measures 30.6cm in diameter. The rim is made flat. Dual circle areas surround a flower motif in the centre, and each circle is filled in with a lotus petal and arabesque motif. A band of geometric pattern is arranged on the inner rim, and arabesque pattern on the body (197 units). This type of design is not widely known in Japan [II-78]. Fig.36-199 is a middle size dish with a diameter of 23cm. The flattened rim is lobed. The inner bottom is decorated with a design of a lion holding a ball, and a band of wave pattern is arranged around the inner rim. Carved vertical stripes cover the body (originally, they may have been intended as lotus petals) (9 units). There are some excavated examples of this type of dish in Japan (from the first half to the middle of the sixteenth century).

Fig.36-200 is an under-glaze cobalt blue large bowl. The inner bottom, the external and inner rim are decorated with designs of chrysanthemum scroll, dragon with arabesque and continuous geometric pattern. The foot-ring carries an under-glaze cobalt blue reign mark inside, which reads 'Made in Zhengde reign era' (42 units). Dating of the Zhengde era falls from 1506 to 1521 and this reign mark can be thought of as the production date [II-79]. Only a few of such bowls have been excavated in Japan.

Fig.36-201 is an under-glaze cobalt blue kendi. This fragment was from the spout in globular form and painted with floral arabesque design (1 unit). In Japan, kendi is extremely rare in excavations and have been unearthed only at a few sites, including Manzaimachi Site, Nagasaki. The National Museum of Indonesia in Jakarta owns a kendi with relatively a similar spout (from the first half to the middle of the sixteenth century).

(2) Vietnamese ceramics

Fig.37-202 is a bottle in iron brown glaze. This is a type of bottle called the '*Nanban-chimaki* flower base' in Japan. A trace of having been formed on a wheel after manually coiling the base is visible inside the lower body. An iron brown glaze covers the exterior to the upper part of the interior. In Japan, many examples were passed down from generation to generation as vases, and there are also excavated examples including at the Sakai Kango-toshi Site in Osaka and Sakaemachi Site in Nagasaki (5 units, the fifteenth to the sixteenth centuries).

(3) Thailand ceramics

Although the examples below are listed under this period, it is thought that not many are dated to the fifteenth century.

Iron-oxide painted stoneware

Fig.38-203 is a bowl with iron-oxide painting. A glued trace of kiln tool with legs is visible on the inner bottom (6 units, the fifteenth-century, Sukhothai ware).

Fig.38-204, 205 are covers of covered boxes with iron-oxide painting. Inside the cover is unglazed (15 units in total, the fifteenth to the sixteenth century). Perhaps these fragments made one piece so should be thought of as such.

8. Period IV-2 (from around late of the 16th to the beginning of the 17th century)
Somba Opu Fort
(1) Chinese ceramics
Under-glaze cobalt blue and other wares
Jingdezhen ware

Fig.39-206 has the inner bottom painted with a flower design, which is probably peony. Referring to the similar object in the Topkapi Palace Museum (No.1531), the interior would be filled with a design of grape and vine. Although it is simplified, the exterior body is decorated with pine and plum tree design according to the Topkapi Palace example. Similar pieces were excavated at Banten Lama Site, as well as in the collection in Lonvek and Ponhea Lueu in Cambodia [II-80].

Fig.39-207 are bowls with over-glaze polychrome enamels decoration. One on left is a fragment of a rise of inner bottom /*man-tou-xin* style and carries an underglaze cobalt-blue design of heron and lotus in the inner bottom. Within a foot-ring, there is a description also in under-glaze cobalt blue, which reads *wan-fu-xiu-tong* 萬福修同. Its body is painted with coloured pattern.

Fig.39-208 is a small white porcelain bowl with an unglazed circular ring in the centre (around the second half of the sixteenth century).

Fig.39-209 is an under-glaze cobalt blue jar with a narrowing lower body. The under-glaze cobalt-blue pattern of lotus petal decorates the bottom [II-81]. The shoulder has *Ru-i* head shape frames within the outlined sections, which is filled with a design of lotus and floral scroll. Continuous linked *Ru-i* head pattern runs around the join to the neck.

A similar piece in the Topkapi Palace Museum suggests that the neck is decorated with a motif of clouds and *Ru-i* head.

Fig.39-210 is a jar with over-glaze polychrome enamels decoration.

Fig.39-211 Upper fragment is a bottle in a shape of a bird.

Fig.40-212 is a small jar with under-glaze cobalt blue decoration. A spray of flower design ornaments the body and the shoulder has a design of saw-teeth like lotus petal or banana leaf. The base is flat.

Fig.40-213 is a jar in different glaze with raised sections. It has a tapering body towards bottom, which is decorated with a lotus petal pattern. Another object with a very close design in the lower body [II-82] also has a similar pattern on the neck and shoulder to the under-glaze cobalt blue jar (Fig.39-209). This suggests that differently decorated jars of Jingdezhen came to the same site (in the sixteenth century).

Under-glaze cobalt blue ware

Zhangzhou ware

Fig.41-214 is a bowl with lined dots pattern. The pattern appears to have simplified the previous example of a Jingdezhen *Lianzi* bowl, which is covered with small flowers (the first half of the sixteenth century) [II-83].

Fig.41-215 is a bowl with a design of flower in the inner bottom. Flowering plants in thick and bold brushwork decorate the exterior body [II-84].

Fig.41-216 is a bowl and the design is too simplified, but possible to read as *shan* 善 .

Fig.41-217 is a bowl with a thick character *fu* 福 in the inner bottom [II-85].

Fig.41-218 is a dish decorated with a motif in thick brushwork. The motif is either a lion holding a ball or Qilin.

Fig.41-219 This dish has a flower motif in the inner bottom.

The inner bottom of Fig.41-220 shows a flower and arabesque pattern goes around the rim, which is slightly folded outwards [II-86].

The inner bottom of Fig.41-221 has double circles both of which are filled with stylized flower motif in thick brush. A flower motif is also placed at each four points on the interior [II-87].

Fig.42-222, 223 are large dishes with flat rim. Six paneled flowers are arranged around the rim over the scale patterned ground. Fig.42-222 shows a design of bird and flowering plant in the inner bottom, while Fig.42-223 is painted with a phoenix and flowering pattern [II-88]. These type of large dishes have been excavated also in Japan.

Buton Wolio Fort

(1) Chinese ceramics

Under-glaze cobalt blue ware (including over-glaze polychrome enamels)

Fig.43-224: There are many of this kind of under-glaze cobalt blue bowls with a rise of inner bottom/*man-tou-xin*.

Fig.43-225, 226 are the type of ware with over-glaze enamels decoration, red for example, over the under-glaze cobalt blue body. Fig.43-225 bears an inscription in under-glaze cobalt blue within foot-ring, which reads *man-fu-you-tong* 萬福攸同. Similar example was found at Somba Opu Fort (Fig.39-207, lower left).

Banten Lama Site
(1) Chinese ceramics
Under-glaze cobalt blue ware and ware with over-glaze polychrome enamels decoration
Jingdezhen ware

Fig.44-227 is a small cup decorated with a design of legendary three sacred mountains floating over water in under-glaze cobalt blue. A wave pattern is painted in under-glaze cobalt blue around the lower body and the foot-ring bears a reign mark of 'Made in the Great Ming dynasty' inside (3 unites, around the second half of the sixteenth century) [II-89].

Fig.44-228 is either a dish or large bowl with over-glaze enamels decoration. The inner bottom of this dish is painted with a similar motif with Fig.44-227, but mainly in red enamel. Lower body shows a design, probably lotus petals. The foot-ring carries a reign mark in under-glaze cobalt blue in an area outlined by double circle, but period is missing (8 units). Production date is also same with Fig.44-227. There is no excavated example of this type of ware in Japan.

Fig.44-229 is an over-glaze enamels decorated bowl. Red, green and yellow enamels were added on a preliminary painted pattern in under-glaze cobalt blue. The body is decorated with a design of alternating lobed panel and flower. On the interior and around the rim, it is arranged with jewels and geometric patterns respectively (20 units, the second half of the sixteenth century). This type of ware is not common in Japan.

Fig.44-230 is an under-glaze cobalt blue bowl (from the 1590s to 1610s). It is decorated with a flower motif in the centre, and grapes pattern on the interior. A pine and plum trees motif appears on the body (31 units) [II-90]. Fig.39-206 from Somba Opu is a similar example.

Chinese stoneware

Fig.45-231 is a three-coloured (sancai) jar with ears. It is a low-fired stoneware. Arabesque pattern is applied on the body. There are several excavated pieces of this kind, the Tradescant type jar, known in Japan (1 unit, the sixteenth to the seventeenth centuries).

(2) Myanmar stoneware

Fig.46-232 are the large dishes in tin based milky glaze and more than two units were unearthed [II-91]. The fragment at the bottom is a large dish in white glaze with green decoration.

9. Period V-1 (around the first half of the 17th century)
Somba Opu Fort
(1) Chinese ceramics

Under-glaze cobalt blue and other wares
Jingdezhen ware

Fig.47-233 is a small cup with under-glaze cobalt blue decoration.

Fig.47-234 is also an under-glaze cobalt blue small cup. Production date is estimated seventeenth century but whether the first half or second half is not clear.

Fig.47-235 is a small bowl in the Kraak style. It is lobed in mold (around the first quarter of the seventeenth century) [II-92].

Fig.47-236, Two fragments on the left are dish with flat rim. The innter bottom is painted with a phoenix and flowering plant design [II-93].

Fig.47-237 is a small dish in the Meizan type, a variety of the Kraak style. It is lobed in mold and the inner bottom is decorated with a treasure pattern. On the exterior, a flower design is painted in the *Cintamani* shaped panels. The exterior has vertically outlined sections and a treasure pattern is arranged space between lines [II-94].

Fig.47-238 is a molded white porcelain dish with lobed flat rim.

Zhangzhou ware

Fig.48-239 is an under-glaze cobalt blue bowl [II-95].

Fig.48-240 is a bowl with a design of heron and lotus on the inner bottom, and lotus motif on the exterior body [II-96].

The inner bottom of Fig.48-241 is divided into two sections by a double ring, which was filled with stylized flower pattern [II-97].

Fig.48-242 is a large deep dish. This type of dish is often found also in Japan. The inner bottom sports a design of phoenix and bamboo. On the interior, four foliated panels are placed at four different directions and space between them is decorated with a pattern of three horizontal lines – somehow it looks like the Chinese hexagram motif. A continuous meander pattern ornaments the rim [II-98].

Fig.48-243 is one of the Kraak style dish and its centre shows a Meizan type decoration [II-99].

Fig.48-244 is a large dish with over-glaze polychrome enamels decoration. The colour had been badly faded and makes it difficult to fully identify the pattern. There is a similar object decorated with a symmetrically painted phoenix and peony in the centre, and on the flat rim alternating design of four paneled flower at each direction and floral plants on the ground filled with scale pattern [II-100].

Fig.48-245 is a large celadon dish.

Fig.48-246 is a small lobed dish made in white porcelain. The Dehua kilns in Fujian province produced this type of lobed dishes, but they were usually formed in mold and leaving base spur marks on the inner bottom or foot-ring. Fig.48-246 was probably fired in other kiln in Fujian around the close period.

Buton Wolio Fort
(1) Chinese ceramics

Jingdezhen and Zhangzhou wares from the 1590s to the first half of the seventeenth century were excavated in a large quantity.

Under-glaze cobalt blue and other wares

Jingdezhen ware

Fig.49-247 is an example of a white porcelain bowl with a character *gui* 貴 in under-glaze cobalt blue inside the foot-ring.

Fig.49-248 include fragments of under-glaze cobalt blue bowls. Bottom left is a small bowl in the Kraak style.

Fig.49-249 is a large bowl with design of a classic Chinese poetic exposition, *Chibifu*. A flower band ornaments around the inner bottom. Externally the body is painted with a poem, which is thought to be a classic Chinese and a human figure and a boat. The base of the foot-ring is planed broad and the base is unglazed (from the 1620s to 1640s).

Fig.49-250/Fig.50-252 are under-glaze cobalt blue dishes with the Kraak style design, the typical designs for European markets. Upper right fragment in Fig.50-252 is a dish of the Meizan type. Upper left of Fig.50-252 is a bowl in the Kraak style and particularly called the monster mask type.

Fig.50-253 are under-glaze cobalt blue dishes with different design. The lower right is one of the Kraak style and resembles to a dish in tulip style but the interior decoration is different (probably the Chongzhen reign period).

Fig.50-254 is an under-glaze cobalt blue ware with under-glaze copper red painting. Similar to Fig.49-249, this has a flat broad foot-ring and the base is unglazed (probably made in the 1620s to 1640s).

Fig.50-255 shows a design of heron and water plants in white slip and cobalt on the iron brown glazed body. This type of decoration is called the Mochibana type in Japan.

Fig.50-256 is an under-glaze cobalt blue covered box (around the second half of the sixteenth to the seventeenth centuries).

Zhangzhou ware

Fig.51-257 shows fragments of dishes from the first half of the seventeenth century. One on the top has a phoenix design in the inner bottom and under-glaze cobalt blue design of meander pattern on the border of the rim. Many similar examples of this type had been excavated also in Japan.

Fig.51-258 is a large celadon dish. The interior is carved with a design of chrysanthemum petals.

Fig.51-259 is a large dish decorated with white base motif in cobalt blue glaze.

Fig.51-260 is a covered box with over-glaze polychrome enamels decoration.

Fig.51-261: Colour tone of glaze and make of the base suggest that this large dish with enamels decoration was made in the middle of the seventeenth century, the final period for a Zhangzhou ware large dish. Same view applied to the large celadon dish shown in Fig.51-262.

Fig.51-262 This large celadon dish has carved line design on the interior.

Dehua ware

The Dehua kiln produced unique white porcelains.

Fig.51-263 is a lobed small dish made in mold (from the late sixteenth to the first half of the seventeenth centuries).

Fig.51-264 is a dish formed in mold. Characteristically this dish has base spur marks on the inner bottom and also on the base of foot-ring. Colour tone of the glaze is unique white, and is called ivory white (the seventeenth century).

Banten Lama Site

(1) Chinese ceramics

Under-glaze cobalt blue ware (including over-glaze polychrome enamels decoration)

Jingdezhen ware

Fig.52-265, 266 are middle size under-glaze cobalt blue dishes with flat mouth rim. Fig.52-265 has arabesque pattern running along the edge of rim, and floral scroll design on the exterior (6 units, from the 1590s to 1630s). The inner bottom of Fig.52-266 is decorated with a design of deer under the tree and water bird with plants on the flat rim (32 units, from the 1590s to 1610s) [II-101].

Fig.52-267 is a middle size under-glaze cobalt blue dish with round body. There are designs of fish jumping out of water on the inner bottom, and treasures on both interior and exterior (93 units). This type of dish has not been excavated in Japan (from the 1590s to 1630s).

Fig.52-268 is an under-glaze cobalt blue large dish. Its interior sports a mountain landscape design. The exterior displays a tree motif (6 unites). In Japan, large dish is rare, and apart from Yuan under-glaze cobalt blue, only a few in the Kraak style of the early Edo period were so far excavated at sites including the Hirado Dutch Trading Post. It is even rare to see designs other than the Kraak style (from the 1590s to 1630s).

Fig.52-269 is an under-glaze cobalt blue dish (about 14.6cm in diameter). The panel decorations on the interior were press molded in relief (34 units). This is also the Meizan type, a variation of the Kraak style. A birds and flowers design is displayed in the inner bottom. Patterns of paneled flower and treasures are alternating on the inside the dish. The exterior is divided into sections, each of which is decorated with under-glaze cobalt blue motif of treasures (from the 1600s to 1630s).

Fig.52-270 are fragments of under-glaze cobalt blue dishes in the Kraak style. Mixture of fine and coarse made the Kraak style dishes were excavated, but Fig.52-270 is a fine example. The outer side of interior is divided into sections – which is a unique feature of the Kraak – painted in with flower and treasure patterns. Around the inner bottom shows an arks/*maribasami* motif accompanied with geometric/*saya* pattern and triangle ground. The exterior also has paneled treasure motif. The panels were first outlined in press mold in relief then given under-glaze cobalt blue painting (41 units of Fig.52-270). The Kraak style dish was sought after in Europe, and we expect to be fired for a long period through orders (from the 1600s to 1630s) [II-102].

Fig.52-271 are fragments of the Kaark style large dish with diameter over 40cm. The inner bottom is covered with a detailed design, which is encircled by arks/*maribasami* motif. Internally and externally, motif panels are distributed in divided sections (17 units, from the 1590s to 1610s) [II-103].

Fig.52-272 is an under-glaze cobalt blue large dish. This is a type of the Kraak style that would carry a tulip design in divided sections on the outer side of interior. One of the characteristics is a band around the inner bottom in which appears a design of chrysanthemums with unique leaves. Although no fragments carrying a tulip design remain, fragment with a mound with grasses was found. This is likely part of the design of a Chinese figure in landscape, which would have been arranged alternately with a tulip design. The inner bottom shows partial design of architectural structure (balustrade), also a typical design composition for a Kraak style large dish with a tulip motif (3 units, the second quarter of the seventeenth century) [II-104].

Fig.52-273 is a white porcelain small cup. A double outlined square within the foot-ring bears an under-glaze cobalt blue reign mark of six characters in two lines, which reads 'Made in the Ming dynasty, Chenghua reign' (1 unit, from the 1600s to 1610s) [II-105].

Fig.52-274 is a cover of under-glaze cobalt blue covered box with a design of crane and clouds on the top, and ivy pattern on the side (1 unit, from the second half of the sixteenth to the beginning of the seventeenth centuries).

Fig.52-275/277 are iron brown glazed boxes and covers decorated with patterns applied in white slip. Fig.52-275 is a cover of a small box. The top is painted with a flower pattern in white base over iron brown glaze body, and its side is incised with vertical lines (3 units). Fig.52-276 and 277 are large covered box decorated with carved vertical stripes on the side in iron brown glaze. Floral arabesque pattern in white base is distributed under the rim (6 unit of Fig.52-276, and 3 units of Fig.52-277, from the late sixteenth century to the first half of the seventeenth centuries).

Fujian ware

In the southern Fujian province, kilns are distributed in Dehua, Anxi and Zhangzhou regions. These kilns produced inferior quality porcelain compared to that of the Jingdezhen type with Dehua ware white porcelain as an exception. This lead to a distribution of some kilns producing low quality porcelain also in the northern Guangdong province. Serious production of under-glaze cobalt blue ware in the southern Fujian started from the second half of the sixteenth century, while the Jingdezhen was gaining a main status as the producer of under-glaze cobalt blue. For this reason, in Banten Lama the southern Fujian porcelain appeared after the period IV-2.

Fig.53-278 is an under-glaze cobalt blue bowl. It is made of relatively white Kaolinite and entirely glazed. Crumbling chaff is attached by firing to the base of foot-ring. The body is decorated with a floral arabesque pattern and the inner bottom displays a flower motif (197 units, the Zhangzhou type ware, from the 1590s to 1630s) [II-106].

Fig.53-279 is a large bowl with over-glaze enamels decoration and a type called *gosu-akae* in Japan. The body was applied with white slip before firing. Glazing around the area close to the foot-ring is sloppy and coarse sand is occasionally attached by firing.

Crudely made body is painted with a lotus pattern chiefly in red enamel. Around the rim it is decorated with paneled motif over the ground pattern (1 unit, the Zhangzhou type ware, from the 1590s to 1630s).

Fig.53-280 is a small under-glaze cobalt blue dish. Condition of the raw body and foot-ring is close to those of Fig.53-278. A flag and tower motif is visible in the inner bottom and geometric pattern distributes around the interior of a gently folded rim (1 unit, from the 1590s to 1630s) [II-107].

Fig.53-281 is an under-glaze cobalt blue dish decorated with a motif – it appears Qilin – in the inner bottom (1 unit, from the 1590s to 1630s, the Zhangzhou type ware).

Fig.53-282 is a large under-glaze cobalt blue dish with a flat mouth rim. It was called as *Gosu-de* in Japan, while European said the Swatow ware. The inner bottom shows a design of phoenix and bamboo, while paneled flower design was arranged on the ground filled with wave pattern. Dishes with this motif were commonly excavated also in Japan, as well as in Hoi An, Vietnam [II-108]. The body is first covered in white slip, painted motifs in cobalt, and finally applied in transparent glaze (371 units, the Zhangzhou type ware, from the 1590s to 1630s).

Fig.53-283 is a white porcelain bottle with long body, so called the Anpin jar. The fragments can be grouped into several types by closely observing rims and bottoms but all is listed up as a whole in this publication (31 units) [II-109].

Dehua ware

Fig.53-284 is a white porcelain lobed dish. The foot-ring was also formed in press mold and this forming method left characteristic wrinkles on the base. Some base spur marks remain in the inner bottom and inside the foot-ring [II-110]. About 14 units of white porcelain bowls in similar spur marks and mold technique were found (late sixteenth to the first half of the seventeenth centuries, the Dehua ware).

Chinese stoneware

Fig.54-285 is a jar in iron brown glaze. Patted trace is left on the shoulder (1 unit, the seventeenth to the eighteenth centuries).

Fig.54-286 is an iron brown glazed dish, probably for light. On the base remained clockwise trace of the string cutting. The interior is covered with iron-based water (27 units, the seventeenth to eighteenth centuries).

Fig.54-287 is a small jar in black glaze. There is a distinctively visible trace of base strips being coiled up in forming. The foot-ring was planed out of the base. The body is covered in black glaze except the base, and glaze on the lip was intentionally removed off to show off the original body (1 unit, the seventeenth century) [II-111].

(2) Vietnamese ceramics

Iron-oxide painted ware

Fig.55-288 is a bowl with iron-oxide decoration. The centre has an unglazed circular ring and iron-oxide painting, and the base is unglazed. This is made in finer base than the example found at Buton Wolio Fort (Fig.67-343), and thought to be older type (1 unit, the seventeenth century).

(3) Hizen ware

Hizen porcelain

In the modern times, stoneware and porcelain were extensively fired in the Hizen region, which extended over modern day Saga and Nagasaki prefectures, Japan. They were called the Karatsu ware and the Imari ware named after the ports from which they were exported. However this publication calls them as the Hizen stoneware and the Hizen porcelain, which reflect the production site more accurately.

Fig.56-289 is a sauce dish. The rim is carved in the shape of chrysanthemum, and the interior is decorated with chrysanthemum petals in underg-laze cobalt blue. Similar sauce dish was excavated at the Kamanotsuji kiln site, Yamauchicho, Saga prefecture. This was intended for the domestic Japanese market and only two other examples apart from Japan were excavated at Banten Lama and Buton Wolio Fort (2 units, from the 1630s to 1640s) [II-112].

Fig.56-290, 291 are dishes with under-glaze cobalt blue decoration. The rim of Fig.56-290 is gently flared up and its border is decorated with a wood grain pattern. The outer interior is ornamented a key-fret pattern (1 unit). Fig.56-291 is painted with a design of peony on rock around which appears a linked *Ru-i* head pattern in under-glaze cobalt blue (2 unites, around the 1640s) [II-113].

Hizen stoneware

Fig.56-292 is a stoneware dish. It was fired with stacking technique using sand balls. Refined white base formed the body, which resulted in egg colour hue. It is likely fired at the Uchinoyama kiln, Ureshino city (1 unit, from the 1610s to 1640s).

Fig.56-293 is a dish in iron brown glaze. The interior has an incised atabesque pattern. Lower body is painted over with iron base water except the base of foot-ring. White spur marks, which could be remains of Kaolinite, were left in the inner bottom and on the base of foot-ring (the second quarter of the seventeenth century). In addition to Fig.56-293, the Mishima style and stoneware with brush stroke decoration were also found (the total 7 units).

(4) Islamic stoneware

A few stoneware, likely made in the West Asia were unearthed.

Fig.57-294 is a bowl with under-glaze cobalt blue decoration. Under-glaze cobalt blue design floral arabesque was applied on the white slip covered body. Inside and outside of the foot-ring is unglazed (1 unit, the sixteenth to seventeenth centuries).

(5) European stoneware

Fig.57-295/297 are albarellos. They are soft-paste stoneware in tin glaze. Fig.57-295 is decorated with a tobacco leaf design in indigo blue enamel. Fragments in Fig.57-296 and 297 are glazed in white tin and come in various size and shapes (The jar with indigo enamel decoration : 17 unites, middle size such as Fig.57-296 : 14 units, and jars with long body : 14 units.) In addition, there are five large sized ware and twelve of smaller size (the Delft ware, the Netherlands, around the seventeenth century).

Fig.57-298 is a salt glazed stoneware ewer with handle. This is a type called the 'alcohol bottle with a bearded man' (40 units, the second half of the sixteenth to the seventeenth centuries) [II-114].

Tirtayasa Site

(1) Chinese ceramics

Under-glaze cobalt blue and other wares

Jingdezhen ware

Fig.58-299 are under-glaze cobalt blue large bowls with slightly folded rim. Fragments decorated with chrysanthemum and bird motifs were excavated (the first half of the seventeenth century).

Fig.58-300 is an under-glaze cobalt blue large bowl. The inner bottom displays a design of floral arabesque within a double circle. Inside the foot-ring bears an inscription *yui-tang-jia-qi* 玉堂佳器 in a double circle (the Chongzhen reign period).

Fig.58-301 left is an under-glaze cobalt blue square dish. The rim is flatly made and there is a poem only part of which can be deciphered as '... *tian* 天 ...'. The foot-ring is planed thick (the Chongzhen reign period).

Fig.58-301 right is either small bowl or small cup with a white base decoration in iron brown glaze. They are the fragments of rim and body. The body was differently glazed externally and internally, the former in iron brown glaze and the latter in transparent glaze. A design in white base was expressed over the external body in iron brown glaze. This type of style is known as the Mochibana type in Japan (the seventeenth century).

Fig.58-302 are the fragments of bottom, rim and side of under-glaze cobalt blue large dishes. The bottom fragment shows a design of deer, flowering plant and rock. The base is unglazed. The fragments of rim and side appear to be the same ware. The rim is lobed and decorated with flowering plant motif and horizontal lines that suggest water (the first half of the seventeenth century).

Zhangzhou ware

Fig.59-303 is a bottom fragment of under-glaze cobalt blue bowl. The inner bottom of this bowl is painted with a floral motif and the external body with floral arabesque pattern (the Zhangzhou type, Fujian province, the first half of the seventeenth century).

Fig.59-304 is a white porcelain large dish. The interior is painted with white slip and decorated with incised patterns. From the base to inside foot-ring is unglazed. Coarse sands are attached by firing to the base of foot-ring. White glaze bears cloudiness because of the insufficient firing (the first half of the seventeenth century) [II-115].

Fig.59-305 is a small lobed cornered square dish with under-glaze cobalt blue decoration. The pattern on the border looks bamboo (the first half of the seventeenth century) [II-116].

Fig.59-306 are fragments of side of an under-glaze cobalt blue large dish. The interior shows an unique bird and flowers design [II-117]. Decoration on the inner bottom is only partially visible but it is highly likely a voyage design (the Zhangzhou type ware, the first half of the seventeenth century).

In summing up, there are only a few late Ming porcelains. Their production sites are Jingdezhen and Zhangzhou area kilns but the latter outnumbers the former. In addition, there are some stoneware thin fragments of Thailand jars of the same period.

10. Period V-2 (around the second half of the 17th century to the beginning of the 18th century)

Trowulan Site

(1) Hizen ware

Hizen porcelain

Fig.20-307 is a white porcelain bowl fired at the Arita kiln, Hizen. This bowl has special features common in the 1650s to 1680s.

Fig.20-308 is a covered small bowl with under-glaze cobalt blue decoration. Pattern is very loosely painted and obscure but it could be clouds and dragon (from 1655 to the 1680s, the Arita kiln).

Fig.20-309, 310 are covers for covered boxes decorated with over-glaze enamels motif. Fig.20-309 was incised with a chrysanthemum pattern around the side after forming. On the white porcelain base, peony spray pattern was first outlined in black, then in-filled with blue enamel. White line appears where the black outline disappears. Fig.20-310 has divided sections by red double lines on white porcelain base. A foliated panel is outlined also in red on the top of the cover within which a red flower pattern is painted in the centre. Colours around the flower motif have been significantly faded but there seems a design of leaves in green or yellow enamel. The side is also decorated with a flower motif in red, green or yellow, but again the colours were badly exfoliated.

As two examples were excavated at this site, Hizen porcelain covered box outstands in the areas of Indonesia. Small bowl with a cover tends to be found more in Cambodia, Laos and Thailand. Apart from bowls, other types were not for Japanese but intended to the Southeast Asian market in the second half of the seventeenth century.

It is noted that Hizen porcelain dated to the first half of the eighteenth century were not excavated at this site, while they were found at Banten Lama and other archaeological sites in Jakarta, as well as Buton Wolio Fort in Sulawesi. This fact suggests that the Dutch East India Company was not trading with this area in the eighteenth century.

After two hundred years in the Meiji period, Hizen porcelain for daily use made its way to Tirtayasa, although in small quantity. Bowls with under-glaze cobalt blue decoration applied with paper stencils were also confirmed in Cambodia and Laos within the Southeast Asia. However, daily use Hizen porcelain bowls stopped with stencil print and no examples with a copper printed design have been found. In Cambodia and Laos in the meantime, the Seto and Mino porcelain with a copperplate transfer ware was becoming a mainstream.

Somba Opu fort

(1) Chinese ceramics

Under-glaze cobalt blue and other wares

Zhangzhou ware

Fig.60-311 (left) is an under-glaze cobalt blue bowl decorated with auspicious characters *shou* 壽. Multiple *shou* characters are arranged on the external body and a continuous flower pattern appears on the inside of the rim. This type of bowl was fired in quantity during the second half of the seventeenth century and the design after the 1660s became looser in comparison to the earlier type in the 1650s. This example looks relatively older and is expected to be the 1650s.

Fig.60-311 (right) is a small dish (the second half of the seventeenth century).

Fig.60-312 is a large dish with an over-glaze enamels decoration. Characteristically fine crackles cover the body and inside the foot-ring is almost unglazed. This kind of feature is often found in dishes of the second half of the seventeenth century, and thought of the southern Fujian origin. Although it is obscure, there is a pattern looks like peony in the inner bottom. This is similar to the dish excavated at the Buton Wolio Fort (Fig.51-261).

(2) Hizen porcelain and stoneware

Hizen porcelain

Fig.61-313 is a dish with a design of flowering plants (around the 1640s).

Fig.61-314 is a dish with unglazed circular ring area in the inner bottom within which shows a character of *hi* 日 in under-glaze cobalt blue [II-118].

Two on the left of Fig.61-315 are the same type, but instead they have a design of fish jumping out of wave (from the 1660s to 1670s).

Fig.61-315 The lower right is a Kraak style dish (before or after the 1660s).

Fig.61-316 is an under-glaze cobalt blue bowl.

In Fig.61-317, five fragments except those in two lower rows on the left are under-glaze cobalt blue large bowl. Inside the rim is decorated with a meander pattern (before or after the 1660s to 1670s). One on the top right is a large bowl with a slightly flat rim (around the 1660s).

Fig.61-318 are dishes in under-glaze cobalt blue decoration. The top right is the Kraak style and inferior quality.

Fig.61-319 is an under-glaze cobalt blue dish in the Kraak style (before or after the 1660s to 1670s).

Fig.62-320 fragments on the left are cover. One on the right is an albarello (from the 1650 to 1670s).

Fig.62-321 is a small dish with an over-glaze polychrome enamels decoration. The colour had been significantly exfoliated, but it appears to have a design of flying bird and cherry branch. This is broadly categorized as the Kakiemon style (from the 1670s to 1690s), and is an unusual example to be excavated in Indonesia.

Fig.62-322 are under-glaze cobalt blue decorated dishes (the second half of the seventeenth century) and probably all was fired in Arita. The large fragment at the bottom is a dish decorated with a *Ru-i* head pattern in the inner bottom. There is a fragment of dish found at Banten Lama, which has an added design of flowering plant on the interior (from the 1650s to 1680s) [II-119].

Fig.63-323 a large fragment at the bottom right is a large dish with an under-glaze cobalt blue decoration (from the 1680s to 1700s) [II-120].

Fig.63-324 the fragment on the left is an under-glaze cobalt blue bottle and the top right is a Kraak style dish.

Buton Wolio Fort

(1) Chinese ceramics

Under-glaze cobalt blue and other wares

Jingdezhen ware

Fig.64-325 shows a collection of fragments of under-glaze cobalt blue bowls. They were made in coarse and possible the Jingdezhen.

Fig.64-326 are under-glaze cobalt blue bowls (fromt the end of the seventeenth century to the beginning of the eighteenth century).

Fig.64-327 is a dish decorated with carved pattern on the interior and continuous geometric motif around the rim in under-glaze cobalt blue. Similar examples were excavated, such as, at Banten Lama (Fig.70-358) (from the end of seventeenth century to the beginning of the eighteenth century).

Fig.64-328 is an under-glaze cobalt blue large dish. They have a unique double foot-ring (from the end of seventeenth century to the beginning of the eighteenth century).

Fig.64-329 is a large dish decorated with over-glaze polychrome enamels design. They also have a characteristic double foot-ring (from the end of seventeenth century to the beginning of the eighteenth century).

Fig.64-330 are three-coloured (sancai) dishes.

Fig.65-331 are bowls and large bowls differently glazed in iron brown on the external and the interior and inside the foot-ring in under-glaze cobalt blue. The fragment on top left is smaller compared to the others and would be a tea or coffee cup for the European market. This type of porcelain in iron brown glaze is usually called the Batavian ware in Europe.

Fig.65-332 are dishes of similar type with Fig.65-331.

Fig.65-333 are also differently glazed dishes with iron brown on one side and either under-glaze cobalt blue or over-glaze enamels on the other.

Fig.65-334 is a cobalt blue large jar with paneled design. Panels contain cobalt blue and under-glaze copper red painting.

Fig.65-335 are large jars decorated with an over-glaze polychrome enamels (the end seventeenth to the beginning of the eighteenth centuries). It is a characteristic to Buton Wolio Fort that it presents many Arita large jars dated to the 1690s to 1730s, both over-glaze enamels and under-glaze cobalt blue. At the same time we need to pay attention to the fact that Jingdezhen large jars of the same period were also found in a big quantity.

(1) Fujian and Guangdong wares

Fig.66-336 are mainly bowls with stamped decoration in under-glaze cobalt blue [II-121]. They need to be given a range in dating from the 1680s to the first half of the eighteenth centuries.

Fig.66-337 is a bowl with stamped decoration in under-glaze cobalt blue. Linked characters of *shou* 壽 are distributed on the body and the inner bottom displays a stamped flower motif. On the slightly folded rim, a continuous design of, possibly, *Ru-i* head is arranged. It is well made for a stamped under-glaze cobalt blue bowl and the glaze remains on the inner bottom. This type is not so common in Japan and further study is awaited on the position of such ware in a history of ceramics.

Fig.66-338 include under-glaze cobalt blue dishes. One on left displays a leaf and poem.

Fig.66-339 is a large under-glaze cobalt blue dish with an unglazed circular ring in the centre.

Fig.66-340 is an under-glaze cobalt blue dish decorated with a stamped motif. It is of inferior quality. The centre has an unglazed circular ring for stacking other ware on at firing. The Siddham script pattern was stamped in under-glaze cobalt blue on the outer interior. This type of coarsely stamped under-glaze cobalt blue made in a great quantity in Fujian and Guangdong provinces during the late seventeenth to the first half of the eighteenth centuries. Some kilns continued to produce such ware even afterwards. There is a similar kind of dish excavated at Banten Lama (Fig.72-376).

Fig.66-341 shows a collection of under-glaze cobalt blue bowls and large bowls with a stamped decoration. One on the upper right was repeatedly stamped with the Siddham scripts. One on the upper left is alternately stamped with a stylized character *shou* 壽 and flower like motif. This type of ware has been found in Japan, for example Okinawa.

Fig.66-342 is a body of white porcelain covered box, probably the Dehua ware.

(2) Vietnamese ceramics

Fig.67-343 is a bowl with stamped iron-oxide painting. The stamped design appears to be chrysanthemum. The base is unglazed and the inner bottom has an unglazed circular ring. Quite a few similar bowls had been found, including Somba Opu Fort and Banten Lama (Fig.55-288). There are many examples also in Japan.

Buton Wolio Fort

(1) Hizen ceramics

Hizen is the main ware during the second half of the seventeenth century with some additional low quality porcelains of Fujian and Guangdong.

Hizen porcelain

Fig.68-344 are some bowls in under-glaze cobalt blue. The fragment on the bottom right shows a design of fish jumping out of water and only one example was found of this design. All are thought the dating enter the period during 1655–the 1680s.

Fig.68–345 are over-glaze enamels decorated bowls. There are dishes of this type among the finds at the southern moat trial excavation (from the 1660s to 1690s).

Fig.68–346 & Fig.69–347 are a collection of under-glaze cobalt blue dishes in the Kraak style. Upper left in Fig.68–346 is poorly made and dated to around the 1650s. The third from left in the upper row in Fig.69–347 is a small dish of the Meizan type, a variation of the Karaak style.

Fig.69–348 are dishes decorated in under-glaze cobalt blue. Centre on the right row shows a phoenix motif and is suspected to be decorated with a design of phoenix and character *shou* 壽.

Fig.69–349 are large celadon dishes. A unique feature is an unglazed circular ring painted in iron slip inside the foot-ring. They are Hizen ware and in particular thought to be fired at the Arita kiln (from the 1650s to 1670s).

Fig.69–350 is an under-glaze cobalt blue decorated large deep bowl usually accompanied with a cover (from the 1660s to 1680s). Similar pieces are known also in the Netherlands and England [II-122].

The left in Fig.69–351 is a large bowl bearing a VOC monogram in the inner bottom (between the 1690s and 1700s). There are other similar large bowls, albeit only a few, with under-glaze cobalt blue VOC monogram in the inner bottom.

Fig.69–352 are a collection of under-glaze cobalt blue decorated fragments including kendi and covered box.

Banten Lama Site
(1) Chinese ceramics
Under-glaze cobalt blue and other wares
Jingdezhen ware

Fig.70–353 is a bowl in under-glaze cobalt blue and colour glazes (*sancai*). On the exterior, it has differently glazed sections in green, yellow, purple and white. A stylized flower attached by *Ru-i* head pattern is displayed in the centre of the bowl with a floral arabesque design on the interior of the rim. The area within the foot-ring is given transparent glaze (79 units, the second half of the seventeenth to the beginning of the eighteenth centuries).

Fig.70–354 is a bowl in colour glazes (*sancai*). Different glaze - green, yellow, purple and white were applied on the body, except the area within the foot-ring. The foot-ring bears a double ring in under-glaze cobalt blue inside (94 units, the second half of the seventeenth to the first half of the eighteenth centuries).

Fig.70–355 is a green glazed bowl with incised decoration. The exterior is covered with carved flower pattern, which looks similar to Fig.70–358 and Fig.71–365 on green glazed body (1 unit, from the second half of the seventeenth to the beginning of the eighteenth centuries).

Fig.70–356 is a large bowl (?) in colour glaze/sancai. The body is incised with pattern and glazed in purple as a main, green and yellow. The foot-ring bears an under-glaze cobalt blue double ring (3 units, from the second half of the seventeenth to the first half of the eighteenth centuries).

Fig.70-357 is a large dish with over-glaze enamels decoration. This dish has a characteristic double foot-ring. Flower pattern in bright green and yellow enamels decorates the interior (7 units). A similar dish was excavated at Tirtayasa Site and the production date can be the second half of the seventeenth century.

Fig.70-358 is an under-glaze cobalt blue dish with incised design. The interior has carved decoration. Both around the inner bottom and the rim are decorated with continuing key-fret patterns, and paneled flowering plant design in under-glaze cobalt blue is arranged in-between them (84 units). This kind of decoration was often used for dishes and bowls, or bottles and jars in the Jingdezhen porcelain dated to the Kangxi era (1662-1722) (from the last quarter of the seventeenth to the first quarter of the eighteenth centuries).

Fig.70-359 is a *sancai* covered box. Green, yellow, purple and white enamels are differently glazed (7 units for covers and 5 units for boxes, the second half of the seventeenth to the first half of the eighteenth centuries).

Fig.70-360 are a collection of coloured dolls. They include human figures in cobalt blue and iron oxide brown glaze, and a bird in green glaze. These kinds of dolls were often made around the Kangxi era (1662-1722) (6 units).

Fig.70-361 is a small under-glaze cobalt blue dish in iron brown glaze. The interior is filled with scattered small plum-like flowers over wave pattern. The centre of foot-ring bears a four-petal flower, which also appears on Fig.71-363.

Fig.71-362 is an under-glaze cobalt blue bowl decorated with chrysanthemum arabesque pattern on the inner bottom and exterior. A band of lotus petal pattern runs around the lower body (144 units). There is a similar piece at Tirtayasa Site.

Fig.71-363 is a under-glaze cobalt blue bowl in iron brown glaze and decorated with an under-glaze cobalt blue flowering arabesque pattern in the inner bottom and on the interior. The exterior is glazed in iron brown colour. There is an under-glaze cobalt blue four-petal flower in the centre of the foot-ring, which is similar to one seen in Fig.70-361.

Fig.71-364 is an under-glaze cobalt blue small bowl. It is decorated with a flower pattern in the centre and bears a mark inside foot-ring, which looks a kind of treasure pattern in under-glaze cobalt blue.

Fig.71-365 is a large bowl and shares a similar design with Fig.70-358. The inner bottom shows a flower motif and the exterior is incised with flower patterns. In and out of the rim, as well as around the inner bottom are arranged with bands of linked jewel design in under-glaze cobalt blue (10 units, the late seventeenth to the first quarter of the eighteenth centuries).

Fig.71-366 shows a cover of covered box decorated in under-glaze cobalt blue. The top of the cover displays a lion holding a ball design (4 units, in large possibility not this period but around the first half of the seventeenth century).

Fujian and Guangdong wares

Fig.72-367 is an under-glaze cobalt blue dish. The inner bottom is decorated with a design of leaf and poem (57 units, the second half of the seventeenth century) [II-123].

Fig.72-368 is a small under-glaze cobalt blue dish. This had been often misidentified for the Early Imari ware because of the similar make of forming and decoration. This dish is decorated with a design of hare in landscape and is glazed overall. Chaffs are attached by firing on the base of foot-ring (13 units of similar kind of ware) [II-124].

Fig.72-369 are under-glaze cobalt blue dishes. They share the same kind of basic works with Fig.72-368 and 377. There are remains of chaffs attached by firing. The interior is decorated with a motif of Chinese figures playing and drinking under a willow tree (14 units, from the second half of the seventeenth to the beginning of the eighteenth centuries) [II-125].

Fig.72-370 is a large celadon dish. Unlike large dishes in the late Ming period, it is a common feature of large dishes of this period that bodies are not applied with white slip and transparent glaze, foot-rings are formed differently and around foot-ring is unglazed. The interior is applied with a carved pattern (133 units, from the middle to late seventeenth century, the Zhangzhou ware type) [II-126].

Fig.72-371 is a large dish in over-glaze polychrome enamels. The coarse body has an unglazed circular ring in the inner bottom and painting in red, green and yellow enamels. The inner bottom displays a flower motif, which is encircled by unglazed ring painted in green. The outer interior is divided and each section is decorated with flowering plant pattern (210 units, from the middle to late seventeenth century, the Zhangzhou ware type).

Fig.72-372 is an under-glaze cobalt blue large dish. The lip of rim is slightly folded outwards. The inner bottom is unglazed around which a simplified arabesque pattern is painted in free and bold brushwork (2 units, from the second half of the seventeenth to the beginning of the eighteenth centuries) [II-127].

Fig.72-373 is an under-glaze cobalt blue dish decorated with a scattered floral design. The space within the foot-ring bears a mark in an under-glaze cobalt blue double ring. The floral design reminds us of the similar example of the Chokichidani kiln, Aria. The assumed date of Chokichidani example is around the 1660s and this dish (Fig.72-373) is viewed to have a similar dating, which is the second half of the seventeenth century (106 units).

Fig.72-374 is a white porcelain cover of a covered box. There are two colours, white and ivory white which is unique to the Dehua porcelain. This is formed in mold and decorated with a carved relief on the exterior (597 units, from the second half of the seventeenth to the first half of the eighteenth centuries).

Fig.72-375 is an under-glaze cobalt blue bowl with a stamped design (53 units, from the late seventeenth to the middle of the eighteenth centuries).

Fig.72-376 is an under-glaze cobalt blue dish with a stamped pattern of the Siddham script and an unglazed circular ring in the inner bottom (50 units, from late seventeenth to the middle of the eighteenth centuries) [II-128].

Fig.72-377 is painted with a landscape design in the centre (57 units, the second half of the seventeenth century) [II-129].

Fig.72-378, 379 are small cup and small dish differently glazed in green and other. The small cup was applied with green glaze at low temperature but originally this could be a porcelain. The interior of Fig.72-378 looks white owing to incomplete firing but it is given transparent glaze (22 units, from the seventeenth to the first half of the eighteenth centuries) [II-130], and could be fired in the southern Fujian province. Fig.72-379 is glazed in green from the interior to the exterior, and inside the foot-ring is applied with transparent glaze (25 units, from the seventeenth to the first half of the eighteenth centuries).

Fig.72-380 is a porcelain covered box in green glaze. Inside is treated with transparent glaze (16 units, from the seventeenth to the eighteenth centuries).

Chinese stonewares

Fig.73-381, 383 are large bowls in iron brown glaze and decorated with iron oxide painting. It is made with refined base in pale brown colour. The glaze is shiny strong brown and painted design presents black brown colour. There is no example of this type of ware known in Japan. The rim is unglazed (7 units).

Fig.73-382 is also a large bowl in iron brown glaze with iron oxide painting (1 unit, from the seventeenth to the eighteenth centuries).

Fig.73-383 is a large bowl in iron brown glaze. It is glazed only on the interior and the bear exterior presents pale brown colour. Originally this appears a cover of jar. Sand spurs are left on the base (14 units, the seventeenth century) [II-131].

Fig.73-384 is a jar in iron brown glaze.

Fig.73-385 is a small dish in iron brown glaze. It is glazed on the interior alone with unglazed rim. A small tongue shaped handle is attached to one side of the rim, which suggests that this is a holder for light (300 units, from the seventeenth to the first half of the eighteenth centuries) [II-132].

(2) Vietnamese ceramics

Iron-oxide painted stoneware

Fig.74-386 is a bowl decorated with iron oxide painting. There is an unglazed circular ring in the centre and the base is unglazed. The interior is drawn a circle line and stamped pattern of chrysanthemum decorates the inner bottom and both sides (66 units, from the second half of the seventeenth century).

(3) Hizen ceramics

Hizen porcelain

Fig.75-387ab & Fig.76-387c are large dishes with over-glaze polychrome enamels decoration. They were formed of white porcelain base. Chrysanthemum motif is painted in the centre. It cannot be confirmed whether a fragment of rim with segmented patterns is from the same dish. However, it is included in this group as there is a high possibility judging from the condition of the base. The exterior is decorated with a arabesque design in enamels. The foot-ring bears a mark within a double lined square (possibly a character *fuku* 福) also in colour. The enamels are green, yellow, purple and black, but red is not used. Characteristic pattern on the body also suggests that this large dish belongs to the middle period of the early over-glaze enamels decorated ware (2 units, around the first half of the 1650s).

Fig.75-388 is a bowl with an under-glaze cobalt blue decoration. The inner bottom shows a motif of carp jumping out of the wave. This type of ware typically carries a design of clouds and dragon, or clouds, dragon and phoenix on the exterior and distribute fish pattern in three different directions on the interior. In the case of even larger bowl, a band of meander pattern is usually arranged inner area of the rim. Dragon's head sometimes replace carp on the inner bottom. This bowl was modeled after a late Ming porcelain and produced in mass widely in the Hizen area at one time for Southeast Asian markets.

Fig.75-389 is a celadon dish. The foot-ring has an unglazed circular ring inside, over which is applied in iron slip. Attached trace of kiln tool remains on this area. The interior is decorated with a carved plant motif (?) (10 units, the second half of the seventeenth century, Hasami kiln) [II-133].

Fig.75-390, 391 are molded dishes with lobed shape and under-glaze cobalt blue decoration. Fig.75-390 has a rim painted in iron and a design of crab on the inner bottom. The interior is decorated with paneled patterns including birds and flowers, while the external is painted with floral arabesque pattern. The foot-ring carries an under-glaze cobalt blue mark of rough character *fuku* 福 inside. More than two spur marks are left around this mark. This dish appeared fired at the Kamanotsuji kiln in Nangawara. Crabs are not a common motif in Hizen porcelain but they appeared on Jingdezhen porcelain of late Ming period excavated at Banten Lama. This dish might have been made to an order, or imported through an intentional selection (6 units, from the 1680s to 1700s). Fig.75-391 is a small fragment of a rim and its unique motif makes us think that this was ordered to the Arita by an European customer who also gave instruction on motif (1 unit, around the 1660s.) [II-134]

Fig.76-392 is a small dish with over-glaze enamels decoration. White porcelain base was molded into lobed shape and the interior is painted with flower motif in red and green enamels. A red circle is drawn on the external (1 unit, from the 1660s to 1690s, the Arita ware).

Fig.76-393 is a dish with flat rim decorated in over-glaze polychrome enamels. The white porcelain base has a painted red double circle around the inner bottom. The floral arabesque pattern on the interior is coloured in red and green(?), and a band of lotus petal pattern is painted in red around the rim. There is also a red circle on the external body (5 units, from 1655 to the 1680s, the Arita ware).

Fig.76-394 is a white porcelain three foots dish. It is formed in mold and the rim is made in the shape of either flower petal or leaf. The base is made to circle and unglazed. For firing, a porcelain kiln tool was put underneath. Foots are pasted with monkey faces made in mold (1 unit, the second half of the seventeenth century, the Arita kiln) [II-135].

Fig.76-395 is a Kraak style dish decorated in under-glaze cobalt blue. Arcs/*maribasami* ornaments were drowned the inner bottom. This type of dish was modeled after late Ming porcelain and produced massively in Hizen for export (48 units, from the 1660s to 1690s).

Fig.76-396 is a large dish in the Kraak style with under-glaze cobalt blue design of bird and flowers in the inner bottom (3 units, from the 1660s to 1680s).

Fig.76-397 is a large dish in the Kraak style with over-glaze polychrome enamels decoration. The body is made in white porcelain base and designs of arcs/*maribasami* is painted in the inner bottom and broken twig on the exterior in red, green, yellow and black outlines but other than red were discoloured (1 unit, from the 1660s to 1670s, Arita ware).

Fig.76-400, 401 are under-glaze cobalt blue decorated large dishes. The rim is carved into foliated shape. The inner bottom displays a design of flower in vase and plant design is painted around it. The exterior is ornamented with a motif of scrolling flowers and leaves in under-glaze cobalt blue. The spur marks were left inside the foot-ring. The motif of flower in vase was often painted on export ware (3 units, from the 1680s to 1690s). Fig.76-401 is a molded dish with a lobed rim. The inner bottom sports a design of plum tree and rock and the outer interior is decorated with paneled plum trees and flowering plant. The exterior is painted with sprays in under-glaze cobalt blue. It is a unique feature of this dish that the lip is painted in cobalt blue (55 units, from the 1670s to 1690s, the Arita ware).

Fig.76-402 appears a barber dish with under-glaze cobalt blue decoration. Characteristic feature of such dish is a slightly upturned edge of the rim. The interior is decorated with a design of birds and flowers.

Fig.76-403 is an under-glaze cobalt blue decorated bowl. There are an early type of five-petal flower in the inner bottom and a landscape design on the exterior. The base bears a reign mark, which reads 'Made in Great Ming Period' in under-glaze cobalt blue (1 unit, from the 1670s to 1680s, the Arita ware).

Fig.76-404/406 are covered boxs with over-glaze polychrome enamels decoration. Fig.76-404 is a cover and decorated with flowering plants on the top and ivies on the side in red, green, and yellow(?) enamels (14 units). Fig.76-405 is a box. It is unknown whether there was a design or not (35 units). Fig.76-406 has an unclear design on the body (34 units, 1655-1680s, the Arita kiln) [II-136].

Fig.76-407 is a covered octagonal large bowl with under-glaze cobalt blue decoration. This bowl was molded in octagonal shape and incised with a pattern on the body. Patterns of swastika/*sayagata* and bundled brushwood are alternately incised on the exterior surface, over which thick in-filling in cobalt blue was applied to raise the patterns. This kind of decoration technique was often used in Arita during the Genroku period (1688-1704) (2 units, from the 1690s to 1700s, the Arita ware).

Fig.76-408 is a large covered bowl decorated with under-glaze cobalt blue design. The exterior is divided into sections and the upper section is painted with peony arabesque motif and the side with plum tree and rock design. Large covered bowl of this type is considered for an export market and there are quite a few heirloom objects in Europe (92 units of in the sense of covered bowl, from the 1660s to the beginning of the eighteenth century, the Arita ware).

Fig.77-409 are over-glaze enamels decorated dishes in middle and large sizes. The inner bottom has red circle within which a remote and serene land is painted in green and black outlines. The interior carries a red stamped pattern as well as a landscape motif in green circle. The glaze was not melted completely and this is a difference from the Arita ware. The motif, stamped remote land, appears in the Chinese Zhangzhou polychrome enamel (the *Gosu-akae* style) and only found in the Yoshida ware of Ureshino city, Saga prefecture in the seventeenth century (18 units, from the 1650s to 1660s) [II-137].

Fig.77-410, 412 are dishes decorated in under-glaze cobalt blue. Fig.77-410 shows a flower motif, probably peony, in the inner bottom with a band of flower pattern painted in the disappearing ink technique around. This kind of ornament and shape are in common with the Arita wares fired at the Chokichidani and Kakiemon kilns. This is thought an Arita ware of the same period (1 unit, 1655-the 1670s). Fig.77-412 has a high foot-ring and a double circle in under-glaze cobalt blue inside. This particular fragment does not show any decoration, but there is a high possibility that others from the same section were decorated (1 unit, from the 1660s to 1690s, the Arita ware).

Fig.76-398, 399 & Fig.77-411 are under-glaze cobalt blue decorated dishes with a curved rim. Fig.77-411 has its inner bottom painted with a design of a rock and the exterior with sprays. There is a double circle in under-glaze cobalt blue inside the foot-ring (44 units, from the 1670s to 1690s). Fig.76-399 is a dish with a foliated rim. Five-petal flower is positioned in the inner bottom of the dish and both sides are decorated with floral arabesque design in under-glaze cobalt blue. This five-petal flower is different from the standardized version, which gained a popularity after the 1690s, and thought as the style of an advent stage (2 units, from the 1680s to 1690s). The inner bottom of Fig.76-398 has a flowering plant design. The interior and exterior are decorated with swirl and plum blossoms and arabesque motifs respectively (1 unit, from the 1680s to 1700s). All are the Arita ware.

Fig.77-413 is an ewer with a handle and under-glaze cobalt blue decoration. Ewers in this shape were made for the European market from the 1660s to 1680s. They were fitted with a metal rim with one-touch operation. The body is decorated with a design of flowers and grasses and layered bands of laurels and fillings run around above and below (1 unit, from the 1660s to 1670s, the Arita ware).

Fig.77-414 is also an ewer with a handle and under-glaze cobalt blue decoration. Landscape painted in three divided sections is the main design of the body and *Ru-i* head pattern goes around the rim (1 unit, from the 1670s to 1680s, the Arita ware) [II-138].

(4) European stoneware

Fig.78-415 is a large bowl with indigo blue painting. Motif is outlined in blue over the tin glazed body and the area within the outline is filled in pale blue. There is one spur mark on exterior side of the rim (2 units, the eighteenth century, the Netherlands).

Fig.78-416 are tiles with indigo blue painting. The upper left is a fragment of one corner and has a popular flower pattern. The lower left looks to have a sailing boat (possibly the second half of the seventeenth century). The lower right is decorated with a landscape within a double circle (the second half of the seventeenth century). All are fired at a Delft kiln.

Fig.78-417 is a stoneware jar with ears in salt glaze and it is decorated in blue enamel (13 units, the seventeenth century).

Tirtayasa Site

(1) Chinese ceramics

Under-glaze cobalt blue and other wares

Jingdezhen ware

Fig.79-418 is an under-glaze cobalt blue large bowl. Decoration of the centre is unknown but a floral scroll pattern decorates both sides while lotus petals ornament the inner side of the rim. The outer side of the rim is painted with a band of meander pattern. Lower part of the body is arranged with pointy lotus petals and the exterior of the foot-ring is decorated with tips of waves? (the second half of the seventeenth century).

Fig.79-419 are the fragments of rim from an under-glaze cobalt blue large bowl or bowl with curved rim. This was more finely decorated than Fig.80-420. The exterior is painted with chrysanthemum arabesque pattern and the inner side of the rim with a pattern of stylized flower in diamond shape in under-glaze cobalt blue (the second half of the seventeenth century) [II-139].

Fig.80-420 is an under-glaze cobalt blue large bowl. The inner bottom and exterior are decorated with a chrysanthemum arabesque design. There is a continuing pattern, which looks like lotus petals in the lower part of the body. The base of the foot-ring is shaved flat (the second half of the seventeenth century).

Fig.80-421 is an under-glaze cobalt blue bowl. It is decorated with a design of insects and flowering tree in the inner bottom and of flowering tree and rock on the exterior. Under-glaze cobalt blue reign mark is inscribed in the centre of the foot-ring, which reads 'Made in the Great Qing dynasty, Kangxi reign' (from the 1660s to 1680s).

Fig.81-422 is an under-glaze cobalt blue bowl decorated with chrysanthemum arabesque in under-glaze cobalt blue outlines on the exterior and inside of the rim. There is also a design in the inner bottom. The decoration is made in so called the pencil drawing technique (the second half of the seventeenth century).

Fig.81-423, 434 are under-glaze cobalt blue bowls that resemble to Fig.79-419.

Fig.81-425 is a base fragment of an under-glaze cobalt blue bowl. The inner bottom is painted with lotus arabesque design, the exterior with arabesque pattern, and the lower body with a lotus petal motif (the second half of the seventeenth century).

Fig.81–426 is an under-glaze cobalt blue large bowl. A flower motif similar to palmetto appears on the exterior and the interior is also decorated with a design in under-glaze cobalt blue, possibly floral arabesque. The base of the foot-ring is shaved flat (the second half of the seventeenth century).

Fig.82–427 is a base fragment of an under-glaze cobalt blue large bowl. There is a *Ru-i* head with arabesque pattern design on the inner bottom. This is possibly the similar type of Fig.82–428.

Fig.82–428 is a base of under-glaze cobalt blue large bowl. The inner bottom displays a character *shou* 壽 in leaving white line inside a flaming *Cintamani*. Design of the *Ru-i* head arabesque decorates the exterior. The base of the foot-ring is shaved flat (the second half of the seventeenth century).

Fig.82–429 is an under-glaze cobalt blue small bowl. It is decorated with designs of lotus in the inner bottom, lotus scroll on the exterior and lotus petals on the lower body. There is a geometric mark framed in a square in the centre of the foot-ring [II-140].

Fig.82–430 & Fig.83–431 are under-glaze cobalt blue large dishes with a double foot-ring [II-141]. The inner bottom is decorated with a design of floral arabesque and the outer interior with a linked *Ru-i* head pattern. Arabesquee pattern goes around the rim and jewel design is painted on the exterior (the second half of the seventeenth century).

Fig.83–432 is a large dish with over-glaze polychrome enamels decoration. Surface from the interior to the exterior distributes a distinctive floral arabesque design in bright green and other enamels. A double foot-ring is a special feature often found in large dishes made during the Kangxi era (the second half of the seventeenth century). Similar examples were excavated at Banten Lama.

Fig.83–433 is also a large dish decorated in over-glaze enamels with a double foot-ring.

Fig.83–434 is a bowl in green glaze. The body is glazed except the base of foot-ring (the second half of the seventeenth century). There is another example with monochrome glaze and it is a bowl in yellow glaze.

Fig.83–435 is a *sancai* bowl in purple, green, yellow and white (transparent) glaze separately painted on the internal and external body. Brown spur marks are left on the inner bottom (the second half of the seventeenth century).

Fig.83–436 & Fig.84–437 are differently glazed (*sancai*) dishes in green, yellow, purple and white (transparent). Within the foot-ring was treated with transparent glaze at the main firing (several units, the second half of the seventeenth century).

Fig.84–438 is an under-glaze cobalt blue dish with a paulownia leaf motif and Chinese poem *wu-tong-yi-ye-luo, tian-xia-jin-qiu* 梧桐一葉落、天下尽皆秋 in the inner bottom (the second half of the seventeenth century).

Fig.84–439 is an under-glaze cobalt blue dish decorated with a design of fishing figure and mountainous landscape in the inner bottom. Decoration on the rim is not identified. The exterior is painted with a branch motif in under-glaze cobalt blue (the second half of the seventeenth century).

Fig.84-440 is an under-glaze cobalt blue dish. The inner bottom is filled with a design of insects, rock, peony and bamboo, and the rim is decorated with arabesque pattern. A design of insects and spray is arranged on the exterior. The base of the foot-ring is shaved even (the second half of the seventeenth century).

Fig.85-441 is an under-glaze cobalt blue dish decorated with dragon and floral arabesque (?) in the inner bottom and stylized flower pattern (?) on the rim. The exterior has broken sprig (?) motif in under-glaze cobalt blue (the second half of the seventeenth century).

Fig.85-442 is an under-glaze cobalt blue dish with a chrysanthemum arabesque pattern in the inner bottom. Partial chrysanthemum arabesque also ornaments around the rim. Spray motif in under-glaze cobalt blue appears on the exterior [II-142].

Fig.85-443 is an under-glaze cobalt blue small cup in iron brown glaze. Under-glaze cobalt blue designs of landscape and stylized flower pattern are painted on the inner bottom and inside the rim. The exterior is given different colour in iron brown glaze (the second half of the seventeenth century).

Fujian and Guangdong wares

Fig.86-444 is an under-glaze cobalt blue bowl. Double circle in the inner bottom and a pattern on the exterior is painted in under-glaze cobalt blue. The inner bottom and base are unglazed (probably the second half of the seventeenth century).

Dehua ware

Fig.86-445 is a white porcelain small cup. The rim is gently flared up and the body is decorated with a relief pattern by press mold. It was badly fired and could be the Dehua ware (probably the second half of the seventeenth century).

Fig.86-446 is a white porcelain covered container missing a cover. The exterior is applied a decoration, which looks like a plum, by press molding. Inner side of the rim is unglazed (the second half of the seventeenth century).

Fig.86-447 is a white porcelain spoon. It was hump molded and the tip of the handle is decorated with a relief pattern (the second half of the seventeenth century) [II-143].

(2) Hizen ceramics

Hizen porcelain

Fig.87-448 is a bottom of a bowl with an under-glaze cobalt blue design of carp jumping out of waves. Because the wave on the inner bottom is very loosely painted, it is thought a later example during 1655 to 1680s, which was the years when bowl with this pattern was produced.

Fig.87-449 is a large bowl decorated with peony design in under-glaze cobalt blue. The exterior sports the peony design. There is another large bowl decorated with much stylized peony design and with the VOC monogram painted in under-glaze cobalt blue in the inner bottom. This bowl is dated to 1690 to the beginning of the eighteenth century, but our example here (Fig.87-449) is an older style (from the 1660s to 1680s).

Fig.87-450 is a large bowl with a design of paneled flowering plants in under-glaze cobalt blue. The exterior is given paneled sections at three directions within which painted flowering plants. A band of meander motif runs around inside the rim and a flowering plant motif is painted in the inner bottom (from the 1660s to 1670s).

Fig.87-451 is a large bowl with an under-glaze cobalt blue peony design. The exterior shows peony flowers and clouds among swirls. The interior has a design that could be flaming jewel (from the 1660s to 1680s).

Fig.88-452 is a large bowl with under-glaze cobalt-blue decoration. Flowering plants motif is painted on the interior. There is also a design encircled with a double ring on the inner bottom. Floral arabesque pattern is describing an arc on the exterior (from the 1660s to 1680s, no photograph).

Fig.88-454 is a small dish with over-glaze polychrome enamels decoration. The rim is lobed and the inner bottom is ornamented with autumn grass pattern in enamels (yellow and others. Majority of the enamels has been exfoliated. From the 1660s to 1680s).

Fig.88-453, 455 are small dishes with designs in under-glaze cobalt blue. There is a landscape design on the inner bottom of Fig.88-455. Firing was insufficient and fine crackles appear over the body (from the 1660s to 1670s). Fig.88-453 displays a bird, grass and water motif in the inner bottom (from the 1660s to 1680s). They are likely for the domestic Japanese market, but Fig.88-455 could be a saucer for an export cup and saucer.

Fig.89-456, 458 are dishes with curved rim and over-glaze enamels decoration of floral arabesque pattern on the interior and lotus petals on the rim (Fig.89-456). The inner bottom and the space around it are painted with flowers and plants in blue and yellow enamels with red circles (missing paints are filled in pencil in the photograph). Insufficient firing resulted in many fine crackles (from the 1660s to 1680s). It is possible that they were intended for export.

Fig.89-457 & Fig.90-462 are dishes with under-glaze cobalt blue decoration. Fig.89-457 has its interior decorated with flowers and exterior with plants like motif, both in under-glaze cobalt blue (from the 1660s to 1680s). The inner bottom and interior of Fig.90-462 are ornamented with flowering plants and scattered paulownia designs in under-glaze cobalt blue. The exterior is given a motif of twig. A character *sei* 製 is written inside the foot-ring and this could be a single mark (from the 1660s to 1680s). They are also considered domestic products.

Fig.89-459 is an under-glaze cobalt blue dish in the Kraak style, but the design is significantly different from Fig.90-460. Details such as flowering plants in the inner bottom, flower pattern around the inside and paneled jewelry motif are dissimilar. However, these two types were excavated together at the same kiln site including the Chokichidani in Arita, they would have co-existed for some time (from the 1660s to 1670s).

In addition to these two examples, fragments of large dishes in the Kraak style were also excavated, although they were not illustrated here. These artifacts suggest a possibility that large, middle and small size were combined depending for usage.

Fig.90-460 is a Kraak style dish with under-glaze cobalt blue decoration. Flowering plant decorates the inner bottom with alternately arranged paneled flower and treasure patterns. The exterior shows simplified panels in rough style. The Kraak style dish is grouped into three sized, large, middle and small. This example is a small size (from the 1660s to 1680s).

Fig.90-461 is a large dish with under-glaze cobalt blue design of paneled flower and grass pattern on the interior. The exterior is decorated with sprigs. Spur marks were left on the base. The design would make this as an export item (from the 1670s to 1680s).

Fig.90-463, 464 are middle size dishes with under-glaze cobalt blue design. Fig.90-463 is missing the inner bottom and the design is unknown, but the twisted flower pattern applied with disappearing ink technique fills the space around the inner bottom (from the 1660s to 1680s). Fig.90-464 is filled with twisted flower. The exterior is arranged with a sprig motif (from the 1670s to 1680s). These dishes were made to the domestic market.

Fig.91-465 is a large celadon dish. The inner bottom is decorated with incised flower design by carving and combing, which is surrounded by an incised meander pattern. A circular ring created within the foot-ring is unglazed but painted with iron contained water. The very centre of the foot-ring is slightly dented. Remaining of kiln tool is attached to the unglazed circular ring and in this case, the tool was made with the same base for the body (from the 1660s to 1680s, the Hasami ware).

Fig.91-466 is a cover of large covered box decorated with an under-glaze cobalt blue design. The top is decorated with bird and flower motif, which is encircled by a band of swirl pattern. The outer area is covered with a peony arabesque design. This kind of large box and cover is not found at Japanese archaeological sites, but because some examples had been excavated at Banten Lama Site [II-144], they would have been intended for export (from the 1660s to 1670s).

Fig.91-467 is a box of a large covered box and cover decorated with peony arabesque pattern in under-glaze cobalt blue (from the 1660s to 1670s). This is also for an export market.

Fig.91-468 is a box of white porcelain covered box and cover made in hump mold. The body is decorated with circle pattern in each section set by relief lines. Around the rim and the receiving part are unglazed (probably the Hizen ware, the second half of the seventeenth century).

Fig.91-469 is a box with the receiving part of covered box and cover with over-glaze enamels decoration. A red outline is drawn on the external around the rim (the second half of the seventeenth century).

Fig.91-470 is an under-glaze cobalt blue decorated bottle. The exterior is painted with flowering plants design (from the 1660s to 1680s).

Fig.91-471 is an under-glaze cobalt blue decorated kendi. The body sports paneled treasure and plum tree pattern in the Kraak style (from the 1660s to 1680s).

(3) Vietnamese ceramics

Iron-oxide painted stoneware

Fig.92-472 is a bowl decorated with stamped chrysanthemum pattern in iron-oxide. Chrysanthemum pattern is stamped in the inner bottom as well as the exterior. There is an unglazed circular ring in the inner bottom and the base is unglazed (the second half of the seventeenth century). Similar bowls had been excavated the archaeological sites including Banten Lama (Fig.74-386).

11. Period VI-1 (around the first half of the 18th century)

Buton Wolio Fort

(1) Chinese ceramics

Under-glaze cobalt blue and other wares

Jingdezhen ware

Fig.93-473 shows a collection of the Kraak style dishes of this period (from the end of the seventeenth century to the first quarter of the eighteenth century).

Fig.93-474 are celadon dishes. The inner bottom is painted with flower and swirl patterns. This type was also excavated at Banten Lama Site (Fig.99-505) and they are likely made for Europe. Covered large bowl was also found at Banten Lama Site (Fig.102-538).

Fig.93-475 are dishes decorated the inner bottom with a variegated design of plum blossoms and ice cracks.

Fig.93-476 are under-glaze cobalt blue dishes with added decoration in over-glaze polychrome enamels. The majority is the Chinese Imari.

Fig.94-478 is an over-glaze polychrome enamels decorated dish with iron brown glaze.

Fig.94-479 are covered containers in iron-brown glaze with over-glaze polychrome enamels decoration.

Fig.94-480 are covered boxes and containers decorated with design in over-glaze polychrome enamels.

Fujian ware

Fig.93-477 is a dish covered with a unique floral arabesque design on the interior. A similar motif dish with similar design was also unearthed at Banten Lama Site (Fig.101-531). There are not a few the Jingdezhen heirloom items in Europe (in the collection of the Hessen State Museum, Darmstadt).

Fig.95-481 are flat dishes with rim. The rim area is in-filled. Similar dishes were also found at Banten Lama (Fig.102-540, 541, from the end of seventeenth century to the first quarter of eighteenth century) [II-145].

Fig.95-482 are a collection of under-glaze cobalt blue bowls. The majority is small round shape. They were made with mold and glaze on the rim was removed (the Dehua ware, from early to the middle of the eighteenth century).

(2) Hizen ceramics

Hizen porcelain

Fig.96-483 are large dishes with peony arabesque design in under-glaze cobalt blue. They were made for foreign markets (from the 1730s to 1750s) [II-146].

Three fragments on left of Fig.96-484 are a cover of over-glaze polychrome enameled jar. One on right is a cover of large octagonal jar with under-glaze cobalt blue design, the same kind of Fig.97-491. Paneled phoenix design decorates the body, and the ground pattern is a distinctive centipede arabesque.

Fig.96-485a & Fig.98-485b is a cover of large jar decorated with over-glaze polychrome enamels motif.

Fig.97-486/488, 492 are large jars with over-glaze polychrome and gold enamels decoration (the *Kinrande* style). Fig.97-487 includes bodies decorated with designs of cow, stone walls, gate, residence and flowering tree. On the neck, ground between the panels is filled with stylised flower pattern and linked diamond shaped panels are arranged on the shoulder [II-147]. Fig.97-487, 488 are large octagonal jars composed flat panels with over-glaze polychrome enamel decoration [II-148].

Fig.97-489 is also a cover of octagonal jar composed flat panels with under-glaze cobalt blue design. Design of hare as a main subject ornaments space between the panels. This cover is a similar type with fragment of large jar decorated with a design of carp climbing up a waterfall (Fig.97-490) [II-149], excavated at the southern moat. Fragment of bottom part shown at lower right in Fig.97-492 is thought a similar type. Fragments of large jar in under-glaze cobalt blue (Fig.97-494) also have a design of carp climbing up a waterfall and thus belong to the same category with Fig.97-490.

Fig.97-491: An octagonal large jar is decorated with centipede arabesque motif in under-glaze cobalt blue. A distinctive pattern of lotus petal in under-glaze cobalt blue runs around the rim.

Fig.98-495 is a large bottle with under-glaze cobalt blue design. There are more than two different kinds. The fragment on the upper left is a bottle with under-glaze cobalt blue design of centipede like arabesque filling between panels and this is possibly a set with Fig.97-491 the large octagonal jar.

Fig.98-496 is a gourd shaped large bottle in over-glaze and gold enamels (the *Kinrande* style) [II-150]. Usually this kind of bottle was made with jars with the same design as a set. It is speculated that Fig.98-496 was also produced to make a set with a large jar decorated with a design of crane and pine tree in over-glaze polychrome enamel for example.

Fig.98-497 is also a large bottle with over-glaze polychrome enamels decoration.

Banten Lama Site

(1) Chinese ceramics

Under-glaze cobalt blue and other wares

Jingdezhen ware

Fig.99-498 is an under-glaze cobalt blue small bowl in iron-oxide glaze. The exterior is covered in iron-oxide glaze and the inner bottom displays a flower basket motif in under-glaze cobalt blue. Space inside the foot-ring bears a mark 'Made by *Ju-yu-tang* 聚玉堂' also in under-glaze cobalt blue (6 units). In China, there are examples with similar 'Made by *Ju-qing-tang* 聚慶堂', but they are not so common. Such kind of shallow dish with a flower basket design in the inner bottom and glazed in iron-oxide on the exterior were popular export ware of this period. Contemporary Hizen porcelain copied, and made small bowl with flower basket design.

Fig.99-499 is an under-glaze cobalt blue small bowl. It is formed in mold and lobed. Molded lines are painted in under-glaze cobalt blue and flowering plant motif is arranged in each section. A flower pattern is placed in the inner bottom, and a small flower pattern also appears in the centre of the foot-ring (12 units, from the end of seventeenth to the first quarter of the eighteenth centuries).

Fig.99-500/502 are under-glaze cobalt blue dishes in the Kraak style. They are modeled after the Kraak style dish of the late Ming period. The inner bottom shows a flower design within arks/*maribasami* ornament. Paneled sections each of which is decorated with designs of flower and treasure are alternately arranged in the space around the inner bottom. The dish Fig.99-501 bears an under-glaze cobalt blue mark outlined by double square. Fig.99-502 has a central double ring in under-glaze cobalt blue within the foot-ring (25 units, from the end of seventeenth to the beginning of the eighteenth century).

Fig.99-503 is a large dish with over-glaze enamels decoration over under-glaze cobalt blue foundation. The interior shows a design of pine tree and bamboo in under-glaze cobalt blue and red was added later (6 units, from the second half of the seventeenth to the beginning of the eighteenth centuries).

Fig.99-504 is an under-glaze cobalt blue covered large bowl with a pair of ears. This type of shape is likely ordered from Europe. In the outside designed a Chinese garden with pine tree etc. (17 units, from the late seventeenth to the first half of eighteenth centuries) [II-151].

Fig.99-505 is under-glaze cobalt blue dish. The inner bottom is painted with flower with vines motif with paneled flower and grasses in the space around it (74 units, from late seventeenth to middle of the eighteenth centuries) [II-152].

Fig.99-506 is an under-glaze cobalt blue small dish in iron-oxide glaze on the exterior. Several motifs are arranged on the interior including flower and linked *Ru-i* head pattern (2 units, from the end of the seventeenth to the first half of the eighteenth centuries).

Fig.100-507 is an under-glaze cobalt blue dish or large bowl. The inner bottom is bulging like a bum like the *man-tou-xin* and the base is made in a shape of *Yunzi* piece container. A cross shaped flower motif decorates the inner bottom surrounded by a continuous *Ru-i* head pattern (1 unit, the eighteenth century) [II-153].

Fig.100-508 is an under-glaze cobalt blue dish. A design of linked *Ru-i* head pattern based around a letter ornaments the inner bottom. The interior closer to the rim is covered with two layers of linked *shou* 壽 character. The exterior also displays a linked *shou* character motif. There is a mark of swirls framed in a double square within the foot-ring (1 unit, around the first half of the eighteenth century).

Fig.100-509 is a bowl decorated in over-glaze polychrome enamels. Red enamel is added after underglaze cobalt-blue painting was fired. The design is for the European taste and this type of ware is called the Chinese Imari in Europe (61 units, around the first half of the eighteen centuries).

Fig.100-510 is a cover decorated in over-glaze polychrome enamels. The exterior has a design of chrysanthemum and plants in under-glaze cobalt blue with red, green and yellow enamels [II-154]. There are not a few bowls and dishes in this kind of the Chinese Imari style decorated with chrysanthemum motif. Because an example of the Arita ware in the *Kinrande* 金襴手 style is known, it is thought the Arita porcelain was modeled (1 unit, the first half of the eighteenth century).

Fig.100-511 is an over-glaze enamels decorated dish. Floral arabesque motif is painted just in red enamel on the interior (50 units, the eighteenth century).

Fig.100-512 is an under-glaze cobalt blue dish with a design of willow tree and landscape in the inner bottom (172 units, from late seventeenth to the first half of the eighteenth century).

Fig.100-513, 514 are cover and body of covered large bowl with over-glaze enamel decoration. They are not a set because the cover and body have different designs of floral arabesque in colour enamels (21 units of Fig.100-514, from the first half to middle eighteenth century) [II-155].

Fig.100-515 is an under-glaze cobalt blue dish with flat rim. The rim is applied with iron-oxide glaze and the interior is covered with a design of plum blossom and ice crack (46 units, the eighteenth century). Probably made in Jingdezhen. There is a similar dish at Buton Wolio Fort (Fig.93-475).

Fig.100-516, 517 are an under-glaze cobalt blue covered box. Fig.100-516 is a cover decorated with flowering plants pattern (128 units of similar pieces). Fig.100-517 is a box decorated with a band of lotus petals around the lover part of the body (85 units, from the second half of the seventeenth to eighteenth centuries).

Fig.101-518, 519 are under-glaze cobalt blue small bowls. In the inner bottom of Fig.101-518 is decrated a flower pattern, while fish pattern are painted in the exterior of Fig.101-519. The space inside the foot-ring bears a mark in under-glaze cobalt blue (6 units of Fig.101-518 and 130 units of Fig.101-519, from the second half of the seventeenth to the first half of the eighteenth centuries).

Fig.101-520 is an under-glaze cobalt blue small bowl decorated with under-glaze cobalt blue motifs, chrysanthemum on the exterior and water birds in the inner bottom (1 unit, from middle to late seventeenth century).

Fig.101-521 is an under-glaze cobalt blue small bowl. Both interior and exterior is ornamented with obscure motifs in under-glaze cobalt blue [II-156]. There are a three star like pattern and horse on the exterior. Dotted motif on Fig.101-521 could be part of the three stars design (32 units, from the second half of the seventeenth to the first half of the eighteenth centuries).

Fig.101-522 is an under-glaze cobalt blue small bowl in iron brown glaze. While the interior has a design in under-glaze cobalt blue, the exterior is covered with iron brown glaze. Flowering plants motif is arranged in the inner bottom and space around it. All around the rim is decorated with variegated design of wave (1 unit, from the last quarter of the seventeenth to the beginning of the eighteenth centuries) [II-157].

Fig.101-523 is an under-glaze cobalt blue small bowl. It is molded to form lotus petals in relief on the side, and the exterior is divided into according to these lotus petals within which painted flowering plant in under-glaze cobalt blue. Arabesque runs above these sections. There is a pine tree in the inner bottom and inside the rim is given a similar wave design of Fig.101-522 [II-158]. The rim is applied with iron brown glaze (9 units, from late seventeenth to the first quarter of the eighteenth centuries).

Fig.101-524 is a small bowl decorated in over-glaze polychrome enamels and in iron brown glaze. The exterior is glazed in iron brown and the rim is brushed with iron oxide glaze. Peony is painted in red in the interior (86 units, from the last quarter of the seventeenth to the first half of the eighteenth centuries).

Fig.101-525 is an under-glaze cobalt blue deep dish. The inner bottom displays a flower motif (?) and the inner side is given a spray decoration. Inside the foot-ring shows a square framed mark in under-glaze cobalt blue (2 units, the second half of the seventeenth century).

Fig.101-526 is an under-glaze cobalt blue small dish. The exterior is ornamented with incised perpendicular stripes. The inner bottom shows a plum tree design and the interior has paneled stylized floral arabesque pattern. This is possibly an accompanied saucer of Fig.101-523 (12 units, from the last quarter of the seventeenth to the first quarter of the eighteenth centuries).

Fig.101-527 is an under-glaze cobalt blue small dish with iron brown glaze on the exterior. Flower motif is centred and the interior is alternately arranged with paneled designs of landscape and flower (463 units, from the last quarter of the seventeenth to the first half of the eighteenth century).

Fig.101-528 is an under-glaze cobalt blue dish with iron brown glaze on the exterior. Several flowering plants are painted on the internal and slanted lattice pattern in under-glaze cobalt blue goes around the internal rim (33 units, from the last quarter of the seventeenth to the first half of the eighteenth centuries).

Fig.101-529 is an under-glaze cobalt blue deep dish with iron brown glaze. The inner bottom is decorated with a design of possibly phoenix (12 units, from the second half of the seventeenth to the first half of the eighteenth centuries).

Fig.101-530 is an under-glaze cobalt blue dish with flat rim. The base is shaved inside only to make a *Yunzi* piece box shape. This kind of base is made to order for the European clients as illustrated in the design drawings of porcelain, which were produced by the Dutch Cornelis Pronk in 1734. Many of such base are made for export porcelain.

Flat plate with flat rim was likely the main tableware for dining in Europe. Iron brown glaze is applied on the lip. The rim is decorated with a design of grape and bamboo (69 units, the first half of the eighteenth century) [II-159].

Fig.101-531 is an under-glaze cobalt blue large dish. The lip is applied with iron brown glaze and floral arabesque pattern is painted on the interior (184 units, from the second half of the seventeenth to the beginning of the eighteenth centuries) [II-160].

Fig.101-532 is an under-glaze cobalt blue large bowl. It is molded into lobed shape. A crab was placed in the inner bottom and surrounded by water plants. The space around the inner bottom already painted with fish and water plants (9 units, the second half of the eighteenth and the beginning of eighteenth centuries) [II-161].

Fig.102-533 is an under-glaze cobalt blue large bowl with iron brown glaze on the exterior. The inner bottom displays a design of wild goose with reed, and the space around the inner side is filled with a flower pattern (16 units, from the second half of the seventeenth to the first quarter of the eighteenth centuries).

Fig.102-534 is an under-glaze cobalt blue large bowl. It is decorated with a band of lotus petal on the lower body and swirl pattern runs around the rim. In the inner bottom is a motif of deformed flower or leaf. The rim is decorated with a band of variant lotus petals (61 units, from late seventeenth to the middle of the eighteenth centuries) [II-162].

Fig.102-535 is a small bowl with over-glaze polychrome enamels decoration and iron brown glaze on both sides. The exterior has grape leaf shaped roundels in transparent glaze, over which over-glaze enamels patterns were painted (64 units, the eighteenth century) [II-163].

Fig.102-536 is an under-glaze cobalt blue dish. The design of Chinese garden with a rock, peony, trees and balustrade fills in the inner bottom of the dish that is encircled by a band of key-fret pattern. The rim is painted with a border of geometric pattern, which was intended for the European markets (92 units, from late seventeenth to the middle of the eighteenth centuries).

Fig.102-537 is an under-glaze cobalt blue dish with flat rim. The base is shaved inside only. Flowering plants are scattered in the interior and slanted lattice pattern surrounds the inner bottom and the rim (337 units, from the early to the middle of the eighteenth century).

Fig.102-538 is a covered large bowl with a similar kind of design with Fig.99-505. Unique flowering plant design is painted within each section that are arranged on the exterior (4 units, from late seventeenth to the middle of the eighteenth centuries) [II-164].

Fig.102-539 is an under-glaze cobalt blue covered large bowl decorated with a design of chrysanthemum arabesque pattern. The lip of the mouth is unglazed (151 unit, from late seventeenth to the first half of the eighteenth centuries) [II-165].

Fig.102-540, 541 are under-glaze cobalt blue dishes with flat rim. Fig.102-540 has an iron brown glazed lip and a design of flower basket in the inner bottom. The inner bottom of Fig.102-541 is decorated with citrus fruits (37 units of Fig.102-540 and 3 units of Fig.102-541, from late seventeenth to the first half of the eighteenth centuries).

Fig.102-542 is an under-glaze cobalt blue dish in the Kraak style (233 unites, the first half of the eighteenth century). This appears to be the later type of the Kraak style than Fig.99-502.

Fujian and Guangdong wares

Fig.103-543 is a bowl with over-glaze polychrome enamels decoration.

Fig.103-544 is a molded bowl with over-glaze polychrome enamels decoration. Glaze on the lip was removed because it was fired with another vessel placed together at the mouths. The exterior is painted with floral arabesque design in red, green and yellow enamels (2 unit, from the second half of the seventeenth to eighteenth centuries, the Dehua ware) [II-166].

Fig.103-545, 546 are spoons. They were formed in mold and entirely glazed. There are remains of chaffs on the base. Fig.103-545 is white porcelain and Fig.103-546 is decorated with flower pattern in over-glaze polychrome enamels. It is possible that production of these types of porcelain spoons began from around the late seventeenth century (124 units of Fig.103-545 and 22 units of Fig.103-546, expected around the eighteenth century, the Dehua ware) [II-167].

Chinese stoneware

Fig.104-547 is a dish in three glazes (*sancai*) with flat rim. This dish has a lobed rim and is decorated with a design of flowering plant expressed with incised lines and red, green, yellow and purple glazes. This is a stoneware, but high fired with colour glazes (3 units) [II-168].

Fig.104-548 is a large bowl with ears in iron brown glaze. The foundation is light brown. This bowl was shaped in mold and applied a relief pattern on the exterior. There remain some granular pressed marks. Both interior and exterior are glazed in iron brown, with the rim left unglazed. In Japan, similar object had been excavated only in Nagasaki (70 units, from the seventeenth to eighteenth centuries).

Fig.104-549 is an unglazed high-fired stoneware ewer with handle. It is usually made in press mold using orange-brown refined base, and fired at the Yixing kiln, Jiangsu province. It originally accompanied a cover and made for tea drinking [II-169]. The body is painted with vermillion slip. This type of the Yixing kiln teapot was exported widely to Europe. The Meissen kiln of Germany made the copies. In Japan, this led to a birth of the Banko ware (10 units, from the seventeenth to nineteenth centuries).

(2) Hizen ceramics

Hizen porcelain

Fig.105-550 is a barber's dish with an over-glaze enamels design. The rim is lobed by molding. The inner bottom is decorated with a flower basket design in red and green enamels (from the second to third quarter of the eighteenth century).

Fig.105-551, 552 are dishes decorated in over-glaze polychrome and gold enamels (the *Kinrande* style). They are the saucers accompanying cups and for an export. Design is painted in red and gold enamels after under-glaze cobalt blue was applied. Fig.105-551 is decorated with a flower pattern in the inner bottom and flowering plant motif on the interior. Fig.105–552 has unglazed circular ring, but a colour enamel paints over the ring. Flower motif is arranged in the inner bottom and the space around the inner bottom is painted with flowering plants within each panel (284 units of Fig.105–551 and 41 units of Fig.105–552, from the 1690s to the first half of the eighteenth century, the Arita ware) [II-170].

Fig.105–553 is an under-glaze cobalt-blue dish in the Kraak style. Iron brown glaze is applied on the lip. The dish is decorated with designs of fruit tree in the inner bottom and panelled flower and grasses are arranged around it. Design expression in both inside and between each panel is variegated from the original Chinese Kraak style (7 units, from the 1690s to 1740s) [II-171].

Fig.105–554 is an under-glaze cobalt blue dish in the Kraak style. Designs around the inner bottom are considerably different from the typical design of Chinese Kraak style. Peony, chrysanthemum and fruit tree are painted in six large panels and flower pattern fills between the panels. The inner bottom appears to illustrate a design of flower basket (4 units, from the 1700s to 1740s, the Arita ware) [II-172].

Fig.105–555 is a large bowl with brim and under-glaze cobalt blue decoration. This was originally accompanied by a cover. The brim is painted with a peony spray motif on the upper space and a band of key-fret pattern runs along the rim. The flat base is unglazed (3 units, The first half of the eighteenth century, the Arita ware).

12. Period VI-2 (around the second half of the 18th century)

Buton Wolio Fort

(1) Chinese ceramics

Under-glaze cobalt blue and other wares

Jingdezhen ware

Fig.106–556 is a dish decorated with the Siddham scripts design. Similar item was excavated also at Banten Lama Site (Fig.108–578).

Fig.106–557 is a dish for the European markets. The design is possibly so called the Willow pattern.

Fig.106–558 is also dish for Europe decorated with so called the Willow pattern similar to the finds at Banten Lama (Fig.109–586).

Fig.106–559 is an irregular shaped dish decorated with over-glaze polychrome enamels design. The polychrome enamels were deteriorated, but they are likely the famille rose types (from the second half of the eighteenth to the first half of the nineteenth centuries).

Fig.106–560 is an under-glaze cobalt blue covered box.

Fujian ware

Fig.107–561 is an under-glaze cobalt blue dish decorated with a design of Lingzhi, narcissus and bamboo. A dish with same motif, probably a Jingdezhen ware, was excavated at Banten Lama (Fig.108-.575) [II-173]. The motif of Lingzhi, narcissus and bamboo was popular in the eighteenth century and also influenced Hizen porcelain. In Japan, the Hizen, the Seto and Mino kilns manufactured bowls and dishes etc. in this motif from the second half of the eighteenth to the middle of the nineteenth centuries.

Fig.107-562 are under-glaze cobalt blue dishes with flared body. The inner bottom is decorated with chrysanthemum and wavy arabesque pattern. A round dish of the same type of design was excavated at Banten Lama (Fig.110-597).

Fig.107-563 are bowls decorated with over-glaze polychrome enamels design. One on left has an unglazed circular ring in the inner bottom.

Fig.107-564 are fragments of rim of bowls decorated with over-glaze polychrome enamels design. Rims are slightly curved. This kind of bowls are dated to the eighteenth century.

Dehua ware

Special features of the Dehua ware of this period are molded shape and glaze removed lip. The Dehua ware was mainly producing white porcelain and only a few under-glaze cobalt blue ware was known until the seventeenth century. However low quality under-glaze cobalt blue ware was made in a great quantity and distributed widely in the eighteenth century

Fig.107-565 and 566 are a collection of under-glaze cobalt blue bowls. They are largely small bowls in round shape, but the one on the upper left shown in Fig.107-566 is differently made and has a folded rim. This would have been accompanied with a cover and used differently from the other group.

Fig.107-567 is an under-glaze cobalt blue small bowl with iron brown glaze. The interior is decorated with a design of Lingzhi, narcissus and bamboo in under-glaze cobalt blue.

Fig.107-568 is an over-glaze enamels decorated dish.

Fig.107-569 are bowls differently glazed in blue on the exterior and transparent on the interior.

Banten Lama Site

(1) Chinese ceramics

Under-glaze cobalt blue and other wares

Jingdezhen ware

Fig.108-570 is a cup with handle decorated with an over-glaze polychrome enamel design. This appears to be a chocolate cup accompanied with a saucer. The exterior is decorated in over-glaze polychrome enamels (1 unit, from the middle to late eighteenth century).

Fig.108-571 is a cup with over-glaze polychrome enamels decoration. This is a drinking cup, for example coffee. The exterior is painted with a sailing boat in black enamel and other colours. Sailing boat was also a frequently painted motif through orders from the European clients in the eighteenth century (1 unit, from the middle to late eighteenth century).

Fig.108-572 is an over-glaze polychrome enamels decorated bowl. The exterior is covered in red enamel over which arranged are white panels with famille rose enamel motif inside. There is a reign mark inside the foot-ring, which reads 'Made in Great Qing, Qianlong reign period' (12 units, from the late of eighteenth to the beginning of nineteenth centuries) [II-174].

Fig.108-573 is a cover decorated in over-glaze polychrome enamels. This could be a cover of a large bowl and is painted with flowering plants in famille rose enamels. A red orchid is painted inside the foot-ring (53 units, from the middle of the eighteenth to the beginning of the nineteenth centuries).

Fig.108-574 is a cover of a large bowl decorated in over-glaze polychrome enamels. Motifs of *Dharmachakra* and character (?) are painted in black enamel (1 unit, from the middle of the eighteenth to the beginning of the nineteenth centuries).

Fig.108-575 is an under-glaze cobalt blue dish decorated with a design of Lingzhi, narcissus and bamboo on both sides. There is a swirl (?) type of mark in under-glaze cobalt blue within a double square frame. There is a slight possibility that this was made in Fujian region (7 units, the eighteenth century). Arita also started to produce dishes with this kind of motif in the second half of the eighteenth century.

Fig.108-576 is a salt dish decorated both sides with over-glaze polychrome enamels design of flower pattern probably in famille rose enamel (?). Such salt dish is included in a service set in Europe (2 units, the eighteenth century).

Fig.108-577 is a white porcelain cover (12 units, the eighteenth century) [II-175].

Fig.108-578 is an under-glaze cobalt blue dish. Production site is either Jingdezhen or Fujian but not precisely identified. The inner bottom displays a character of *shou* 壽 (?) and the space around it is filled with repeated the Siddham characters (80 units, the eighteenth century). Although a dish from Buton Wolio (Fig.106-556) is a similar type, shape of rim and material present small differences. This is likely produced later than Fig.106-556.

Fig.109-579 is an under-glaze cobalt blue small bowl decorated with designs of landscape on exterior and rock and water in the inner bottom (86 units, the eighteenth century).

Fig.109-580 is an under-glaze cobalt blue small bowl. Similar design of Fig.109-584 is painted on the exterior. Inside the foot-ring bears a mark in under-glaze cobalt blue which reads *ruo-shen-zhen-zang* 若深珍藏 (42 units, from the middle to late eighteenth century).

Fig.109-581 is an under-glaze cobalt blue small bowl decorated with floral arabesque pattern on the exterior and in the inner bottom (9 units) [II-176].

Fig.109-582 is an under-glaze cobalt blue small bowl decorated with a design of Lingzhi, narcissus and bamboo [II-177]. There is a mark in under-glaze cobalt blue inside the foot-ring (25 units, from the second half of the eighteenth to the beginning of the nineteenth centuries).

Fig.109-583 is an under-glaze cobalt blue small bowl. The base is shaved to make a *Yunzi* piece container. Floral arabesque design decorates the exterior. It is extremely small. Relatively many of this kind of small bowls have been found in Okinawa in Japan, and the Tsuboya ware originated in Okinawa made stoneware copies from around the eighteenth to nineteenth centuries. It is assumedly used for strong alcohol drinks such as *awamori*, an indigenous alcohol drink in Okinawa. The purpose of this type of small bowls found at Banten Lama is unknown, but there are not many excavated (2 units, from the second half of the eighteenth to around nineteenth centuries).

Fig.109-584 is an under-glaze cobalt blue dish decorated with patterns modeled after bronze vessels on the inner bottom and side (61 units, from middle to late eighteenth century).

Fig.109-585 an under-glaze cobalt blue dish with a scattered flower motif on the inner bottom, which is encircled by linked *Ru-i* head pattern or it is called the *Rinpo/* Dharmachakra pattern in Japan. The rim is filled with detailed border pattern, which was favoured in Europe (1 unit, the eighteenth century) [II-178].

Fig.109-586 is an under-glaze cobalt blue dish with flat rim. The design is so called the Willow pattern. The inner bottom displays Chinese landscape with a willow tree in the inner bottom. There are layers of bands with waves and geometric patterns from the centre towards the rim. This is also a typical motif targeting Europe. Remains of spur marks on the base replicate spur marks in Arita-fired Hizen porcelain and occasionally found in Chinese porcelain for the European markets (149 units, from middle to late eighteenth century).

Fig.109-587, 588 are under-glaze cobalt blue large bowl and cover. Fig.109-587 is a cover and decorated mainly with a design of bird and flowering plant. The rim is painted with a band of key-fret pattern and flowers within. This decoration on the rim seems the same kind as the dish Fig.102-536 (25 units in the same types). Fig.109-588 is a body decorated with flower and grasses. The exterior of the rim has the same motif as the cover, but the interior is also applied with a band of key-fert pattern (14 units, the eighteenth century) [II-179].

Fig.109-589 is an under-glaze cobalt blue cover decorated with a design of floral arabesque drawn only in outlines (15 units, around the second half of the eighteenth century) [II-180].

Fujian ware

Fig.110-590 is an under-glaze cobalt blue bowl decorated with a design of character *shou* and peony arabesque. This kind of large bowls come with variety of designs (36 units, the eighteenth century) [II-181]. Made in the southern region of Fujian province.

Fig.110-591, 592 are molded under-glaze cobalt blue small bowls. Characteristically the glaze on the lip is removed. Fig.110-591 has an arrangement of circle and dot design around the rim, and Fig.110-592 roundels and slanted lattice ground (215 units of Fig.110-592, the eighteenth century, the Dehua ware) [II-182].

Fig.110-593 is a white porcelain small bowl. It is formed in press mold and the lip was removed of glazing [II-183]. There are other versions simply decorated with blue enamel on the same foundation (588 units, from the second half of the eighteenth to the first half of the nineteenth centuries, the Dehua ware).

Fig.110-594 is decorated with a design of Chinese figure in the inner bottom. Under-glaze cobalt blue mark which reads *he-mei* 和美 is centrally placed inside the foot-ring (30 units, the eighteenth century) [II-184].

Fig.110-595, 596 are under-glaze cobalt blue dishes. Fig.110-595 sports a design of crane in the inner bottom and bears a mark *yuan-yu* 源裕 inside the foot-ring (103 units, the eighteenth century). Fig.110-596 has its inner bottom filled with flower pattern (19 units, the eighteenth century).

Floral arabesque motif fills in the inner bottom of Fig.110-597. There is a mark in under-glaze cobalt blue inside the foot-ring, which reads '?-*xing* 興 ?' ('?' representing an illegible character) (265 units, the eighteenth century) [II-185].

Fig.110-598 displays a design of dragon in the inner bottom and a mark inside the foot-ring (43 similar units, the eighteenth century).

Fig.110-599 is decorated with a design of dragon and clouds. There is a mark inside the foot-ring (12 units, from middle to late eighteenth century) [II-186]. They were fired at regional kilns in the southern Fujian province.

Fig.110-600 is under-glaze cobalt blue dish, which was formed in press mold and its lip is removed of glaze. The inner bottom is decorated with a dragon like motif in under-glaze cobalt blue (245 units, the eighteenth century, the Dehua ware) [II-187].

Chinese stoneware

Fig.111-601 is a flowerpot in green glaze. It is thinly made with fine base. One on the right is molded in a round shape. The exterior is glazed in green (11 units, from the second half of the seventeenth to the eighteenth centuries) [II-188].

Fig.111-602 is a high fired unglazed stoneware ewer. The fragment is a handle and the spout is attached at the right angle (10 units, the seventeenth to the eighteenth centuries) [II-189].

(2) Hizen ceramics and other wares

Hizen stoneware and other wares

Fig.112-603 is a stoneware cooking pot with ears. The ear is attached to the curved rim. Small horn shaped legs are pasted at the side of unglazed base. There are two versions in glazing on the light brown body, transparent glaze and iron oxide glaze. This type of cooking pot with ears was made in Kansai and are common in Japan (16 units, the eighteenth century) [II-190].

Fig.112-604 is a jar in brown glaze. The fragments are the shoulder part and base (the right in the picture). The inside shows a lattice trace from patted forming. Both sides are glazed in iron oxide [II-191]. The early Hizen jars had wave pattern trace of patted forming. At Banten Lama found one thin fragment with patted trace in wave pattern and this may contribute export Hizen stoneware to go back years (1 unit, probably the eighteenth century).

(3) European ceramics

Fig.113-605 is a dish with indigo blue painting. A design of peacock (?) and others are painted in blue enamel on white glaze. The base is coarse soft paste stoneware. The glaze on the base of foot-ring had been removed owing to the usage (6 units, possibly the eighteenth century, the Netherlands).

13. Period VII-1 (around the first half of the 19th century)

Buton Wolio Fort

(1) Chinese ceramics

Under-glaze cobalt blue ware

Jingdezhen ware

Fig.114-606 is an under-glaze cobalt blue bowl (from the beginning to middle nineteenth century).

Fig.114-607 are under-glaze cobalt blue bowls with a design of stylized floral arabesque and a curved rim. The inner bottom is also decorated with floral pattern. This type of bowl is common in Japan and influenced porcelain produced at the Nankin-sarayama kiln in Satsuma (around the end of Edo period).

Fig.114-608 is an under-glaze cobalt blue dish with a floral arabesque pattern. It is not clear whether this type is identified as Jingdezhen or Fujian.

Fig.114-609 is a covered large bowl decorated with under-glaze cobalt blue design of floral arabesque in so called the pencil drawing technique (from the late eighteenth to middle of the nineteenth centuries).

Banten Lama Site

(1) Chinese ceramics

Under-glaze cobalt blue ware

Jingdezhen ware

Fig.115-610 is an under-glaze cobalt blue bowl. The external body is painted with lotus petal motif and the inner bottom displays a floral pattern. The foot-ring carries a reign mark in under-glaze cobalt blue that reads 'Made in Great Qing, Jiaqing reign era' (4 units, the first half of the nineteenth century) [II-192].

Fujian ware

Fig.116-611 is an under-glaze cobalt blue bowl. It is not certain of its origin, either Jingdezhen or Fujian. The exterior is filled with a floral arabesque design. There is a mark in under-glaze cobalt blue inside the foot-ring. In Japan, this type of ware can be mostly found in Okinawa, but there are some examples also excavated at other archaeological sites (2 units, from the first half to the middle of the nineteenth century).

Fig.116-612 is an under-glaze cobalt blue large bowl. On the exterior, it is decorated with floral arabesque pattern (20 units, Fujian type ware. from the middle of the eighteenth to the beginning of the nineteenth century) [II-193].

Fig.116-613 is an under-glaze cobalt blue spoon. An arabesque motif is painted inside (38 units, from the second half of the eighteenth to the first half of the nineteenth centuries) [II-194].

(2) European ceramics

Fig.117-614 is a bottle with handle. There is an incised mark on the shoulder (29 units, from the eighteenth to middle of the nineteenth centuries).

Tirtayasa Site

(1) Chinese ceramics

Under-graze cobalt blue ware

Possible Fujian and Guangdong wares

Fig.118-615 is an under-glaze cobalt blue bowl with curved rim. There is a central double ring in the inner bottom and the inside of the rim is painted with a band in cobalt. On the exterior, it is decorated loose floral arabesque. It is not certain of its origin, either Jingdezhen or Fujian (from the early to middle of the nineteenth century).

14. Period VII-2 (around the second half of the 19th century)

Buton Wolio Fort

(1) Hizen type porcelain

Fig.119-616 shows some the Hizen type bowls with stencil paper printed decoration in under-glaze cobalt blue from Meiji to Taisho periods. From the pattern, they can be identified as the Tobe ware from Ehime Prefecture.

(2) European stoneware

Fig.120-617/619 are the European stoneware. Chinese ceramics sharply dropped after the second half of the nineteenth century and tableware was taken over by the European stoneware.

Banten Lama Site

(1) European stoneware

Fig.121-620 is a cup decorated with the Alpine pattern in blue by copper plate transfer technique. There is a mark, similar to Fig.121-622, transferred inside the foot-ring.

Fig.121-621 are dishes with a willow pattern in copper plate transfer technique. The fragment at the bottom is a Petrus Regout ware, the Netherlands. Others are British made (middle of the nineteenth century).

Fig.121-622 is a saucer decorated with a blue design in copper plate transfer technique. On the base, there is a mark of 'ADAMS & SONS' (the Adams & Sons ware, England).

Fig.121-623 is a dish decorated in copper plate transfer technique. It shows an oriental pattern in blue enamel. There is another dish with different design in the centre and in green enamel. An 'ORIENTAL' mark is transferred inside the foot-ring

(29 units). It was fired at the Petrus Regout kiln in Maastricht, the Netherlands.

Fig.121-624 is a dish with underglaze black decoration by copper plate transfer. The foot-ring bears a mark which shows '- ADAMS' inside (the second half of the nineteenth century, England).

Fig.121-625 is a dish decorated with a relief pattern and a design transferred in copper plate. The flowering plant in relief is coloured in purple (or red), yellow, yellow-green and light blue (10 units). There is also a white porcelain dish in the same shape (11 units, from the middle to late nineteenth century, possibly England).

Fig.121-626 is a dish with over-glaze polychrome enamels decoration. The interior shows a design of flower and grasses in green, blue and red [II-195]. This is a saucer to accompany a cup (47 units).

Chapter II Note

1 Figs.45 and 46, Idemitsu Museum of Art 1982. Dated to the Southern Dynasties period (420-589).

2 P.42, Cixi-shi Bowuguan (ed.) 2002. Dated to the Tang Dynasty period.

3 195, Adhyatman 1981. The ninth to tenth centuries.

4 Colour plate 10, Cixi shi Bowuguan (ed.) 2002. Date is given as the Tang Dynasty period.

5 Similar lobed dishes in *Bachi*/Japanese plectrum shape decorated with incised pattern were excavated at the Yuezhou and Silongkou kilns (P.82 of Zhejiang Province Antique Archaeology Institute et al. 2002).

6 The jar in the Shanghai Museum is similar and covered with long neck and four ears (Shanghai Renmin Meisu Chupanshe 1981, Fig.203). It is dated to the Northern Sung period.

7 Covered jar with ears in the Haiyan Museum in China resembles to this jar (Fig.165, Shanghai Renmin Meisu Chupanshe 1981). The Five Dynasties period.

8 Similar example is Fig.248 in Shogakukan 1976a-11, with an applied figure pattern.

9 There are similar pieces including one excavated at the Shomyoji Temple, Kanazawa-ku, Yokohama-shi (an Important Cultural Property. Shogakukan 1981, Fig.33) and in the Cargo rescued from off Sinan, Korea (Gunnip Chungan Banmurguan 1977, Figs.59, 60).

10 The Seikado Bunko Art Museum owns a similar bowl, which is reportedly as a heirloom of the Konoike family (an Important Cultural Property. Heibonsha (ed.) 1997, Fig.71).

11 Similar objects can be found among the Cargo salvaged from off Sinan (Fig.107-109, Gunnip Chungan Banmurguan 1977).

12 Although with a different pattern on the exterior, there is a similar bowl with a high stem (Fig.121, Xianggang Daxue Fung Ping-shan Bowuguan 1992).

13 This is a bottle with bulging round body, narrow neck and wide open mouth (the *yu-hu-chun* shape), called the Gaignières-Fonthill Vase (Shogakukan 1981, Fig.43).

14 Fig.96 in National Museum of Vietnamese History 2005 is a similar example and dated to the eleventh to the thirteenth centuries. Another one shown in Fig.75 Machida City Museum (ed.) 1993 is dated to the thirteenth to the fourteenth centuries.

15 Similar examples include Fig.41, Aichiken Tōji Shiryōkan 1987 (the thirteenth to the fourteenth centuries) and Fig.94 in National Museum of Vietnamese History 2005 (the eleventh to the thirteenth centuries).

16 Fig.87 in Machida City Museum (ed.) 1993 is a similar dish, which is decorated with a peony design in the inner bottom and dated to the fourteenth to the fifteenth centuries.

17 Fig.43 in Machida City Museum (ed.) 1993 has a resemblance and the date is the thirteenth to the fourteenth centuries.

18 The Dehua type Anxi Kuidou kiln produced similar works.

19 An ewer found in the Cargo salvaged from Sinan off-shore shares likeness (Gunnip Chungan Banmurguan 1977, Fig.163). This ewer is 24.1cm in height and a ring is fixed on the cover for attaching a metal handle later.

20 The Topkapi Palace Museum owns a similar work (Krahl & Ayers 1986-556) dated to the middle of the fourteenth century. Diameter 45.5cm.

21 Fig.12 in Miksic & Kamei 2010, says from the Trowulan Site, is a same kind of octagonal cover of jar.

22 Similar pieces are Fig.4 in Miksic & Kamei 2010 and Fig.5 in Heibonsha (ed.) 1995.

23 Other excavated same kind of cover of a round shape jars are an under-glaze cobalt blue jar with red glaze from Baoding in Hebei province (Shogakukan 1981, Fig.52), and another from the Katsuren Gusuku Site, Okinawa (Kamei et al. 2005, pp.149, 150).

24 For similar example, a complete pair with a cover was found in Baoding, Hebei province (Fig.52, Shogakukan 1981). In addition there is a body only in the Percival David Collection in the British Museum, and a thin fragment of body was excavated at the Olon Sum Site in Mongolia (Kamei et al. 2009, Fig.9). We have little knowledge of other example excavated outside of the Chinese Continent.

25 Only similar work known today is one owned by the Yangzhou Antique Shop, which is fitted with metalwork on the upper part (Kamei et al. 2005, p.124).

26 The National Museum of History in Taiwan has a similar piece (Guoli Lishi Bowuguang 1992, Fig.65, Height is 26.0cm).

27 Resembled work of Fig.6-55 is Fig.266 in Shogakukan 1981 (height 24.7cm). Similar floral arabesque pattern on the shoulder of Fig.6-56 appears in Fig.154 also in Shogakukan 1981.

28 See Fig.265 in Shogakukan 1981 for a similar example (diameter 45.0 - 46.0cm).

29 The shipwreck was discovered off the coast of Cu Lao Cham in Central Vietnam.

30 The salvaged example off Hoi An (Butterfield 2000) has a six petals flower as well as a different style of design in the inner bottom. The outline around the inner bottom is a single and looks broadly painted.

31 Basins in Machida City Museum (ed.) 1993 (Fig.27-31) also have unglazed interior. Although shape is very different, it is possible for these examples and ours have the same purpose.

32 The upper body shape is not known, but the bottom part looks alike to the celadon jar in Fig.82 in National Museum of Vietnamese History 2005 (16.0cm in diameter) dated to the eleventh to thirteenth centuries.

33 A similar work appears to be a large bowl attached with small clay balls such as Fig.50 in Machida City Museum (ed.) 1993.

34 A relatively similar example is a dish with incised flower pattern in brown glaze in Fig.113, Machida City Museum (ed.) 1993. This dish is dated to the fifteenth to the sixteenth centuries, but our dish is possibly older.

35 Fig.109 in Machida City Museum (ed.) 1993 is a similar example and production date is the thirteenth to the fourteenth centuries. The British Museum has also a similar bowl, but it is with flared rim and closer to the *tenmoku* shape.

36 A similar object is a large bowl in Fig.126 (35.3cm in diameter), Machida City Museum (ed.) 1993. It is dated to the fourteenth to the fifteenth centuries.

37 Similar bowl is Fig.136, Machida City Museum (ed.) 1993, dated to the fourteenth century (diameter is 16.2cm).

38 This resembles to an under-glaze cobalt blue ware shown in Fig.147 in Machida City Museum (ed.) 1993.

39 Fig.134 and 135 in Machida City Museum (ed.) 1993 look similar.

40 In Islamic ceramic world, these kinds of white glazed ceramic tiles with indigo painting are known from the thirteenth to the fifteenth centuries (Shogakukan 1984, p.218). Many of these tiles are hexagonal or star shaped.

41 Similar object is shown in p.96 in Adhyatman & Abu Ridho 1984, which is given a dating of the fourteenth century.

42 Jingdezhen kiln is the largest porcelain production center after the Ming dynasty period around Jingdezhen City in Jiangxi Province.

43 The National Palace Museum in Taipei owns a similar piece, which is made in the beginning of Ming period (Fig.28, Guoli Gugong Bowuyuan 1990 illustration 28, diameter is 19.6cm). The Taipei example is an imperial class quality.

44 There is a heirloom object of under-glaze cobalt blue ware covered jar in the collection of Shoudou Museum, China, which was originally excavated in Beijing (Kamei et al. 2005, p.21, total height is 65.5cm) and dated to around Hongwu era (1368-98), although there is a view to categorize this as copper red painting. Another example of copper red painting is in the Umezawa Memorial Museum (an Important Cultural Property, Fig.22, Heibonsha 1995, in height of 51.2cm), and an example of under-glaze cobalt blue was found in Jingdezhen.

45 A similar bottle is in the collection of the Matsuoka Museum of Art (42.0cm in height), which is made in around the Yongle era (1403-1424).

46 A similar piece is introduced in Fig.145, Machida City Museum (ed.) 1993. Its arabesque pattern is less sketchy, and its shape also suggests a possibility that it is older than our example and dated to the fourteen century.

47 One of the prominent examples of such design appears on the mouth of a bottle with a dragon motif named Byakue, a heirloom object in Japan (Yabe 1978, 11, height is 28.7cm). The lotus pattern is also closer to Jingdezhen and in an old style. This can be a key reference to Vietnamese under-glaze cobalt blue ware of the middle to late fourteenth century. No.179 to be introduced later in this chapter is a fragment of this type of bottle. Another example, a bottle with a globular body with narrow long neck (the *yu-hu-chun* shape) with a meander and earlier style lotus patterns is Fig.232 in National Museum of Vietnamese History 2005. This publication date it to the fifteenth to the sixteenth

centuries, but the pattern and shape suggests a high possibility of its being around the second half of the fourteenth century.

48 A similar object was excavated at the Kofukumon Gate, Shichan-una, Shuri Fort in Okinawa (Fig.11, No.29 in Okinawaken Maizôbunkazai Centre 2001a). Although the object is identified as Chinese, it is likely Vietnamese origin.

49 A basin decorated with a design of bird and tree in Fig.144, Shogakukan 1984 is a similar piece and from the fifteenth to the sixteenth centuries.

50 A similar large jar is in the Sano Art Museum (height: 39.5cm) listed in Fig.78 of Hiebonsha (ed.) 1978. Similar to a bottle with year mark of 1450 in the Topkapi Palace Museum, the Sano Art Museum piece has later feature in the design, lotus sub-petal and vein painted on the peony arabesque leaf. Our jar is older.

51 In the National Museum of Vietnamese History there is a similar object (National Museum of Vietnamese History 2005, Fig.223), which lower border of stand and upper narrow part is painted in iron slip. It is dated to the fifteenth century.

52 This large dish resembles to the object in the National Museum of Indonesia (Heibonsha 1978, Fig.85).

53 A similar dish decorated with fish and alga in the inner bottom and treasure motif on the outer interior is introduced in Fig.153, Machida City Museum (ed.) 1993 which is dated to the fifteenth to the sixteenth centuries.

54 A similar object is Fig.209, Machida City Museum (ed.) 1993, which is dated to the fifteenth to the sixteenth centuries.

55 Other similar excavated example is published in Fig.302 upper right in Shogakukan 1984.

56 There is another similar finding from Trowulan in Fig.259, Machida City Museum (ed.) 1993. The internal main decoration is different.

57 A jar decorated with incised ribbed pattern on the body and lotus motif on the shoulder exists. This jar is with an inner cover and the rim is unglazed (Shogakukan 1984, Fig.80, Si Satachanalai ware, the fifteenth century, 13.3cm in mouth diameter).

58 An example of similar piece is among the salvaged cargo from the Nangyang Shipwreck (Mukai 2012, Fig.34), and expected date is the first half of the fifteenth century.

59 Similar works of the left is in the collection of the Tokyo National Museum (Fig.26, Heibonsha 1978, Large bowl, Sukhothai ware, 26.0cm in diameter, fifteenth century) and in the salvaged material from the Turiang Shipwreck (Fig.24, Mukai 2012).

60 Similar vessels are included in the cargo from the Longquan Shipwreck (Mukai 2012, Fig.48), and it is highly possible that they are the Sukohthai ware made in the middle of the fifteenth century.

61 A similar piece is in the National Museum of Bangkok, which is introduced in Fig.220, Shogakukan 1984 (height 50.0cm, Si Satachanalai ware, thirteenth to fourteenth centuries). Later research suggests that this is Ban Bang Phun ware, Suphan Buri Province and the date is estimated around the first half of the fifteenth century (Takashima 2013).

62 A similar work is shown in Fig.1 in Mukai 2012.

63 This resembles to No.1421, p.164 in Butterfield 2000 (in later the cargo salvaged off Hoi An).

64 Similar object is Fig.1353 in the cargo salvaged off Hoi An (Butterfield 2000), and Machida

City Museum (ed.) 1993, Fig.178 dated to the sixteenth century.

65 One of the Tokyo National Museum Collection (fifteenth to sixteenth centuries, Fig.152 in Machida City Museum 1993) looks very similar to this large dish as far as judging from a photograph.

66 Fig.218 in National Museum of Vietnamese History 2005 is similar. This example is dated to the fifteenth century, but the lotus sub-petal painted on the lower part suggests that the date can be the second half of the fifteenth century.

67 Fig.14 in National Museum of Vietnamese History 1995 shows similar decoration of raised dragon motif in black clay, which is given a date of fifteenth to sixteenth centuries.

68 A same type of bowl was excavated at the Aramaki Honmura Site, Yamanashi Prefecture, Japan (Fig.195 in Tokyo Kokuritsu Hakubutsukan 1975 and p.53 in Ohashi 1981).

69 Fig.228 in Goddio et al. 2002 shows a similar work from the Lena Cargo Shipwreck.

70 This is the sunken ship cargo, which was salvaged off Palawan Island, the Philippines. The ship is assumed to sunk around the Hongzhi reign period (1488-1505).

71 Fig.67 and 115 (Goddio et al. 2002, French edition).

72 The design is close to the floral arabesque decorating the external of bowl from the Lena Cargo, shown in Fig.188, Goddio et al. 2002.

73 This kind of motif also can be found, although in more quick brushwork, in the Lena Cargo, Fig.183 in Goddio et al. 2002.

74 Similar design but more roughly painted can be found among the Lena Cargo (Goddio et al. 2002) and also introduced in the Topkapi Palace Museum as Fig.720, Krahl & Ayers 1986 (Afterwards, all reference number of the collection of the Topkapi Palace is used in this book.). It is dated to the second half of the fifteenth to the beginning of the sixteenth centuries.

75 This resembles to a persimmon-shaped covered box for incense with iron brown painting in the collection of the Nezu Art Institute (Shogakukan 1984, Fig.330, Si Satachanalai ware).

76 The right is possibly a body part fragment of a bottle introduced in Fig.64, Shogakukan 1984 (gourd-shaped bottle decorated with an iron-brown painting motif of flower and grasses in mat white glaze, Idemitsu Museum of Art 1982).

77 A similar piece is a jar decorated with a lion and peony design in coloured glaze/*sancai*, Fig.243 in Shogakukan 1976b.

78 The Topkapi Palace Museum owns similar dishes shown in Fig.781 and 782, and dated to the beginning of the sixteenth century. The lotus petal and flower motif on the inner bottom is also a simplified version of Fig.682.

79 Dish decorated with a similar dragon and arabesque pattern is also in the Topkapi Palace Museum (Fig.785, 787 and 788), and they are dated to the beginning of the sixteenth century.

80 Lonvek is the capital of Cambodia after the abandonment of Angkor in the middle fifteenth century. Ponhea Lueu was the outer port facing the Tonlé Sap River.

81 Similar example is Fig.824 in the Topkapi Palace Museum. Its height is 29-30cm and date is from the first half to the middle of the sixteenth century.

82 An example of heirloom object is illustrated at the upper left in page 195 collection in Tan

Xue-hui et al.1998, but this also resembles to Fig.824 in the Topkapi Palace Museum.

83 Resembled works were made at the Anxi Kuidou kiln in Fujian province (p.77 in Ceng 2001).

84 The Pinghe Nansheng Huazailou kiln in Fujian province produced similar works (p.61 in Ceng 2001).

85 This type of vessel was made at the Anxi Kuidou kiln in Fujian province.

86 Fig.1 in Adhyatman 1999 is a similar piece.

87 Fig.7 in Adhyatman 1999 is a similar work.

88 For similar example see Adhyatman 1999, Fig.50 for No.222 and Fig.46 for No.223.

89 Although similar but different era work was excavated at the site of Dutch Trading Post in Hirado, Nagasaki Prefecture (Fig.20-27 in Hirado-shi Kyoiku-iinkai 1988), only a few known in Japan.

90 Same kind of bowl was excavated also at the archaeological site of Sakaemachi, Nagasaki-shi (Fig.36−51 in Nagasaki-shi Maizobunkazai Chosa Kyogikai1993). The Topkapi Palace Museum owns the similar heirloom object (Fig.1531), which is dated to the beginning of the seventeenth century.

91 An example in Japan was excavated at the Dutch Trading Post in Hirado (Fig.21-35, Hirado-shi Kyoiku-iinkai 1988). The characteristics resembles the upper left of Fig.117 or Fig.120−2 in Sasaki et al.2004. The example in the lower of Fig.46−232 is thought the later dating because rough manufacturing of the bottom and no glazing.

92 The jewel design on the exterior resembles to the salvaged cargo from the Dutch ship Witte Leeuw, which sank off Saint Helena in 1613, shown as Fig.8852 in Pijl-Ketel 1982, and the internal pattern is closer to Fig.1495 in the Topkapi Palace Museum collection.

93 Similar work can be found in p.172 in Pijl-Ketel 1982, the salvaged from the sunken ship Witte Leeuw.

94 This is similar to Fig.5175 in Pijl-Ketel 1982, salvaged from the sunken ship Witte Leeuw.

95 There are many example of excavated similar works in Japan, and also found at the Zhangpu Pinshui kiln in Fujian.

96 Similar pieces are found at the Pinghe Nansheng Huazailou kiln in Fujian, Fig.115 in Adhyatman 1999 and p.208 in Pijl-Ketel 1982, salvaged from the Witte Leeuw.

97 This under-glaze cobalt blue pattern looks very close to the pattern in the inner bottom decorating the over-glaze polychrome enamels dish shown as Fig.180 in Adhyatman 1999.

98 Similar examples are introduced in p.201 in Pijl-Ketel 1982 and Fig.71 in Adhyatman 1999.

99 The *Meizande* is a type of the Kraak style with jewel shaped panels and a design of arc lines/*maribasami* motif around the inner bottom. Many are small dishes and in particular those made in the Jingdezhen had been excavated in Japan in quantity. A similar example is No.341 in Kyūshū Ceramic Museum 2003, which diameter measures 26.8cm.

100 Adhyatman 1999, Fig.197.

101 A similar dish was excavated in No.12 pit, section 2 of Sakaemachi Site, Nagasaki-shi, Japan. The Casa-Museu Dr. Anastácio Gonçalves in Lisbon, Portugal owns a heirloom object of similar look (p.83 in Pinto 1996). Both of these examples have foliated rim.

102 This type of the Kraak dishes are not often excavated in China, probably owing to the

fact that they were export items. However, some have been reportedly found in graves in Guangchang county, Jiangxi (pp.86-89 in Yao et al.1990). This can be special as the place is close to the production site. These examples were found in tombs with year inscription, and are mainly the Kraak style dishes produced from 1608 (Wanli 36) to 1645 (Southern Ming, Honguang 1).

103 Similar examples are few in Japan except the Dutch Trading Post in Hirado.

104 Tulip designs for large dishes come in great varieties. The closest design to this fragment is the large dish Fig.1609 in the collection of the Topkapi Palace Museum, which is 48.0cm in diameter. In Japan, fragments with different type of tulip designs were excavated including a small quantity from the Dutch Trading Post Site in Dejima, Nagasaki (Fig.37-3 in Nagasaki-shi Kyoiku-iinkai 1986).

105 A similar object was excavated from the foundation soil under the stone wall along the coast at the Dutch Trading Post in Hirado, which was built in around 1616. The reign mark 'Made in the Ming dynasty, Chenghua reign' framed within a double square is also found in a work excavated at the Sumitomo Copper Refinery Site in Osaka (Fig.24-341/343 in Osaka-shi Bunkazai Kyokai 1998). The Eisei-bunko Museum has a heirloom cup with a design of circled dragons in colour enamels, which is dated to the Qing Dynasty Yongzheng reign.

106 Many examples were excavated also in Japan and often accompanied with stuck up Hizen stoneware in preparation of firing using clay balls.

107 In addition to Japan where not a small volume was excavated, there are excavated examples also in Hoi An in Vietnam. Similar works were found in the Zhaoan-Xian kiln, Zhangzhou (Fujian-sheng Bowuguang 1997).

108 Hoi An is the port city in Quàng Nam, Central Vietnam, which was under the control of the Nguyen Lord.

109 It was named after the Anpin (Zeelandia) Fort in Taiwan. This type of jar was widely distributed over the regions from Japan to Southeast Asia during the end of sixteenth to the seventeenth centuries. An old example is the one excavated at the Dutch Trading Post in Hirado, and the later example was found among the Vung Tau cargo, which was shipwrecked around the 1690s.

110 The rim of this dish is foliated with pointy edges. This shape of dish with decoration in over-glaze polychrome enamels was excavated in Osaka city (Mori 1993, however the over-glaze polychrome dish is not Vietnamese but the Dehua ware.). In addition, white porcelain bowls, which were similarly formed in hump mold as well as fired in stuck system using clay balls were unearthed in Nagasaki (Fig.18-8 in Nagasaki-shi Kyoiku-iinkai 1997) and Okinawa (Ohashi 1999a), Japan.

111 A similar jar can be found in Page 116 in Nezu Institute of Fine Arts 1993. The Nezu example refers the tea caddy named *Reiki* (Legendary tortoise) illustrated in the "Taishô meikikan" (Dictionary of masterpieces from Taishô era) as a resembled ware. *Reiki* was said once in possession of Kobori Enshû.

112 This sauce dish was confirmed in 1989, which demonstrated the possibility that Hizen porcelain was exported already in the 1640s.

113 Middle size dishes with a wood grain design on the flared up rim such as Fig.56-290 were also found at several kilns active around the 1640s including No.3 of Yanbeta and Sarukawa (Fig.74-1/4 in Ohashi et al.1988). They were also for export, and Banten Lama is the only site abroad so far from which this type of dish was excavated.

114 In Japan, they were excavated in Nagasaki and Hirado.

115 Similar work was included among the artifacts damaged by the Meireki Great Fire, which was excavated at the Yurakuchô Icchôme site, Tokyo (Musashi Bunkazai Kenkyujo 2015).

116 Similar pieces were found at the Huazailou kiln, Zhangzhou.

117 The large dish decorated with a voyage design shown in Fig.150 in Harrisson 1979 and Fig.87 in Adhyatman 1999 resemble to this large dish.

118 Similar work was unearthed at the Beaterio de la Compania de Jesus Site, Manila under the Spanish rule (Nogami et al. 2005).

119 Kyūshū Ceramic Museum 1990, Fig.288.

120 Similar pieces are excavated at the Pasar Ikan Site, which stands at the site of Dutch East India Company warehouse in Jakarta (Kyūshū Ceramic Museum 1990, Fig.217) and Fig.399 also in Kyūshū Ceramic Museum 1991.

121 Decoration technique to apply a stamped under-glaze cobalt blue pattern on exterior is called 'stamped under-glaze cobalt blue' in China and practiced at the sites in Fujian and Guangdong regions. A large volume was excavated also in Japan, for example Nagasaki, Okinawa and also at the Doshômachi Site, Osaka (from a pit in soil to set the fire site of 1723, Mori 1993). The Old City of Fengshan in Zuoying (Fig.56, p.835 in Zang et al.1993), Taiwan also presented similar work.

122 See Fig.204 in Jörg 2003

123 Similar dishes were unearthed in the Old City of Fengshan in Zuoying located on the west coast of Southern Taiwan. The Old City was founded after Zheng Cheng-gong/Koxinga entered into Taiwan in 1661 and also at the Zhucuo kiln, the Zhangzhou or Anxi kiln, Anxi (Fig.3-5 in Ye 1990). The example found in the Old City is painted with a leaf and inscribed 'Wrought in the Yimao year winter of Taiping era (estimated 1675)'. Dishes with a leaf painting and this same inscription were found at the Shuiwei kiln, Dapu-xian, Guangdong (p.4 in Yang 1990), and a report informs another examples of fragments inscribed with 'the Jiwei year of Taiping era', 'the Gengshen year of Taiping era'. It is highly possible that Jiwei year suggests 1679 and Gengshen year as 1680.

124 Similar work was found at the Old City of Fengshan in Zuoying.

125 Such custom of playing a game of 'paper, stone and scissors' losers have to drink alcohol was also depicted as a design in a Jingdezhen ware large dish in the collection of the Topkapi Palace Museum (No.3248 and 3249), which is dated to the Kangxi reign period (1662-1722). Similar custom was taken as a design also in over-glaze polychrome enamel decorated porcelain made in Arita by the beginning of the eighteenth century. There is no excavated example in Japan.

126 This kind of celadon dish has rarely been excavated in Japan, but some are in the collections in Southeast Asia and the Topkapi Palace Museum.

127 There is no example of similar work in Japan but found in the Old City of Fengshan and

Lop Buri, which is an archaeological site of royal palace in the Central Thailand (Chandavij 1989).

128 These kind of dishes in middle and large sizes have hardly been excavated in Japan, but they were excavated in Southeast Asia, for example at Lop Buri Site in Thailand.

129 Similar work was included in the Vung Tau Cargo, sunk off Con Dao Island, Southern Vietnam in around 1690 (Jörg & Flecker 2003).

130 Covered boxes in green glaze which looks soft paste owing to incomplete firing were included in the Hatcher Cargo (the Hatcher Junk) (around 1643–1646), a commercial salvaged goods (Sheaf 1988).

131 Similar bowl was unearthed in the Old City of Fengshan in Zuoying.

132 A similar example was among the salvaged Vung Tau Cargo, is different that a handle is pasted from inside of the rim. Fig.97 in Zang et al. 1993 from the Old City of Fengshan also has a handle pasted on the interior.

133 This kind of celadon large dish was also excavated in Indonesia. In addition, two heirloom items have been confirmed in Turkey (Ohashi 1998).

134 The Gemeentemuseum Den Haag owns a similar dish, which is in irregular shape and decorated with a design of a sailing boat in under-glaze cobalt blue (longest diameter 16.0cm, fig.28 in Arita Porcelain Park 1993) and a correction in the Groningen Museum (Fig.44 in Kyushu Ceramic Museum 1983). The Burghley House in England also has a resembled dish (Fig.44 in Burghley House 1983). The heirloom in Den Haag bears a painting in the style of Frederik van Frytom, a Dutch ceramic painter, in the inner bottom.

135 No similar work has been identified but the monkey face legs look close to tripod legs attached to celadon dish made in the middle of the seventeenth century.

136 These covered boxes have been also excavated in Japan, but excavated at higher rate in Indonesia, and a significant volume have been excavated when counting Chinese porcelain and Vietnamese ceramics also. The reason for this is said that they were highly sought after as container of lime mixed with areca nut for chewing, which was popular in this region.

137 The first discovered example was among the artifacts from the Pasar Ikan, Indonesia (Fig.148, 149 in Kyūshū Ceramic Museum 1990). Great volume was found in Indonesia and quite a few were also found at Banten Lama (Kyūshū Ceramic Museum 1990, Fig.290). There are excavated examples in Japan but a few. Up until present, Indonesia has the most and for this reason they were thought to be export items.

138 There is a similar ewer in Europe, which is attached with a silver cover bearing the year mark of 1689 (Nagabuchi 1997). Not a few heirloom items remain today.

139 The Topkapi Palace Museum owns a resembled piece (no.2029).

140 The Topkapi Palace Museum owns a similar bowl (no.2051).

141 The Topkapi Palace Museum owns a same kind of dish (no.2099).

142 There is a similar dish in the Topkapi Palace Museum (no.2030).

143 The similar spoon in the salvaged Vung Tau Cargo (Fig.93 in Jörg & Flecker 2001) retains the pointy spoon section.

144 Fig.309–311 in Kyūshū Ceramic Museum 1990.

145 The Topkapi Palace Museum also owns a dish with the same folded rim and in-filling but different design in the centre (Fig.2610).

146 This is close to the design of Fig.132 in Kyūshū Ceramic Museum 1995.

147 Examples of large octagonal jar with this kind of design are in the USUI collection (Fig.143, Nihon Keizai Shinbunsha 2009) and a jar of Fig.190 in Kyushu Ceramic Museum 2000 is not formed in the technique of combination of flat panels..

148 The Kambara Collection has a similar object (owned by Arita-cho, Fig.5 Arita-chô Kyôiku Iinkai 2008) and its total height is 78.9cm.

149 Object in the same group is an octagonal jar with a design of carp climbing up a waterfall and pine with bamboo in under-glaze cobalt blue in the Toguri Museum of Art (Fig.218, Toguri Museum of Art 1991. Height is 58.2cm) or Fig.5 in Ko-Imari Chôsa Iinkai 1959 (Height is 59.2cm).

150 The design of arabesque tied with a cord is close to the large jar decorated with a crane and pine tree motif in the Kyūshū Ceramic Museum (total height 68.5cm, Fig.150 & 151 in Ohashi 2011).

151 There is similar shape of ware with over-glaze polychrome enamels decoration in Portuguese (p.226 in Pinto 1996), also in European stoneware.

152 Similar piece was excavated at the Lop Buri Site. In addition, the Topkapi Palace Museum owns a cup and saucer (Fig.2208).

153 The same design but more loosely manufactured is found among artifacts from the Lop Buri Site.

154 This resembles to a cover of sugar container at the Topkapi Palace Museum (Fig.2977 ibid.). Dated to around 1700 to 1725.

155 Fig.100–513 looks close to Fig.2871 in the collection of the Topkapi Palace Museum, dated around 1710 to 1740.

156 There is a similar ware among the salvaged Vung Tau Cargo (Jörg & Flecker 2001) from which the design in the inner bottom appears fish jumping out of water, although it is more simply painted.

157 Combination of this kind of pattern with flowering plant motif is alike to the salvaged ceramics among the Vung Tau Cargo.

158 Similar decoration technique of outlining pressed lotus petal shape in under-glaze cobalt blue is also found in the salvaged Vung Tau Cargo. Lotus petal was replaced by linked turtle shell on the Vung Tau Cargo. This example may be a variation of linked turtle shell motif, although our example does not have the lower part.

159 This is similar to the dish in the Topkapi Palace Museum (Fig.2439).

160 This is a unique flower motif and the similar piece is housed in the Topkapi Palace Museum (Fig.2054).

161 A similar work is in the Topkapi Palace Museum (Fig.2203).

162 Same type of bowl was excavated at the Lop Buri Site, and there are also similar examples in Indonesia.

163 The original state was unknown because colours were exfoliated or discoloured. Fig.3313 at the Topkapi Palace Museum suggests that panels originally had a painting of flowering

plant in famille rose enamels. The Topkapi example is in iron brown glaze with gold. Similar piece was excavated at the Lop Buri.

164 No.2193 in the Topkapi Palace Museum is a similar object.

165 A cover with the same kind of design is owned by the Topkapi Palace Museum (Fig.2198).

166 A same type of bowl was found at the Lop Buri Site (Chandavij 1989).

167 There is a similar piece in the Vung Tau Cargo, which sunk in around 1690.

168 This type of colour glazed (*sancai*) ware is not found in Japan, but there is an example in the Natinoal Museum of Indonesia, Jakarta. Although it is not lobed, another example is introduced as a Vietnamese stoneware (Aichi-ken Toji Shiryokan 1987). Date is from the sixteenth to the seventeenth centuries, but judging from the technique, the eighteenth century is more likely. Vietnam has not been confirmed as a production site either, and we should like to consider the southern China as a possibility. A similar example is included in the salvaged cargo from the Cape of Ca Mau at the south point of Vietnam (Fig.145). It was accompanied with a Jingdezhen porcelain with a mark of Yongzheng.

169 In Japan, the similar object was excavated at the Iwashita Site in Nagasaki (Fig.31 & 32 in Nagasaki-ken Kyoiku-iinkai 1984) together with Hizen ceramics dated to the second half of the seventeenth to the beginning of the eighteenth centuries. The same kind was also included in the commercial salvaged 'the Naking cargo' (estimated from the Gerdermarsen, sunk in 1752), to be dated around 1750. Also it is found in the Old City of Fengshan.

170 In Japan, saucers with this kind of over-glaze polychrome enamels painting were excavated to some extent at the Hagi Castle Town Site, Yamaguchi (Fig.56, p.93 in Yamaguchi-ken Maizo-bunkazai Center 2002 is a base of polychorme enamels). Indonesia and Amsterdam, the Netherlands also have excavated examples (Fig.267-272 in Kyushu Ceramic Museum 2000). There are a number of heirlooms in Europe.

171 The same kind was unearthed at the Pasar Ikan Site (Fig.222 in Kyushu Ceramic Museum 1990), the Mr. and Mrs. Shindo Collection in Jakarta (Fig.53-56, Kyūshū Ceramic Museum 1990) as well as at the Dejima in Nagasaki, Japan. It is confirmed at the Hiekoba kiln Site in Arita (Fig.2-I-i in Ohashi 1995).

172 The Mr. and Mrs. Shindo Collection has a similar object.

173 The Topkapi Palace Museum owns a Jingdezhen version (No.2543).

174 This type of bowls is occasionally excavated in various places of Japan including Nagasaki.

175 Such unique shape with Cintamani shaped knob is popular in porcelain for Thailand. The Portuguese example is an over-glaze enamels ware, but has a cover of similar shape.

176 Similar ware was excavated at the Lop Buri Site (Chandavij 1989) and also among the belongings reportedly owned by Baisao, who died in 1763 (p.22 in Saga Kenritsu Hakubutsukan 1983). There are some excavated in Japan, for example Okinawa and Nagasaki.

177 Small cups and bowls with this design were unearthed relatively in big volume mainly in Okinawa and Nagasaki but also in other areas in Japan. The Hizen porcelain also introduced this design on its bowls and dishes, and the Seto-Mino region made under-glaze cobalt blue porcelain with this design in a great quantity in the nineteenth century.

178 Dish with a close look design is Fig.2595 at the Topkapi Palace Museum, which is dated to

around 1750 to 1770.

179 Similar shape in smaller size is Fig.2641 in the collection of the Topkapi Palace Museum, which is dated to around 1750 to 1780.

180 Another piece with resemblance was excavated at the Lop Buri and the Topkapi Palace Museum also has a similar piece (No.2394), dated to around 1720 to 1750.

181 While a large quantity was found in Okinawa, Japan, a small volume was also excavated in Nagasaki. There are many examples in Southeast Asia such as the Old City of Fengshan.

182 Both are found in Okinawa in quantity and also common in Southeast Asia. Fig.110-592 was unearthed at the Old City of Fengshan in Zuoying, Taiwan and No.2647 in the Topkapi Palace Museum.

183 This type was most excavated in Okinawa, Japan, but also occasionally found in other regions. The Old City of Fengshan in Zuoying is another place to have found a similar piece, which suggests many were distributed widely in Southeast Asia.

184 This kind of dish is found through excavation in Okinawa, Japan (Fig.26-13 in Okinawa Kenritsu Maizo-bunkazai Center 2001).

185 There is a similar in the Dehua ware (pp.88-97 in Xu 1990).

186 The Topkaki Palace Museum owns a similar work (Fig.2611). It is interesting to found such common ware found its way into the Topkapi.

187 Apart from Okinawa and Nagasaki, there is only a few excavated in Japan, but there are in a great volume in Southeast Asia such as the Old City of Fengshan in Zuoying. Also, found among the commercial salvaged 'Nankin cargo' (estimated cargo from the Gerdermarsen, sunk in 1752, Fig.88 in Jörg 1986) and it is dated to around 1750.

188 Although this kind of stoneware in green glaze had been excavated in Nagasaki, not many are known in Japan.

189 Similar pieces are included in the Vung Tau Cargo and artifacts found at the Old City of Fengshan in Zuoying. Also in Japan a heirloom object reportedly owned by Baisao (d.1763) exists.

190 It was found in Cape Town in South Africa apart from Japan. The Dutch power was over two places.

191 This is the first Hizen jar formed in this kind of patting method confirmed outside Japan, but since then another work was excavated in the Netherlands (unreported data, but the author observed in the Archaeological Service in Amsterdam).

192 Bowls with this kind of design are also occasionally found in Japan. Many were unearthed in Okinawa in particular (Fig. 28-31 in Okinawa Kenritsu Maizo-bunkazai Center 2001c, and Fig.29-25 in Okinawa-ken Kyoiku-iinkai 1999), and there is only a few at Banten Lama.

193 It is not common in Japan but quite a few were found in the Old City of of Fengshan in Zuoying, Hoi An and Lop Buri sites etc.

194 Okinawa and Nagasaki presented a small volume and examples were found also in the Lop Buri Site.

195 Similar work is in the group of finds at the Uwamachi Site, Nagasaki City (Nagamatsu 1993). It is thought a product of the Adams & Sons, England.

III. Chronology and special features of ceramics

We have been involved with classifying and analyzing a great many excavated ceramics data in Indonesia since 1989. The research started with the Banten Lama Site then Tirtayasa Site, Somba Opu Fort, Buton Wolio Fort and Trowulan Site in the order of research.

Important outcomes of our researches have been published accordingly. This publication divides the outcomes into 14 periods from I-1 to VII-2 and introduces them with additional commentaries consulting with types and production sites.

Looking this through, one can have a general view of trade ceramics at each period in Indonesia, except earthenware, but because it will cover such wider area, we are going to discuss the special features across the five sites below.

1. Rise and fall of the sites

The dates of trade ceramics will make us understood around when these sites came into existence, were active and declined.

1-1 Trowulan Site

Regarding the Trowulan Site, which prospered earliest among these five sites, we analyzed Chinese, Vietnamese and Thailand ceramics during the period of the Majapahit Kingdom and before. Excavated artifacts from this site also include ceramics from the post-Majapahit period, a small number of the late Ming Chinese ceramics (the second half of the sixteenth to the first half of seventeenth centuries), nine Hizen ware including porcelain covered box dated to the second half of the seventeenth century, and a small quantity of Chinese porcelain from the second half of the seventeenth to the eighteenth centuries. There were also the nineteenth century Chinese porcelain as well as Europeans. Life continued in this area after the kingdom disappeared, for which reason a small quantity of trade ceramics was still unearthed after the Majapahit period. However, excavation trend is significantly different compared to the kingdom period in terms of volume and quality. Because of this reason, ceramics from the later period is omitted in this publication except Hizen ware.

Quantity and volume of excavated Chinese, Vietnamese and Thailand ceramics focused on the period II (the late thirteenth to fourteenth centuries) and III (fifteenth to the beginning of sixteenth centuries). This supports the view that the Majapahit Kingdom prospered in the fourteenth and fifteenth centuries. It is a reasonable argument that the kingdom began in the late thirteenth century. Excavation of Chinese porcelain and Vietnamese under-glaze cobalt blue, albeit in small quantity, dated to the late fifteenth to the beginning of sixteenth centuries endorse the view that the kingdom fell in the beginning of the sixteenth century.

Through a comparison with the cargo salvaged from off Hoi An, a well-known shipwreck data of the second half of fifteenth to the beginning of sixteenth centuries [III-1], it was understood the Vietnamese ceramics which share similarities with the Hoi An Cargo are in the newest group of all the Vietnamese ceramics excavated from the Trowulan Site. Many other pieces are older. A bulbous/*Tian-qiu* 天球 bottle with a neck bearing a reign mark of 'Made in Đại Hòa 大和 8 (1450)' in the collection of the Topkapi Palace Museum in Turkey provides an important standard for dating Vietnamese ceramics, and the finds from the Trowulan are older than that. For under-glaze cobalt-blue ware, many appear to be dated to the first half of fifteenth century. Many of white porcelain, celadon, and iron-oxide painted wares can be dated to the fourteenth century. When it comes to the fifteenth century, Thailand celadon and stoneware decorated with iron-oxide painting increased in addition to Vietnamese under-glaze cobalt blue. Chinese Longquan celadon ware was also excavated in great quantity, but it is the special feature of the Trowulan Site that ceramics from Southeast Asia – under-glaze cobalt blue, celadon and iron-oxide decorated wares – also increased in the fifteenth century.

By studying within the duration of the Majapahit Kingdom, the trade ceramics dated to the end of the thirteenth to fourteenth centuries consist of high quality celadon basins, large bowls and bottles including Longquan celadon lead by *Jiuhai* 酒海 jars to no small extent. A great number of high quality Jingdezhen under-glaze cobalt blue large jars dated to the second half of fourteenth century (late Yuan and early Ming dynasties) are also found. Cizhou ware in turquoise blue glaze and large jar with under-glaze iron decoration also fell into the fourteenth century. Notable feature of the fourteenth century in comparison to the fifteenth is that Chinese high class large jars and bottles, ranging from celadon, under-glaze cobalt blue, copper brown, copper-red painting, white porcelain, turquoise blue glaze and iron-oxide decoration, are included in a great quantity. This feature continued until the reign of Emperor Hongwu of Ming dynasty (1368-98). Examples of prestigious bottles fired in the imperial kiln during the Ming dynasty after the Hongwu Emperor are bulbous/*Tian-qiu* bottle 天球瓶 or *Meiping* from the Emperor Youngle reign (1403-24). Officially fired under-glaze cobalt blue bowls had been also unearthed but they are also up to the Youngle reign period.

It is also noted that secondly burnt marks are visible in many of the under-glaze cobalt blue and other type of wares, that are dated to the second half of fourteenth to the beginning of fifteenth centuries, excavated from the Trowulan Site. This leads us to think a possibility of a great fire. A historical record mentions that the Hayam Wuruk King (ruled: 1350–89) was a wise ruler, but an internal conflict appeared to arise in the beginning of fifteenth century. Zheng He recorded strife between the kings of the east and the west when called at Java during his first voyage.

It was highly likely that the fire suggested from the remaining marks on the ceramics was caused by such strife. Fukami Sumio points out in his study [III-2] that when Zheng He stopped in Majapahit at his first voyage (1405-07), one hundred and seventy of his staffs were killed by the internal conflict. This record reveals that there were two palaces – east and west – in the capital and they caused the internal strife. Judging from the record, we can speculate that the palace(s) or prestigious ceramic storage was burnt down during this internal strife.

Fukami notes that the strife did not necessarily weaken the kingdom. He also accounts that the past historians misinterpreted historical documents and that China was receiving many tributary visits up to the 1450's. The Majapahit is written as *Zhaowa*/Java 爪哇 in Chinese and during the fifteenth century, Java sent tributary delegations to China 11 times in the 1400's, 7 times in the 1410's, 14 times in the 1420's, 7 times (actually it was 8 times) in the 1430's, 8 times in the 1440's, 3 times in the 1450's, twice in the 1460's, no visits in the 1470's and 80's, twice in the 1490's. This suggests that the Majapahit was continuing tributary trade with the Ming Dynasty until the first half of the 1450's. We can also see that such trade existed until the 1460's and there was a gap of more than twenty years when no trade was made in the second half of the fifteenth century. The Ryukyu Kingdom was also sending tributary delegations to China but they decreased the frequency in the 1440's. There is a view that a fall of delegations by the Majapahit after the 1450's was thus caused under the Ming's circumstance that they placed restrictions and were more reluctant to receive delegations owing to worsening financial situation.

However, Fukami accounts that it is natural to think the Majapahit itself must have some reasons for not sending delegations to the Ming for 30 years from 1465. He continues that the Malacca and the Ayutthaya were taking Majapahit's position in the second half of the fifteenth century, in particular after the 1460's. This may explain the reason why Vietnamese and Thailand ceramics are found in Laos [III-3], while they can be hardly seen in Indonesia, including Trowulan. Many Longquan celadon excavated at Trowulan Site demonstrate the tributary trade continued until before the 1460's. This is to say, the majority of celadon bowls and dishes date up to the middle of the fifteenth century, and on the contrary examples (of celadon) from the second half is a lot less. There are Jingdezhen under-glaze cobalt blue ware that can be dated to the beginning of the fifteenth century, as well as some salvaged objects from the Lena Cargo shipwreck dated to the late fifteenth to the early sixteenth centuries [III-4]. However, no obvious example between these periods has not been identified.

This volume of excavated Chinese celadon and under-glaze cobalt blue ware clearly follow the change in frequency of delegations. When we focus on the second half of the fifteenth century, Longquan celadon bowls and dishes from the Trowulan Site account for only less than 1% of the 1,120 units listed under the fifteenth century. Jingdezhen under-glaze cobalt blue ware porcelain accounts for about 44% of 263 units, but most of these are estimate to be from Hongzhi reign period (1488-1505).

1-2 Somba Opu Fort

We now move to the main palace of the Gowa Kingdom/Sultanate, the Somba Opu Fort. From the fact that a small quantity of the Jingdezhen ware in under-glaze cobalt blue ware, Thailand celadon and stoneware with iron-oxide painting dated to the first half of the fifteenth century, it is thought that the fort became king's residence from around this period. We see that the activities in the fort became active in the III-2 period (the second half of the fifteenth to early sixteenth century) because Jingdezhen porcelain increased, Vietnamese under-glaze cobalt blue ware and Thailand ceramics appeared. In the IV period (late fifteenth to sixteenth centuries) a great number of Jingdezhen porcelain was excavated, but Vietnamese and Thailand ware, those types found in Vientiane of Laos, almost disappeared. This might be considered because Vietnamese and Thailand ceramics stopped distributing in the islands of Indonesia in the sixteenth century after the Majapahit Kingdom disappeared. Further attention is needed on this point, whether Vietnamese and Thailand ceramics dated to after the sixteenth century would emerge in Indonesia.

More porcelain made in the Zhangzhou was excavated than Jingdezhen porcelain in V-1 period (first half of the seventeenth century).

During V-2 period (second half of the 17th century) some low-quality porcelain made in the southern Fujian province were found, but the volume of Hizen porcelain increased. Ikuta Shigeru argues that the Gowa Kingdom was founded by the Makassar people based in Gowa (Makassar) around 1530 [III-5]. However, by studying the excavated ceramics, it is possible that certain authority was already forming a stronghold in this region already in the fifteenth century. Volume of Chinese porcelain increased from the sixteenth century, because the Gowa Kingdom launched a trade and was pirating once they unified the peninsula, as Ikuta explained. After the seventeenth century set in, the Gowa Sultanate attacked the south coast of Kalimantan, Sumbawa Island and Lombok Island. In the seventeenth century, the English and the Danish East India Companies and France as well made inroads into the Gowa against the Dutch East India Company (VOC). According to Ikuta again, the VOC opened a trading post (in Gowa), but the Gowa Sultanate refused VOC's policy of monopolizing trade and they came to stand against each other.

When in 1641 the Dutch gained a control of Malacca, many of Portuguese living in Malacca moved to the Gowa where they began to base upon. VOC took an advantage of it when Arung Palakka, a leader of the Bugis people rebelled against the Sultan of Gowa in 1660. In 1666, the Dutch allied with the Bugis people to attack the Gowa and forced the Sultan Hasanuddin (ruled: 1653-69) to surrender after heated battle. Although Hasanuddin resisted, but was obliged to retire after all in 1669. The fort came into the possession of the VOC, and all European and Malay were forced out from the Gowa. Latest dated ceramics excavated from Somba Opu Fort are the Hizen porcelain from before and after the 1660s. This proves the history that the Sultanate of Gowa came to an end in 1669.

When the Banten Sultanate was fell by the Dutch attack in 1682, substantial volume of Jingdezhen porcelain dated to the 1670's to the 80's was brought in, as the Tirtayasa Site demonstrates. However, the Gowa Sultanate was destroyed by the Dutch before Chinese porcelain began to export in the 1670's to the early 80's, before the lifting of the Great Clearance issued in 1684. This can be the reason why the ceramics recovered from the Somba Opu Fort ends with Hizen porcelain.

1-3 Buton Wolio Fort

This section will discuss ceramics excavated at the Wolio Fort, the residential fort for sultans of the Buton Sultanate and located in the southeast part of Sulawesi. Buton was Islamized in 1540 and continued until the modern days as an Islamic nation ruled by sultan.

Many of the studied ceramics were dated to after the sixteenth century and this endorses the history of the sultanate after 1540. Also, included in those ceramics are a small amount of high quality Longquan celadon dated to the thirteenth to the first half of the fifteenth centuries (Fig.23-99 left) as well as Vietnamese under-glaze cobalt blue wares from the first half of the fifteenth century (Fig.27-150) which belongs to the period III-1.

What can we know from these high quality Longquan celadon made in the fourteenth century? The first written record of Buton appeared in *Nagarakertagama* (1365), the eulogy of Majapahit, written by a Buddhist court poet Prapanca under the reign of Hayam Wuruk of the Majapahit. Prapanca listed Buton as a territory along with Bantaen, Luwu, Talawud Islands, Makassar, Banggai and Selayar [III-6]. From this record, we can assume that Buton was within a political position to be able to reach to the Chinese porcelain.

However, no Jingdezhen under-glaze cobalt blue ware dated to the second half of the fifteenth century to the beginning of the sixteenth century have not been found at the Wolio Fort. During this period, the Gowa Kingdom in neighbour started to thrive and this type of porcelain was excavated at the Somba Opu Fort, a stronghold of the Gowa Kingdom. This suggests that the Gowa Kingdom flourished earlier than the Buton. Because ceramics with secure date to the second half of the fifteenth century were not found at the Wolio Fort, it is possible that distribution of Chinese ceramics had been interrupted under certain circumstances until the foundation of Islamic rule. Excavated Chinese porcelain supports a view that the Buton Kingdom was Islamized around 1540. From this point to modern day, the Sultanate of Buton had continued, even though, its detailed history is unknown because there are only a few records available on this sultanate. However, from the abundant of imported porcelain, we can see that the sultanate was at its highest power in the seventeenth and eighteenth centuries. Most of this rich Chinese porcelain in quality and quantity cannot be found in any archaeological sites of the Edo period in Japan, but they are most similar to the artifacts found at Banten Lama Site in Java. This is presumably because the Dutch East India Company brought Chinese porcelain to both sultanates.

Buton Wolio Fort: period II-2 (14th century)

A small quantity of Longquan celadon had been excavated. A fragment of either wine jar/*Jiu-hai* Jar or large bottle in celadon glaze (Fig.23-99 left) is decorated with ribbed lotus flower petals carved on the exterior. Fig.23-99 on the right is a fragment of Cizhou ware jar decorated with an iron-oxide painting. This appears to be the same kind of Fig.6–56 that was excavated at Trowulan Site. Dated to the fourteenth century, both are the luxury items and a symbol of prestige in comparison to ordinary trade ceramics such as bowls and dishes.

As these examples demonstrate, import ceramics of this period are rather unique and different from bowls and dishes of later period. As introduced earlier, the Buton was first recorded in the *Nagarakertagama* written under the reign of Hayam Wuruk King of Java as being a territory of the Majapahit Kingdom. While high quality celadon ware and the Cizhou ware with iron-oxide painting dated to the second half of the fourteenth to the beginning of the fifteenth centuries were found in the Buton, there is no example of Chinese ceramics dated afterwards. Also in Trowulan Site of the Majapahit Kingdom good quality Chinese porcelain dated up to the beginning of the fifteenth century were found, but no later examples of such porcelain were identified. Are these two phenomena related each other?

In Trowulan Site, unique Vietnamese ceramics including ceramic tiles replaced Chinese porcelain, but this is not the case for the Buton. This says, disappearing of prestigious Chinese ceramics in the fifteenth century in both Buton and Trowulan may be resulted from circumstances in China.

Buton Wolio Fort: period IV (from the end of 15th century to the beginning of the 17th century)

Under-glaze cobalt blue bowls and dishes from Jingdezhen are the main finds from the period IV-1 (the first half of the sixteenth century). Some wares with over-glaze polychrome enamels decoration are also found.

Jingdezhen bowls and dishes in under-glaze cobalt blue continued to be the major objects into the period IV-2 (second half of the sixteenth century), and a few under-glaze cobalt blue ware from Zhangzhou, Fujian started to appear.

Jar with ears in black glaze made in Thailand was also excavated.

In addition to these widely distributed ceramics, some are given special prestigious roles, for example a jar in colour glaze within raised outlines/Fahua (Fig.35–194). This is a fragment of shoulder and judging from its characteristic red base, it is highly likely fired in northern China, possibly Shanxi province. Much is still unknown about the production site of ceramics glazed in Fahua. This fragment has a design of flower bunch within the frame in the shape of *Ru-i* head. Jewel string design fills the space between *Ru-i* heads frames. As far as my personal view goes, similar combination of *Ru-i* head pattern and jewel string design usually appear to decorate bottles. There is one example of a jar with the similar design in the collection of the National Museum of Indonesia, Jakarta. This jar has a narrow mouth and was found in the Eastern Kalimantan [III-7]. But the jewel string design on this jar is a lot simpler. It is speculated that this fragment came from a jar with wide mouth also judging from the condition of interior. In any case, design composition of this jar is a superior standard for this type of Fahua ceramics even comparing with heirloom examples. This leads us to think that this jar was fired sometime in the fifteenth and sixteenth centuries when the Fahua technique reached at its height.

In addition, Thailand, Myanmar and Chinese wares were also excavated at Buton Wolio Fort.

Buton Wolio Fort: period V-1 (around the first half of the 17th century)

The volume of excavated ceramics increased. In particular the Jingdezhen and Zhangzhou porcelain were unearthed in great quantity. Rich varieties of wares were found, not only bowls and dishes but also large dishes, small bowls, covered boxes and bottles. White porcelain bowls and dishes (Fig.51-263, 264), as well as covered boxes fired at the Dehua kilns and the Anping jars from Fujian province were also included. Also excavated were, although only one example each, a Hizen ware sauce dish decorated in under-glaze cobalt blue and a Delft albarello jar in white glaze. The Hizen ware sauce dish is not for an export market, and this is the second example confirmed outside Japan after one excavated at Banten Lama Site (Fig.56-289).

Three-coloured (*sancai*) jar, called the Tradescant jar, should rather be included in the period IV (the sixteenth century). It was made in the southern China.

For the sixteenth to the seventeenth centuries, iron-brown glazed jars from the southern China and high fired, unglazed pottery jars from Thailand are the general type of ceramics excavated at Banten Lama. Although precise date is unknown, it is highly possible that they were made around the late Ming period.

Another example is a high fired unglazed pottery jars produced at the Sing Buri kilns, Thailand. An example excavated at an archaeological site in Sakai, Osaka contained sulfur inside. The Sing Buri ware were thickly made, and thought to have widely distributed during the second half of the sixteenth to the seventeenth centuries as a gunpowder container such as potassium nitrate and sulfur [III-8].

Some of the examples of Myanmar stoneware are the fragments of a large dish in milky glaze, as well as fragments of a large jar with white decoration in black glaze. There are only a limited number of excavated Myanmar stoneware both in Indonesia and Japan. The former was found in a small quantity in Hirado and Nagasaki, Japan. The latter has recently been excavated in the Funai-cho, a medieval time territory of the Otomo Lord in Oita prefecture.

There is one Hizen stoneware dish in green glaze, which is undoubtedly dated to the middle of the seventeenth century. This dish was fired using sand spurs and is older than a large two-coloured dish of the second half of the seventeenth century often found in Indonesia and Southeast Asia. A small quantity of Hizen ware from the same period had been excavated in Banten Lama. Largest volume of artifacts was from the seventeenth century, followed by the eighteenth century.

Buton Wolio Fort: period V-2 (around the second half of the 17th century)

This period saw a plunge of the Jingdezhen and Zhangzhou porcelain. The Hizen porcelain took their place were excavated in a great number. Because, this owes to the fact that the export of Chinese porcelain dramatically decreased by the civil war after

1644 and consequently finds of Chinese porcelain sharply fell until the 1670s.

Zheng Chenggong/Koxinga and his fellows were actively involved with trade, while resisting against the Qing dynasty. Under such circumstances, considerable amount of inferior ceramics fired in Fujian and Guangdong, which would have had close ties with Zheng Chenggong, were unearthed. (Fig.66-338 etc.) These types of under-glaze cobalt blue are usually not found in Japan, and were perhaps traded illegally.

The majority of Hizen porcelain belong to this period were made after the 1660s. Low quality ceramics from the Yoshida kiln, Ureshino and others were seen at Banten Lama and Pasar Ikan Sites (Jakarta). However, such ceramics cannot be found at Wolio Fort. Only a few of inferior quality with estimated date of the 1650s have been found here, for example the upper left of Fig.68-346. Therefore, there is no large dish in over-glaze enamels decoration from the 1650s, which was found at Banten Lama Site. Large dish in celadon glaze fired in Arita outnumber those made in Hasami, Nagasaki Prefecture. Most of the Hizen ware appears to come from the Arita kilns. This is to say that many are luxury items. The quality is similar to that of Tirtayasa Site [III-9] in that point.

However, referring to the Hizen porcelain, a dish with a design of five-petals flower or similar dated to the end of 1670s - the beginnig of 80s (Fig.90-464) had not been found at Wolio Fort, although it was excavated at Tirtayasa. A bowl from earlier period (Fig.68-344, lower right) has finer and clearer design compared to the example decorated with the similar design of carp jumping out of water in the inner bottom from Tirtayasa (Fig.87-448). Because of this reason, the Wolio bowl is older type than Tirtayasa's. Many the Arita large jars and bottles dated to the first half of the eighteenth century were excavated at Wolio Fort during the following period (VI-1), and the situation is slightly different from Banten Lama, where tableware continued to be the main objects. This is to say that at Wolio Fort, many of the Arita porcelain were made from the 1660s - 1670s and Chinese porcelain increased from the 1680s. The Arita porcelain dated to the 1680s to 1690s are hardly seen now, except one example of Fig.69-347 lower left. Then suddenly more than 90 units of large jars and large bottles from the first quarter of the eighteenth century came to appear. Apart from the large jars and bottles, there is a large dish with under-glaze cobalt blue decoration (Fig.96-483), but this could be prestigious goods, therefore it was possibly presented by the Dutch and not acquired through general distribution. Tableware of this period had been replaced by the Jingdezhen and Fujian ware (porcelain).

Buton Wolio Fort: period VI (around the 18th century)

The Jingdezhen porcelain were excavated in great volume again in the period VI-1. This can be explained by the fact that export of Chinese porcelain recommenced upon, the travel and trade permission decree was issued in China in 1684. The Jingdezhen ware found from this period is expectedly dated to the 1680s to the first half of the eighteenth century. Most various kinds and types of porcelain were excavated in this period throughout the duration of this site. Large jars are prominent among the finds.

The Hizen porcelain, which came in second in terms of quantity, are mostly for the European market in comparison to the period V-2. Ninety out of 111 the Hizen porcelain are large jars and large bottles. After the 1690s into the first half of the eighteenth century, large jars were fired in Arita. They were over 50 cm in height, and accompanied flower vases as a set piece. Following explanation might be a possible reason why orders of those five-piece set of jars and vases started to come in Arita.

The official export of Japanese porcelain by the Dutch declined following the Nagasaki trade amount restrictions decree, issued by the Tokugawa Shogunate (Bakufu) in 1685. Dealing amount of the private trade was also fixed, but the Dutch was mainly exporting the porcelain through this private trade. Because the Bakufu imposed a restriction on trade amount to the Dutch East India Company (VOC), it had to concentrate on exporting highly profitable goods, leaving goods with low profit rate to the private trades [III-10].

Until then, VOC tended to limit the private trading as an official notice in 1667 stated "the private trading is permitted only when there is an extra room in a ship. Shipping charges and taxes must be paid at least 20% and maximum 30% according to the freight volume" [III-11]. They became less conscious of volume because an amount of trade for the private trades was fixed in 1685, which may have contributed to increase of the private trades.

Exporting the five-piece set of large jars and vases would have probably started around this time, entwined with demands from the European market. That a set of jars and vases were exported privately is demonstrated by the figures; 2,256 jars and 1,286 vases, 9,619 jars and 4,076 vases, and 2,180 jars and 1,490 vases were exported in 1709, 1711 and 1712 respectively. As we can see from these figures, jars always outnumbered vases and in 1709 and 1712, jars and vases are in a ration of three to two. This is the same ratio of the five-piece set and we can assume that many of the jars and vases recorded in this document was acquired to be sold as a five-piece set.

The private trade was growing to an extent that in 1696 the Bakufu even built two dedicated warehouses in Dejima. It is estimated that the private trade was thriving until 1723, and these periods just includes dates when the Augustus II the Strong Great of Dresden was enthusiastically collecting the Japanese porcelain. We can sum up the reasons for new demands of a five-piece set of large jars and vases for export; while porcelain export was shifting to the private trade after the Nagasaki trade amount restriction decree in 1685, the VOC began to accept orders of large items; demand for decorative larger porcelain increased in Europe under the Orientalism. Size was getting larger and larger under such circumstances [III-12].

In addition to large jars and vases, there are a few large plates and cups with saucers for the European market (for coffee and tee). For Chinese, low-quality porcelain in under-glaze cobalt blue decoration from Fujian and Guangdong were found in large quantities, in particular under-glaze cobalt blue with stamped decoration was unique to this period.

The Hizen porcelain disappeared in the period VI-2 except one example. Jingdezhen porcelain also decreased while cheaper ware, for example bowls from Fujian and Guangdong or the Dehua small bowls (Fig.107-565/569) made in mold, were excavated in great amount. This is to say that high-quality porcelain for the European market was rare now.

Buton Wolio Fort: period VII (the 19th century)

The period VII saw further decrease of excavated volume of porcelain. However, a small volume was still unearthed in comparison to the situation at Banten Lama that was destroyed by the Dutch in 1809. Sharp drop at Buton Wolio could be caused by a halt of the Dutch ceramic trade resulting from dissolution of the VOC in 1799.

The second half of the nineteenth century is a period when the Chinese porcelain plunged and the European ceramics were growing instead. Obviously identified the Chinese porcelain had disappeared among the finds at Wolio Fort. The European stoneware and the Hizen bowls with stencil print designs in under-glaze cobalt blue were found in small quantity to replace the Chinese. This is also a period when excavated ceramics dramatically dropped in volume as a whole.

As we have seen, significant volume of excavated ceramics at the Wolio Fort centred around the seventeenth to eighteenth centuries. Its rich variety makes them similar to those found at Banten Lama, although the latter presented richer varieties.

It is highly suggested that many ceramics were dated to the seventeenth to eighteenth centuries because they, and in particular Jingdezhen and Arita, were brought in by the VOC during its very active trading period. The Wolio Fort and Somba Opu Fort were both located in Sulawesi, but ceramics can tell us their different histories.

1-4 Banten Lama Site

Ceramics predate the fifteenth century were hardly found. If there were, they were Chinese, Thailand and Vietnamese.

Banten Lama: period IV & V-1 (from around the 16th to the first half of the 17th century)

Only a small quantity of the Jingdezhen porcelain was found in the period IV-1, and it accounts for only 1% of the entire volume. Ceramics dated to the period V-1 (the second half of the sixteenth to the first half of the seventeenth centuries) to VI (the eighteenth century) account for 89% of all and these figures endorse the history of the Banten Sultanate. Chinese porcelain dated after the 1590s stands out in the period V-1. The Jingdezhen occupies 35% but in addition, the Zhangzhou ware (southern Fujian province) joined and accounts for 45% of the entire finds. This was the time when the England entered into trading in Asia following the Dutch. The Jingdezhen and Zhangzhou porcelain are different in quality, former the high and latter the poor. Such different quality would have presented different price. Those who could not afford expensive Jingdezhen under-glaze cobalt blue would have bought cheaper porcelain from Fujian province, and created more demands for under-glaze cobalt-blue porcelain. Bowls, small dishes, and inferior quality middle and large size dishes from Zhangzhou were fairly equally distributed both in Southeast Asia and Japan. On the other hand, only a few the Kraak style large dishes, large bowls and bottles that were fired in great quantity at Jingdezhen for the European markets were found in the Southeast Asia compared to Europe.

Banten Lama: period V-2 (second half of the 17th to the early 18th centuries

As many as 1,017 Japanese Hizen porcelain were found in this period and this largely owed to the Chinese civil war caused by a political shift from the Ming to the Qing dynasties after 1644. The Qing Dynasty banned foreign trade in order to block the Zheng Chenggong/Koxinga family's activities at sea. This blockade continued until the Zheng family surrendered in 1683. During these periods, the Hizen porcelain was exported to Europe via Southeast Asia in place of the Chinese porcelain. This is not to say that export of Chinese ware completely stopped from 1644 to 1684, but regional porcelain such as the Guangdong ware along with a small number of Jingdezhen by was distributed in Southeast Asia by the illegal trade. However, it is very difficult to identify and select pre-1684 ceramics among the Kangxi style at this stage. For this reason, we included any Kangxi style porcelain in this period and this resulted in a high proportion of the Chinese porcelain.

True picture is that there were less the Chinese porcelain than the Hizen porcelain before 1684, in particular before the 1670s. The majority representing this period at Somba Opu Fort in the Gowa Sultanate, which fell in 1669, was the Hizen porcelain. Tirtayasa Site, which eliminated in 1682, began to acquire many the Chinese porcelain from around the 1670s but the Hizen porcelain still outnumbered the Chinese. This makes us to think that the export of the Chinese porcelain recommenced almost immediately after the travel and trade permission decree was announced.

Main salvaged cargo from the *Oosterland*, the Dutch ship, which shipwrecked at Cape Town in 1697 was the Chinese Jingdezhen porcelain and there was only a small volume of Arita. The salvaged cargo from the Vung Tau that was navigating around 1690s [III-13] could be similarly good material to understand the situation after the Chinese porcelain export started again. When we look at the material from 1684 to the early eighteenth century from Banten Lama Site, there is an increase of the Jingdezhen porcelain for the European market. The same can be said to the Hizen porcelain.

What this means is that Jingdezhen and Hizen were no longer for the Southeast Asian market. This market was taken over by the Fujian and Guangdong provinces. Instead, Jingdezhen and Arita shifted to Europe and many of such wares (the Jingdezhen and Arita porcelains for European market) was excavated in Banten Lama.

Banten Lama: period VI (the 18th century)

Proportion of the Hizen porcelain of this period significantly decreased to 3%, although it still maintained a considerable volume during the period VI-1 (first half of the eighteenth century). Characteristically the Hizen porcelain for the Southeast Asian market is no longer included and instead those for Europe seem to be transported by the Dutch vessels. The Jingdezhen porcelain is also under the same circumstances.

For example, a bowl and cover in the Chinese Imari style with over-glaze polychrome enamels decoration (Fig.100–509, 510), which was thought to be made for Europe to compete with Arita, can only be found at the sites in Asia, close association with the Dutch such as Buton Wolio Fort as another example (Fig.93–476). As unique products of Jingdezhen, there is a stemmed bowl differently glazed in brown and transparency with an under-glaze cobalt blue decoration (Fig.99–498), as well as a cup and saucer with over-glaze polychrome enamels decoration in brown glaze. There are also many examples of polychrome enamel decoration in a transparent glaze section over brown ground. They are called the Batavian ware in Europe and widely found in Europe. The Topkapi Palace Museum in Turkey also owns a number of examples. Many of the Batavian ware was made in the late seventeenth to the eighteenth centuries and some were excavated also at Buton Wolio Fort (Fig.94–478, 479). On the other hand, set-pieces of jars and flower vases in large and small sizes made in Arita and Jingdezhen for Europe during this period were hardly found at Banten Lama, although they were found at Buton Wolio Fort. Like in Japan, there seemed no custom to decorate walls with porcelain in Banten Lama. This seems to reflect a difference with European architectural structure, which usually have higher ceilings.

Fujian and Guangdong continued to export porcelain to the Southeast Asia and they accounted for 36% of the entire finds at this site of this period. The nucleus is porcelain produced in the southern Fujian, in particular the Dehua kilns. Distinctive products of the Dehua kiln are bowls and dishes formed in hump mold with unglazed rim (Fig.110–591/ 593, 600). They come in different glaze and decorations – under-glaze cobalt blue, white glaze, over-glaze enamels paintings, brown glaze, blue glaze, etc. They must have been produced in mass and cheaply available. These wares were widely distributed from the Southeast Asia, Taiwan and Japan, where significant volume of such the Dehua ware was excavated in Okinawa and Nagasaki. Until the period V-2, the Fujian and Guangdong porcelain usually had pale brown or grey tint caused by inferior base and incomplete firing. However, their bodies became white even to compete with Jingdezhen in the period VI and in particular after the middle of the eighteenth century.

Banten Lama: period VII (late 18th to the 19th century)

This is the final period of Banten Lama and the palace was destroyed by the Dutch. Thus, the excavated material dated to this period accounted for only 9% of the entire artifacts at the same site. There were few the Jingdezhen porcelain and the Fujian and Guangdong types porcelain occupied, but we need to pay attention that the European tableware (stoneware) became the main objects in the second half of the nineteenth century. Because this tendency was observed also in Buton and Trowulan not only in Banten Lama, it appears that many the European stoneware flew in entire parts of Indonesia.

1-5 Tirtayasa Site

Through a study of the ceramics excavated at the Tirtayasa Site, we learn that the majority of porcelain is dated to the second half of the seventeenth century (period V-2) with a little mixture of older porcelain from the final Ming period. There is also a very small quantity of porcelain made after the eighteenth century, but they are of low quality and should be considered as everyday goods belonged to the following generations who had nothing to do with the royal villa life. Looking at the porcelain dated to the second half of the seventeenth century by production sites, the majority is the Hizen and the Jingdezhen wares, with a very few the Fujian and Guangdong. Vietnamese bowls with stamped patterns are equally insignificant in number. At Banten Lama, Fujian and Guangdong porcelain occupied higher ratio under this period [III-14]. Such difference can be explained by the reasons that Banten Lama lasted longer and relatively different class of people lived in the royal villa. It may be telling us that because Tirtayasa existed only for a short time, main inhabitants were the sultan and his people. This indicates while the Jingdezhen and Hizen porcelain were valued at the time, those from Fujian and Guangdong, as well as the Vietnamese bowls with iron painting were low quality – in different words, cheap – and had a different market.

Production date of the Hizen porcelain mostly falls into the 1660s to 1680s. Among them, dishes with five-petal flower decoration could be of the late 1670s earliest, and highly likely in the 1680s. The date close to December 1682, when the Tirtayasa Villa was attacked by the Dutch, is speculated. Regarding Chinese Jingdezhen, the majority is made during the Kangxi reign period and before recommencing of full-scale export in 1684.

The dish with under-glaze cobalt blue design of paulownia leaf and poem (Fig.84-438) could be dated as early as the 1660s–70s considering that the similar examples from the Fujian and Guangdong kilns are given year mark of 1675, 1679 and 1680 [III-15]. This period coincides with the time when the Qing Dynasty banned trades by issuing a decree in 1661. Because the Chinese porcelain hardly made way to Japan and there seemed only a few exported, it had been hard to identify porcelain that is certainly dated to this period.

Regarding the Hizen porcelain, main production site is Arita, Saga Prefecture, but there are also celadon dishes from Hasami, Nagasaki Prefecture.

Many porcelain products from the 1660s to 1680s, in particular bowls and dishes are decorated with the same and made in the same shape. This is true to both Hizen and Chinese and they were likely owned in a set as tableware.

The Hizen porcelain is divided into two categories, those intended for export and others for domestic market. This is also the case at Banten Lama and the Pasar Ikan Sites [III-16] and can be a unique feature of the Hizen porcelain of the second half of the seventeenth century. We learn from this fact that whoever it was – the Chinese or Dutch – not only made to order porcelain for export, but also selected and exported suitable ones among the Arita products originally intended for domestic distribution. This phenomenon stopped, however, after the Chinese procelain began to be exported again in full-scale as a result of the decree in 1684 after which Hizen (Arita) lost its tableware market over Jingdezhen.

We can also take it into consideration that the Tirtayasa Villa was owned by the Tirtayasa Great Sultan, who resisted to the Dutch. It is quite possible that the Chinese vessels transported ceramics rather than the Dutch. Therefore, there might be just a few export porcelain ordered by the Dutch for the European market and more the Hizen porcelain for Japanese domestic market.

In any case, ceramics data from this site play an important role in dating the Tirtayasa Villa, and at the same time provide valuable information to explain the real picture of ceramic trading in Southeast Asia in the seventeenth century.

2. Essential aspects of the trade ceramics excavated in Indonesia

We are now going to discuss special features of contents of ceramics excavated in Indonesia.

We start with the points worth attention in regard to the Chinese ceramics.

2-1 Ceramics from Trowulan Site

A special feature observed at Trowulan Site is that not a small number of Chinese ceramics pre-date an establishment of the Majapahit Kingdom.

Earlier examples include a bowl in celadon glaze, the Yuezhou ware bowls and a Changsha ware dish (Fig.1-11) dated to the ninth to tenth centuries. Another example (Fig.1-1) might be even earlier. There is a document recording *Heling* in Java made a first formal visit to China in 640. It is also recorded that the Southeast Asian islands intermittently sent tributes to the Sui and the Tang Dynasties. We need to examine the possibilities in relation to these records. The *San-fo-chi*/Shrivijaya began to present a tribute to the Song Dynasty (960-1279). In the eastern Java Sindok (ruled: 927-947), an influential person in the former the Mataram Kingdom came to the throne, and Airlangga King founded the Kediri Kingdom in the early eleventh century. The Yuezhou celadon ware of this period represents not only bowls but also rare jar with ears (Fig.1-05, 06). In addition, there is white porcelain (Fig.1-07/10). They prove that the trade with China was beginning to grow and also that objects to show one's prestige started to come in. These porcelains also inform us that the region exercised political and financial power to a certain degree already before the establishment of the Majapahit Kingdom.

Fig.6-52 is fragment of an under-glaze red and blue covered jar, excavated at Trowulan Site.

Similar fragments were found in the past as a pair in Baoding, Hebei province, China with at the Olon Sum Site in Mongol, and that's all. It is important that they were found not in China but in Indonesia across the ocean. Many variety kinds of fourteenth century under-glaze cobalt blue wares in the Yuan style were found. Examples include rough quality bowls and small bottles (Fig.5-39, 40) as well as a number of large bowls, dishes and basins (Fig.5-43) in large size. In addition, there are high-level porcelain with under-glaze copper red painting (Fig.6-53) and in white glaze. There is no other example of a single site known in the world with ceramics in such rich variety. This period coincides with the time when the Prime Minister Gajah Mada (d: 1364) was in charge.

Along with a number of white porcelain large bowls and dishes in the Shu-fu style (Fig.3-23, 24 & Fig.5-36, 37), a bowl decorated with a green painting on the similar white porcelain base (Fig.11-108) was found at Trowulan Site.

Under-glaze cobalt blue with over-glaze polychrome enamels decoration (*doucai*) is famous among the Jingdezhen porcelain, and such *doucai* ware was excavated at the imperial kiln site from the Chenghua reign period (1464-87) in Zushan, Jingdezhen [III-17]. However, other over-glaze enamels decorated ware (*wucai*) dated to the first half of the fifteenth century has not been found. There is another example decorated in just green enamel only, which is a bowl with a dragon design bearing a year mark of 'Made in Great Ming Hongzhi reign period' (1488-1505) [III-18]. Published commentary on this bowl notes, that "there seems another one with year mark of Chenghua reign period". But the item from Trowulan in mention here is different from those in imperial kiln quality and no other similar piece has been identified. This can be an important data when considering of the beginning of *wucai* technique in Jingdezhen.

2-2 Ceramic slabs with iron-oxide paintings from Trowulan Site

We analysed the ceramics tiles with iron paintings and identified them to the Cizhou ware, although they had been long identified as the Vietnamese.

During the first survey to sort out the artifacts in January 2012, we noticed that these ceramic slabs were fired at the Cizhou kiln in China, because their patters were markedly different from those found in the Vietnamese under-glaze cobalt blue, but more close to the Cizhou ware jars, bottles and others. We needed to be cautious if no other type of the Cizhou ware had been excavated at this site, but learned at the second survey that some jars and bowls with iron-oxide decoration and in turquoise blue glaze had been unearthed. They were dated to the fourteenth century, and the iron-oxide painted ceramic slabs are also estimated to have the same date judging from the pattern. Most of the Vietnamese under-glaze cobalt blue ceramic slabs are dated to around the first half of the fifteenth century, a different date for the Trowulan slabs. Focusing on the shape, iron-oxide decorated ceramic slabs are in square and closer to the Chinese square tiles. On the other hand, many of the Vietnamese under-glaze cobalt blue ceramic slabs take more complicated shapes, and look very different from the Chinese tiles. There are only a few examples of the fourteenth to fifteenth century ceramic tiles left today, except two Jingdezhen porcelain pieces with under-glaze cobalt blue decoration, which are in the collection of the British Museum [III-19].

These two tiles have the same patterns and in square shape demonstrating difference from multifarious shape of Vietnamese under-glaze cobalt blue ceramic slabs. The British Museum tiles follow most general shape for the East Asian tiles and thought to be made during the first half of the fifteenth century. They are decorated with an under-glaze cobalt blue design in graduated shading. Similar representation of design is also observed in the Vietnamese under-glaze cobalt blue ceramic slabs, which also have similar patterns with the Jingdezhen ceramic tiles. This makes us to think that some of the Vietnamese ceramic slabs were influenced by the early fifteenth century Jingdezhen tiles. This is to say, diverse the Vietnamese under-glaze cobalt blue ceramic slabs made in the first half of the fifteenth century were made to order on the fourteenth century the Cizhou ceramic slabs with iron-oxide decoration as samples. Its patterns were modeled after the Jingdezhen under-glaze cobalt blue porcelain or ceramic tiles, and shapes followed the local architectural ornamentation.

It is highly speculated that the loss of the royal palace by fire caused by the civil war in the Majapahit in the early fifteenth century contributed to the orders of the Vietnamese under-glaze cobalt blue ceramic slabs.

The Vietnamese ceramic slabs are rarely excavated, and also I have no other information of the Cizhou tiles than Trowulan Site. Meanwhile a small quantity of the Islamic stoneware tiles with blue decoration in white glaze (Fig.10-93/95) as well as stoneware tiles in blue glaze (Fig.10-96/98) were excavated at this site. There are the previous examples of the Islamic stoneware tiles dated to before the fourteenth century. They might have been transported by Muslim merchants who were leading the trades during the thirteenth to the fourteenth centuries in period of the Mongol Empire. Excavated Islamic tiles are divided into two types. One type is with frames around the edge, and this type is also found in the Vietnamese under-glaze cobalt blue ceramic slabs. Another type is square and simply coloured in blue glaze. How exactly these two different types were used is still unknown, but in the Middle and Near East there is an example of arranging blue glazed tiles between tiles with cobalt-blue decoration. This would be a subject of future research, but such arrangement might have given a reference for the Majapahit when ordering the Cizhou tiles in the fourteenth century. Fig.7-58/63 are slabs with frames decorated with iron-oxide paintings, and Fig.7-64/67 are the tiles in iron glaze. Both slabs and titles were building materials, but they were likely used for different purposes. Tiles would have covered floors but examples from the Middle and Near East suggests a possibility of slabs and tiles decorating walls together [III-20]. Ceramic slabs were glazed also on sides, therefore they could have faced walls just as seen in the Great Mosque of Demak. These two categories – slabs and tiles – follow the estimates that there were two types of stoneware as Cizhou and Islam.

While the Cizhou ceramic slabs with iron-oxide paining are square in principle, the Vietnamese ceramic slabs dated to the first half of the fifteenth century come in various shapes. The latter was presumably ordered to replace the Cizhou ceramic slabs during the period III-1 (first half of the fifteenth century). Reasons behind this are not explained yet, but Trowulan Site also saw an increase of the Vietnamese under-glaze cobalt blue in this period, and there are richer varieties of shape. The artifacts reveal that ceramic slabs with over-glaze polychrome enamels decoration joined in the fifteenth century

(Fig.15-137). Judging from the patterns, the core of these slabs can be dated to the first half of the fifteenth century, or middle of the fifteenth century at the latest, and they are estimated to have brought in Trowulan sometime before the construction of the Great Mosque of Demak in the second half of the fifteenth century (there are four different views regarding the construction date between 1466 to 1506). However, because 'Demak was the only sultan ruled vassal within the Majapahit Kingdom already in the second half of the fourteenth century' [III-21], Muslim traders could be involved. We can imagine that the Islamic slabs and tiles were imported, consumed and developed in the Majapahit Kingdom.

Taking it into an account that the dynasty ended in 1478 under the reign of Brawijaya V (ruled: 1466-1478), the father of Raden Patah who built the Great Mosque of Demak, it seems appropriate that the order of the Vietnamese under-glaze cobalt blue ceramic slabs terminated in the middle of the fifteenth century. On the point that the Vietnamese under-glaze cobalt blue ceramic slabs (Mayuyama called them ceramic tiles) were limited to the northern and eastern Java, Mayuyama indicated an exchange between the Majapahit and the Champa Kingdom with particularly close relationships during the reigns of King Kertawijaya (ruled 1447-51), the seventh king of the Majapahit who married to Muslim Darawati of Champa, and of Brawijaya V, the last king of the Majapahit Kingdom. It has to be mentioned, though, the Vietnamese under-glaze cobalt blue ceramic slabs are in great variety and some could be dated slightly earlier. The middle of the fifteenth century is the latest production dates we could assume.

After the Majapahit Kingdom fell, Raden Patah built up national prosperity as the sultan of Demak and constructed the Great Mosque of Demak. He took and transported some of the building materials from the former palace of Majapahit. This explains why the Vietnamese under-glaze cobalt blue ceramic slabs that resembled to those found at Trowulan Site were used in the Great Mosque. It is natural that the older, fourteenth century the Islamic ceramic slabs or the Cizhou ceramic slabs with iron-oxide decoration cannot be found in the Great Mosque of Demak, because they would have been highly likely disappeared from the palace of Majapahit already in the fifteenth century. But there is an earlier mentioned example of the Minaret Mosque in Kudus, northeast of Demak whose gate is decorated with a ceramic slab with iron-oxide decoration possibly from Cizhou [III-22]. It is in oblong shape and different from the more complex and varied shape of the Vietnamese under-glaze cobalt blue slab.

Some of the variegated Vietnamese ceramic slabs share special decorative features such as gradual filling and patterns with the Jingdezhen under-glaze cobalt blue tiles dated to the first half of the fifteenth century (in the collection of the British Museum). For example, Fig.51-262 in the Sakai & Ohashi 2014 and Fig.15-135 in this publication also demonstrates gradual filling in the floral arabesque pattern [III-23]. They are more similar to the designs of the Jingdezhen under-glaze cobalt blue tiles, while the pattern of Fig.15-136 is closer to decorations in Vietnamese under-glaze cobalt blue large dish.

2-3 The transitional period after the fifteenth century

At Trowulan Site, no the imperial kiln quality was found among the Chinese porcelains produced after the Yongle reign period (1403-24). Chinese view on the position of Indonesia might have shifted. This period rather gave a higher weight to the Vietnamese and the Thailand ceramics. The Vietnamese ceramics was distributed to some extent in Trowulan in the fourteenth century, but their significant period was the fifteenth century. The Thailand ceramics joined in the distribution in the first half of the fifteenth century. However, the sixteenth century had a different picture. The Vietnamese large dishes of under-glaze cobalt blue and over-glaze polychrome enamels decoration were not found at the Somba Opu Fort nor Buton Wolio Fort during the sixteenth century, while many of them were found in Laos. Similarly, only a few Thailand ceramics with iron-oxide painting were found at Banten Lama, although there are many left in Laos. We learn from this situation that different ceramic distribution was working in the Southeast Asia between the fifteenth and sixteenth centuries. The situation of Laos could fit in its history that their national power was growing in the sixteenth century. High-fired unglazed jar from Sing Buri, Thailand and tin glazed large stoneware dish fired in Myanmar, both dated to the second half of the sixteenth century were excavated at Banten Lama. Because these two types of wares are not familiar at the other archaeological sites, they may suggest Banten's relationship with its trading partners, when it was beginning to flourish as an Islamic nation in the Western Java. These two types of ware have been unearthed in Japan as well, although in a small quantity.

Focusing on the sixteenth century, bowls and large bowls in under-glaze cobalt blue and over-glaze polychrome enamels decorations fired in Jingdezhen were found at Somba Opu Fort in Gowa, Sulawesi as well as at Wolio Fort in Buton. Artifacts from these two sites share a lot of similarities. They also have much number in common with the archaeological finds in Cambodia and Laos of the Indochina Peninsula. On the other hand, they are not so familiar in Japan where smaller dishes and bowls tend to be the mainstream. This difference probably owes to eating styles of each culture.

Hardly any Chinese porcelain of the imperial kiln class of the fifteenth century, in particular after the Yongle reign period, was excavated in Indonesia. High quality the *Ko-akae* style ware with a mark "Made by *Chen Shou Liu* 陳守劉" were unearthed one at each in Cambodia and Laos, but not in Trowulan. However, bowl and dish in the *Ko-akae* style and with polychrome enamels decoration of semi-quality were excavated. Furthermore, bowl with gold decoration, which resembles to the Jiajing period style of the second half of the sixteenth century was also seen in Laos, but no such example has been identified in Indonesia. Regarding the Zhangzhou kiln, its under-glaze cobalt blue ware began to appear from the second half of the sixteenth century but there is not so many earlier types compared to Laos. The Zhangzhou ware increases its presence in the first half of the seventeenth century.

In this period, the Dutch East India Company was actively exporting the Kraak style under-glaze cobalt blue dishes, or large bowls and bottles fired in Jingdezhen.

These wares have been excavated also in Indonesia. The Kraak style dish decorated with a tulip design that originated in the Chongzhen era (1628-44) was unearthed in Banten Lama. Large bowl decorated with a scene and poetic exposition *Chi-bi-fu* fired in the Chongzhen era are often found in Japan and the Indochina peninsula and also had been excavated at Buton Wolio Fort (Fig.49-249). On the contrary, ware with unglazed circular foot-ring or small dish with unglazed base and curved rim dated to the Chongzhen era have been found in Japan, Vietnam and Laos, but not in Indonesia.

Naturally, under-glaze cobalt blue or polychrome enamels decorated wares represented by the *Ko-sometsuke* and *Shonzui* styles ware that were especially ordered by Japanese tea practitioners have not been excavated anywhere outside Japan.

2-4 Japanese Hizen wares

We already reported the characteristics of export Hizen ware in an exhibition catalogue "Hizen wares abroad: The 10th anniversary special exhibition" published in 1990. An outline is discussed below with some new information, which was discovered after the publication.

In Indonesia, there are a few findings of the Hizen stoneware, while the Hizen porcelain also found sauce dish (Fig.56-289) or mid dish etc. of around the 1640s. These shards support a record of the Dutch East India Company that a Chinese junk exported rough porcelains from Nagasaki to Cambodia via Ayutthaya in 1647. The Hizen porcelain in this period has no special products for export, but all of exported one was selected from the domestic market. The same condition is confirmed on the Hizen stoneware, such as whitish mid dish (Fig.56-292) fired with sand balls stacking technique, likely in the Uchinoyama kiln, Ureshino City. Because the oldest dating of these ceramics is the 1610s and an earlier possibility than the export of porcelain in 1647, we can consider the export in chance of the Red seal ship trade period before the national isolation of Japan.

The Chinese civil war in 1644 caused by a political shift seriously affected the distribution of trade ceramics in Southeast Asia. The export of Chinese porcelain dramatically dropped after this year, and Chinese vessels assumedly started to transport the Hizen ware to the Indochina peninsula and Indonesia already around 1647.

Volume of excavated Hizen porcelain increased in the 1650s. Those obviously dated to the 1650s are roughly made under-glaze cobalt blue dish in the Kraak style, dish with a design of character of *hi* 日 and phoenix in under-glaze cobalt blue, large dishes with over-glaze enamels decoration made in Arita (Fig.75-387) and in Yoshida, Hizen (Fig.77-409). They could be even dated to the first half of 1650s. These dishes were made for export markets except the large dish of Arita. Such export porcelain began to appear from the 1650s. Dish decorated with a character of *hi* 日 and phoenix design is not so commonly seen in Indonesia but many were found in Vietnam. Fig.61-314 has an unglazed ring area in the inner bottom and there is a good chance that this was made in Hasami rather than in Arita. In Vietnam, we find more typical type of dish with a design of character of *hi* 日 and phoenix made in Arita. Dish with a design of character of *hi* 日 and phoenix and with unglazed ring area was excavated also in Hoi An, and there is also one in the Philippines, although it is not clear if the Philippine example was originally decorated with phoenix design.

The Dutch East India Company took a step to get seriously involved with exporting the Hizen porcelain after China banned trading at sea in 1656, because there was no prospect for Chinese porcelain to be exported. The most typical Hizen ware for export is an under-glaze cobalt blue bowl decorated with a design of dragon and crowd (dragon and phoenix) with carp jumping out of water, destined for Southeast Asia. This type of dish was excavated in the Southeast Asian nations including Vietnam, Thailand, Cambodia, Laos and Malaysia. Also in Indonesia, examples were found at the Somba Opu Fort, Buton Wolio Fort, Banten Lama and Tirtayasa to a few degrees. The design of carp jumping out of waves changes according to period and there are old and new types. Comparing the artifacts from those four sites, the pattern of Tirtayasa's is more rough (Fig.87-448) and thought to be the newest.

Bowls belong to this group are usually decorated with a Chinese design of carp jumping out of waves at the inner bottom, called the *araiso* pattern. However Hizen arranged the design and replaced carp with dragon head or dragon. Such arranged design was found in Vietnam and Ayutthaya, Thailand. In Indonesia however, only the carp version has been confirmed. In addition to the design of carp jumping out of wave, large bowls decorated with other designs were extensively made for Southeast Asia during the late 1650s to 1660s and excavated in the nations of this region. Buton Wolio Fort presented some (Fig.68-344, 345) but many were unearthed from Tirtayasa (Fig.87-449/Fig.88-452). The Tirtayasa bowl is later than the bowl collected at the Fukiagehama, Kagoshima Prefecture, Japan and given a date of the 1660s-70s. Another typical export ware is the Kraak style dish. This style was mainly sought after by the Dutch East India Company rather than made for Southeast Asia and transported widely to Europe. We analyze at this stage that low quality the Kraak style dishes with simplified design were exported chiefly to Southeast Asia. Examples through excavation in Indonesia came from Somba Opu Fort (Fig.61-318, upper right), Buton Wolio Fort (Fig.68-346, upper left), Pasar Ikan as well as Banten Lama [III-24], but there is no piece excavated at Tirtayasa.

From the late 1650s the Dutch East India Company ordered Hizen to make the Karrak style dish for the European market, and they were much closer to the Jingdezhen Kraak style of the late Ming period. They were excavated at Somba Opu Fort (Fig.61-319), Buton Wolio Fort (Fig.68-346, middle left is the Meizan type, Fig.69-347, second from right in the upper row is the Meizan type, the one in the bottom row is dated to the late seventeenth to the beginning of eighteenth centuries), Banten Lama (Fig.76-395/397) and Tirtayasa (Fig.89-459, Fig.90-460). Because of more simplified designs, most found at the Tirtayasa would be dated to later period and nothing can be as early as the 1650s.

The Great Sultan Tirtayasa acceded the throne in 1651 and developed a major irrigation system in the Tirtayasa region from 1663. His sultanate was at war with the Dutch in 1677 and then a civil war broke out. The Great Sultan abdicated the throne to his son Sultan Haji in 1678 and relocated to the Tirtayasa Villa. Because the son allied with the Dutch, the Great Sultan captured the Surosowan Palace in February 1682, which led Sultan Haji to flee. However, in March of the same year, the Dutch force invaded the Surosowan Palace, and the Tirtayasa Villa also fell in the end of 1682. The Great Sultan gave in to Sultan Haji in March 1683 [III-25].

The Hizen porcelain (found at Tirtayasa) possibly helps to reaffirm the speculated dates of the Tirtayasa Villa, that it existed between 1663 and 1682. There is one type of ware found in a big quantity only in Banten Lama and Tirtayasa from the 1660s to 1670s – that is a small dish. Fig.76-392/394, Fig.77-410/412 are from Banten Lama, and Fig.88-453/455, Fig.89-456/458 are of Tirtayasa. These small dishes are not particularly for the Southeast Asian taste, nor they have distinguished features as the export ware. If we say, dish with flat rims (Fig.89-456, 458) could be for export. Fig.89-456 and Fig.76-393 (Banten Lama) are the same type. Fig.88-454 also look similar to Fig.76-392 (Banten Lama), and interior of Fig.90-463, 464 is decorated with a design in disappearing ink technique. The decoration in disappearing ink technique is rare in Southeast Asia. Fig.90-464 has a four or five petals flower motif in the inner bottom thus is perhaps later. This kind of motif is also for Japanese taste. Hizen porcelain with a five petals flower design arranged in the inner bottom is rarely found outside Japan. Apart from the piece from Banten Lama (Fig.76-399, 403), only few examples are two small bowls with under-glaze cobalt blue decoration found in a site near the Temple Mayor in Mexico [III-26]. Heirloom objects are also comparatively few. Looking at large dish, those from Tirtayasa (Fig.90-461) and Banten Lama (Fig.76-401) show relative similarities. Type of large celadon dish (Fig.91-465) is found particularly in Indonesia, if within Southeast Asia and excavated at Buton Wolio Fort (Fig.69-349) and Banten Lama (Fig.75-389). Fig.75-389 from Banten Lama and Fig.91-465 from Tirtayasa share some features – a sunken central area within the unglazed circular ring inside the foot-ring, carved relief pattern on the inner bottom, and colour tone of glaze. They were fired at Hasami, Nagasaki Prefecture and dated to the 1660s to 1670s, if we need to be more precise, around the 1670s.

It is noted that more large dishes dated to the second half of the seventeenth century were found in Indonesia, compared to Vietnam, Thailand, Cambodia and Laos. They include dishes in celadon glaze, under-glaze cobalt blue in the Kraak style and Hizen stoneware dishes as well as those with over-glaze enamels decoration. In particular difference from Vietnam is outstanding where bowls and small dishes are the main vessel type. Such difference may be resulted from eating habit in each regions.

Cover of large covered box with under-glaze cobalt blue decoration (Fig.91-466, 467) have been confirmed only in Indonesia within Southeast Asia and they were unearthed at Banten Lama [III-27].

As some examples were excavated in Trowulan, Banten Lama (Fig.76-404/406) and

Tirtayasa (Fig.91-468, 469), small covered box is more common in Indonesia. Although such type has been found also in Thailand and Cambodia, it appears covered small bowl or small bottle are rather more familiar in these regions.

As we have seen, Hizen porcelain excavated at Banten Lama and Tirtayasa share many common features. This would support the history of both places, that Tirtayasa was separated from Banten Lama.

The Chinese porcelain, in particular the Jingdezhen ware, was excavated in a great quantity along with the Hizen ware. Many of the Jingdezhen porcelain demonstrates characteristics of the Kangxi reign period (1662-1722). Latest possible production date of these porcelain could be 1682, the year when Tirtayasa fell. Then when could be the earliest? Considering that there is a large bowl with the year mark 'Made in Great Qing, Kangxi reign period' (Fig.80-421), the earliest date would be after 1661. Similar large bowls of Fig.80-420 are known from the fourth layer of the Chinese Mansion/ Tojin-yashiki in Nagasaki (illustration No.12, Fig.54, 55 in Ogiura 2013). A significant volume of Chinese porcelain was excavated from the lower layer of leveled ground before the construction of the mansion, and their main dates are from 1685 to 1688. These similar Chinese porcelains suggest a good chance that the large bowl from Tirtayasa could be dated very close to 1682. Many Hizen bowls excavated along with Chinese porcelain are decorated with a design of carp jumping out of wave in under-glaze cobalt blue. The design is very loosely painted and makes us to date them to the 1670s to 80s. Also excavated were the bowls decorated with printed design with paper stencils. This is another feature to make us to suggest a date as after the 1670s. There is one celadon bowl decorated with an under-glaze cobalt blue flower with five petals in the innre bottom. Five-petal flower appeared after the 1680s. Thinking all of these factors, there is no evidence to deny a speculation of dating them mostly to 1685-1688 [III-28]. More than one dish with the European landscape design was also unearthed and these dishes are also produced after the 1680s. Although there are some small cups with older appearance, the main component is quite likely made in the 1680s with 1688 as latest year.

The Chinese porcelain from Tirtayasa includes a similar example to the piece excavated at the Chinese Mansion (Fig.80-420), but the others are in better quality. High quality perhaps relates to the nature of the site of Tirtayasa as a royal villa and the porcelain group does not go back much beyond 1682. A number of dishes and bowls in three-colour glazes (*sancai*) (Fig.83-435/Fig.84-437) were excavated at Buton Wolio fort (Fig.64-330) and Banten Lama (Fig.70-353, 354, 359). In addition, large dishes with double foot-rings (Fig.82-430 & Fig.83-432, 433) were also unearthed at Buton Wolio Fort (Fig.64-328, 329) and Banten Lama (Fig.70-357). These tendencies of ceramics are the common characteristics shared in Indonesia of this period.

Another feature of the artifacts from the period V-2 is the Vietnamese bowl with stamped pattern. Although small in number, this type of ware was excavated at different sites including Buton Wolio Fort (Fig.67-343), Banten Lama (Fig.74-386) and Tirtayasa (Fig.92-472). It was the Hizen porcelain that was mainly distributed around the 1650s to 70s, but the Chinese porcelain also have been traded in this period, possibly porcelain from Fujian region such as small dish as well as bowl with a design of auspicious character *shou* 壽 excavated at the Somba Opu fort (Fig.60-311). The latter has a flower band decoration inside the rim and character *shou* 壽 arranged on the exterior. Decorating inside the rim is an old style. The character *shou* is also obviously in older style when comparing it to the one written on a bowl found at the Chinese Mansion site. In fact, it may be even older than the shipwrecked material from around the 1660s, which were collected at the Fukiagehama in Kagoshima Prefecture. There is a bowl with the same design that was burnt in the Edo Fort by the Great Fire of Meireki in 1657, and this bowl has a rim inside which is undecorated. Fig.60-311 is strikingly similar to the bowl found in Vientiane, Laos in the points that the rim is not curved and a band of flower design decorates inside the rim. The Vientiane bowl with a character *shou* 壽 design retains the bottom and bears a mark 'Precious receptacle for the Jade Hall' *yu-tang-jia-qi* 玉堂佳器 in the inner bottom (Ohashi 2016). From this, date of Somba Opu Fort bowl is estimated before 1657 and an earliest possibility is the second half of the 1640s.

Another Chinese porcelain that was likely distributed in the 1650s to 70s is dish with a leaf design made in Fujian. The examples of dishes with leaf and magnolia motif are Fig.66 338 left from Buton Wolio fort and Fig.72-367 from Banten Lama. The old type of dish was excavated at the Old City of Fengshan in Zuoyin, Taiwan, and it was inscribed 'Winter of the Yimao year in Taiping Era 太平年興、乙卯冬記' (presumably 1675). The small dish written Taiping Era 太平年興 was also found at the same archaeological site. It is generally thought that these ware is associated with the cargo recovered from the Vung Tau, a ship sunk probably in the 1690s. The Vung Tau version has a slightly different design, and a poem *yi-ye-yao-qiu-qi xin-chun-zai-fang-fei* 一葉約秋気、新春再芳菲 as well as magnolia are added. All of the dishes of this type excavated at Buton Wolio Fort and Banten Lama were added magnolia. They will not go back to the 1670s and assumed to be dated to the 1680s to 90s.

As we have seen, new manufuctured Chinese porcelain was hardly circulated before the 1670s, more precisely from 1644 to the 1660s.

The Hizen (Arita) porcelain fired as late as the first half of the eighteenth century was still excavated only in Indonesia among Southeast Asian countries, but they were rather for Europe than for Indonesia. This is probably because the Dutch vessels with cargo always called at their base Batavia (Jakarta today) on route to Europe. The Hizen porcelain of this period was also unearthed in Cape Town, South Africa, which was the important call point after Batavia.

An extensive volume of ceramics excavated from the five archaeological sites reveals transformation of ceramic distribution in this region during the thirteenth to the nineteenth centuries. They also shed light on significant features of ceramics distributed to Indonesia through comparison with other regions.

Chapter III Note

1 See footnote 29, chapter II.

2 Fukami 2014.

3 See Shimizu 2014 for the Vietnamese ceramics. PL.15-18 and 20-28 are the Vietnamese porcelain presumably dated to around the sixteenth century, which types are not represented at Trowulan Site.

4 See footnote 70, chapter II.

5 Ikuta & Ishizawa 2009.

6 p.241 in Ishi (ed.) 1991

7 Fig.270 in Adhyatman 1981, height 20 cm, dated as the 15th century.

8 Ōhashi 2004.

9 Sakai (ed.) 2000, 2004 and 2007

10 Yamawaki 1988, pp.335–391

11 Yamawaki 1988, p.389.

12 Ohashi 2004a & p.10 in Ohashi 2011

13 Jorg 2001.

14 Ohashi & Sakai 1999.

15 Ohashi 1999, pp.50–53.

16 Fig.108-264 in Kyushu Ceramic Museum 1990.

17 Jingdezhen-shi 1993

18 Shogakukan 1976b-63, 64.

19 The Trustees of British Museum 1995.

20 Fig.7 in Carswell 1999 is a wall of Muladye Mosque, built by the 6th sultan of the Ottoman, Mulat II, in Edirne, around 1435.

21 Mayuyama 1977.

22 Sakai 2015.

23 Fig.11 and 12 in Sakai 2009 appear to be the similar type.

24 P.97 and 129, Kyūshū Ceramic Museum 1990.

25 Halwany 1993

26 Fig.19–22 & Fig.20–9 in Nogami 2013.

27 Fig.310 and 311, Kyūshū Ceramic Museum 1990.

28 Ôgiura 2013.

IV Ceramic trade and history

In this final chapter of this publication, we would review the achievements of the researches at Trowulan and four royal capital sites from the viewpoint of the ceramic trade history.

1. A revised history of each royal capital

The five archaeological sites associate with the Majapahit Kingdom (Trowulan Site), the Banten Sultanate (Banten Lama and Tirtayasa Sites), the Gowa Sultanate (Somba Opu Fort) and the Buton Sultanate (Wolio Fort). Among those four kingdoms/sultanates, Buton is hardly known of its beginning and end outside the local community. Other three kingdoms/sultanates are, however, well known within the framework of Indonesian history or that of the Archipelago of Southeast Asian. Broad sense of time and history is almost a general knowledge [IV-1].

In particular, the chronological outlook of the Majapahit Kingdom and the Banten Sultanate in Java has become an open knowledge, because records and related archaeological sites remain relatively in good order. The origin of the Majapahit is founding of a kingdom by 'Raden Wijaya who took an advantage of the Mongolian Invasions'. A popular narrative history tells that his chosen capital Trowulan took its name from the local fruit product *maja*, because it was bitter [IV-2]. It is also a common knowledge in the history of Java or of Indonesia that the pre-Islamic classical Javanese culture (Hindu-Java) is divided into the Central Java period and Eastern Java period, and the former represented by the Borobudur was destroyed by a great eruption of the Mount Merapi in the tenth century which led to the beginning of the latter.

The year 1527 is close to the foundation of the Banten Sultanate and also the year when the Portuguese confirmed that the Sunda Kelapa (Jakarta in today) was occupied by the Muslims. From this information, the foundation of the Banten Sultanate was slightly earlier than 1527. This year is known as the founding year of the Jakarta city today. Founding of the Banten Sultanate at the beginning of the sixteenth century is another common knowledge along with a Muslim saint Sunan Gunung Jati, who is identified with Fatahillah, the founding father of Banten.

Such general view of the period significantly differs from the period I-1 (ninth to thirteenth centuries) in this publication. The excavation at Trowulan revealed variety of ceramics of this period including the Yuezhou celadon ware, the Changsha ware with iron-oxide painting in yellow glaze and the Jingdezhen qingbai porcelain. In addition, not a few superior quality products were included. Obviously Trowulan was importing a high quality Chinese ceramics even before 'Raden Wijaya tasted bitter *maja*'. The volume and continuing status of ceramics of each period makes it certain that the place bore significance already by the eleventh century when the first bating place was built at the sacred mountain Penanggungan.

Another issue is that many of the Yuezhou celadon ware and the Changsha ware were the products of the Tang period. It is mentioned earlier that the Eastern Java period began with the great eruption of Mount Merapi in the tenth century, however, these ceramics are older. Although a few in number, archaeological sites during the Central Java period also exist relatively close to Trowulan [IV-3]. Therefore, it was known that the Hindu-Java culture had been spread in the Eastern Java even in the Central Java period prior to the tenth century. Ceramics fragments, however, inform us the possible picture that Trowulan was in function as one of the strongholds of the Eastern Java. This says that the *maja* fruit in Trowulan was bitter far before Raden Wijaya tasted them.

The Yuezhou celadon and the Changsha ware are included in the main three types in the ceramic trade, which is generally thought began in the ninth century. Other key Chinese ceramics is the Xingzhou ware white porcelain as well as the Islamic blue glaze stoneware. A group of ceramics including those already mentioned plus the Gongxian ware had been recovered from a shipwreck off Belitung Island on the east coast of southern Sumatera [IV-4]. They were not confirmed among the ceramic fragments we studied, but they are expected to be discovered in the Eastern Java. However, it is unlikely that the first imported ceramics into the Central Java were passed down the generation and carried to the eastern part, if the immigration was prompted by the great eruption.

Another equally significant factor is that the Changsha ware was also excavated at Banten Lama. The Banten Girang (the Upper Banten) Site was the stronghold during the pre-Islamic period, and was located ten kilometres upstream on the Banten River. It is natural to think that all trade ceramics brought to Bante Girang passed through Banten Lama at the estuary. The excavation research in Girang unearthed the Guangdong type blue glaze stoneware that was included in the early trade ceramics, and this clearly demonstrates that the Sunda Strait area at the west edge of Java Island was a part of the trade network of this period. Although the base moved within a short distance unlike Trowulan, the region as a whole was not separated in the ninth century and after the sixteenth century [IV-5].

In addition, it is also important that the ceramics belong to the period II-1 (late thirteenth to the fourteenth centuries) and to the period II-2 (the second half of the fourteenth century) were found at Somba Opu and Wolio respectively.

According to the legend of the Gowa Kingdom, it was the fourteenth king who converted to Islam in the beginning of the seventeenth century. Giving twenty years to one generation, it is estimated that the first king Tumanurung reigned in the beginning of the fourteenth century. Setting aside whether individual kings existed or not, the foundation date of the kingdom which was passed down through generations does not largely contradict to the beginning of importing trade ceramics. We need to pay attention to the fact that a white porcelain covered box made in the southern Fujian province (Fig.22-29) closely resembles to the excavated item of Trowulan.

As earlier mentioned, Wolio was traditionally adopting pre-Islamic names for the kings which were similar to the Hindu-Java culture. The Longquan celadon and the Cizhou ware with iron-oxide painting found at Wolio look closer to the ceramic fragments excavated at Trowulan. One thing is that Wolio is missing ceramics dated to the following period III-2 (the second half of the fifteenth to the beginning of the sixteenth centuries). On contrary, the Jingdezhen ware, the Vietnamese under-glaze cobalt blue ware and the stoneware with iron-oxide painting from Si Satachanalai, Thailand were imported to Somba Opu of the same period. What is the reason behind this big difference? While Wolio followed Trowulan in its tendency of declining, Somba Opu on the contrary was deeply involved with ceramic trade of this period. Unlike Buton, fourteen pre-Islamic kings of the Gowa hardly carried elements of Hindu-Java culture in their names. Somba Opu had continuity from older period similar to Trowulan and Banten Lama, but Wolio lacked the connection to the ceramic trade in those times. It may be resulted from whether one had a closer unified relationship with the Majapahit or not.

In any case, ceramic fragments from Trowulan and four capital sites clearly revealed a long history continued from the older times beyond the general understanding. The political and social backgrounds, which made the early ceramic trade possible, were rarely recorded and only obscure oral tradition was passed through generations. However, the ceramic fragments shed light on the historical continuity from the older past. They also tell us a story of general history of this region that the port cities were used for long period of time as the base.

2. Relation with the western Islamic worlds

The four capital sites were the capital of Muslim kingdoms/sultanates and it is natural that they had a close relationship with the western Islamic worlds centred around the Mecca [IV-6]. The Majapahit Kingdom with Trowulan as its capital worshipped the Hindu but the Samudera Pasai, the oldest Islam kingdom in the Southeast Asia was already established in Aceh at the north edge of Sumatra by 1297, the right after the foundation of the Majapahit Kingdom. By 1368 under the reign of the King Hayam Wuruk, a Muslim community was already established in Trowulan [IV-7]. We are going to review the situation through a history of ceramic trade.

The western Islamic world has been producing Islamic stoneware. They are tin glazed stoneware with its origin going back to Mesopotamia and Egypt. The low fired and soft paste Islamic stoneware was not transported to the other Asian regions where the Chinese ceramics were competing. The western Islamic worlds were rather a consumer of the Chinese and the East Asian ceramics.

This tradition went back to the early ceramic trade era (the ninth to tenth centuries) when the Muslim merchants from west, such as Persian and Arabian were visiting Southeast Asia and East Asia on the Dhow ships. Fragments of jars with applied decoration in turquoise or cobalt blue glaze, or of amphora had been universally found at archaeological port sites in East Asia and wider area of Asia of this period. They were also found among the cargo, which sunk off the Belitung Island as mentioned earlier. It is highly possible that they were also transported to Java, but not included in the fragments from Trowulan and four capital sites we had analaysed. It is an additional note that fragments of the Islamic ware in blue glaze and decorated with multiple glaze incised lines (three glazed Islamic ware/*sancai*) were excavated along with the Yuezhou celadon ware at the Lobu Tua Site in Barus, west coast of North Sumatra [IV-8].

During the middle ceramic trade period (the eleventh to thirteenth centuries) that follows the early period, while accepting the Longquan celadon ware, the western Islamic worlds developed own stoneware culture. One of the examples is the luster ware, which imitated metal sheen, and another is glazed tiles that would advance as architectural ornamentation. There is no evidence that both of the luster ware and glazed tiles were certainly brought over to the East.

In the late ceramic trade period (the fourteenth to eighteenth centuries) there was a constant cultural contact with the Indian Ocean Rim particularly and technological exchange between Islamic stoneware and eastern Asian ceramics became prominent. The first step of creation of the under-glaze cobalt blue ware by mixing the Chinese white porcelain technique with the cobalt-blue decoration on white glaze of Islam stoneware is a milestone. The Zhizheng style under-glaze cobalt blue ware from the Yuan Dynasty period is the complete form, and it is well known that many of this superior quality under-glaze cobalt blue ware imported to the western Islamic world.

The Topkapi Palace Museum in Istanbul, Turkey and the Sheikh Safi Mausoleum in Ardabil, Iran have famous collection of these under-glaze cobalt blue ware, but their collections were formed some centuries after the production. On the other hand, an extensive amount of the Zhizheng style under-glaze cobalt blue ware fragments were excavated at the Firuzshah Kotala [IV-9], an archaeological palace site of the Islamic Tughlaq Dynasty in Delhi, India are more significant. That is because the palace was founded in 1354 and destroyed in 1398. These years correspond to the time around the Zhizheng period (1341-1367) when the under-glaze cobalt blue porcelain was fired. This fact makes it hard to think that they were passed down at other place. In addition, fragments of the abbreviate style under-glaze cobalt blue ware also found at this palace site along with the contemporary Zhizheng style of superior quality. The majority of Yuan under-glaze cobalt blue ware in the abbreviate style were found in Southeast Asia such as the Philippines, and they are not found along with the Zhizheng style. Therefore, it has been understood that Yuan under-glaze cobalt blue ware in both styles were distributed to different supply places, although they were produced in the same period. Delhi is an extremely rear case of mixing both together, but also at Trowulan we had confirmed the Zhizheng style as in this publication together with a great quantity of the Yuan under-glaze cobalt blue ware in the abbreviate style [IV-10]. The Yuan under-glaze cobalt blue ware found at Firuzshah Kotla and Trowulan bear extreme resemblance in terms of assortment. In addition, there is no possibility that fragments at Trowulan were brought in at the later time. This information indicates that they also share the real import date.

Such connection of Trowulan's fragments with the western Islamic worlds is also visible in other aspects, that are the tiles with blue decoration on white ground (Fig.10–93/95) and the square tiles in turquoise blue glaze (Fig.10–96/98). Both are brought into Trowulan around the fourteenth century, but while the former was produced around the time of the Yuan under-glaze cobalt blue ware or a bit later, the latter already appeared by the thirteenth century in the western Islamic world. They consist of only a tiny proportion in the ceramic fragments from Trowulan, but undoubtedly originate in the west. Furthermore, they form the prototype of northern Vietnamese tiles, which were ordered at a considerable volume in the first half of the fifteenth century. This kind of situation sufficiently suggests the relation of Trowulan, which was already formed at the peak of the Majapahit Kingdom in the second half of the fourteenth century, with the Muslim society [IV-11].

The stoneware dish decorated with indigo-blue painting over white ground excavated at Banten Lama (Fig.57–294) is very important that it had taken over Trowulan's position. This fragment of dish is decorated with an unique continuous leave design on the outer area of internal, and I would consider as a product in the Safavid Dynasty [IV-12]. The Dutch East India Company ordered the Safavid Dynasty imitation of the Chinese under-glaze cobalt blue ware to replace the real one, and such products were found also in East Asia. However, this Banten Lama dish has only little similarity in patterns with the Chinese under-glaze cobalt blue ware, and colour development of cobalt gives different impression. This dish is suspected to be the sixteenth century product.

It was mentioned in the earlier chapter that the Dutch record of 1596 reveals that there were many Asian traders in Banten and the Persians were included. Every Persians were not necessarily had a direct contact with the Safavid Dynasty, but at least a Persian scholar of Islamic study settled in Ayutthaya in the seventeenth century [IV-13]. This makes us think that the number of Persian visitors to Southeast Asia during the sixteenth to seventeenth centuries were by no means small. The Mughal Empire was controlling the Indian subcontinent of the time. Their official language was the Persian and a number of Persian immigrated to India. The Islamic culture in India is deeply related to the early Islamic culture in Southeast Asia. Accepting the Persian value was, except the Shia Islam, natural in Southeast Asia[IV-14].

The Banten Sultanate was an Islamic state and the founding father Fatahillah was a Muslim scholar who completed the Hajj. It is no surprise that products of the Safavid, which was founded in the beginning of the sixteenth century and had its peak time in the first half of the seventeenth century, were taken into Banten. It is suspected that the same kind of thing was happening in the Aceh Sultanate directly facing the Indian Ocean. The Islamic ceramics, a stoneware, in particular tableware was no match for the Chinese ceramics, but the Islamic culture and Muslim trade activities behind was reaching deep into the Southeast Asian Islands.

3. Indonesian society: the reception of Hizen ware

We first came to be interested in the ceramic fragments excavated in Indonesia because of the unrecorded significant volume of the Hizen ceramics found at Banten Lama. Furthermore, we were able to confirm the Hizen ware at any archaeological sites of the seventeenth and eighteenth centuries in Indonesia. That is not limited to the sites in Java, but the same applies also to Somba Opu in Sulawesi and Wolio in Buton. Although this publication did not include it, not a few Hizen ware is also known at Aceh at the northern end of Sumatra. They include the unique Hizen stoneware large bowls with two colours and brush marks which were excavated at multiple occasions.

In this section, we are going to consider the position of the Hizen ware at Trowulan bearing it in mind to avoid repetition from the previous chapter.

At Trowulan, we confirmed the Hizen white porcelain bowl (Fig.20-307), the underglaze cobalt blue decorated small bowl with a cover (Fig.20-308) and a couple of covered boxes with overglaze polychrome enamels decoration (Fig.20-309, 310). Those Hizen accounted for only a fraction among the large volume of fragments, and the production year of the second half of the seventeenth century is not related to the general timeframe of Trowulan. Despite of all, one cannot deny that the Hizen ware was brought in Trowulan.

Like many other older kingdoms in Indonesia, we do not have much information on how exactly the Majapahit Kingdom ended. It is said that newly emerging Islamic port cities such as Demak in the Central Java united and attacked Trowulan. Although it was assumed in the 1520s, the fact is not confirmed. Ceramic fragments of the second half of the fourteenth century bear to no small extent traces of secondary firing, which would indicate the civil war at the time of Zheng He's visit. However, we did not confirm such traces on the fragments of the beginning of the sixteenth century. Moreover, the Vietnamese glazed tiles still in the Great Mosque of Demak were likely to be carried to Trowulan first, but they do not show any of such trace of fire. Above all, the later Muslim generation of Java thought that Raden Patah, the first sultan of Demak had a lineage from the Majapahit kings. At this stage, we can only assume that Trowulan disappeared without any particular force after the 1520s (Map 2).

Demak was the leader among the Islamic port cities in Java, but it went into decline caused by the internal strife in the middle of the sixteenth century before taking over the Majapahit and establishing its sovereignty in Java. The Pajang located inland of Central Java and the Mataram contested over the position to succeed, and the Mataram won in the late sixteenth century to unify the Central and Eastern Java by the 1620s. There is a high possibility that Trowulan region was under the influence of Surabaya, one of the Islamic port cities in those years, but with no particular role. This situation continued to around the time when Surabaya was united by the Mataram in 1625. Hardly no ceramics deserving special mention were distributed into Trowulan after the beginning of the sixteenth century. The Mataram was at the height in the first half of the seventeenth century and attacked Batavia twice in the 1620s. The Mataram kept its influence for a while afterwards until 1674 when Trunojoyo's rebellion broke out in the Madura Island of Eastern Java in relation to the Makassar War. Surabaya fell under control of the rebel force in the following year. The Sultan of the Mataram sought assistance from the Dutch East India Company and the Dutch army recaptured Surabaya in 1677. Since then the Mataram Sultanate ceded the north coast region of Java including Surabaya to the Dutch.

If Hizen ware was brought into Trowulan during 1655 to 1680, Trowulan was then experiencing changeover of its ruler through disturbances out of the stable situation under sovereignty of the Mataram. Now, we are going to consider the supplier and buyer of Hizen ceramics during those years.

The principle importing ports in Indonesia of the Hizen ware in this time were Batavia and Banten. The former of course served the Dutch who carried the cargo from Nagasaki via Zeelandia in Taiwan but after losing Zeelandia in 1661 by the attack from Zheng Chenggong, they shipped directly to Batavia. The Banten was in principle used by the vessels associated with the Zheng Kingdom in Taiwan, but the Banten and the England vessels in part also imported Hizen ware to this port from Anping (former Zeelandia) or Amoy.

The inland route to reach Trowulan region from these ports is most likely via Surabaya which directly connect to the Brantas River, although from the port at the north coast of Java for example Tuban is also a possibility as it was in the Majapahit era. The question then is the transport from Batavia and Banten to these ports, and here Kure Katsutoshi revealed a very interesting fact in his recent research based on the Dutch historical documents [IV-15].

To begin with, the Dutch shipped porcelains from Batavia to Jepara, a port in the Central Java from 1636, and to Gresik in the suburb of Surabaya from the following year. The monetary value did not become clear before Hizen ware occupied the majority of the shipments after 1661, but while the shipments to Jepara outnumbered in the 1660s, Gresik was receiving more after the 1670s (Graph 1). The total value of transport to Gresik until 1681 grew more than 20% as a result. When we compare the value with copper (also Japanese origin) to both ports in the same period, the total sum to Jepara was close to three times. Jepara was the outer port of the Mataram Palace, and the market here is the central government of the Mataram. Demand for copper there was far larger than in Gresik, which was away from the palace. Porcelain in particular created a large market in the Eastern Java after the 1670s.

In the meantime, the Dutch frequently saw and recorded the activities of vessels sent by the Zheng Kingdom after 1670 at the north coast of Java Island. For example, a vessel being built by the order of the *shahbandar* of the Banten at Rembang, the eastern point of the Central Java, in 1671 was sold to the Zheng, or the Zheng ordered to build a ship at Gresik in 1672. It is also recorded that many of the Overseas Chinese who cooperated at the ports were from Taiwan.

There is no doubt that the Great Sultan of Tirtayasa, the Banten was extending his activities in this region in opposition to the Dutch. It was prompted by the Gowa's defeat at the Makassar War. The Great Sultan had a son-in-law, a Muslim scholar Sheikh Yusuf who was the member of the royal family of the Gowa, and the Sultan had a good reason to try to rally. This is to say that the Dutch certainly carried very likely the Hizen porcelain to the Eastern Java, and we need to pay attention that the Banten and the Zheng also had a good chance.

Then who was buying the Hizen porcelain in the Eastern Java? The important point is that Gresik and Surabaya were not merely the window to the Eastern Javanese market, but they were the joint of trade linking with the east part of Indonesia such as Java, Sulawesi and Maluku (the Spice) Islands. They had been traditionally exporting rice from Java, and importing spice and marine products from the eastern Indonesia. It is highly possible that fair amount of the seventeenth century ceramics found at Somba Opu and Buton Wolio were among those carried via Surabaya and Gresik. The Trunojoyo Rebellion was caused by an aristocrat from the Madura Island jointly with aristocrats from Surabaya and exiled from the Gowa. In the background, there was a feeling of resistance against friendly the Dutch policy taken by the sultan of Mataram. Madura, Surabaya and the Gowa were traditionally forming a marine trade zone and competing with the Mataram and their resistance is undoubted.

Considering these circumstances, aristocrats and merchants who were involved with the trade in this region were quite possibly purchasing porcelain. However, they were based in Gresik or Surabaya and it is hard to think of their direct contact with Trowulan, which was located over sixty kilometres inland. Aristocrats should have been in Mojokerto, a town close from Trowulan, but they were not living in then farming village of Trowulan.

By reviewing the excavated the Hizen porcelain, they are small products such as bowls, small bowls and covered boxes. In addition, the volume is very small. It is discussed in the Chapter III, no products from the later period was found. This leads us to think that they were brought in at some exceptional occasions in a small quantity. The size also suggests that they were easy to carry. Then, it is reasonable to think that owners outside, for example aristocrats in Mojokerto carried with them at a special visit to Trawulan. Special occasions can be visits to early Muslim cemeteries left in Trowulan, for example the tomb of the Princess Champa [IV-16]. Whatever the reasons are, there certainly was a plenty of supply of the Hizen ware in Java Island to the extent that they could be transported to an inland farming village.

4. Mass produced ceramics for daily life and the Overseas Chinese communities

Trowulan, Tirtayasa and Somba Opu completed their role as the centre of political power before the late seventeenth century. But when investigating the ceramic fragments excavated at long lasted Banten Lama and Buton Wolio, the maximum volume was found at the period VI-2 (around the second half of the eighteenth century) at both sites.

The Banten Sultanate had its height during period of the Great Sultan of Tirtayasa, and became dependent on the Dutch East India Company after the internal strife in 1683. The Buton, on the other hand, was the key sultanate and it became a serious issue that between the Gowa and the Dutch, who they would support at the Makassar War. But after this, they disappeared from the general history. We observed a big gap between the excavated volume of ceramic fragments and active periods of each sultanates. This does not apply only to the Banten and the Buton, but the majority of kingdoms (most of them are Islamic sultanate) in the Archipelago of Southeast Asia closed their active time in the second half of the seventeenth century. Therefore, European historians are thinking that until the 1680s in this region 'the Age of Commerce' has been finished but already enter into new 'the Age of Development' [IV-17].

That a significant volume of fragments dated to the eighteenth century, in particular the second half, is not a special phenomenon to Banten Lama and Buton Wolio. For example, port city sites related to the Aceh Sultanate at the northern end of Sumatra, or archaeological sites in association with the Johor Sultanate located at the southern tip of the Malay Peninsula and other places are in the similar situation. This phenomenon is not limited to the Archipelago but can be observed at many port city sites including Lop Buri in Thailand, the Old City of Fengshan in Zuoying of Taiwan, and Pho Hien in Vietnam [IV-18]. The major part of ceramic fragments excavated at these sites are not the local products but the Fujian ceramics from China. That is, they are the trade ceramics and we may say that 'the Age of Commerce' indeed became active in the second half of the eighteenth century. One thing needs special attention is that the Fujian ceramics of the second half of the eighteenth century demonstrates significant difference from the previous products. First, despite that a great number was imported, they consist of only a few kinds majority of which are tableware bowls and dishes. Decorations are simple and conventional and frequently formed in mold. This means that they are mass produced common ware and largely different from the ceramics with antique value displayed in museums.

Some of the kilns in Fujian were already exporting this kind of common ceramics since the seventeenth century. The low quality white porcelain Anping jar (Fig.53-283) was first formed upper and bottom halves separately and later joined them together, and the under-glaze cobalt blue wares were decorated in stamped motifs (Fig.66-336, 340). But such ware was a special existing in this period and not a majority. Most of the ceramics imported to Southeast Asia in the second half of the eighteenth century were the mass production type of common ware. In Trowulan, which had long been a farming village, estimated fifty-five units/individual numbers of such ware had been excavated and this accounts for 0.7% of total 7,754 estimated units/individual numbers.

We would like to analyze the meaning of this type of the Fujian ceramic in low quality.

Grazed ceramics take variety of different forms but they are simply divided into bowl, dish and others (Table 1). Bowls and dishes are categorized in tableware and others include any other types. Entire fragments excavated at Trowulan consist of

41.9% bowls, 38.0% dishes and 20.1% others. Ratios of bowl and dish are very close, but when we focus on the main period (late thirteenth to the beginning of the sixteenth centuries), that accounts for 94% of the entire periods, dish occupies the maximum share except the first half of the fourteenth century.

Dish form (mid & large dishes) is the most important shape of tableware in large part of present Southeast Asia except Vietnam and their staple food rice is in principle served in a dish. Bowl is to serve soup included curry and noodle and the secondary shape. Many numbers of dishes in Trowulan as a whole indicate that they were used as tableware for such purposes. However, there is only a small possibility that bowls and dishes were actually used as a everyday tableware. That is because the Hindu religious thinking of clean/unclean took control over the style of traditional meals particularly in the Majapahit era and disposable banana leaves would have been used at each meal likely in modern South India. Ceramics would had been treasured and treated as if furnishings except when being used at special ritual meals. Even with that purpose, dishes with eye-catching decoration and pattern were at a superior position. The ratio given earlier reflects the different usage of ware.

Going back to the eighteenth century common ware, the ratio at Trowulan of this period is 47.1% of bowl, 32.9% of dish and 20.0% of others. Obviously bowl increased and came close to the half of the entire amount. It is hard to think that eating habit of the people in the same region fundamentally changed in the eighteenth century comparing to the Majapahit era, and another factor for this change should be considered. We do not have a full statistic to compare but in regard to the eighteenth century common ware, we recognize a tendency that the ration of bowl is higher both at Banten Lama [IV-19] and Buton Wolio.

When we try to give a logical explanation to this phenomenon, an introduction of other dietary culture is presumed. The most feasible reason of heavy use of bowls is migration of the Chinese. The first big wave of immigration of the Chinese into Southeast Asia is the middle of the seventeenth century around the transitional period from the Ming to Qing Dynasties. Then, there was a bigger wave in the second half of the eighteenth century. Majority of Chinese who settled in the islands were from the southern Fujian. They naturally first settled in port cities and it is Surabaya in this region. They began to move to the inlands and there is a big chance that this happened in the second half of the eighteenth century.

The Overseas Chinese brought in their own tableware as well as food culture, which influenced the locals. Bowl oriented tableware was accepted by part of the locals who were mainly using dishes [IV-20]. But this was observed in cities in principle, and it is not likely that the same situation affected the farming society of Trowulan. With only a few exception, the majority part of villagers were likely to be carrying on with their traditional eating habit and just having some dishes for the family [IV-21].

Then how do we understand the excavated common ware of the second half of the eighteenth century? As long as the locals in Trowulan had a limited use of them, we could only think that they were brought in by the visitors. As we discussed in the earlier section how Hizen porcelain was carried in, we cannot think of any other reasons that they were taken in by city dwellers nearby such as Mojokerto at the time of their pilgrimage to Islamic tombs. This would be the only reasonable possibility unless the eighteenth century residences in Trowulan had a special link to port cities, like in the previous century.

Migration of the Chinese from the Southern Fujian in the second half of the eighteenth century is a major social change also observed in other islands as well as the Javanese society. From the view point of ceramic trade, this phenomenon marked a visible trace of incoming of an enormous volume of the Fujian type inferior porcelain. In case of Trowulan, only under the special circumstances that it was a place to receive early Islamic culture, the large influence permeated in the part of farming village. Buton Wolio had a similar condition. The Wolio Fort was the central part of the continuing Buton Sultanate and the residents were the royal family and aristocrats only. Bau-bau port city outside the fort, however, was thriving with marine products trading and more Chinese were involved with the business and settling in. Under such circumstances, great volume of the Fujian type common ware was taken into the fort.

The Chinese immigration further grew in large scale around from the middle of the nineteenth century. Banten Lama and Buton Wolio present a comprehensive situation to understand the Chinese immigrants and their related ceramics. While the amount of ceramic fragments radically decrease at the latter, a certain volume with the European ceramics as the mainstream was excavated at Banten Lama. Although the palace in Banten was destroyed and the sultanate vanished in the beginning of the nineteenth century, Banten Lama still kept its role as a small port town and the Chinese continued to live there, albeit a few, until the late nineteenth century. Ceramics used by the Chinese then was not the Fujian common ware of even worse quality, but had been shifted to the European. One can think of the possibility that the Chinese in Bau-bau also changed the ceramics but it was not brought into the fort probably because their relation to aristocrats inside the fort was significantly weaken.

The ceramic fragments excavated at these sites inform us that the lifestyle of the Chinese immigrated in the European colonies changed through adopting conditions of each settlement.

Chapter IV Note
1 Gajah Mada of the Majapahit, Tirtayasa of the Banten and Hasanuddin of the Gowa are the officially recognized national heroes by the Indonesian government, and their names have been adopted to various public places such as universities and major roads.
2 The real meaning of this narrative history is not that simple in strict sense, for example what 'bitterness' symbolizes, but it is understood in general that Majapahit simply signifies 'bitter maja'
3 The Dinoyo Inscription of AD 760 was found in an area near the Malang Plateau, which

is 50 kilometers southeastward from Trowulan. There remains the Badut Temple in the Central Javanese style in the neighbourhood.

4 It is a Dhow ship called 'Batu Hitam (the Black Stone)'. Judging from the position of discovery off Belitung Island, it is highly speculated that this ship was sailing to Java as the first destination (Krahl et al. 2011).

5 Ceramic fragments from the periods I-2 (thirteenth-fourteenth centuries), II-1 (late thirteenth to fourteenth centuries) and III-2 (late fifteenth to the beginning of sixteenth centuries) are missing at Banten Lama, but those were found at Banten Girang (Guillot et al. 1994).

6 The Great Sultan of Tirtayasa fought the internal strife of the Banten Sultanate against his own son. The son took his nickname Sultan Haji, because he was a Muslim who completed the pilgrimage to Mecca (Hajj).

7 The Islam cemetery bearing 1368 as the oldest year was located in the southern region Troloyo, Trowulan.

8 Guillot et al.1998 (Morimoto 2006 for selected translation).

9 Smart 1975 and Misugi 1987.

10 No.44-46 of pp.16, Sakai & Ōhashi 2014.

11 Glazed tiles of the western Islamic world obviously originated in the region of Persian culture, but the author thinks that they were brought via the Islamic culture area in the northwest India (Sakai 2015).

12 Almost identical pattern is confirmed in the interior of the white stoneware bowl with cobalt blue decoration owned by the Reza Abbasi Museum in Teheran, Iran.

13 It is Sheikh Ahmad Qomi, who came to Ayutthaya in 1631.

14 For example, sultans of the fifteenth century Malacca took the Persian title 'shah' over generations, which origin directly goes back to the Islamic sultanates in India.

15 Kure 2016.

16 It is a Muslim tomb left in Trowulan, which carries the year of 1448. This tomb is believed to be of the Princess of Champa, who links the Majapahit king and newly emerged Muslim power such as Demak, but there is no certain evidence to prove it.

17 Reid 1988 and others.

18 Pho Hien is a port city archaeological site located in Northern Vietnam. It was the outer port of the Trinh Lords who controlled the Northern Vietnam in the seventeenth and eighteenth centuries. The trading post of the Dutch East India Company was also located here.

19 Sakai 2002 pp.90-91 Much number of the Overseas Chinese had been migrated in Banten Lama around mid the 17th century.

20 For example, noodles were one of the Chinese food cultures accepted by the locals. However in Indonesia noodles and soup are generally separated to suit with the tropical climate and both of them are served in respective bowls. In the continent of Southeast Asia using custom of bowl for noodle is more higher than Indonesia, but container for rice is basically dish, and glutinous rice, the stable diet in Northeast Thailand and Lao, is entered into cylindrical bamboo container.

21 Coffee is common in faming villages today, but in the eighteenth century it was forcefully began to be planted in some area as export products, and farmers was not likely to have drunk it.

Bibliography

Adhyatman, Sumarah, *Antique Ceramics found in Indonesia, Jakarta*: The Ceramic Society of Indonesia, 1981.

Adhyatman, Sumarah, *Zhangzhou (Swatow) Ceramics, Sixteenth to Seventeenth Centuries Found in Indonesia*, Jakarta: The Ceramic Society of Indonesia, 1999.

Adhyatman, Sumarah & Abu Ridho, *Tempayan di Indonesia /Martavans in Indonesia*, 2nd ed., Jakarta: The Ceramic Society of Indonesia, 1984.

Aichiken Tôji Shiryôkan, *Kikakuten: Tônan Ajia no Yakimono* [Special exhibition: Southeast Asian Ceramics]. Aichi Prefectural Ceramic Museum, 1987.

Arita-chô Kyôiku Iinkai, *Ôshûkizoku o Miryôshita Ko-Imari –Kanbara korekushon* [Old Imari which Enchanted European Nobles – from the Kanbara Collection]. Arita-cho Board of Education, 2008.

Arita Porcelain Park, *Tojiki no tozai koryu-ten* [a exhibition of ceramic exchange between the East and West], 1993.

Burghley House, *The Exhibition of Burghley House porcelain*, 1983.

Butterfield Auctioneers Corp, *Treasures from The Hoi An Hoard: Important Vietnamese Ceramics from a Late 15th/Early 16th Century Cargo*, 2000.

Carswell, John, *Iznik Pottery*, The Trustees of The British Museum, 1998.

Ceng Fan, *Fujian Taoci Kaogu Gailun* [Outline of ceramic archaeology in Fujian], Fujian-sheng Ditu Chubanshe, 2001.

Chandavij, Natthapatra, *Ceramics from Excavations Lop Buri 1986-1987*. Bangkok: Fine Arts Department, 1989.

Chiyoda City Board of Education, *Edojô no Kôkogaku II Dai-II bunsatsu* [Edo Castle Archaeology II, No. II, separate volume]. Chiyoda City Board of Education, 2011.

Christie's Limited, *The Hatcher Porcelain Cargo*, 1988.

Cixi-shi Bowuguan (ed.), *Shanglinhu Yue Yao* [Yue ware kiln site of Shanglinhu]. Cixi City Museum, Cultural Relics Press, 2002.

Duppoizat, Marie-France & Naniek Harkantiningsih, *Catalogue of the Chinese Style Ceramics of Majapahit, Tentative Inventory*, Cahier d'Archipel 36, Paris: Association Archipel, 2007.

Fukami Sumio, 'Jûgo Seiki no Majapahit' [Majapahit in the Fifteenth Century], *Jûshi-jûgo Seiki Kaiiki Ajia ni okeru Vietnam Tôji no Ugoki – Vietnam, Ryukyu, Majapahit*. Institute of International Culture Bulletin, Shōwa Women's University Vol.21, 2014.

Fujian-sheng Bowuguang, *Zhangzhou Yao* [the Zhangzhou Ware], Fujian Renmin Chupanshe, 1997.

Gabbert, Gunhild, *Chinesisches Porzellan im Museum für Kunsthandwerk Frankfurt am Main* [Chinese porcelains in Museum Angewandte Kunst, Fraunkfurt], Frankfurt am Main, 1977.

Goddio, Franck et al., *Tresor de Porcelaines: L'etrange Voyage de la Jonque Lena*, London: Periplus Publishing Ltd., 2002.

Guillot, Claude, *The Sultanate of Banten*, Jakarta: Gramedia, 1990.

Guillot, Claude, Lukman Nurhakim & Sonny Wibisono, *Banten avant l'Islam : Etude archeologique de Banten Girang (Java-Indonesie) 932?-1526*, Paris: Publications de l'Ecole Francaise d'Extreme-Orient, 1994.

Guillot, Claude, Daniel Perret & Naniek H. Wibisono, *Lobu Tua: Sejarah Awal Barus* [Lobu Tua: the early history of Barus], Jakarta: Yayasan Obor, 1998.

Gunnip Chungan Banmurguan, *Sinan Haedi Munwu* [Treasures from the Seabed of Sinan]. National Museum of Korea, Seoul, 1977.

Guoli Gugong Bowuyuan, *Ming-dai Chunian Ciqi Tezhan Tulu* [Catalogue of special exhibition: Early Ming porcelains]. National Palace Museum, Taipei, 1990.

Guoli Lishi Bowuguang, *Chungguo Ming Tao Zhan* [Exhibition of Masterpieces of Chinese ceramics. National Museum of History, Taipei, 1992.

Guy, John, 'The Vietnamese Wall Tiles of Majapahit',*Transactions of the Oriental Ceramics Society* 53 (1988-89), 1989.

Guy, John, *Ceramic Tradition of South East Asia*, Singapore: Oxford University Press, 1989.

Halwany Michrob, 1993. *Laporan Hasil Penelitian Arkeologi Situs Tirtayasa dan Situs Pagedongan* [Archaeological Study Report of Tirtayasa & Pagedongan Sites], Banten: SPSP Jabar-DKI-Lampung.

Harrison, Barbara, *Swatow In Het Princessehof (Trades Wares from China of the late Ming Dynasty)*, Leeuwarden, 1979.

Hasan M. Ambary, Hasan Djafar, Mundardjito, *Laporan Penelitian Arkeologi Banten 1976* [Archaeological Research Report of Banten 1976], Jakarta: Pusat Penelitian Purbakara dan Peninggalan Nasional [National Ancient and Ruins Research Centre], 1978.

Hasan M. Ambary, Halwany Michrob & John Miksic (ed.), *Catalogue of Sites, Monuments and Artifacts of Banten*. Jakarta: Directorate for Protection and Development of Historical and Archaeological Heritage, 1988.

Heibonsha (ed.), *Tôjitaikei 47 Thai, Vietnam no Tôji* [Compendium of Ceramics: Ceramics of Thailand and Vietnam]. Heibonsha, 1978.

Heibonsha (ed.), *Chûgoku no Tôji 8 Gen, Min no Seika* [Chinese Ceramics 8, the Yuan and the Ming Under-glaze cobalt blue wares]. Heibonsha, 1995.

Heibonsha (ed.), *Chûgoku no Tôji 4 Seiji* [Chinese Ceramics 4, Celadon ware]. Heibonsha, 1997.

Hirado-shi Kyoiku-iinkai, *Hirado Oranda Shokan-ato* [The Dutch Trading Post ruins in Hirado], 1988.

Ho Chuimei, *Ancient Ceramic Kiln Technology In Asia*, Hong Kong University, 1990.

Idemitsu Museum of Art, *Kinnen Hakken no Kama-ato Shutsudo Chûgoku Tôjiki Ten* [Exhibition of Chinese ceramics recently excavated from kiln sites]. Idemitsu Museum of Art, 1982.

Ikuta Shigeru and Ishizawa Yoshiaki, *Sekai no Rekishi 13 Tônan Ajia no Dentô to Hatten* [World History 13, Tradition and Development of Southeast Asia]. Chûkô Bunko, 2009.

Institute of International Culture, Shōwa Women's University, *Vietnam Hoi-An chiiki no Kôkogakuteki Kenkyû* [Archaeological Research in the Hoi An district, Vietnam]. Institute of International Culture, Shōwa Women's University, 2002.

Ishii Yoneo (ed.), *Indonesia no jiten* [the Encyclopaedia of Indonesia], Dohosha Pub., 1991.

Jingdezhen-shi Taoci Kaogu Yanjiusuo, Xu-shi Yisuguang, *Cheng-yao Yizhen – Jingdezhen Zhushan chutu Chenghua-guanyao Ciqi* [A legacy of Chenghua – Imperial Chenghua porcelains excavated at Zhushan, Jingdezhen]. Jingdezhen Ceramics Archaeology Institute, Hong Kong Xu Museum of Art, 1993.

Jörg, C.J.A., *The Geldermalsen History and Porcelain*, Groningen: Kemper Publishers, 1986.

Jörg, C.J.A., *Fine & Curious: Japanese Export Porcelain in Dutch Collections*, Hotei Pub., 2003.

Jörg, C.J.A. & Michael Flecker, *Porcelain from the Vung Tau Wreck: The Hallstrom Excavation*, Sun Tree Pub., 2001.

Kamei Meitoku et al., *Ashû Kotôji Kenkyû* II [Research on Asian Historical Ceramics II]. Ashû Kotôji Gakkai, 2005.

Kamei Meitoku et al., *Ashû Kotôji Kenkyû* III [Research on Asian Historical Ceramics III]. Ashû Kotôji Gakkai, 2008.

Kamei Meitoku et al., *Karakorum Iseki Shutsudo Tôji Chôsa Houkokusho II* [Excavation Report on Ceramics from the Karakorum Archaeological Site II]. Senshû Daigaku Bungakubu Ajia Kôkogaku Kenkyûshitsu, 2009.

Krahl, R. & J. Ayers, *Chinese Ceramics in The Topkapi Sarayi Museum Istanbul, A Complete Catalogue*, Sotheby's Publications, 1986.

Krahl, Regina, John Guy, J. Keith Wilson & Julian Raby, *Shipwrecked Tang Treasures and Monsoon Winds*, Washington: Smithsonian Books, 2011.

Ko-Imari Chôsa Iinkai (ed.), *Ko-Imari*. 1959.

Kure Katsutoshi, 'Taiwan Teishi – Chûgoku Nanbu – Tounan Ajia o Musubu Shojyôken to Oranda Higashi Indo Kaisha' [Conditions that Connect the Zheng family, Southern China and Southeast Asia and the Dutch East India Company], *Bôekitôji to Bunkenshiryô kara Higashi Ajia, Tounan Ajia no Rekishi o Kangaeru – Jûroku seiki, Jûnana seiki o Chûshin to shita Kaiiki ni okeru Hito, Mono no Nagare*. Rikkyo Daigaku Ajia Chiiki Kenkyujo, 2016.

Kyōto National Museum, *Nihonjin ga Kononda Chûgoku Tôji* [Chinese Ceramics: the most popular works among Japanese nationals]. Kyoto National Museum, 1991.

Kyūshū Ceramic Museum, *Umi o Watatta Hizen no Yakimono-ten* [Exhibition of Hizen Ceramics Abroad the Seas]. Kyūshū Ceramic Museum, 1990.

Kyūshū Ceramic Museum, *Shibata Korekushon II* [Shibata Collection II]. Kyūshū Ceramic Museum, 1991.

Kyūshū Ceramic Museum, *Shibata Korekushon IV* [Shibata Collection IV]. Kyūshū Ceramic Museum, 1995.

Kyūshū Ceramic Museum, *Ko-Imari no Michi* [The Voyage of Old-Imari Porcelain]. Kyūshū Ceramic Museum, 2000.

Kyūshū Ceramic Museum, *Hakuu Korekushon Hyaku-sen* [Selected 100 works from the Hakuu Collection]. Kyūshū Ceramic Museum, 2003.

Machida City Museum (ed.), *Vietnam Tôji* [Vietnamese Ceramics]. Machida City Museum, 1993.

Machida City Museum (ed.), *Masuda Korekushon Vietnam Tôji no Nisennen* [Masuda Collection: 2000 years of Vietnamese ceramics]. Machida City Museum, 2013.

Mayuyama Yasuhiko, *Demak Kaikyôjiin no Annan Seika Tôsen ni tsuite* [On Vietnamese Underglaze cobalt blue ceramic tiles in the Demak Great Mosque]. Tôyô Tôji 4, 1977.

Mayuyama Yasuhiko, *Majapahit Outoato Shutsudo no Gendai Seika-jihen* [Yuan under-glaze cobalt blue porcelain fragments found at the Majapahit capital site], Gen no Sometsuke-ten –

Jūyon seiki no Keitokuchin-yô. The Museum of Oriental Ceramics, Osaka, 1985.

Miksic, John and Kamei Meitoku, *Indonesia Trowulan Iseki Hakkutsu Tôji no Kenkyû – Singapore Daigaku Tônan Ajia Kenkyûshitsu Hokanshiryô/Research on Ceramics Discovered at the Trowulan site in Indonesia*, Senshū University Asian Archaeological Team & Southeast Asian Studies Programme, National University of Singapore, 2010.

Misugi Takatoshi, *Sekai no Sometsuke (4)* [Underglaze cobalt-blue ware from the world (4)]. Dôhôsha, 1987.

Mori Tsuyoshi, 'Osaka de tsukawareta Vetonamu-sei tojiki [Vietnamese ceramics used in Osaka]', *Ashibi*, 40, Osakashi Bunkazai Kyokai, 1992.

Mori Tsuyoshi, 'Edo-jidai no karamono to wamono [the Chinese ware and the Japanese ware in the Edo period]', *Ashibi*, 43, Osaka-shi Bunkazai-kyokai, 1993.

Morimoto Asako, 'Sumatera Nishikaigan Barus no Robu Tua Iseki' [Lobu Tua Site in Barus on the west coast of Sumatera], *Kindai Kôko* 55. Kanazawa University, Study of Archaeology, 2006.

Mukai Kou, *Kanazawa Daigaku Bunkashigengaku Kenkyû dai Go gou Thai Tôjiki no Hennen Kenkyû* [Kanazawa University Cultural Resource Studies No.5 Study of Thailand Ceramics Chronology]. Kanazawa University, Center for Cultural Resource Studies, 2012.

Musashi Bunkazai Kenkyujo, *Yurakucho Yicchome iseki* [Yurakucho Yicchome Site], 2015.

Nagafuchi Tomoko, 'Yusyutsu-sareta Hizen-tojiki no nagare (nentsuki bin, tsubo rui) [the Chronology of exported Hizen ware (dated bottle and jar etc.)]', *the Shibata Collection V*, Kyushu Ceramic Museum, 1997.

Nagamatsu Minoru, 'Hakkutsu-sareta syokubunka no yofuka nitsuite [Regarding Excavated Westernization of Eating Culture], *Nagasaki Dejima no Syokubunka*, Shinwa Bank, 1993.

Nagasaki-ken Kyoiku-iinkai, *Kyushu Odan-jidoshado kensetsu nitomonau maizo-bunkazai kinkyu-chosa hookkusyo* [the rescue investigation report of under-ground cultural properties related construction of the Kyushu Odan Highway], 1984.

Nagasaki-shi Kyoiku-iinkai, *Dejima Oranda Shokan-ato han-i kakunin chosa hookkusho* [Investigation Roport for areal confirmation of the Dutch Trading Post in Dejima], 1986.

Nagasaki-shi Kyoiku-iinkai, *Tsukimachi Iseki* [Tsukimachi Site], 1997.

Nagasaki-shi Maizo-bunkazai Chosa Kyogikai, *Sakaemachi Iseki* [Sakaemachi Site], 1993.

National Museum of Vietnamese History, *Bat Trang Ceramics 14th-19th Centuries*, Hanoi: 1995.

National Museum of Vietnamese History, *2000 years of Vietnamese ceramics*, Hanoi: 2005.

Nihon Keizai Shimbunsha, *Eikoku David Korekushon Chûgoku Tôjikiten* [Exhibition of Sir Percival David Chinese Ceramics Collection in England], Japan Financial Times (Nikkei), 1980.

Nihon Keizai Shimbunsha, *Paris ni Saita Ko-imari no Hana* [The flower of Ko-Imari ware blooming in Paris], Japan Financial Times (Nikkei), 2009.

Nezu Institute of Fine Arts, *Nanban Shimamono* [Namban and Objects from the South Seas], Nezu Museum, 1993.

Nogami Takenori, 'Gareon-boeki to Hizen-jiki [the Galleon trade and Hizen porcelain]', *Toyotoji*, 42, pp.141-176, 2013.

Nogami Takenori, Alfredo B. Orogo, Nida T. Cuevas, Tanaka Kazuhiko & Hong Xiao-chun,

'Gareon-sen de hakobareta Hizen-jiki' [Hizen porcelains carried by Galleon ships], *the Journal of Underwater Archaeological Studies*, no.1, 2005

Ôgiura Masayoshi, *Tôjin Yashiki Ato* [The Chinese Mansion Site]. Nagasakishi Kyôiku Iinkai, 2013.

Ôhashi Kôji, 'Jugo-juroku seiki niokeru Nihon syutsudo no seika-wan ni kansuru hennen-shian [A chronological hypothesis for under-glaze cobalt blue bowl found in Japan during 15th-16th centuries] (1)', *Hakusui*, 8, 1981.

Ôhashi Kôji, 'Kaigai-yusyutsu sareta Hizen toki no tokushitsu nitsuite [Regarding characteristics of exported Hizen stoneware]', *Ôcho no Kokogaku*, Yuzankaku, 1995.

Ôhashi Kôji, 'Toruko de hakenshita Hizen no seiji [the Hizen celadon found in Turkey]', *Menome*, 259, Ribun Pub., 1998.

Ôhashi Kôji, 'Minmatsu-Shindai niokeru Chugoku Fukkensho Tokkayou-kei jiki nitsuite [Regarding the Dehua type porcelain, Fujian in the late Ming and Qing periods]', *Osaka-shi Bunkazai-kyokai Kenkyu-kiyo*, 2, pp.241-248, 1999a.

Ôhashi Kôji, 'Aki Nidai' [Two Autumn Subjects], *Me no Me*, no.279, 1999b.

Ôhashi Kôji, *Umi o Watatta Tôjiki* [Ceramics that Crossed the Seas]. Yoshikawa Kôbunkan, 2004a.

Ôhashi Kôji, 'Nihon-jiki, Tokugawa Shogun to Oshu-ouko no Imari [Japanese porcelain, Imari ware of the Tokugawa Shoguns and European royality/nobility]', *JIKI*, Faenza City & the Japan Foundation, 2004b.

Ôhashi Kôji, '17seiki-kohan, Chugoku jiki no ryo wo koeta Hizen jiki no ryutsu [the late 17th century, the distribution of Hizen porcelain, surpassed quantity of Chinese porcelain]', *Chugoku tojiki no kokogaku*, 4, pp.63-84, Yuzankaku, 2016.

Ôhashi Kôji (ed.), *Umi wo watatta Ko-Imari, ceramic road* [the old-Imari abroad, the ceramic road], Seigansha, 2011.

Ôhashi Kôji and Sakai Takashi, 'Indonesia Banten Iseki Shutsudo no Tôjiki' [Ceramics from the site of Banten in Indonesia]. *Kokuritsu Rekishi Minzoku Hakubutsukan Kenkyû Hôkoku*, no.82, 1999.

Ôhashi Kôji et al., *Arita-cho shi ishigama-hen* [the History of Arita-cho, volume of stone kiln], Arita, 1988.

Okinawa-ken Kyoiku-iinkai, *Kiyuna Kaizuka & Kiyuna Gusuku* [Kiyuna shell mound and gusuku], 1999.

Okinawaken Maizôbunkazai Centre, *Shurijô – Shichanuuna, Youmotsuza, Zuisenmon, Roukokumon, Koufukumon, Kobikimon Hakkutsuchôsa Houkokusho* [Shurijo Castle – Excavation Report of Shichanuuna, Youmotsuza, Zuisenmon gate, Roukokumon gate, Kôfukumon gate, and Kobikimon gate sites]. Okinawaken Maizôbunkazai Centre, 2001a.

Okinawa-ken Maizôbunkazai Centre, *Syuri-jo ato, kanriyou doro chiku hakkutsu chosa hokkusyo* [the Shuri Castle, a excavation research report of the management road district], 2001b.

Okinawa-ken Maizôbunkazai Centre, *Tenkai-ji ato I* [Tenkai-ji temple ruins I], 2001c.

Osaka-shi Bunkazai Kyokai, *Sumitomo Dofukisho-ato Hakkutsu-chosa hokokusho* [Excavation Research Report of the Sumitomo Cupper Refinery ruins], 1998.

Pigeaud, Theodore Gauthier Th. (trans.), *Java in the 14th Century: A Study in Cultural History*

The Nagara-Kertagama by Rakawi, Prapanca of Majapahit, 1356 A.D., ACLS History E-Book Project, 2006.

Pijl-Ketel, C.L. van der, *The Ceramic load of the 'Witte Leeuw'*, Amsterdam: Rijksmuseum, 1982.

Pinto De Matos, Maria Antonia, *Chinese Export Porcelain: From The Museum of Anastacio Goncalves, Lisbon*, 1996.

Reid, Anthony, *Southeast Asia in the Age of Commerce 1450-1680*, New Haven: Yale Univ. Press, 1988.

Sakai Takashi, *Koshi kokka Banten to toji-boeki* [Banten, A Port City Nation and Its Ceramic Trade], Doseisha, 2002.

Sakai Takashi, 'Indonesia, Trowulan Iseki to Vietnam Tairu' [A Preliminary Study of Vietnamese Decorated Tiles Found in Java, Indonesia (2)], *Kanazawa Daigaku Kôkogaku Kiyô*, no.30. Kanazawa Daigaku Bungakubu Kôkogaku kôza, 2009.

Sakai Takashi, 'Indonesia, Trowulan Shutsudo no Tairu' [Glazed Tiles Excavated at Trowulan Site, Indonesia], Tôyô Tôji no.44. 2015.

Sakai Takashi (ed.), *Banten, Tirtayasa Iseki Hakkutsu Chôsa Houkokusho* [Excavation Report on Banten and Tirtayasa Archaeological Site]. Institute of Asian, Studies, Sophia University and National Archaeology Study Center, Indonesia, 2000.

Sakai Takashi (ed.), *Umi no Shirukurôdo no Kyoten Banten, Tirtayasa Iseki no Tôjibôeki no Kenkyû* [Research on trade ceramics found at Banten and Tirtayasa Archaeological sites, the Foothold of the Sea Silk Road]. Nara Shirukurôdohaku Kinen Kokusaikôryû Zaidan Shirukurôdogaku Kenkyû Centre, 2004.

Sakai Takashi (ed.), *Banten, Tirtayasa Iseki, Buton Wolio-jôato Hakkutsu Chôsa Houkokusho* [Excavation Report on the Banten, Tirtayasa Site and Buton Wolio Fort]. Association of Asian Cultural Properties Cooperation, 2007.

Sakai Takashi and Ôhashi Kôji, *Indoneshia, Trowulan Iseki Shutsudo no Tôjiki* [Ceramics found in the Trowulan Site, Indonesia], monograph series 15. Institute of Asian Studies, Sophia University, 2014.

Saga Kenritsu Hakubutsukan, *Baisao*, 1983.

Sasaki Tatsuo, Nogami Tateki and Sasaki Hanae, 'Myanmar kama-ato chosa to saisyu tojiki' [Investigations on kiln sites and surface ceramics in Myanmar], *Kanazawa Daigaku Kokogaku Kiyo*, 27, pp.147-246, 2004.

Serrurier, L., 'Kaar Van Oud-Banten In Geroudheid, begracht door wijlen Mr. L. Serruirier (met eene inleideng van Dr. H. Brendes)', *TBG* 45, Batavia: 1902.

Shanghai Renmin Meisu Chupanshe, *Chungguo Taoci Chuanji 4 Yue-yao* [Complete works of Chinese ceramics 4, Yue kiln], Shanghai People's Fine Arts Publishing House, 1981

Sheaf, Colin & Kiburn, Richard, *The Hatcher Porcelain Cargoes, The Complete Record*, Oxford, 1988.

Shimizu Naho, 'Vientiane Kyûshigaichinai Shutsudo no Hizen Tôjiki' [Hizen ceramics found in the old town district in Vientiane], *Sekai ni Yushutsusareta Hizen Tôjiki*. Kyushu Kinsei Tôjigakkai, 2010.

Shimizu Naho, 'Laos Shutsudo no Vietnam Tôji' [Vietnamese ceramics found in Laos], *Jûyon-Jûgo Seiki Kaiiki Ajia ni Okeru Vietnam Tôji no Ugoki – Vietnam, Ryukyu, Majapahit-*.

Institute of International Culture Bulletin, Shōwa Women's University Vol.21, 2014, 109-124.

Shimizu Naho and Laos National Museum, 'Laos Xiangkhouang-kennai Bukkyôjiin ni okeru Hakkutsu chôsa' [Excavation research at Buddhist temples in Xiangkhouang province, Laos], *Tônan Ajia Kôkogaku* 34. Japanese Society for Southeast Asian Archaeology, 2014.

Shogakukan, *Sekai Tôji Zenshû 11 Zui-Tou* [Ceramics of the World 11, the Sui and Tang Dynasties]. Shogakukan, 1976a.

Shogakukan, *Sekai Tôji Zenshû 14 Min* [Ceramics of the World 14, the Ming Dynasty]. Shogakukan, 1976b.

Shogakukan, *Sekai Tôji Zenshû 13 Ryo, Kin-Gen* [Ceramics of the World 13, the Liao, Jin and Yuan Dynasties]. Shogakukan, 1981.

Shogakukan, *Sekai Tôji Zenshû 16 Nankai* [Ceramics of the World 16, Southeast Asia]. Shogakukan, 1984.

Smart, Ellen, 'Fourteenth Century Chinese Porcelain from a Tughlaq Palace in Delhi', *Transactions of the Oriental Ceramic Society*, vol. 51, 1975.

Takashima Hiroyuki, '(5) Muyû Inkamon Tsubo' [(5) Unglazed jars with Stamped Designs], *Kogoshima Jingû Shozou Tôjiki no Kenkyû*. Kagoshima Jingû Shozou Tôjiki Chôsadan, 2013.

Tan Xue-hui et al., *Chungguo Min-dai Ciqi Mulu* [Catalogue of Chinese porcelain from Ming period]. Nanfan Pub., 1998.

The Trustees of The British Museum, *Islamic Tiles-Venetia Porter-*, Northampton: Interlink Books, 1995.

Tokyo Kokuritsu Hakubutsukan [Tokyo National Museum], *Nihon syutsudo-no Chugoku-toji* [Chinese ceramics found in Japan], 1975.

Toguri Museum of Art, *Nihon-toji meihin zuroku* [the Catalogue of fine Japanese ceramics], 1998.

Woodward, C.S., *Oriental Ceramics at The Cape of Good Hope 1652-1795*, Taylor & Francis, 1974.

Xianggang Daxue Fung Ping-shan Bowuguan, *Jingdezhen Chutu Taoci* [Excavated ceramics from Jingdezhen], University Museum and Art Gallery, the University of Hong Kong, 1992.

Xu Ben-zhang, Shitan Dehua-yao qinghua zhuangshi yisi ji yingxiang [a essay of decorative art and influence of the Dehua under-glaze cobalt blue porcelain], Ho Chuimei (ed.) *Ancient Ceramic Kiln Technology in Asia*, 1990.

Yabe Yoshiaki, *Tôji-taikei 47 Thai, Vietnam no Tôji* [Compendium of Ceramics: Ceramics of Thailand and Vietnam]. Heibonsha, 1978.

Yamaguchi-ken Maizo-bunkazai Center, *Hagi-jo ato (Sotobori-chiku) I* [the Hagi Fort ruins, the outer moat district I], 2002.

Yamawaki Teijirô, 'Bôekihen – Tou-Ransen no Imariyaki Yushutsu' [Trade – Imari ware export by Chinese and Dutch vessels], *Aritachôshi Shougyô-hen I*. Saga-ken Aritachô, 1988.

Yang Shao-xiang, 'Guangdong qinghua ciqi chutan [a primary study of Guangdong under-glaze cobalt blue porcelain]', Ho Chuimei (ed.) *Ancient Ceramic Kiln Technology in Asia*, 1990.

Yao Cheng-qing, Sun Jing-min and Yao Lian-hong, 'Shi-tan Guangchang Jinianmu chutude qinghua cipan [An essay for under-glaze cobalt blue large dish found in the dated tomb of Guangchang]', *Jiangsi Wenwu*, 2, 1990.

Ye Qing-lin, ʻAnxi qinghua ciqide chubu yanjiu [a primary study for Anxi under-glaze cobalt blue ware]ʼ , Ho Chuimei (ed.) *Ancient Ceramic Kiln Technology in Asia*, 1990.

Zang Zhen-hua, Gao You-de & Liu Yi-chang, ʻZuoying Qing-dai Fengshan-xian Jiucheng Juluode Shijueʼ [Prospecting trial excavation at the Old City of Fengshan County of Qing Era in Zuoying], *Bulletin of the Institute of History and Philology 64-3*, Academia Sinica, 1993.

Zhejiang Province Antique Archaeology Institute, School of Archaeology and Museology of Peking University, Cixi City Cultural Properties Authority, *Yue ware kiln site of Silongkou*, Cultural Relics Press, 2002.

Zhungguo Guangxi Zhuang-zu Zizhiqu Bowuguan [Museum of Guangxi Zhuang Autonomous Region], National Museum of Vietnamese History et al., *Yuenan Chushui Taoci* [Salvaged Vietnamese ceramics], 2009.

Acknowledgements

Research on the ceramic sherds excavated from Trowulan Site began in 2012. Several years earlier, the outdoor ceramic stores on the premises of the Trowulan Museum took us by surprise when we first came across it. Three or four years prior to our first collaboration work for this ceramic shards at the site, the late Professor Kamei Meitoku had asked me if I would join a collaborative research project at Trowulan, however, the Indonesian partner was not yet able to invite us to participate. When the possibility to collaborate finally emerged, Professor Kamei sadly became unwell.

We owe great deal of thanks to Professor Naniek H. Wibisono from the National Archaeology Study Centre for enabling us to participate in the academic study of such a vast quantity of ceramics. Our collaboration works with her started in the study of Banten Lama over a quarter of a century ago. This publication can be said to be a summary of research conducted over the last 25 years. However, Naniek H. Wibisono also guided Professor Mikami Tsugio around Banten Lama during his visit, and this has also informed the research presented here.

It is not only to Professor Kamei and Professor Mikami, but also to Dr. Hasan M. Ambary, Dr. Halwany Michrab and Mr. Abu Ridho, to whom we owe great deal of gratitude in our understanding of Banten Lama. Sadly, they are all deceased. The initial intention of this publication is to pay tribute to these remarkable scholars. At the same time, we hope it can be a gift from all of us to help the younger generation in the field of the ceramic trade study, in particular of Indonesia.

In this publication, Chapters I and IV are written by Sakai Takashi and II and III by Ôhashi Kôji. English translation was provided by Uchida Hiromi and Professor Nicole Rousmaniere. In addition, last but certainly not least, we would like to express our deep gratitude to Mr. Takimoto Tadashi and colleagues at the Association of Asian Cultural Properties Cooperation.

January, 2018
Sakai Takashi

──────── 編者・著者・訳者紹介 ────────

坂井　隆（さかい たかし）

1954年東京都生まれ。2003年上智大学大学院より博士号（地域研究）授与。国立台湾大学芸術史研究所（大学院）教授。

主書に『「伊万里」からアジアが見える―海の陶磁路と日本―』（講談社 1998年）、『港市国家バンテンと陶磁貿易』（同成社 2002年）、『世界の考古学　東南アジアの考古学』（共著 同成社 1998年）、『イスラームと文化財』（共著 新泉社 2015年）、『水中文化遺産―海から蘇る歴史―』（共著 勉誠社 2017年）などがある。

大橋康二（おおはし こうじ）

1948年神奈川県生まれ。青山学院大学院文学研究科史学専攻修士課程修了。佐賀県立九州陶磁文化館館長を経て、現在、同館名誉顧問。佐賀大学非常勤講師。東洋陶磁学会常任委員長、NPO法人アジア文化財協力協会理事長、近世陶磁研究会会長。

主著に『古伊万里の文様』（理工学社 1994年）、『世界をリードした磁器窯・肥前窯』（新泉社 2004年）、『海を渡った陶磁器』（吉川弘文館 2004年）、『将軍と鍋島・柿右衛門』（雄山閣 2007年）、『年代別蕎麦猪口大事典』（講談社 2009年）などがある。

Nicole Coolidge Rousmaniere（ニコール クーリッジ ルマニエール）

IFAC Handa Curator of Japanese Arts, British Museum

2018 年 1 月 20 日　初版発行 《検印省略》

インドネシアの王都出土の肥前陶磁
—トロウラン遺跡ほか—

編　者　坂井　隆

著　者　坂井　隆／大橋康二

発行者　宮田哲男

発行所　株式会社 雄山閣

東京都千代田区富士見 2-6-9

ＴＥＬ　03-3262-3231 ／ＦＡＸ　03-3262-6938

ＵＲＬ　http://www.yuzankaku.co.jp

e-mail　info@yuzankaku.co.jp

振　替　00130-5-1685

印刷・製本　株式会社ティーケー出版印刷

ISBN978-4-639-02489-7 C3022
N.D.C.224　320p　27cm

表1 トロウラン遺跡出土陶磁器集計表　Table 1　Ceramic Shards found in Trowulan

中 国 China

時期区分 period		越州 Yue 青磁 Celadon 碗	皿	他	長沙 Changsha 黄釉鉄彩 碗	皿	他	同安 Tongan 青磁 碗	皿	他	龍泉 Longquan 青磁 碗	皿	他	景徳鎮 青白磁 Yinqing 碗	皿	他	白磁 White 碗	皿	他	青花 U.glaze cobalt 碗	皿	他	釉裏紅 U.glaze copper 碗	皿	他	瑠璃釉 Blue 碗	皿	他	五彩 Polychrome 碗	皿	他	その他 青磁 Celadon 碗	皿	他	青白磁 Yinqing 碗	皿	他	白磁 White 碗	皿	他	褐釉 Brown 他	磁州 鉄絵 Iron paint 碗	皿	他	陶板 slab	翡翠釉 Turquoise 碗	皿	他	徳化 白磁 White 碗	皿	他	漳州 青花 U.glaze cobalt 碗	皿	他	福建・広東 青花 碗	皿	他	福建 青磁 Celadon 碗	皿	他	白磁 White 碗	皿	他	五彩 Polychrome 碗	皿	他	総計 total
I	9-10c	5	1		1																											1																																			
	10-11c	21	14	2																																																															
	11-12c							1						1																								1																													
	12-13c									3	12			1	2	7																						49			3																										
	小計 s.total	26	15	2	1					3	13			2	2	7																1						50			3																										125
I-2	13-14c										32	13								16															21	1		16						1																							101
	小計 s.total										32	13								16															21	1		16						1																							101
II	14c										15	192	36	14	12	5	36	11		64	35	79			6													893	99	22	3	43	8					27																				1,600
	小計 s.total										15	192	36	14	12	5	36	11		64	35	79			6													893	99	22	3	43	8					27																				1,600
II-2	late 14c											89			9		22	9	1	100	27	52	1			2									87	5	9	471	6	108				2													1	14								1,015
	小計 s.total											89			9		22	9	1	100	27	52	1			2									87	5	9	471	6	108				2													1	14								1,015
III	15c										802	318					2	1		116	86	62	2			2									2	2					44													1						1						1,441
	小計 s.total										802	318					2	1		116	86	62	2			2									2	2					44													1						1						1,441
IV	16-17c																			24	15	2																																17	39	3	1						101
	小計 s.total																			24	15	2																																17	39	3	1						101
IV-2	18c																			14																													1											33	22		70
	小計 s.total																			14																													1											33	22		70
総計 total		26	15	2	1			3			862	612	36	16	23	28	60	21	1	304	163	209			9				2	2		1			1	87	5	975	573	44	159	43	8					27	2					1	17	39	3	1			33	22	2	14	1	4,453

東南アジア Southeast Asia ／ イスラム Islam ／ 日本 Japan

時期区分 period		ベトナム 白磁 White 碗	皿	他	青磁 Celadon 碗	皿	他	鉄釉 Iron 碗	皿	他	白濁釉 Milky 碗	皿	他	緑釉 Green 碗	皿	他	鉄絵 Iron paint 碗	皿	他	青花 U.glaze cobalt 碗	皿	他	陶板 slab	五彩 Polychrome 碗	皿	他	陶板 slab	他 Others 形象 sculpture	タイ 青磁 Celadon 碗	皿	他	鉄絵 Iron paint 碗	皿	他	黒釉 Black 他	無釉 No glaze 他	イスラム 白釉藍彩 Blue & white 陶板	肥前 染付 U.glaze cobalt 碗	皿	他	色絵 Polychrome 碗	皿	他	白磁 White 碗	皿	他	総計 total
I	9-10c										1			1																																	
	10-11c						1																																								
	11-12c						?																																								
	12-13c		1		1	1								1																																	6
	小計 s.total		1		1	1					1			1																																	6
I-2	13-14c	14				2		7	1		4			2			2		1	2																											35
	小計 s.total	14				2		7	1		4			2			2		1	2																											35
II	14c	17					3			2																											8										30
	小計 s.total	17					3			2																											8										30
II-2	late 14c	85	1	20	3	5		9			1						5	2	1	165	53	33														18											401
	小計 s.total	85	1	20	3	5		9			1						5	2	1	165	53	33														18											401
III	15c	8					1							6			78	3		344	577	604	171	1	3	1	2		163	530	28	34	213	8	26	19											2,820
	小計 s.total	8					1							6			78	3		344	577	604	171	1	3	1	2		163	530	28	34	213	8	26	19											2,820
IV	16-17c																																					1	3		4	1					9
	小計 s.total																																					1	3		4	1					9
IV-2	18c																																														
	小計 s.total																																														
総計 total		124	2	22	15	7		3	14			9		1			85	3	4	165	53	35	344	577	604	171	1	3	1	2	18	163	530	28	34	213	8	26	19	8	1	3		4	1		3,301

＊数字は推定個体数である。基本的には底部もしくは口縁部が残っている陶片の個数である。 # The figures are estimated individuals units, counted by botom/edge parts shards only.

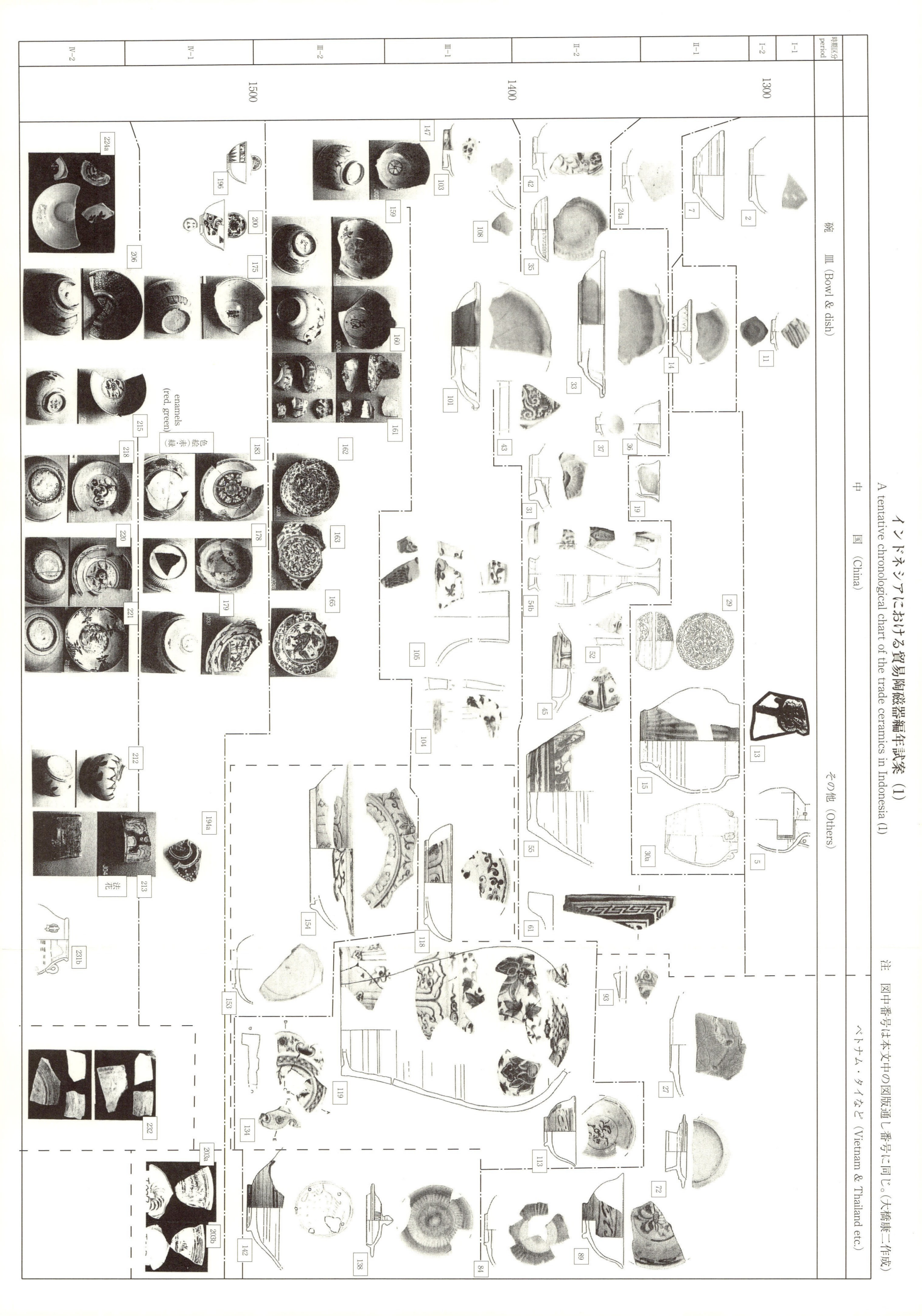

インドネシアにおける貿易陶磁器編年試案 (1)

A tentative chronological chart of the trade ceramics in Indonesia (1)

注 図中番号は本文中の図版通し番号に同じ。(大橋康二作成)

編年区分 period		中 国 (China)	ベトナム・タイなど (Vietnam & Thailand etc.)
		碗 皿 (Bowl & dish) その他 (Others)	

period							
時期区分	IV-2	V-1	V-2	VI-1	VI-2	VII-1	VII-2

1600　1700　1800

中国 (China)

肥前 (Hizen)

ヨーロッパ (Europe)

中国 (China)

碗 (Bowl)　皿 (Dish)

その他 (Others)

肥前 (Hizen)　ベトナム (Vietnam)　イスラム (Islam)　ヨーロッパ (Europe)

百寿文 / Bai shou motif

色絵 enamels

肥前系 (Hizen type)